WESTERN CLASSICS COLLECTION VOLUME I

Riders of the Purple Sage, The Light of Western Stars, The Rainbow Trail

ZANE GREY

CONTENTS

RIDERS OF THE
PURPLE SAGE

❧ I ❧

LASSITER

A SHARP CLIP-CROP of iron-shod hoofs deadened and died away, and clouds of yellow dust drifted from under the cottonwoods out over the sage.

Jane Withersteen gazed down the wide purple slope with dreamy and troubled eyes. A rider had just left her and it was his message that held her thoughtful and almost sad, awaiting the churchmen who were coming to resent and attack her right to befriend a Gentile.

She wondered if the unrest and strife that had lately come to the little village of Cottonwoods was to involve her. And then she sighed, remembering that her father had founded this remotest border settlement of southern Utah and that he had left it to her. She owned all the ground and many of the cottages. Withersteen House was hers, and the great ranch, with its thousands of cattle, and the swiftest horses of the sage. To her belonged Amber Spring, the water which gave verdure and beauty to the village and made living possible on that wild purple upland waste. She could not escape being involved by whatever befell Cottonwoods.

That year, 1871, had marked a change which had been gradually coming in the lives of the peace-loving Mormons of the border. Glaze—Stone Bridge—Sterling, villages to the north, had risen against the invasion of Gentile settlers and the forays of rustlers. There had been opposition to the one and fighting with the other. And now Cottonwoods had begun to wake and bestir itself and grown hard.

Jane prayed that the tranquillity and sweetness of her life would not be permanently disrupted. She meant to do so much more for her people than she had done. She wanted the sleepy quiet pastoral days to last always. Trouble between the Mormons and the Gentiles of the community would make her unhappy. She was Mormon-born, and she was a friend to poor and unfortunate Gentiles. She wished only to go on doing good and being happy. And she thought of what that great ranch meant to her. She loved it all—the grove of cottonwoods, the old stone house, the amber-tinted water, and the droves of shaggy, dusty horses and mustangs, the sleek, clean-limbed, blooded racers, and the browsing herds of cattle and the lean, sun-browned riders of the sage.

While she waited there she forgot the prospect of untoward change. The bray of a lazy burro broke the afternoon quiet, and it was comfortingly suggestive of the drowsy farmyard, and the open corrals, and the green alfalfa fields. Her clear sight intensified the purple sage-slope as it rolled before her. Low swells of prairie-like ground sloped up to the west. Dark, lonely cedar-trees, few and far between, stood out strikingly, and at long distances ruins of red rocks. Farther on, up the gradual slope, rose a broken wall, a huge monument, looming dark purple and stretching its solitary, mystic way, a wavering line that faded in the north. Here to the westward was the light and color and beauty. Northward the slope descended to a dim line of canyons from which rose an up-flinging of the earth, not mountainous, but a vast heave of purple uplands, with ribbed and fan-shaped walls, castle-crowned cliffs, and gray escarpments. Over it all crept the lengthening, waning afternoon shadows.

The rapid beat of hoofs recalled Jane Withersteen to the question at hand. A group of riders cantered up the lane, dismounted, and threw their bridles. They were seven in number, and Tull, the leader, a tall, dark man, was an elder of Jane's church.

"Did you get my message?" he asked, curtly.

"Yes," replied Jane.

"I sent word I'd give that rider Venters half an hour to come down to the village. He didn't come."

"He knows nothing of it;" said Jane. "I didn't tell him. I've been waiting here for you."

"Where is Venters?"

"I left him in the courtyard."

"Here, Jerry," called Tull, turning to his men, "take the gang and fetch Venters out here if you have to rope him."

The dusty-booted and long-spurred riders clanked noisily into the grove of cottonwoods and disappeared in the shade.

"Elder Tull, what do you mean by this?" demanded Jane. "If you must arrest Venters you might have the courtesy to wait till he leaves my home. And if you do arrest him it will be adding insult to injury. It's absurd to accuse Venters of being mixed up in that shooting fray in the village last night. He was with me at the time. Besides, he let me take charge of his guns. You're only using this as a pretext. What do you mean to do to Venters?"

"I'll tell you presently," replied Tull. "But first tell me why you defend this worthless rider?"

"Worthless!" exclaimed Jane, indignantly. "He's nothing of the kind. He was the best rider I ever had. There's not a reason why I shouldn't champion him and every reason why I should. It's no little shame to me, Elder Tull, that through my friendship he has roused the enmity of my people and become an outcast. Besides I owe him eternal gratitude for saving the life of little Fay."

"I've heard of your love for Fay Larkin and that you intend to adopt her. But—Jane Withersteen, the child is a Gentile!"

"Yes. But, Elder, I don't love the Mormon children any less because I love a Gentile child. I shall adopt Fay if her mother will give her to me."

"I'm not so much against that. You can give the child Mormon teaching," said Tull. "But I'm sick of seeing this fellow Venters hang around you. I'm going to put a stop to it. You've so much love to throw away on these beggars of Gentiles that I've an idea you might love Venters."

Tull spoke with the arrogance of a Mormon whose power could not be brooked and with the passion of a man in whom jealousy had kindled a consuming fire.

4

"Maybe I do love him," said Jane. She felt both fear and anger stir her heart. "I'd never thought of that. Poor fellow! he certainly needs some one to love him."

"This'll be a bad day for Venters unless you deny that," returned Tull, grimly.

Tull's men appeared under the cottonwoods and led a young man out into the lane. His ragged clothes were those of an outcast. But he stood tall and straight, his wide shoulders flung back, with the muscles of his bound arms rippling and a blue flame of defiance in the gaze he bent on Tull.

For the first time Jane Withersteen felt Venters's real spirit. She wondered if she would love this splendid youth. Then her emotion cooled to the sobering sense of the issue at stake.

"Venters, will you leave Cottonwoods at once and forever?" asked Tull, tensely.

"Why?" rejoined the rider.

"Because I order it."

Venters laughed in cool disdain.

The red leaped to Tull's dark cheek.

"If you don't go it means your ruin," he said, sharply.

"Ruin!" exclaimed Venters, passionately. "Haven't you already ruined me? What do you call ruin? A year ago I was a rider. I had horses and cattle of my own. I had a good name in Cottonwoods. And now when I come into the village to see this woman you set your men on me. You hound me. You trail me as if I were a rustler. I've no more to lose—except my life."

"Will you leave Utah?"

"Oh! I know," went on Venters, tauntingly, "it galls you, the idea of beautiful Jane Withersteen being friendly to a poor Gentile. You want her all yourself. You're a wiving Mormon. You have use for her—and Withersteen House and Amber Spring and seven thousand head of cattle!"

Tull's hard jaw protruded, and rioting blood corded the veins of his neck.

"Once more. Will you go?"

"NO!"

"Then I'll have you whipped within an inch of your life," replied Tull, harshly. "I'll turn you out in the sage. And if you ever come back you'll get worse."

Venters's agitated face grew coldly set and the bronze changed

Jane impulsively stepped forward. "Oh! Elder Tull!" she cried. "You won't do that!"

Tull lifted a shaking finger toward her.

"That'll do from you. Understand, you'll not be allowed to hold this boy to a friendship that's offensive to your Bishop. Jane Withersteen, your father left you wealth and power. It has turned your head. You haven't yet come to see the place of Mormon women. We've reasoned with you, borne with you. We've patiently waited. We've let you have your fling, which is more than I ever saw granted to a Mormon woman. But you haven't come to your senses. Now, once for all, you can't have any further friendship with Venters. He's going to be whipped, and he's got to leave Utah!"

"Oh! Don't whip him! It would be dastardly!" implored Jane, with slow certainty of her failing courage.

Tull always blunted her spirit, and she grew conscious that she had feigned a boldness which she did not possess. He loomed up now in different guise, not as a jealous suitor, but embodying the mysterious despotism she had known from childhood—the power of her creed.

"Venters, will you take your whipping here or would you rather go out in the sage?" asked Tull. He smiled a flinty smile that was more than inhuman, yet seemed to give out of its dark aloofness a gleam of righteousness.

"I'll take it here—if I must," said Venters. "But by God!—Tull you'd better kill me outright. That'll be a dear whipping for you and your praying Mormons. You'll make me another Lassiter!"

The strange glow, the austere light which radiated from Tull's face, might have been a holy joy at the spiritual conception of exalted duty. But there was something more in him, barely hidden, a something personal and sinister, a deep of himself, an engulfing abyss. As his religious mood was fanatical and inexorable, so would his physical hate be merciless.

"Elder, I—I repent my words," Jane faltered. The religion in her, the long habit of obedience, of humility, as well as agony of fear, spoke in her voice. "Spare the boy!" she whispered.

"You can't save him now," replied Tull stridently.

Her head was bowing to the inevitable. She was grasping the truth, when suddenly there came, in inward constriction, a hardening of gentle forces within her breast. Like a steel bar it was stiffening all that had been soft and weak in her. She felt a birth in her of something new and unintelligible. Once more her strained gaze sought the sage-slopes. Jane Withersteen loved that wild and purple wilderness. In times of sorrow it had been her strength, in happiness its beauty was her continual delight. In her extremity she found herself murmuring, "Whence cometh my help!" It was a prayer, as if forth from those lonely purple reaches and walls of red and clefts of blue might ride a fearless man, neither creed-bound nor creed-mad, who would hold up a restraining hand in the faces of her ruthless people.

The restless movements of Tull's men suddenly quieted down. Then followed a low whisper, a rustle, a sharp exclamation.

"Look!" said one, pointing to the west.

"A rider!"

Jane Withersteen wheeled and saw a horseman, silhouetted against the western sky, coming riding out of the sage. He had ridden down from the left, in the golden glare of the sun, and had been unobserved till close at hand. An answer to her prayer!

"Do you know him? Does any one know him?" questioned Tull, hurriedly.

His men looked and looked, and one by one shook their heads.

"He's come from far," said one.

"Thet's a fine hoss," said another.

"A strange rider."

"Huh! he wears black leather," added a fourth.

With a wave of his hand, enjoining silence, Tull stepped forward in such a way that he concealed Venters.

The rider reined in his mount, and with a lithe forward-slipping action appeared to reach the ground in one long step. It was a peculiar movement in its quickness and inasmuch that while performing it the rider did not swerve in the slightest from a square front to the group before him.

"Look!" hoarsely whispered one of Tull's companions. "He packs two black-butted guns —low down—they're hard to see—black akin them black chaps."

"A gun-man!" whispered another. "Fellers, careful now about movin' your hands."

The stranger's slow approach might have been a mere leisurely manner of gait or the cramped short steps of a rider unused to walking; yet, as well, it could have been the guarded advance of one who took no chances with men.

"Hello, stranger!" called Tull. No welcome was in this greeting only a gruff curiosity.

The rider responded with a curt nod. The wide brim of a black sombrero cast a dark shade over his face. For a moment he closely regarded Tull and his comrades, and then, halting in his slow walk, he seemed to relax.

"Evenin', ma'am," he said to Jane, and removed his sombrero with quaint grace.

Jane, greeting him, looked up into a face that she trusted instinctively and which riveted her attention. It had all the characteristics of the range rider's—the leanness, the red burn of the sun, and the set changelessness that came from years of silence and solitude. But it was not these which held her, rather the intensity of his gaze, a strained weariness, a piercing wistfulness of keen, gray sight, as if the man was forever looking for that which he never found. Jane's subtle woman's intuition, even in that brief instant, felt a sadness, a hungering, a secret.

"Jane Withersteen, ma'am?" he inquired.

"Yes," she replied.

"The water here is yours?"

"Yes."

"May I water my horse?"

"Certainly. There's the trough."

"But mebbe if you knew who I was—" He hesitated, with his glance on the listening men. "Mebbe you wouldn't let me water him—though I ain't askin' none for myself."

"Stranger, it doesn't matter who you are. Water your horse. And if you are thirsty and hungry come into my house."

"Thanks, ma'am. I can't accept for myself—but for my tired horse—"

Trampling of hoofs interrupted the rider. More restless movements on the part of Tull's men broke up the little circle, exposing the prisoner Venters.

"Mebbe I've kind of hindered somethin'—for a few moments, perhaps?" inquired the rider.

"Yes," replied Jane Withersteen, with a throb in her voice.

She felt the drawing power of his eyes; and then she saw him look at the bound Venters, and at the men who held him, and their leader.

"In this here country all the rustlers an' thieves an' cut-throats an' gun-throwers an' all-round no-good men jest happen to be Gentiles. Ma'am, which of the no-good class does that young feller belong to?"

"He belongs to none of them. He's an honest boy."

"You KNOW that, ma'am?"

"Yes—yes."

"Then what has he done to get tied up that way?"

His clear and distinct question, meant for Tull as well as for Jane Withersteen, stilled the restlessness and brought a momentary silence.

"Ask him," replied Jane, her voice rising high.

The rider stepped away from her, moving out with the same slow, measured stride in which he had approached, and the fact that his action placed her wholly to one side, and him no nearer to Tull and his men, had a penetrating significance.

"Young feller, speak up," he said to Venters.

"Here stranger, this's none of your mix," began Tull. "Don't try any interference. You've been asked to drink and eat. That's more than you'd have got in any other village of the Utah border. Water your horse and be on your way."

"Easy—easy—I ain't interferin' yet," replied the rider. The tone of his voice had undergone a change. A different man had spoken. Where, in addressing Jane, he had been mild and gentle, now, with his first speech to Tull, he was dry, cool, biting. "I've lest stumbled

7

onto a queer deal. Seven Mormons all packin' guns, an' a Gentile tied with a rope, an' a woman who swears by his honesty! Queer, ain't that?"

"Queer or not, it's none of your business," retorted Tull.

"Where I was raised a woman's word was law. I ain't quite outgrowed that yet."

Tull fumed between amaze and anger.

"Meddler, we have a law here something different from woman's whim—Mormon law!... Take care you don't transgress it."

"To hell with your Mormon law!"

The deliberate speech marked the rider's further change, this time from kindly interest to an awakening menace. It produced a transformation in Tull and his companions. The leader gasped and staggered backward at a blasphemous affront to an institution he held most sacred. The man Jerry, holding the horses, dropped the bridles and froze in his tracks. Like posts the other men stood watchful-eyed, arms hanging rigid, all waiting.

"Speak up now, young man. What have you done to be roped that way?"

"It's a damned outrage!" burst out Venters. "I've done no wrong. I've offended this Mormon Elder by being a friend to that woman."

"Ma'am, is it true—what he says?" asked the rider of Jane, but his quiveringly alert eyes never left the little knot of quiet men.

"True? Yes, perfectly true," she answered.

"Well, young man, it seems to me that bein' a friend to such a woman would be what you wouldn't want to help an' couldn't help.... What's to be done to you for it?"

"They intend to whip me. You know what that means—in Utah!"

"I reckon," replied the rider, slowly.

With his gray glance cold on the Mormons, with the restive bit-champing of the horses, with Jane failing to repress her mounting agitations, with Venters standing pale and still, the tension of the moment tightened. Tull broke the spell with a laugh, a laugh without mirth, a laugh that was only a sound betraying fear.

"Come on, men!" he called.

Jane Withersteen turned again to the rider.

"Stranger, can you do nothing to save Venters?"

"Ma'am, you ask me to save him—from your own people?"

"Ask you? I beg of you!"

"But you don't dream who you're askin'."

"Oh, sir, I pray you—save him!"

"These are Mormons, an' I..."

"At—at any cost—save him. For I—I care for him!"

Tull snarled. "You love-sick fool! Tell your secrets. There'll be a way to teach you what you've never learned.... Come men out of here!"

"Mormon, the young man stays," said the rider.

Like a shot his voice halted Tull.

"What!"

"Who'll keep him? He's my prisoner!" cried Tull, hotly. "Stranger, again I tell you—don't mix here. You've meddled enough. Go your way now or—"

"Listen!... He stays."

Absolute certainty, beyond any shadow of doubt, breathed in the rider's low voice.

"Who are you? We are seven here."

The rider dropped his sombrero and made a rapid movement, singular in that it left him

8

somewhat crouched, arms bent and stiff, with the big black gun-sheaths swung round to the fore.

"LASSITER!"

It was Venters's wondering, thrilling cry that bridged the fateful connection between the rider's singular position and the dreaded name.

Tull put out a groping hand. The life of his eyes dulled to the gloom with which men of his fear saw the approach of death. But death, while it hovered over him, did not descend, for the rider waited for the twitching fingers, the downward flash of hand that did not come. Tull, gathering himself together, turned to the horses, attended by his pale comrades.

2

COTTONWOODS

Venters appeared too deeply moved to speak the gratitude his face expressed. And Jane turned upon the rescuer and gripped his hands. Her smiles and tears seemingly dazed him. Presently as something like calmness returned, she went to Lassiter's weary horse.

"I will water him myself," she said, and she led the horse to a trough under a huge old cottonwood. With nimble fingers she loosened the bridle and removed the bit. The horse snorted and bent his head. The trough was of solid stone, hollowed out, moss-covered and green and wet and cool, and the clear brown water that fed it spouted and splashed from a wooden pipe.

"He has brought you far to-day?"

"Yes, ma'am, a matter of over sixty miles, mebbe seventy."

"A long ride—a ride that—Ah, he is blind!"

"Yes, ma'am," replied Lassiter.

"What blinded him?"

"Some men once roped an' tied him, an' then held white-iron close to his eyes."

"Oh! Men? You mean devils.... Were they your enemies—Mormons?"

"Yes, ma'am."

"To take revenge on a horse! Lassiter, the men of my creed are unnaturally cruel. To my everlasting sorrow I confess it. They have been driven, hated, scourged till their hearts have hardened. But we women hope and pray for the time when our men will soften."

"Beggin' your pardon, ma'am—that time will never come."

"Oh, it will!... Lassiter, do you think Mormon women wicked? Has your hand been against them, too?"

"No. I believe Mormon women are the best and noblest, the most long-sufferin', and the blindest, unhappiest women on earth."

"Ah!" She gave him a grave, thoughtful look. "Then you will break bread with me?"

Lassiter had no ready response, and he uneasily shifted his weight from one leg to another, and turned his sombrero round and round in his hands. "Ma'am," he began, presently, "I reckon your kindness of heart makes you overlook things. Perhaps I ain't well

10

known hereabouts, but back up North there's Mormons who'd rest uneasy in their graves at the idea of me sittin' to table with you."

"I dare say. But—will you do it, anyway?" she asked.

"Mebbe you have a brother or relative who might drop in an' be offended, an' I wouldn't want to—"

"I've not a relative in Utah that I know of. There's no one with a right to question my actions." She turned smilingly to Venters. "You will come in, Bern, and Lassiter will come in. We'll eat and be merry while we may."

"I'm only wonderin' if Tull an' his men'll raise a storm down in the village," said Lassiter, in his last weakening stand.

"Yes, he'll raise the storm—after he has prayed," replied Jane. "Come."

She led the way, with the bridle of Lassiter's horse over her arm. They entered a grove and walked down a wide path shaded by great low-branching cottonwoods. The last rays of the setting sun sent golden bars through the leaves. The grass was deep and rich, welcome contrast to sage-tired eyes. Twittering quail darted across the path, and from a tree-top somewhere a robin sang its evening song, and on the still air floated the freshness and murmur of flowing water.

The home of Jane Withersteen stood in a circle of cottonwoods, and was a flat, long, red-stone structure with a covered court in the center through which flowed a lively stream of amber-colored water. In the massive blocks of stone and heavy timbers and solid doors and shutters showed the hand of a man who had builded against pillage and time; and in the flowers and mosses lining the stone-bedded stream, in the bright colors of rugs and blankets on the court floor, and the cozy corner with hammock and books and the clean-linened table, showed the grace of a daughter who lived for happiness and the day at hand.

Jane turned Lassiter's horse loose in the thick grass. "You will want him to be near you," she said, "or I'd have him taken to the alfalfa fields." At her call appeared women who began at once to bustle about, hurrying to and fro, setting the table. Then Jane, excusing herself, went within.

She passed through a huge low ceiled chamber, like the inside of a fort, and into a smaller one where a bright wood-fire blazed in an old open fireplace, and from this into her own room. It had the same comfort as was manifested in the home-like outer court; moreover, it was warm and rich in soft hues.

Seldom did Jane Withersteen enter her room without looking into her mirror. She knew she loved the reflection of that beauty which since early childhood she had never been allowed to forget. Her relatives and friends, and later a horde of Mormon and Gentile suitors, had fanned the flame of natural vanity in her. So that at twenty-eight she scarcely thought at all of her wonderful influence for good in the little community where her father had left her practically its beneficent landlord, but cared most for the dream and the assurance and the allurement of her beauty. This time, however, she gazed into her glass with more than the usual happy motive, without the usual slight conscious smile. For she was thinking of more than the desire to be fair in her own eyes, in those of her friend; she wondered if she were to seem fair in the eyes of this Lassiter, this man whose name had crossed the long, wild brakes of stone and plains of sage, this gentle-voiced, sad-faced man who was a hater and a killer of Mormons. It was not now her usual half-conscious vain obsession that actuated her as she hurriedly changed her riding-dress to one of white, and then looked long at the stately form with its gracious contours, at the fair face with its strong chin and full firm lips, at the dark-blue, proud, and passionate eyes.

"If by some means I can keep him here a few days, a week—he will never kill another

Mormon," she mused. "Lassiter!... I shudder when I think of that name, of him. But when I look at the man I forget who he is—I almost like him. I remember only that he saved Bern. He has suffered. I wonder what it was—did he love a Mormon woman once? How splendidly he championed us poor misunderstood souls! Somehow he knows—much."

Jane Withersteen joined her guests and bade them to her board. Dismissing her woman, she waited upon them with her own hands. It was a bountiful supper and a strange company. On her right sat the ragged and half-starved Venters; and though blind eyes could have seen what he counted for in the sum of her happiness, yet he looked the gloomy outcast his allegiance had made him, and about him there was the shadow of the ruin presaged by Tull. On her left sat black-leather-garbed Lassiter looking like a man in a dream. Hunger was not with him, nor composure, nor speech, and when he twisted in frequent unquiet movements the heavy guns that he had not removed knocked against the table-legs. If it had been otherwise possible to forget the presence of Lassiter those telling little jars would have rendered it unlikely. And Jane Withersteen talked and smiled and laughed with all the dazzling play of lips and eyes that a beautiful, daring woman could summon to her purpose.

When the meal ended, and the men pushed back their chairs, she leaned closer to Lassiter and looked square into his eyes.

"Why did you come to Cottonwoods?"

Her question seemed to break a spell. The rider arose as if he had just remembered himself and had tarried longer than his wont.

"Ma'am, I have hunted all over the southern Utah and Nevada for—somethin'. An' through your name I learned where to find it—here in Cottonwoods."

"My name! Oh, I remember. You did know my name when you spoke first. Well, tell me where you heard it and from whom?"

"At the little village—Glaze, I think it's called—some fifty miles or more west of here. An' I heard it from a Gentile, a rider who said you'd know where to tell me to find—"

"What?" she demanded, imperiously, as Lassiter broke off.

"Milly Erne's grave," he answered low, and the words came with a wrench.

Venters wheeled in his chair to regard Lassiter in amazement, and Jane slowly raised herself in white, still wonder.

"Milly Erne's grave?" she echoed, in a whisper. "What do you know of Milly Erne, my best-beloved friend—who died in my arms? What were you to her?"

"Did I claim to be anythin'?" he inquired. "I know people—relatives—who have long wanted to know where she's buried, that's all."

"Relatives? She never spoke of relatives, except a brother who was shot in Texas. Lassiter, Milly Erne's grave is in a secret burying-ground on my property."

"Will you take me there?... You'll be offendin' Mormons worse than by breakin' bread with me."

"Indeed yes, but I'll do it. Only we must go unseen. To-morrow, perhaps."

"Thank you, Jane Withersteen," replied the rider, and he bowed to her and stepped backward out of the court.

"Will you not stay—sleep under my roof?" she asked.

"No, ma'am, an' thanks again. I never sleep indoors. An' even if I did there's that gatherin' storm in the village below. No, no. I'll go to the sage. I hope you won't suffer none for your kindness to me."

"Lassiter," said Venters, with a half-bitter laugh, "my bed too, is the sage. Perhaps we may meet out there."

"Mebbe so. But the sage is wide an' I won't be near. Good night."

At Lassiter's low whistle the black horse whinnied, and carefully picked his blind way out of the grove. The rider did not bridle him, but walked beside him, leading him by touch of hand and together they passed slowly into the shade of the cottonwoods.

"Jane, I must be off soon," said Venters. "Give me my guns. If I'd had my guns—"

"Either my friend or the Elder of my church would be lying dead," she interposed.

"Tull would be—surely."

"Oh, you fierce-blooded, savage youth! Can't I teach you forebearance, mercy? Bern, it's divine to forgive your enemies. 'Let not the sun go down upon thy wrath.'"

"Hush! Talk to me no more of mercy or religion—after to-day. To-day this strange coming of Lassiter left me still a man, and now I'll die a man!... Give me my guns."

Silently she went into the house, to return with a heavy cartridge-belt and gun-filled sheath and a long rifle; these she handed to him, and as he buckled on the belt she stood before him in silent eloquence.

"Jane," he said, in gentler voice, "don't look so. I'm not going out to murder your churchman. I'll try to avoid him and all his men. But can't you see I've reached the end of my rope? Jane, you're a wonderful woman. Never was there a woman so unselfish and good. Only you're blind in one way.... Listen!"

From behind the grove came the clicking sound of horses in a rapid trot.

"Some of your riders," he continued. "It's getting time for the night shift. Let us go out to the bench in the grove and talk there."

It was still daylight in the open, but under the spreading cottonwoods shadows were obscuring the lanes. Venters drew Jane off from one of these into a shrub-lined trail, just wide enough for the two to walk abreast, and in a roundabout way led her far from the house to a knoll on the edge of the grove. Here in a secluded nook was a bench from which, through an opening in the tree-tops, could be seen the sage-slope and the wall of rock and the dim lines of canyons. Jane had not spoken since Venters had shocked her with his first harsh speech; but all the way she had clung to his arm, and now, as he stopped and laid his rifle against the bench, she still clung to him.

"Jane, I'm afraid I must leave you."

"Bern!" she cried.

"Yes, it looks that way. My position is not a happy one—I can't feel right—I've lost all—"

"I'll give you anything you—"

"Listen, please. When I say loss I don't mean what you think. I mean loss of good-will, good name—that which would have enabled me to stand up in this village without bitterness. Well, it's too late.... Now, as to the future, I think you'd do best to give me up. Tull is implacable. You ought to see from his intention to-day that—But you can't see. Your blindness—your damned religion!... Jane, forgive me—I'm sore within and something rankles. Well, I fear that invisible hand will turn its hidden work to your ruin."

"Invisible hand? Bern!"

"I mean your Bishop." Venters said it deliberately and would not release her as she started back. "He's the law. The edict went forth to ruin me. Well, look at me! It'll now go forth to compel you to the will of the Church."

"You wrong Bishop Dyer. Tull is hard, I know. But then he has been in love with me for years."

"Oh, your faith and your excuses! You can't see what I know—and if you did see it you'd not admit it to save your life. That's the Mormon of you. These elders and bishops will do absolutely any deed to go on building up the power and wealth of their church, their empire. Think of what they've done to the Gentiles here, to me—think of Milly Erne's fate!"

ZANE GREY

"What do you know of her story?"

"I know enough—all, perhaps, except the name of the Mormon who brought her here. But I must stop this kind of talk."

She pressed his hand in response. He helped her to a seat beside him on the bench. And he respected a silence that he divined was full of woman's deep emotion beyond his understanding.

It was the moment when the last ruddy rays of the sunset brightened momentarily before yielding to twilight. And for Venters the outlook before him was in some sense similar to a feeling of his future, and with searching eyes he studied the beautiful purple, barren waste of sage. Here was the unknown and the perilous. The whole scene impressed Venters as a wild, austere, and mighty manifestation of nature. And as it somehow reminded him of his prospect in life, so it suddenly resembled the woman near him, only in her there were greater beauty and peril, a mystery more unsolvable, and something nameless that numbed his heart and dimmed his eye.

"Look! A rider!" exclaimed Jane, breaking the silence. "Can that be Lassiter?"

Venters moved his glance once more to the west. A horseman showed dark on the sky-line, then merged into the color of the sage.

"It might be. But I think not—that fellow was coming in. One of your riders, more likely. Yes, I see him clearly now. And there's another."

"I see them, too."

"Jane, your riders seem as many as the bunches of sage. I ran into five yesterday 'way down near the trail to Deception Pass. They were with the white herd."

"You still go to that canyon? Bern, I wish you wouldn't. Oldring and his rustlers live somewhere down there."

"Well, what of that?"

"Tull has already hinted to your frequent trips into Deception Pass."

"I know." Venters uttered a short laugh. "He'll make a rustler of me next. But, Jane, there's no water for fifty miles after I leave here, and the nearest is in the canyon. I must drink and water my horse. There! I see more riders. They are going out."

"The red herd is on the slope, toward the Pass."

Twilight was fast falling. A group of horsemen crossed the dark line of low ground to become more distinct as they climbed the slope. The silence broke to a clear call from an incoming rider, and, almost like the peal of a hunting-horn, floated back the answer. The outgoing riders moved swiftly, came sharply into sight as they topped a ridge to show wild and black above the horizon, and then passed down, dimming into the purple of the sage.

"I hope they don't meet Lassiter," said Jane.

"So do I," replied Venters. "By this time the riders of the night shift know what happened to-day. But Lassiter will likely keep out of their way."

"Bern, who is Lassiter? He's only a name to me—a terrible name."

"Who is he? I don't know, Jane. Nobody I ever met knows him. He talks a little like a Texan, like Milly Erne. Did you note that?"

"Yes. How strange of him to know of her! And she lived here ten years and has been dead two. Bern, what do you know of Lassiter? Tell me what he has done—why you spoke of him to Tull—threatening to become another Lassiter yourself?"

"Jane, I only heard things, rumors, stories, most of which I disbelieved. At Glaze his name was known, but none of the riders or ranchers I knew there ever met him. At Stone Bridge I never heard him mentioned. But at Sterling and villages north of there he was spoken of often. I've never been in a village which he had been known to visit. There were many conflicting stories about him and his doings. Some said he had shot up this and that Mormon village, and others denied it. I'm inclined to believe he has, and you know how Mormons hide the truth. But there was one feature about Lassiter upon which all agree—that he was what riders in this country call a gun-man. He's a man with a marvelous quickness and accuracy in the use of a Colt. And now that I've seen him I know more. Lassiter was born without fear. I watched him with eyes which saw him my friend. I'll never forget the moment I recognized him from what had been told me of his crouch before the draw. It was then I yelled his name. I believe that yell saved Tull's life. At any rate, I know this, between Tull and death then there was not the breadth of the littlest hair. If he or any of his men had moved a finger downward—"

Venters left his meaning unspoken, but at the suggestion Jane shuddered.

The pale afterglow in the west darkened with the merging of twilight into night. The sage now spread out black and gloomy. One dim star glimmered in the southwest sky. The sound of trotting horses had ceased, and there was silence broken only by a faint, dry pattering of cottonwood leaves in the soft night wind.

Into this peace and calm suddenly broke the high-keyed yelp of a coyote, and from far off in the darkness came the faint answering note of a trailing mate.

"Hello! the sage-dogs are barking," said Venters.

"I don't like to hear them," replied Jane. "At night, sometimes when I lie awake, listening to the long mourn or breaking bark or wild howl, I think of you asleep somewhere in the sage, and my heart aches."

"Jane, you couldn't listen to sweeter music, nor could I have a better bed."

"Just think! Men like Lassiter and you have no home, no comfort, no rest, no place to lay your weary heads. Well!... Let us be patient. Tull's anger may cool, and time may help us. You might do some service to the village—who can tell? Suppose you discovered the long-unknown hiding-place of Oldring and his band, and told it to my riders? That would disarm Tull's ugly hints and put you in favor. For years my riders have trailed the tracks of stolen cattle. You know as well as I how dearly we've paid for our ranges in this wild country. Oldring drives our cattle down into the network of deceiving canyons, and somewhere far to the north or east he drives them up and out to Utah markets. If you will spend time in Deception Pass try to find the trails."

"Jane, I've thought of that. I'll try."

"I must go now. And it hurts, for now I'll never be sure of seeing you again. But to-morrow, Bern?"

"To-morrow surely. I'll watch for Lassiter and ride in with him."

"Good night."

Then she left him and moved away, a white, gliding shape that soon vanished in the shadows.

Venters waited until the faint slam of a door assured him she had reached the house, and then, taking up his rifle, he noiselessly slipped through the bushes, down the knoll, and on under the dark trees to the edge of the grove. The sky was now turning from gray to blue; stars had begun to lighten the earlier blackness; and from the wide flat sweep before him blew a cool wind, fragrant with the breath of sage. Keeping close to the edge of the cottonwoods, he went swiftly and silently westward. The grove was long, and he had not reached the end when he heard something that brought him to a halt. Low padded thuds told him horses were coming this way. He sank down in the gloom, waiting, listening. Much before he had expected, judging from sound, to his amazement he descried horsemen near at hand. They were riding along the border of the sage, and instantly he knew the hoofs of the horses were muffled. Then the pale starlight afforded him indistinct sight of the riders. But his eyes were keen and used to the dark, and by peering closely he recognized the huge bulk and black-bearded visage of Oldring and the lithe, supple form of the rustler's lieutenant, a masked rider. They passed on; the darkness swallowed them. Then, farther out on the sage, a dark, compact body of horsemen went by, almost without sound, almost like specters, and they, too, melted into the night.

3

AMBER SPRING

No UNUSUAL CIRCUMSTANCES was it for Oldring and some of his men to visit Cottonwoods in the broad light of day, but for him to prowl about in the dark with the hoofs of his horses muffled meant that mischief was brewing. Moreover, to Venters the presence of the masked rider with Oldring seemed especially ominous. For about this man there was mystery, he seldom rode through the village, and when he did ride through it was swiftly; riders seldom met by day on the sage, but wherever he rode there always followed deeds as dark and mysterious as the mask he wore. Oldring's band did not confine themselves to the rustling of cattle.

Venters lay low in the shade of the cottonwoods, pondering this chance meeting, and not for many moments did he consider it safe to move on. Then, with sudden impulse, he turned the other way and went back along the grove. When he reached the path leading to Jane's home he decided to go down to the village. So he hurried onward, with quick soft steps. Once beyond the grove he entered the one and only street. It was wide, lined with tall poplars, and under each row of trees, inside the foot-path, were ditches where ran the water from Jane Withersteen's spring.

Between the trees twinkled lights of cottage candles, and far down flared bright windows of the village stores. When Venters got closer to these he saw knots of men standing together in earnest conversation. The usual lounging on the corners and benches and steps was not in evidence. Keeping in the shadow Venters went closer and closer until he could hear voices. But he could not distinguish what was said. He recognized many Mormons, and looked hard for Tull and his men, but looked in vain. Venters concluded that the rustlers had not passed along the village street. No doubt these earnest men were discussing Lassiter's coming. But Venters felt positive that Tull's intention toward himself that day had not been and would not be revealed.

So Venters, seeing there was little for him to learn, began retracing his steps. The church was dark, Bishop Dyer's home next to it was also dark, and likewise Tull's cottage. Upon almost any night at this hour there would be lights here, and Venters marked the unusual omission.

As he was about to pass out of the street to skirt the grove, he once more slunk down at the sound of trotting horses. Presently he descried two mounted men riding toward him. He hugged the shadow of a tree. Again the starlight, brighter now, aided him, and he made out Tull's stalwart figure, and beside him the short, froglike shape of the rider Jerry. They were silent, and they rode on to disappear.

Venters went his way with busy, gloomy mind, revolving events of the day, trying to reckon those brooding in the night. His thoughts overwhelmed him. Up in that dark grove dwelt a woman who had been his friend. And he skulked about her home, gripping a gun stealthily as an Indian, a man without place or people or purpose. Above her hovered the shadow of grim, hidden, secret power. No queen could have given more royally out of a bounteous store than Jane Withersteen gave her people, and likewise to those unfortunates whom her people hated. She asked only the divine right of all women—freedom; to love and to live as her heart willed. And yet prayer and her hope were vain.

"For years I've seen a storm clouding over her and the village of Cottonwoods," muttered Venters, as he strode on. "Soon it'll burst. I don't like the prospects." That night the villagers whispered in the street—and night-riding rustlers muffled horses—and Tull was at work in secret—and out there in the sage hid a man who meant something terrible—Lassiter!

Venters passed the black cottonwoods, and, entering the sage, climbed the gradual slope. He kept his direction in line with a western star. From time to time he stopped to listen and heard only the usual familiar bark of coyote and sweep of wind and rustle of sage. Presently a low jumble of rocks loomed up darkly somewhat to his right, and, turning that way, he whistled softly. Out of the rocks glided a dog that leaped and whined about him. He climbed over rough, broken rock, picking his way carefully, and then went down. Here it was darker, and sheltered from the wind. A white object guided him. It was another dog, and this one was asleep, curled up between a saddle and a pack. The animal awoke and thumped his tail in greeting. Venters placed the saddle for a pillow, rolled in his blankets, with his face upward to the stars. The white dog snuggled close to him. The other whined and pattered a few yards to the rise of ground and there crouched on guard. And in that wild covert Venters shut his eyes under the great white stars and intense vaulted blue, bitterly comparing their loneliness to his own, and fell asleep.

When he awoke, day had dawned and all about him was bright steel-gray. The air had a cold tang. Arising, he greeted the fawning dogs and stretched his cramped body, and then, gathering together bunches of dead sage sticks, he lighted a fire. Strips of dried beef held to the blaze for a moment served him and the dogs. He drank from a canteen. There was nothing else in his outfit; he had grown used to a scant fire. Then he sat over the fire, palms outspread, and waited. Waiting had been his chief occupation for months, and he scarcely knew what he waited for unless it was the passing of the hours. But now he sensed action in the immediate present; the day promised another meeting with Lassiter and Jane, perhaps news of the rustlers; on the morrow he meant to take the trail to Deception Pass.

And while he waited he talked to his dogs. He called them Ring and Whitie; they were sheep-dogs, half collie, half deerhound, superb in build, perfectly trained. It seemed that in his fallen fortunes these dogs understood the nature of their value to him, and governed their affection and faithfulness accordingly. Whitie watched him with somber eyes of love, and Ring, crouched on the little rise of ground above, kept tireless guard. When the sun rose, the white dog took the place of the other, and Ring went to sleep at his master's feet.

By and by Venters rolled up his blankets and tied them and his meager pack together, then climbed out to look for his horse. He saw him, presently, a little way off in the sage, and went to fetch him. In that country, where every rider boasted of a fine mount and was eager for a race, where thoroughbreds dotted the wonderful grazing ranges, Venters rode a horse that was sad proof of his misfortunes.

Then, with his back against a stone, Venters faced the east, and, stick in hand and idle blade, he waited. The glorious sunlight filled the valley with purple fire. Before him, to left, to right, waving, rolling, sinking, rising, like low swells of a purple sea, stretched the sage. Out of the grove of cottonwoods, a green patch on the purple, gleamed the dull red of Jane Withersteen's old stone house. And from there extended the wide green of the village gardens and orchards marked by the graceful poplars; and farther down shone the deep, dark richness of the alfalfa fields. Numberless red and black and white dots speckled the sage, and these were cattle and horses.

So, watching and waiting, Venters let the time wear away. At length he saw a horse rise above a ridge, and he knew it to be Lassiter's black. Climbing to the highest rock, so that he would show against the sky-line, he stood and waved his hat. The almost instant turning of Lassiter's horse attested to the quickness of that rider's eye. Then Venters climbed down, saddled his horse, tied on his pack, and, with a word to his dogs, was about to ride out to meet Lassiter, when he concluded to wait for him there, on higher ground, where the outlook was commanding.

It had been long since Venters had experienced friendly greeting from a man. Lassiter's warmed in him something that had grown cold from neglect. And when he had returned it, with a strong grip of the iron hand that held his, and met the gray eyes, he knew that Lassiter and he were to be friends.

"Venters, let's talk awhile before we go down there," said Lassiter, slipping his bridle. "I ain't in no hurry. Them's sure fine dogs you've got." With a rider's eye he took in the points of Venter's horse, but did not speak his thought. "Well, did anythin' come off after I left you last night?"

Venters told him about the rustlers.

"I was snug hid in the sage," replied Lassiter, "an' didn't see or hear no one. Oldrin's got a high hand here, I reckon. It's no news up in Utah how he holes in canyons an' leaves no track." Lassiter was silent a moment. "Me an' Oldrin' wasn't exactly strangers some years back when he drove cattle into Bostil's Ford, at the head of the Rio Virgin. But he got harassed there an' now he drives some place else."

"Lassiter, you knew him? Tell me, is he Mormon or Gentile?"

"I can't say. I've knowed Mormons who pretended to be Gentiles."

"No Mormon ever pretended that unless he was a rustler," declared Venters.

"Mebbe so."

"It's a hard country for any one, but hardest for Gentiles. Did you ever know or hear of a Gentile prospering in a Mormon community?"

"I never did."

"Well, I want to get out of Utah. I've a mother living in Illinois. I want to go home. It's eight years now."

The older man's sympathy moved Venters to tell his story. He had left Quincy, run off to seek his fortune in the gold fields had never gotten any farther than Salt Lake City, wandered here and there as helper, teamster, shepherd, and drifted southward over the divide and across the barrens and up the rugged plateau through the passes to the last border settlements. Here he became a rider of the sage, had stock of his own, and for a time prospered, until chance threw him in the employ of Jane Withersteen.

"Lassiter, I needn't tell you the rest."

"Well, it'd be no news to me. I know Mormons. I've seen their women's strange love en' patience en' sacrifice an' silence en' whet I call madness for their idea of God. An' over against that I've seen the tricks of men. They work hand in hand, all together, an' in the dark. No man can hold out against them, unless he takes to packin' guns. For Mormons are slow to kill. That's the only good I ever seen in their religion. Venters, take this from me, these Mormons ain't just right in their minds. Else could a Mormon marry one woman when he already has a wife, an' call it duty?"

"Lassiter, you think as I think," returned Venters.

"How'd it come then that you never throwed a gun on Tull or some of them?" inquired the rider, curiously.

"Jane pleaded with me, begged me to be patient, to overlook. She even took my guns from me. I lost all before I knew it," replied Venters, with the red color in his face. "But, Lassiter, listen. Out of the wreck I saved a Winchester, two Colts, and plenty of shells. I packed these down into Deception Pass. There, almost every day for six months, I have practiced with my rifle till the barrel burnt my hands. Practised the draw—the firing of a Colt, hour after hour!"

"Now that's interestin' to me," said Lassiter, with a quick uplift of his head and a concentration of his gray gaze on Venters. "Could you throw a gun before you began that practisin'?"

"Yes. And now..." Venters made a lightning-swift movement.

Lassiter smiled, and then his bronzed eyelids narrowed till his eyes seemed mere gray slits. "You'll kill Tull!" He did not question; he affirmed.

"I promised Jane Withersteen I'd try to avoid Tull. I'll keep my word. But sooner or later Tull and I will meet. As I feel now, if he even looks at me I'll draw!"

"I reckon so. There'll be hell down there, presently." He paused a moment and flicked a sage-brush with his quirt. "Venters, seein' as you're considerable worked up, tell me Milly Erne's story."

Venters's agitation stilled to the trace of suppressed eagerness in Lassiter's query.

"Milly Erne's story? Well, Lassiter, I'll tell you what I know. Milly Erne had been in Cottonwoods years when I first arrived there, and most of what I tell you happened before my arrival. I got to know her pretty well. She was a slip of a woman, and crazy on religion. I conceived an idea that I never mentioned—I thought she was at heart more Gentile than Mormon. But she passed as a Mormon, and certainly she had the Mormon woman's locked lips. You know, in every Mormon village there are women who seem mysterious to us, but about Milly there was more than the ordinary mystery. When she came to Cottonwoods she had a beautiful little girl whom she loved passionately. Milly was not known openly in Cottonwoods as a Mormon wife. That she really was a Mormon wife I have no doubt. Perhaps the Mormon's other wife or wives would not acknowledge Milly. Such things happen in these villages. Mormon wives wear yokes, but they get jealous. Well, whatever had brought Milly to this country—love or madness of religion—she repented of it. She gave up teaching the village school. She quit the church. And she began to fight Mormon upbringing for her baby girl. Then the Mormons put on the screws—slowly, as is their way. At last the child disappeared. 'Lost' was the report. The child was stolen, I know that. So do you. That wrecked Milly Erne. But she lived on in hope. She became a slave. She worked her heart and soul and life out to get back her child. She never heard of it again. Then she sank.... I can see her now, a frail thing, so transparent you could almost look through her—white like ashes—and her eyes!... Her eyes have always haunted me. She had one real friend—Jane Withersteen. But Jane couldn't mend a broken heart, and Milly died."

For moments Lassiter did not speak, or turn his head.

"The man!" he exclaimed, presently, in husky accents.

"I haven't the slightest idea who the Mormon was," replied Venters; "nor has any Gentile in Cottonwoods."

"Does Jane Withersteen know?"

"Yes. But a red-hot running-iron couldn't burn that name out of her!"

Without further speech Lassiter started off, walking his horse and Venters followed with his dogs. Half a mile down the slope they entered a luxuriant growth of willows, and soon came into an open space carpeted with grass like deep green velvet. The rushing of water and singing of birds filled their ears. Venters led his comrade to a shady bower and showed him Amber Spring. It was a magnificent outburst of clear, amber water pouring from a dark, stone-lined hole. Lassiter knelt and drank, lingered there to drink again. He made no comment, but Venters did not need words. Next to his horse a rider of the sage loved a spring. And this spring was the most beautiful and remarkable known to the upland riders of southern Utah. It was the spring that made old Withersteen a feudal lord and now enabled his daughter to return the toll which her father had exacted from the toilers of the sage.

The spring gushed forth in a swirling torrent, and leaped down joyously to make its swift way along a willow-skirted channel. Moss and ferns and lilies overhung its green banks. Except for the rough-hewn stones that held and directed the water, this willow thicket and glade had been left as nature had made it.

Below were artificial lakes, three in number, one above the other in banks of raised earth, and round about them rose the lofty green-foliaged shafts of poplar trees. Ducks dotted the glassy surface of the lakes; a blue heron stood motionless on a water-gate; kingfishers darted with shrieking flight along the shady banks; a white hawk sailed above; and from the trees and shrubs came the song of robins and cat-birds. It was all in strange contrast to the endless slopes of lonely sage and the wild rock environs beyond. Venters thought of the woman who loved the birds and the green of the leaves and the murmur of the water.

Next on the slope, just below the third and largest lake, were corrals and a wide stone barn and open sheds and coops and pens. Here were clouds of dust, and cracking sounds of hoofs, and romping colts and heehawing burros. Neighing horses trampled to the corral fences. And on the little windows of the barn projected bobbing heads of bays and blacks and sorrels. When the two men entered the immense barnyard, from all around the din increased. This welcome, however, was not seconded by the several men and boys who vanished on sight.

Venters and Lassiter were turning toward the house when Jane appeared in the lane leading a horse. In riding-skirt and blouse she seemed to have lost some of her statuesque proportions, and looked more like a girl rider than the mistress of Withersteen. She was brightly smiling, and her greeting was warmly cordial.

"Good news," she announced. "I've been to the village. All is quiet. I expected—I don't know what. But there's no excitement. And Tull has ridden out on his way to Glaze."

"Tull gone?" inquired Venters, with surprise. He was wondering what could have taken Tull away. Was it to avoid another meeting with Lassiter that he went? Could it have any connection with the probable nearness of Oldring and his gang?

"Gone, yes, thank goodness," replied Jane. "Now I'll have peace for a while. Lassiter, I want you to see my horses. You are a rider, and you must be a judge of horseflesh. Some of mine have Arabian blood. My father got his best strain in Nevada from Indians who claimed their horses were bred down from the original stock left by the Spaniards."

"Well, ma'am, the one you've been ridin' takes my eye," said Lassiter, as he walked round the racy, clean-limbed, and fine-pointed roan.

"Where are the boys?" she asked, looking about. "Jerd, Paul, where are you? Here, bring out the horses."

The sound of dropping bars inside the barn was the signal for the horses to jerk their heads in the windows, to snort and stamp. Then they came pounding out of the door, a file of thoroughbreds, to plunge about the barnyard, heads and tails up, manes flying. They halted afar off, squared away to look, came slowly forward with whinnies for their mistress, and doubtful snorts for the strangers and their horses.

"Come—come—come," called Jane, holding out her hands. "Why, Bells—Wrangle, where are your manners? Come, Black Star—come, Night. Ah, you beauties! My racers of the sage!"

Only two came up to her; those she called Night and Black Star. Venters never looked at them without delight. The first was soft dead black, the other glittering black, and they were perfectly matched in size, both being high and long-bodied, wide through the shoulders, with lithe, powerful legs. That they were a woman's pets showed in the gloss of skin, the fineness of mane. It showed, too, in the light of big eyes and the gentle reach of eagerness.

"I never seen their like," was Lassiter's encomium, "an' in my day I've seen a sight of horses. Now, ma'am, if you was wantin' to make a long an' fast ride across the sage—say to elope—"

Lassiter ended there with dry humor, yet behind that was meaning. Jane blushed and made arch eyes at him.

"Take care, Lassiter, I might think that a proposal," she replied, gaily. "It's dangerous to propose elopement to a Mormon woman. Well, I was expecting you. Now will be a good hour to show you Milly Erne's grave. The day-riders have gone, and the night-riders haven't come in. Bern, what do you make of that? Need I worry? You know I have to be made to worry."

"Well, it's not usual for the night shift to ride in so late," replied Venters, slowly, and his glance sought Lassiter's. "Cattle are usually quiet after dark. Still, I've known even a coyote to stampede your white herd."

"I refuse to borrow trouble. Come," said Jane.

They mounted, and, with Jane in the lead, rode down the lane, and, turning off into a cattle trail, proceeded westward. Venters's dogs trotted behind them. On this side of the ranch the outlook was different from that on the other; the immediate foreground was rough and the sage more rugged and less colorful; there were no dark-blue lines of canyons to hold the eye, nor any uprearing rock walls. It was a long roll and slope into gray obscurity. Soon Jane left the trail and rode into the sage, and presently she dismounted and threw her bridle. The men did likewise. Then, on foot, they followed her, coming out at length on the rim of a low escarpment. She passed by several little ridges of earth to halt before a faintly defined mound. It lay in the shade of a sweeping sage-brush close to the edge of the promontory; and a rider could have jumped his horse over it without recognizing a grave.

"Here!"

She looked sad as she spoke, but she offered no explanation for the neglect of an unmarked, uncared-for grave. There was a little bunch of pale, sweet lavender daisies, doubtless planted there by Jane.

"I only come here to remember and to pray," she said. "But I leave no trail!"

A grave in the sage! How lonely this resting-place of Milly Erne! The cottonwoods or the alfalfa fields were not in sight, nor was there any rock or ridge or cedar to lend contrast to the monotony. Gray slopes, tinging the purple, barren and wild, with the wind waving the sage, swept away to the dim horizon.

Lassiter looked at the grave and then out into space. At that moment he seemed a figure of bronze.

Jane touched Venters's arm and led him back to the horses.

"Bern!" cried Jane, when they were out of hearing. "Suppose Lassiter were Milly's husband—the father of that little girl lost so long ago!"

"It might be, Jane. Let us ride on. If he wants to see us again he'll come."

So they mounted and rode out to the cattle trail and began to climb. From the height of the ridge, where they had started down, Venters looked back. He did not see Lassiter, but his glance, drawn irresistibly farther out on the gradual slope, caught sight of a moving cloud of dust.

"Hello, a rider!"

"Yes, I see," said Jane.

"That fellow's riding hard. Jane, there's something wrong."

"Oh yes, there must be.... How he rides!"

The horse disappeared in the sage, and then puffs of dust marked his course.

"He's short-cut on us—he's making straight for the corrals."

Venters and Jane galloped their steeds and reined in at the turning of the lane. This lane led down to the right of the grove. Suddenly into its lower entrance flashed a bay horse. Then Venters caught the fast rhythmic beat of pounding hoofs. Soon his keen eye recognized the swing of the rider in his saddle.

"It's Judkins, your Gentile rider!" he cried. "Jane, when Judkins rides like that it means hell!"

4

DECEPTION PASS

THE RIDER THUNDERED up and almost threw his foam-flecked horse in the sudden stop. He was a giant form, and with fearless eyes.

"Judkins, you're all bloody!" cried Jane, in affright. "Oh, you've been shot!"

"Nothin' much Miss Withersteen. I got a nick in the shoulder. I'm some wet an' the hoss's been throwin' lather, so all this ain't blood."

"What's up?" queried Venters, sharply.

"Rustlers sloped off with the red herd."

"Where are my riders?" demanded Jane.

"Miss Withersteen, I was alone all night with the herd. At daylight this mornin' the rustlers rode down. They began to shoot at me on sight. They chased me hard an' far, burnin' powder all the time, but I got away."

"Jud, they meant to kill you," declared Venters.

"Now I wonder," returned Judkins. "They wanted me bad. An' it ain't regular for rustlers to waste time chasin' one rider."

"Thank heaven you got away," said Jane. "But my riders—where are they?"

"I don't know. The night-riders weren't there last night when I rode down, en' this mornin' I met no day-riders."

"Judkins! Bern, they've been set upon—killed by Oldring's men!"

"I don't think so," replied Venters, decidedly. "Jane, your riders haven't gone out in the sage."

"Bern, what do you mean?" Jane Withersteen turned deathly pale.

"You remember what I said about the unseen hand?"

"Oh!... Impossible!"

"I hope so. But I fear—" Venters finished, with a shake of his head.

"Bern, you're bitter; but that's only natural. We'll wait to see what's happened to my riders. Judkins, come to the house with me. Your wound must be attended to."

"Jane, I'll find out where Oldring drives the herd," vowed Venters.

"No, no! Bern, don't risk it now—when the rustlers are in such shooting mood."

"I'm going. Jud, how many cattle in that red herd?"

"Twenty-five hundred head."

"Whew! What on earth can Oldring do with so many cattle? Why, a hundred head is a big steal. I've got to find out."

"Don't go," implored Jane.

"Bern, you want a hoss thet can run. Miss Withersteen, if it's not too bold of me to advise, make him take a fast hoss or don't let him go."

"Yes, yes, Judkins. He must ride a horse that can't be caught. Which one—Black Star —Night?"

"Jane, I won't take either," said Venters, emphatically. "I wouldn't risk losing one of your favorites."

"Wrangle, then?"

"Thet's the hoss," replied Judkins. "Wrangle can outrun Black Star an' Night. You'd never believe it, Miss Withersteen, but I know. Wrangle's the biggest en' fastest hoss on the sage."

"Oh no, Wrangle can't beat Black Star. But, Bern, take Wrangle if you will go. Ask Jerd for anything you need. Oh, be watchful, careful.... God speed you."

She clasped his hand, turned quickly away, and went down a lane with the rider.

Venters rode to the barn, and, leaping off, shouted for Jerd. The boy came running. Venters sent him for meat, bread, and dried fruits, to be packed in saddlebags. His own horse he turned loose into the nearest corral. Then he went for Wrangle. The giant sorrel had earned his name for a trait the opposite of amiability. He came readily out of the barn, but once in the yard he broke from Venters, and plunged about with ears laid back. Venters had to rope him, and then he kicked down a section of fence, stood on his hind legs, crashed down and fought the rope. Jerd returned to lend a hand.

"Wrangle don't git enough work," said Jerd, as the big saddle went on. "He's unruly when he's corralled, an' wants to run. Wait till he smells the sage!"

"Jerd, this horse is an iron-jawed devil. I never straddled him but once. Run? Say, he's swift as wind!"

When Venters's boot touched the stirrup the sorrel bolted, giving him the rider's flying mount. The swing of this fiery horse recalled to Venters days that were not really long past, when he rode into the sage as the leader of Jane Withersteen's riders. Wrangle pulled hard on a tight rein. He galloped out of the lane, down the shady border of the grove, and hauled up at the watering-trough, where he pranced and champed his bit. Venters got off and filled his canteen while the horse drank. The dogs, Ring and Whitie, came trotting up for their drink. Then Venters remounted and turned Wrangle toward the sage.

A wide, white trail wound away down the slope. One keen, sweeping glance told Venters that there was neither man nor horse nor steer within the limit of his vision, unless they were lying down in the sage. Ring loped in the lead and Whitie loped in the rear. Wrangle settled gradually into an easy swinging canter, and Venters's thoughts, now that the rush and flurry of the start were past, and the long miles stretched before him, reverted to a calm reckoning of late singular coincidences.

There was the night ride of Tull's, which, viewed in the light of subsequent events, had a look of his covert machinations; Oldring and his Masked Rider and his rustlers riding muffled horses; the report that Tull had ridden out that morning with his man Jerry on the trail to Glaze, the strange disappearance of Jane Withersteen's riders, the unusually determined attempt to kill the one Gentile still in her employ, an intention frustrated, no doubt, only by Judkin's magnificent riding of her racer, and lastly the driving of the red herd. These events, to Venters's color of mind, had a dark relationship. Remembering Jane's accusation of bitterness, he tried hard to put aside his rancor in judging Tull. But it was bitter knowledge that made him see the truth. He had felt the shadow of an unseen hand; he had watched till he saw its dim outline, and then he had traced it to a man's hate, to the rivalry of a Mormon Elder, to the power of a Bishop, to the long, far-reaching arm of a terrible creed. That unseen hand had made its first move against Jane Withersteen. Her riders had been called in, leaving her without help to drive seven thousand head of cattle. But to Venters it seemed extraordinary that the power which had called in these riders had left so many cattle to be driven by rustlers and harried by wolves. For hand in glove with that power was an insatiate greed; they were one and the same.

"What can Oldring do with twenty-five hundred head of cattle?" muttered Venters. "Is he a Mormon? Did he meet Tull last night? It looks like a black plot to me. But Tull and his churchmen wouldn't ruin Jane Withersteen unless the Church was to profit by that ruin. Where does Oldring come in? I'm going to find out about these things."

Wrangle did the twenty-five miles in three hours and walked little of the way. When he had gotten warmed up he had been allowed to choose his own gait. The afternoon had well advanced when Venters struck the trail of the red herd and found where it had grazed the night before. Then Venters rested the horse and used his eyes. Near at hand were a cow and a calf and several yearlings, and farther out in the sage some straggling steers. He caught a glimpse of coyotes skulking near the cattle. The slow sweeping gaze of the rider failed to find other living things within the field of sight. The sage about him was breast-high to his horse, oversweet with its warm, fragrant breath, gray where it waved to the light, darker where the wind left it still, and beyond the wonderful haze-purple lent by distance. Far across that wide waste began the slow lift of uplands through which Deception Pass cut its tortuous many-canyoned way.

Venters raised the bridle of his horse and followed the broad cattle trail. The crushed sage resembled the path of a monster snake. In a few miles of travel he passed several cows and calves that had escaped the drive. Then he stood on the last high bench of the slope with the floor of the valley beneath. The opening of the canyon showed in a break of the sage, and the cattle trail paralleled it as far as he could see. That trail led to an undiscovered point where Oldring drove cattle into the pass, and many a rider who had followed it had never returned. Venters satisfied himself that the rustlers had not deviated from their usual course, and then he turned at right angles off the cattle trail and made for the head of the pass.

The sun lost its heat and wore down to the western horizon, where it changed from white to gold and rested like a huge ball about to roll on its golden shadows down the slope. Venters watched the lengthening of the rays and bars, and marveled at his own league-long shadow. The sun sank. There was instant shading of brightness about him, and he saw a kind of cold purple bloom creep ahead of him to cross the canyon, to mount the opposite slope and chase and darken and bury the last golden flare of sunlight.

Venters rode into a trail that he always took to get down into the canyon. He dismounted and found no tracks but his own made days previous. Nevertheless he sent the dog Ring ahead and waited. In a little while Ring returned. Whereupon Venters led his horse on to the break in the ground.

The opening into Deception Pass was one of the remarkable natural phenomena in a country remarkable for vast slopes of sage, uplands insulated by gigantic red walls, and deep canyons of mysterious source and outlet. Here the valley floor was level, and here opened a narrow chasm, a ragged vent in yellow walls of stone. The trail down the five hundred feet of sheer depth always tested Venters's nerve. It was bad going for even a burro. But Wrangle, as Venters led him, snorted defiance or disgust rather than fear, and, like a hobbled horse on the jump, lifted his ponderous iron-shod fore hoofs and crashed down over the first rough step. Venters warmed to greater admiration of the sorrel; and, giving him a loose bridle, he stepped down foot by foot. Oftentimes the stones and shale started by Wrangle buried Venters to his knees; again he was hard put to it to dodge a rolling boulder, there were times when he could not see Wrangle for dust, and once he and the horse rode a sliding shelf of yellow, weathered cliff. It was a trail on which there could be no stops, and, therefore, if perilous, it was at least one that did not take long in the descent.

Venters breathed lighter when that was over, and felt a sudden assurance in the success of his enterprise. For at first it had been a reckless determination to achieve something at any cost, and now it resolved itself into an adventure worthy of all his reason and cunning, and keenness of eye and ear.

Pinyon pines clustered in little clumps along the level floor of the pass. Twilight had gathered under the walls. Venters rode into the trail and up the canyon. Gradually the trees and caves and objects low down turned black, and this blackness moved up the walls till night enfolded the pass, while day still lingered above. The sky darkened; and stars began to show, at first pale and then bright. Sharp notches of the rim-wall, biting like teeth into the blue, were landmarks by which Venters knew where his camping site lay. He had to feel his way through a thicket of slender oaks to a spring where he watered Wrangle and drank himself. Here he unsaddled and turned Wrangle loose, having no fear that the horse would leave the thick, cool grass adjacent to the spring. Next he satisfied his own hunger, fed Ring and Whitie and, with them curled beside him, composed himself to await sleep.

There had been a time when night in the high altitude of these Utah uplands had been satisfying to Venters. But that was before the oppression of enemies had made the change in his mind. As a rider guarding the herd he had never thought of the night's wildness and loneliness; as an outcast, now when the full silence set in, and the deep darkness, and trains of radiant stars shone cold and calm, he lay with an ache in his heart. For a year he had lived as a black fox, driven from his kind. He longed for the sound of a voice, the touch of a hand. In the daytime there was riding from place to place, and the gun practice to which something drove him, and other tasks that at least necessitated action, at night, before he won sleep, there was strife in his soul. He yearned to leave the endless sage slopes, the wilderness of canyons, and it was in the lonely night that this yearning grew unbearable. It was then that he reached forth to feel Ring or Whitie, immeasurably grateful for the love and companionship of two dogs.

On this night the same old loneliness beset Venters, the old habit of sad thought and burning unquiet had its way. But from it evolved a conviction that his useless life had undergone a subtle change. He had sensed it first when Wrangle swung him up to the high saddle, he knew it now when he lay in the gateway of Deception Pass. He had no thrill of adventure, rather a gloomy perception of great hazard, perhaps death. He meant to find Oldring's retreat. The rustlers had fast horses, but none that could catch Wrangle. Venters knew no rustler could creep upon him at night when Ring and Whitie guarded his hiding-place. For the rest, he had eyes and ears, and a long rifle and an unerring aim, which he meant to use. Strangely his foreshadowing of change did not hold a thought of the killing of Tull. It related only to what was to happen to him in Deception Pass; and he could no more lift the veil of that mystery than tell where the trails led to in that unexplored canyon. Moreover, he did not care. And at length, tired out by stress of thought, he fell asleep.

When his eyes unclosed, day had come again, and he saw the rim of the opposite wall tipped with the gold of sunrise. A few moments sufficed for the morning's simple camp duties. Near at hand he found Wrangle, and to his surprise the horse came to him. Wrangle was one of the horses that left his viciousness in the home corral. What he wanted was to be free of mules and burros and steers, to roll in dust-patches, and then to run down the wide, open, windy sage-plains, and at night browse and sleep in the cool wet grass of a springhole. Jerd knew the sorrel when he said of him, "Wait till he smells the sage!"

Venters saddled and led him out of the oak thicket, and, leaping astride, rode up the canyon, with Ring and Whitie trotting behind. An old grass-grown trail followed the course of a shallow wash where flowed a thin stream of water. The canyon was a hundred rods wide, its yellow walls were perpendicular; it had abundant sage and a scant growth of oak and pinon. For five miles it held to a comparatively straight bearing, and then began a heightening of rugged walls and a deepening of the floor. Beyond this point of sudden change in the character of the canyon Venters had never explored, and here was the real door to the intricacies of Deception Pass.

He reined Wrangle to a walk, halted now and then to listen, and then proceeded cautiously with shifting and alert gaze. The canyon assumed proportions that dwarfed those of its first ten miles. Venters rode on and on, not losing in the interest of his wide surroundings any of his caution or keen search for tracks or sight of living thing. If there ever had been a trail here, he could not find it. He rode through sage and clumps of pinon trees and grassy plots where long-petaled purple lilies bloomed. He rode through a dark constriction of the pass no wider than the lane in the grove at Cottonwoods. And he came out into a great amphitheater into which jutted huge towering corners of a confluence of intersecting canyons.

Venters sat his horse, and, with a rider's eye, studied this wild cross-cut of huge stone gullies. Then he went on, guided by the course of running water. If it had not been for the main stream of water flowing north he would never have been able to tell which of those many openings was a continuation of the pass. In crossing this amphitheater he went by the mouths of five canyons, fording little streams that flowed into the larger one. Gaining the outlet which he took to be the pass, he rode on again under over hanging walls. One side was dark in shade, the other light in sun. This narrow passageway turned and twisted and opened into a valley that amazed Venters.

Here again was a sweep of purple sage, richer than upon the higher levels. The valley was miles long, several wide, and inclosed by unscalable walls. But it was the background of this valley that so forcibly struck him. Across the sage-flat rose a strange up-flinging of yellow rocks. He could not tell which were close and which were distant. Scrawled mounds of stone, like mountain waves, seemed to roll up to steep bare slopes and towers.

In this plain of sage Venters flushed birds and rabbits, and when he had proceeded about a mile he caught sight of the bobbing white tails of a herd of running antelope. He rode along the edge of the stream which wound toward the western end of the slowly looming mounds of stone. The high slope retreated out of sight behind the nearer protection. To Venters the valley appeared to have been filled in by a mountain of melted stone that had hardened in strange shapes of rounded outline. He followed the stream till he lost it in a deep cut. Therefore Venters quit the dark slit which baffled further search in that direction, and rode out along the curved edge of stone where it met the sage. It was not long before he came to a low place, and here Wrangle readily climbed up.

All about him was ridgy roll of wind-smoothed, rain-washed rock. Not a tuft of grass or a bunch of sage colored the dull rust-yellow. He saw where, to the right, this uneven flow of stone ended in a blunt wall. Leftward, from the hollow that lay at his feet, mounted a gradual slow-swelling slope to a great height topped by leaning, cracked, and ruined crags. Not for some time did he grasp the wonder of that acclivity. It was no less than a mountain-side, glistening in the sun like polished granite, with cedar-trees springing as if by magic out of the denuded surface. Winds had swept it clear of weathered shale, and rains had washed it free of dust. Far up the curved slope its beautiful lines broke to meet the vertical rim-wall, to lose its grace in a different order and color of rock, a stained yellow cliff of cracks and caves and seamed crags. And straight before Venters was a scene less striking but more significant to his keen survey. For beyond a mile of the bare, hummocky rock began the valley of sage, and the mouths of canyons, one of which surely was another gateway into the pass.

He got off his horse, and, giving the bridle to Ring to hold, he commenced a search for the cleft where the stream ran. He was not successful and concluded the water dropped into an underground passage. Then he returned to where he had left Wrangle, and led him down off the stone to the sage. It was a short ride to the opening canyons. There was no reason for a choice of which one to enter. The one he rode into was a clear, sharp shaft in yellow stone a thousand feet deep, with wonderful wind-worn caves low down and high above buttressed and turreted ramparts. Farther on Venters came into a region where deep indentations marked the line of canyon walls. These were huge, cove-like blind pockets extending back to a sharp corner with a dense growth of underbrush and trees.

Venters penetrated into one of these offshoots, and, as he had hoped, he found abundant grass. He had to bend the oak saplings to get his horse through. Deciding to make this a hiding-place if he could find water, he worked back to the limit of the shelving walls. In a little cluster of silver spruces he found a spring. This inclosed nook seemed an ideal place to leave his horse and to camp at night, and from which to make stealthy trips on foot. The thick grass hid his trail; the dense growth of oaks in the opening would serve as a barrier to keep Wrangle in, if, indeed, the luxuriant browse would not suffice for that. So Venters, leaving Whitie with the horse, called Ring to his side, and, rifle in hand, worked his way out to the open. A careful photographing in mind of the formation of the bold outlines of rimrock assured him he would be able to return to his retreat even in the dark.

Bunches of scattered sage covered the center of the canyon, and among these Venters threaded his way with the step of an Indian. At intervals he put his hand on the dog and stopped to listen. There was a drowsy hum of insects, but no other sound disturbed the warm midday stillness. Venters saw ahead a turn, more abrupt than any yet. Warily he rounded this corner, once again to halt bewildered.

The canyon opened fan-shaped into a great oval of green and gray growths. It was the hub of an oblong wheel, and from it, at regular distances, like spokes, ran the outgoing canyons. Here a dull red color predominated over the fading yellow. The corners of wall bluntly rose, scarred and scrawled, to taper into towers and serrated peaks and pinnacled domes.

Venters pushed on more heedfully than ever. Toward the center of this circle the sage-brush grew smaller and farther apart He was about to sheer off to the right, where thickets and jumbles of fallen rock would afford him cover, when he ran right upon a broad cattle trail. Like a road it was, more than a trail, and the cattle tracks were fresh. What surprised him more, they were wet! He pondered over this feature. It had not rained. The only solution to this puzzle was that the cattle had been driven through water, and water deep enough to wet their legs.

Suddenly Ring growled low. Venters rose cautiously and looked over the sage. A band of straggling horsemen were riding across the oval. He sank down, startled and trembling. "Rustlers!" he muttered. Hurriedly he glanced about for a place to hide. Near at hand there was nothing but sage-brush. He dared not risk crossing the open patches to reach the rocks. Again he peeped over the sage. The rustlers—four—five—seven—eight in all, were approaching, but not directly in line with him. That was relief for a cold deadness which seemed to be creeping inward along his veins. He crouched down with bated breath and held the bristling dog.

He heard the click of iron-shod hoofs on stone, the coarse laughter of men, and then voices gradually dying away. Long moments passed. Then he rose. The rustlers were riding into a canyon. Their horses were tired, and they had several pack animals; evidently they had traveled far. Venters doubted that they were the rustlers who had driven the red herd. Oldring's band had split. Venters watched these horsemen disappear under a bold canyon wall.

The rustlers had come from the northwest side of the oval. Venters kept a steady gaze in that direction, hoping, if there were more, to see from what canyon they rode. A quarter of an hour went by. Reward for his vigilance came when he descried three more mounted men, far over to the north. But out of what canyon they had ridden it was too late to tell. He watched the three ride across the oval and round the jutting red corner where the others had gone.

"Up that canyon!" exclaimed Venters. "Oldring's den! I've found it!"

A knotty point for Venters was the fact that the cattle tracks all pointed west. The broad trail came from the direction of the canyon into which the rustlers had ridden, and undoubtedly the cattle had been driven out of it across the oval. There were no tracks pointing the other way. It had been in his mind that Oldring had driven the red herd toward the rendezvous, and not from it. Where did that broad trail come down into the pass, and where did it lead? Venters knew he wasted time in pondering the question, but it held a fascination not easily dispelled. For many years Oldring's mysterious entrance and exit to Deception Pass had been all-absorbing topics to sage-riders.

All at once the dog put an end to Venters's pondering. Ring sniffed the air, turned slowly in his tracks with a whine, and then growled. Venters wheeled. Two horsemen were within a hundred yards, coming straight at him. One, lagging behind the other, was Oldring's Masked Rider.

Venters cunningly sank, slowly trying to merge into sage-brush. But, guarded as his action was, the first horse detected it. He stopped short, snorted, and shot up his ears. The rustler bent forward, as if keenly peering ahead. Then, with a swift sweep, he jerked a gun from its sheath and fired.

The bullet zipped through the sage-brush. Flying bits of wood struck Venters, and the hot, stinging pain seemed to lift him in one leap. Like a flash the blue barrel of his rifle gleamed level and he shot once—twice.

The foremost rustler dropped his weapon and toppled from his saddle, to fall with his foot catching in a stirrup. The horse snorted wildly and plunged away, dragging the rustler through the sage.

The Masked Rider huddled over his pommel slowly swaying to one side, and then, with a faint, strange cry, slipped out of the saddle.

✿ 5 ✿

THE MASKED RIDER

VENTERS LOOKED QUICKLY from the fallen rustlers to the canyon where the others had disappeared. He calculated on the time needed for running horses to return to the open, if their riders heard shots. He waited breathlessly. But the estimated time dragged by and no riders appeared. Venters began presently to believe that the rifle reports had not penetrated into the recesses of the canyon, and felt safe for the immediate present.

He hurried to the spot where the first rustler had been dragged by his horse. The man lay in deep grass, dead, jaw fallen, eyes protruding—a sight that sickened Venters. The first man at whom he had ever aimed a weapon he had shot through the heart. With the clammy sweat oozing from every pore Venters dragged the rustler in among some boulders and covered him with slabs of rock. Then he smoothed out the crushed trail in grass and sage. The rustler's horse had stopped a quarter of a mile off and was grazing.

When Venters rapidly strode toward the Masked Rider not even the cold nausea that gripped him could wholly banish curiosity. For he had shot Oldring's infamous lieutenant, whose face had never been seen. Venters experienced a grim pride in the feat. What would Tull say to this achievement of the outcast who rode too often to Deception Pass?

Venters's curious eagerness and expectation had not prepared him for the shock he received when he stood over a slight, dark figure. The rustler wore the black mask that had given him his name, but he had no weapons. Venters glanced at the drooping horse, there were no gun-sheaths on the saddle.

"A rustler who didn't pack guns!" muttered Venters. "He wears no belt. He couldn't pack guns in that rig.... Strange!"

A low, gasping intake of breath and a sudden twitching of body told Venters the rider still lived.

"He's alive!... I've got to stand here and watch him die. And I shot an unarmed man."

Shrinkingly Venters removed the rider's wide sombrero and the black cloth mask. This action disclosed bright chestnut hair, inclined to curl, and a white, youthful face. Along the lower line of cheek and jaw was a clear demarcation, where the brown of tanned skin met the white that had been hidden from the sun.

31

"Oh, he's only a boy!... What! Can he be Oldring's Masked Rider?"

The boy showed signs of returning consciousness. He stirred; his lips moved; a small brown hand clenched in his blouse.

Venters knelt with a gathering horror of his deed. His bullet had entered the rider's right breast, high up to the shoulder. With hands that shook, Venters untied a black scarf and ripped open the blood-wet blouse.

First he saw a gaping hole, dark red against a whiteness of skin, from which welled a slender red stream. Then the graceful, beautiful swell of a woman's breast!

"A woman!" he cried. "A girl!... I've killed a girl!"

She suddenly opened eyes that transfixed Venters. They were fathomless blue. Consciousness of death was there, a blended terror and pain, but no consciousness of sight. She did not see Venters. She stared into the unknown.

Then came a spasm of vitality. She writhed in a torture of reviving strength, and in her convulsions she almost tore from Ventner's grasp. Slowly she relaxed and sank partly back. The ungloved hand sought the wound, and pressed so hard that her wrist half buried itself in her bosom. Blood trickled between her spread fingers. And she looked at Venters with eyes that saw him.

He cursed himself and the unerring aim of which he had been so proud. He had seen that look in the eyes of a crippled antelope which he was about to finish with his knife. But in her it had infinitely more—a revelation of mortal spirit. The instinctive bringing to life was there, and the divining helplessness and the terrible accusation of the stricken.

"Forgive me! I didn't know!" burst out Venters.

"You shot me—you've killed me!" she whispered, in panting gasps. Upon her lips appeared a fluttering, bloody froth. By that Venters knew the air in her lungs was mixing with blood. "Oh, I knew—it would—come—some day!... Oh, the burn!... Hold me—I'm sinking—it's all dark.... Ah, God!... Mercy—"

Her rigidity loosened in one long quiver and she lay back limp, still, white as snow, with closed eyes.

Venters thought then that she died. But the faint pulsation of her breast assured him that life yet lingered. Death seemed only a matter of moments, for the bullet had gone clear through her. Nevertheless, he tore sageleaves from a bush, and, pressing them tightly over her wounds, he bound the black scarf round her shoulder, tying it securely under her arm. Then he closed the blouse, hiding from his sight that blood-stained, accusing breast.

"What—now?" he questioned, with flying mind. "I must get out of here. She's dying—but I can't leave her."

He rapidly surveyed the sage to the north and made out no animate object. Then he picked up the girl's sombrero and the mask. This time the mask gave him as great a shock as when he first removed it from her face. For in the woman he had forgotten the rustler, and this black strip of felt-cloth established the identity of Oldring's Masked Rider. Venters had solved the mystery. He slipped his rifle under her, and, lifting her carefully upon it, he began to retrace his steps. The dog trailed in his shadow. And the horse, that had stood drooping by, followed without a call. Venters chose the deepest tufts of grass and clumps of sage on his return. From time to time he glanced over his shoulder. He did not rest. His concern was to avoid jarring the girl and to hide his trail. Gaining the narrow canyon, he turned and held close to the wall till he reached his hiding-place. When he entered the dense thicket of oaks he was hard put to it to force a way through. But he held his burden almost upright, and by slipping side wise and bending the saplings he got in. Through sage and grass he hurried to the grove of silver spruces.

32

He laid the girl down, almost fearing to look at her. Though marble pale and cold, she was living. Venters then appreciated the tax that long carry had been to his strength. He sat down to rest. Whitie sniffed at the pale girl and whined and crept to Venters's feet. Ring lapped the water in the runway of the spring.

Presently Venters went out to the opening, caught the horse and, leading him through the thicket, unsaddled him and tied him with a long halter. Wrangle left his browsing long enough to whinny and toss his head. Venters felt that he could not rest easily till he had secured the other rustler's horse; so, taking his rifle and calling for Ring, he set out. Swiftly yet watchfully he made his way through the canyon to the oval and out to the cattle trail. What few tracks might have betrayed him he obliterated, so only an expert tracker could have trailed him. Then, with many a wary backward glance across the sage, he started to round up the rustler's horse. This was unexpectedly easy. He led the horse to lower ground, out of sight from the opposite side of the oval along the shadowy western wall, and so on into his canyon and secluded camp.

The girl's eyes were open; a feverish spot burned in her cheeks she moaned something unintelligible to Venters, but he took the movement of her lips to mean that she wanted water. Lifting her head, he tipped the canteen to her lips. After that she again lapsed into unconsciousness or a weakness which was its counterpart. Venters noted, however, that the burning flush had faded into the former pallor.

The sun set behind the high canyon rim, and a cool shade darkened the walls. Venters fed the dogs and put a halter on the dead rustlers horse. He allowed Wrangle to browse free. This done, he cut spruce boughs and made a lean-to for the girl. Then, gently lifting her upon a blanket, he folded the sides over her. The other blanket he wrapped about his shoulders and found a comfortable seat against a spruce-tree that upheld the little shack. Ring and Whitie lay near at hand, one asleep, the other watchful.

Venters dreaded the night's vigil. At night his mind was active, and this time he had to watch and think and feel beside a dying girl whom he had all but murdered. A thousand excuses he invented for himself, yet not one made any difference in his act or his self-reproach.

It seemed to him that when night fell black he could see her white face so much more plainly.

"She'll go, presently," he said, "and be out of agony—thank God!"

Every little while certainty of her death came to him with a shock; and then he would bend over and lay his ear on her breast. Her heart still beat.

The early night blackness cleared to the cold starlight. The horses were not moving, and no sound disturbed the deathly silence of the canyon.

"I'll bury her here," thought Venters, "and let her grave be as much a mystery as her life was."

For the girl's few words, the look of her eyes, the prayer, had strangely touched Venters.

"She was only a girl," he soliloquized. "What was she to Oldring? Rustlers don't have wives nor sisters nor daughters. She was bad—that's all. But somehow... well, she may not have willingly become the companion of rustlers. That prayer of hers to God for mercy!... Life is strange and cruel. I wonder if other members of Oldring's gang are women? Likely enough. But what was his game? Oldring's Mask Rider! A name to make villagers hide and lock their doors. A name credited with a dozen murders, a hundred forays, and a thousand stealings of cattle. What part did the girl have in this? It may have served Oldring to create mystery."

Hours passed. The white stars moved across the narrow strip of dark-blue sky above. The

ZANE GREY

silence awoke to the low hum of insects. Venters watched the immovable white face, and as he watched, hour by hour waiting for death, the infamy of her passed from his mind. He thought only of the sadness, the truth of the moment. Whoever she was—whatever she had done—she was young and she was dying.

The after-part of the night wore on interminably. The starlight failed and the gloom blackened to the darkest hour. "She'll die at the gray of dawn," muttered Venters, remembering some old woman's fancy. The blackness paled to gray, and the gray lightened and day peeped over the eastern rim. Venters listened at the breast of the girl. She still lived. Did he only imagine that her heart beat stronger, ever so slightly, but stronger? He pressed his ear closer to her breast. And he rose with his own pulse quickening.

"If she doesn't die soon—she's got a chance—the barest chance to live," he said.

He wondered if the internal bleeding had ceased. There was no more film of blood upon her lips. But no corpse could have been whiter. Opening her blouse, he untied the scarf, and carefully picked away the sage leaves from the wound in her shoulder. It had closed. Lifting her lightly, he ascertained that the same was true of the hole where the bullet had come out. He reflected on the fact that clean wounds closed quickly in the healing upland air. He recalled instances of riders who had been cut and shot apparently to fatal issues; yet the blood had clotted, the wounds closed, and they had recovered. He had no way to tell if internal hemorrhage still went on, but he believed that it had stopped. Otherwise she would surely not have lived so long. He marked the entrance of the bullet, and concluded that it had just touched the upper lobe of her lung. Perhaps the wound in the lung had also closed. As he began to wash the blood stains from her breast and carefully rebandage the wound, he was vaguely conscious of a strange, grave happiness in the thought that she might live.

Broad daylight and a hint of sunshine high on the cliff-rim to the west brought him to consideration of what he had better do. And while busy with his few camp tasks he revolved the thing in his mind. It would not be wise for him to remain long in his present hiding-place. And if he intended to follow the cattle trail and try to find the rustlers he had better make a move at once. For he knew that rustlers, being riders, would not make much of a day's or night's absence from camp for one or two of their number; but when the missing ones failed to show up in reasonable time there would be a search. And Venters was afraid of that.

"A good tracker could trail me," he muttered. "And I'd be cornered here. Let's see. Rustlers are a lazy set when they're not on the ride. I'll risk it. Then I'll change my hiding-place."

He carefully cleaned and reloaded his guns. When he rose to go he bent a long glance down upon the unconscious girl. Then ordering Whitie and Ring to keep guard, he left the camp.

The safest cover lay close under the wall of the canyon, and here through the dense thickets Venters made his slow, listening advance toward the oval. Upon gaining the wide opening he decided to cross it and follow the left wall till he came to the cattle trail. He scanned the oval as keenly as if hunting for antelope. Then, stooping, he stole from one cover to another, taking advantage of rocks and bunches of sage, until he had reached the thickets under the opposite wall. Once there, he exercised extreme caution in his surveys of the ground ahead, but increased his speed when moving. Dodging from bush to bush, he passed the mouths of two canyons, and in the entrance of a third canyon he crossed a wash of swift clear water, to come abruptly upon the cattle trail.

It followed the low bank of the wash, and, keeping it in sight, Venters hugged the line of sage and thicket. Like the curves of a serpent the canyon wound for a mile or more and then opened into a valley. Patches of red showed clear against the purple of sage, and farther out on the level dotted strings of red led away to the wall of rock.

"Ha, the red herd!" exclaimed Venters.

Then dots of white and black told him there were cattle of other colors in this inclosed valley. Oldring, the rustler, was also a rancher. Venters's calculating eye took count of stock that outnumbered the red herd.

"What a range!" went on Venters. "Water and grass enough for fifty thousand head, and no riders needed!"

After his first burst of surprise and rapid calculation Venters lost no time there, but slunk again into the sage on his back trail. With the discovery of Oldring's hidden cattle-range had come enlightenment on several problems. Here the rustler kept his stock, here was Jane Withersteen's red herd; here were the few cattle that had disappeared from the Cottonwoods slopes during the last two years. Until Oldring had driven the red herd his thefts of cattle for that time had not been more than enough to supply meat for his men. Of late no drives had been reported from Sterling or the villages north. And Venters knew that the riders had wondered at Oldring's inactivity in that particular field. He and his band had been active enough in their visits to Glaze and Cottonwoods; they always had gold; but of late the amount gambled away and drunk and thrown away in the villages had given rise to much conjecture. Oldring's more frequent visits had resulted in new saloons, and where there had formerly been one raid or shooting fray in the little hamlets there were now many. Perhaps Oldring had another range farther on up the pass, and from there drove the cattle to distant Utah towns where he was little known But Venters came finally to doubt this. And, from what he had learned in the last few days, a belief began to form in Venters's mind that Oldring's intimidations of the villages and the mystery of the Masked Rider, with his alleged evil deeds, and the fierce resistance offered any trailing riders, and the rustling of cattle—these things were only the craft of the rustler-chief to conceal his real life and purpose and work in Deception Pass.

And like a scouting Indian Venters crawled through the sage of the oval valley, crossed trail after trail on the north side, and at last entered the canyon out of which headed the cattle trail, and into which he had watched the rustlers disappear.

If he had used caution before, now he strained every nerve to force himself to creeping stealth and to sensitiveness of ear. He crawled along so hidden that he could not use his eyes except to aid himself in the toilsome progress through the brakes and ruins of cliff-wall. Yet from time to time, as he rested, he saw the massive red walls growing higher and wilder, more looming and broken. He made note of the fact that he was turning and climbing. The sage and thickets of oak and brakes of alder gave place to pinyon pine growing out of rocky soil. Suddenly a low, dull murmur assailed his ears. At first he thought it was thunder, then the slipping of a weathered slope of rock. But it was incessant, and as he progressed it filled out deeper and from a murmur changed into a soft roar.

"Falling water," he said. "There's volume to that. I wonder if it's the stream I lost."

The roar bothered him, for he could hear nothing else. Likewise, however, no rustlers could hear him. Emboldened by this and sure that nothing but a bird could see him, he arose from his hands and knees to hurry on. An opening in the pinyons warned him that he was nearing the height of slope.

He gained it, and dropped low with a burst of astonishment. Before him stretched a short canyon with rounded stone floor bare of grass or sage or tree, and with curved, shelving walls. A broad rippling stream flowed toward him, and at the back of the canyon waterfall burst from a wide rent in the cliff, and, bounding down in two green steps, spread into a long white sheet.

If Venters had not been indubitably certain that he had entered the right canyon his astonishment would not have been so great. There had been no breaks in the walls, no side canyons entering this one where the rustlers' tracks and the cattle trail had guided him, and, therefore, he could not be wrong. But here the canyon ended, and presumably the trails also.

"That cattle trail headed out of here," Venters kept saying to himself. "It headed out. Now what I want to know is how on earth did cattle ever get in here?"

If he could be sure of anything it was of the careful scrutiny he had given that cattle track, every hoofmark of which headed straight west. He was now looking east at an immense round boxed corner of canyon down which tumbled a thin, white veil of water, scarcely twenty yards wide. Somehow, somewhere, his calculations had gone wrong. For the first time in years he found himself doubting his rider's skill in finding tracks, and his memory of what he had actually seen. In his anxiety to keep under cover he must have lost himself in this offshoot of Deception Pass, and thereby in some unaccountable manner, missed the canyon with the trails. There was nothing else for him to think. Rustlers could not fly, nor cattle jump down thousand-foot precipices. He was only proving what the sage-riders had long said of this labyrinthine system of deceitful canyons and valleys—trails led down into Deception Pass, but no rider had ever followed them.

On a sudden he heard above the soft roar of the waterfall an unusual sound that he could not define. He dropped flat behind a stone and listened. From the direction he had come swelled something that resembled a strange muffled pounding and splashing and ringing. Despite his nerve the chill sweat began to dampen his forehead. What might not be possible in this stonewalled maze of mystery? The unnatural sound passed beyond him as he lay gripping his rifle and fighting for coolness. Then from the open came the sound, now distinct and different. Venters recognized a hobble-bell of a horse, and the cracking of iron on submerged stones, and the hollow splash of hoofs in water.

Relief surged over him. His mind caught again at realities, and curiosity prompted him to peep from behind the rock.

In the middle of the stream waded a long string of packed burros driven by three superbly mounted men. Had Venters met these dark-clothed, dark-visaged, heavily armed men anywhere in Utah, let alone in this robbers' retreat, he would have recognized them as rustlers. The discerning eye of a rider saw the signs of a long, arduous trip. These men were packing in supplies from one of the northern villages. They were tired, and their horses were almost played out, and the burros plodded on, after the manner of their kind when exhausted, faithful and patient, but as if every weary, splashing, slipping step would be their last.

All this Venters noted in one glance. After that he watched with a thrilling eagerness. Straight at the waterfall the rustlers drove the burros, and straight through the middle, where the water spread into a fleecy, thin film like dissolving smoke. Following closely, the rustlers rode into this white mist, showing in bold black relief for an instant, and then they vanished.

Venters drew a full breath that rushed out in brief and sudden utterance.

"Good Heaven! Of all the holes for a rustler!... There's a cavern under that waterfall, and a passageway leading out to a canyon beyond. Oldring hides in there. He needs only to guard a trail leading down from the sage-flat above. Little danger of this outlet to the pass being discovered. I stumbled on it by luck, after I had given up. And now I know the truth of what puzzled me most—why that cattle trail was wet!"

He wheeled and ran down the slope, and out to the level of the sage-brush. Returning, he had no time to spare, only now and then, between dashes, a moment when he stopped to cast sharp eyes ahead. The abundant grass left no trace of his trail. Short work he made of the distance to the circle of canyons. He doubted that he would ever see it again; he knew he never wanted to; yet he looked at the red corners and towers with the eyes of a rider picturing landmarks never to be forgotten.

Here he spent a panting moment in a slow-circling gaze of the sage-oval and the gaps between the bluffs. Nothing stirred except the gentle wave of the tips of the brush. Then he pressed on past the mouths of several canyons and over ground new to him, now close under the eastern wall. This latter part proved to be easy traveling, well screened from possible observation from the north and west, and he soon covered it and felt safer in the deepening shade of his own canyon. Then the huge, notched bulge of red rim loomed over him, a mark by which he knew again the deep cove where his camp lay hidden. As he penetrated the thicket, safe again for the present, his thoughts reverted to the girl he had left there. The afternoon had far advanced. How would he find her? He ran into camp, frightening the dogs.

The girl lay with wide-open, dark eyes, and they dilated when he knelt beside her. The flush of fever shone in her cheeks. He lifted her and held water to her dry lips, and felt an inexplicable sense of lightness as he saw her swallow in a slow, choking gulp. Gently he laid her back.

"Who—are—you?" she whispered, haltingly.

"I'm the man who shot you," he replied.

"You'll—not—kill me—now?"

"No, no."

"What—will—you—do—with me?"

"When you get better—strong enough—I'll take you back to the canyon where the rustlers ride through the waterfall."

As with a faint shadow from a flitting wing overhead, the marble whiteness of her face seemed to change.

"Don't—take—me—back—there!"

❧ 6 ❧

THE MILL-WHEEL OF STEERS

MEANTIME, at the ranch, when Judkins's news had sent Venters on the trail of the rustlers, Jane Withersteen led the injured man to her house and with skilled fingers dressed the gunshot wound in his arm.

"Judkins, what do you think happened to my riders?"

"I—I d rather not say," he replied.

"Tell me. Whatever you'll tell me I'll keep to myself. I'm beginning to worry about more than the loss of a herd of cattle. Venters hinted of—but tell me, Judkins."

"Well, Miss Withersteen, I think as Venters thinks—your riders have been called in."

"Judkins!... By whom?"

"You know who handles the reins of your Mormon riders."

"Do you dare insinuate that my churchmen have ordered in my riders?"

"I ain't insinuatin' nothin', Miss Withersteen," answered Judkins, with spirit. "I know what I'm talking about. I didn't want to tell you."

"Oh, I can't believe that! I'll not believe it! Would Tull leave my herds at the mercy of rustlers and wolves just because—because—? No, no! It's unbelievable."

"Yes, thet particular thing's onheard of around Cottonwoods But, beggin' pardon, Miss Withersteen, there never was any other rich Mormon woman here on the border, let alone one thet's taken the bit between her teeth."

That was a bold thing for the reserved Judkins to say, but it did not anger her. This rider's crude hint of her spirit gave her a glimpse of what others might think. Humility and obedience had been hers always. But had she taken the bit between her teeth? Still she wavered. And then, with quick spurt of warm blood along her veins, she thought of Black Star when he got the bit fast between his iron jaws and ran wild in the sage. If she ever started to run! Jane smothered the glow and burn within her, ashamed of a passion for freedom that opposed her duty.

"Judkins, go to the village," she said, "and when you have learned anything definite about my riders please come to me at once."

When he had gone Jane resolutely applied her mind to a number of tasks that of late had been neglected. Her father had trained her in the management of a hundred employees and the working of gardens and fields; and to keep record of the movements of cattle and riders. And beside the many duties she had added to this work was one of extreme delicacy, such as required all her tact and ingenuity. It was an unobtrusive, almost secret aid which she rendered to the Gentile families of the village. Though Jane Withersteen never admitted so to herself, it amounted to no less than a system of charity. But for her invention of numberless kinds of employment, for which there was no actual need, these families of Gentiles, who had failed in a Mormon community, would have starved.

In aiding these poor people Jane thought she deceived her keen churchmen, but it was a kind of deceit for which she did not pray to be forgiven. Equally as difficult was the task of deceiving the Gentiles, for they were as proud as they were poor. It had been a great grief to her to discover how these people hated her people; and it had been a source of great joy that through her they had come to soften in hatred. At any time this work called for a clearness of mind that precluded anxiety and worry; but under the present circumstances it required all her vigor and obstinate tenacity to pin her attention upon her task.

Sunset came, bringing with the end of her labor a patient calmness and power to wait that had not been hers earlier in the day. She expected Judkins, but he did not appear. Her house was always quiet; to-night, however, it seemed unusually so. At supper her women served her with a silent assiduity; it spoke what their sealed lips could not utter—the sympathy of Mormon women. Jerd came to her with the key of the great door of the stone stable, and to make his daily report about the horses. One of his daily duties was to give Black Star and Night and the other racers a ten-mile run. This day it had been omitted, and the boy grew confused in explanations that she had not asked for. She did inquire if he would return on the morrow, and Jerd, in mingled surprise and relief, assured her he would always work for her. Jane missed the rattle and trot, canter and gallop of the incoming riders on the hard trails. Dusk shaded the grove where she walked; the birds ceased singing; the wind sighed through the leaves of the cottonwoods, and the running water murmured down its stone-bedded channel. The glimmering of the first star was like the peace and beauty of the night. Her faith welled up in her heart and said that all would soon be right in her little world. She pictured Venters about his lonely camp-fire sitting between his faithful dogs. She prayed for his safety, for the success of his undertaking.

Early the next morning one of Jane's women brought in word that Judkins wished to speak to her. She hurried out, and in her surprise to see him armed with rifle and revolver, she forgot her intention to inquire about his wound.

"Judkins! Those guns? You never carried guns."

"It's high time, Miss Withersteen," he replied. "Will you come into the grove? It ain't jest exactly safe for me to be seen here."

She walked with him into the shade of the cottonwoods.

"What do you mean?"

"Miss Withersteen, I went to my mother's house last night. While there, some one knocked, an' a man asked for me. I went to the door. He wore a mask. He said I'd better not ride any more for Jane Withersteen. His voice was hoarse an' strange, disguised I reckon, like his face. He said no more, an' ran off in the dark."

"Did you know who he was?" asked Jane, in a low voice.

"Yes."

Jane did not ask to know; she did not want to know; she feared to know. All her calmness fled at a single thought.

"Thet's why I'm packin' guns," went on Judkins. "For I'll never quit ridin' for you, Miss Withersteen, till you let me go."

"Judkins, do you want to leave me?"

"Do I look thet way? Give me a hoss—a fast hoss, an' send me out on the sage."

"Oh, thank you, Judkins! You're more faithful than my own people. I ought not accept your loyalty—you might suffer more through it. But what in the world can I do? My head whirls. The wrong to Venters—the stolen herd—these masks, threats, this coil in the dark! I can't understand! But I feel something dark and terrible closing in around me."

"Miss Withersteen, it's all simple enough," said Judkins, earnestly. "Now please listen— an' beggin' your pardon—jest turn thet deaf Mormon ear aside, an' let me talk clear an' plain in the other. I went around to the saloons an' the stores an' the loafin' places yesterday. All your riders are in. There's talk of a vigilance band organized to hunt down rustlers. They call themselves 'The Riders.' Thet's the report—thet's the reason given for your riders leavin' you. Strange thet only a few riders of other ranchers joined the band! An' Tull's man, Jerry Card— he's the leader. I seen him en' his hoss. He 'ain't been to Glaze. I'm not easy to fool on the looks of a hoss thet's traveled the sage. Tull an' Jerry didn't ride to Glaze!... Well, I met Blake en' Dorn, both good friends of mine, usually, as far as their Mormon lights will let 'em go. But these fellers couldn't fool me, an' they didn't try very hard. I asked them, straight out like a man, why they left you like thet. I didn't forget to mention how you nursed Blake's poor old mother when she was sick, an' how good you was to Dorn's kids. They looked ashamed, Miss Withersteen. An' they jest froze up—thet dark set look thet makes them strange an' different to me. But I could tell the difference between thet first natural twinge of conscience an' the later look of some secret thing. An' the difference I caught was thet they couldn't help themselves. They hadn't no say in the matter. They looked as if their bein' unfaithful to you was bein' faithful to a higher duty. An' there's the secret. Why it's as plain as—as sight of my gun here."

"Plain!... My herds to wander in the sage—to be stolen! Jane Withersteen a poor woman! Her head to be brought low and her spirit broken!... Why, Judkins, it's plain enough."

"Miss Withersteen, let me get what boys I can gather, an' hold the white herd. It's on the slope now, not ten miles out—three thousand head, an' all steers. They're wild, an' likely to stampede at the pop of a jack-rabbit's ears. We'll camp right with them, en' try to hold them."

"Judkins, I'll reward you some day for your service, unless all is taken from me. Get the boys and tell Jerd to give you pick of my horses, except Black Star and Night. But—do not shed blood for my cattle nor heedlessly risk your lives."

Jane Withersteen rushed to the silence and seclusion of her room, and there could not longer hold back the bursting of her wrath. She went stone-blind in the fury of a passion that had never before showed its power. Lying upon her bed, sightless, voiceless, she was a writhing, living flame. And she tossed there while her fury burned and burned, and finally burned itself out.

Then, weak and spent, she lay thinking, not of the oppression that would break her, but of this new revelation of self. Until the last few days there had been little in her life to rouse passions. Her forefathers had been Vikings, savage chieftains who bore no cross and brooked no hindrance to their will. Her father had inherited that temper; and at times, like antelope fleeing before fire on the slope, his people fled from his red rages. Jane Withersteen realized that the spirit of wrath and war had lain dormant in her. She shrank from black depths hitherto unsuspected. The one thing in man or woman that she scorned above all scorn, and which she could not forgive, was hate. Hate headed a flaming pathway straight to hell. All in a flash, beyond her control there had been in her a birth of fiery hate. And the man who had dragged her peaceful and loving spirit to this degradation was a minister of God's word, an Elder of her church, the counselor of her beloved Bishop.

The loss of herds and ranges, even of Amber Spring and the Old Stone House, no longer concerned Jane Withersteen, she faced the foremost thought of her life, what she now considered the mightiest problem—the salvation of her soul.

She knelt by her bedside and prayed; she prayed as she had never prayed in all her life—prayed to be forgiven for her sin to be immune from that dark, hot hate; to love Tull as her minister, though she could not love him as a man; to do her duty by her church and people and those dependent upon her bounty; to hold reverence of God and womanhood inviolate.

When Jane Withersteen rose from that storm of wrath and prayer for help she was serene, calm, sure—a changed woman. She would do her duty as she saw it, live her life as her own truth guided her. She might never be able to marry a man of her choice, but she certainly never would become the wife of Tull. Her churchmen might take her cattle and horses, ranges and fields, her corrals and stables, the house of Withersteen and the water that nourished the village of Cottonwoods; but they could not force her to marry Tull, they could not change her decision or break her spirit. Once resigned to further loss, and sure of herself, Jane Withersteen attained a peace of mind that had not been hers for a year. She forgave Tull, and felt a melancholy regret over what she knew he considered duty, irrespective of his personal feeling for her. First of all, Tull, as he was a man, wanted her for himself; and secondly, he hoped to save her and her riches for his church. She did not believe that Tull had been actuated solely by his minister's zeal to save her soul. She doubted her interpretation of one of his dark sayings—that if she were lost to him she might as well be lost to heaven. Jane Withersteen's common sense took arms against the binding limits of her religion; and she doubted that her Bishop, whom she had been taught had direct communication with God—would damn her soul for refusing to marry a Mormon. As for Tull and his churchmen, when they had harassed her, perhaps made her poor, they would find her unchangeable, and then she would get back most of what she had lost. So she reasoned, true at last to her faith in all men, and in their ultimate goodness.

The clank of iron hoofs upon the stone courtyard drew her hurriedly from her retirement. There, beside his horse, stood Lassiter, his dark apparel and the great black gun-sheaths contrasting singularly with his gentle smile. Jane's active mind took up her interest in him and her half-determined desire to use what charm she had to foil his evident design in visiting Cottonwoods. If she could mitigate his hatred of Mormons, or at least keep him from killing more of them, not only would she be saving her people, but also be leading back this bloodspiller to some semblance of the human.

"Mornin', ma'am," he said, black sombrero in hand.

"Lassiter I'm not an old woman, or even a madam," she replied, with her bright smile. "If you can't say Miss Withersteen—call me Jane."

"I reckon Jane would be easier. First names are always handy for me."

"Well, use mine, then. Lassiter, I'm glad to see you. I'm in trouble."

Then she told him of Judkins's return, of the driving of the red herd, of Venters's departure on Wrangle, and the calling-in of her riders.

"'Pears to me you're some smilin' an' pretty for a woman with so much trouble," he remarked.

"Lassiter! Are you paying me compliments? But, seriously I've made up my mind not to be miserable. I've lost much, and I'll lose more. Nevertheless, I won't be sour, and I hope I'll never be unhappy—again."

Lassiter twisted his hat round and round, as was his way, and took his time in replying.

"Women are strange to me. I got to back-trailin' myself from them long ago. But I'd like a game woman. Might I ask, seein' as how you take this trouble, if you're goin' to fight?"

"Fight! How? Even if I would, I haven't a friend except that boy who doesn't dare stay in the village."

"I make bold to say, ma'am—Jane—that there's another, if you want him."

"Lassiter!... Thank you. But how can I accept you as a friend? Think! Why, you'd ride down into the village with those terrible guns and kill my enemies—who are also my churchmen."

"I reckon I might be riled up to jest about that," he replied, dryly.

She held out both hands to him.

"Lassiter! I'll accept your friendship—be proud of it—return it—if I may keep you from killing another Mormon."

"I'll tell you one thing," he said, bluntly, as the gray lightning formed in his eyes. "You're too good a woman to be sacrificed as you're goin' to be.... No, I reckon you an' me can't be friends on such terms."

In her earnestness she stepped closer to him, repelled yet fascinated by the sudden transition of his moods. That he would fight for her was at once horrible and wonderful.

"You came here to kill a man—the man whom Milly Erne—"

"The man who dragged Milly Erne to hell—put it that way!... Jane Withersteen, yes, that's why I came here. I'd tell so much to no other livin' soul.... There're things such a woman as you'd never dream of—so don't mention her again. Not till you tell me the name of the man!"

"Tell you! I? Never!"

"I reckon you will. An' I'll never ask you. I'm a man of strange beliefs an' ways of thinkin', an' I seem to see into the future an' feel things hard to explain. The trail I've been followin' for so many years was twisted en' tangled, but it's straightenin' out now. An', Jane Withersteen, you crossed it long ago to ease poor Milly's agony. That, whether you want or not, makes Lassiter your friend. But you cross it now strangely to mean somethin to me—God knows what!—unless by your noble blindness to incite me to greater hatred of Mormon men."

Jane felt swayed by a strength that far exceeded her own. In a clash of wills with this man she would go to the wall. If she were to influence him it must be wholly through womanly allurement. There was that about Lassiter which commanded her respect. She had abhorred his name; face to face with him, she found she feared only his deeds. His mystic suggestion, his foreshadowing of something that she was to mean to him, pierced deep into her mind. She believed fate had thrown in her way the lover or husband of Milly Erne. She believed that through her an evil man might be reclaimed. His allusion to what he called her blindness terrified her. Such a mistaken idea of his might unleash the bitter, fatal mood she sensed in him. At any cost she must placate this man; she knew the die was cast, and that if Lassiter did not soften to a woman's grace and beauty and wiles, then it would be because she could not make him.

"I reckon you'll hear no more such talk from me," Lassiter went on, presently. "Now, Miss Jane, I rode in to tell you that your herd of white steers is down on the slope behind them big ridges. An' I seen somethin' goin' on that'd be mighty interestin' to you, if you could see it. Have you a field-glass?"

"Yes, I have two glasses. I'll get them and ride out with you. Wait, Lassiter, please," she said, and hurried within. Sending word to Jerd to saddle Black Star and fetch him to the court, she then went to her room and changed to the riding-clothes she always donned when going into the sage. In this male attire her mirror showed her a jaunty, handsome rider. If she expected some little need of admiration from Lassiter, she had no cause for disappointment.

The gentle smile that she liked, which made of him another person, slowly overspread his face.

"If I didn't take you for a boy!" he exclaimed. "It's powerful queer what difference clothes make. Now I've been some scared of your dignity, like when the other night you was all in white but in this rig—"

Black Star came pounding into the court, dragging Jerd half off his feet, and he whistled at Lassiter's black. But at sight of Jane all his defiant lines seemed to soften, and with tosses of his beautiful head he whipped his bridle.

"Down, Black Star, down," said Jane.

He dropped his head, and, slowly lengthening, he bent one foreleg, then the other, and sank to his knees. Jane slipped her left foot in the stirrup, swung lightly into the saddle, and Black Star rose with a ringing stamp. It was not easy for Jane to hold him to a canter through the grove, and like the wind he broke when he saw the sage. Jane let him have a couple of miles of free running on the open trail, and then she coaxed him in and waited for her companion. Lassiter was not long in catching up, and presently they were riding side by side. It reminded her how she used to ride with Venters. Where was he now? She gazed far down the slope to the curved purple lines of Deception Pass and involuntarily shut her eyes with a trembling stir of nameless fear.

"We'll turn off here," Lassiter said, "en' take to the sage a mile or so. The white herd is behind them big ridges."

"What are you going to show me?" asked Jane. "I'm prepared—don't be afraid."

He smiled as if he meant that bad news came swiftly enough without being presaged by speech.

When they reached the lee of a rolling ridge Lassiter dismounted, motioning to her to do likewise. They left the horses standing, bridles down. Then Lassiter, carrying the field-glasses began to lead the way up the slow rise of ground. Upon nearing the summit he halted her with a gesture.

"I reckon we'd see more if we didn't show ourselves against the sky," he said. "I was here less than an hour ago. Then the herd was seven or eight miles south, an' if they ain't bolted yet—"

"Lassiter!... Bolted?"

"That's what I said. Now let's see."

Jane climbed a few more paces behind him and then peeped over the ridge. Just beyond began a shallow swale that deepened and widened into a valley and then swung to the left. Following the undulating sweep of sage, Jane saw the straggling lines and then the great body of the white herd. She knew enough about steers, even at a distance of four or five miles, to realize that something was in the wind. Bringing her field-glass into use, she moved it slowly from left to right, which action swept the whole herd into range. The stragglers were restless; the more compactly massed steers were browsing. Jane brought the glass back to the big sentinels of the herd, and she saw them trot with quick steps, stop short and toss wide horns, look everywhere, and then trot in another direction.

"Judkins hasn't been able to get his boys together yet," said Jane. "But he'll be there soon. I hope not too late. Lassiter, what's frightening those big leaders?"

"Nothin' jest on the minute," replied Lassiter. "Them steers are quietin' down. They've been scared, but not bad yet. I reckon the whole herd has moved a few miles this way since I was here."

"They didn't browse that distance—not in less than an hour. Cattle aren't sheep."

"No, they jest run it, en' that looks bad."

"Lassiter, what frightened them?" repeated Jane, impatiently.

"Put down your glass. You'll see at first better with a naked eye. Now look along them ridges on the other side of the herd, the ridges where the sun shines bright on the sage.... That's right. Now look en' look hard en' wait."

Long-drawn moments of straining sight rewarded Jane with nothing save the low, purple rim of ridge and the shimmering sage.

"It's begun again!" whispered Lassiter, and he gripped her arm. "Watch.... There, did you see that?"

"No, no. Tell me what to look for?"

"A white flash—a kind of pin-point of quick light—a gleam as from sun shinin' on somethin' white."

Suddenly Jane's concentrated gaze caught a fleeting glint. Quickly she brought her glass to bear on the spot. Again the purple sage, magnified in color and size and wave, for long moments irritated her with its monotony. Then from out of the sage on the ridge flew up a broad, white object, flashed in the sunlight and vanished. Like magic it was, and bewildered Jane.

"What on earth is that?"

"I reckon there's some one behind that ridge throwin' up a sheet or a white blanket to reflect the sunshine."

"Why?" queried Jane, more bewildered than ever.

"To stampede the herd," replied Lassiter, and his teeth clicked.

"Ah!" She made a fierce, passionate movement, clutched the glass tightly, shook as with the passing of a spasm, and then dropped her head. Presently she raised it to greet Lassiter with something like a smile. "My righteous brethren are at work again," she said, in scorn. She had stifled the leap of her wrath, but for perhaps the first time in her life a bitter derision curled her lips. Lassiter's cool gray eyes seemed to pierce her. "I said I was prepared for anything; but that was hardly true. But why would they—anybody stampede my cattle?"

"That's a Mormon's godly way of bringin' a woman to her knees."

"Lassiter, I'll die before I ever bend my knees. I might be led I won't be driven. Do you expect the herd to bolt?"

"I don't like the looks of them big steers. But you can never tell. Cattle sometimes stampede as easily as buffalo. Any little flash or move will start them. A rider gettin' down an' walkin' toward them sometimes will make them jump an' fly. Then again nothin' seems to scare them. But I reckon that white flare will do the biz. It's a new one on me, an' I've seen some ridin' an' rustlin'. It jest takes one of them God-fearin' Mormons to think of devilish tricks."

"Lassiter, might not this trick be done by Oldring's men?" asked Jane, ever grasping at straws.

"It might be, but it ain't," replied Lassiter. "Oldring's an honest thief. He don't skulk behind ridges to scatter your cattle to the four winds. He rides down on you, an' if you don't like it you can throw a gun."

Jane bit her tongue to refrain from championing men who at the very moment were proving to her that they were little and mean compared even with rustlers.

"Look!... Jane, them leadin' steers have bolted. They're drawin' the stragglers, an' that'll pull the whole herd."

Jane was not quick enough to catch the details called out by Lassiter, but she saw the line of cattle lengthening. Then, like a stream of white bees pouring from a huge swarm, the steers stretched out from the main body. In a few moments, with astonishing rapidity, the whole herd got into motion. A faint roar of trampling hoofs came to Jane's ears, and gradually swelled; low, rolling clouds of dust began to rise above the sage.

"It's a stampede, an' a hummer," said Lassiter.

"Oh, Lassiter! The herd's running with the valley! It leads into the canyon! There's a straight jump-off!"

"I reckon they'll run into it, too. But that's a good many miles yet. An', Jane, this valley swings round almost north before it goes east. That stampede will pass within a mile of us."

The long, white, bobbing line of steers streaked swiftly through the sage, and a funnel-shaped dust-cloud arose at a low angle. A dull rumbling filled Jane's ears.

"I'm thinkin' of millin' that herd," said Lassiter. His gray glance swept up the slope to the west. "There's some specks an' dust way off toward the village. Mebbe that's Judkins an' his boys. It ain't likely he'll get here in time to help. You'd better hold Black Star here on this high ridge."

He ran to his horse and, throwing off saddle-bags and tightening the cinches, he leaped astride and galloped straight down across the valley.

Jane went for Black Star and, leading him to the summit of the ridge, she mounted and faced the valley with excitement and expectancy. She had heard of milling stampeded cattle, and knew it was a feat accomplished by only the most daring riders.

The white herd was now strung out in a line two miles long. The dull rumble of thousands of hoofs deepened into continuous low thunder, and as the steers swept swiftly closer the thunder became a heavy roll. Lassiter crossed in a few moments the level of the valley to the eastern rise of ground and there waited the coming of the herd. Presently, as the head of the white line reached a point opposite to where Jane stood, Lassiter spurred his black into a run.

Jane saw him take a position on the off side of the leaders of the stampede, and there he rode. It was like a race. They swept on down the valley, and when the end of the white line neared Lassiter's first stand the head had begun to swing round to the west. It swung slowly and stubbornly, yet surely, and gradually assumed a long, beautiful curve of moving white. To Jane's amaze she saw the leaders swinging, turning till they headed back toward her and up the valley. Out to the right of these wild plunging steers ran Lassiter's black, and Jane's keen eye appreciated the fleet stride and sure-footedness of the blind horse. Then it seemed that the herd moved in a great curve, a huge half-moon with the points of head and tail almost opposite, and a mile apart But Lassiter relentlessly crowded the leaders, sheering them to the left, turning them little by little. And the dust-blinded wild followers plunged on madly in the tracks of their leaders. This ever-moving, ever-changing curve of steers rolled toward Jane and when below her, scarce half a mile, it began to narrow and close into a circle. Lassiter had ridden parallel with her position, turned toward her, then aside, and now he was riding directly away from her, all the time pushing the head of that bobbing line inward.

It was then that Jane, suddenly understanding Lassiter's feat stared and gasped at the riding of this intrepid man. His horse was fleet and tireless, but blind. He had pushed the leaders around and around till they were about to turn in on the inner side of the end of that line of steers. The leaders were already running in a circle; the end of the herd was still running almost straight. But soon they would be wheeling. Then, when Lassiter had the circle formed, how would he escape? With Jane Withersteen prayer was as ready as praise; and she prayed for this man's safety. A circle of dust began to collect. Dimly, as through a yellow veil, Jane saw Lassiter press the leaders inward to close the gap in the sage. She lost sight of him in the dust, again she thought she saw the black, riderless now, rear and drag himself and fall. Lassiter had been thrown—lost! Then he reappeared running out of the dust into the sage. He had escaped, and she breathed again.

Spellbound, Jane Withersteen watched this stupendous millwheel of steers. Here was the milling of the herd. The white running circle closed in upon the open space of sage. And the dust circles closed above into a pall. The ground quaked and the incessant thunder of pounding hoofs rolled on. Jane felt deafened, yet she thrilled to a new sound. As the circle of sage lessened the steers began to bawl, and when it closed entirely there came a great upheaval in the center, and a terrible thumping of heads and clicking of horns. Bawling, climbing, goring, the great mass of steers on the inside wrestled in a crashing din, heaved and groaned under the pressure. Then came a deadlock. The inner strife ceased, and the hideous roar and crash. Movement went on in the outer circle, and that, too, gradually stilled. The white herd had come to a stop, and the pall of yellow dust began to drift away on the wind.

Jane Withersteen waited on the ridge with full and grateful heart. Lassiter appeared, making his weary way toward her through the sage. And up on the slope Judkins rode into sight with his troop of boys. For the present, at least, the white herd would be looked after.

When Lassiter reached her and laid his hand on Black Star's mane, Jane could not find speech.

"Killed—my—hoss," he panted.

"Oh! I'm sorry," cried Jane. "Lassiter! I know you can't replace him, but I'll give you any one of my racers—Bells, or Night, even Black Star."

"I'll take a fast hoss, Jane, but not one of your favorites," he replied. "Only—will you let me have Black Star now an' ride him over there an' head off them fellers who stampeded the herd?"

He pointed to several moving specks of black and puffs of dust in the purple sage.

"I can head them off with this hoss, an' then—"

"Then, Lassiter?"

"They'll never stampede no more cattle."

"Oh! No! No!... Lassiter, I won't let you go!"

But a flush of fire flamed in her cheeks, and her trembling hands shook Black Star's bridle, and her eyes fell before Lassiter's.

✿ 7 ✿

THE DAUGHTER OF WITHERSTEEN

"Lassiter, will you be my rider?" Jane had asked him.

"I reckon so," he had replied.

Few as the words were, Jane knew how infinitely much they implied. She wanted him to take charge of her cattle and horse and ranges, and save them if that were possible. Yet, though she could not have spoken aloud all she meant, she was perfectly honest with herself. Whatever the price to be paid, she must keep Lassiter close to her; she must shield from him the man who had led Milly Erne to Cottonwoods. In her fear she so controlled her mind that she did not whisper this Mormon's name to her own soul, she did not even think it. Besides, beyond this thing she regarded as a sacred obligation thrust upon her, was the need of a helper, of a friend, of a champion in this critical time. If she could rule this gun-man, as Venters had called him, if she could even keep him from shedding blood, what strategy to play his flame and his presence against the game of oppression her churchmen were waging against her? Never would she forget the effect on Tull and his men when Venters shouted Lassiter's name. If she could not wholly control Lassiter, then what she could do might put off the fatal day.

One of her safe racers was a dark bay, and she called him Bells because of the way he struck his iron shoes on the stones. When Jerd led out this slender, beautifully built horse Lassiter suddenly became all eyes. A rider's love of a thoroughbred shone in them. Round and round Bells he walked, plainly weakening all the time in his determination not to take one of Jane's favorite racers.

"Lassiter, you're half horse, and Bells sees it already," said Jane, laughing. "Look at his eyes. He likes you. He'll love you, too. How can you resist him? Oh, Lassiter, but Bells can run! It's nip and tuck between him and Wrangle, and only Black Star can beat him. He's too spirited a horse for a woman. Take him. He's yours."

"I jest am weak where a hoss's concerned," said Lassiter. "I'll take him, an' I'll take your orders, ma'am."

"Well, I'm glad, but never mind the ma'am. Let it still be Jane."

From that hour, it seemed, Lassiter was always in the saddle, riding early and late, and

47

coincident with his part in Jane's affairs the days assumed their old tranquillity. Her intelligence told her this was only the lull before the storm, but her faith would not have it so.

She resumed her visits to the village, and upon one of these she encountered Tull. He greeted her as he had before any trouble came between them, and she, responsive to peace if not quick to forget, met him halfway with manner almost cheerful. He regretted the loss of her cattle; he assured her that the vigilantes which had been organized would soon rout the rustlers; when that had been accomplished her riders would likely return to her.

"You've done a headstrong thing to hire this man Lassiter," Tull went on, severely. "He came to Cottonwoods with evil intent."

"I had to have somebody. And perhaps making him my rider may turn out best in the end for the Mormons of Cottonwoods."

"You mean to stay his hand?"

"I do—if I can."

"A woman like you can do anything with a man. That would be well, and would atone in some measure for the errors you have made."

He bowed and passed on. Jane resumed her walk with conflicting thoughts. She resented Elder Tull's cold, impassive manner that looked down upon her as one who had incurred his just displeasure. Otherwise he would have been the same calm, dark-browed, impenetrable man she had known for ten years. In fact, except when he had revealed his passion in the matter of the seizing of Venters, she had never dreamed he could be other than the grave, reproving preacher. He stood out now a strange, secretive man. She would have thought better of him if he had picked up the threads of their quarrel where they had parted. Was Tull what he appeared to be? The question flung itself in-voluntarily over Jane Withersteen's inhibitive habit of faith without question. And she refused to answer it. Tull could not fight in the open. Venters had said, Lassiter had said, that her Elder shirked fight and worked in the dark. Just now in this meeting Tull had ignored the fact that he had sued, exhorted, demanded that she marry him. He made no mention of Venters. His manner was that of the minister who had been outraged, but who overlooked the frailties of a woman. Beyond question he seemed unutterably aloof from all knowledge of pressure being brought to bear upon her, absolutely guiltless of any connection with secret power over riders, with night journeys, with rustlers and stampedes of cattle. And that convinced her again of unjust suspicions. But it was convincement through an obstinate faith. She shuddered as she accepted it, and that shudder was the nucleus of a terrible revolt.

Jane turned into one of the wide lanes leading from the main street and entered a huge, shady yard. Here were sweet-smelling clover, alfalfa, flowers, and vegetables, all growing in happy confusion. And like these fresh green things were the dozens of babies, tots, toddlers, noisy urchins, laughing girls, a whole multitude of children of one family. For Collier Brandt, the father of all this numerous progeny, was a Mormon with four wives.

The big house where they lived was old, solid, picturesque the lower part built of logs, the upper of rough clapboards, with vines growing up the outside stone chimneys. There were many wooden-shuttered windows, and one pretentious window of glass proudly curtained in white. As this house had four mistresses, it likewise had four separate sections, not one of which communicated with another, and all had to be entered from the outside.

In the shade of a wide, low, vine-roofed porch Jane found Brandt's wives entertaining Bishop Dyer. They were motherly women, of comparatively similar ages, and plain-featured, and just at this moment anything but grave. The Bishop was rather tall, of stout build, with iron-gray hair and beard, and eyes of light blue. They were merry now; but Jane had seen them when they were not, and then she feared him as she had feared her father.

The women flocked around her in welcome.

"Daughter of Withersteen," said the Bishop, gaily, as he took her hand, "you have not been prodigal of your gracious self of late. A Sabbath without you at service! I shall reprove Elder Tull."

"Bishop, the guilt is mine. I'll come to you and confess," Jane replied, lightly; but she felt the undercurrent of her words.

"Mormon love-making!" exclaimed the Bishop, rubbing his hands. "Tull keeps you all to himself."

"No. He is not courting me."

"What? The laggard! If he does not make haste I'll go a-courting myself up to Withersteen House."

There was laughter and further bantering by the Bishop, and then mild talk of village affairs, after which he took his leave, and Jane was left with her friend, Mary Brandt.

"Jane, you're not yourself. Are you sad about the rustling of the cattle? But you have so many, you are so rich."

Then Jane confided in her, telling much, yet holding back her doubts of fear.

"Oh, why don't you marry Tull and be one of us?

"But, Mary, I don't love Tull," said Jane, stubbornly.

"I don't blame you for that. But, Jane Withersteen, you've got to choose between the love of man and love of God. Often we Mormon women have to do that. It's not easy. The kind of happiness you want I wanted once. I never got it, nor will you, unless you throw away your soul. We've all watched your affair with Venters in fear and trembling. Some dreadful thing will come of it. You don't want him hanged or shot—or treated worse, as that Gentile boy was treated in Glaze for fooling round a Mormon woman. Marry Tull. It's your duty as a Mormon. You'll feel no rapture as his wife—but think of Heaven! Mormon women don't marry for what they expect on earth. Take up the cross, Jane. Remember your father found Amber Spring, built these old houses, brought Mormons here, and fathered them. You are the daughter of Withersteen!"

Jane left Mary Brandt and went to call upon other friends. They received her with the same glad welcome as had Mary, lavished upon her the pent-up affection of Mormon women, and let her go with her ears ringing of Tull, Venters, Lassiter, of duty to God and glory in Heaven.

"Verily," murmured Jane, "I don't know myself when, through all this, I remain unchanged—nay, more fixed of purpose."

She returned to the main street and bent her thoughtful steps toward the center of the village. A string of wagons drawn by oxen was lumbering along. These "sage-freighters," as they were called, hauled grain and flour and merchandise from Sterling, and Jane laughed suddenly in the midst of her humility at the thought that they were her property, as was one of the three stores for which they freighted goods. The water that flowed along the path at her feet, and turned into each cottage-yard to nourish garden and orchard, also was hers, no less her private property because she chose to give it free. Yet in this village of Cottonwoods, which her father had founded and which she maintained she was not her own mistress; she was not able to abide by her own choice of a husband. She was the daughter of Withersteen. Suppose she proved it, imperiously! But she quelled that proud temptation at its birth.

Nothing could have replaced the affection which the village people had for her; no power could have made her happy as the pleasure her presence gave. As she went on down the street past the stores with their rude platform entrances, and the saloons where tired horses stood with bridles dragging, she was again assured of what was the bread and wine of life to her—that she was loved. Dirty boys playing in the ditch, clerks, teamsters, riders, loungers on the corners, ranchers on dusty horses, little girls running errands, and women hurrying to the stores all looked up at her coming with glad eyes.

Jane's various calls and wandering steps at length led her to the Gentile quarter of the village. This was at the extreme southern end, and here some thirty Gentile families lived in huts and shacks and log-cabins and several dilapidated cottages. The fortunes of these inhabitants of Cottonwoods could be read in their abodes. Water they had in abundance, and therefore grass and fruit-trees and patches of alfalfa and vegetable gardens. Some of the men and boys had a few stray cattle, others obtained such intermittent employment as the Mormons reluctantly tendered them. But none of the families was prosperous, many were very poor, and some lived only by Jane Withersteen's beneficence.

As it made Jane happy to go among her own people, so it saddened her to come in contact with these Gentiles. Yet that was not because she was unwelcome; here she was gratefully received by the women, passionately by the children. But poverty and idleness, with their attendant wretchedness and sorrow, always hurt her. That she could alleviate this distress more now than ever before proved the adage that it was an ill wind that blew nobody good. While her Mormon riders were in her employ she had found few Gentiles who would stay with her, and now she was able to find employment for all the men and boys. No little shock was it to have man after man tell her that he dare not accept her kind offer.

"It won't do," said one Carson, an intelligent man who had seen better days. "We've had our warning. Plain and to the point! Now there's Judkins, he packs guns, and he can use them, and so can the daredevil boys he's hired. But they've little responsibility. Can we risk having our homes burned in our absence?"

Jane felt the stretching and chilling of the skin of her face as the blood left it.

"Carson, you and the others rent these houses?" she asked.

"You ought to know, Miss Withersteen. Some of them are yours."

"I know?... Carson, I never in my life took a day's labor for rent or a yearling calf or a bunch of grass, let alone gold."

"Bivens, your store-keeper, sees to that."

"Look here, Carson," went on Jane, hurriedly, and now her cheeks were burning. "You and Black and Willet pack your goods and move your families up to my cabins in the grove. They're far more comfortable than these. Then go to work for me. And if aught happens to you there I'll give you money—gold enough to leave Utah!"

The man choked and stammered, and then, as tears welled into his eyes, he found the use of his tongue and cursed. No gentle speech could ever have equaled that curse in eloquent expression of what he felt for Jane Withersteen. How strangely his look and tone reminded her of Lassiter!

"No, it won't do," he said, when he had somewhat recovered himself. "Miss Withersteen, there are things that you don't know, and there's not a soul among us who can tell you."

"I seem to be learning many things, Carson. Well, then, will you let me aid you—say till better times?"

"Yes, I will," he replied, with his face lighting up. "I see what it means to you, and you know what it means to me. Thank you! And if better times ever come, I'll be only too happy to work for you."

"Better times will come. I trust God and have faith in man. Good day, Carson."

The lane opened out upon the sage-inclosed alfalfa fields, and the last habitation, at the end of that lane of hovels, was the meanest. Formerly it had been a shed; now it was a home. The broad leaves of a wide-spreading cottonwood sheltered the sunken roof of weathered boards. Like an Indian hut, it had one floor. Round about it were a few scanty rows of vegetables, such as the hand of a weak woman had time and strength to cultivate. This little dwelling-place was just outside the village limits, and the widow who lived there had to carry her water from the nearest irrigation ditch. As Jane Withersteen entered the unfenced yard a child saw her, shrieked with joy, and came tearing toward her with curls flying. This child was a little girl of four called Fay. Her name suited her, for she was an elf, a sprite, a creature so fairy-like and beautiful that she seemed unearthly.

"Muvver sended for oo," cried Fay, as Jane kissed her, "an' oo never tome."

"I didn't know, Fay; but I've come now."

Fay was a child of outdoors, of the garden and ditch and field, and she was dirty and ragged. But rags and dirt did not hide her beauty. The one thin little bedraggled garment she wore half covered her fine, slim body. Red as cherries were her cheeks and lips; her eyes were violet blue, and the crown of her childish loveliness was the curling golden hair. All the children of Cottonwoods were Jane Withersteen's friends, she loved them all. But Fay was dearest to her. Fay had few playmates, for among the Gentile children there were none near her age, and the Mormon children were forbidden to play with her. So she was a shy, wild, lonely child.

"Muvver's sick," said Fay, leading Jane toward the door of the hut.

Jane went in. There was only one room, rather dark and bare, but it was clean and neat. A woman lay upon a bed.

"Mrs. Larkin, how are you?" asked Jane, anxiously.

"I've been pretty bad for a week, but I'm better now."

"You haven't been here all alone—with no one to wait on you?"

"Oh no! My women neighbors are kind. They take turns coming in."

"Did you send for me?"

"Yes, several times."

"But I had no word—no messages ever got to me."

"I sent the boys, and they left word with your women that I was ill and would you please come."

A sudden deadly sickness seized Jane. She fought the weakness, as she fought to be above suspicious thoughts, and it passed, leaving her conscious of her utter impotence. That, too, passed as her spirit rebounded. But she had again caught a glimpse of dark underhand domination, running its secret lines this time into her own household. Like a spider in the blackness of night an unseen hand had begun to run these dark lines, to turn and twist them about her life, to plait and weave a web. Jane Withersteen knew it now, and in the realization further coolness and sureness came to her, and the fighting courage of her ancestors.

"Mrs. Larkin, you're better, and I'm so glad," said Jane. "But may I not do something for you—a turn at nursing, or send you things, or take care of Fay?"

"You're so good. Since my husband's been gone what would have become of Fay and me but for you? It was about Fay that I wanted to speak to you. This time I thought surely I'd die, and I was worried about Fay. Well, I'll be around all right shortly, but my strength's gone and I won't live long. So I may as well speak now. You remember you've been asking me to let you take Fay and bring her up as your daughter?"

"Indeed yes, I remember. I'll be happy to have her. But I hope the day—"

"Never mind that. The day'll come—sooner or later. I refused your offer, and now I'll tell you why."

"I know why," interposed Jane. "It's because you don't want her brought up as a Mormon."

"No, it wasn't altogether that." Mrs. Larkin raised her thin hand and laid it appealingly on Jane's. "I don't like to tell you. But—it's this: I told all my friends what you wanted. They know you, care for you, and they said for me to trust Fay to you. Women will talk, you know. It got to the ears of Mormons—gossip of your love for Fay and your wanting her. And it came straight back to me, in jealousy, perhaps, that you wouldn't take Fay as much for love of her as because of your religious duty to bring up another girl for some Mormon to marry."

"That's a damnable lie!" cried Jane Withersteen.

"It was what made me hesitate," went on Mrs. Larkin, "but I never believed it at heart. And now I guess I'll let you—"

"Wait! Mrs. Larkin, I may have told little white lies in my life, but never a lie that mattered, that hurt any one. Now believe me. I love little Fay. If I had her near me I'd grow to worship her. When I asked for her I thought only of that love.... Let me prove this. You and Fay come to live with me. I've such a big house, and I'm so lonely. I'll help nurse you, take care of you. When you're better you can work for me. I'll keep little Fay and bring her up— without Mormon teaching. When she's grown, if she should want to leave me, I'll send her, and not empty-handed, back to Illinois where you came from. I promise you."

"I knew it was a lie," replied the mother, and she sank back upon her pillow with something of peace in her white, worn face. "Jane Withersteen, may Heaven bless you! I've been deeply grateful to you. But because you're a Mormon I never felt close to you till now. I don't know much about religion as religion, but your God and my God are the same."

❧ 8 ❧

SURPRISE VALLEY

BACK IN THAT STRANGE CANYON, which Venters had found indeed a valley of surprises, the wounded girl's whispered appeal, almost a prayer, not to take her back to the rustlers crowned the events of the last few days with a confounding climax. That she should not want to return to them staggered Venters. Presently, as logical thought returned, her appeal confirmed his first impression—that she was more unfortunate than bad—and he experienced a sensation of gladness. If he had known before that Oldring's Masked Rider was a woman his opinion would have been formed and he would have considered her abandoned. But his first knowledge had come when he lifted a white face quivering in a convulsion of agony; he had heard God's name whispered by blood-stained lips; through her solemn and awful eyes he had caught a glimpse of her soul. And just now had come the entreaty to him, "Don't—take—me—back—there!"

Once for all Venters's quick mind formed a permanent conception of this poor girl. He based it, not upon what the chances of life had made her, but upon the revelation of dark eyes that pierced the infinite, upon a few pitiful, halting words that betrayed failure and wrong and misery, yet breathed the truth of a tragic fate rather than a natural leaning to evil.

"What's your name?" he inquired.

"Bess," she answered.

"Bess what?"

"That's enough—just Bess."

The red that deepened in her cheeks was not all the flush of fever. Venters marveled anew, and this time at the tint of shame in her face, at the momentary drooping of long lashes. She might be a rustler's girl, but she was still capable of shame, she might be dying, but she still clung to some little remnant of honor.

"Very well, Bess. It doesn't matter," he said. "But this matters—what shall I do with you?"

"Are—you—a rider?" she whispered.

"Not now. I was once. I drove the Withersteen herds. But I lost my place—lost all I owned —and now I'm—I'm a sort of outcast. My name's Bern Venters."

"You won't—take me—to Cottonwoods—or Glaze? I'd be—hanged."

"No, indeed. But I must do something with you. For it's not safe for me here. I shot that rustler who was with you. Sooner or later he'll be found, and then my tracks. I must find a safer hiding-place where I can't be trailed."

"Leave me—here."

"Alone—to die!"

"Yes."

"I will not." Venters spoke shortly with a kind of ring in his voice.

"What—do you want—to do—with me?" Her whispering grew difficult, so low and faint that Venters had to stoop to hear her.

"Why, let's see," he replied, slowly. "I'd like to take you some place where I could watch by you, nurse you, till you're all right."

"And—then?"

"Well, it'll be time to think of that when you're cured of your wound. It's a bad one. And —Bess, if you don't want to live—if you don't fight for life—you'll never—"

"Oh! I want—to live! I'm afraid—to die. But I'd rather—die—than go back—to—to—"

"To Oldring?" asked Venters, interrupting her in turn.

Her lips moved in an affirmative.

"I promise not to take you back to him or to Cottonwoods or to Glaze."

The mournful earnestness of her gaze suddenly shone with unutterable gratitude and wonder. And as suddenly Venters found her eyes beautiful as he had never seen or felt beauty. They were as dark blue as the sky at night. Then the flashing changed to a long, thoughtful look, in which there was a wistful, unconscious searching of his face, a look that trembled on the verge of hope and trust.

"I'll try—to live," she said. The broken whisper just reached his ears. "Do what—you want—with me."

"Rest then—don't worry—sleep," he replied.

Abruptly he arose, as if words had been decision for him, and with a sharp command to the dogs he strode from the camp. Venters was conscious of an indefinite conflict of change within him. It seemed to be a vague passing of old moods, a dim coalescing of new forces, a moment of inexplicable transition. He was both cast down and uplifted. He wanted to think and think of the meaning, but he resolutely dispelled emotion. His imperative need at present was to find a safe retreat, and this called for action.

So he set out. It still wanted several hours before dark. This trip he turned to the left and wended his skulking way southward a mile or more to the opening of the valley, where lay the strange scrawled rocks. He did not, however, venture boldly out into the open sage, but clung to the right-hand wall and went along that till its perpendicular line broke into the long incline of bare stone.

Before proceeding farther he halted, studying the strange character of this slope and realizing that a moving black object could be seen far against such background. Before him ascended a gradual swell of smooth stone. It was hard, polished, and full of pockets worn by centuries of eddying rain-water. A hundred yards up began a line of grotesque cedar-trees, and they extended along the slope clear to its most southerly end. Beyond that end Venters wanted to get, and he concluded the cedars, few as they were, would afford some cover.

Therefore he climbed swiftly. The trees were farther up than he had estimated, though he had from long habit made allowance for the deceiving nature of distances in that country. When he gained the cover of cedars he paused to rest and look, and it was then he saw how the trees sprang from holes in the bare rock. Ages of rain had run down the slope, circling, eddying in depressions, wearing deep round holes. There had been dry seasons, accumulations of dust, wind-blown seeds, and cedars rose wonderfully out of solid rock. But these were not beautiful cedars. They were gnarled, twisted into weird contortions, as if growth were torture, dead at the tops, shrunken, gray, and old. Theirs had been a bitter fight, and Venters felt a strange sympathy for them. This country was hard on trees—and men.

He slipped from cedar to cedar, keeping them between him and the open valley. As he progressed, the belt of trees widened and he kept to its upper margin. He passed shady pockets half full of water, and, as he marked the location for possible future need, he reflected that there had been no rain since the winter snows. From one of these shady holes a rabbit hopped out and squatted down, laying its ears flat.

Venters wanted fresh meat now more than when he had only himself to think of. But it would not do to fire his rifle there. So he broke off a cedar branch and threw it. He crippled the rabbit, which started to flounder up the slope. Venters did not wish to lose the meat, and he never allowed crippled game to escape, to die lingeringly in some covert. So after a careful glance below, and back toward the canyon, he began to chase the rabbit.

The fact that rabbits generally ran uphill was not new to him. But it presently seemed singular why this rabbit, that might have escaped downward, chose to ascend the slope. Venters knew then that it had a burrow higher up. More than once he jerked over to seize it, only in vain, for the rabbit by renewed effort eluded his grasp. Thus the chase continued on up the bare slope. The farther Venters climbed the more determined he grew to catch his quarry. At last, panting and sweating, he captured the rabbit at the foot of a steeper grade. Laying his rifle on the bulge of rising stone, he killed the animal and slung it from his belt.

Before starting down he waited to catch his breath. He had climbed far up that wonderful smooth slope, and had almost reached the base of yellow cliff that rose skyward, a huge scarred and cracked bulk. It frowned down upon him as if to forbid further ascent. Venters bent over for his rifle, and, as he picked it up from where it leaned against the steeper grade, he saw several little nicks cut in the solid stone.

They were only a few inches deep and about a foot apart. Venters began to count them— one—two—three—four—on up to sixteen. That number carried his glance to the top of his first bulging bench of cliff-base. Above, after a more level offset, was still steeper slope, and the line of nicks kept on, to wind round a projecting corner of wall.

A casual glance would have passed by these little dents; if Venters had not known what they signified he would never have bestowed upon them the second glance. But he knew they had been cut there by hand, and, though age-worn, he recognized them as steps cut in the rock by the cliff-dwellers. With a pulse beginning to beat and hammer away his calmness, he eyed that indistinct line of steps, up to where the buttress of wall hid further sight of them. He knew that behind the corner of stone would be a cave or a crack which could never be suspected from below. Chance, that had sported with him of late, now directed him to a probable hiding-place. Again he laid aside his rifle, and, removing boots and belt, he began to walk up the steps. Like a mountain goat, he was agile, sure-footed, and he mounted the first bench without bending to use his hands. The next ascent took grip of fingers as well as toes, but he climbed steadily, swiftly, to reach the projecting corner, and slipped around it. Here he faced a notch in the cliff. At the apex he turned abruptly into a ragged vent that split the ponderous wall clear to the top, showing a narrow streak of blue sky.

At the base this vent was dark, cool, and smelled of dry, musty dust. It zigzagged so that he could not see ahead more than a few yards at a time. He noticed tracks of wildcats and rabbits in the dusty floor. At every turn he expected to come upon a huge cavern full of little square stone houses, each with a small aperture like a staring dark eye. The passage lightened and widened, and opened at the foot of a narrow, steep, ascending chute.

Venters had a moment's notice of the rock, which was of the same smoothness and hardness as the slope below, before his gaze went irresistibly upward to the precipitous walls of this wide ladder of granite. These were ruined walls of yellow sandstone, and so split and splintered, so overhanging with great sections of balancing rim, so impending with tremendous crumbling crags, that Venters caught his breath sharply, and, appalled, he instinctively recoiled as if a step upward might jar the ponderous cliffs from their foundation. Indeed, it seemed that these ruined cliffs were but awaiting a breath of wind to collapse and come tumbling down. Venters hesitated. It would be a foolhardy man who risked his life under the leaning, waiting avalanches of rock in that gigantic split. Yet how many years had they leaned there without falling! At the bottom of the incline was an immense heap of weathered sandstone all crumbling to dust, but there were no huge rocks as large as houses, such as rested so lightly and frightfully above, waiting patiently and inevitably to crash down. Slowly split from the parent rock by the weathering process, and carved and sculptured by ages of wind and rain, they waited their moment. Venters felt how foolish it was for him to fear these broken walls; to fear that, after they had endured for thousands of years, the moment of his passing should be the one for them to slip. Yet he feared it.

"What a place to hide!" muttered Venters. "I'll climb—I'll see where this thing goes. If only I can find water!"

With teeth tight shut he essayed the incline. And as he climbed he bent his eyes downward. This, however, after a little grew impossible; he had to look to obey his eager, curious mind. He raised his glance and saw light between row on row of shafts and pinnacles and crags that stood out from the main wall. Some leaned against the cliff, others against each other; many stood sheer and alone; all were crumbling, cracked, rotten. It was a place of yellow, ragged ruin. The passage narrowed as he went up; it became a slant, hard for him to stick on; it was smooth as marble. Finally he surmounted it, surprised to find the walls still several hundred feet high, and a narrow gorge leading down on the other side. This was a divide between two inclines, about twenty yards wide. At one side stood an enormous rock. Venters gave it a second glance, because it rested on a pedestal. It attracted closer attention. It was like a colossal pear of stone standing on its stem. Around the bottom were thousands of little nicks just distinguishable to the eye. They were marks of stone hatchets. The cliff-dwellers had chipped and chipped away at this boulder till it rested its tremendous bulk upon a mere pin-point of its surface. Venters pondered. Why had the little stone-men hacked away at that big boulder? It bore no semblance to a statue or an idol or a godhead or a sphinx. Instinctively he put his hands on it and pushed; then his shoulder and heaved. The stone seemed to groan, to stir, to grate, and then to move. It tipped a little downward and hung balancing for a long instant, slowly returned, rocked slightly, groaned, and settled back to its former position.

Venters divined its significance. It had been meant for defense. The cliff-dwellers, driven by dreaded enemies to this last stand, had cunningly cut the rock until it balanced perfectly, ready to be dislodged by strong hands. Just below it leaned a tottering crag that would have toppled, starting an avalanche on an acclivity where no sliding mass could stop. Crags and pinnacles, splintered cliffs, and leaning shafts and monuments, would have thundered down to block forever the outlet to Deception Pass.

"That was a narrow shave for me," said Venters, soberly. "A balancing rock! The cliff-dwellers never had to roll it. They died, vanished, and here the rock stands, probably little changed.... But it might serve another lonely dweller of the cliffs. I'll hide up here somewhere, if I can only find water."

He descended the gorge on the other side. The slope was gradual, the space narrow, the course straight for many rods. A gloom hung between the up-sweeping walls. In a turn the passage narrowed to scarce a dozen feet, and here was darkness of night. But light shone ahead; another abrupt turn brought day again, and then wide open space.

Above Venters loomed a wonderful arch of stone bridging the canyon rims, and through the enormous round portal gleamed and glistened a beautiful valley shining under sunset gold reflected by surrounding cliffs. He gave a start of surprise. The valley was a cove a mile long, half that wide, and its enclosing walls were smooth and stained, and curved inward, forming great caves. He decided that its floor was far higher than the level of Deception Pass and the intersecting canyons. No purple sage colored this valley floor. Instead there were the white of aspens, streaks of branch and slender trunk glistening from the green of leaves, and the darker green of oaks, and through the middle of this forest, from wall to wall, ran a winding line of brilliant green which marked the course of cottonwoods and willows.

"There's water here—and this is the place for me," said Venters. "Only birds can peep over those walls, I've gone Oldring one better."

Venters waited no longer, and turned swiftly to retrace his steps. He named the canyon Surprise Valley and the huge boulder that guarded the outlet Balancing Rock. Going down he did not find himself attended by such fears as had beset him in the climb; still, he was not easy in mind and could not occupy himself with plans of moving the girl and his outfit until he had descended to the notch. There he rested a moment and looked about him. The pass was darkening with the approach of night. At the corner of the wall, where the stone steps turned, he saw a spur of rock that would serve to hold the noose of a lasso. He needed no more aid to scale that place. As he intended to make the move under cover of darkness, he wanted most to be able to tell where to climb up. So, taking several small stones with him, he stepped and slid down to the edge of the slope where he had left his rifle and boots. He placed the stones some yards apart. He left the rabbit lying upon the bench where the steps began. Then he addressed a keen-sighted, remembering gaze to the rim-wall above. It was serrated, and between two spears of rock, directly in line with his position, showed a zigzag crack that at night would let through the gleam of sky. This settled, he put on his belt and boots and prepared to descend. Some consideration was necessary to decide whether or not to leave his rifle there. On the return, carrying the girl and a pack, it would be added encumbrance; and after debating the matter he left the rifle leaning against the bench. As he went straight down the slope he halted every few rods to look up at his mark on the rim. It changed, but he fixed each change in his memory. When he reached the first cedar-tree, he tied his scarf upon a dead branch, and then hurried toward camp, having no more concern about finding his trail upon the return trip.

Darkness soon emboldened and lent him greater speed. It occurred to him, as he glided into the grassy glade near camp and head the whinny of a horse, that he had forgotten Wrangle. The big sorrel could not be gotten into Surprise Valley. He would have to be left here.

Venters determined at once to lead the other horses out through the thicket and turn them loose. The farther they wandered from this canyon the better it would suit him. He easily descried Wrangle through the gloom, but the others were not in sight. Venters whistled low for the dogs, and when they came trotting to him he sent them out to search for the horses, and followed. It soon developed that they were not in the glade nor the thicket. Venters grew cold and rigid at the thought of rustlers having entered his retreat. But the thought passed, for the demeanor of Ring and Whitie reassured him. The horses had wandered away.

Under the clump of silver spruces a denser mantle of darkness, yet not so thick that Venter's night-practiced eyes could not catch the white oval of a still face. He bent over it with a slight suspension of breath that was both caution lest he frighten her and chill uncertainty of feeling lest he find her dead. But she slept, and he arose to renewed activity.

He packed his saddle-bags. The dogs were hungry, they whined about him and nosed his busy hands; but he took no time to feed them nor to satisfy his own hunger. He slung the saddlebags over his shoulders and made them secure with his lasso. Then he wrapped the blankets closer about the girl and lifted her in his arms. Wrangle whinnied and thumped the ground as Venters passed him with the dogs. The sorrel knew he was being left behind, and was not sure whether he liked it or not. Venters went on and entered the thicket. Here he had to feel his way in pitch blackness and to wedge his progress between the close saplings. Time meant little to him now that he had started, and he edged along with slow side movement till he got clear of the thicket. Ring and Whitie stood waiting for him. Taking to the open aisles and patches of the sage, he walked guardedly, careful not to stumble or step in dust or strike against spreading sage-branches.

If he were burdened he did not feel it. From time to time, when he passed out of the black lines of shade into the wan starlight, he glanced at the white face of the girl lying in his arms. She had not awakened from her sleep or stupor. He did not rest until he cleared the black gate of the canyon. Then he leaned against a stone breast-high to him and gently released the girl from his hold. His brow and hair and the palms of his hands were wet, and there was a kind of nervous contraction of his muscles. They seemed to ripple and string tense. He had a desire to hurry and no sense of fatigue. A wind blew the scent of sage in his face. The first early blackness of night passed with the brightening of the stars. Somewhere back on his trail a coyote yelped, splitting the dead silence. Venters's faculties seemed singularly acute.

He lifted the girl again and pressed on. The valley better traveling than the canyon. It was lighter, freer of sage, and there were no rocks. Soon, out of the pale gloom shone a still paler thing, and that was the low swell of slope. Venters mounted it and his dogs walked beside him. Once upon the stone he slowed to snail pace, straining his sight to avoid the pockets and holes. Foot by foot he went up. The weird cedars, like great demons and witches chained to the rock and writhing in silent anguish, loomed up with wide and twisting naked arms. Venters crossed this belt of cedars, skirted the upper border, and recognized the tree he had marked, even before he saw his waving scarf.

Here he knelt and deposited the girl gently, feet first and slowly laid her out full length. What he feared was to reopen one of her wounds. If he gave her a violent jar, or slipped and fell! But the supreme confidence so strangely felt that night admitted no such blunders.

The slope before him seemed to swell into obscurity to lose its definite outline in a misty, opaque cloud that shaded into the over-shadowing wall. He scanned the rim where the serrated points speared the sky, and he found the zigzag crack. It was dim, only a shade lighter than the dark ramparts, but he distinguished it, and that served.

Lifting the girl, he stepped upward, closely attending to the nature of the path under his feet. After a few steps he stopped to mark his line with the crack in the rim. The dogs clung closer to him. While chasing the rabbit this slope had appeared interminable to him; now, burdened as he was, he did not think of length or height or toil. He remembered only to avoid a misstep and to keep his direction. He climbed on, with frequent stops to watch the rim, and before he dreamed of gaining the bench he bumped his knees into it, and saw, in the dim gray light, his rifle and the rabbit. He had come straight up without mishap or swerving off his course, and his shut teeth unlocked.

As he laid the girl down in the shallow hollow of the little ridge with her white face upturned, she opened her eyes. Wide, staring black, at once like both the night and the stars, they made her face seem still whiter.

"Is—it—you?" she asked, faintly.

"Yes," replied Venters.

"Oh! Where—are we?"

"I'm taking you to a safe place where no one will ever find you. I must climb a little here and call the dogs. Don't be afraid. I'll soon come for you."

She said no more. Her eyes watched him steadily for a moment and then closed. Venters pulled off his boots and then felt for the little steps in the rock. The shade of the cliff above obscured the point he wanted to gain, but he could see dimly a few feet before him. What he had attempted with care he now went at with surpassing lightness. Buoyant, rapid, sure, he attained the corner of wall and slipped around it. Here he could not see a hand before his face, so he groped along, found a little flat space, and there removed the saddle-bags. The lasso he took back with him to the corner and looped the noose over the spur of rock.

"Ring—Whitie—come," he called, softly.

Low whines came up from below.

"Here! Come, Whitie—Ring," he repeated, this time sharply.

Then followed scraping of claws and pattering of feet; and out of the gray gloom below him swiftly climbed the dogs to reach his side and pass beyond.

Venters descended, holding to the lasso. He tested its strength by throwing all his weight upon it. Then he gathered the girl up, and, holding her securely in his left arm, he began to climb, at every few steps jerking his right hand upward along the lasso. It sagged at each forward movement he made, but he balanced himself lightly during the interval when he lacked the support of a taut rope. He climbed as if he had wings, the strength of a giant, and knew not the sense of fear. The sharp corner of cliff seemed to cut out of the darkness. He reached it and the protruding shelf, and then, entering the black shade of the notch, he moved blindly but surely to the place where he had left the saddle-bags. He heard the dogs, though he could not see them. Once more he carefully placed the girl at his feet. Then, on hands and knees, he went over the little flat space, feeling for stones. He removed a number, and, scraping the deep dust into a heap, he unfolded the outer blanket from around the girl and laid her upon this bed. Then he went down the slope again for his boots, rifle, and the rabbit, and, bringing also his lasso with him, he made short work of that trip.

"Are—you—there?" The girl's voice came low from the blackness.

"Yes," he replied, and was conscious that his laboring breast made speech difficult.

"Are we—in a cave?"

"Yes."

"Oh, listen!... The waterfall!... I hear it! You've brought me back!"

Venters heard a murmuring moan that one moment swelled to a pitch almost softly shrill and the next lulled to a low, almost inaudible sigh.

"That's—wind blowing—in the—cliffs," he panted. "You're far from Oldring's—canyon."

The effort it cost him to speak made him conscious of extreme lassitude following upon great exertion. It seemed that when he lay down and drew his blanket over him the action was the last before utter prostration. He stretched inert, wet, hot, his body one great strife of throbbing, stinging nerves and bursting veins. And there he lay for a long while before he felt that he had begun to rest.

Rest came to him that night, but no sleep. Sleep he did not want. The hours of strained effort were now as if they had never been, and he wanted to think. Earlier in the day he dismissed an inexplicable feeling of change; but now, when there was no longer demand on his cunning and strength and he had time to think, he could not catch the illusive thing that had sadly perplexed as well as elevated his spirit.

59

Above him, through a V-shaped cleft in the dark rim of the cliff, shone the lustrous stars that had been his lonely accusers for a long, long year. To-night they were different. He studied them. Larger, whiter, more radiant they seemed; but that was not the difference he meant. Gradually it came to him that the distinction was not one he saw, but one he felt. In this he divined as much of the baffling change as he thought would be revealed to him then. And as he lay there, with the singing of the cliff-winds in his ears, the white stars above the dark, bold vent, the difference which he felt was that he was no longer alone.

SILVER SPRUCE AND ASPENS

THE REST of that night seemed to Venters only a few moments of starlight, a dark overcasting of sky, an hour or so of gray gloom, and then the lighting of dawn.

When he had bestirred himself, feeding the hungry dogs and breaking his long fast, and had repacked his saddle-bags, it was clear daylight, though the sun had not tipped the yellow wall in the east. He concluded to make the climb and descent into Surprise Valley in one trip. To that end he tied his blanket upon Ring and gave Whitie the extra lasso and the rabbit to carry. Then, with the rifle and saddle-bags slung upon his back, he took up the girl. She did not awaken from heavy slumber.

That climb up under the rugged, menacing brows of the broken cliffs, in the face of a grim, leaning boulder that seemed to be weary of its age-long wavering, was a tax on strength and nerve that Venters felt equally with something sweet and strangely exulting in its accomplishment. He did not pause until he gained the narrow divide and there he rested. Balancing Rock loomed huge, cold in the gray light of dawn, a thing without life, yet it spoke silently to Venters: "I am waiting to plunge down, to shatter and crash, roar and boom, to bury your trail, and close forever the outlet to Deception Pass!"

On the descent of the other side Venters had easy going, but was somewhat concerned because Whitie appeared to have succumbed to temptation, and while carrying the rabbit was also chewing on it. And Ring evidently regarded this as an injury to himself, especially as he had carried the heavier load. Presently he snapped at one end of the rabbit and refused to let go. But his action prevented Whitie from further misdoing, and then the two dogs pattered down, carrying the rabbit between them.

Venters turned out of the gorge, and suddenly paused stock-still, astounded at the scene before him. The curve of the great stone bridge had caught the sunrise, and through the magnificent arch burst a glorious stream of gold that shone with a long slant down into the center of Surprise Valley. Only through the arch did any sunlight pass, so that all the rest of the valley lay still asleep, dark green, mysterious, shadowy, merging its level into walls as misty and soft as morning clouds.

Venters then descended, passing through the arch, looking up at its tremendous height and sweep. It spanned the opening to Surprise Valley, stretching in almost perfect curve from rim to rim. Even in his hurry and concern Venters could not but feel its majesty, and the thought came to him that the cliff-dwellers must have regarded it as an object of worship.

Down, down, down Venters strode, more and more feeling the weight of his burden as he descended, and still the valley lay below him. As all other canyons and coves and valleys had deceived him, so had this deep, nestling oval. At length he passed beyond the slope of weathered stone that spread fan-shape from the arch, and encountered a grassy terrace running to the right and about on a level with the tips of the oaks and cottonwoods below. Scattered here and there upon this shelf were clumps of aspens, and he walked through them into a glade that surpassed in beauty and adaptability for a wild home, any place he had ever seen. Silver spruces bordered the base of a precipitous wall that rose loftily. Caves indented its surface, and there were no detached ledges or weathered sections that might dislodge a stone. The level ground, beyond the spruces, dropped down into a little ravine. This was one dense line of slender aspens from which came the low splashing of water. And the terrace, lying open to the west, afforded unobstructed view of the valley of green treetops.

For his camp Venters chose a shady, grassy plot between the silver spruces and the cliff. Here, in the stone wall, had been wonderfully carved by wind or washed by water several deep caves above the level of the terrace. They were clean, dry, roomy.

He cut spruce boughs and made a bed in the largest cave and laid the girl there. The first intimation that he had of her being aroused from sleep or lethargy was a low call for water.

He hurried down into the ravine with his canteen. It was a shallow, grass-green place with aspens growing up everywhere. To his delight he found a tiny brook of swift-running water. Its faint tinge of amber reminded him of the spring at Cottonwoods, and the thought gave him a little shock. The water was so cold it made his fingers tingle as he dipped the canteen. Having returned to the cave, he was glad to see the girl drink thirstily. This time he noted that she could raise her head slightly without his help.

"You were thirsty," he said. "It's good water. I've found a fine place. Tell me—how do you feel?"

"There's pain—here," she replied, and moved her hand to her left side.

"Why, that's strange! Your wounds are on your right side. I believe you're hungry. Is the pain a kind of dull ache—a gnawing?"

"It's like—that."

"Then it's hunger." Venters laughed, and suddenly caught himself with a quick breath and felt again the little shock. When had he laughed? "It's hunger," he went on. "I've had that gnaw many a time. I've got it now. But you mustn't eat. You can have all the water you want, but no food just yet."

"Won't I—starve?"

"No, people don't starve easily. I've discovered that. You must lie perfectly still and rest and sleep—for days."

"My hands—are dirty; my face feels—so hot and sticky; my boots hurt." It was her longest speech as yet, and it trailed off in a whisper.

"Well, I'm a fine nurse!"

It annoyed him that he had never thought of these things. But then, awaiting her death and thinking of her comfort were vastly different matters. He unwrapped the blanket which covered her. What a slender girl she was! No wonder he had been able to carry her miles and pack her up that slippery ladder of stone. Her boots were of soft, fine leather, reaching clear to her knees. He recognized the make as one of a boot-maker in Sterling. Her spurs, that he had stupidly neglected to remove, consisted of silver frames and gold chains, and the rowels, large as silver dollars, were fancifully engraved. The boots slipped off rather hard. She wore heavy woollen rider's stockings, half length, and these were pulled up over the ends of her short trousers. Venters took off the stockings to note her little feet were red and swollen. He bathed them. Then he removed his scarf and bathed her face and hands.

"I must see your wounds now," he said, gently.

She made no reply, but watched him steadily as he opened her blouse and untied the bandage. His strong fingers trembled a little as he removed it. If the wounds had reopened! A chill struck him as he saw the angry red bullet-mark, and a tiny stream of blood winding from it down her white breast. Very carefully he lifted her to see that the wound in her back had closed perfectly. Then he washed the blood from her breast, bathed the wound, and left it unbandaged, open to the air.

Her eyes thanked him.

"Listen," he said, earnestly. "I've had some wounds, and I've seen many. I know a little about them. The hole in your back has closed. If you lie still three days the one in your breast will close and you'll be safe. The danger from hemorrhage will be over."

He had spoken with earnest sincerity, almost eagerness.

"Why—do you—want me—to get well?" she asked, wonderingly.

The simple question seemed unanswerable except on grounds of humanity. But the circumstances under which he had shot this strange girl, the shock and realization, the waiting for death, the hope, had resulted in a condition of mind wherein Venters wanted her to live more than he had ever wanted anything. Yet he could not tell why. He believed the killing of the rustler and the subsequent excitement had disturbed him. For how else could he explain the throbbing of his brain, the heat of his blood, the undefined sense of full hours, charged, vibrant with pulsating mystery where once they had dragged in loneliness?

"I shot you," he said, slowly, "and I want you to get well so I shall not have killed a woman. But—for your own sake, too—"

A terrible bitterness darkened her eyes, and her lips quivered.

"Hush," said Venters. "You've talked too much already."

In her unutterable bitterness he saw a darkness of mood that could not have been caused by her present weak and feverish state. She hated the life she had led, that she probably had been compelled to lead. She had suffered some unforgivable wrong at the hands of Oldring. With that conviction Venters felt a shame throughout his body, and it marked the rekindling of fierce anger and ruthlessness. In the past long year he had nursed resentment. He had hated the wilderness—the loneliness of the uplands. He had waited for something to come to pass. It had come. Like an Indian stealing horses he had skulked into the recesses of the canyons. He had found Oldring's retreat; he had killed a rustler; he had shot an unfortunate girl, then had saved her from this unwitting act, and he meant to save her from the consequent wasting of blood, from fever and weakness. Starvation he had to fight for her and for himself. Where he had been sick at the letting of blood, now he remembered it in grim, cold calm. And as he lost that softness of nature, so he lost his fear of men. He would watch for Oldring, biding his time, and he would kill this great black-bearded rustler who had held a girl in bondage, who had used her to his infamous ends.

Venters surmised this much of the change in him—idleness had passed; keen, fierce vigor flooded his mind and body; all that had happened to him at Cottonwoods seemed remote and hard to recall; the difficulties and perils of the present absorbed him, held him in a kind of spell.

First, then, he fitted up the little cave adjoining the girl's room for his own comfort and use. His next work was to build a fireplace of stones and to gather a store of wood. That done, he spilled the contents of his saddle-bags upon the grass and took stock. His outfit consisted of a small-handled axe, a hunting-knife, a large number of cartridges for rifle or revolver, a tin plate, a cup, and a fork and spoon, a quantity of dried beef and dried fruits, and small canvas bags containing tea, sugar, salt, and pepper. For him alone this supply would have been bountiful to begin a sojourn in the wilderness, but he was no longer alone. Starvation in the uplands was not an unheard-of thing; he did not, however, worry at all on that score, and feared only his possible inability to supply the needs of a woman in a weakened and extremely delicate condition.

If there was no game in the valley—a contingency he doubted—it would not be a great task for him to go by night to Oldring's herd and pack out a calf. The exigency of the moment was to ascertain if there were game in Surprise Valley. Whitie still guarded the dilapidated rabbit, and Ring slept near by under a spruce. Venters called Ring and went to the edge of the terrace, and there halted to survey the valley.

He was prepared to find it larger than his unstudied glances had made it appear; for more than a casual idea of dimensions and a hasty conception of oval shape and singular beauty he had not had time. Again the felicity of the name he had given the valley struck him forcibly. Around the red perpendicular walls, except under the great arc of stone, ran a terrace fringed at the cliff-base by silver spruces; below that first terrace sloped another wider one densely overgrown with aspens, and the center of the valley was a level circle of oaks and alders, with the glittering green line of willows and cottonwood dividing it in half. Venters saw a number and variety of birds flitting among the trees. To his left, facing the stone bridge, an enormous cavern opened in the wall; and low down, just above the tree-tops, he made out a long shelf of cliff-dwellings, with little black, staring windows or doors. Like eyes they were, and seemed to watch him. The few cliff-dwellings he had seen—all ruins—had left him with haunting memory of age and solitude and of something past. He had come, in a way, to be a cliff-dweller himself, and those silent eyes would look down upon him, as if in surprise that after thousands of years a man had invaded the valley. Venters felt sure that he was the only white man who had ever walked under the shadow of the wonderful stone bridge, down into that wonderful valley with its circle of caves and its terraced rings of silver spruce and aspens.

The dog growled below and rushed into the forest. Venters ran down the declivity to enter a zone of light shade streaked with sunshine. The oak-trees were slender, none more than half a foot thick, and they grew close together, intermingling their branches. Ring came running back with a rabbit in his mouth. Venters took the rabbit and, holding the dog near him, stole softly on. There were fluttering of wings among the branches and quick bird-notes, and rustling of dead leaves and rapid patterings. Venters crossed well-worn trails marked with fresh tracks; and when he had stolen on a little farther he saw many birds and running quail, and more rabbits than he could count. He had not penetrated the forest of oaks for a hundred yards, had not approached anywhere near the line of willows and cottonwoods which he knew grew along a stream. But he had seen enough to know that Surprise Valley was the home of many wild creatures.

Venters returned to camp. He skinned the rabbits, and gave the dogs the one they had quarreled over, and the skin of this he dressed and hung up to dry, feeling that he would like to keep it. It was a particularly rich, furry pelt with a beautiful white tail. Venters remembered that but for the bobbing of that white tail catching his eye he would not have espied the rabbit, and he would never have discovered Surprise Valley. Little incidents of chance like this had turned him here and there in Deception Pass; and now they had assumed to him the significance and direction of destiny.

His good fortune in the matter of game at hand brought to his mind the necessity of keeping it in the valley. Therefore he took the axe and cut bundles of aspens and willows, and packed them up under the bridge to the narrow outlet of the gorge. Here he began fashioning a fence, by driving aspens into the ground and lacing them fast with willows. Trip after trip he made down for more building material, and the afternoon had passed when he finished the work to his satisfaction. Wildcats might scale the fence, but no coyote could come in to search for prey, and no rabbits or other small game could escape from the valley.

Upon returning to camp he set about getting his supper at ease, around a fine fire, without hurry or fear of discovery. After hard work that had definite purpose, this freedom and comfort gave him peculiar satisfaction. He caught himself often, as he kept busy round the camp-fire, stopping to glance at the quiet form in the cave, and at the dogs stretched cozily near him, and then out across the beautiful valley. The present was not yet real to him.

While he ate, the sun set beyond a dip in the rim of the curved wall. As the morning sun burst wondrously through a grand arch into this valley, in a golden, slanting shaft, so the evening sun, at the moment of setting, shone through a gap of cliffs, sending down a broad red burst to brighten the oval with a blaze of fire. To Venters both sunrise and sunset were unreal.

A cool wind blew across the oval, waving the tips of oaks, and while the light lasted, fluttering the aspen leaves into millions of facets of red, and sweeping the graceful spruces. Then with the wind soon came a shade and a darkening, and suddenly the valley was gray. Night came there quickly after the sinking of the sun. Venters went softly to look at the girl. She slept, and her breathing was quiet and slow. He lifted Ring into the cave, with stern whisper for him to stay there on guard. Then he drew the blanket carefully over her and returned to the camp-fire.

Though exceedingly tired, he was yet loath to yield to lassitude, but this night it was not from listening, watchful vigilance; it was from a desire to realize his position. The details of his wild environment seemed the only substance of a strange dream. He saw the darkening rims, the gray oval turning black, the undulating surface of forest, like a rippling lake, and the spear-pointed spruces. He heard the flutter of aspen leaves and the soft, continuous splash of falling water. The melancholy note of a canyon bird broke clear and lonely from the high cliffs. Venters had no name for this night singer, and he had never seen one, but the few notes, always pealing out just at darkness, were as familiar to him as the canyon silence. Then they ceased, and the rustle of leaves and the murmur of water hushed in a growing sound that Venters fancied was not of earth. Neither had he a name for this, only it was inexpressibly wild and sweet. The thought came that it might be a moan of the girl in her last outcry of life, and he felt a tremor shake him. But no! This sound was not human, though it was like despair. He began to doubt his sensitive perceptions, to believe that he half-dreamed what he thought he heard. Then the sound swelled with the strengthening of the breeze, and he realized it was the singing of the wind in the cliffs.

By and by a drowsiness overcame him, and Venters began to nod, half asleep, with his back against a spruce. Rousing himself and calling Whitie, he went to the cave. The girl lay barely visible in the dimness. Ring crouched beside her, and the patting of his tail on the stone assured Venters that the dog was awake and faithful to his duty. Venters sought his own bed of fragrant boughs; and as he lay back, somehow grateful for the comfort and safety, the night seemed to steal away from him and he sank softly into intangible space and rest and slumber.

Venters awakened to the sound of melody that he imagined was only the haunting echo of dream music. He opened his eyes to another surprise of this valley of beautiful surprises.

Out of his cave he saw the exquisitely fine foliage of the silver spruces crossing a round space of blue morning sky; and in this lacy leafage fluttered a number of gray birds with black and white stripes and long tails. They were mocking-birds, and they were singing as if they wanted to burst their throats. Venters listened. One long, silver-tipped branch dropped almost to his cave, and upon it, within a few yards of him, sat one of the graceful birds. Venters saw the swelling and quivering of its throat in song. He arose, and when he slid down out of his cave the birds fluttered and flew farther away.

Venters stepped before the opening of the other cave and looked in. The girl was awake, with wide eyes and listening look, and she had a hand on Ring's neck.

"Mocking-birds!" she said.

"Yes," replied Venters, "and I believe they like our company."

"Where are we?"

"Never mind now. After a little I'll tell you."

"The birds woke me. When I heard them—and saw the shiny trees—and the blue sky— and then a blaze of gold dropping down—I wondered—"

She did not complete her fancy, but Venters imagined he understood her meaning. She appeared to be wandering in mind. Venters felt her face and hands and found them burning with fever. He went for water, and was glad to find it almost as cold as if flowing from ice. That water was the only medicine he had, and he put faith in it. She did not want to drink, but he made her swallow, and then he bathed her face and head and cooled her wrists.

The day began with the heightening of the fever. Venters spent the time reducing her temperature, cooling her hot cheeks and temples. He kept close watch over her, and at the least indication of restlessness, that he knew led to tossing and rolling of the body, he held her tightly, so no violent move could reopen her wounds. Hour after hour she babbled and laughed and cried and moaned in delirium; but whatever her secret was she did not reveal it. Attended by something somber for Venters, the day passed. At night in the cool winds the fever abated and she slept.

The second day was a repetition of the first. On the third he seemed to see her wither and waste away before his eyes. That day he scarcely went from her side for a moment, except to run for fresh, cool water; and he did not eat. The fever broke on the fourth day and left her spent and shrunken, a slip of a girl with life only in her eyes. They hung upon Venters with a mute observance, and he found hope in that.

To rekindle the spark that had nearly flickered out, to nourish the little life and vitality that remained in her, was Venters's problem. But he had little resource other than the meat of the rabbits and quail; and from these he made broths and soups as best he could, and fed her with a spoon. It came to him that the human body, like the human soul, was a strange thing and capable of recovering from terrible shocks. For almost immediately she showed faint signs of gathering strength. There was one more waiting day, in which he doubted, and spent long hours by her side as she slept, and watched the gentle swell of her breast rise and fall in breathing, and the wind stir the tangled chestnut curls. On the next day he knew that she would live.

Upon realizing it he abruptly left the cave and sought his accustomed seat against the trunk of a big spruce, where once more he let his glance stray along the sloping terraces. She would live, and the somber gloom lifted out of the valley, and he felt relief that was pain. Then he roused to the call of action, to the many things he needed to do in the way of making camp fixtures and utensils, to the necessity of hunting food, and the desire to explore the valley.

But he decided to wait a few more days before going far from camp, because he fancied that the girl rested easier when she could see him near at hand. And on the first day her languor appeared to leave her in a renewed grip of life. She awoke stronger from each short slumber; she ate greedily, and she moved about in her bed of boughs; and always, it seemed to Venters, her eyes followed him. He knew now that her recovery would be rapid. She talked about the dogs, about the caves, the valley, about how hungry she was, till Venters silenced her, asking her to put off further talk till another time. She obeyed, but she sat up in her bed, and her eyes roved to and fro, and always back to him.

Upon the second morning she sat up when he awakened her, and would not permit him to bathe her face and feed her, which actions she performed for herself. She spoke little, however, and Venters was quick to catch in her the first intimations of thoughtfulness and curiosity and appreciation of her situation. He left camp and took Whitie out to hunt for rabbits. Upon his return he was amazed and somewhat anxiously concerned to see his invalid sitting with her back to a corner of the cave and her bare feet swinging out. Hurriedly he approached, intending to advise her to lie down again, to tell her that perhaps she might overtax her strength. The sun shone upon her, glinting on the little head with its tangle of bright hair and the small, oval face with its pallor, and dark-blue eyes underlined by dark-blue circles. She looked at him and he looked at her. In that exchange of glances he imagined each saw the other in some different guise. It seemed impossible to Venters that this frail girl could be Oldring's Masked Rider. It flashed over him that he had made a mistake which presently she would explain.

"Help me down," she said.

"But—are you well enough?" he protested. "Wait—a little longer."

"I'm weak—dizzy. But I want to get down."

He lifted her—what a light burden now!—and stood her upright beside him, and supported her as she essayed to walk with halting steps. She was like a stripling of a boy; the bright, small head scarcely reached his shoulder. But now, as she clung to his arm, the rider's costume she wore did not contradict, as it had done at first, his feeling of her femininity. She might be the famous Masked Rider of the uplands, she might resemble a boy; but her outline, her little hands and feet, her hair, her big eyes and tremulous lips, and especially a something that Venters felt as a subtle essence rather than what he saw, proclaimed her sex.

She soon tired. He arranged a comfortable seat for her under the spruce that overspread the camp-fire.

"Now tell me—everything," she said.

He recounted all that had happened from the time of his discovery of the rustlers in the canyon up to the present moment.

"You shot me—and now you've saved my life?"

"Yes. After almost killing you I've pulled you through."

"Are you glad?"

"I should say so!"

Her eyes were unusually expressive, and they regarded him steadily; she was unconscious of that mirroring of her emotions and they shone with gratefulness and interest and wonder and sadness.

"Tell me—about yourself?" she asked.

He made this a briefer story, telling of his coming to Utah, his various occupations till he became a rider, and then how the Mormons had practically driven him out of Cottonwoods, an outcast.

Then, no longer able to withstand his own burning curiosity, he questioned her in turn.

"Are you Oldring's Masked Rider?"

ZANE GREY

"Yes," she replied, and dropped her eyes.

"I knew it—I recognized your figure—and mask, for I saw you once. Yet I can't believe it!... But you never were really that rustler, as we riders knew him? A thief—a marauder—a kidnapper of women—a murderer of sleeping riders!"

"No! I never stole—or harmed any one—in all my life. I only rode and rode—"

"But why—why?" he burst out. "Why the name? I understand Oldring made you ride. But the black mask—the mystery—the things laid to your hands—the threats in your infamous name—the night-riding credited to you—the evil deeds deliberately blamed on you and acknowledged by rustlers—even Oldring himself! Why? Tell me why?"

"I never knew that," she answered low. Her drooping head straightened, and the large eyes, larger now and darker, met Venters's with a clear, steadfast gaze in which he read truth. It verified his own conviction.

"Never knew? That's strange! Are you a Mormon?"

"No."

"Is Oldring a Mormon?"

"No."

"Do you—care for him?"

"Yes. I hate his men—his life—sometimes I almost hate him!"

Venters paused in his rapid-fire questioning, as if to brace him self to ask for a truth that would be abhorrent for him to confirm, but which he seemed driven to hear.

"What are—what were you to Oldring?"

Like some delicate thing suddenly exposed to blasting heat, the girl wilted; her head dropped, and into her white, wasted cheeks crept the red of shame.

Venters would have given anything to recall that question. It seemed so different—his thought when spoken. Yet her shame established in his mind something akin to the respect he had strangely been hungering to feel for her.

"D—n that question!—forget it!" he cried, in a passion of pain for her and anger at himself. "But once and for all—tell me—I know it, yet I want to hear you say so—you couldn't help yourself?"

"Oh no."

"Well, that makes it all right with me," he went on, honestly. "I—I want you to feel that... you see—we've been thrown together—and—and I want to help you—not hurt you. I thought life had been cruel to me, but when I think of yours I feel mean and little for my complaining. Anyway, I was a lonely outcast. And now!... I don't see very clearly what it all means. Only we are here—together. We've got to stay here, for long, surely till you are well. But you'll never go back to Oldring. And I'm sure helping you will help me, for I was sick in mind. There's something now for me to do. And if I can win back your strength—then get you away, out of this wild country—help you somehow to a happier life—just think how good that'll be for me!"

68

❧ 10 ❧

LOVE

DURING ALL THESE waiting days Venters, with the exception of the afternoon when he had built the gate in the gorge, had scarcely gone out of sight of camp and never out of hearing. His desire to explore Surprise Valley was keen, and on the morning after his long talk with the girl he took his rifle and, calling Ring, made a move to start. The girl lay back in a rude chair of boughs he had put together for her. She had been watching him, and when he picked up the gun and called the dog Venters thought she gave a nervous start.

"I'm only going to look over the valley," he said.

"Will you be gone long?"

"No," he replied, and started off. The incident set him thinking of his former impression that, after her recovery from fever, she did not seem at ease unless he was close at hand. It was fear of being alone, due, he concluded, most likely to her weakened condition. He must not leave her much alone.

As he strode down the sloping terrace, rabbits scampered before him, and the beautiful valley quail, as purple in color as the sage on the uplands, ran fleetly along the ground into the forest. It was pleasant under the trees, in the gold-flecked shade, with the whistle of quail and twittering of birds everywhere. Soon he had passed the limit of his former excursions and entered new territory. Here the woods began to show open glades and brooks running down from the slope, and presently he emerged from shade into the sunshine of a meadow. The shaking of the high grass told him of the running of animals, what species he could not tell, but from Ring's manifest desire to have a chase they were evidently some kind wilder than rabbits. Venters approached the willow and cottonwood belt that he had observed from the height of slope. He penetrated it to find a considerable stream of water and great half-submerged mounds of brush and sticks, and all about him were old and new gnawed circles at the base of the cottonwoods.

"Beaver!" he exclaimed. "By all that's lucky! The meadow's full of beaver! How did they ever get here?"

Beaver had not found a way into the valley by the trail of the cliff-dwellers, of that he was

69

certain; and he began to have more than curiosity as to the outlet or inlet of the stream. When he passed some dead water, which he noted was held by a beaver dam, there was a current in the stream, and it flowed west. Following its course, he soon entered the oak forest again, and passed through to find himself before massed and jumbled ruins of cliff wall. There were tangled thickets of wild plum-trees and other thorny growths that made passage extremely laborsome. He found innumerable tracks of wildcats and foxes. Rustlings in the thick undergrowth told him of stealthy movements of these animals. At length his further advance appeared futile, for the reason that the stream disappeared in a split at the base of immense rocks over which he could not climb. To his relief he concluded that though beaver might work their way up the narrow chasm where the water rushed, it would be impossible for men to enter the valley there.

This western curve was the only part of the valley where the walls had been split asunder, and it was a wildly rough and inaccessible corner. Going back a little way, he leaped the stream and headed toward the southern wall. Once out of the oaks he found again the low terrace of aspens, and above that the wide, open terrace fringed by silver spruces. This side of the valley contained the wind or water worn caves. As he pressed on, keeping to the upper terrace, cave after cave opened out of the cliff; now a large one, now a small one. Then yawned, quite suddenly and wonderfully above him, the great cavern of the cliff-dwellers.

It was still a goodly distance, and he tried to imagine, if it appeared so huge from where he stood, what it would be when he got there. He climbed the terrace and then faced a long, gradual ascent of weathered rock and dust, which made climbing too difficult for attention to anything else. At length he entered a zone of shade, and looked up. He stood just within the hollow of a cavern so immense that he had no conception of its real dimensions. The curved roof, stained by ages of leakage, with buff and black and rust-colored streaks, swept up and loomed higher and seemed to soar to the rim of the cliff. Here again was a magnificent arch, such as formed the grand gateway to the valley, only in this instance it formed the dome of a cave instead of the span of a bridge.

Venters passed onward and upward. The stones he dislodged rolled down with strange, hollow crack and roar. He had climbed a hundred rods inward, and yet he had not reached the base of the shelf where the cliff-dwellings rested, a long half-circle of connected stone house, with little dark holes that he had fancied were eyes. At length he gained the base of the shelf, and here found steps cut in the rock. These facilitated climbing, and as he went up he thought how easily this vanished race of men might once have held that stronghold against an army. There was only one possible place to ascend, and this was narrow and steep.

Venters had visited cliff-dwellings before, and they had been in ruins, and of no great character or size but this place was of proportions that stunned him, and it had not been desecrated by the hand of man, nor had it been crumbled by the hand of time. It was a stupendous tomb. It had been a city. It was just as it had been left by its builders. The little houses were there, the smoke-blackened stains of fires, the pieces of pottery scattered about cold hearths, the stone hatchets; and stone pestles and mealing-stones lay beside round holes polished by years of grinding maize—lay there as if they had been carelessly dropped yesterday. But the cliff-dwellers were gone!

Dust! They were dust on the floor or at the foot of the shelf, and their habitations and utensils endured. Venters felt the sublimity of that marvelous vaulted arch, and it seemed to gleam with a glory of something that was gone. How many years had passed since the cliff-dwellers gazed out across the beautiful valley as he was gazing now? How long had it been since women ground grain in those polished holes? What time had rolled by since men of an unknown race lived, loved, fought, and died there? Had an enemy destroyed them? Had disease destroyed them, or only that greatest destroyer—time? Venters saw a long line of blood-red hands painted low down upon the yellow roof of stone. Here was strange portent, if not an answer to his queries. The place oppressed him. It was light, but full of a transparent gloom. It smelled of dust and musty stone, of age and disuse. It was sad. It was solemn. It had the look of a place where silence had become master and was now irrevocable and terrible and could not be broken. Yet, at the moment, from high up in the carved crevices of the arch, floated down the low, strange wail of wind—a knell indeed for all that had gone.

Venters, sighing, gathered up an armful of pottery, such pieces as he thought strong enough and suitable for his own use, and bent his steps toward camp. He mounted the terrace at an opposite point to which he had left. He saw the girl looking in the direction he had gone. His footsteps made no sound in the deep grass, and he approached close without her being aware of his presence. Whitie lay on the ground near where she sat, and he manifested the usual actions of welcome, but the girl did not notice them. She seemed to be oblivious to everything near at hand. She made a pathetic figure drooping there, with her sunny hair contrasting so markedly with her white, wasted cheeks and her hands listlessly clasped and her little bare feet propped in the framework of the rude seat. Venters could have sworn and laughed in one breath at the idea of the connection between this girl and Oldring's Masked Rider. She was the victim of more than accident of fate—a victim to some deep plot the mystery of which burned him. As he stepped forward with a half-formed thought that she was absorbed in watching for his return, she turned her head and saw him. A swift start, a change rather than rush of blood under her white cheeks, a flashing of big eyes that fixed their glance upon him, transformed her face in that single instant of turning, and he knew she had been watching for him, that his return was the one thing in her mind. She did not smile; she did not flush; she did not look glad. All these would have meant little compared to her indefinite expression. Venters grasped the peculiar, vivid, vital something that leaped from her face. It was as if she had been in a dead, hopeless clamp of inaction and feeling, and had been suddenly shot through and through with quivering animation. Almost it was as if she had returned to life.

And Venters thought with lightning swiftness, "I've saved her—I've unlinked her from that old life—she was watching as if I were all she had left on earth—she belongs to me!" The thought was startlingly new. Like a blow it was in an unprepared moment. The cheery salutation he had ready for her died unborn and he tumbled the pieces of pottery awkwardly on the grass while some unfamiliar, deep-seated emotion, mixed with pity and glad assurance of his power to succor her, held him dumb.

"What a load you had!" she said. "Why, they're pots and crocks! Where did you get them?"

Venters laid down his rifle, and, filling one of the pots from his canteen, he placed it on the smoldering campfire.

"Hope it'll hold water," he said, presently. "Why, there's an enormous cliff-dwelling just across here. I got the pottery there. Don't you think we needed something? That tin cup of mine has served to make tea, broth, soup—everything."

"I noticed we hadn't a great deal to cook in."

She laughed. It was the first time. He liked that laugh, and though he was tempted to look at her, he did not want to show his surprise or his pleasure.

"Will you take me over there, and all around in the valley—pretty soon, when I'm well?" she added.

71

"Indeed I shall. It's a wonderful place. Rabbits so thick you can't step without kicking one out. And quail, beaver, foxes, wildcats. We're in a regular den. But—haven't you ever seen a cliff-dwelling?"

"No. I've heard about them, though. The—the men say the Pass is full of old houses and ruins."

"Why, I should think you'd have run across one in all your riding around," said Venters. He spoke slowly, choosing his words carefully, and he essayed a perfectly casual manner, and pretended to be busy assorting pieces of pottery. She must have no cause again to suffer shame for curiosity of his. Yet never in all his days had he been so eager to hear the details of anyone's life.

"When I rode—I rode like the wind," she replied, "and never had time to stop for anything."

"I remember that day I—I met you in the Pass—how dusty you were, how tired your horse looked. Were you always riding?"

"Oh, no. Sometimes not for months, when I was shut up in the cabin."

Venters tried to subdue a hot tingling.

"You were shut up, then?" he asked, carelessly.

"When Oldring went away on his long trips—he was gone for months sometimes—he shut me up in the cabin."

"What for?"

"Perhaps to keep me from running away. I always threatened that. Mostly, though, because the men got drunk at the villages. But they were always good to me. I wasn't afraid."

"A prisoner! That must have been hard on you?"

"I liked that. As long as I can remember I've been locked up there at times, and those times were the only happy ones I ever had. It's a big cabin, high up on a cliff, and I could look out. Then I had dogs and pets I had tamed, and books. There was a spring inside, and food stored, and the men brought me fresh meat. Once I was there one whole winter."

It now required deliberation on Venters's part to persist in his unconcern and to keep at work. He wanted to look at her, to volley questions at her.

"As long as you can remember—you've lived in Deception Pass?" he went on.

"I've a dim memory of some other place, and women and children; but I can't make anything of it. Sometimes I think till I'm weary."

"Then you can read—you have books?"

"Oh yes, I can read, and write, too, pretty well. Oldring is educated. He taught me, and years ago an old rustler lived with us, and he had been something different once. He was always teaching me."

"So Oldring takes long trips," mused Venters. "Do you know where he goes?"

"No. Every year he drives cattle north of Sterling—then does not return for months. I heard him accused once of living two lives—and he killed the man. That was at Stone Bridge."

Venters dropped his apparent task and looked up with an eagerness he no longer strove to hide.

"Bess," he said, using her name for the first time, "I suspected Oldring was something besides a rustler. Tell me, what's his purpose here in the Pass? I believe much that he has done was to hide his real work here."

"You're right. He's more than a rustler. In fact, as the men say, his rustling cattle is now only a bluff. There's gold in the canyons!"

"Ah!"

"Yes, there's gold, not in great quantities, but gold enough for him and his men. They wash for gold week in and week out. Then they drive a few cattle and go into the villages to drink and shoot and kill—to bluff the riders."

"Drive a few cattle! But, Bess, the Withersteen herd, the red herd—twenty-five hundred head! That's not a few. And I tracked them into a valley near here."

"Oldring never stole the red herd. He made a deal with Mormons. The riders were to be called in, and Oldring was to drive the herd and keep it till a certain time—I won't know when—then drive it back to the range. What his share was I didn't hear."

"Did you hear why that deal was made?" queried Venters.

"No. But it was a trick of Mormons. They're full of tricks. I've heard Oldring's men tell about Mormons. Maybe the Withersteen woman wasn't minding her halter! I saw the man who made the deal. He was a little, queer-shaped man, all humped up. He sat his horse well. I heard one of our men say afterward there was no better rider on the sage than this fellow. What was the name? I forget."

"Jerry Card?" suggested Venters.

"That's it. I remember—it's a name easy to remember—and Jerry Card appeared to be on fair terms with Oldring's men."

"I shouldn't wonder," replied Venters, thoughtfully. Verification of his suspicions in regard to Tull's underhand work—for the deal with Oldring made by Jerry Card assuredly had its inception in the Mormon Elder's brain, and had been accomplished through his orders—revived in Venters a memory of hatred that had been smothered by press of other emotions. Only a few days had elapsed since the hour of his encounter with Tull, yet they had been forgotten and now seemed far off, and the interval one that now appeared large and profound with incalculable change in his feelings. Hatred of Tull still existed in his heart, but it had lost its white heat. His affection for Jane Withersteen had not changed in the least; nevertheless, he seemed to view it from another angle and see it as another thing—what, he could not exactly define. The recalling of these two feelings was to Venters like getting glimpses into a self that was gone; and the wonder of them—perhaps the change which was too illusive for him—was the fact that a strange irritation accompanied the memory and a desire to dismiss it from mind. And straightway he did dismiss it, to return to thoughts of his significant present.

"Bess, tell me one more thing," he said. "Haven't you known any women—any young people?"

"Sometimes there were women with the men; but Oldring never let me know them. And all the young people I ever saw in my life was when I rode fast through the villages."

Perhaps that was the most puzzling and thought-provoking thing she had yet said to Venters. He pondered, more curious the more he learned, but he curbed his inquisitive desires, for he saw her shrinking on the verge of that shame, the causing of which had occasioned him such self-reproach. He would ask no more. Still he had to think, and he found it difficult to think clearly. This sad-eyed girl was so utterly different from what it would have been reason to believe such a remarkable life would have made her. On this day he had found her simple and frank, as natural as any girl he had ever known. About her there was something sweet. Her voice was low and well modulated. He could not look into her face, meet her steady, unabashed, yet wistful eyes, and think of her as the woman she had confessed herself. Oldring's Masked Rider sat before him, a girl dressed as a man. She had been made to ride at the head of infamous forays and drives. She had been imprisoned for many months of her life in an obscure cabin. At times the most vicious of men had been her companions; and the vilest of women, if they had not been permitted to approach her, had, at least, cast their shadows over her. But—but in spite of all this—there thundered at Venters some truth that lifted its voice higher than the clamoring facts of dishonor, some truth that was the very life of her beautiful eyes; and it was innocence.

In the days that followed, Venters balanced perpetually in mind this haunting conception of innocence over against the cold and sickening fact of an unintentional yet actual gift. How could it be possible for the two things to be true? He believed the latter to be true, and he would not relinquish his conviction of the former; and these conflicting thoughts augmented the mystery that appeared to be a part of Bess. In those ensuing days, however, it became clear as clearest light that Bess was rapidly regaining strength; that, unless reminded of her long association with Oldring, she seemed to have forgotten it; that, like an Indian who lives solely from moment to moment, she was utterly absorbed in the present.

Day by day Venters watched the white of her face slowly change to brown, and the wasted cheeks fill out by imperceptible degrees. There came a time when he could just trace the line of demarcation between the part of her face once hidden by a mask and that left exposed to wind and sun. When that line disappeared in clear bronze tan it was as if she had been washed clean of the stigma of Oldring's Masked Rider. The suggestion of the mask always made Venters remember; now that it was gone he seldom thought of her past. Occasionally he tried to piece together the several stages of strange experience and to make a whole. He had shot a masked outlaw the very sight of whom had been ill omen to riders; he had carried off a wounded woman whose bloody lips quivered in prayer; he had nursed what seemed a frail, shrunken boy; and now he watched a girl whose face had become strangely sweet, whose dark-blue eyes were ever upon him without boldness, without shyness, but with a steady, grave, and growing light. Many times Venters found the clear gaze embarrassing to him, yet, like wine, it had an exhilarating effect. What did she think when she looked at him so? Almost he believed she had no thought at all. All about her and the present there in Surprise Valley, and the dim yet subtly impending future, fascinated Venters and made him thoughtful as all his lonely vigils in the sage had not.

Chiefly it was the present that he wished to dwell upon; but it was the call of the future which stirred him to action. No idea had he of what that future had in store for Bess and him. He began to think of improving Surprise Valley as a place to live in, for there was no telling how long they would be compelled to stay there. Venters stubbornly resisted the entering into his mind of an insistent thought that, clearly realized, might have made it plain to him that he did not want to leave Surprise Valley at all. But it was imperative that he consider practical matters; and whether or not he was destined to stay long there, he felt the immediate need of a change of diet. It would be necessary for him to go farther afield for a variety of meat, and also that he soon visit Cottonwoods for a supply of food.

It occurred again to Venters that he could go to the canyon where Oldring kept his cattle, and at little risk he could pack out some beef. He wished to do this, however, without letting Bess know of it till after he had made the trip. Presently he hit upon the plan of going while she was asleep.

That very night he stole out of camp, climbed up under the stone bridge, and entered the outlet to the Pass. The gorge was full of luminous gloom. Balancing Rock loomed dark and leaned over the pale descent. Transformed in the shadowy light, it took shape and dimensions of a spectral god waiting—waiting for the moment to hurl himself down upon the tottering walls and close forever the outlet to Deception Pass. At night more than by day

Venters felt something fearful and fateful in that rock, and that it had leaned and waited through a thousand years to have somehow to deal with his destiny.

"Old man, if you must roll, wait till I get back to the girl, and then roll!" he said, aloud, as if the stones were indeed a god.

And those spoken words, in their grim note to his ear, as well as contents to his mind, told Venters that he was all but drifting on a current which he had not power nor wish to stem.

Venters exercised his usual care in the matter of hiding tracks from the outlet, yet it took him scarcely an hour to reach Oldring's cattle. Here sight of many calves changed his original intention, and instead of packing out meat he decided to take a calf out alive. He roped one, securely tied its feet, and swung it over his shoulder. Here was an exceedingly heavy burden, but Venters was powerful—he could take up a sack of grain and with ease pitch it over a pack-saddle—and he made long distance without resting. The hardest work came in the climb up to the outlet and on through to the valley. When he had accomplished it, he became fired with another idea that again changed his intention. He would not kill the calf, but keep it alive. He would go back to Oldring's herd and pack out more calves. Thereupon he secured the calf in the best available spot for the moment and turned to make a second trip.

When Venters got back to the valley with another calf, it was close upon daybreak. He crawled into his cave and slept late. Bess had no inkling that he had been absent from camp nearly all night, and only remarked solicitously that he appeared to be more tired than usual, and more in the need of sleep. In the afternoon Venters built a gate across a small ravine near camp, and here corralled the calves; and he succeeded in completing his task without Bess being any the wiser.

That night he made two more trips to Oldring's range, and again on the following night, and yet another on the next. With eight calves in his corral, he concluded that he had enough; but it dawned upon him then that he did not want to kill one. "I've rustled Oldring's cattle," he said, and laughed. He noted then that all the calves were red. "Red!" he exclaimed. "From the red herd. I've stolen Jane Withersteen's cattle!... That's about the strangest thing yet."

One more trip he undertook to Oldring's valley, and this time he roped a yearling steer and killed it and cut out a small quarter of beef. The howling of coyotes told him he need have no apprehension that the work of his knife would be discovered. He packed the beef back to camp and hung it upon a spruce-tree. Then he sought his bed.

On the morrow he was up bright and early, glad that he had a surprise for Bess. He could hardly wait for her to come out. Presently she appeared and walked under the spruce. Then she approached the camp-fire. There was a tinge of healthy red in the bronze of her cheeks, and her slender form had begun to round out in graceful lines.

"Bess, didn't you say you were tired of rabbit?" inquired Venters. "And quail and beaver?"

"Indeed I did."

"What would you like?"

"I'm tired of meat, but if we have to live on it I'd like some beef."

"Well, how does that strike you?" Venters pointed to the quarter hanging from the spruce-tree. "We'll have fresh beef for a few days, then we'll cut the rest into strips and dry it."

"Where did you get that?" asked Bess, slowly.

"I stole that from Oldring."

"You went back to the canyon—you risked—" While she hesitated the tinge of bloom faded out of her cheeks.

"It wasn't any risk, but it was hard work."

"I'm sorry I said I was tired of rabbit. Why! How—When did you get that beef?"

"Last night."

"While I was asleep?"

"Yes."

"I woke last night sometime—but I didn't know."

Her eyes were widening, darkening with thought, and whenever they did so the steady, watchful, seeing gaze gave place to the wistful light. In the former she saw as the primitive woman without thought; in the latter she looked inward, and her gaze was the reflection of a troubled mind. For long Venters had not seen that dark change, that deepening of blue, which he thought was beautiful and sad. But now he wanted to make her think.

"I've done more than pack in that beef," he said. "For five nights I've been working while you slept. I've got eight calves corralled near a ravine. Eight calves, all alive and doing fine!"

"You went five nights!"

All that Venters could make of the dilation of her eyes, her slow pallor, and her exclamation, was fear—fear for herself or for him.

"Yes. I didn't tell you, because I knew you were afraid to be left alone."

"Alone?" She echoed his word, but the meaning of it was nothing to her. She had not even thought of being left alone. It was not, then, fear for herself, but for him. This girl, always slow of speech and action, now seemed almost stupid. She put forth a hand that might have indicated the groping of her mind. Suddenly she stepped swiftly to him, with a look and touch that drove from him any doubt of her quick intelligence or feeling.

"Oldring has men watch the herds—they would kill you. You must never go again!"

When she had spoken, the strength and the blaze of her died, and she swayed toward Venters.

"Bess, I'll not go again," he said, catching her.

She leaned against him, and her body was limp and vibrated to a long, wavering tremble. Her face was upturned to his. Woman's face, woman's eyes, woman's lips—all acutely and blindly and sweetly and terribly truthful in their betrayal! But as her fear was instinctive, so was her clinging to this one and only friend.

Venters gently put her from him and steadied her upon her feet; and all the while his blood raced wild, and a thrilling tingle unsteadied his nerve, and something—that he had seen and felt in her—that he could not understand—seemed very close to him, warm and rich as a fragrant breath, sweet as nothing had ever before been sweet to him.

With all his will Venters strove for calmness and thought and judgment unbiased by pity, and reality unswayed by sentiment. Bess's eyes were still fixed upon him with all her soul bright in that wistful light. Swiftly, resolutely he put out of mind all of her life except what had been spent with him. He scorned himself for the intelligence that made him still doubt. He meant to judge her as she had judged him. He was face to face with the inevitableness of life itself. He saw destiny in the dark, straight path of her wonderful eyes. Here was the simplicity, the sweetness of a girl contending with new and strange and enthralling emotions here the living truth of innocence; here the blind terror of a woman confronted with the thought of death to her savior and protector. All this Venters saw, but, besides, there was in Bess's eyes a slow-dawning consciousness that seemed about to break out in glorious radiance.

"Bess, are you thinking?" he asked.

"Yes—oh yes!"

"Do you realize we are here alone—man and woman?"

"Yes."

"Have you thought that we may make our way out to civilization, or we may have to stay here—alone—hidden from the world all our lives?"

"I never thought—till now."

"Well, what's your choice—to go—or to stay here—alone with me?"

"Stay!" New-born thought of self, ringing vibrantly in her voice, gave her answer singular power.

Venters trembled, and then swiftly turned his gaze from her face—from her eyes. He knew what she had only half divined—that she loved him.

❧ II ❧

FAITH AND UNFAITH

AT JANE WITHERSTEEN'S home the promise made to Mrs. Larkin to care for little Fay had begun to be fulfilled. Like a gleam of sunlight through the cottonwoods was the coming of the child to the gloomy house of Withersteen. The big, silent halls echoed with childish laughter. In the shady court, where Jane spent many of the hot July days, Fay's tiny feet pattered over the stone flags and splashed in the amber stream. She prattled incessantly. What difference, Jane thought, a child made in her home! It had never been a real home, she discovered. Even the tidiness and neatness she had so observed, and upon which she had insisted to her women, became, in the light of Fay's smile, habits that now lost their importance. Fay littered the court with Jane's books and papers, and other toys her fancy improvised, and many a strange craft went floating down the little brook.

And it was owing to Fay's presence that Jane Withersteen came to see more of Lassiter. The rider had for the most part kept to the sage. He rode for her, but he did not seek her except on business; and Jane had to acknowledge in pique that her overtures had been made in vain. Fay, however, captured Lassiter the moment he first laid eyes on her.

Jane was present at the meeting, and there was something about it which dimmed her sight and softened her toward this foe of her people. The rider had clanked into the court, a tired yet wary man, always looking for the attack upon him that was inevitable and might come from any quarter; and he had walked right upon little Fay. The child had been beautiful even in her rags and amid the surroundings of the hovel in the sage, but now, in a pretty white dress, with her shining curls brushed and her face clean and rosy, she was lovely. She left her play and looked up at Lassiter.

If there was not an instinct for all three of them in that meeting, an unreasoning tendency toward a closer intimacy, then Jane Withersteen believed she had been subject to a queer fancy. She imagined any child would have feared Lassiter. And Fay Larkin had been a lonely, a solitary elf of the sage, not at all an ordinary child, and exquisitely shy with strangers. She watched Lassiter with great, round, grave eyes, but showed no fear. The rider gave Jane a favorable report of cattle and horses; and as he took the seat to which she invited him, little Fay edged as much as half an inch nearer. Jane replied to his look of inquiry and told Fay's story. The rider's gray, earnest gaze troubled her. Then he turned to Fay and smiled in a way that made Jane doubt her sense of the true relation of things. How could Lassiter smile so at a child when he had made so many children fatherless? But he did smile, and to the gentleness she had seen a few times he added something that was infinitely sad and sweet. Jane's intuition told her that Lassiter had never been a father, but if life ever so blessed him he would be a good one. Fay, also, must have found that smile singularly winning. For she edged closer and closer, and then, by way of feminine capitulation, went to Jane, from whose side she bent a beautiful glance upon the rider.

Lassiter only smiled at her.

Jane watched them, and realized that now was the moment she should seize, if she was ever to win this man from his hatred. But the step was not easy to take. The more she saw of Lassiter the more she respected him, and the greater her respect the harder it became to lend herself to mere coquetry. Yet as she thought of her great motive, of Tull, and of that other whose name she had schooled herself never to think of in connection with Milly Erne's avenger, she suddenly found she had no choice. And her creed gave her boldness far beyond the limit to which vanity would have led her.

"Lassiter, I see so little of you now," she said, and was conscious of heat in her cheeks.

"I've been riding hard," he replied.

"But you can't live in the saddle. You come in sometimes. Won't you come here to see me —oftener?"

"Is that an order?"

"Nonsense! I simply ask you to come to see me when you find time."

"Why?"

The query once heard was not so embarrassing to Jane as she might have imagined. Moreover, it established in her mind a fact that there existed actually other than selfish reasons for her wanting to see him. And as she had been bold, so she determined to be both honest and brave.

"I've reasons—only one of which I need mention," she answered. "If it's possible I want to change you toward my people. And on the moment I can conceive of little I wouldn't do to gain that end."

How much better and freer Jane felt after that confession! She meant to show him that there was one Mormon who could play a game or wage a fight in the open.

"I reckon," said Lassiter, and he laughed.

It was the best in her, if the most irritating, that Lassiter always aroused.

"Will you come?" She looked into his eyes, and for the life of her could not quite subdue an imperiousness that rose with her spirit. "I never asked so much of any man—except Bern Venters."

"'Pears to me that you'd run no risk, or Venters, either. But mebbe that doesn't hold good for me."

"You mean it wouldn't be safe for you to be often here? You look for ambush in the cottonwoods?"

"Not that so much."

At this juncture little Fay sidled over to Lassiter.

"Has oo a little dirl?" she inquired.

"No, lassie," replied the rider.

Whatever Fay seemed to be searching for in Lassiter's sun-reddened face and quiet eyes she evidently found. "Oo tan tom to see me," she added, and with that, shyness gave place to friendly curiosity. First his sombrero with its leather band and silver ornaments commanded her attention; next his quirt, and then the clinking, silver spurs. These held her for some time, but presently, true to childish fickleness, she left off playing with them to look for something else. She laughed in glee as she ran her little hands down the slippery, shiny surface of Lassiter's leather chaps. Soon she discovered one of the hanging gun—sheaths, and she dragged it up and began tugging at the huge black handle of the gun. Jane Withersteen repressed an exclamation. What significance there was to her in the little girl's efforts to dislodge that heavy weapon! Jane Withersteen saw Fay's play and her beauty and her love as most powerful allies to her own woman's part in a game that suddenly had acquired a strange zest and a hint of danger. And as for the rider, he appeared to have forgotten Jane in the wonder of this lovely child playing about him. At first he was much the shyer of the two. Gradually her confidence overcame his backwardness, and he had the temerity to stroke her golden curls with a great hand. Fay rewarded his boldness with a smile, and when he had gone to the extreme of closing that great hand over her little brown one, she said, simply, "I like oo!"

Sight of his face then made Jane oblivious for the time to his character as a hater of Mormons. Out of the mother longing that swelled her breast she divined the child hunger in Lassiter.

He returned the next day, and the next; and upon the following he came both at morning and at night. Upon the evening of this fourth day Jane seemed to feel the breaking of a brooding struggle in Lassiter. During all these visits he had scarcely a word to say, though he watched her and played absent-mindedly with Fay. Jane had contented herself with silence. Soon little Fay substituted for the expression of regard, "I like oo," a warmer and more generous one, "I love oo."

Thereafter Lassiter came oftener to see Jane and her little protegee. Daily he grew more gentle and kind, and gradually developed a quaintly merry mood. In the morning he lifted Fay upon his horse and let her ride as he walked beside her to the edge of the sage. In the evening he played with the child at an infinite variety of games she invented, and then, oftener than not, he accepted Jane's invitation to supper. No other visitor came to Withersteen House during those days. So that in spite of watchfulness he never forgot, Lassiter began to show he felt at home there. After the meal they walked into the grove of cottonwoods or up by the lakes, and little Fay held Lassiter's hand as much as she held Jane's. Thus a strange relationship was established, and Jane liked it. At twilight they always returned to the house, where Fay kissed them and went in to her mother. Lassiter and Jane were left alone.

Then, if there were anything that a good woman could do to win a man and still preserve her self-respect, it was something which escaped the natural subtlety of a woman determined to allure. Jane's vanity, that after all was not great, was soon satisfied with Lassiter's silent admiration. And her honest desire to lead him from his dark, blood-stained path would never have blinded her to what she owed herself. But the driving passion of her religion, and its call to save Mormons' lives, one life in particular, bore Jane Withersteen close to an infringement of her womanhood. In the beginning she had reasoned that her appeal to Lassiter must be through the senses. With whatever means she possessed in the way of adornment she enhanced her beauty. And she stooped to artifices that she knew were unworthy of her, but which she deliberately chose to employ. She made of herself a girl in every variable mood wherein a girl might be desirable. In those moods she was not above the methods of an inexperienced though natural flirt. She kept close to him whenever opportunity afforded; and she was forever playfully, yet passionately underneath the surface, fighting him for possession of the great black guns. These he would never yield to her. And so in that manner their hands were often and long in contact. The more of simplicity that she sensed in him the greater the advantage she took.

She had a trick of changing—and it was not altogether voluntary—from this gay, thoughtless, girlish coquettishness to the silence and the brooding, burning mystery of a woman's mood. The strength and passion and fire of her were in her eyes, and she so used them that Lassiter had to see this depth in her, this haunting promise more fitted to her years than to the flaunting guise of a wilful girl.

The July days flew by. Jane reasoned that if it were possible for her to be happy during such a time, then she was happy. Little Fay completely filled a long aching void in her heart. In fettering the hands of this Lassiter she was accomplishing the greatest good of her life, and to do good even in a small way rendered happiness to Jane Withersteen. She had attended the regular Sunday services of her church; otherwise she had not gone to the village for weeks. It was unusual that none of her churchmen or friends had called upon her of late; but it was neglect for which she was glad. Judkins and his boy riders had experienced no difficulty in driving the white herd. So these warm July days were free of worry, and soon Jane hoped she had passed the crisis; and for her to hope was presently to trust, and then to believe. She thought often of Venters, but in a dreamy, abstract way. She spent hours teaching and playing with little Fay. And the activity of her mind centered around Lassiter. The direction she had given her will seemed to blunt any branching off of thought from that straight line. The mood came to obsess her.

In the end, when her awakening came, she learned that she had builded better than she knew. Lassiter, though kinder and gentler than ever, had parted with his quaint humor and his coldness and his tranquillity to become a restless and unhappy man. Whatever the power of his deadly intent toward Mormons, that passion now had a rival, the one equally burning and consuming. Jane Withersteen had one moment of exultation before the dawn of a strange uneasiness. What if she had made of herself a lure, at tremendous cost to him and to her, and all in vain!

That night in the moonlit grove she summoned all her courage and, turning suddenly in the path, she faced Lassiter and leaned close to him, so that she touched him and her eyes looked up to his.

"Lassiter!... Will you do anything for me?"

In the moonlight she saw his dark, worn face change, and by that change she seemed to feel him immovable as a wall of stone.

Jane slipped her hands down to the swinging gun-sheaths, and when she had locked her fingers around the huge, cold handles of the guns, she trembled as with a chilling ripple over all her body.

"May I take your guns?"

"Why?" he asked, and for the first time to her his voice carried a harsh note. Jane felt his hard, strong hands close round her wrists. It was not wholly with intent that she leaned toward him, for the look of his eyes and the feel of his hands made her weak.

"It's no trifle—no woman's whim—it's deep—as my heart. Let me take them?"

"Why?"

"I want to keep you from killing more men—Mormons. You must let me save you from more wickedness—more wanton bloodshed—" Then the truth forced itself falteringly from her lips. "You must—let—help me to keep my vow to Milly Erne. I swore to her—as she lay dying—that if ever any one came here to avenge her—I swore I would stay his hand. Perhaps I—I alone can save the—the man who—who—Oh, Lassiter!... I feel that I can't change you—then soon you'll be out to kill—and you'll kill by instinct—and among the Mormons you kill will be the one—who... Lassiter, if you care a little for me—let me—for my sake—let me take your guns!"

As if her hands had been those of a child, he unclasped their clinging grip from the handles of his guns, and, pushing her away, he turned his gray face to her in one look of terrible realization and then strode off into the shadows of the cottonwoods.

When the first shock of her futile appeal to Lassiter had passed, Jane took his cold, silent condemnation and abrupt departure not so much as a refusal to her entreaty as a hurt and stunned bitterness for her attempt at his betrayal. Upon further thought and slow consideration of Lassiter's past actions, she believed he would return and forgive her. The man could not be hard to a woman, and she doubted that he could stay away from her. But at the point where she had hoped to find him vulnerable she now began to fear he was proof against all persuasion. The iron and stone quality that she had early suspected in him had actually cropped out as an impregnable barrier. Nevertheless, if Lassiter remained in Cottonwoods she would never give up her hope and desire to change him. She would change him if she had to sacrifice everything dear to her except hope of heaven. Passionately devoted as she was to her religion, she had yet refused to marry a Mormon. But a situation had developed wherein self paled in the great white light of religious duty of the highest order. That was the leading motive, the divinely spiritual one; but there were other motives, which, like tentacles, aided in drawing her will to the acceptance of a possible abnegation. And through the watches of that sleepless night Jane Withersteen, in fear and sorrow and doubt, came finally to believe that if she must throw herself into Lassiter's arms to make him abide by "Thou shalt not kill!" she would yet do well.

In the morning she expected Lassiter at the usual hour, but she was not able to go at once to the court, so she sent little Fay. Mrs. Larkin was ill and required attention. It appeared that the mother, from the time of her arrival at Withersteen House, had relaxed and was slowly losing her hold on life. Jane had believed that absence of worry and responsibility coupled with good nursing and comfort would mend Mrs. Larkin's broken health. Such, however, was not the case.

When Jane did get out to the court, Fay was there alone, and at the moment embarking on a dubious voyage down the stone-lined amber stream upon a craft of two brooms and a pillow. Fay was as delightfully wet as she could possibly wish to get.

Clatter of hoofs distracted Fay and interrupted the scolding she was gleefully receiving from Jane. The sound was not the light-spirited trot that Bells made when Lassiter rode him into the outer court. This was slower and heavier, and Jane did not recognize in it any of her other horses. The appearance of Bishop Dyer startled Jane. He dismounted with his rapid, jerky motion flung the bridle, and, as he turned toward the inner court and stalked up on the stone flags, his boots rang. In his authoritative front, and in the red anger unmistakably flaming in his face, he reminded Jane of her father.

"Is that the Larkin pauper?" he asked, bruskly, without any greeting to Jane.

"It's Mrs. Larkin's little girl," replied Jane, slowly.

"I hear you intend to raise the child?"

"Yes."

"Of course you mean to give her Mormon bringing-up?"

"No."

His questions had been swift. She was amazed at a feeling that some one else was replying for her.

"I've come to say a few things to you." He stopped to measure her with stern, speculative eye.

Jane Withersteen loved this man. From earliest childhood she had been taught to revere and love bishops of her church. And for ten years Bishop Dyer had been the closest friend and counselor of her father, and for the greater part of that period her own friend and Scriptural teacher. Her interpretation of her creed and her religious activity in fidelity to it, her acceptance of mysterious and holy Mormon truths, were all invested in this Bishop. Bishop Dyer as an entity was next to God. He was God's mouthpiece to the little Mormon community at Cottonwoods. God revealed himself in secret to this mortal.

And Jane Withersteen suddenly suffered a paralyzing affront to her consciousness of reverence by some strange, irresistible twist of thought wherein she saw this Bishop as a man. And the train of thought hurdled the rising, crying protests of that other self whose poise she had lost. It was not her Bishop who eyed her in curious measurement. It was a man who tramped into her presence without removing his hat, who had no greeting for her, who had no semblance of courtesy. In looks, as in action, he made her think of a bull stamping cross-grained into a corral. She had heard of Bishop Dyer forgetting the minister in the fury of a common man, and now she was to feel it. The glance by which she measured him in turn momentarily veiled the divine in the ordinary. He looked a rancher; he was booted, spurred, and covered with dust; he carried a gun at his hip, and she remembered that he had been known to use it. But during the long moment while he watched her there was nothing commonplace in the slow-gathering might of his wrath.

"Brother Tull has talked to me," he began. "It was your father's wish that you marry Tull, and my order. You refused him?"

"Yes."

"You would not give up your friendship with that tramp Venters?"

"No."

"But you'll do as I order!" he thundered. "Why, Jane Withersteen, you are in danger of becoming a heretic! You can thank your Gentile friends for that. You face the damning of your soul to perdition."

In the flux and reflux of the whirling torture of Jane's mind, that new, daring spirit of hers vanished in the old habitual order of her life. She was a Mormon, and the Bishop regained ascendance.

"It's well I got you in time, Jane Withersteen. What would your father have said to these goings-on of yours? He would have put you in a stone cage on bread and water. He would have taught you something about Mormonism. Remember, you're a born Mormon. There have been Mormons who turned heretic—damn their souls!—but no born Mormon ever left us yet. Ah, I see your shame. Your faith is not shaken. You are only a wild girl." The Bishop's tone softened. "Well, it's enough that I got to you in time.... Now tell me about this Lassiter. I hear strange things."

"What do you wish to know?" queried Jane.

"About this man. You hired him?"

"Yes, he's riding for me. When my riders left me I had to have any one I could get."

"Is it true what I hear—that he's a gun-man, a Mormon-hater, steeped in blood?"

"True—terribly true, I fear."

"But what's he doing here in Cottonwoods? This place isn't notorious enough for such a man. Sterling and the villages north, where there's universal gun-packing and fights every day—where there are more men like him, it seems to me they would attract him most. We're only a wild, lonely border settlement. It's only recently that the rustlers have made killings here. Nor have there been saloons till lately, nor the drifting in of outcasts. Has not this gun-man some special mission here?"

Jane maintained silence.

"Tell me," ordered Bishop Dyer, sharply.

"Yes," she replied.

"Do you know what it is?"

"Yes."

"Tell me that."

"Bishop Dyer, I don't want to tell."

He waved his hand in an imperative gesture of command. The red once more leaped to his face, and in his steel-blue eyes glinted a pin-point of curiosity.

"That first day," whispered Jane, "Lassiter said he came here to find—Milly Erne's grave!"

With downcast eyes Jane watched the swift flow of the amber water. She saw it and tried to think of it, of the stones, of the ferns; but, like her body, her mind was in a leaden vise. Only the Bishop's voice could release her. Seemingly there was silence of longer duration than all her former life.

"For what—else?" When Bishop Dyer's voice did cleave the silence it was high, curiously shrill, and on the point of breaking. It released Jane's tongue, but she could not lift her eyes.

"To kill the man who persuaded Milly Erne to abandon her home and her husband—and her God!"

With wonderful distinctness Jane Withersteen heard her own clear voice. She heard the water murmur at her feet and flow on to the sea; she heard the rushing of all the waters in the world. They filled her ears with low, unreal murmurings—these sounds that deadened her brain and yet could not break the long and terrible silence. Then, from somewhere—from an immeasurable distance—came a slow, guarded, clinking, clanking step. Into her it shot electrifying life. It released the weight upon her numbed eyelids. Lifting her eyes she saw—ashen, shaken, stricken—not the Bishop but the man! And beyond him, from round the corner came that soft, silvery step. A long black boot with a gleaming spur swept into sight—and then Lassiter! Bishop Dyer did not see, did not hear: he stared at Jane in the throes of sudden revelation.

"Ah, I understand!" he cried, in hoarse accents. "That's why you made love to this Lassiter—to bind his hands!"

It was Jane's gaze riveted upon the rider that made Bishop Dyer turn. Then clear sight failed her. Dizzily, in a blur, she saw the Bishop's hand jerk to his hip. She saw gleam of blue and spout of red. In her ears burst a thundering report. The court floated in darkening circles around her, and she fell into utter blackness.

The darkness lightened, turned to slow-drifting haze, and lifted. Through a thin film of blue smoke she saw the rough-hewn timbers of the court roof. A cool, damp touch moved across her brow. She smelled powder, and it was that which galvanized her suspended thought. She moved, to see that she lay prone upon the stone flags with her head on Lassiter's knee, and he was bathing her brow with water from the stream. The same swift glance, shifting low, brought into range of her sight a smoking gun and splashes of blood.

"Ah-h!" she moaned, and was drifting, sinking again into darkness, when Lassiter's voice arrested her.

"It's all right, Jane. It's all right."

"Did—you—kill—him?" she whispered.

"Who? That fat party who was here? No. I didn't kill him."

"Oh!... Lassiter!"

"Say! It was queer for you to faint. I thought you were such a strong woman, not faintish like that. You're all right now—only some pale. I thought you'd never come to. But I'm awkward round women folks. I couldn't think of anythin'."

"Lassiter!... the gun there!... the blood!"

"So that's troublin' you. I reckon it needn't. You see it was this way. I come round the house an' seen that fat party an' heard him talkin' loud. Then he seen me, an' very impolite goes straight for his gun. He oughtn't have tried to throw a gun on me—whatever his reason was. For that's meetin' me on my own grounds. I've seen runnin' molasses that was quicker 'n him. Now I didn't know who he was, visitor or friend or relation of yours, though I seen he was a Mormon all over, an' I couldn't get serious about shootin'. So I winged him—put a bullet through his arm as he was pullin' at his gun. An' he dropped the gun there, an' a little blood. I told him he'd introduced himself sufficient, an' to please move out of my vicinity. An' he went."

Lassiter spoke with slow, cool, soothing voice, in which there was a hint of levity, and his touch, as he continued to bathe her brow, was gentle and steady. His impassive face, and the kind gray eyes, further stilled her agitation.

"He drew on you first, and you deliberately shot to cripple him—you wouldn't kill him—you—Lassiter?"

"That's about the size of it."

Jane kissed his hand.

All that was calm and cool about Lassiter instantly vanished.

"Don't do that! I won't stand it! An' I don't care a damn who that fat party was."

He helped Jane to her feet and to a chair. Then with the wet scarf he had used to bathe her face he wiped the blood from the stone flags and, picking up the gun, he threw it upon a couch. With that he began to pace the court, and his silver spurs jangled musically, and the great gun-sheaths softly brushed against his leather chaps.

"So—it's true—what I heard him say?" Lassiter asked, presently halting before her. "You made love to me—to bind my hands?"

"Yes," confessed Jane. It took all her woman's courage to meet the gray storm of his glance.

"All these days that you've been so friendly an' like a pardner—all these evenin's that have been so bewilderin' to me—your beauty—an'—an' the way you looked an' came close to me—they were woman's tricks to bind my hands?"

"Yes."

"An' your sweetness that seemed so natural, an' your throwin' little Fay an' me so much together—to make me love the child—all that was for the same reason?"

"Yes."

Lassiter flung his arms—a strange gesture for him.

"Mebbe it wasn't much in your Mormon thinkin', for you to play that game. But to ring the child in—that was hellish!"

Jane's passionate, unheeding zeal began to loom darkly.

"Lassiter, whatever my intention in the beginning, Fay loves you dearly—and I—I've grown to—to like you."

"That's powerful kind of you, now," he said. Sarcasm and scorn made his voice that of a stranger. "An' you sit there an' look me straight in the eyes! You're a wonderful strange woman, Jane Withersteen."

"I'm not ashamed, Lassiter. I told you I'd try to change you."

"Would you mind tellin' me just what you tried?"

"I tried to make you see beauty in me and be softened by it. I wanted you to care for me so that I could influence you. It wasn't easy. At first you were stone-blind. Then I hoped you'd love little Fay, and through that come to feel the horror of making children fatherless."

"Jane Withersteen, either you're a fool or noble beyond my understandin'. Mebbe you're both. I know you're blind. What you meant is one thing—what you did was to make me love you."

"Lassiter!"

"I reckon I'm a human bein', though I never loved any one but my sister, Milly Erne. That was long—"

"Oh, are you Milly's brother?"

"Yes, I was, an' I loved her. There never was any one but her in my life till now. Didn't I tell you that long ago I back-trailed myself from women? I was a Texas ranger till—till Milly left home, an' then I became somethin' else—Lassiter! For years I've been a lonely man set on one thing. I came here an' met you. An' now I'm not the man I was. The change was gradual, an' I took no notice of it. I understand now that never-satisfied longin' to see you, listen to you, watch you, feel you near me. It's plain now why you were never out of my thoughts. I've had no thoughts but of you. I've lived an' breathed for you. An' now when I know what it means—what you've done—I'm burnin' up with hell's fire!"

"Oh, Lassiter—no—no—you don't love me that way!" Jane cased.

"If that's what love is, then I do."

"Forgive me! I didn't mean to make you love me like that. Oh, what a tangle of our lives! You—Milly Erne's brother! And I—heedless, mad to melt your heart toward Mormons. Lassiter, I may be wicked but not wicked enough to hate. If I couldn't hate Tull, could I hate you?"

"After all, Jane, mebbe you're only blind—Mormon blind. That only can explain what's close to selfishness—"

"I'm not selfish. I despise the very word. If I were free—"

"But you're not free. Not free of Mormonism. An' in playin' this game with me you've been unfaithful."

"Un faithful!" faltered Jane.

"Yes, I said unfaithful. You're faithful to your Bishop an' unfaithful to yourself. You're false to your womanhood an' true to your religion. But for a savin' innocence you'd have made yourself low an' vile—betrayin' yourself, betrayin' me—all to bind my hands an' keep me from snuffin' out Mormon life. It's your damned Mormon blindness."

"Is it vile—is it blind—is it only Mormonism to save human life? No, Lassiter, that's God's law, divine, universal for all Christians."

"The blindness I mean is blindness that keeps you from seein' the truth. I've known many good Mormons. But some are blacker than hell. You won't see that even when you know it. Else, why all this blind passion to save the life of that—that...."

Jane shut out the light, and the hands she held over her eyes trembled and quivered against her face.

"Blind—yes, en' let me make it clear en' simple to you," Lassiter went on, his voice losing its tone of anger. "Take, for instance, that idea of yours last night when you wanted my guns. It was good an' beautiful, an' showed your heart—but—why, Jane, it was crazy. Mind I'm assumin' that life to me is as sweet as to any other man. An' to preserve that life is each man's first an' closest thought. Where would any man be on this border without guns? Where, especially, would Lassiter be? Well, I'd be under the sage with thousands of other men now livin' an' sure better men than me. Gun-packin' in the West since the Civil War has growed into a kind of moral law. An' out here on this border it's the difference between a man an' somethin' not a man. Look what your takin' Venters's guns from him all but made him! Why, your churchmen carry guns. Tull has killed a man an' drawed on others. Your Bishop has shot a half dozen men, an' it wasn't through prayers of his that they recovered. An' to-day he'd have shot me if he'd been quick enough on the draw. Could I walk or ride down into Cottonwoods without my guns? This is a wild time, Jane Withersteen, this year of our Lord eighteen seventy-one."

"No time—for a woman!" exclaimed Jane, brokenly. "Oh, Lassiter, I feel helpless—lost—and don't know where to turn. If I am blind—then—I need some one—a friend—you, Lassiter—more than ever!"

"Well, I didn't say nothin' about goin' back on you, did I?"

✌ 12 ✌

THE INVISIBLE HAND

JANE RECEIVED a letter from Bishop Dyer, not in his own handwriting, which stated that the abrupt termination of their interview had left him in some doubt as to her future conduct. A slight injury had incapacitated him from seeking another meeting at present, the letter went on to say, and ended with a request which was virtually a command, that she call upon him at once.

The reading of the letter acquainted Jane Withersteen with the fact that something within her had all but changed. She sent no reply to Bishop Dyer nor did she go to see him. On Sunday she remained absent from the service—for the second time in years—and though she did not actually suffer there was a dead-lock of feelings deep within her, and the waiting for a balance to fall on either side was almost as bad as suffering. She had a gloomy expectancy of untoward circumstances, and with it a keen-edged curiosity to watch developments. She had a half-formed conviction that her future conduct—as related to her churchmen—was beyond her control and would be governed by their attitude toward her. Something was changing in her, forming, waiting for decision to make it a real and fixed thing. She had told Lassiter that she felt helpless and lost in the fateful tangle of their lives; and now she feared that she was approaching the same chaotic condition of mind in regard to her religion. It appalled her to find that she questioned phases of that religion. Absolute faith had been her serenity. Though leaving her faith unshaken, her serenity had been disturbed, and now it was broken by open war between her and her ministers. That something within her—a whisper—which she had tried in vain to hush had become a ringing voice, and it called to her to wait. She had transgressed no laws of God. Her churchmen, however invested with the power and the glory of a wonderful creed, however they sat in inexorable judgment of her, must now practice toward her the simple, common, Christian virtue they professed to preach, "Do unto others as you would have others do unto you!"

Jane Withersteen, waiting in darkness of mind, remained faithful still. But it was darkness that must soon be pierced by light. If her faith were justified, if her churchmen were trying only to intimidate her, the fact would soon be manifest, as would their failure, and then she would redouble her zeal toward them and toward what had been the best work of her life—work for the welfare and happiness of those among whom she lived, Mormon and Gentile alike. If that secret, intangible power closed its coils round her again, if that great invisible hand moved here and there and everywhere, slowly paralyzing her with its mystery and its inconceivable sway over her affairs, then she would know beyond doubt that it was not chance, nor jealousy, nor intimidation, nor ministerial wrath at her revolt, but a cold and calculating policy thought out long before she was born, a dark, immutable will of whose empire she and all that was hers was but an atom.

Then might come her ruin. Then might come her fall into black storm. Yet she would rise again, and to the light. God would be merciful to a driven woman who had lost her way.

A week passed. Little Fay played and prattled and pulled at Lassiter's big black guns. The rider came to Withersteen House oftener than ever. Jane saw a change in him, though it did not relate to his kindness and gentleness. He was quieter and more thoughtful. While playing with Fay or conversing with Jane he seemed to be possessed of another self that watched with cool, roving eyes, that listened, listened always as if the murmuring amber stream brought messages, and the moving leaves whispered something. Lassiter never rode Bells into the court any more, nor did he come by the lane or the paths. When he appeared it was suddenly and noiselessly out of the dark shadow of the grove.

"I left Bells out in the sage," he said, one day at the end of that week. "I must carry water to him."

"Why not let him drink at the trough or here?" asked Jane, quickly.

"I reckon it'll be safer for me to slip through the grove. I've been watched when I rode in from the sage."

"Watched? By whom?"

"By a man who thought he was well hid. But my eyes are pretty sharp. An', Jane," he went on, almost in a whisper, "I reckon it'd be a good idea for us to talk low. You're spied on here by your women."

"Lassiter!" she whispered in turn. "That's hard to believe. My women love me."

"What of that?" he asked. "Of course they love you. But they're Mormon women."

Jane's old, rebellious loyalty clashed with her doubt.

"I won't believe it," she replied, stubbornly.

"Well then, just act natural an' talk natural, an' pretty soon—give them time to hear us—pretend to go over there to the table, en' then quick-like make a move for the door en' open it."

"I will," said Jane, with heightened color. Lassiter was right; he never made mistakes; he would not have told her unless he positively knew. Yet Jane was so tenacious of faith that she had to see with her own eyes, and so constituted that to employ even such small deceit toward her women made her ashamed, and angry for her shame as well as theirs. Then a singular thought confronted her that made her hold up this simple ruse—which hurt her, though it was well justified—against the deceit she had wittingly and eagerly used toward Lassiter. The difference was staggering in its suggestion of that blindness of which he had accused her. Fairness and justice and mercy, that she had imagined were anchor-cables to hold fast her soul to righteousness had not been hers in the strange, biased duty that had so exalted and confounded her.

Presently Jane began to act her little part, to laugh and play with Fay, to talk of horses and cattle to Lassiter. Then she made deliberate mention of a book in which she kept records of all pertaining to her stock, and she walked slowly toward the table, and when near the door she suddenly whirled and thrust it open. Her sharp action nearly knocked down a woman who had undoubtedly been listening.

"Hester," said Jane, sternly, "you may go home, and you need not come back."

Jane shut the door and returned to Lassiter. Standing unsteadily, she put her hand on his arm. She let him see that doubt had gone, and how this stab of disloyalty pained her.

"Spies! My own women!... Oh, miserable!" she cried, with flashing, tearful eyes.

"I hate to tell you," he replied. By that she knew he had long spared her. "It's begun again —that work in the dark."

"Nay, Lassiter—it never stopped!"

So bitter certainty claimed her at last, and trust fled Withersteen House and fled forever. The women who owed much to Jane Withersteen changed not in love for her, nor in devotion to their household work, but they poisoned both by a thousand acts of stealth and cunning and duplicity. Jane broke out once and caught them in strange, stone-faced, unhesitating falsehood. Thereafter she broke out no more. She forgave them because they were driven. Poor, fettered, and sealed Hagars, how she pitied them! What terrible thing bound them and locked their lips, when they showed neither consciousness of guilt toward their benefactress nor distress at the slow wearing apart of long-established and dear ties?

"The blindness again!" cried Jane Withersteen. "In my sisters as in me!... O God!"

There came a time when no words passed between Jane and her women. Silently they went about their household duties, and secretly they went about the underhand work to which they had been bidden. The gloom of the house and the gloom of its mistress, which darkened even the bright spirit of little Fay, did not pervade these women. Happiness was not among them, but they were aloof from gloom. They spied and listened; they received and sent secret messengers; and they stole Jane's books and records, and finally the papers that were deeds of her possessions. Through it all they were silent, rapt in a kind of trance. Then one by one, without leave or explanation or farewell, they left Withersteen House, and never returned.

Coincident with this disappearance Jane's gardeners and workers in the alfalfa fields and stable men quit her, not even asking for their wages. Of all her Mormon employees about the great ranch only Jerd remained. He went on with his duty, but talked no more of the change than if it had never occurred.

"Jerd," said Jane, "what stock you can't take care of turn out in the sage. Let your first thought be for Black Star and Night. Keep them in perfect condition. Run them every day and watch them always."

Though Jane Withersteen gave them such liberality, she loved her possessions. She loved the rich, green stretches of alfalfa, and the farms, and the grove, and the old stone house, and the beautiful, ever-faithful amber spring, and every one of a myriad of horses and colts and burros and fowls down to the smallest rabbit that nipped her vegetables; but she loved best her noble Arabian steeds. In common with all riders of the upland sage Jane cherished two material things —the cold, sweet, brown water that made life possible in the wilderness and the horses which were a part of that life. When Lassiter asked her what Lassiter would be without his guns he was assuming that his horse was part of himself. So Jane loved Black Star and Night because it was her nature to love all beautiful creatures—perhaps all living things; and then she loved them because she herself was of the sage and in her had been born and bred the rider's instinct to rely on his four-footed brother. And when Jane gave Jerd the order to keep her favorites trained down to the day it was a half-conscious admission that presaged a time when she would need her fleet horses.

Jane had now, however, no leisure to brood over the coils that were closing round her.

Mrs. Larkin grew weaker as the August days began; she required constant care; there was little Fay to look after; and such household work as was imperative. Lassiter put Bells in the stable with the other racers, and directed his efforts to a closer attendance upon Jane. She welcomed the change. He was always at hand to help, and it was her fortune to learn that his boast of being awkward around women had its root in humility and was not true.

His great, brown hands were skilled in a multiplicity of ways which a woman might have envied. He shared Jane's work, and was of especial help to her in nursing Mrs. Larkin. The woman suffered most at night, and this often broke Jane's rest. So it came about that Lassiter would stay by Mrs. Larkin during the day, when she needed care, and Jane would make up the sleep she lost in night-watches. Mrs. Larkin at once took kindly to the gentle Lassiter, and, without ever asking who or what he was, praised him to Jane. "He's a good man and loves children," she said. How sad to hear this truth spoken of a man whom Jane thought lost beyond all redemption! Yet ever and ever Lassiter towered above her, and behind or through his black, sinister figure shone something luminous that strangely affected Jane. Good and evil began to seem incomprehensibly blended in her judgment. It was her belief that evil could not come forth from good; yet here was a murderer who dwarfed in gentleness, patience, and love any man she had ever known.

She had almost lost track of her more outside concerns when early one morning Judkins presented himself before her in the courtyard.

Thin, hard, burnt, bearded, with the dust and sage thick on him, with his leather wristbands shining from use, and his boots worn through on the stirrup side, he looked the rider of riders. He wore two guns and carried a Winchester.

Jane greeted him with surprise and warmth, set meat and bread and drink before him; and called Lassiter out to see him. The men exchanged glances, and the meaning of Lassiter's keen inquiry and Judkins's bold reply, both unspoken, was not lost upon Jane.

"Where's your hoss?" asked Lassiter, aloud.

"Left him down the slope," answered Judkins. "I footed it in a ways, an' slept last night in the sage. I went to the place you told me you 'moss always slept, but didn't strike you."

"I moved up some, near the spring, an' now I go there nights."

"Judkins—the white herd?" queried Jane, hurriedly.

"Miss Withersteen, I make proud to say I've not lost a steer. Fer a good while after thet stampede Lassiter milled we hed no trouble. Why, even the sage dogs left us. But it's begun agin—thet flashin' of lights over ridge tips, an' queer puffin' of smoke, en' then at night strange whistles en' noises. But the herd's acted magnificent. An' my boys, say, Miss Withersteen, they're only kids, but I ask no better riders. I got the laugh in the village fer takin' them out. They're a wild lot, an' you know boys hev more nerve than grown men, because they don't know what danger is. I'm not denyin' there's danger. But they glory in it, an' mebbe I like it myself—anyway, we'll stick. We're goin' to drive the herd on the far side of the first break of Deception Pass. There's a great round valley over there, an' no ridges or piles of rocks to aid these stampeders. The rains are due. We'll hev plenty of water fer a while. An' we can hold thet herd from anybody except Oldrin'. I come in fer supplies. I'll pack a couple of burros an' drive out after dark to-night."

"Judkins, take what you want from the store-room. Lassiter will help you. I—I can't thank you enough... but—wait."

Jane went to the room that had once been her father's, and from a secret chamber in the thick stone wall she took a bag of gold, and, carrying it back to the court, she gave it to the rider.

"There, Judkins, and understand that I regard it as little for your loyalty. Give what is fair to your boys, and keep the rest. Hide it. Perhaps that would be wisest."

"Oh... Miss Withersteen!" ejaculated the rider. "I couldn't earn so much in—in ten years. It's not right—I oughtn't take it."

"Judkins, you know I'm a rich woman. I tell you I've few faithful friends. I've fallen upon evil days. God only knows what will become of me and mine! So take the gold."

She smiled in understanding of his speechless gratitude, and left him with Lassiter. Presently she heard him speaking low at first, then in louder accents emphasized by the thumping of his rifle on the stones. "As infernal a job as even you, Lassiter, ever heerd of."

"Why, son," was Lassiter's reply, "this breakin' of Miss Withersteen may seem bad to you, but it ain't bad—yet. Some of these wall-eyed fellers who look jest as if they was walkin' in the shadow of Christ himself, right down the sunny road, now they can think of things en' do things that are really hell-bent."

Jane covered her ears and ran to her own room, and there like caged lioness she paced to and fro till the coming of little Fay reversed her dark thoughts.

The following day, a warm and muggy one threatening rain awhile Jane was resting in the court, a horseman clattered through the grove and up to the hitching-rack. He leaped off and approached Jane with the manner of a man determined to execute difficult mission, yet fearful of its reception. In the gaunt, wiry figure and the lean, brown face Jane recognized one of her Mormon riders, Blake. It was he of whom Judkins had long since spoken. Of all the riders ever in her employ Blake owed her the most, and as he stepped before her, removing his hat and making manly efforts to subdue his emotion, he showed that he remembered.

"Miss Withersteen, mother's dead," he said.

"Oh—Blake!" exclaimed Jane, and she could say no more.

"She died free from pain in the end, and she's buried—resting at last, thank God!... I've come to ride for you again, if you'll have me. Don't think I mentioned mother to get your sympathy. When she was living and your riders quit, I had to also. I was afraid of what might be done—said to her.... Miss Withersteen, we can't talk of—of what's going on now—"

"Blake, do you know?"

"I know a great deal. You understand, my lips are shut. But without explanation or excuse I offer my services. I'm a Mormon—I hope a good one. But—there are some things!... It's no use, Miss Withersteen, I can't say any more—what I'd like to. But will you take me back?"

"Blake!... You know what it means?"

"I don't care. I'm sick of—of—I'll show you a Mormon who'll be true to you!"

"But, Blake—how terribly you might suffer for that!"

"Maybe. Aren't you suffering now?"

"God knows indeed I am!"

"Miss Withersteen, it's a liberty on my part to speak so, but I know you pretty well—know you'll never give in. I wouldn't if I were you. And I—I must—Something makes me tell you the worst is yet to come. That's all. I absolutely can't say more. Will you take me back—let me ride for you—show everybody what I mean?"

"Blake, it makes me happy to hear you. How my riders hurt me when they quit!" Jane felt the hot tears well to her eyes and splash down upon her hands. "I thought so much of them —tried so hard to be good to them. And not one was true. You've made it easy to forgive. Perhaps many of them really feel as you do, but dare not return to me. Still, Blake, I hesitate to take you back. Yet I want you so much."

"Do it, then. If you're going to make your life a lesson to Mormon women, let me make mine a lesson to the men. Right is right. I believe in you, and here's my life to prove it."

"You hint it may mean your life!" said Jane, breathless and low.

"We won't speak of that. I want to come back. I want to do what every rider aches in his secret heart to do for you.... Miss Withersteen, I hoped it'd not be necessary to tell you that my mother on her deathbed told me to have courage. She knew how the thing galled me— she told me to come back.... Will you take me?"

"God bless you, Blake! Yes, I'll take you back. And will you—will you accept gold from me?"

"Miss Withersteen!"

"I just gave Judkins a bag of gold. I'll give you one. If you will not take it you must not come back. You might ride for me a few months—weeks—days till the storm breaks. Then you'd have nothing, and be in disgrace with your people. We'll forearm you against poverty, and me against endless regret. I'll give you gold which you can hide—till some future time."

"Well, if it pleases you," replied Blake. "But you know I never thought of pay. Now, Miss Withersteen, one thing more. I want to see this man Lassiter. Is he here?"

"Yes, but, Blake—what—Need you see him? Why?" asked Jane, instantly worried. "I can speak to him—tell him about you."

"That won't do. I want to—I've got to tell him myself. Where is he?"

"Lassiter is with Mrs. Larkin. She is ill. I'll call him," answered Jane, and going to the door she softly called for the rider. A faint, musical jingle preceded his step—then his tall form crossed the threshold.

"Lassiter, here's Blake, an old rider of mine. He has come back to me and he wishes to speak to you."

Blake's brown face turned exceedingly pale.

"Yes, I had to speak to you," he said, swiftly. "My name's Blake. I'm a Mormon and a rider. Lately I quit Miss Withersteen. I've come to beg her to take me back. Now I don't know you; but I know—what you are. So I've this to say to your face. It would never occur to this woman to imagine—let alone suspect me to be a spy. She couldn't think it might just be a low plot to come here and shoot you in the back. Jane Withersteen hasn't that kind of a mind.... Well, I've not come for that. I want to help her—to pull a bridle along with Judkins and—and you. The thing is—do you believe me?"

"I reckon I do," replied Lassiter. How this slow, cool speech contrasted with Blake's hot, impulsive words! "You might have saved some of your breath. See here, Blake, cinch this in your mind. Lassiter has met some square Mormons! An' mebbe—"

"Blake," interrupted Jane, nervously anxious to terminate a colloquy that she perceived was an ordeal for him. "Go at once and fetch me a report of my horses."

"Miss Withersteen!... You mean the big drove—down in the sage-cleared fields?"

"Of course," replied Jane. "My horses are all there, except the blooded stock I keep here."

"Haven't you heard—then?"

"Heard? No! What's happened to them?"

"They're gone, Miss Withersteen, gone these ten days past. Dorn told me, and I rode down to see for myself."

"Lassiter—did you know?" asked Jane, whirling to him.

"I reckon so.... But what was the use to tell you?"

It was Lassiter turning away his face and Blake studying the stone flags at his feet that brought Jane to the understanding of what she betrayed. She strove desperately, but she could not rise immediately from such a blow.

"My horses! My horses! What's become of them?"

"Dorn said the riders report another drive by Oldring.... And I trailed the horses miles down the slope toward Deception Pass."

"My red herd's gone! My horses gone! The white herd will go next. I can stand that. But if I lost Black Star and Night, it would be like parting with my own flesh and blood. Lassiter—Blake—am I in danger of losing my racers?"

"A rustler—or—or anybody stealin' hosses of yours would most of all want the blacks," said Lassiter. His evasive reply was affirmative enough. The other rider nodded gloomy acquiescence.

"Oh! Oh!" Jane Withersteen choked, with violent utterance.

"Let me take charge of the blacks?" asked Blake. "One more rider won't be any great help to Judkins. But I might hold Black Star and Night, if you put such store on their value."

"Value! Blake, I love my racers. Besides, there's another reason why I mustn't lose them. You go to the stables. Go with Jerd every day when he runs the horses, and don't let them out of your sight. If you would please me—win my gratitude, guard my black racers."

When Blake had mounted and ridden out of the court Lassiter regarded Jane with the smile that was becoming rarer as the days sped by.

"'Pears to me, as Blake says, you do put some store on them hosses. Now I ain't gainsayin' that the Arabians are the handsomest hosses I ever seen. But Bells can beat Night, an' run neck en' neck with Black Star."

"Lassiter, don't tease me now. I'm miserable—sick. Bells is fast, but he can't stay with the blacks, and you know it. Only Wrangle can do that."

"I'll bet that big raw-boned brute can more'n show his heels to your black racers. Jane, out there in the sage, on a long chase, Wrangle could kill your favorites."

"No, no," replied Jane, impatiently. "Lassiter, why do you say that so often? I know you've teased me at times, and I believe it's only kindness. You're always trying to keep my mind off worry. But you mean more by this repeated mention of my racers?"

"I reckon so." Lassiter paused, and for the thousandth time in her presence moved his black sombrero round and round, as if counting the silver pieces on the band. "Well, Jane, I've sort of read a little that's passin' in your mind."

"You think I might fly from my home—from Cottonwoods—from the Utah border?"

"I reckon. An' if you ever do an' get away with the blacks I wouldn't like to see Wrangle left here on the sage. Wrangle could catch you. I know Venters had him. But you can never tell. Mebbe he hasn't got him now.... Besides—things are happenin', an' somethin' of the same queer nature might have happened to Venters."

"God knows you're right!... Poor Bern, how long he's gone! In my trouble I've been forgetting him. But, Lassiter, I've little fear for him. I've heard my riders say he's as keen as a wolf.... As to your reading my thoughts—well, your suggestion makes an actual thought of what was only one of my dreams. I believe I dreamed of flying from this wild borderland, Lassiter. I've strange dreams. I'm not always practical and thinking of my many duties, as you said once. For instance—if I dared—if I dared I'd ask you to saddle the blacks and ride away with me—and hide me."

"Jane!"

The rider's sunburnt face turned white. A few times Jane had seen Lassiter's cool calm broken—when he had met little Fay, when he had learned how and why he had come to love both child and mistress, when he had stood beside Milly Erne's grave. But one and all they could not be considered in the light of his present agitation. Not only did Lassiter turn white

—not only did he grow tense, not only did he lose his coolness, but also he suddenly, violently, hungrily took her into his arms and crushed her to his breast.

"Lassiter!" cried Jane, trembling. It was an action for which she took sole blame. Instantly, as if dazed, weakened, he released her. "Forgive me!" went on Jane. "I'm always forgetting your—your feelings. I thought of you as my faithful friend. I'm always making you out more than human... only, let me say—I meant that—about riding away. I'm wretched, sick of this— this—Oh, something bitter and black grows on my heart!"

"Jane, the hell—of it," he replied, with deep intake of breath, "is you can't ride away. Mebbe realizin' it accounts for my grabbin' you—that way, as much as the crazy boy's rapture your words gave me. I don't understand myself.... But the hell of this game is—you can't ride away."

"Lassiter!... What on earth do you mean? I'm an absolutely free woman."

"You ain't absolutely anythin' of the kind.... I reckon I've got to tell you!"

"Tell me all. It's uncertainty that makes me a coward. It's faith and hope—blind love, if you will, that makes me miserable. Every day I awake believing—still believing. The day grows, and with it doubts, fears, and that black bat hate that bites hotter and hotter into my heart. Then comes night—I pray—I pray for all, and for myself—I sleep—and I awake free once more, trustful, faithful, to believe—to hope! Then, O my God! I grow and live a thousand years till night again!... But if you want to see me a woman, tell me why I can't ride away—tell me what more I'm to lose—tell me the worst."

"Jane, you're watched. There's no single move of yours, except when you're hid in your house, that ain't seen by sharp eyes. The cottonwood grove's full of creepin', crawlin' men. Like Indians in the grass. When you rode, which wasn't often lately, the sage was full of sneakin' men. At night they crawl under your windows into the court, an' I reckon into the house. Jane Withersteen, you know, never locked a door! This here grove's a hummin' bee-hive of mysterious happenin's. Jane, it ain't so much that these soles keep out of my way as me keepin' out of theirs. They're goin' to try to kill me. That's plain. But mebbe I'm as hard to shoot in the back as in the face. So far I've seen fit to watch only. This all means, Jane, that you're a marked woman. You can't get away—not now. Mebbe later, when you're broken, you might. But that's sure doubtful. Jane, you're to lose the cattle that's left—your home an' ranch—an' Amber Spring. You can't even hide a sack of gold! For it couldn't be slipped out of the house, day or night, an' hid or buried, let alone be rid off with. You may lose all. I'm tellin' you, Jane, hopin' to prepare you, if the worst does come. I told you once before about that strange power I've got to feel things."

"Lassiter, what can I do?"

"Nothin', I reckon, except know what's comin' an' wait an' be game. If you'd let me make a call on Tull, an' a long-deferred call on—"

"Hush!... Hush!" she whispered.

"Well, even that wouldn't help you any in the end."

"What does it mean? Oh, what does it mean? I am my father's daughter—a Mormon, yet I can't see! I've not failed in religion—in duty. For years I've given with a free and full heart. When my father died I was rich. If I'm still rich it's because I couldn't find enough ways to become poor. What am I, what are my possessions to set in motion such intensity of secret oppression?"

"Jane, the mind behind it all is an empire builder."

"But, Lassiter, I would give freely—all I own to avert this—this wretched thing. If I gave —that would leave me with faith still. Surely my—my churchmen think of my soul? If I lose my trust in them—"

95

"Child, be still!" said Lassiter, with a dark dignity that had in it something of pity. "You are a woman, fine en' big an' strong, an' your heart matches your size. But in mind you're a child. I'll say a little more—then I'm done. I'll never mention this again. Among many thousands of women you're one who has bucked against your churchmen. They tried you out, an' failed of persuasion, an' finally of threats. You meet now the cold steel of a will as far from Christlike as the universe is wide. You're to be broken. Your body's to be held, given to some man, made, if possible, to bring children into the world. But your soul?... What do they care for your soul?"

✹ 13 ✸

SOLITUDE AND STORM

IN HIS HIDDEN valley Venters awakened from sleep, and his ears rang with innumerable melodies from full-throated mockingbirds, and his eyes opened wide upon the glorious golden shaft of sunlight shining through the great stone bridge. The circle of cliffs surrounding Surprise Valley lay shrouded in morning mist, a dim blue low down along the terraces, a creamy, moving cloud along the ramparts. The oak forest in the center was a plumed and tufted oval of gold.

He saw Bess under the spruces. Upon her complete recovery of strength she always rose with the dawn. At the moment she was feeding the quail she had tamed. And she had begun to tame the mocking-birds. They fluttered among the branches overhead and some left off their songs to flit down and shyly hop near the twittering quail. Little gray and white rabbits crouched in the grass, now nibbling, now laying long ears flat and watching the dogs.

Venters's swift glance took in the brightening valley, and Bess and her pets, and Ring and Whitie. It swept over all to return again and rest upon the girl. She had changed. To the dark trousers and blouse she had added moccasins of her own make, but she no longer resembled a boy. No eye could have failed to mark the rounded contours of a woman. The change had been to grace and beauty. A glint of warm gold gleamed from her hair, and a tint of red shone in the clear dark brown of cheeks. The haunting sweetness of her lips and eyes, that earlier had been illusive, a promise, had become a living fact. She fitted harmoniously into that wonderful setting; she was like Surprise Valley—wild and beautiful.

Venters leaped out of his cave to begin the day.

He had postponed his journey to Cottonwoods until after the passing of the summer rains. The rains were due soon. But until their arrival and the necessity for his trip to the village he sequestered in a far corner of mind all thought of peril, of his past life, and almost that of the present. It was enough to live. He did not want to know what lay hidden in the dim and distant future. Surprise Valley had enchanted him. In this home of the cliff-dwellers there were peace and quiet and solitude, and another thing, wondrous as the golden morning shaft of sunlight, that he dared not ponder over long enough to understand.

The solitude he had hated when alone he had now come to love. He was assimilating

97

something from this valley of gleams and shadows. From this strange girl he was assimilating more.

The day at hand resembled many days gone before. As Venters had no tools with which to build, or to till the terraces, he remained idle. Beyond the cooking of the simple fare there were no tasks. And as there were no tasks, there was no system. He and Bess began one thing, to leave it; to begin another, to leave that; and then do nothing but lie under the spruces and watch the great cloud-sails majestically move along the ramparts, and dream and dream. The valley was a golden, sunlit world. It was silent. The sighing wind and the twittering quail and the singing birds, even the rare and seldom-occurring hollow crack of a sliding weathered stone, only thickened and deepened that insulated silence.

Venters and Bess had vagrant minds.

"Bess, did I tell you about my horse Wrangle?" inquired Venters.

"A hundred times," she replied.

"Oh, have I? I'd forgotten. I want you to see him. He'll carry us both."

"I'd like to ride him. Can he run?"

"Run? He's a demon. Swiftest horse on the sage! I hope he'll stay in that canyon."

"He'll stay."

They left camp to wander along the terraces, into the aspen ravines, under the gleaming walls. Ring and Whitie wandered in the fore, often turning, often trotting back, open-mouthed and solemn-eyed and happy. Venters lifted his gaze to the grand archway over the entrance to the valley, and Bess lifted hers to follow his, and both were silent. Sometimes the bridge held their attention for a long time. To-day a soaring eagle attracted them.

"How he sails!" exclaimed Bess. "I wonder where his mate is?"

"She's at the nest. It's on the bridge in a crack near the top. I see her often. She's almost white."

They wandered on down the terrace, into the shady, sun-flecked forest. A brown bird fluttered crying from a bush. Bess peeped into the leaves. "Look! A nest and four little birds. They're not afraid of us. See how they open their mouths. They're hungry."

Rabbits rustled the dead brush and pattered away. The forest was full of a drowsy hum of insects. Little darts of purple, that were running quail, crossed the glades. And a plaintive, sweet peeping came from the coverts. Bess's soft step disturbed a sleeping lizard that scampered away over the leaves. She gave chase and caught it, a slim creature of nameless color but of exquisite beauty.

"Jewel eyes," she said. "It's like a rabbit—afraid. We won't eat you. There—go."

Murmuring water drew their steps down into a shallow shaded ravine where a brown brook brawled softly over mossy stones. Multitudes of strange, gray frogs with white spots and black eyes lined the rocky bank and leaped only at close approach. Then Venters's eye descried a very thin, very long green snake coiled round a sapling. They drew closer and closer till they could have touched it. The snake had no fear and watched them with scintillating eyes.

"It's pretty," said Bess. "How tame! I thought snakes always ran."

"No. Even the rabbits didn't run here till the dogs chased them."

On and on they wandered to the wild jumble of massed and broken fragments of cliff at the west end of the valley. The roar of the disappearing stream dinned in their ears. Into this maze of rocks they threaded a tortuous way, climbing, descending, halting to gather wild plums and great lavender lilies, and going on at the will of fancy. Idle and keen perceptions guided them equally.

"Oh, let us climb there!" cried Bess, pointing upward to a small space of terrace left green and shady between huge abutments of broken cliff. And they climbed to the nook and rested and looked out across the valley to the curling column of blue smoke from their campfire. But the cool shade and the rich grass and the fine view were not what they had climbed for. They could not have told, although whatever had drawn them was well-satisfying. Light, sure-footed as a mountain goat, Bess pattered down at Venters's heels; and they went on, calling the dogs, eyes dreamy and wide, listening to the wind and the bees and the crickets and the birds.

Part of the time Ring and Whitie led the way, then Venters, then Bess; and the direction was not an object. They left the sun-streaked shade of the oaks, brushed the long grass of the meadows, entered the green and fragrant swaying willows, to stop, at length, under the huge old cottonwoods where the beavers were busy.

Here they rested and watched. A dam of brush and logs and mud and stones backed the stream into a little lake. The round, rough beaver houses projected from the water. Like the rabbits, the beavers had become shy. Gradually, however, as Venters and Bess knelt low, holding the dogs, the beavers emerged to swim with logs and gnaw at cottonwoods and pat mud walls with their paddle-like tails, and, glossy and shiny in the sun, to go on with their strange, persistent industry. They were the builders. The lake was a mud-hole, and the immediate environment a scarred and dead region, but it was a wonderful home of wonderful animals.

"Look at that one—he puddles in the mud," said Bess. "And there! See him dive! Hear them gnawing! I'd think they'd break their teeth. How's it they can stay out of the water and under the water?"

And she laughed.

Then Venters and Bess wandered farther, and, perhaps not all unconsciously this time, wended their slow steps to the cave of the cliff-dwellers, where she liked best to go.

The tangled thicket and the long slant of dust and little chips of weathered rock and the steep bench of stone and the worn steps all were arduous work for Bess in the climbing. But she gained the shelf, gasping, hot of cheek, glad of eye, with her hand in Venters's. Here they rested. The beautiful valley glittered below with its millions of wind-turned leaves bright-faced in the sun, and the mighty bridge towered heavenward, crowned with blue sky. Bess, however, never rested for long. Soon she was exploring, and Venters followed; she dragged forth from corners and shelves a multitude of crudely fashioned and painted pieces of pottery, and he carried them. They peeped down into the dark holes of the kivas, and Bess gleefully dropped a stone and waited for the long-coming hollow sound to rise. They peeped into the little globular houses, like mud-wasp nests, and wondered if these had been store-places for grain, or baby cribs, or what; and they crawled into the larger houses and laughed when they bumped their heads on the low roofs, and they dug in the dust of the floors. And they brought from dust and darkness armloads of treasure which they carried to the light. Flints and stones and strange curved sticks and pottery they found; and twisted grass rope that crumbled in their hands, and bits of whitish stone which crushed to powder at a touch and seemed to vanish in the air.

"That white stuff was bone," said Venters, slowly. "Bones of a cliff-dweller."

"No!" exclaimed Bess.

"Here's another piece. Look!... Whew! dry, powdery smoke! That's bone."

Then it was that Venters's primitive, childlike mood, like a savage's, seeing, yet unthinking, gave way to the encroachment of civilized thought. The world had not been made for a single day's play or fancy or idle watching. The world was old. Nowhere could be gotten a better idea of its age than in this gigantic silent tomb. The gray ashes in Venters's

ZANE GREY

hand had once been bone of a human being like himself. The pale gloom of the cave had shadowed people long ago. He saw that Bess had received the same shock—could not in moments such as this escape her feeling living, thinking destiny.

"Bern, people have lived here," she said, with wide, thoughtful eyes.

"Yes," he replied.

"How long ago?"

"A thousand years and more."

"What were they?"

"Cliff-dwellers. Men who had enemies and made their homes high out of reach."

"They had to fight?"

"Yes."

"They fought for—what?"

"For life. For their homes, food, children, parents—for their women!"

"Has the world changed any in a thousand years?"

"I don't know—perhaps a little."

"Have men?"

"I hope so—I think so."

"Things crowd into my mind," she went on, and the wistful light in her eyes told Venters the truth of her thoughts. "I've ridden the border of Utah. I've seen people—know how they live—but they must be few of all who are living. I had my books and I studied them. But all that doesn't help me any more. I want to go out into the big world and see it. Yet I want to stay here more. What's to become of us? Are we cliff-dwellers? We're alone here. I'm happy when I don't think. These—these bones that fly into dust—they make me sick and a little afraid. Did the people who lived here once have the same feelings as we have? What was the good of their living at all? They're gone! What's the meaning of it all—of us?"

"Bess, you ask more than I can tell. It's beyond me. Only there was laughter here once— and now there's silence. There was life—and now there's death. Men cut these little steps, made these arrow-heads and mealing-stones, plaited the ropes we found, and left their bones to crumble in our fingers. As far as time is concerned it might all have been yesterday. We're here to-day. Maybe we're higher in the scale of human beings—in intelligence. But who knows? We can't be any higher in the things for which life is lived at all."

"What are they?"

"Why—I suppose relationship, friendship—love."

"Love!"

"Yes. Love of man for woman—love of woman for man. That's the nature, the meaning, the best of life itself."

She said no more. Wistfulness of glance deepened into sadness.

"Come, let us go," said Venters.

Action brightened her. Beside him, holding his hand she slipped down the shelf, ran down the long, steep slant of sliding stones, out of the cloud of dust, and likewise out of the pale gloom.

"We beat the slide," she cried.

The miniature avalanche cracked and roared, and rattled itself into an inert mass at the base of the incline. Yellow dust like the gloom of the cave, but not so changeless, drifted away on the wind; the roar clapped in echo from the cliff, returned, went back, and came again to die in the hollowness. Down on the sunny terrace there was a different atmosphere. Ring and Whitie leaped around Bess. Once more she was smiling, gay, and thoughtless, with the dream-mood in the shadow of her eyes.

"Bess, I haven't seen that since last summer. Look!" said Venters, pointing to the scalloped edge of rolling purple clouds that peeped over the western wall. "We're in for a storm."

"Oh, I hope not. I'm afraid of storms."

"Are you? Why?"

"Have you ever been down in one of these walled-up pockets in a bad storm?"

"No, now I think of it, I haven't."

"Well, it's terrible. Every summer I get scared to death and hide somewhere in the dark. Storms up on the sage are bad, but nothing to what they are down here in the canyons. And in this little valley—why, echoes can rap back and forth so quick they'll split our ears."

"We're perfectly safe here, Bess."

"I know. But that hasn't anything to do with it. The truth is I'm afraid of lightning and thunder, and thunder-claps hurt my head. If we have a bad storm, will you stay close to me?"

"Yes."

When they got back to camp the afternoon was closing, and it was exceedingly sultry. Not a breath of air stirred the aspen leaves, and when these did not quiver the air was indeed still. The dark-purple clouds moved almost imperceptibly out of the west.

"What have we for supper?" asked Bess.

"Rabbit."

"Bern, can't you think of another new way to cook rabbit?" went on Bess, with earnestness.

"What do you think I am—a magician?" retorted Venters.

"I wouldn't dare tell you. But, Bern, do you want me to turn into a rabbit?"

There was a dark-blue, merry flashing of eyes and a parting of lips; then she laughed. In that moment she was naive and wholesome.

"Rabbit seems to agree with you," replied Venters. "You are well and strong—and growing very pretty."

Anything in the nature of compliment he had never before said to her, and just now he responded to a sudden curiosity to see its effect. Bess stared as if she had not heard aright, slowly blushed, and completely lost her poise in happy confusion.

"I'd better go right away," he continued, "and fetch supplies from Cottonwoods."

A startlingly swift change in the nature of her agitation made him reproach himself for his abruptness.

"No, no, don't go!" she said. "I didn't mean—that about the rabbit. I—I was only trying to be—funny. Don't leave me all alone!"

"Bess, I must go sometime."

"Wait then. Wait till after the storms."

The purple cloud-bank darkened the lower edge of the setting sun, crept up and up, obscuring its fiery red heart, and finally passed over the last ruddy crescent of its upper rim.

The intense dead silence awakened to a long, low, rumbling roll of thunder.

"Oh!" cried Bess, nervously.

"We've had big black clouds before this without rain," said Venters. "But there's no doubt about that thunder. The storms are coming. I'm glad. Every rider on the sage will hear that thunder with glad ears."

Venters and Bess finished their simple meal and the few tasks around the camp, then faced the open terrace, the valley, and the west, to watch and await the approaching storm.

It required keen vision to see any movement whatever in the purple clouds. By infinitesimal degrees the dark cloud-line merged upward into the golden-red haze of the afterglow of sunset. A shadow lengthened from under the western wall across the valley. As straight and rigid as steel rose the delicate spear-pointed silver spruces; the aspen leaves, by nature pendant and quivering, hung limp and heavy; no slender blade of grass moved. A gentle splashing of water came from the ravine. Then again from out of the west sounded the low, dull, and rumbling roll of thunder.

A wave, a ripple of light, a trembling and turning of the aspen leaves, like the approach of a breeze on the water, crossed the valley from the west; and the lull and the deadly stillness and the sultry air passed away on a cool wind.

The night bird of the canyon, with clear and melancholy notes announced the twilight. And from all along the cliffs rose the faint murmur and moan and mourn of the wind singing in the caves. The bank of clouds now swept hugely out of the western sky. Its front was purple and black, with gray between, a bulging, mushrooming, vast thing instinct with storm. It had a dark, angry, threatening aspect. As if all the power of the winds were pushing and piling behind, it rolled ponderously across the sky. A red flare burned out instantaneously, flashed from the west to east, and died. Then from the deepest black of the purple cloud burst a boom. It was like the bowling of a huge boulder along the crags and ramparts, and seemed to roll on and fall into the valley to bound and bang and boom from cliff to cliff.

"Oh!" cried Bess, with her hands over her ears. "What did I tell you?"

"Why, Bess, be reasonable!" said Venters.

"I'm a coward."

"Not quite that, I hope. It's strange you're afraid. I love a storm."

"I tell you a storm down in these canyons is an awful thing. I know Oldring hated storms. His men were afraid of them. There was one who went deaf in a bad storm, and never could hear again."

"Maybe I've lots to learn, Bess. I'll lose my guess if this storm isn't bad enough. We're going to have heavy wind first, then lightning and thunder, then the rain. Let's stay out as long as we can."

The tips of the cottonwoods and the oaks waved to the east, and the rings of aspens along the terraces twinkled their myriad of bright faces in fleet and glancing gleam. A low roar rose from the leaves of the forest, and the spruces swished in the rising wind. It came in gusts, with light breezes between. As it increased in strength the lulls shortened in length till there was a strong and steady blow all the time, and violent puffs at intervals, and sudden whirling currents. The clouds spread over the valley, rolling swiftly and low, and twilight faded into a sweeping darkness. Then the singing of the wind in the caves drowned the swift roar of rustling leaves; then the song swelled to a mourning, moaning wail; then with the gathering power of the wind the wail changed to a shriek. Steadily the wind strengthened and constantly the strange sound changed.

The last bit of blue sky yielded to the on-sweep of clouds. Like angry surf the pale gleams of gray, amid the purple of that scudding front, swept beyond the eastern rampart of the valley. The purple deepened to black. Broad sheets of lightning flared over the western wall. There were not yet any ropes or zigzag streaks darting down through the gathering darkness. The storm center was still beyond Surprise Valley.

"Listen!... Listen!" cried Bess, with her lips close to Venters's ear. "You'll hear Oldring's knell!"

"What's that?"

"Oldring's knell. When the wind blows a gale in the caves it makes what the rustlers call Oldring's knell. They believe it bodes his death. I think he believes so, too. It's not like any sound on earth.... It's beginning. Listen!"

The gale swooped down with a hollow unearthly howl. It yelled and pealed and shrilled and shrieked. It was made up of a thousand piercing cries. It was a rising and a moving sound. Beginning at the western break of the valley, it rushed along each gigantic cliff, whistling into the caves and cracks, to mount in power, to bellow a blast through the great stone bridge. Gone, as into an engulfing roar of surging waters, it seemed to shoot back and begin all over again.

It was only wind, thought Venters. Here sped and shrieked the sculptor that carved out the wonderful caves in the cliffs. It was only a gale, but as Venters listened, as his ears became accustomed to the fury and strife, out of it all or through it or above it pealed low and perfectly clear and persistently uniform a strange sound that had no counterpart in all the sounds of the elements. It was not of earth or of life. It was the grief and agony of the gale. A knell of all upon which it blew!

Black night enfolded the valley. Venters could not see his companion, and knew of her presence only through the tightening hold of her hand on his arm. He felt the dogs huddle closer to him. Suddenly the dense, black vault overhead split asunder to a blue-white, dazzling streak of lightning. The whole valley lay vividly clear and luminously bright in his sight. Upreared, vast and magnificent, the stone bridge glimmered like some grand god of storm in the lightning's fire. Then all flashed black again—blacker than pitch—a thick, impenetrable coal-blackness. And there came a ripping, crashing report. Instantly an echo resounded with clapping crash. The initial report was nothing to the echo. It was a terrible, living, reverberating, detonating crash. The wall threw the sound across, and could have made no greater roar if it had slipped in avalanche. From cliff to cliff the echo went in crashing retort and banged in lessening power, and boomed in thinner volume, and clapped weaker and weaker till a final clap could not reach across the waiting cliff.

In the pitchy darkness Venters led Bess, and, groping his way, by feel of hand found the entrance to her cave and lifted her up. On the instant a blinding flash of lightning illumined the cave and all about him. He saw Bess's face white now with dark, frightened eyes. He saw the dogs leap up, and he followed suit. The golden glare vanished; all was black; then came the splitting crack and the infernal din of echoes.

Bess shrank closer to him and closer, found his hands, and pressed them tightly over her ears, and dropped her face upon his shoulder, and hid her eyes.

Then the storm burst with a succession of ropes and streaks and shafts of lightning, playing continuously, filling the valley with a broken radiance; and the cracking shots followed each other swiftly till the echoes blended in one fearful, deafening crash.

Venters looked out upon the beautiful valley—beautiful now as never before—mystic in its transparent, luminous gloom, weird in the quivering, golden haze of lightning. The dark spruces were tipped with glimmering lights; the aspens bent low in the winds, as waves in a tempest at sea; the forest of oaks tossed wildly and shone with gleams of fire. Across the valley the huge cavern of the cliff-dwellers yawned in the glare, every little black window as clear as at noonday; but the night and the storm added to their tragedy. Flung arching to the black clouds, the great stone bridge seemed to bear the brunt of the storm. It caught the full fury of the rushing wind. It lifted its noble crown to meet the lightnings. Venters thought of the eagles and their lofty nest in a niche under the arch. A driving pall of rain, black as the clouds, came sweeping on to obscure the bridge and the gleaming walls and the shining valley. The lightning played incessantly, streaking down through opaque darkness of rain. The roar of the wind, with its strange knell and the re-crashing echoes, mingled with the roar of the flooding rain, and all seemingly were deadened and drowned in a world of sound.

In the dimming pale light Venters looked down upon the girl. She had sunk into his arms, upon his breast, burying her face. She clung to him. He felt the softness of her, and the warmth, and the quick heave of her breast. He saw the dark, slender, graceful outline of her form. A woman lay in his arms! And he held her closer. He who had been alone in the sad, silent watches of the night was not now and never must be again alone. He who had yearned for the touch of a hand felt the long tremble and the heart-beat of a woman. By what strange chance had she come to love him! By what change—by what marvel had she grown into a treasure!

No more did he listen to the rush and roar of the thunder-storm. For with the touch of clinging hands and the throbbing bosom he grew conscious of an inward storm—the tingling of new chords of thought, strange music of unheard, joyous bells sad dreams dawning to wakeful delight, dissolving doubt, resurging hope, force, fire, and freedom, unutterable sweetness of desire. A storm in his breast—a storm of real love.

❧ 14 ❧

WEST WIND

WHEN THE STORM abated Venters sought his own cave, and late in the night, as his blood cooled and the stir and throb and thrill subsided, he fell asleep.

With the breaking of dawn his eyes unclosed. The valley lay drenched and bathed, a burnished oval of glittering green. The rain-washed walls glistened in the morning light. Waterfalls of many forms poured over the rims. One, a broad, lacy sheet, thin as smoke, slid over the western notch and struck a ledge in its downward fall, to bound into broader leap, to burst far below into white and gold and rosy mist.

Venters prepared for the day, knowing himself a different man.

"It's a glorious morning," said Bess, in greeting.

"Yes. After the storm the west wind," he replied.

"Last night was I—very much of a baby?" she asked, watching him.

"Pretty much."

"Oh, I couldn't help it!"

"I'm glad you were afraid."

"Why?" she asked, in slow surprise.

"I'll tell you some day," he answered, soberly. Then around the camp-fire and through the morning meal he was silent; afterward he strolled thoughtfully off alone along the terrace. He climbed a great yellow rock raising its crest among the spruces, and there he sat down to face the valley and the west.

"I love her!"

Aloud he spoke—unburdened his heart—confessed his secret. For an instant the golden valley swam before his eyes, and the walls waved, and all about him whirled with tumult within.

"I love her!... I understand now."

Reviving memory of Jane Withersteen and thought of the complications of the present amazed him with proof of how far he had drifted from his old life. He discovered that he hated to take up the broken threads, to delve into dark problems and difficulties. In this beautiful valley he had been living a beautiful dream. Tranquillity had come to him, and the joy of solitude, and interest in all the wild creatures and crannies of this incomparable valley —and love. Under the shadow of the great stone bridge God had revealed Himself to Venters.

"The world seems very far away," he muttered, "but it's there—and I'm not yet done with it. Perhaps I never shall be.... Only—how glorious it would be to live here always and never think again!"

Whereupon the resurging reality of the present, as if in irony of his wish, steeped him instantly in contending thought. Out of it all he presently evolved these things: he must go to Cottonwoods; he must bring supplies back to Surprise Valley; he must cultivate the soil and raise corn and stock, and, most imperative of all, he must decide the future of the girl who loved him and whom he loved. The first of these things required tremendous effort, the last one, concerning Bess, seemed simply and naturally easy of accomplishment. He would marry her. Suddenly, as from roots of poisonous fire, flamed up the forgotten truth concerning her. It seemed to wither and shrivel up all his joy on its hot, tearing way to his heart. She had been Oldring's Masked Rider. To Venters's question, "What were you to Oldring?" she had answered with scarlet shame and drooping head.

"What do I care who she is or what she was!" he cried, passionately. And he knew it was not his old self speaking. It was this softer, gentler man who had awakened to new thoughts in the quiet valley. Tenderness, masterful in him now, matched the absence of joy and blunted the knife-edge of entering jealousy. Strong and passionate effort of will, surprising to him, held back the poison from piercing his soul.

"Wait!... Wait!" he cried, as if calling. His hand pressed his breast, and he might have called to the pang there. "Wait! It's all so strange—so wonderful. Anything can happen. Who am I to judge her? I'll glory in my love for her. But I can't tell it—can't give up to it."

Certainly he could not then decide her future. Marrying her was impossible in Surprise Valley and in any village south of Sterling. Even without the mask she had once worn she would easily have been recognized as Oldring's Rider. No man who had ever seen her would forget her, regardless of his ignorance as to her sex. Then more poignant than all other argument was the fact that he did not want to take her away from Surprise Valley. He resisted all thought of that. He had brought her to the most beautiful and wildest place of the uplands; he had saved her, nursed her back to strength, watched her bloom as one of the valley lilies; he knew her life there to be pure and sweet—she belonged to him, and he loved her. Still these were not all the reasons why he did not want to take her away. Where could they go? He feared the rustlers—he feared the riders—he feared the Mormons. And if he should ever succeed in getting Bess safely away from these immediate perils, he feared the sharp eyes of women and their tongues, the big outside world with its problems of existence. He must wait to decide her future, which, after all, was deciding his own. But between her future and his something hung impending. Like Balancing Rock, which waited darkly over the steep gorge, ready to close forever the outlet to Deception Pass, that nameless thing, as certain yet intangible as fate, must fall and close forever all doubts and fears of the future.

"I've dreamed," muttered Venters, as he rose. "Well, why not?... To dream is happiness! But let me just once see this clearly wholly; then I can go on dreaming till the thing falls. I've got to tell Jane Withersteen. I've dangerous trips to take. I've work here to make comfort for this girl. She's mine. I'll fight to keep her safe from that old life. I've already seen her forget it. I love her. And if a beast ever rises in me I'll burn my hand off before I lay it on her with shameful intent. And, by God! sooner or later I'll kill the man who hid her and kept her in Deception Pass!"

As he spoke the west wind softly blew in his face. It seemed to soothe his passion. That west wind was fresh, cool, fragrant, and it carried a sweet, strange burden of far-off things—tidings of life in other climes, of sunshine asleep on other walls—of other places where reigned peace. It carried, too, sad truth of human hearts and mystery—of promise and hope unquenchable. Surprise Valley was only a little niche in the wide world whence blew that burdened wind. Bess was only one of millions at the mercy of unknown motive in nature and life. Content had come to Venters in the valley; happiness had breathed in the slow, warm air; love as bright as light had hovered over the walls and descended to him; and now on the west wind came a whisper of the eternal triumph of faith over doubt.

"How much better I am for what has come to me!" he exclaimed. "I'll let the future take care of itself. Whatever falls, I'll be ready."

Venters retraced his steps along the terrace back to camp, and found Bess in the old familiar seat, waiting and watching for his return.

"I went off by myself to think a little," he explained.

"You never looked that way before. What—what is it? Won't you tell me?"

"Well, Bess, the fact is I've been dreaming a lot. This valley makes a fellow dream. So I forced myself to think. We can't live this way much longer. Soon I'll simply have to go to Cottonwoods. We need a whole pack train of supplies. I can get—"

"Can you go safely?" she interrupted.

"Why, I'm sure of it. I'll ride through the Pass at night. I haven't any fear that Wrangle isn't where I left him. And once on him—Bess, just wait till you see that horse!"

"Oh, I want to see him—to ride him. But—but, Bern, this is what troubles me," she said. "Will—will you come back?"

"Give me four days. If I'm not back in four days you'll know I'm dead. For that only shall keep me."

"Oh!"

"Bess, I'll come back. There's danger—I wouldn't lie to you—but I can take care of myself."

"Bern, I'm sure—oh, I'm sure of it! All my life I've watched hunted men. I can tell what's in them. And I believe you can ride and shoot and see with any rider of the sage. It's not—not that I—fear."

"Well, what is it, then?"

"Why—why—why should you come back at all?"

"I couldn't leave you here alone."

"You might change your mind when you get to the village—among old friends—"

"I won't change my mind. As for old friends—" He uttered a short, expressive laugh.

"Then—there—there must be a—a woman!" Dark red mantled the clear tan of temple and cheek and neck. Her eyes were eyes of shame, upheld a long moment by intense, straining search for the verification of her fear. Suddenly they drooped, her head fell to her knees, her hands flew to her hot cheeks.

"Bess—look here," said Venters, with a sharpness due to the violence with which he checked his quick, surging emotion.

As if compelled against her will—answering to an irresistible voice—Bess raised her head, looked at him with sad, dark eyes, and tried to whisper with tremulous lips.

"There's no woman," went on Venters, deliberately holding her glance with his. "Nothing on earth, barring the chances of life, can keep me away."

Her face flashed and flushed with the glow of a leaping joy; but like the vanishing of a gleam it disappeared to leave her as he had never beheld her.

"I am nothing—I am lost—I am nameless!"

"Do you want me to come back?" he asked, with sudden stern coldness. "Maybe you want to go back to Oldring!"

That brought her erect, trembling and ashy pale, with dark, proud eyes and mute lips refuting his insinuation.

"Bess, I beg your pardon. I shouldn't have said that. But you angered me. I intend to work —to make a home for you here—to be a—a brother to you as long as ever you need me. And you must forget what you are—were—I mean, and be happy. When you remember that old life you are bitter, and it hurts me."

"I was happy—I shall be very happy. Oh, you're so good that—that it kills me! If I think, I can't believe it. I grow sick with wondering why. I'm only a let me say it—only a lost, nameless—girl of the rustlers. Oldring's Girl, they called me. That you should save me—be so good and kind—want to make me happy—why, it's beyond belief. No wonder I'm wretched at the thought of your leaving me. But I'll be wretched and bitter no more. I promise you. If only I could repay you even a little—"

"You've repaid me a hundredfold. Will you believe me?"

"Believe you! I couldn't do else."

"Then listen!... Saving you, I saved myself. Living here in this valley with you, I've found myself. I've learned to think while I was dreaming. I never troubled myself about God. But God, or some wonderful spirit, has whispered to me here. I absolutely deny the truth of what you say about yourself. I can't explain it. There are things too deep to tell. Whatever the terrible wrongs you've suffered, God holds you blameless. I see that—feel that in you every moment you are near me. I've a mother and a sister 'way back in Illinois. If I could I'd take you to them—to-morrow."

"If it were true! Oh, I might—I might lift my head!" she cried.

"Lift it then—you child. For I swear it's true."

She did lift her head with the singular wild grace always a part of her actions, with that old unconscious intimation of innocence which always tortured Venters, but now with something more—a spirit rising from the depths that linked itself to his brave words.

"I've been thinking—too," she cried, with quivering smile and swelling breast. "I've discovered myself—too. I'm young—I'm alive —I'm so full—oh! I'm a woman!"

"Bess, I believe I can claim credit of that last discovery—before you," Venters said, and laughed.

"Oh, there's more—there's something I must tell you."

"Tell it, then."

"When will you go to Cottonwoods?"

"As soon as the storms are past, or the worst of them."

"I'll tell you before you go. I can't now. I don't know how I shall then. But it must be told. I'd never let you leave me without knowing. For in spite of what you say there's a chance you mightn't come back."

Day after day the west wind blew across the valley. Day after day the clouds clustered gray and purple and black. The cliffs sang and the caves rang with Oldring's knell, and the lightning flashed, the thunder rolled, the echoes crashed and crashed, and the rains flooded the valley. Wild flowers sprang up everywhere, swaying with the lengthening grass on the terraces, smiling wanly from shady nooks, peeping wondrously from year-dry crevices of the walls. The valley bloomed into a paradise. Every single moment, from the breaking of the gold bar through the bridge at dawn on to the reddening of rays over the western wall, was one of colorful change. The valley swam in thick, transparent haze, golden at dawn, warm and white at noon, purple in the twilight. At the end of every storm a rainbow curved down into the leaf-bright forest to shine and fade and leave lingeringly some faint essence of its rosy iris in the air.

Venters walked with Bess, once more in a dream, and watched the lights change on the walls, and faced the wind from out of the west.

Always it brought softly to him strange, sweet tidings of far-off things. It blew from a place that was old and whispered of youth. It blew down the grooves of time. It brought a story of the passing hours. It breathed low of fighting men and praying women. It sang clearly the song of love. That ever was the burden of its tidings—youth in the shady woods, waders through the wet meadows, boy and girl at the hedgerow stile, bathers in the booming surf, sweet, idle hours on grassy, windy hills, long strolls down moonlit lanes—everywhere in far-off lands, fingers locked and bursting hearts and longing lips—from all the world tidings of unquenchable love.

Often, in these hours of dreams he watched the girl, and asked himself of what was she dreaming? For the changing light of the valley reflected its gleam and its color and its meaning in the changing light of her eyes. He saw in them infinitely more than he saw in his dreams. He saw thought and soul and nature—strong vision of life. All tidings the west wind blew from distance and age he found deep in those dark-blue depths, and found them mysteries solved. Under their wistful shadow he softened, and in the softening felt himself grow a sadder, a wiser, and a better man.

While the west wind blew its tidings, filling his heart full, teaching him a man's part, the days passed, the purple clouds changed to white, and the storms were over for that summer.

"I must go now," he said.

"When?" she asked.

"At once—to-night."

"I'm glad the time has come. It dragged at me. Go—for you'll come back the sooner."

Late in the afternoon, as the ruddy sun split its last flame in the ragged notch of the western wall, Bess walked with Venters along the eastern terrace, up the long, weathered slope, under the great stone bridge. They entered the narrow gorge to climb around the fence long before built there by Venters. Farther than this she had never been. Twilight had already fallen in the gorge. It brightened to waning shadow in the wider ascent. He showed her Balancing Rock, of which he had often told her, and explained its sinister leaning over the outlet. Shuddering, she looked down the long, pale incline with its closed-in, toppling walls.

"What an awful trail! Did you carry me up here?"

"I did, surely," replied he.

"It frightens me, somehow. Yet I never was afraid of trails. I'd ride anywhere a horse could go, and climb where he couldn't. But there's something fearful here. I feel as—as if the place was watching me."

"Look at this rock. It's balanced here—balanced perfectly. You know I told you the cliff-dwellers cut the rock, and why. But they're gone and the rock waits. Can't you see—feel how it waits here? I moved it once, and I'll never dare again. A strong heave would start it. Then it would fall and bang, and smash that crag, and jar the walls, and close forever the outlet to Deception Pass!"

"Ah! When you come back I'll steal up here and push and push with all my might to roll the rock and close forever the outlet to the Pass!" She said it lightly, but in the undercurrent of her voice was a heavier note, a ring deeper than any ever given mere play of words.

"Bess!... You can't dare me! Wait till I come back with supplies—then roll the stone."

"I—was—in—fun." Her voice now throbbed low. "Always you must be free to go when you will. Go now... this place presses on me—stifles me."

"I'm going—but you had something to tell me?"

"Yes.... Will you—come back?"

"I'll come if I live."

"But—but you mightn't come?"

"That's possible, of course. It'll take a good deal to kill me. A man couldn't have a faster horse or keener dog. And, Bess, I've guns, and I'll use them if I'm pushed. But don't worry."

"I've faith in you. I'll not worry until after four days. Only—because you mightn't come—I must tell you—"

She lost her voice. Her pale face, her great, glowing, earnest eyes, seemed to stand alone out of the gloom of the gorge. The dog whined, breaking the silence.

"I must tell you—because you mightn't come back," she whispered. "You must know what—what I think of your goodness—of you. Always I've been tongue-tied. I seemed not to be grateful. It was deep in my heart. Even now—if I were other than I am—I couldn't tell you. But I'm nothing—only a rustler's girl—nameless—infamous. You've saved me—and I'm —I'm yours to do with as you like.... With all my heart and soul—I love you!"

❧ 15 ❧

SHADOWS ON THE SAGE-SLOPE

IN THE CLOUDY, threatening, waning summer days shadows lengthened down the sage-slope, and Jane Withersteen likened them to the shadows gathering and closing in around her life.

Mrs. Larkin died, and little Fay was left an orphan with no known relative. Jane's love redoubled. It was the saving brightness of a darkening hour. Fay turned now to Jane in childish worship. And Jane at last found full expression for the mother-longing in her heart. Upon Lassiter, too, Mrs. Larkin's death had some subtle reaction. Before, he had often, without explanation, advised Jane to send Fay back to any Gentile family that would take her in. Passionately and reproachfully and wonderingly Jane had refused even to entertain such an idea. And now Lassiter never advised it again, grew sadder and quieter in his contemplation of the child, and infinitely more gentle and loving. Sometimes Jane had a cold, inexplicable sensation of dread when she saw Lassiter watching Fay. What did the rider see in the future? Why did he, day by day, grow more silent, calmer, cooler, yet sadder in prophetic assurance of something to be?

No doubt, Jane thought, the rider, in his almost superhuman power of foresight, saw behind the horizon the dark, lengthening shadows that were soon to crowd and gloom over him and her and little Fay. Jane Withersteen awaited the long-deferred breaking of the storm with a courage and embittered calm that had come to her in her extremity. Hope had not died. Doubt and fear, subservient to her will, no longer gave her sleepless nights and tortured days. Love remained. All that she had loved she now loved the more. She seemed to feel that she was defiantly flinging the wealth of her love in the face of misfortune and of hate. No day passed but she prayed for all—and most fervently for her enemies. It troubled her that she had lost, or had never gained, the whole control of her mind. In some measure reason and wisdom and decision were locked in a chamber of her brain, awaiting a key. Power to think of some things was taken from her. Meanwhile, abiding a day of judgment, she fought ceaselessly to deny the bitter drops in her cup, to tear back the slow, the intangibly slow growth of a hot, corrosive lichen eating into her heart.

On the morning of August 10th, Jane, while waiting in the court for Lassiter, heard a clear, ringing report of a rifle. It came from the grove, somewhere toward the corrals. Jane glanced out in alarm. The day was dull, windless, soundless. The leaves of the cottonwoods drooped, as if they had foretold the doom of Withersteen House and were now ready to die and drop and decay. Never had Jane seen such shade. She pondered on the meaning of the report. Revolver shots had of late cracked from different parts of the grove—spies taking snap-shots at Lassiter from a cowardly distance! But a rifle report meant more. Riders seldom used rifles. Judkins and Venters were the exceptions she called to mind. Had the men who hounded her hidden in her grove, taken to the rifle to rid her of Lassiter, her last friend? It was probable—it was likely. And she did not share his cool assumption that his death would never come at the hands of a Mormon. Long had she expected it. His constancy to her, his singular reluctance to use the fatal skill for which he was famed—both now plain to all Mormons—laid him open to inevitable assassination. Yet what charm against ambush and aim and enemy he seemed to bear about him! No, Jane reflected, it was not charm; only a wonderful training of eye and ear, and sense of impending peril. Nevertheless that could not forever avail against secret attack.

That moment a rustling of leaves attracted her attention; then the familiar clinking accompaniment of a slow, soft, measured step, and Lassiter walked into the court.

"Jane, there's a fellow out there with a long gun," he said, and, removing his sombrero, showed his head bound in a bloody scarf.

"I heard the shot; I knew it was meant for you. Let me see—you can't be badly injured?"

"I reckon not. But mebbe it wasn't a close call!... I'll sit here in this corner where nobody can see me from the grove." He untied the scarf and removed it to show a long, bleeding furrow above his left temple.

"It's only a cut," said Jane. "But how it bleeds! Hold your scarf over it just a moment till I come back."

She ran into the house and returned with bandages; and while she bathed and dressed the wound Lassiter talked.

"That fellow had a good chance to get me. But he must have flinched when he pulled the trigger. As I dodged down I saw him run through the trees. He had a rifle. I've been expectin' that kind of gun play. I reckon now I'll have to keep a little closer hid myself. These fellers all seem to get chilly or shaky when they draw a bead on me, but one of them might jest happen to hit me."

"Won't you go away—leave Cottonwoods as I've begged you to—before some one does happen to hit you?" she appealed to him.

"I reckon I'll stay."

"But, oh, Lassiter—your blood will be on my hands!"

"See here, lady, look at your hands now, right now. Aren't they fine, firm, white hands? Aren't they bloody now? Lassiter's blood! That's a queer thing to stain your beautiful hands. But if you could only see deeper you'd find a redder color of blood. Heart color, Jane!"

"Oh!... My friend!"

"No, Jane, I'm not one to quit when the game grows hot, no more than you. This game, though, is new to me, an' I don't know the moves yet, else I wouldn't have stepped in front of that bullet."

"Have you no desire to hunt the man who fired at you—to find him—and—and kill him?"

"Well, I reckon I haven't any great hankerin' for that."

"Oh, the wonder of it!... I knew—I prayed—I trusted. Lassiter, I almost gave—all myself to soften you to Mormons. Thank God, and thank you, my friend.... But, selfish woman that I am, this is no great test. What's the life of one of those sneaking cowards to such a man as you? I think of your great hate toward him who—I think of your life's implacable purpose. Can it be—"

"Wait!... Listen!" he whispered. "I hear a hoss."

He rose noiselessly, with his ear to the breeze. Suddenly he pulled his sombrero down over his bandaged head and, swinging his gun-sheaths round in front, he stepped into the alcove.

"It's a hoss—comin' fast," he added.

Jane's listening ear soon caught a faint, rapid, rhythmic beat of hoofs. It came from the sage. It gave her a thrill that she was at a loss to understand. The sound rose stronger, louder. Then came a clear, sharp difference when the horse passed from the sage trail to the hard-packed ground of the grove. It became a ringing run—swift in its bell-like clatterings, yet singular in longer pause than usual between the hoofbeats of a horse.

"It's Wrangle!... It's Wrangle!" cried Jane Withersteen. "I'd know him from a million horses!"

Excitement and thrilling expectancy flooded out all Jane Withersteen's calm. A tight band closed round her breast as she saw the giant sorrel flit in reddish-brown flashes across the openings in the green. Then he was pounding down the lane—thundering into the court—crashing his great iron-shod hoofs on the stone flags. Wrangle it was surely, but shaggy and wild-eyed, and sage-streaked, with dust-caked lather staining his flanks. He reared and crashed down and plunged. The rider leaped off, threw the bridle, and held hard on a lasso looped round Wrangle's head and neck. Janet's heart sank as she tried to recognize Venters in the rider. Something familiar struck her in the lofty stature in the sweep of powerful shoulders. But this bearded, longhaired, unkempt man, who wore ragged clothes patched with pieces of skin, and boots that showed bare legs and feet—this dusty, dark, and wild rider could not possibly be Venters.

"Whoa, Wrangle, old boy! Come down. Easy now. So—so—so. You're home, old boy, and presently you can have a drink of water you'll remember."

In the voice Jane knew the rider to be Venters. He tied Wrangle to the hitching-rack and turned to the court.

"Oh, Bern!... You wild man!" she exclaimed.

"Jane—Jane, it's good to see you! Hello, Lassiter! Yes, it's Venters."

Like rough iron his hard hand crushed Jane's. In it she felt the difference she saw in him. Wild, rugged, unshorn—yet how splendid! He had gone away a boy—he had returned a man. He appeared taller, wider of shoulder, deeper-chested, more powerfully built. But was that only her fancy—he had always been a young giant—was the change one of spirit? He might have been absent for years, proven by fire and steel, grown like Lassiter, strong and cool and sure. His eyes—were they keener, more flashing than before? —met hers with clear, frank, warm regard, in which perplexity was not, nor discontent, nor pain.

"Look at me long as you like," he said, with a laugh. "I'm not much to look at. And, Jane, neither you nor Lassiter, can brag. You're paler than I ever saw you. Lassiter, here, he wears a bloody bandage under his hat. That reminds me. Some one took a flying shot at me down in the sage. It made Wrangle run some.... Well, perhaps you've more to tell me than I've got to tell you."

Briefly, in few words, Jane outlined the circumstances of her undoing in the weeks of his absence.

Under his beard and bronze she saw his face whiten in terrible wrath.

"Lassiter—what held you back?"

No time in the long period of fiery moments and sudden shocks had Jane Withersteen ever beheld Lassiter as calm and serene and cool as then.

"Jane had gloom enough without my addin' to it by shootin' up the village," he said.

As strange as Lassiter's coolness was Venters's curious, intent scrutiny of them both, and under it Jane felt a flaming tide wave from bosom to temples.

"Well—you're right," he said, with slow pause. "It surprises me a little, that's all."

Jane sensed then a slight alteration in Venters, and what it was, in her own confusion, she could not tell. It had always been her intention to acquaint him with the deceit she had fallen to in her zeal to move Lassiter. She did not mean to spare herself. Yet now, at the moment, before these riders, it was an impossibility to explain.

Venters was speaking somewhat haltingly, without his former frankness. "I found Oldring's hiding-place and your red herd. I learned—I know—I'm sure there was a deal between Tull and Oldring." He paused and shifted his position and his gaze. He looked as if he wanted to say something that he found beyond him. Sorrow and pity and shame seemed to contend for mastery over him. Then he raised himself and spoke with effort. "Jane I've cost you too much. You've almost ruined yourself for me. It was wrong, for I'm not worth it. I never deserved such friendship. Well, maybe it's not too late. You must give me up. Mind, I haven't changed. I am just the same as ever. I'll see Tull while I'm here, and tell him to his face."

"Bern, it's too late," said Jane.

"I'll make him believe!" cried Venters, violently.

"You ask me to break our friendship?"

"Yes. If you don't, I shall."

"Forever?"

"Forever!"

Jane sighed. Another shadow had lengthened down the sage slope to cast further darkness upon her. A melancholy sweetness pervaded her resignation. The boy who had left her had returned a man, nobler, stronger, one in whom she divined something unbending as steel. There might come a moment later when she would wonder why she had not fought against his will, but just now she yielded to it. She liked him as well—nay, more, she thought, only her emotions were deadened by the long, menacing wait for the bursting storm.

Once before she had held out her hand to him—when she gave it; now she stretched it tremblingly forth in acceptance of the decree circumstance had laid upon them. Venters bowed over it kissed it, pressed it hard, and half stifled a sound very like a sob. Certain it was that when he raised his head tears glistened in his eyes.

"Some—women—have a hard lot," he said, huskily. Then he shook his powerful form, and his rags lashed about him. "I'll say a few things to Tull—when I meet him."

"Bern—you'll not draw on Tull? Oh, that must not be! Promise me—"

"I promise you this," he interrupted, in stern passion that thrilled while it terrorized her. "If you say one more word for that plotter I'll kill him as I would a mad coyote!"

Jane clasped her hands. Was this fire-eyed man the one whom she had once made as wax to her touch? Had Venters become Lassiter and Lassiter Venters?

"I'll—say no more," she faltered.

"Jane, Lassiter once called you blind," said Venters. "It must be true. But I won't upbraid you. Only don't rouse the devil in me by praying for Tull! I'll try to keep cool when I meet him. That's all. Now there's one more thing I want to ask of you—the last. I've found a valley down in the Pass. It's a wonderful place. I intend to stay there. It's so hidden I believe no one can find it. There's good water, and browse, and game. I want to raise corn and stock. I need to take in supplies. Will you give them to me?"

"Assuredly. The more you take the better you'll please me—and perhaps the less my—my enemies will get."

"Venters, I reckon you'll have trouble packin' anythin' away," put in Lassiter.

"I'll go at night."

"Mebbe that wouldn't be best. You'd sure be stopped. You'd better go early in the mornin'—say, just after dawn. That's the safest time to move round here."

"Lassiter, I'll be hard to stop," returned Venters, darkly.

"I reckon so."

"Bern," said Jane, "go first to the riders' quarters and get yourself a complete outfit. You're a—a sight. Then help yourself to whatever else you need—burros, packs, grain, dried fruits, and meat. You must take coffee and sugar and flour—all kinds of supplies. Don't forget corn and seeds. I remember how you used to starve. Please—please take all you can pack away from here. I'll make a bundle for you, which you mustn't open till you're in your valley. How I'd like to see it! To judge by you and Wrangle, how wild it must be!"

Jane walked down into the outer court and approached the sorrel. Upstarting, he laid back his ears and eyed her.

"Wrangle—dear old Wrangle," she said, and put a caressing hand on his matted mane. "Oh, he's wild, but he knows me! Bern, can he run as fast as ever?"

"Run? Jane, he's done sixty miles since last night at dark, and I could make him kill Black Star right now in a ten-mile race."

"He never could," protested Jane. "He couldn't even if he was fresh."

"I reckon mebbe the best hoss'll prove himself yet," said Lassiter, "an', Jane, if it ever comes to that race I'd like you to be on Wrangle."

"I'd like that, too," rejoined Venters. "But, Jane, maybe Lassiter's hint is extreme. Bad as your prospects are, you'll surely never come to the running point."

"Who knows!" she replied, with mournful smile.

"No, no, Jane, it can't be so bad as all that. Soon as I see Tull there'll be a change in your fortunes. I'll hurry down to the village.... Now don't worry."

Jane retired to the seclusion of her room. Lassiter's subtle forecasting of disaster, Venters's forced optimism, neither remained in mind. Material loss weighed nothing in the balance with other losses she was sustaining. She wondered dully at her sitting there, hands folded listlessly, with a kind of numb deadness to the passing of time and the passing of her riches. She thought of Venters's friendship. She had not lost that, but she had lost him. Lassiter's friendship—that was more than love—it would endure, but soon he, too, would be gone. Little Fay slept dreamlessly upon the bed, her golden curls streaming over the pillow. Jane had the child's worship. Would she lose that, too? And if she did, what then would be left? Conscience thundered at her that there was left her religion. Conscience thundered that she should be grateful on her knees for this baptism of fire; that through misfortune, sacrifice, and suffering her soul might be fused pure gold. But the old, spontaneous, rapturous spirit no more exalted her. She wanted to be a woman—not a martyr. Like the saint of old who mortified his flesh, Jane Withersteen had in her the temper for heroic martyrdom, if by sacrificing herself she could save the souls of others. But here the damnable verdict blistered her that the more she sacrificed herself the blacker grew the souls of her churchmen. There was something terribly wrong with her soul, something terribly wrong with her churchmen and her religion. In the whirling gulf of her thought there was yet one shining light to guide her, to sustain her in her hope; and it was that, despite her errors and her frailties and her blindness, she had one absolute and unfaltering hold on ultimate and supreme justice. That was love. "Love your enemies as yourself!" was a divine word, entirely free from any church or creed.

Jane's meditations were disturbed by Lassiter's soft, tinkling step in the court. Always he wore the clinking spurs. Always he was in readiness to ride. She passed out and called him into the huge, dim hall.

"I think you'll be safer here. The court is too open," she said.

"I reckon," replied Lassiter. "An' it's cooler here. The day's sure muggy. Well, I went down to the village with Venters."

"Already! Where is he?" queried Jane, in quick amaze.

"He's at the corrals. Blake's helpin' him get the burros an' packs ready. That Blake is a good fellow."

"Did—did Bern meet Tull?"

"I guess he did," answered Lassiter, and he laughed dryly.

"Tell me! Oh, you exasperate me! You're so cool, so calm! For Heaven's sake, tell me what happened!"

"First time I've been in the village for weeks," went on Lassiter, mildly. "I reckon there 'ain't been more of a show for a long time. Me an' Venters walkin' down the road! It was funny. I ain't sayin' anybody was particular glad to see us. I'm not much thought of hereabouts, an' Venters he sure looks like what you called him, a wild man. Well, there was some runnin' of folks before we got to the stores. Then everybody vamoosed except some surprised rustlers in front of a saloon. Venters went right in the stores an' saloons, an' of course I went along. I don't know which tickled me the most—the actions of many fellers we met, or Venters's nerve. Jane, I was downright glad to be along. You see that sort of thing is my element, an' I've been away from it for a spell. But we didn't find Tull in one of them places. Some Gentile feller at last told Venters he'd find Tull in that long buildin' next to Parsons's store. It's a kind of meetin'-room; and sure enough, when we peeped in, it was half full of men.

"Venters yelled: 'Don't anybody pull guns! We ain't come for that!' Then he tramped in, an' I was some put to keep alongside him. There was a hard, scrapin' sound of feet, a loud cry, an' then some whisperin', an' after that stillness you could cut with a knife. Tull was there, an' that fat party who once tried to throw a gun on me, an' other important-lookin' men, en' that little frog-legged feller who was with Tull the day I rode in here. I wish you could have seen their faces, 'specially Tull's an' the fat party's. But there ain't no use of me tryin' to tell you how they looked.

"Well, Venters an' I stood there in the middle of the room with that batch of men all in front of us, en' not a blamed one of them winked an eyelash or moved a finger. It was natural, of course, for me to notice many of them packed guns. That's a way of mine, first noticin' them things. Venters spoke up, an' his voice sort of chilled an' cut, en' he told Tull he had a few things to say."

Here Lassiter paused while he turned his sombrero round and round, in his familiar habit, and his eyes had the look of a man seeing over again some thrilling spectacle, and under his red bronze there was strange animation.

"Like a shot, then, Venters told Tull that the friendship between you an' him was all over, an' he was leaving your place. He said you'd both of you broken off in the hope of propitiatin' your people, but you hadn't changed your mind otherwise, an' never would.

"Next he spoke up for you. I ain't goin' to tell you what he said. Only—no other woman who ever lived ever had such tribute! You had a champion, Jane, an' never fear that those thick-skulled men don't know you now. It couldn't be otherwise. He spoke the ringin', lightnin' truth.... Then he accused Tull of the underhand, miserable robbery of a helpless woman. He told Tull where the red herd was, of a deal made with Oldrin', that Jerry Card had made the deal. I thought Tull was goin' to drop, an' that little frog-legged cuss, he looked some limp an' white. But Venters's voice would have kept anybody's legs from bucklin'. I was stiff myself. He went on an' called Tull—called him every bad name ever known to a rider, an' then some. He cursed Tull. I never hear a man get such a cursin'. He laughed in scorn at the idea of Tull bein' a minister. He said Tull an' a few more dogs of hell builded their empire out of the hearts of such innocent an' God-fearin' women as Jane Withersteen. He called Tull a binder of women, a callous beast who hid behind a mock mantle of righteousness—an' the last an' lowest coward on the face of the earth. To prey on weak women through their religion—that was the last unspeakable crime!

"Then he finished, an' by this time he'd almost lost his voice. But his whisper was enough. 'Tull,' he said, 'she begged me not to draw on you to-day. She would pray for you if you burned her at the stake.... But listen!... I swear if you and I ever come face to face again, I'll kill you!'

"We backed out of the door then, an' up the road. But nobody follered us."

Jane found herself weeping passionately. She had not been conscious of it till Lassiter ended his story, and she experienced exquisite pain and relief in shedding tears. Long had her eyes been dry, her grief deep; long had her emotions been dumb. Lassiter's story put her on the rack; the appalling nature of Venters's act and speech had no parallel as an outrage; it was worse than bloodshed. Men like Tull had been shot, but had one ever been so terribly denounced in public? Over-mounting her horror, an uncontrollable, quivering passion shook her very soul. It was sheer human glory in the deed of a fearless man. It was hot, primitive instinct to live—to fight. It was a kind of mad joy in Venters's chivalry. It was close to the wrath that had first shaken her in the beginning of this war waged upon her.

"Well, well, Jane, don't take it that way," said Lassiter, in evident distress. "I had to tell you. There's some things a feller jest can't keep. It's strange you give up on hearin' that, when all this long time you've been the gamest woman I ever seen. But I don't know women. Mebbe there's reason for you to cry. I know this—nothin' ever rang in my soul an' so filled it as what Venters did. I'd like to have done it, but—I'm only good for throwin' a gun, en' it seems you hate that.... Well, I'll be goin' now."

"Where?"

"Venters took Wrangle to the stable. The sorrel's shy a shoe, an' I've got to help hold the big devil an' put on another."

"Tell Bern to come for the pack I want to give him—and—and to say good-by," called Jane, as Lassiter went out.

Jane passed the rest of that day in a vain endeavor to decide what and what not to put in the pack for Venters. This task was the last she would ever perform for him, and the gifts were the last she would ever make him. So she picked and chose and rejected, and chose again, and often paused in sad revery, and began again, till at length she filled the pack.

It was about sunset, and she and Fay had finished supper and were sitting in the court, when Venters's quick steps rang on the stones. She scarcely knew him, for he had changed the tattered garments, and she missed the dark beard and long hair. Still he was not the Venters of old. As he came up the steps she felt herself pointing to the pack, and heard herself speaking words that were meaningless to her. He said good-by; he kissed her, released her, and turned away. His tall figure blurred in her sight, grew dim through dark, streaked vision, and then he vanished.

Twilight fell around Withersteen House, and dusk and night. Little Fay slept; but Jane lay with strained, aching eyes. She heard the wind moaning in the cottonwoods and mice squeaking in the walls. The night was interminably long, yet she prayed to hold back the dawn. What would another day bring forth? The blackness of her room seemed blacker for the sad, entering gray of morning light. She heard the chirp of awakening birds, and fancied she caught a faint clatter of hoofs. Then low, dull distant, throbbed a heavy gunshot. She had expected it, was waiting for it; nevertheless, an electric shock checked her heart, froze the very living fiber of her bones. That vise-like hold on her faculties apparently did not relax for a long time, and it was a voice under her window that released her.

"Jane!... Jane!" softly called Lassiter.

She answered somehow.

"It's all right. Venters got away. I thought mebbe you'd heard that shot, en' I was worried some."

"What was it—who fired?"

"Well—some fool feller tried to stop Venters out there in the sage—an' he only stopped lead!... I think it'll be all right. I haven't seen or heard of any other fellers round. Venters'll go through safe. An', Jane, I've got Bells saddled, an' I'm going to trail Venters. Mind, I won't show myself unless he falls foul of somebody an' needs me. I want to see if this place where he's goin' is safe for him. He says nobody can track him there. I never seen the place yet I couldn't track a man to. Now, Jane, you stay indoors while I'm gone, an' keep close watch on Fay. Will you?"

"Yes! Oh yes!"

"An' another thing, Jane," he continued, then paused for long—"another thing—if you ain't here when I come back—if you're gone—don't fear, I'll trail you—I'll find you out."

"My dear Lassiter, where could I be gone—as you put it?" asked Jane, in curious surprise.

"I reckon you might be somewhere. Mebbe tied in an old barn—or corralled in some gulch—or chained in a cave! Milly Erne was—till she give in! Mebbe that's news to you.... Well, if you're gone I'll hunt for you."

"No, Lassiter," she replied, sadly and low. "If I'm gone just forget the unhappy woman whose blinded selfish deceit you repaid with kindness and love."

She heard a deep, muttering curse, under his breath, and then the silvery tinkling of his spurs as he moved away.

Jane entered upon the duties of that day with a settled, gloomy calm. Disaster hung in the dark clouds, in the shade, in the humid west wind. Blake, when he reported, appeared without his usual cheer; and Jerd wore a harassed look of a worn and worried man. And when Judkins put in appearance, riding a lame horse, and dismounted with the cramp of a rider, his dust-covered figure and his darkly grim, almost dazed expression told Jane of dire calamity. She had no need of words.

"Miss Withersteen, I have to report—loss of the—white herd," said Judkins, hoarsely.

"Come, sit down, you look played out," replied Jane, solicitously. She brought him brandy and food, and while he partook of refreshments, of which he appeared badly in need, she asked no questions.

"No one rider—could hev done more—Miss Withersteen," he went on, presently.

"Judkins, don't be distressed. You've done more than any other rider. I've long expected to lose the white herd. It's no surprise. It's in line with other things that are happening. I'm grateful for your service."

"Miss Withersteen, I knew how you'd take it. But if anythin', that makes it harder to tell.

You see, a feller wants to do so much fer you, an' I'd got fond of my job. We led the herd a ways off to the north of the break in the valley. There was a big level an' pools of water an' tip-top browse. But the cattle was in a high nervous condition. Wild—as wild as antelope! You see, they'd been so scared they never slept, I ain't a goin' to tell you of the many tricks that were pulled off out there in the sage. But there wasn't a day for weeks thet the herd didn't get started to run. We allus managed to ride 'em close an' drive 'em back an' keep 'em bunched. Honest, Miss Withersteen, them steers was thin. They was thin when water and grass was everywhere. Thin at this season—thet'll tell you how your steers was pestered. Fer instance, one night a strange runnin' streak of fire run right through the herd. That streak was a coyote—with an oiled an' blazin' tail! Fer I shot it an' found out. We had hell with the herd that night, an' if the sage an' grass hadn't been wet—we, hosses, steers, an' all would hev burned up. But I said I wasn't goin' to tell you any of the tricks.... Strange now, Miss Withersteen, when the stampede did come it was from natural cause—jest a whirlin' devil of dust. You've seen the like often. An' this wasn't no big whirl, fer the dust was mostly settled. It had dried out in a little swale, an' ordinarily no steer would ever hev run fer it. But the herd was nervous en' wild. An' jest as Lassiter said, when that bunch of white steers got to movin' they was as bad as buffalo. I've seen some buffalo stampedes back in Nebraska, an' this bolt of the steers was the same kind.

"I tried to mill the herd jest as Lassiter did. But I wasn't equal to it, Miss Withersteen. I don't believe the rider lives who could hev turned thet herd. We kept along of the herd fer miles, an' more 'n one of my boys tried to get the steers a-millin'. It wasn't no use. We got off level ground, goin' down, an' then the steers ran somethin' fierce. We left the little gullies an' washes level-full of dead steers. Finally I saw the herd was makin' to pass a kind of low pocket between ridges. There was a hog-back—as we used to call 'em—a pile of rocks stickin' up, and I saw the herd was goin' to split round it, or swing out to the left. An' I wanted 'em to go to the right so mebbe we'd be able to drive 'em into the pocket. So, with all my boys except three, I rode hard to turn the herd a little to the right. We couldn't budge 'em. They went on en' split round the rocks, en' the most of 'em was turned sharp to the left by a deep wash we hedn't seen—hed no chance to see.

"The other three boys—Jimmy Vail, Joe Willis, an' thet little Cairns boy—a nervy kid! they, with Cairns leadin', tried to buck thet herd round to the pocket. It was a wild, fool idee. I couldn't do nothin'. The boys got hemmed in between the steers an' the wash—thet they hedn't no chance to see, either. Vail an' Willis was run down right before our eyes. An' Cairns, who rode a fine hoss, he did some ridin'. I never seen equaled, en' would hev beat the steers if there'd been any room to run in. I was high up an' could see how the steers kept spillin' by twos an' threes over into the wash. Cairns put his hoss to a place thet was too wide fer any hoss, an' broke his neck an' the hoss's too. We found that out after, an' as fer Vail an' Willis— two thousand steers ran over the poor boys. There wasn't much left to pack home fer buryin'!... An', Miss Withersteen, thet all happened yesterday, en' I believe, if the white herd didn't run over the wall of the Pass, it's runnin' yet."

On the morning of the second day after Judkins's recital, during which time Jane remained indoors a prey to regret and sorrow for the boy riders, and a new and now strangely insistent fear for her own person, she again heard what she had missed more than she dared honestly confess—the soft, jingling step of Lassiter. Almost overwhelming relief surged through her, a feeling as akin to joy as any she could have been capable of in those gloomy hours of shadow, and one that suddenly stunned her with the significance of what Lassiter had come to mean to her. She had begged him, for his own sake, to leave Cottonwoods. She might yet beg that, if her weakening courage permitted her to dare absolute loneliness and helplessness, but she realized now that if she were left alone her life would become one long, hideous nightmare.

When his soft steps clinked into the hall, in answer to her greeting, and his tall, black-garbed form filled the door, she felt an inexpressible sense of immediate safety. In his presence she lost her fear of the dim passageways of Withersteen House and of every sound. Always it had been that, when he entered the court or the hall, she had experienced a distinctly sickening but gradually lessening shock at sight of the huge black guns swinging at his sides. This time the sickening shock again visited her, it was, however, because a revealing flash of thought told her that it was not alone Lassiter who was thrillingly welcome, but also his fatal weapons. They meant so much. How she had fallen—how broken and spiritless must she be—to have still the same old horror of Lassiter's guns and his name, yet feel somehow a cold, shrinking protection in their law and might and use.

"Did you trail Venters—find his wonderful valley?" she asked, eagerly.

"Yes, an' I reckon it's sure a wonderful place."

"Is he safe there?"

"That's been botherin' me some. I tracked him an' part of the trail was the hardest I ever tackled. Mebbe there's a rustler or somebody in this country who's as good at trackin' as I am. If that's so Venters ain't safe."

"Well—tell me all about Bern and his valley."

To Jane's surprise Lassiter showed disinclination for further talk about his trip. He appeared to be extremely fatigued. Jane reflected that one hundred and twenty miles, with probably a great deal of climbing on foot, all in three days, was enough to tire any rider. Moreover, it presently developed that Lassiter had returned in a mood of singular sadness and preoccupation. She put it down to a moodiness over the loss of her white herd and the now precarious condition of her fortune.

Several days passed, and as nothing happened, Jane's spirits began to brighten. Once in her musings she thought that this tendency of hers to rebound was as sad as it was futile. Meanwhile, she had resumed her walks through the grove with little Fay.

One morning she went as far as the sage. She had not seen the slope since the beginning of the rains, and now it bloomed a rich deep purple. There was a high wind blowing, and the sage tossed and waved and colored beautifully from light to dark. Clouds scudded across the sky and their shadows sailed darkly down the sunny slope.

Upon her return toward the house she went by the lane to the stables, and she had scarcely entered the great open space with its corrals and sheds when she saw Lassiter hurriedly approaching. Fay broke from her and, running to a corral fence, began to pat and pull the long, hanging ears of a drowsy burro.

One look at Lassiter armed her for a blow.

Without a word he led her across the wide yard to the rise of the ground upon which the stable stood.

"Jane—look!" he said, and pointed to the ground.

Jane glanced down, and again, and upon steadier vision made out splotches of blood on the stones, and broad, smooth marks in the dust, leading out toward the sage.

"What made these?" she asked.

"I reckon somebody has dragged dead or wounded men out to where there was hosses in the sage."

"Dead—or—wounded—men!"

"I reckon—Jane, are you strong? Can you bear up?"

His hands were gently holding hers, and his eyes—suddenly she could no longer look into them. "Strong?" she echoed, trembling. "I—I will be."

Up on the stone-flag drive, nicked with the marks made by the iron-shod hoofs of her racers, Lassiter led her, his grasp ever growing firmer.

"Where's Blake—and—and Jerb?" she asked, haltingly.

"I don't know where Jerb is. Bolted, most likely," replied Lassiter, as he took her through the stone door. "But Blake—poor Blake! He's gone forever!... Be prepared, Jane."

With a cold prickling of her skin, with a queer thrumming in her ears, with fixed and staring eyes, Jane saw a gun lying at her feet with chamber swung and empty, and discharged shells scattered near.

Outstretched upon the stable floor lay Blake, ghastly white—dead—one hand clutching a gun and the other twisted in his bloody blouse.

"Whoever the thieves were, whether your people or rustlers—Blake killed some of them!" said Lassiter.

"Thieves?" whispered Jane.

"I reckon. Hoss-thieves!... Look!" Lassiter waved his hand toward the stalls.

The first stall—Bells's stall—was empty. All the stalls were empty. No racer whinnied and stamped greeting to her. Night was gone! Black Star was gone!

❧ 16 ❧

GOLD

As Lassiter had reported to Jane, Venters "went through" safely, and after a toilsome journey reached the peaceful shelter of Surprise Valley. When finally he lay wearily down under the silver spruces, resting from the strain of dragging packs and burros up the slope and through the entrance to Surprise Valley, he had leisure to think, and a great deal of the time went in regretting that he had not been frank with his loyal friend, Jane Withersteen.

But, he kept continually recalling, when he had stood once more face to face with her and had been shocked at the change in her and had heard the details of her adversity, he had not had the heart to tell her of the closer interest which had entered his life. He had not lied; yet he had kept silence.

Bess was in transports over the stores of supplies and the outfit he had packed from Cottonwoods. He had certainly brought a hundred times more than he had gone for; enough, surely, for years, perhaps to make permanent home in the valley. He saw no reason why he need ever leave there again.

After a day of rest he recovered his strength and shared Bess's pleasure in rummaging over the endless packs, and began to plan for the future. And in this planning, his trip to Cottonwoods, with its revived hate of Tull and consequent unleashing of fierce passions, soon faded out of mind. By slower degrees his friendship for Jane Withersteen and his contrition drifted from the active preoccupation of his present thought to a place in memory, with more and more infrequent recalls.

And as far as the state of his mind was concerned, upon the second day after his return, the valley, with its golden hues and purple shades, the speaking west wind and the cool, silent night, and Bess's watching eyes with their wonderful light, so wrought upon Venters that he might never have left them at all.

That very afternoon he set to work. Only one thing hindered him upon beginning, though it in no wise checked his delight, and that in the multiplicity of tasks planned to make a paradise out of the valley he could not choose the one with which to begin. He had to grow into the habit of passing from one dreamy pleasure to another, like a bee going from flower to flower in the valley, and he found this wandering habit likely to extend to his labors. Nevertheless, he made a start.

At the outset he discovered Bess to be both a considerable help in some ways and a very great hindrance in others. Her excitement and joy were spurs, inspirations; but she was utterly impracticable in her ideas, and she flitted from one plan to another with bewildering vacillation. Moreover, he fancied that she grew more eager, youthful, and sweet; and he marked that it was far easier to watch her and listen to her than it was to work. Therefore he gave her tasks that necessitated her going often to the cave where he had stored his packs.

Upon the last of these trips, when he was some distance down the terrace and out of sight of camp, he heard a scream, and then the sharp barking of the dogs.

For an instant he straightened up, amazed. Danger for her had been absolutely out of his mind. She had seen a rattlesnake—or a wildcat. Still she would not have been likely to scream at sight of either; and the barking of the dogs was ominous. Dropping his work, he dashed back along the terrace. Upon breaking through a clump of aspens he saw the dark form of a man in the camp. Cold, then hot, Venters burst into frenzied speed to reach his guns. He was cursing himself for a thoughtless fool when the man's tall form became familiar and he recognized Lassiter. Then the reversal of emotions changed his run to a walk; he tried to call out, but his voice refused to carry; when he reached camp there was Lassiter staring at the white-faced girl. By that time Ring and Whitie had recognized him.

"Hello, Venters! I'm makin' you a visit," said Lassiter, slowly. "An' I'm some surprised to see you've a—a young feller for company."

One glance had sufficed for the keen rider to read Bess's real sex, and for once his cool calm had deserted him. He stared till the white of Bess's cheeks flared into crimson. That, if it were needed, was the concluding evidence of her femininity, for it went fittingly with her sun-tinted hair and darkened, dilated eyes, the sweetness of her mouth, and the striking symmetry of her slender shape.

"Heavens! Lassiter!" panted Venters, when he caught his breath. "What relief—it's only you! How—in the name of all that's wonderful—did you ever get here?"

"I trailed you. We—I wanted to know where you was, if you had a safe place. So I trailed you."

"Trailed me," cried Venters, bluntly.

"I reckon. It was some of a job after I got to them smooth rocks. I was all day trackin' you up to them little cut steps in the rock. The rest was easy."

"Where's your hoss? I hope you hid him."

"I tied him in them queer cedars down on the slope. He can't be seen from the valley."

"That's good. Well, well! I'm completely dumfounded. It was my idea that no man could track me in here."

"I reckon. But if there's a tracker in these uplands as good as me he can find you."

"That's bad. That'll worry me. But, Lassiter, now you're here I'm glad to see you. And—and my companion here is not a young fellow!... Bess, this is a friend of mine. He saved my life once."

The embarrassment of the moment did not extend to Lassiter. Almost at once his manner, as he shook hands with Bess, relieved Venters and put the girl at ease. After Venters's words and one quick look at Lassiter, her agitation stilled, and, though she was shy, if she were conscious of anything out of the ordinary in the situation, certainly she did not show it.

"I reckon I'll only stay a little while," Lassiter was saying. "An' if you don't mind troublin', I'm hungry. I fetched some biscuits along, but they're gone. Venters, this place is sure the wonderfullest ever seen. Them cut steps on the slope! That outlet into the gorge! An' it's like climbin' up through hell into heaven to climb through that gorge into this valley! There's a queer-lookin' rock at the top of the passage. I didn't have time to stop. I'm wonderin' how you ever found this place. It's sure interestin'."

During the preparation and eating of dinner Lassiter listened mostly, as was his wont, and occasionally he spoke in his quaint and dry way. Venters noted, however, that the rider showed an increasing interest in Bess. He asked her no questions, and only directed his attention to her while she was occupied and had no opportunity to observe his scrutiny. It seemed to Venters that Lassiter grew more and more absorbed in his study of Bess, and that he lost his coolness in some strange, softening sympathy. Then, quite abruptly, he arose and announced the necessity for his early departure. He said good-by to Bess in a voice gentle and somewhat broken, and turned hurriedly away. Venters accompanied him, and they had traversed the terrace, climbed the weathered slope, and passed under the stone bridge before either spoke again.

Then Lassiter put a great hand on Venters's shoulder and wheeled him to meet a smoldering fire of gray eyes.

"Lassiter, I couldn't tell Jane! I couldn't," burst out Venters, reading his friend's mind. "I tried. But I couldn't. She wouldn't understand, and she has troubles enough. And I love the girl!"

"Venters, I reckon this beats me. I've seen some queer things in my time, too. This girl—who is she?"

"I don't know."

"Don't know! What is she, then?"

"I don't know that, either. Oh, it's the strangest story you ever heard. I must tell you. But you'll never believe."

"Venters, women were always puzzles to me. But for all that, if this girl ain't a child, an' as innocent, I'm no fit person to think of virtue an' goodness in anybody. Are you goin' to be square with her?"

"I am—so help me God!"

"I reckoned so. Mebbe my temper oughtn't led me to make sure. But, man, she's a woman in all but years. She's sweeter 'n the sage."

"Lassiter, I know, I know. And the hell of it is that in spite of her innocence and charm she's—she's not what she seems!"

"I wouldn't want to—of course, I couldn't call you a liar, Venters," said the older man.

"What's more, she was Oldring's Masked Rider!"

Venters expected to floor his friend with that statement, but he was not in any way prepared for the shock his words gave. For an instant he was astounded to see Lassiter stunned; then his own passionate eagerness to unbosom himself, to tell the wonderful story, precluded any other thought.

"Son, tell me all about this," presently said Lassiter as he seated himself on a stone and wiped his moist brow.

Thereupon Venters began his narrative at the point where he had shot the rustler and Oldring's Masked Rider, and he rushed through it, telling all, not holding back even Bess's unreserved avowal of her love or his deepest emotions.

"That's the story," he said, concluding. "I love her, though I've never told her. If I did tell her I'd be ready to marry her, and that seems impossible in this country. I'd be afraid to risk taking her anywhere. So I intend to do the best I can for her here."

"The longer I live the stranger life is," mused Lassiter, with downcast eyes. "I'm reminded of somethin' you once said to Jane about hands in her game of life. There's that unseen hand of power, an' Tull's black hand, an' my red one, an' your indifferent one, an' the girl's little brown, helpless one. An', Venters there's another one that's all-wise an' all-wonderful. That's the hand guidin' Jane Withersteen's game of life!... Your story's one to daze a far clearer head than mine. I can't offer no advice, even if you asked for it. Mebbe I can help you. Anyway, I'll hold Oldrin' up when he comes to the village an' find out about this girl. I knew the rustler years ago. He'll remember me."

"Lassiter, if I ever meet Oldring I'll kill him!" cried Venters, with sudden intensity.

"I reckon that'd be perfectly natural," replied the rider.

"Make him think Bess is dead—as she is to him and that old life."

"Sure, sure, son. Cool down now. If you're goin' to begin pullin' guns on Tull an' Oldrin' you want to be cool. I reckon, though, you'd better keep hid here. Well, I must be leavin'."

"One thing, Lassiter. You'll not tell Jane about Bess? Please don't!"

"I reckon not. But I wouldn't be afraid to bet that after she'd got over anger at your secrecy—Venters, she'd be furious once in her life!—she'd think more of you. I don't mind sayin' for myself that I think you're a good deal of a man."

In the further ascent Venters halted several times with the intention of saying good-by, yet he changed his mind and kept on climbing till they reached Balancing Rock. Lassiter examined the huge rock, listened to Venters's idea of its position and suggestion, and curiously placed a strong hand upon it.

"Hold on!" cried Venters. "I heaved at it once and have never gotten over my scare."

"Well, you do seem uncommon nervous," replied Lassiter, much amused. "Now, as for me, why I always had the funniest notion to roll stones! When I was a kid I did it, an' the bigger I got the bigger stones I'd roll. Ain't that funny? Honest—even now I often get off my hoss just to tumble a big stone over a precipice, en' watch it drop, en' listen to it bang an' boom. I've started some slides in my time, an' don't you forget it. I never seen a rock I wanted to roll as bad as this one! Wouldn't there jest be roarin', crashin' hell down that trail?"

"You'd close the outlet forever!" exclaimed Venters. "Well, good-by, Lassiter. Keep my secret and don't forget me. And be mighty careful how you get out of the valley below. The rustlers' canyon isn't more than three miles up the Pass. Now you've tracked me here, I'll never feel safe again."

In his descent to the valley, Venters's emotion, roused to stirring pitch by the recital of his love story, quieted gradually, and in its place came a sober, thoughtful mood. All at once he saw that he was serious, because he would never more regain his sense of security while in the valley. What Lassiter could do another skilful tracker might duplicate. Among the many riders with whom Venters had ridden he recalled no one who could have taken his trail at Cottonwoods and have followed it to the edge of the bare slope in the pass, let alone up that glistening smooth stone. Lassiter, however, was not an ordinary rider. Instead of hunting cattle tracks he had likely spent a goodly portion of his life tracking men. It was not improbable that among Oldring's rustlers there was one who shared Lassiter's gift for trailing. And the more Venters dwelt on this possibility the more perturbed he grew.

Lassiter's visit, moreover, had a disquieting effect upon Bess, and Venters fancied that she entertained the same thought as to future seclusion. The breaking of their solitude, though by a well-meaning friend, had not only dispelled all its dream and much of its charm, but had instilled a canker of fear. Both had seen the footprint in the sand.

Venters did no more work that day. Sunset and twilight gave way to night, and the canyon bird whistled its melancholy notes, and the wind sang softly in the cliffs, and the camp-fire blazed and burned down to red embers. To Venters a subtle difference was apparent in all of these, or else the shadowy change had been in him. He hoped that on the morrow this slight depression would have passed away.

In that measure, however, he was doomed to disappointment. Furthermore, Bess reverted to a wistful sadness that he had not observed in her since her recovery. His attempt to cheer her out of it resulted in dismal failure, and consequently in a darkening of his own mood. Hard work relieved him; still, when the day had passed, his unrest returned. Then he set to deliberate thinking, and there came to him the startling conviction that he must leave Surprise Valley and take Bess with him. As a rider he had taken many chances, and as an adventurer in Deception Pass he had unhesitatingly risked his life, but now he would run no preventable hazard of Bess's safety and happiness, and he was too keen not to see that hazard. It gave him a pang to think of leaving the beautiful valley just when he had the means to establish a permanent and delightful home there. One flashing thought tore in hot temptation through his mind—why not climb up into the gorge, roll Balancing Rock down the trail, and close forever the outlet to Deception Pass? "That was the beast in me—showing his teeth!" muttered Venters, scornfully. "I'll just kill him good and quick! I'll be fair to this girl, if it's the last thing I do on earth!"

Another day went by, in which he worked less and pondered more and all the time covertly watched Bess. Her wistfulness had deepened into downright unhappiness, and that made his task to tell her all the harder. He kept the secret another day, hoping by some chance she might grow less moody, and to his exceeding anxiety she fell into far deeper gloom. Out of his own secret and the torment of it he divined that she, too, had a secret and the keeping of it was torturing her. As yet he had no plan thought out in regard to how or when to leave the valley, but he decided to tell her the necessity of it and to persuade her to go. Furthermore, he hoped his speaking out would induce her to unburden her own mind.

"Bess, what's wrong with you?" he asked.

"Nothing," she answered, with averted face.

Venters took hold of her gently, though masterfully, forced her to meet his eyes.

"You can't look at me and lie," he said. "Now—what's wrong with you? You're keeping something from me. Well, I've got a secret, too, and I intend to tell it presently."

"Oh—I have a secret. I was crazy to tell you when you came back. That's why I was so silly about everything. I kept holding my secret back—gloating over it. But when Lassiter came I got an idea—that changed my mind. Then I hated to tell you."

"Are you going to now?"

"Yes—yes. I was coming to it. I tried yesterday, but you were so cold. I was afraid. I couldn't keep it much longer."

"Very well, most mysterious lady, tell your wonderful secret."

"You needn't laugh," she retorted, with a first glimpse of reviving spirit. "I can take the laugh out of you in one second."

"It's a go."

She ran through the spruces to the cave, and returned carrying something which was manifestly heavy. Upon nearer view he saw that whatever she held with such evident importance had been bound up in a black scarf he well remembered. That alone was sufficient to make him tingle with curiosity.

"Have you any idea what I did in your absence?" she asked.

"I imagine you lounged about, waiting and watching for me," he replied, smiling. "I've my share of conceit, you know."

"You're wrong. I worked. Look at my hands." She dropped on her knees close to where he sat, and, carefully depositing the black bundle, she held out her hands. The palms and inside of her fingers were white, puckered, and worn.

"Why, Bess, you've been fooling in the water," he said.

"Fooling? Look here!" With deft fingers she spread open the black scarf, and the bright sun shone upon a dull, glittering heap of gold.

"Gold!" he ejaculated.

"Yes, gold! See, pounds of gold! I found it—washed it out of the stream—picked it out grain by grain, nugget by nugget!"

"Gold!" he cried.

"Yes. Now—now laugh at my secret!"

For a long minute Venters gazed. Then he stretched forth a hand to feel if the gold was real.

"Gold!" he almost shouted. "Bess, there are hundreds—thousands of dollars' worth here!"

He leaned over to her, and put his hand, strong and clenching now, on hers.

"Is there more where this came from?" he whispered.

"Plenty of it, all the way up the stream to the cliff. You know I've often washed for gold. Then I've heard the men talk. I think there's no great quantity of gold here, but enough for—for a fortune for you."

"That—was—your—secret!"

"Yes. I hate gold. For it makes men mad. I've seen them drunk with joy and dance and fling themselves around. I've seen them curse and rave. I've seen them fight like dogs and roll in the dust. I've seen them kill each other for gold."

"Is that why you hated to tell me?"

"Not—not altogether." Bess lowered her head. "It was because I knew you'd never stay here long after you found gold."

"You were afraid I'd leave you?"

"Yes.

"Listen!... You great, simple child! Listen... You sweet, wonderful, wild, blue-eyed girl! I was tortured by my secret. It was that I knew we—we must leave the valley. We can't stay here much longer. I couldn't think how we'd get away—out of the country—or how we'd live, if we ever got out. I'm a beggar. That's why I kept my secret. I'm poor. It takes money to make way beyond Sterling. We couldn't ride horses or burros or walk forever. So while I knew we must go, I was distracted over how to go and what to do. Now! We've gold! Once beyond Sterling, we'll be safe from rustlers. We've no others to fear.

"Oh! Listen! Bess!" Venters now heard his voice ringing high and sweet, and he felt Bess's cold hands in his crushing grasp as she leaned toward him pale, breathless. "This is how much I'd leave you! You made me live again! I'll take you away—far away from this wild country. You'll begin a new life. You'll be happy. You shall see cities, ships, people. You shall have anything your heart craves. All the shame and sorrow of your life shall be forgotten—as if they had never been. This is how much I'd leave you here alone—you sad-eyed girl. I love you! Didn't you know it? How could you fail to know it? I love you! I'm free! I'm a man—a man you've made—no more a beggar!... Kiss me! This is how much I'd leave you here alone —you beautiful, strange, unhappy girl. But I'll make you happy. What—what do I care for— your past! I love you! I'll take you home to Illinois—to my mother. Then I'll take you to far places. I'll make up all you've lost. Oh, I know you love me—knew it before you told me. And it changed my life. And you'll go with me, not as my companion as you are here, nor my sister, but, Bess, darling!... As my wife!"

17

WRANGLE'S RACE RUN

THE PLAN eventually decided upon by the lovers was for Venters to go to the village, secure a horse and some kind of a disguise for Bess, or at least less striking apparel than her present garb, and to return post-haste to the valley. Meanwhile, she would add to their store of gold. Then they would strike the long and perilous trail to ride out of Utah. In the event of his inability to fetch back a horse for her, they intended to make the giant sorrel carry double. The gold, a little food, saddle blankets, and Venters's guns were to compose the light outfit with which they would make the start.

"I love this beautiful place," said Bess. "It's hard to think of leaving it."

"Hard! Well, I should think so," replied Venters. "Maybe—in years—" But he did not complete in words his thought that might be possible to return after many years of absence and change.

Once again Bess bade Venters farewell under the shadow of Balancing Rock, and this time it was with whispered hope and tenderness and passionate trust. Long after he had left her, all down through the outlet to the Pass, the clinging clasp of her arms, the sweetness of her lips, and the sense of a new and exquisite birth of character in her remained hauntingly and thrillingly in his mind. The girl who had sadly called herself nameless and nothing had been marvelously transformed in the moment of his avowal of love. It was something to think over, something to warm his heart, but for the present it had absolutely to be forgotten so that all his mind could be addressed to the trip so fraught with danger.

He carried only his rifle, revolver, and a small quantity of bread and meat, and thus lightly burdened, he made swift progress down the slope and out into the valley. Darkness was coming on, and he welcomed it. Stars were blinking when he reached his old hiding-place in the split of canyon wall, and by their aid he slipped through the dense thickets to the grassy enclosure. Wrangle stood in the center of it with his head up, and he appeared black and of gigantic proportions in the dim light. Venters whistled softly, began a slow approach, and then called. The horse snorted and, plunging away with dull, heavy sound of hoofs, he disappeared in the gloom. "Wilder than ever!" muttered Venters. He followed the sorrel into the narrowing split between the walls, and presently had to desist because he could not see a foot in advance. As he went back toward the open Wrangle jumped out of an ebony shadow of cliff and like a thunderbolt shot huge and black past him down into the starlit glade. Deciding that all attempts to catch Wrangle at night would be useless, Venters repaired to the shelving rock where he had hidden saddle and blanket, and there went to sleep.

The first peep of day found him stirring, and as soon as it was light enough to distinguish objects, he took his lasso off his saddle and went out to rope the sorrel. He espied Wrangle at the lower end of the cove and approached him in a perfectly natural manner. When he got near enough, Wrangle evidently recognized him, but was too wild to stand. He ran up the glade and on into the narrow lane between the walls. This favored Venters's speedy capture of the horse, so, coiling his noose ready to throw, he hurried on. Wrangle let Venters get to within a hundred feet and then he broke. But as he plunged by, rapidly getting into his stride, Venters made a perfect throw with the rope. He had time to brace himself for the shock; nevertheless, Wrangle threw him and dragged him several yards before halting.

"You wild devil," said Venters, as he slowly pulled Wrangle up. "Don't you know me? Come now—old fellow—so—so—"

Wrangle yielded to the lasso and then to Venters's strong hand. He was as straggly and wild-looking as a horse left to roam free in the sage. He dropped his long ears and stood readily to be saddled and bridled. But he was exceedingly sensitive, and quivered at every touch and sound. Venters led him to the thicket, and, bending the close saplings to let him squeeze through, at length reached the open. Sharp survey in each direction assured him of the usual lonely nature of the canyon, then he was in the saddle, riding south.

Wrangle's long, swinging canter was a wonderful ground-gainer. His stride was almost twice that of an ordinary horse; and his endurance was equally remarkable. Venters pulled him in occasionally, and walked him up the stretches of rising ground and along the soft washes. Wrangle had never yet shown any indication of distress while Venters rode him. Nevertheless, there was now reason to save the horse, therefore Venters did not resort to the hurry that had characterized his former trip. He camped at the last water in the Pass. What distance that was to Cottonwoods he did not know; he calculated, however, that it was in the neighborhood of fifty miles.

Early in the morning he proceeded on his way, and about the middle of the forenoon reached the constricted gap that marked the southerly end of the Pass, and through which led the trail up to the sage-level. He spied out Lassiter's tracks in the dust, but no others, and dismounting, he straightened out Wrangle's bridle and began to lead him up the trail. The short climb, more severe on beast than on man, necessitated a rest on the level above, and during this he scanned the wide purple reaches of slope.

Wrangle whistled his pleasure at the smell of the sage. Remounting, Venters headed up the white trail with the fragrant wind in his face. He had proceeded for perhaps a couple of miles when Wrangle stopped with a suddenness that threw Venters heavily against the pommel.

"What's wrong, old boy?" called Venters, looking down for a loose shoe or a snake or a foot lamed by a picked-up stone. Unrewarded, he raised himself from his scrutiny. Wrangle stood stiff head high, with his long ears erect. Thus guided, Venters swiftly gazed ahead to make out a dust-clouded, dark group of horsemen riding down the slope. If they had seen him, it apparently made no difference in their speed or direction.

"Wonder who they are!" exclaimed Venters. He was not disposed to run. His cool mood tightened under grip of excitement as he reflected that, whoever the approaching riders were, they could not be friends. He slipped out of the saddle and led Wrangle behind the tallest sage-brush. It might serve to conceal them until the riders were close enough for him to see who they were; after that he would be indifferent to how soon they discovered him.

After looking to his rifle and ascertaining that it was in working order, he watched, and as he watched, slowly the force of a bitter fierceness, long dormant, gathered ready to flame into life. If those riders were not rustlers he had forgotten how rustlers looked and rode. On they came, a small group, so compact and dark that he could not tell their number. How unusual that their horses did not see Wrangle! But such failure, Venters decided, was owing to the speed with which they were traveling. They moved at a swift canter affected more by rustlers than by riders. Venters grew concerned over the possibility that these horsemen would actually ride down on him before he had a chance to tell what to expect. When they were within three hundred yards he deliberately led Wrangle out into the trail.

Then he heard shouts, and the hard scrape of sliding hoofs, and saw horses rear and plunge back with up-flung heads and flying manes. Several little white puffs of smoke appeared sharply against the black background of riders and horses, and shots rang out. Bullets struck far in front of Venters, and whipped up the dust and then hummed low into the sage. The range was great for revolvers, but whether the shots were meant to kill or merely to check advance, they were enough to fire that waiting ferocity in Venters. Slipping his arm through the bridle, so that Wrangle could not get away, Venters lifted his rifle and pulled the trigger twice.

He saw the first horseman lean sideways and fall. He saw another lurch in his saddle and heard a cry of pain. Then Wrangle, plunging in fright, lifted Venters and nearly threw him. He jerked the horse down with a powerful hand and leaped into the saddle. Wrangle plunged again, dragging his bridle, that Venters had not had time to throw in place. Bending over with a swift movement, he secured it and dropped the loop over the pommel. Then, with grinding teeth, he looked to see what the issue would be.

The band had scattered so as not to afford such a broad mark for bullets. The riders faced Venters, some with red-belching guns. He heard a sharper report, and just as Wrangle plunged again he caught the whim of a leaden missile that would have hit him but for Wrangle's sudden jump. A swift, hot wave, turning cold, passed over Venters. Deliberately he picked out the one rider with a carbine, and killed him. Wrangle snorted shrilly and bolted into the sage. Venters let him run a few rods, then with iron arm checked him.

Five riders, surely rustlers, were left. One leaped out of the saddle to secure his fallen comrade's carbine. A shot from Venters, which missed the man but sent the dust flying over him made him run back to his horse. Then they separated. The crippled rider went one way; the one frustrated in his attempt to get the carbine rode another, Venters thought he made out a third rider, carrying a strange-appearing bundle and disappearing in the sage. But in the rapidity of action and vision he could not discern what it was. Two riders with three horses swung out to the right. Afraid of the long rifle—a burdensome weapon seldom carried by rustlers or riders—they had been put to rout.

Suddenly Venters discovered that one of the two men last noted was riding Jane Withersteen's horse Bells—the beautiful bay racer she had given to Lassiter. Venters uttered a savage outcry. Then the small, wiry, frog-like shape of the second rider, and the ease and grace of his seat in the saddle—things so strikingly incongruous—grew more and more familiar in Venters's sight.

"Jerry Card!" cried Venters.

It was indeed Tull's right-hand man. Such a white hot wrath inflamed Venters that he fought himself to see with clearer gaze.

"It's Jerry Card!" he exclaimed, instantly. "And he's riding Black Star and leading Night!"

The long-kindling, stormy fire in Venters's heart burst into flame. He spurred Wrangle, and as the horse lengthened his stride Venters slipped cartridges into the magazine of his rifle till it was once again full. Card and his companion were now half a mile or more in advance, riding easily down the slope. Venters marked the smooth gait, and understood it when Wrangle galloped out of the sage into the broad cattle trail, down which Venters had once tracked Jane Withersteen's red herd. This hard-packed trail, from years of use, was as clean and smooth as a road. Venters saw Jerry Card look back over his shoulder, the other rider did likewise. Then the three racers lengthened their stride to the point where the swinging canter was ready to break into a gallop.

"Wrangle, the race's on," said Venters, grimly. "We'll canter with them and gallop with them and run with them. We'll let them set the pace."

Venters knew he bestrode the strongest, swiftest, most tireless horse ever ridden by any rider across the Utah uplands. Recalling Jane Withersteen's devoted assurance that Night could run neck and neck with Wrangle, and Black Star could show his heels to him, Venters wished that Jane were there to see the race to recover her blacks and in the unqualified superiority of the giant sorrel. Then Venters found himself thankful that she was absent, for he meant that race to end in Jerry Card's death. The first flush, the raging of Venters's wrath, passed, to leave him in sullen, almost cold possession of his will. It was a deadly mood, utterly foreign to his nature, engendered, fostered, and released by the wild passions of wild men in a wild country. The strength in him then—the thing rife in him that was not hate, but something as remorseless—might have been the fiery fruition of a whole lifetime of vengeful quest. Nothing could have stopped him.

Venters thought out the race shrewdly. The rider on Bells would probably drop behind and take to the sage. What he did was of little moment to Venters. To stop Jerry Card, his evil hidden career as well as his present flight, and then to catch the blacks—that was all that concerned Venters. The cattle trail wound for miles and miles down the slope. Venters saw with a rider's keen vision ten, fifteen, twenty miles of clear purple sage. There were no on-coming riders or rustlers to aid Card. His only chance to escape lay in abandoning the stolen horses and creeping away in the sage to hide. In ten miles Wrangle could run Black Star and Night off their feet, and in fifteen he could kill them outright. So Venters held the sorrel in, letting Card make the running. It was a long race that would save the blacks.

In a few miles of that swinging canter Wrangle had crept appreciably closer to the three horses. Jerry Card turned again, and when he saw how the sorrel had gained, he put Black Star to a gallop. Night and Bells, on either side of him, swept into his stride.

Venters loosened the rein on Wrangle and let him break into a gallop. The sorrel saw the horses ahead and wanted to run. But Venters restrained him. And in the gallop he gained more than in the canter. Bells was fast in that gait, but Black Star and Night had been trained to run. Slowly Wrangle closed the gap down to a quarter of a mile, and crept closer and closer.

Jerry Card wheeled once more. Venters distinctly saw the red flash of his red face. This time he looked long. Venters laughed. He knew what passed in Card's mind. The rider was trying to make out what horse it happened to be that thus gained on Jane Withersteen's peerless racers. Wrangle had so long been away from the village that not improbably Jerry had forgotten. Besides, whatever Jerry's qualifications for his fame as the greatest rider of the sage, certain it was that his best point was not far-sightedness. He had not recognized Wrangle. After what must have been a searching gaze he got his comrade to face about. This action gave Venters amusement. It spoke so surely of the facts that neither Card nor the rustler actually knew their danger. Yet if they kept to the trail—and the last thing such men would do would be to leave it—they were both doomed.

This comrade of Card's whirled far around in his saddle, and he even shaded his eyes from the sun. He, too, looked long. Then, all at once, he faced ahead again and, bending lower in the saddle, began to fling his right arm up and down. That flinging Venters knew to be the lashing of Bells. Jerry also became active. And the three racers lengthened out into a run.

"Now, Wrangle!" cried Venters. "Run, you big devil! Run!"

Venters laid the reins on Wrangle's neck and dropped the loop over the pommel. The sorrel needed no guiding on that smooth trail. He was surer-footed in a run than at any other fast gait, and his running gave the impression of something devilish. He might now have been actuated by Venters's spirit; undoubtedly his savage running fitted the mood of his rider. Venters bent forward swinging with the horse, and gripped his rifle. His eye measured the distance between him and Jerry Card.

In less than two miles of running Bells began to drop behind the blacks, and Wrangle began to overhaul him. Venters anticipated that the rustler would soon take to the sage. Yet he did not. Not improbably he reasoned that the powerful sorrel could more easily overtake Bells in the heavier going outside of the trail. Soon only a few hundred yards lay between Bells and Wrangle. Turning in his saddle, the rustler began to shoot, and the bullets beat up little whiffs of dust. Venters raised his rifle, ready to take snap shots, and waited for favorable opportunity when Bells was out of line with the forward horses. Venters had it in him to kill these men as if they were skunk-bitten coyotes, but also he had restraint enough to keep from shooting one of Jane's beloved Arabians.

No great distance was covered, however, before Bells swerved to the left, out of line with Black Star and Night. Then Venters, aiming high and waiting for the pause between Wrangle's great strides, began to take snap shots at the rustler. The fleeing rider presented a broad target for a rifle, but he was moving swiftly forward and bobbing up and down. Moreover, shooting from Wrangle's back was shooting from a thunderbolt. And added to that was the danger of a low-placed bullet taking effect on Bells. Yet, despite these considerations, making the shot exceedingly difficult, Venters's confidence, like his implacability, saw a speedy and fatal termination of that rustler's race. On the sixth shot the rustler threw up his arms and took a flying tumble off his horse. He rolled over and over, hunched himself to a half-erect position, fell, and then dragged himself into the sage. As Venters went thundering by he peered keenly into the sage, but caught no sign of the man. Bells ran a few hundred yards, slowed up, and had stopped when Wrangle passed him.

Again Venters began slipping fresh cartridges into the magazine of his rifle, and his hand was so sure and steady that he did not drop a single cartridge. With the eye of a rider and the judgment of a marksman he once more measured the distance between him and Jerry Card. Wrangle had gained, bringing him into rifle range. Venters was hard put to it now not to shoot, but thought it better to withhold his fire. Jerry, who, in anticipation of a running fusillade, had huddled himself into a little twisted ball on Black Star's neck, now surmising that this pursuer would make sure of not wounding one of the blacks, rose to his natural seat in the saddle.

In his mind perhaps, as certainly as in Venters's, this moment was the beginning of the real race.

Venters leaned forward to put his hand on Wrangle's neck, then backward to put it on his flank. Under the shaggy, dusty hair trembled and vibrated and rippled a wonderful muscular activity. But Wrangle's flesh was still cold. What a cold-blooded brute thought Venters, and felt in him a love for the horse he had never given to any other. It would not have been humanly possible for any rider, even though clutched by hate or revenge or a passion to save a loved one or fear of his own life, to be astride the sorrel to swing with his swing, to see his magnificent stride and hear the rapid thunder of his hoofs, to ride him in that race and not glory in the ride.

So, with his passion to kill still keen and unabated, Venters lived out that ride, and drank a rider's sage-sweet cup of wildness to the dregs.

When Wrangle's long mane, lashing in the wind, stung Venters in the cheek, the sting added a beat to his flying pulse. He bent a downward glance to try to see Wrangle's actual stride, and saw only twinkling, darting streaks and the white rush of the trail. He watched the sorrel's savage head, pointed level, his mouth still closed and dry, but his nostrils distended as if he were snorting unseen fire. Wrangle was the horse for a race with death. Upon each side Venters saw the sage merged into a sailing, colorless wall. In front sloped the lay of ground with its purple breadth split by the white trail. The wind, blowing with heavy, steady blast into his face, sickened him with enduring, sweet odor, and filled his ears with a hollow, rushing roar.

Then for the hundredth time he measured the width of space separating him from Jerry Card. Wrangle had ceased to gain. The blacks were proving their fleetness. Venters watched Jerry Card, admiring the little rider's horsemanship. He had the incomparable seat of the upland rider, born in the saddle. It struck Venters that Card had changed his position, or the position of the horses. Presently Venters remembered positively that Jerry had been leading Night on the right-hand side of the trail. The racer was now on the side to the left. No—it was Black Star. But, Venters argued in amaze, Jerry had been mounted on Black Star. Another clearer, keener gaze assured Venters that Black Star was really riderless. Night now carried Jerry Card.

"He's changed from one to the other!" ejaculated Venters, realizing the astounding feat with unstinted admiration. "Changed at full speed! Jerry Card, that's what you've done unless I'm drunk on the smell of sage. But I've got to see the trick before I believe it."

Thenceforth, while Wrangle sped on, Venters glued his eyes to the little rider. Jerry Card rode as only he could ride. Of all the daring horsemen of the uplands, Jerry was the one rider fitted to bring out the greatness of the blacks in that long race. He had them on a dead run, but not yet at the last strained and killing pace. From time to time he glanced backward, as a wise general in retreat calculating his chances and the power and speed of pursuers, and the moment for the last desperate burst. No doubt, Card, with his life at stake, gloried in that race, perhaps more wildly than Venters. For he had been born to the sage and the saddle and the wild. He was more than half horse. Not until the last call—the sudden up-flashing instinct of self-preservation—would he lose his skill and judgment and nerve and the spirit of that race. Venters seemed to read Jerry's mind. That little crime-stained rider was actually thinking of his horses, husbanding their speed, handling them with knowledge of years, glorying in their beautiful, swift, racing stride, and wanting them to win the race when his own life hung suspended in quivering balance. Again Jerry whirled in his saddle and the sun flashed red on his face. Turning, he drew Black Star closer and closer toward Night, till they ran side by side, as one horse. Then Card raised himself in the saddle, slipped out of the stirrups, and, somehow twisting himself, leaped upon Black Star. He did not even lose the swing of the horse. Like a leech he was there in the other saddle, and as the horses separated, his right foot, that had been apparently doubled under him, shot down to catch the stirrup. The grace and dexterity and daring of that rider's act won something more than admiration from Venters.

For the distance of a mile Jerry rode Black Star and then changed back to Night. But all Jerry's skill and the running of the blacks could avail little more against the sorrel.

Venters peered far ahead, studying the lay of the land. Straightaway for five miles the trail stretched, and then it disappeared in hummocky ground. To the right, some few rods, Venters saw a break in the sage, and this was the rim of Deception Pass. Across the dark cleft gleamed the red of the opposite wall. Venters imagined that the trail went down into the Pass somewhere north of those ridges. And he realized that he must and would overtake Jerry Card in this straight course of five miles.

Cruelly he struck his spurs into Wrangle's flanks. A light touch of spur was sufficient to make Wrangle plunge. And now, with a ringing, wild snort, he seemed to double up in muscular convulsions and to shoot forward with an impetus that almost unseated Venters. The sage blurred by, the trail flashed by, and the wind robbed him of breath and hearing. Jerry Card turned once more. And the way he shifted to Black Star showed he had to make his last desperate running. Venters aimed to the side of the trail and sent a bullet puffing the dust beyond Jerry. Venters hoped to frighten the rider and get him to take to the sage. But Jerry returned the shot, and his ball struck dangerously close in the dust at Wrangle's flying feet. Venters held his fire then, while the rider emptied his revolver. For a mile, with Black Star leaving Night behind and doing his utmost, Wrangle did not gain; for another mile he gained little, if at all. In the third he caught up with the now galloping Night and began to gain rapidly on the other black.

Only a hundred yards now stretched between Black Star and Wrangle. The giant sorrel thundered on—and on—and on. In every yard he gained a foot. He was whistling through his nostrils, wringing wet, flying lather, and as hot as fire. Savage as ever, strong as ever, fast as ever, but each tremendous stride jarred Venters out of the saddle! Wrangle's power and spirit and momentum had begun to run him off his legs. Wrangle's great race was nearly won—and run. Venters seemed to see the expanse before him as a vast, sheeted, purple plain sliding under him. Black Star moved in it as a blur. The rider, Jerry Card, appeared a mere dot bobbing dimly. Wrangle thundered on—on—on! Venters felt the increase in quivering, straining shock after every leap. Flecks of foam flew into Venters's eyes, burning him, making him see all the sage as red. But in that red haze he saw, or seemed to see, Black Star suddenly riderless and with broken gait. Wrangle thundered on to change his pace with a violent break. Then Venters pulled him hard. From run to gallop, gallop to canter, canter to trot, trot to walk, and walk to stop, the great sorrel ended his race.

Venters looked back. Black Star stood riderless in the trail. Jerry Card had taken to the sage. Far up the white trail Night came trotting faithfully down. Venters leaped off, still half blind, reeling dizzily. In a moment he had recovered sufficiently to have a care for Wrangle. Rapidly he took off the saddle and bridle. The sorrel was reeking, heaving, whistling, shaking. But he had still the strength to stand, and for him Venters had no fears.

As Venters ran back to Black Star he saw the horse stagger on shaking legs into the sage and go down in a heap. Upon reaching him Venters removed the saddle and bridle. Black Star had been killed on his legs, Venters thought. He had no hope for the stricken horse. Black Star lay flat, covered with bloody froth, mouth wide, tongue hanging, eyes glaring, and all his beautiful body in convulsions.

Unable to stay there to see Jane's favorite racer die, Venters hurried up the trail to meet the other black. On the way he kept a sharp lookout for Jerry Card. Venters imagined the rider would keep well out of range of the rifle, but, as he would be lost on the sage without a horse, not improbably he would linger in the vicinity on the chance of getting back one of the blacks. Night soon came trotting up, hot and wet and run out. Venters led him down near the others, and unsaddling him, let him loose to rest. Night wearily lay down in the dust and rolled, proving himself not yet spent.

Then Venters sat down to rest and think. Whatever the risk, he was compelled to stay where he was, or comparatively near, for the night. The horses must rest and drink. He must find water. He was now seventy miles from Cottonwoods, and, he believed, close to the canyon where the cattle trail must surely turn off and go down into the Pass. After a while he rose to survey the valley.

He was very near to the ragged edge of a deep canyon into which the trail turned. The ground lay in uneven ridges divided by washes, and these sloped into the canyon. Following the canyon line, he saw where its rim was broken by other intersecting canyons, and farther down red walls and yellow cliffs leading toward a deep blue cleft that he made sure was Deception Pass. Walking out a few rods to a promontory, he found where the trail went down. The descent was gradual, along a stone-walled trail, and Venters felt sure that this was the place where Oldring drove cattle into the Pass. There was, however, no indication at all that he ever had driven cattle out at this point. Oldring had many holes to his burrow.

In searching round in the little hollows Venters, much to his relief, found water. He composed himself to rest and eat some bread and meat, while he waited for a sufficient time to elapse so that he could safely give the horses a drink. He judged the hour to be somewhere around noon. Wrangle lay down to rest and Night followed suit. So long as they were down Venters intended to make no move. The longer they rested the better, and the safer it would be to give them water. By and by he forced himself to go over to where Black Star lay, expecting to find him dead. Instead he found the racer partially if not wholly recovered. There was recognition, even fire, in his big black eyes. Venters was overjoyed. He sat by the black for a long time. Black Star presently labored to his feet with a heave and a groan, shook himself, and snorted for water. Venters repaired to the little pool he had found, filled his sombrero, and gave the racer a drink. Black Star gulped it at one draught, as if it were but a drop, and pushed his nose into the hat and snorted for more. Venters now led Night down to drink, and after a further time Black Star also. Then the blacks began to graze.

The sorrel had wandered off down the sage between the trail and the canyon. Once or twice he disappeared in little swales. Finally Venters concluded Wrangle had grazed far enough, and, taking his lasso, he went to fetch him back. In crossing from one ridge to another he saw where the horse had made muddy a pool of water. It occurred to Venters then that Wrangle had drunk his fill, and did not seem the worse for it, and might be anything but easy to catch. And, true enough, he could not come within roping reach of the sorrel. He tried for an hour, and gave up in disgust. Wrangle did not seem so wild as simply perverse. In a quandary Venters returned to the other horses, hoping much, yet doubting more, that when Wrangle had grazed to suit himself he might be caught.

As the afternoon wore away Venters's concern diminished, yet he kept close watch on the blacks and the trail and the sage. There was no telling of what Jerry Card might be capable. Venters sullenly acquiesced to the idea that the rider had been too quick and too shrewd for him. Strangely and doggedly, however, Venters clung to his foreboding of Card's downfall.

The wind died away; the red sun topped the far distant western rise of slope; and the long, creeping purple shadows lengthened. The rims of the canyons gleamed crimson and the deep clefts appeared to belch forth blue smoke. Silence enfolded the scene.

It was broken by a horrid, long-drawn scream of a horse and the thudding of heavy hoofs. Venters sprang erect and wheeled south. Along the canyon rim, near the edge, came Wrangle, once more in thundering flight.

Venters gasped in amazement. Had the wild sorrel gone mad? His head was high and

ZANE GREY

twisted, in a most singular position for a running horse. Suddenly Venters descried a frog-like shape clinging to Wrangle's neck. Jerry Card! Somehow he had straddled Wrangle and now stuck like a huge burr. But it was his strange position and the sorrel's wild scream that shook Venters's nerves. Wrangle was pounding toward the turn where the trail went down. He plunged onward like a blind horse. More than one of his leaps took him to the very edge of the precipice.

Jerry Card was bent forward with his teeth fast in the front of Wrangle's nose! Venters saw it, and there flashed over him a memory of this trick of a few desperate riders. He even thought of one rider who had worn off his teeth in this terrible hold to break or control desperate horses. Wrangle had indeed gone mad. The marvel was what guided him. Was it the half-brute, the more than half-horse instinct of Jerry Card? Whatever the mystery, it was true. And in a few more rods Jerry would have the sorrel turning into the trail leading down into the canyon.

"No—Jerry!" whispered Venters, stepping forward and throwing up the rifle. He tried to catch the little humped, frog-like shape over the sights. It was moving too fast; it was too small. Yet Venters shot once... twice... the third time... four times... five! all wasted shots and precious seconds!

With a deep-muttered curse Venters caught Wrangle through the sights and pulled the trigger. Plainly he heard the bullet thud. Wrangle uttered a horrible strangling sound. In swift death action he whirled, and with one last splendid leap he cleared the canyon rim. And he whirled downward with the little frog-like shape clinging to his neck!

There was a pause which seemed never ending, a shock, and an instant's silence.

Then up rolled a heavy crash, a long roar of sliding rocks dying away in distant echo, then silence unbroken.

Wrangle's race was run.

❧ 18 ❧

OLDRING'S KNELL

SOME FORTY HOURS or more later Venters created a commotion in Cottonwoods by riding down the main street on Black Star and leading Bells and Night. He had come upon Bells grazing near the body of a dead rustler, the only incident of his quick ride into the village.

Nothing was farther from Venters's mind than bravado. No thought came to him of the defiance and boldness of riding Jane Withersteen's racers straight into the arch-plotter's stronghold. He wanted men to see the famous Arabians; he wanted men to see them dirty and dusty, bearing all the signs of having been driven to their limit; he wanted men to see and to know that the thieves who had ridden them out into the sage had not ridden them back. Venters had come for that and for more—he wanted to meet Tull face to face; if not Tull, then Dyer; if not Dyer, then anyone in the secret of these master conspirators. Such was Venters's passion. The meeting with the rustlers, the unprovoked attack upon him, the spilling of blood, the recognition of Jerry Card and the horses, the race, and that last plunge of mad Wrangle—all these things, fuel on fuel to the smoldering fire, had kindled and swelled and leaped into living flame. He could have shot Dyer in the midst of his religious services at the altar; he could have killed Tull in front of wives and babes.

He walked the three racers down the broad, green-bordered village road. He heard the murmur of running water from Amber Spring. Bitter waters for Jane Withersteen! Men and women stopped to gaze at him and the horses. All knew him; all knew the blacks and the bay. As well as if it had been spoken, Venters read in the faces of men the intelligence that Jane Withersteen's Arabians had been known to have been stolen. Venters reined in and halted before Dyer's residence. It was a low, long, stone structure resembling Withersteen House. The spacious front yard was green and luxuriant with grass and flowers; gravel walks led to the huge porch; a well-trimmed hedge of purple sage separated the yard from the church grounds; birds sang in the trees; water flowed musically along the walks; and there were glad, careless shouts of children. For Venters the beauty of this home, and the serenity and its apparent happiness, all turned red and black. For Venters a shade overspread the lawn, the flowers, the old vine-clad stone house. In the music of the singing birds, in the murmur of the running water, he heard an ominous sound. Quiet beauty—sweet music—

innocent laughter! By what monstrous abortion of fate did these abide in the shadow of Dyer?

Venters rode on and stopped before Tull's cottage. Women stared at him with white faces and then flew from the porch. Tull himself appeared at the door, bent low, craning his neck. His dark face flashed out of sight; the door banged; a heavy bar dropped with a hollow sound.

Then Venters shook Black Star's bridle, and, sharply trotting, led the other horses to the center of the village. Here at the intersecting streets and in front of the stores he halted once more. The usual lounging atmosphere of that prominent corner was not now in evidence. Riders and ranchers and villagers broke up what must have been absorbing conversation. There was a rush of many feet, and then the walk was lined with faces.

Venters's glance swept down the line of silent stone-faced men. He recognized many riders and villagers, but none of those he had hoped to meet. There was no expression in the faces turned toward him. All of them knew him, most were inimical, but there were few who were not burning with curiosity and wonder in regard to the return of Jane Withersteen's racers. Yet all were silent. Here were the familiar characteristics—masked feeling—strange secretiveness—expressionless expression of mystery and hidden power.

"Has anybody here seen Jerry Card?" queried Venters, in a loud voice.

In reply there came not a word, not a nod or shake of head, not so much as dropping eye or twitching lip—nothing but a quiet, stony stare.

"Been under the knife? You've a fine knife-wielder here—one Tull, I believe!... Maybe you've all had your tongues cut out?"

This passionate sarcasm of Venters brought no response, and the stony calm was as oil on the fire within him.

"I see some of you pack guns, too!" he added, in biting scorn. In the long, tense pause, strung keenly as a tight wire, he sat motionless on Black Star. "All right," he went on. "Then let some of you take this message to Tull. Tell him I've seen Jerry Card! ... Tell him Jerry Card will never return!"

Thereupon, in the same dead calm, Venters backed Black Star away from the curb, into the street, and out of range. He was ready now to ride up to Withersteen House and turn the racers over to Jane.

"Hello, Venters!" a familiar voice cried, hoarsely, and he saw a man running toward him. It was the rider Judkins who came up and gripped Venters's hand. "Venters, I could hev dropped when I seen them hosses. But thet sight ain't a marker to the looks of you. What's wrong? Hev you gone crazy? You must be crazy to ride in here this way—with them hosses —talkie' thet way about Tull en' Jerry Card."

"Jud, I'm not crazy—only mad clean through," replied Venters.

"Mad, now, Bern, I'm glad to hear some of your old self in your voice. Fer when you come up you looked like the corpse of a dead rider with fire fer eyes. You hed thet crowd too stiff fer throwin' guns. Come, we've got to hev a talk. Let's go up the lane. We ain't much safe here."

Judkins mounted Bells and rode with Venters up to the cottonwood grove. Here they dismounted and went among the trees.

"Let's hear from you first," said Judkins. "You fetched back them hosses. Thet is the trick. An', of course, you got Jerry the same as you got Horne."

"Horne!"

"Sure. He was found dead yesterday all chewed by coyotes, en' he'd been shot plumb center."

"Where was he found?"

"At the split down the trail—you know where Oldring's cattle trail runs off north from the trail to the pass."

"That's where I met Jerry and the rustlers. What was Horne doing with them? I thought Horne was an honest cattle-man."

"Lord—Bern, don't ask me thet! I'm all muddled now tryin' to figure things."

Venters told of the fight and the race with Jerry Card and its tragic conclusion.

"I knowed it! I knowed all along that Wrangle was the best hoss!" exclaimed Judkins, with his lean face working and his eyes lighting. "Thet was a race! Lord, I'd like to hev seen Wrangle jump the cliff with Jerry. An' thet was good-by to the grandest hoss an' rider ever on the sage!... But, Bern, after you got the hosses why'd you want to bolt right in Tull's face?"

"I want him to know. An' if I can get to him I'll—"

"You can't get near Tull," interrupted Judkins. "Thet vigilante bunch hev taken to bein' bodyguard for Tull an' Dyer, too."

"Hasn't Lassiter made a break yet?" inquired Venters, curiously.

"Naw!" replied Judkins, scornfully. "Jane turned his head. He's mad in love over her— follers her like a dog. He ain't no more Lassiter! He's lost his nerve, he doesn't look like the same feller. It's village talk. Everybody knows it. He hasn't thrown a gun, an' he won't!"

"Jud, I'll bet he does," replied Venters, earnestly. "Remember what I say. This Lassiter is something more than a gun-man. Jud, he's big—he's great!... I feel that in him. God help Tull and Dyer when Lassiter does go after them. For horses and riders and stone walls won't save them."

"Wal, hev it your way, Bern. I hope you're right. Nat'rully I've been some sore on Lassiter fer gittin' soft. But I ain't denyin' his nerve, or whatever's great in him thet sort of paralyzes people. No later 'n this mornin' I seen him saunterin' down the lane, quiet an' slow. An' like his guns he comes black—black, thet's Lassiter. Wal, the crowd on the corner never batted an eye, en' I'll gamble my hoss thet there wasn't one who hed a heartbeat till Lassiter got by. He went in Snell's saloon, an' as there wasn't no gun play I had to go in, too. An' there, darn my pictures, if Lassiter wasn't standin' to the bar, drinking en' talkin' with Oldrin'."

"Oldring!" whispered Venters. His voice, as all fire and pulse within him, seemed to freeze.

"Let go my arm!" exclaimed Judkins. "Thet's my bad arm. Sure it was Oldrin'. What the hell's wrong with you, anyway? Venters, I tell you somethin's wrong. You're whiter 'n a sheet. You can't be scared of the rustler. I don't believe you've got a scare in you. Wal, now, jest let me talk. You know I like to talk, an' if I'm slow I allus git there sometime. As I said, Lassiter was talkie' chummy with Oldrin'. There wasn't no hard feelin's. An' the gang wasn't payin' no pertic'lar attention. But like a cat watchin' a mouse I hed my eyes on them two fellers. It was strange to me, thet confab. I'm gittin' to think a lot, fer a feller who doesn't know much. There's been some queer deals lately an' this seemed to me the queerest. These men stood to the bar alone, an' so close their big gun-hilts butted together. I seen Oldrin' was some surprised at first, an' Lassiter was cool as ice. They talked, an' presently at somethin' Lassiter said the rustler bawled out a curse, an' then he jest fell up against the bar, an' sagged there. The gang in the saloon looked around an' laughed, an' thet's about all. Finally Oldrin' turned, and it was easy to see somethin' hed shook him. Yes, sir, thet big rustler—you know he's as broad as he is long, an' the powerfulest build of a man—yes, sir, the nerve had been taken out of him. Then, after a little, he began to talk an' said a lot to Lassiter, an' by an' by it didn't take much of an eye to see thet Lassiter was gittin' hit hard. I never seen him anyway but cooler 'n ice—till then. He seemed to be hit harder 'n Oldrin', only he didn't roar out thet way. He jest kind of sunk in, an' looked an' looked, an' he didn't see a livin' soul in thet saloon. Then he sort of come to, an' shakin' hands—mind you, shakin' hands with Oldrin'—he went out. I couldn't help thinkin' how easy even a boy could hev dropped the great gun-man then!... Wal, the rustler stood at the bar fer a long time, en' he was seein' things far off, too; then he come to an' roared fer whisky, an' gulped a drink thet was big enough to drown me."

"Is Oldring here now?" whispered Venters. He could not speak above a whisper. Judkins's story had been meaningless to him.

"He's at Snell's yet. Bern, I hevn't told you yet thet the rustlers hev been raisin' hell. They shot up Stone Bridge an' Glaze, an' fer three days they've been here drinkin' an' gamblin' an' throwin' of gold. These rustlers hev a pile of gold. If it was gold dust or nugget gold I'd hev reason to think, but it's new coin gold, as if it had jest come from the United States treasury. An' the coin's genuine. Thet's all been proved. The truth is Oldrin's on a rampage. A while back he lost his Masked Rider, an' they say he's wild about thet. I'm wonderin' if Lassiter could hev told the rustler anythin' about thet little masked, hard-ridin' devil. Ride! He was most as good as Jerry Card. An', Bern, I've been wonderin' if you know—"

"Judkins, you're a good fellow," interrupted Venters. "Some day I'll tell you a story. I've no time now. Take the horses to Jane."

Judkins stared, and then, muttering to himself, he mounted Bells, and stared again at Venters, and then, leading the other horses, he rode into the grove and disappeared.

Once, long before, on the night Venters had carried Bess through the canyon and up into Surprise Valley, he had experienced the strangeness of faculties singularly, tinglingly acute. And now the same sensation recurred. But it was different in that he felt cold, frozen, mechanical incapable of free thought, and all about him seemed unreal, aloof, remote. He hid his rifle in the sage, marking its exact location with extreme care. Then he faced down the lane and strode toward the center of the village. Perceptions flashed upon him, the faint, cold touch of the breeze, a cold, silvery tinkle of flowing water, a cold sun shining out of a cold sky, song of birds and laugh of children, coldly distant. Cold and intangible were all things in earth and heaven. Colder and tighter stretched the skin over his face; colder and harder grew the polished butts of his guns; colder and steadier became his hands as he wiped the clammy sweat from his face or reached low to his gun-sheaths. Men meeting him in the walk gave him wide berth. In front of Bevin's store a crowd melted apart for his passage, and their faces and whispers were faces and whispers of a dream. He turned a corner to meet Tull face to face, eye to eye. As once before he had seen this man pale to a ghastly, livid white so again he saw the change. Tull stopped in his tracks, with right hand raised and shaking. Suddenly it dropped, and he seemed to glide aside, to pass out of Venters's sight. Next he saw many horses with bridles down—all clean-limbed, dark bays or blacks—rustlers' horses! Loud voices and boisterous laughter, rattle of dice and scrape of chair and clink of gold, burst in mingled din from an open doorway. He stepped inside.

With the sight of smoke-hazed room and drinking, cursing, gambling, dark-visaged men, reality once more dawned upon Venters.

His entrance had been unnoticed, and he bent his gaze upon the drinkers at the bar. Dark-clothed, dark-faced men they all were, burned by the sun, bow-legged as were most riders of the sage, but neither lean nor gaunt. Then Venters's gaze passed to the tables, and swiftly it swept over the hard-featured gamesters, to alight upon the huge, shaggy, black head of the rustler chief.

"Oldring!" he cried, and to him his voice seemed to split a bell in his ears.

It stilled the din.

That silence suddenly broke to the scrape and crash of Oldring's chair as he rose; and then, while he passed, a great gloomy figure, again the thronged room stilled in silence yet deeper.

"Oldring, a word with you!" continued Venters.

"Ho! What's this?" boomed Oldring, in frowning scrutiny.

"Come outside, alone. A word for you—from your Masked Rider!"

Oldring kicked a chair out of his way and lunged forward with a stamp of heavy boot that jarred the floor. He waved down his muttering, rising men.

Venters backed out of the door and waited, hearing, as no sound had ever before struck into his soul, the rapid, heavy steps of the rustler.

Oldring appeared, and Venters had one glimpse of his great breadth and bulk, his gold-buckled belt with hanging guns, his high-top boots with gold spurs. In that moment Venters had a strange, unintelligible curiosity to see Oldring alive. The rustler's broad brow, his large black eyes, his sweeping beard, as dark as the wing of a raven, his enormous width of shoulder and depth of chest, his whole splendid presence so wonderfully charged with vitality and force and strength, seemed to afford Venters an unutterable fiendish joy because for that magnificent manhood and life he meant cold and sudden death.

"Oldring, Bess is alive! But she's dead to you—dead to the life you made her lead—dead as you will be in one second!"

Swift as lightning Venters's glance dropped from Oldring's rolling eyes to his hands. One of them, the right, swept out, then toward his gun—and Venters shot him through the heart.

Slowly Oldring sank to his knees, and the hand, dragging at the gun, fell away. Venters's strangely acute faculties grasped the meaning of that limp arm, of the swaying hulk, of the gasp and heave, of the quivering beard. But was that awful spirit in the black eyes only one of vitality?

"Man—why—didn't—you—wait? Bess—was—" Oldring's whisper died under his beard, and with a heavy lurch he fell forward.

Bounding swiftly away, Venters fled around the corner, across the street, and, leaping a hedge, he ran through yard, orchard, and garden to the sage. Here, under cover of the tall brush, he turned west and ran on to the place where he had hidden his rifle. Securing that, he again set out into a run, and, circling through the sage, came up behind Jane Withersteen's stable and corrals. With laboring, dripping chest, and pain as of a knife thrust in his side, he stopped to regain his breath, and while resting his eyes roved around in search of a horse. Doors and windows of the stable were open wide and had a deserted look. One dejected, lonely burro stood in the near corral. Strange indeed was the silence brooding over the once happy, noisy home of Jane Withersteen's pets.

He went into the corral, exercising care to leave no tracks, and led the burro to the watering-trough. Venters, though not thirsty, drank till he could drink no more. Then, leading the burro over hard ground, he struck into the sage and down the slope.

He strode swiftly, turning from time to time to scan the slope for riders. His head just topped the level of sage-brush, and the burro could not have been seen at all. Slowly the green of Cottonwoods sank behind the slope, and at last a wavering line of purple sage met the blue of sky.

To avoid being seen, to get away, to hide his trail—these were the sole ideas in his mind as he headed for Deception Pass, and he directed all his acuteness of eye and ear, and the keenness of a rider's judgment for distance and ground, to stern accomplishment of the task. He kept to the sage far to the left of the trail leading into the Pass. He walked ten miles and looked back a thousand times. Always the graceful, purple wave of sage remained wide and lonely, a clear, undotted waste. Coming to a stretch of rocky ground, he took advantage of it to cross the trail and then continued down on the right. At length he persuaded himself that he would be able to see riders mounted on horses before they could see him on the little burro, and he rode bareback.

Hour by hour the tireless burro kept to his faithful, steady trot. The sun sank and the long shadows lengthened down the slope. Moving veils of purple twilight crept out of the hollows and, mustering and forming on the levels, soon merged and shaded into night. Venters guided the burro nearer to the trail, so that he could see its white line from the ridges, and rode on through the hours.

Once down in the Pass without leaving a trail, he would hold himself safe for the time being. When late in the night he reached the break in the sage, he sent the burro down ahead of him, and started an avalanche that all but buried the animal at the bottom of the trail. Bruised and battered as he was, he had a moment's elation, for he had hidden his tracks. Once more he mounted the burro and rode on. The hour was the blackest of the night when he made the thicket which inclosed his old camp. Here he turned the burro loose in the grass near the spring, and then lay down on his old bed of leaves.

He felt only vaguely, as outside things, the ache and burn and throb of the muscles of his body. But a dammed-up torrent of emotion at last burst its bounds, and the hour that saw his release from immediate action was one that confounded him in the reaction of his spirit. He suffered without understanding why. He caught glimpses into himself, into unlit darkness of soul. The fire that had blistered him and the cold which had frozen him now united in one torturing possession of his mind and heart, and like a fiery steed with ice-shod feet, ranged his being, ran rioting through his blood, trampling the resurging good, dragging ever at the evil.

Out of the subsiding chaos came a clear question. What had happened? He had left the valley to go to Cottonwoods. Why? It seemed that he had gone to kill a man—Oldring! The name riveted his consciousness upon the one man of all men upon earth whom he had wanted to meet. He had met the rustler. Venters recalled the smoky haze of the saloon, the dark-visaged men, the huge Oldring. He saw him step out of the door, a splendid specimen of manhood, a handsome giant with purple-black and sweeping beard. He remembered inquisitive gaze of falcon eyes. He heard himself repeating: "OLDRING, BESS IS ALIVE! BUT SHE'S DEAD TO YOU," and he felt himself jerk, and his ears throbbed to the thunder of a gun, and he saw the giant sink slowly to his knees. Was that only the vitality of him—that awful light in the eyes—only the hard-dying life of a tremendously powerful brute? A broken whisper, strange as death: "MAN—WHY—DIDN'T—YOU WAIT! BESS—WAS—" And Oldring plunged face forward, dead.

"I killed him," cried Venters, in remembering shock. "But it wasn't THAT. Ah, the look in his eyes and his whisper!"

Herein lay the secret that had clamored to him through all the tumult and stress of his emotions. What a look in the eyes of a man shot through the heart! It had been neither hate nor ferocity nor fear of men nor fear of death. It had been no passionate glinting spirit of a fearless foe, willing shot for shot, life for life, but lacking physical power. Distinctly recalled now, never to be forgotten, Venters saw in Oldring's magnificent eyes the rolling of great, glad surprise—softness—love! Then came a shadow and the terrible superhuman striving of his spirit to speak. Oldring shot through the heart, had fought and forced back death, not for a moment in which to shoot or curse, but to whisper strange words.

What words for a dying man to whisper! Why had not Venters waited? For what? That was no plea for life. It was regret that there was not a moment of life left in which to speak. Bess was—Herein lay renewed torture for Venters. What had Bess been to Oldring? The old question, like a specter, stalked from its grave to haunt him. He had overlooked, he had forgiven, he had loved and he had forgotten; and now, out of the mystery of a dying man's whisper rose again that perverse, unsatisfied, jealous uncertainty. Bess had loved that splendid, black-crowned giant—by her own confession she had loved him; and in Venters's soul again flamed up the jealous hell. Then into the clamoring hell burst the shot that had killed Oldring, and it rang in a wild fiendish gladness, a hateful, vengeful joy. That passed to the memory of the love and light in Oldring's eyes and the mystery in his whisper. So the changing, swaying emotions fluctuated in Venters's heart.

This was the climax of his year of suffering and the crucial struggle of his life. And when the gray dawn came he rose, a gloomy, almost heartbroken man, but victor over evil passions. He could not change the past; and, even if he had not loved Bess with all his soul, he had grown into a man who would not change the future he had planned for her. Only, and once for all, he must know the truth, know the worst, stifle all these insistent doubts and subtle hopes and jealous fancies, and kill the past by knowing truly what Bess had been to Oldring. For that matter he knew—he had always known, but he must hear it spoken. Then, when they had safely gotten out of that wild country to take up a new and an absorbing life, she would forget, she would be happy, and through that, in the years to come, he could not but find life worth living.

All day he rode slowly and cautiously up the Pass, taking time to peer around corners, to pick out hard ground and grassy patches, and to make sure there was no one in pursuit. In the night sometime he came to the smooth, scrawled rocks dividing the valley, and here set the burro at liberty. He walked beyond, climbed the slope and the dim, starlit gorge. Then, weary to the point of exhaustion, he crept into a shallow cave and fell asleep.

In the morning, when he descended the trail, he found the sun was pouring a golden stream of light through the arch of the great stone bridge. Surprise Valley, like a valley of dreams, lay mystically soft and beautiful, awakening to the golden flood which was rolling away its slumberous bands of mist, brightening its walled faces.

While yet far off he discerned Bess moving under the silver spruces, and soon the barking of the dogs told him that they had seen him. He heard the mocking-birds singing in the trees, and then the twittering of the quail. Ring and Whitie came bounding toward him, and behind them ran Bess, her hands outstretched.

"Bern! You're back! You're back!" she cried, in joy that rang of her loneliness.

"Yes, I'm back," he said, as she rushed to meet him.

She had reached out for him when suddenly, as she saw him closely, something checked her, and as quickly all her joy fled, and with it her color, leaving her pale and trembling.

"Oh! What's happened?"

"A good deal has happened, Bess. I don't need to tell you what. And I'm played out. Worn out in mind more than body."

"Dear—you look strange to me!" faltered Bess.

"Never mind that. I'm all right. There's nothing for you to be scared about. Things are going to turn out just as we have planned. As soon as I'm rested we'll make a break to get out of the country. Only now, right now, I must know the truth about you."

"Truth about me?" echoed Bess, shrinkingly. She seemed to be casting back into her mind for a forgotten key. Venters himself, as he saw her, received a pang.

"Yes—the truth. Bess, don't misunderstand. I haven't changed that way. I love you still. I'll love you more afterward. Life will be just as sweet—sweeter to us. We'll be—be married as soon as ever we can. We'll be happy—but there's a devil in me. A perverse, jealous devil! Then I've queer fancies. I forgot for a long time. Now all those fiendish little whispers of doubt and faith and fear and hope come torturing me again. I've got to kill them with the truth."

"I'll tell you anything you want to know," she replied, frankly.

"Then by Heaven! we'll have it over and done with!... Bess—did Oldring love you?"

"Certainly he did."

"Did—did you love him?"

"Of course. I told you so."

"How can you tell it so lightly?" cried Venters, passionately. "Haven't you any sense of—of—" He choked back speech. He felt the rush of pain and passion. He seized her in rude, strong hands and drew her close. He looked straight into her dark-blue eyes. They were shadowing with the old wistful light, but they were as clear as the limpid water of the spring. They were earnest, solemn in unutterable love and faith and abnegation. Venters shivered. He knew he was looking into her soul. He knew she could not lie in that moment; but that she might tell the truth, looking at him with those eyes, almost killed his belief in purity.

"What are—what were you to—to Oldring?" he panted, fiercely.

"I am his daughter," she replied, instantly.

Venters slowly let go of her. There was a violent break in the force of his feeling—then creeping blankness.

"What—was it—you said?" he asked, in a kind of dull wonder.

"I am his daughter."

"Oldring's daughter?" queried Venters, with life gathering in his voice.

"Yes."

With a passionately awakening start he grasped her hands and drew her close.

"All the time—you've been Oldring's daughter?"

"Yes, of course all the time—always."

"But Bess, you told me—you let me think—I made out you were—a—so—so ashamed."

"It is my shame," she said, with voice deep and full, and now the scarlet fired her cheek. "I told you—I'm nothing—nameless—just Bess, Oldring's girl!"

"I know—I remember. But I never thought—" he went on, hurriedly, huskily. "That time —when you lay dying—you prayed—you—somehow I got the idea you were bad."

"Bad?" she asked, with a little laugh.

She looked up with a faint smile of bewilderment and the absolute unconsciousness of a child. Venters gasped in the gathering might of the truth. She did not understand his meaning.

"Bess! Bess!" He clasped her in his arms, hiding her eyes against his breast. She must not see his face in that moment. And he held her while he looked out across the valley. In his dim and blinded sight, in the blur of golden light and moving mist, he saw Oldring. She was the rustler's nameless daughter. Oldring had loved her. He had so guarded her, so kept her from women and men and knowledge of life that her mind was as a child's. That was part of the secret—part of the mystery. That was the wonderful truth. Not only was she not bad, but good, pure, innocent above all innocence in the world—the innocence of lonely girlhood.

He saw Oldring's magnificent eyes, inquisitive, searching, softening. He saw them flare in amaze, in gladness, with love, then suddenly strain in terrible effort of will. He heard Oldring whisper and saw him sway like a log and fall. Then a million bellowing, thundering voices—gunshots of conscience, thunderbolts of remorse—dinned horribly in his ears. He had killed Bess's father. Then a rushing wind filled his ears like a moan of wind in the cliffs, a knell indeed—Oldring's knell.

He dropped to his knees and hid his face against Bess, and grasped her with the hands of a drowning man.

"My God!... My God!... Oh, Bess!... Forgive me! Never mind what I've done—what I've thought. But forgive me. I'll give you my life. I'll live for you. I'll love you. Oh, I do love you as no man ever loved a woman. I want you to know—to remember that I fought a fight for you—however blind I was. I thought—I thought—never mind what I thought—but I loved you—I asked you to marry me. Let that—let me have that to hug to my heart. Oh, Bess, I was driven! And I might have known! I could not rest nor sleep till I had this mystery solved. God! how things work out!"

"Bern, you're weak—trembling—you talk wildly," cried Bess. "You've overdone your strength. There's nothing to forgive. There's no mystery except your love for me. You have come back to me!"

And she clasped his head tenderly in her arms and pressed it closely to her throbbing breast.

❧ 19 ❧

FAY

AT THE HOME of Jane Withersteen Little Fay was climbing Lassiter's knee.

"Does oo love me?" she asked.

Lassiter, who was as serious with Fay as he was gentle and loving, assured her in earnest and elaborate speech that he was her devoted subject. Fay looked thoughtful and appeared to be debating the duplicity of men or searching for a supreme test to prove this cavalier.

"Does oo love my new muvver?" she asked, with bewildering suddenness.

Jane Withersteen laughed, and for the first time in many a day she felt a stir of her pulse and warmth in her cheek.

It was a still drowsy summer of afternoon, and the three were sitting in the shade of the wooded knoll that faced the sage-slope. Little Fay's brief spell of unhappy longing for her mother—the childish, mystic gloom—had passed, and now where Fay was there were prattle and laughter and glee. She had emerged from sorrow to be the incarnation of joy and loveliness. She had grown supernaturally sweet and beautiful. For Jane Withersteen the child was an answer to prayer, a blessing, a possession infinitely more precious than all she had lost. For Lassiter, Jane divined that little Fay had become a religion.

"Does oo love my new muvver?" repeated Fay.

Lassiter's answer to this was a modest and sincere affirmative.

"Why don't oo marry my new muvver an' be my favver?"

Of the thousands of questions put by little Fay to Lassiter this was the first he had been unable to answer.

"Fay—Fay, don't ask questions like that," said Jane.

"Why?"

"Because," replied Jane. And she found it strangely embarrassing to meet the child's gaze. It seemed to her that Fay's violet eyes looked through her with piercing wisdom.

"Oo love him, don't oo?"

"Dear child—run and play," said Jane, "but don't go too far. Don't go from this little hill."

Fay pranced off wildly, joyous over freedom that had not been granted her for weeks.

"Jane, why are children more sincere than grown-up persons?" asked Lassiter.

"Are they?"

"I reckon so. Little Fay there—she sees things as they appear on the face. An Indian does that. So does a dog. An' an Indian an' a dog are most of the time right in what they see. Mebbe a child is always right."

"Well, what does Fay see?" asked Jane.

"I reckon you know. I wonder what goes on in Fay's mind when she sees part of the truth with the wise eyes of a child, an' wantin' to know more, meets with strange falseness from you? Wait! You are false in a way, though you're the best woman I ever knew. What I want to say is this. Fay has taken you're pretendin' to—to care for me for the thing it looks on the face. An' her little formin' mind asks questions. An' the answers she gets are different from the looks of things. So she'll grow up gradually takin' on that falseness, an' be like the rest of the women, an' men, too. An' the truth of this falseness to life is proved by your appearin' to love me when you don't. Things aren't what they seem."

"Lassiter, you're right. A child should be told the absolute truth. But—is that possible? I haven't been able to do it, and all my life I've loved the truth, and I've prided myself upon being truthful. Maybe that was only egotism. I'm learning much, my friend. Some of those blinding scales have fallen from my eyes. And—and as to caring for you, I think I care a great deal. How much, how little, I couldn't say. My heart is almost broken, Lassiter. So now is not a good time to judge of affection. I can still play and be merry with Fay. I can still dream. But when I attempt serious thought I'm dazed. I don't think. I don't care any more. I don't pray!... Think of that, my friend! But in spite of my numb feeling I believe I'll rise out of all this dark agony a better woman, with greater love of man and God. I'm on the rack now; I'm senseless to all but pain, and growing dead to that. Sooner or later I shall rise out of this stupor. I'm waiting the hour."

"It'll soon come, Jane," replied Lassiter, soberly. "Then I'm afraid for you. Years are terrible things, an' for years you've been bound. Habit of years is strong as life itself. Somehow, though, I believe as you—that you'll come out of it all a finer woman. I'm waitin', too. An' I'm wonderin'—I reckon, Jane, that marriage between us is out of all human reason?"

"Lassiter!... My dear friend!... It's impossible for us to marry!"

"Why—as Fay says?" inquired Lassiter, with gentle persistence.

"Why! I never thought why. But it's not possible. I am Jane, daughter of Withersteen. My father would rise out of his grave. I'm of Mormon birth. I'm being broken. But I'm still a Mormon woman. And you—you are Lassiter!"

"Mebbe I'm not so much Lassiter as I used to be."

"What was it you said? Habit of years is strong as life itself! You can't change the one habit—the purpose of your life. For you still pack those black guns! You still nurse your passion for blood."

A smile, like a shadow, flickered across his face.

"No."

"Lassiter, I lied to you. But I beg of you—don't you lie to me. I've great respect for you. I believe you're softened toward most, perhaps all, my people except—But when I speak of your purpose, your hate, your guns, I have only him in mind. I don't believe you've changed."

For answer he unbuckled the heavy cartridge-belt, and laid it with the heavy, swing gun-sheaths in her lap.

"Lassiter!" Jane whispered, as she gazed from him to the black, cold guns. Without them he appeared shorn of strength, defenseless, a smaller man. Was she Delilah? Swiftly, conscious of only one motive—refusal to see this man called craven by his enemies—she rose, and with blundering fingers buckled the belt round his waist where it belonged.

"Lassiter, I am a coward."

"Come with me out of Utah—where I can put away my guns an' be a man," he said. "I reckon I'll prove it to you then! Come! You've got Black Star back, an' Night an' Bells. Let's take the racers an' little Fay, en' race out of Utah. The hosses an' the child are all you have left. Come!"

"No, no, Lassiter. I'll never leave Utah. What would I do in the world with my broken fortunes and my broken heart? I'll never leave these purple slopes I love so well."

"I reckon I ought to 've knowed that. Presently you'll be livin' down here in a hovel, en' presently Jane Withersteen will be a memory. I only wanted to have a chance to show you how a man—any man—can be better 'n he was. If we left Utah I could prove—I reckon I could prove this thing you call love. It's strange, an' hell an' heaven at once, Jane Withersteen. 'Pears to me that you've thrown away your big heart on love—love of religion an' duty an' churchmen, an' riders an' poor families an' poor children! Yet you can't see what love is— how it changes a person!... Listen, an' in tellin' you Milly Erne's story I'll show you how love changed her.

"Milly an' me was children when our family moved from Missouri to Texas, an' we growed up in Texas ways same as if we'd been born there. We had been poor, an' there we prospered. In time the little village where we went became a town, an' strangers an' new families kept movin' in. Milly was the belle them days. I can see her now, a little girl no bigger 'n a bird, an' as pretty. She had the finest eyes, dark blue-black when she was excited, an' beautiful all the time. You remember Milly's eyes! An' she had light-brown hair with streaks of gold, an' a mouth that every feller wanted to kiss.

"An' about the time Milly was the prettiest an' the sweetest, along came a young minister who began to ride some of a race with the other fellers for Milly. An' he won. Milly had always been strong on religion, an' when she met Frank Erne she went in heart an' soul for the salvation of souls. Fact was, Milly, through study of the Bible an' attendin' church an' revivals, went a little out of her head. It didn't worry the old folks none, an' the only worry to me was Milly's everlastin' prayin' an' workin' to save my soul. She never converted me, but we was the best of comrades, an' I reckon no brother an' sister ever loved each other better. Well, Frank Erne an me hit up a great friendship. He was a strappin' feller, good to look at, an' had the most pleasin' ways. His religion never bothered me, for he could hunt an' fish an' ride an' be a good feller. After buffalo once, he come pretty near to savin' my life. We got to be thick as brothers, an' he was the only man I ever seen who I thought was good enough for Milly. An' the day they were married I got drunk for the only time in my life.

"Soon after that I left home—it seems Milly was the only one who could keep me home— an' I went to the bad, as to prosperin' I saw some pretty hard life in the Pan Handle, an' then I went North. In them days Kansas an' Nebraska was as bad, come to think of it, as these days right here on the border of Utah. I got to be pretty handy with guns. An' there wasn't many riders as could beat me ridin'. An' I can say all modest-like that I never seen the white man who could track a hoss or a steer or a man with me. Afore I knowed it two years slipped by, an' all at once I got homesick, en' purled a bridle south.

"Things at home had changed. I never got over that homecomin'. Mother was dead an' in her grave. Father was a silent, broken man, killed already on his feet. Frank Erne was a ghost of his old self, through with workin', through with preachin', almost through with livin', an' Milly was gone!... It was a long time before I got the story. Father had no mind left, an' Frank Erne was afraid to talk. So I had to pick up whet 'd happened from different people.

"It 'pears that soon after I left home another preacher come to the little town. An' he an' Frank become rivals. This feller was different from Frank. He preached some other kind of religion, and he was quick an' passionate, where Frank was slow an' mild. He went after people, women specially. In looks he couldn't compare to Frank Erne, but he had power over women. He had a voice, an' he talked an' talked an' preached an' preached. Milly fell under his influence. She became mightily interested in his religion. Frank had patience with her, as was his way, an' let her be as interested as she liked. All religions were devoted to one God, he said, an' it wouldn't hurt Milly none to study a different point of view. So the new preacher often called on Milly, an' sometimes in Frank's absence. Frank was a cattle-man between Sundays.

"Along about this time an incident come off that I couldn't get much light on. A stranger come to town, an' was seen with the preacher. This stranger was a big man with an eye like blue ice, an' a beard of gold. He had money, an' he 'peared a man of mystery, an' the town went to buzzin' when he disappeared about the same time as a young woman known to be mightily interested in the new preacher's religion. Then, presently, along comes a man from somewheres in Illinois, en' he up an' spots this preacher as a famous Mormon proselyter. That riled Frank Erne as nothin' ever before, an' from rivals they come to be bitter enemies. An' it ended in Frank goin' to the meetin'-house where Milly was listenin', en' before her en' everybody else he called that preacher—called him, well, almost as hard as Venters called Tull here sometime back. An' Frank followed up that call with a hosswhippin', en' he drove the proselyter out of town.

"People noticed, so 'twas said, that Milly's sweet disposition changed. Some said it was because she would soon become a mother, en' others said she was pinin' after the new religion. An' there was women who said right out that she was pinin' after the Mormon. Anyway, one mornin' Frank rode in from one of his trips, to find Milly gone. He had no real near neighbors—livin' a little out of town—but those who was nearest said a wagon had gone by in the night, an' they thought it stopped at her door. Well, tracks always tell, an' there was the wagon tracks an' hoss tracks an' man tracks. The news spread like wildfire that Milly had run off from her husband. Everybody but Frank believed it an' wasn't slow in tellin' why she run off. Mother had always hated that strange streak of Milly's, takin' up with the new religion as she had, an' she believed Milly ran off with the Mormon. That hastened mother's death, an' she died unforgivin'. Father wasn't the kind to bow down under disgrace or misfortune but he had surpassin' love for Milly, an' the loss of her broke him.

"From the minute I heard of Milly's disappearance I never believed she went off of her own free will. I knew Milly, an' I knew she couldn't have done that. I stayed at home awhile, tryin' to make Frank Erne talk. But if he knowed anythin' then he wouldn't tell it. So I set out to find Milly. An' I tried to get on the trail of that proselyter. I knew if I ever struck a town he'd visited that I'd get a trail. I knew, too, that nothin' short of hell would stop his proselytin'. An' I rode from town to town. I had a blind faith that somethin' was guidin' me. An' as the weeks an' months went by I growed into a strange sort of a man, I guess. Anyway, people were afraid of me. Two years after that, way over in a corner of Texas, I struck a town where my man had been. He'd jest left. People said he came to that town without a woman. I back-trailed my man through Arkansas an' Mississippi, an' the old trail got hot again in Texas. I found the town where he first went after leavin' home. An' here I got track of Milly. I found a cabin where she had given birth to her baby. There was no way to tell whether she'd been kept a prisoner or not. The feller who owned the place was a mean, silent sort of a skunk, an' as I was leavin' I jest took a chance an' left my mark on him. Then I went home again.

"It was to find I hadn't any home, no more. Father had been dead a year. Frank Erne still lived in the house where Milly had left him. I stayed with him awhile, an' I grew old watchin' him. His farm had gone to weed, his cattle had strayed or been rustled, his house weathered till it wouldn't keep out rain nor wind. An' Frank set on the porch and whittled sticks, an' day by day wasted away. There was times when he ranted about like a crazy man, but mostly he was always sittin' an' starin' with eyes that made a man curse. I figured Frank had a secret fear that I needed to know. An' when I told him I'd trailed Milly for near three years an' had got trace of her, an' saw where she'd had her baby, I thought he would drop dead at my feet. An' when he'd come round more natural-like he begged me to give up the trail. But he wouldn't explain. So I let him alone, an' watched him day en' night.

"An' I found there was one thing still precious to him, an' it was a little drawer where he kept his papers. This was in the room where he slept. An' it 'peered he seldom slept. But after bein' patient I got the contents of that drawer an' found two letters from Milly. One was a long letter written a few months after her disappearance. She had been bound an' gagged an' dragged away from her home by three men, an' she named them—Hurd, Metzger, Slack. They was strangers to her. She was taken to the little town where I found trace of her two years after. But she didn't send the letter from that town. There she was penned in. 'Peared that the proselytes, who had, of course, come on the scene, was not runnin' any risks of losin' her. She went on to say that for a time she was out of her head, an' when she got right again all that kept her alive was the baby. It was a beautiful baby, she said, an' all she thought an' dreamed of was somehow to get baby back to its father, an' then she'd thankfully lay down and die. An' the letter ended abrupt, in the middle of a sentence, en' it wasn't signed.

"The second letter was written more than two years after the first. It was from Salt Lake City. It simply said that Milly had heard her brother was on her trail. She asked Frank to tell her brother to give up the search because if he didn't she would suffer in a way too horrible to tell. She didn't beg. She just stated a fact an' made the simple request. An' she ended that letter by sayin' she would soon leave Salt Lake City with the man she had come to love, en' would never be heard of again.

"I recognized Milly's handwritin', an' I recognized her way of puttin' things. But that second letter told me of some great change in her. Ponderin' over it, I felt at last she'd either come to love that feller an' his religion, or some terrible fear made her lie an' say so. I couldn't be sure which. But, of course, I meant to find out. I'll say here, if I'd known Mormons then as I do now I'd left Milly to her fate. For mebbe she was right about what she'd suffer if I kept on her trail. But I was young an' wild them days. First I went to the town where she'd first been taken, an' I went to the place where she'd been kept. I got that skunk who owned the place, an' took him out in the woods, an' made him tell all he knowed. That wasn't much as to length, but it was pure hell's-fire in substance. This time I left him some incapacitated for any more skunk work short of hell. Then I hit the trail for Utah.

"That was fourteen years ago. I saw the incomin' of most of the Mormons. It was a wild country an' a wild time. I rode from town to town, village to village, ranch to ranch, camp to camp. I never stayed long in one place. I never had but one idea. I never rested. Four years went by, an' I knowed every trail in northern Utah. I kept on an' as time went by, an' I'd begun to grow old in my search, I had firmer, blinder faith in whatever was guidin' me. Once I read about a feller who sailed the seven seas an' traveled the world, an' he had a story to tell, an' whenever he seen the man to whom he must tell that story he knowed him on sight. I was like that, only I had a question to ask. An' always I knew the man of whom I must ask. So I never really lost the trail, though for many years it was the dimmest trail ever followed by any man.

"Then come a change in my luck. Along in Central Utah I rounded up Hurd, an' I whispered somethin' in his ear, an' watched his face, an' then throwed a gun against his bowels. An' he died with his teeth so tight shut I couldn't have pried them open with a knife. Slack an' Metzger that same year both heard me whisper the same question, an' neither would they speak a word when they lay dyin'. Long before I'd learned no man of this breed or class—or God knows what—would give up any secrets! I had to see in a man's fear of death the connections with Milly Erne's fate. An' as the years passed at long intervals I would find such a man.

"So as I drifted on the long trail down into southern Utah my name preceded me, an' I had to meet a people prepared for me, an' ready with guns. They made me a gun-man. An' that suited me. In all this time signs of the proselyter an' the giant with the blue-ice eyes an' the gold beard seemed to fade dimmer out of the trail. Only twice in ten years did I find a trace of that mysterious man who had visited the proselyter at my home village. What he had to do with Milly's fate was beyond all hope for me to learn, unless my guidin' spirit led me to him! As for the other man, I knew, as sure as I breathed en' the stars shone en' the wind blew, that I'd meet him some day.

"Eighteen years I've been on the trail. An' it led me to the last lonely villages of the Utah border. Eighteen years!... I feel pretty old now. I was only twenty when I hit that trail. Well, as I told you, back here a ways a Gentile said Jane Withersteen could tell me about Milly Erne an' show me her grave!"

The low voice ceased, and Lassiter slowly turned his sombrero round and round, and appeared to be counting the silver ornaments on the band. Jane, leaning toward him, sat as if petrified, listening intently, waiting to hear more. She could have shrieked, but power of tongue and lips were denied her. She saw only this sad, gray, passion-worn man, and she heard only the faint rustling of the leaves.

"Well, I came to Cottonwoods," went on Lassiter, "an' you showed me Milly's grave. An' though your teeth have been shut tighter 'n them of all the dead men lyin' back along that trail, jest the same you told me the secret I've lived these eighteen years to hear! Jane, I said you'd tell me without ever me askin'. I didn't need to ask my question here. The day, you remember, when that fat party throwed a gun on me in your court, an'—"

"Oh! Hush!" whispered Jane, blindly holding up her hands.

"I seen in your face that Dyer, now a bishop, was the proselyter who ruined Milly Erne."

For an instant Jane Withersteen's brain was a whirling chaos and she recovered to find herself grasping at Lassiter like one drowning. And as if by a lightning stroke she sprang from her dull apathy into exquisite torture.

"It's a lie! Lassiter! No, no!" she moaned. "I swear—you're wrong!"

"Stop! You'd perjure yourself! But I'll spare you that. You poor woman! Still blind! Still faithful!... Listen. I know. Let that settle it. An' I give up my purpose!"

"What is it—you say?"

"I give up my purpose. I've come to see an' feel differently. I can't help poor Milly. An' I've outgrowed revenge. I've come to see I can be no judge for men. I can't kill a man jest for hate. Hate ain't the same with me since I loved you and little Fay."

"Lassiter! You mean you won't kill him?" Jane whispered.

"No."

"For my sake?"

"I reckon. I can't understand, but I'll respect your feelin's."

"Because you—oh, because you love me?... Eighteen years! You were that terrible Lassiter! And now—because you love me?"

"That's it, Jane."

"Oh, you'll make me love you! How can I help but love you? My heart must be stone. But —oh, Lassiter, wait, wait! Give me time. I'm not what I was. Once it was so easy to love. Now it's easy to hate. Wait! My faith in God—some God—still lives. By it I see happier times for you, poor passion-swayed wanderer! For me—a miserable, broken woman. I loved your sister Milly. I will love you. I can't have fallen so low—I can't be so abandoned by God—that I've no love left to give you. Wait! Let us forget Milly's sad life. Ah, I knew it as no one else on earth! There's one thing I shall tell you—if you are at my death-bed, but I can't speak now."

"I reckon I don't want to hear no more," said Lassiter.

Jane leaned against him, as if some pent-up force had rent its way out, she fell into a paroxysm of weeping. Lassiter held her in silent sympathy. By degrees she regained composure, and she was rising, sensible of being relieved of a weighty burden, when a sudden start on Lassiter's part alarmed her.

"I heard hosses—hosses with muffled hoofs!" he said; and he got up guardedly.

"Where's Fay?" asked Jane, hurriedly glancing round the shady knoll. The bright-haired child, who had appeared to be close all the time, was not in sight.

"Fay!" called Jane.

No answering shout of glee. No patter of flying feet. Jane saw Lassiter stiffen.

"Fay—oh—Fay!" Jane almost screamed.

The leaves quivered and rustled; a lonesome cricket chirped in the grass, a bee hummed by. The silence of the waning afternoon breathed hateful portent. It terrified Jane. When had silence been so infernal?

"She's—only—strayed—out—of earshot," faltered Jane, looking at Lassiter.

Pale, rigid as a statue, the rider stood, not in listening, searching posture, but in one of doomed certainty. Suddenly he grasped Jane with an iron hand, and, turning his face from her gaze, he strode with her from the knoll.

"See—Fay played here last—a house of stones an' sticks.... An' here's a corral of pebbles with leaves for hosses," said Lassiter, stridently, and pointed to the ground. "Back an' forth she trailed here.... See, she's buried somethin'—a dead grasshopper—there's a tombstone... here she went, chasin' a lizard—see the tiny streaked trail... she pulled bark off this cottonwood... look in the dust of the path—the letters you taught her—she's drawn pictures of birds en' hosses an' people.... Look, a cross! Oh, Jane, your cross!"

Lassiter dragged Jane on, and as if from a book read the meaning of little Fay's trail. All the way down the knoll, through the shrubbery, round and round a cottonwood, Fay's vagrant fancy left records of her sweet musings and innocent play. Long had she lingered round a bird-nest to leave therein the gaudy wing of a butterfly. Long had she played beside the running stream sending adrift vessels freighted with pebbly cargo. Then she had wandered through the deep grass, her tiny feet scarcely turning a fragile blade, and she had dreamed beside some old faded flowers. Thus her steps led her into the broad lane. The little dimpled imprints of her bare feet showed clean-cut in the dust they went a little way down the lane; and then, at a point where they stopped, the great tracks of a man led out from the shrubbery and returned.

❦ 20 ❦

LASSITER'S WAY

FOOTPRINTS TOLD the story of little Fay's abduction. In anguish Jane Withersteen turned speechlessly to Lassiter, and, confirming her fears, she saw him gray-faced, aged all in a moment, stricken as if by a mortal blow.

Then all her life seemed to fall about her in wreck and ruin.

"It's all over," she heard her voice whisper. "It's ended. I'm going—I'm going—"

"Where?" demanded Lassiter, suddenly looming darkly over her.

"To—to those cruel men—"

"Speak names!" thundered Lassiter.

"To Bishop Dyer—to Tull," went on Jane, shocked into obedience.

"Well—what for?"

"I want little Fay. I can't live without her. They've stolen her as they stole Milly Erne's child. I must have little Fay. I want only her. I give up. I'll go and tell Bishop Dyer—I'm broken. I'll tell him I'm ready for the yoke—only give me back Fay—and—and I'll marry Tull!"

"Never!" hissed Lassiter.

His long arm leaped at her. Almost running, he dragged her under the cottonwoods, across the court, into the huge hall of Withersteen House, and he shut the door with a force that jarred the heavy walls. Black Star and Night and Bells, since their return, had been locked in this hall, and now they stamped on the stone floor.

Lassiter released Jane and like a dizzy man swayed from her with a hoarse cry and leaned shaking against a table where he kept his rider's accoutrements. He began to fumble in his saddlebags. His action brought a clinking, metallic sound—the rattling of gun-cartridges. His fingers trembled as he slipped cartridges into an extra belt. But as he buckled it over the one he habitually wore his hands became steady. This second belt contained two guns, smaller than the black ones swinging low, and he slipped them round so that his coat hid them. Then he fell to swift action. Jane Withersteen watched him, fascinated but uncomprehending and she saw him rapidly saddle Black Star and Night. Then he drew her into the light of the huge windows, standing over her, gripping her arm with fingers like cold steel.

153

"Yes, Jane, it's ended—but you're not goin' to Dyer!... I'm goin' instead!"

Looking at him—he was so terrible of aspect—she could not comprehend his words. Who was this man with the face gray as death, with eyes that would have made her shriek had she the strength, with the strange, ruthlessly bitter lips? Where was the gentle Lassiter? What was this presence in the hall, about him, about her—this cold, invisible presence?

"Yes, it's ended, Jane," he was saying, so awfully quiet and cool and implacable, "an' I'm goin' to make a little call. I'll lock you in here, an' when I get back have the saddle-bags full of meat an bread. An' be ready to ride!"

"Lassiter!" cried Jane.

Desperately she tried to meet his gray eyes, in vain, desperately she tried again, fought herself as feeling and thought resurged in torment, and she succeeded, and then she knew.

"No—no—no!" she wailed. "You said you'd foregone your vengeance. You promised not to kill Bishop Dyer."

"If you want to talk to me about him—leave off the Bishop. I don't understand that name, or its use."

"Oh, hadn't you foregone your vengeance on—on Dyer?

"Yes."

"But—your actions—your words—your guns—your terrible looks!... They don't seem foregoing vengeance?"

"Jane, now it's justice."

"You'll—kill him?"

"If God lets me live another hour! If not God—then the devil who drives me!"

"You'll kill him—for yourself—for your vengeful hate?"

"No!"

"For Milly Erne's sake?"

"No."

"For little Fay's?"

"No!"

"Oh—for whose?"

"For yours!"

"His blood on my soul!" whispered Jane, and she fell to her knees. This was the long-pending hour of fruition. And the habit of years—the religious passion of her life—leaped from lethargy, and the long months of gradual drifting to doubt were as if they had never been. "If you spill his blood it'll be on my soul—and on my father's. Listen." And she clasped his knees, and clung there as he tried to raise her. "Listen. Am I nothing to you?"

"Woman—don't trifle at words! I love you! An' I'll soon prove it."

"I'll give myself to you—I'll ride away with you—marry you, if only you'll spare him?"

His answer was a cold, ringing, terrible laugh.

"Lassiter—I'll love you. Spare him!"

"No."

She sprang up in despairing, breaking spirit, and encircled his neck with her arms, and held him in an embrace that he strove vainly to loosen. "Lassiter, would you kill me? I'm fighting my last fight for the principles of my youth—love of religion, love of father. You don't know—you can't guess the truth, and I can't speak ill. I'm losing all. I'm changing. All I've gone through is nothing to this hour. Pity me—help me in my weakness. You're strong again—oh, so cruelly, coldly strong! You're killing me. I see you—feel you as some other Lassiter! My master, be merciful—spare him!"

His answer was a ruthless smile.

She clung the closer to him, and leaned her panting breast on him, and lifted her face to his. "Lassiter, I do love you! It's leaped out of my agony. It comes suddenly with a terrible blow of truth. You are a man! I never knew it till now. Some wonderful change came to me when you buckled on these guns and showed that gray, awful face. I loved you then. All my life I've loved, but never as now. No woman can love like a broken woman. If it were not for one thing—just one thing—and yet! I can't speak it—I'd glory in your manhood—the lion in you that means to slay for me. Believe me—and spare Dyer. Be merciful—great as it's in you to be great.... Oh, listen and believe—I have nothing, but I'm a woman—a beautiful woman, Lassiter—a passionate, loving woman—and I love you! Take me—hide me in some wild place—and love me and mend my broken heart. Spare him and take me away."

She lifted her face closer and closer to his, until their lips nearly touched, and she hung upon his neck, and with strength almost spent pressed and still pressed her palpitating body to his.

"Kiss me!" she whispered, blindly.

"No—not at your price!" he answered. His voice had changed or she had lost clearness of hearing.

"Kiss me!... Are you a man? Kiss me and save me!"

"Jane, you never played fair with me. But now you're blisterin' your lips—blackenin' your soul with lies!"

"By the memory of my mother—by my Bible—no! No, I have no Bible! But by my hope of heaven I swear I love you!"

Lassiter's gray lips formed soundless words that meant even her love could not avail to bend his will. As if the hold of her arms was that of a child's he loosened it and stepped away.

"Wait! Don't go! Oh, hear a last word!... May a more just and merciful God than the God I was taught to worship judge me—forgive me—save me! For I can no longer keep silent!... Lassiter, in pleading for Dyer I've been pleading more for my father. My father was a Mormon master, close to the leaders of the church. It was my father who sent Dyer out to proselyte. It was my father who had the blue-ice eye and the beard of gold. It was my father you got trace of in the past years. Truly, Dyer ruined Milly Erne—dragged her from her home —to Utah—to Cottonwoods. But it was for my father! If Milly Erne was ever wife of a Mormon that Mormon was my father! I never knew—never will know whether or not she was a wife. Blind I may be, Lassiter—fanatically faithful to a false religion I may have been but I know justice, and my father is beyond human justice. Surely he is meeting just punishment—somewhere. Always it has appalled me—the thought of your killing Dyer for my father's sins. So I have prayed!"

"Jane, the past is dead. In my love for you I forgot the past. This thing I'm about to do ain't for myself or Milly or Fay. It's not because of anythin' that ever happened in the past, but for what is happenin' right now. It's for you!... An' listen. Since I was a boy I've never thanked God for anythin'. If there is a God—an' I've come to believe it—I thank Him now for the years that made me Lassiter!... I can reach down en' feel these big guns, en' know what I can do with them. An', Jane, only one of the miracles Dyer professes to believe in can save him!"

Again for Jane Withersteen came the spinning of her brain in darkness, and as she whirled in endless chaos she seemed to be falling at the feet of a luminous figure—a man— Lassiter—who had saved her from herself, who could not be changed, who would slay rightfully. Then she slipped into utter blackness.

When she recovered from her faint she became aware that she was lying on a couch near the window in her sitting-room. Her brow felt damp and cold and wet, some one was chafing her hands; she recognized Judkins, and then saw that his lean, hard face wore the hue and look of excessive agitation.

"Judkins!" Her voice broke weakly.

"Aw, Miss Withersteen, you're comin' round fine. Now jest lay still a little. You're all right; everythin's all right."

"Where is—he?"

"Who?"

"Lassiter!"

"You needn't worry none about him."

"Where is he? Tell me—instantly."

"Wal, he's in the other room patchin' up a few triflin' bullet holes."

"Ah!... Bishop' Dyer?"

"When I seen him last—a matter of half an hour ago, he was on his knees. He was some busy, but he wasn't prayin'!"

"How strangely you talk! I'll sit up. I'm—well, strong again. Tell me. Dyer on his knees! What was he doing?"

"Wal, beggin' your pardon fer blunt talk, Miss Withersteen, Dyer was on his knees an' not prayin'. You remember his big, broad hands? You've seen 'em raised in blessin' over old gray men an' little curly-headed children like—like Fay Larkin! Come to think of thet, I disremember ever hearin' of his liftin' his big hands in blessin' over a woman. Wal, when I seen him last—jest a little while ago—he was on his knees, not prayin', as I remarked—an' he was pressin' his big hands over some bigger wounds."

"Man, you drive me mad! Did Lassiter kill Dyer?"

"Yes."

"Did he kill Tull?"

"No. Tull's out of the village with most of his riders. He's expected back before evenin'. Lassiter will hev to git away before Tull en' his riders come in. It's sure death fer him here. An' wuss fer you, too, Miss Withersteen. There'll be some of an uprisin' when Tull gits back."

"I shall ride away with Lassiter. Judkins, tell me all you saw—all you know about this killing." She realized, without wonder or amaze, how Judkins's one word, affirming the death of Dyer—that the catastrophe had fallen—had completed the change whereby she had been molded or beaten or broken into another woman. She felt calm, slightly cold, strong as she had not been strong since the first shadow fell upon her.

"I jest saw about all of it, Miss Withersteen, an' I'll be glad to tell you if you'll only hev patience with me," said Judkins, earnestly. "You see, I've been pecooliarly interested, an' nat'rully I'm some excited. An' I talk a lot thet mebbe ain't necessary, but I can't help thet.

"I was at the meetin'-house where Dyer was holdin' court. You know he allus acts as magistrate an' judge when Tull's away. An' the trial was fer tryin' what's left of my boy riders —thet helped me hold your cattle—fer a lot of hatched-up things the boys never did. We're used to thet, an' the boys wouldn't hev minded bein' locked up fer a while, or hevin' to dig ditches, or whatever the judge laid down. You see, I divided the gold you give me among all my boys, an' they all hid it, en' they all feel rich. Howsomever, court was adjourned before the judge passed sentence. Yes, ma'm, court was adjourned some strange an' quick, much as if lightnin' hed struck the meetin'-house.

"I hed trouble attendin' the trial, but I got in. There was a good many people there, all my boys, an' Judge Dyer with his several clerks. Also he hed with him the five riders who've been guardin' him pretty close of late. They was Carter, Wright, Jengessen, an' two new riders from Stone Bridge. I didn't hear their names, but I heard they was handy men with guns an' they looked more like rustlers than riders. Anyway, there they was, the five all in a row.

"Judge Dyer was tellin' Willie Kern, one of my best an' steadiest boys—Dyer was tellin' him how there was a ditch opened near Willie's home lettin' water through his lot, where it hadn't ought to go. An' Willie was tryin' to git a word in to prove he wasn't at home all the day it happened—which was true, as I know—but Willie couldn't git a word in, an' then Judge Dyer went on layin' down the law. An' all to onct he happened to look down the long room. An' if ever any man turned to stone he was thet man.

"Nat'rully I looked back to see what hed acted so powerful strange on the judge. An' there, half-way up the room, in the middle of the wide aisle, stood Lassiter! All white an' black he looked, an' I can't think of anythin' he resembled, onless it's death. Venters made thet same room some still an' chilly when he called Tull; but this was different. I give my word, Miss Withersteen, thet I went cold to my very marrow. I don't know why. But Lassiter had a way about him thet's awful. He spoke a word—a name—I couldn't understand it, though he spoke clear as a bell. I was too excited, mebbe. Judge Dyer must hev understood it, an' a lot more thet was mystery to me, for he pitched forrard out of his chair right onto the platform.

"Then them five riders, Dyer's bodyguards, they jumped up, an' two of them thet I found out afterward were the strangers from Stone Bridge, they piled right out of a winder, so quick you couldn't catch your breath. It was plain they wasn't Mormons.

"Jengessen, Carter, an' Wright eyed Lassiter, for what must hev been a second an' seemed like an hour, an' they went white en' strung. But they didn't weaken nor lose their nerve.

"I hed a good look at Lassiter. He stood sort of stiff, bendin' a little, an' both his arms were crooked an' his hands looked like a hawk's claws. But there ain't no tellin' how his eyes looked. I know this, though, an' thet is his eyes could read the mind of any man about to throw a gun. An' in watchin' him, of course, I couldn't see the three men go fer their guns. An' though I was lookin' right at Lassiter—lookin' hard—I couldn't see how he drawed. He was quicker 'n eyesight—thet's all. But I seen the red spurtin' of his guns, en' heard his shots jest the very littlest instant before I heard the shots of the riders. An' when I turned, Wright an' Carter was down, en' Jengessen, who's tough like a steer, was pullin' the trigger of a wabblin' gun. But it was plain he was shot through, plumb center. An' sudden he fell with a crash, an' his gun clattered on the floor.

"Then there was a hell of a silence. Nobody breathed. Sartin I didn't, anyway. I saw Lassiter slip a smokin' gun back in a belt. But he hadn't throwed either of the big black guns, an' I thought thet strange. An' all this was happenin' quick—you can't imagine how quick.

"There come a scrapin' on the floor an' Dyer got up, his face like lead. I wanted to watch Lassiter, but Dyer's face, onct I seen it like thet, glued my eyes. I seen him go fer his gun—why, I could hev done better, quicker—an' then there was a thunderin' shot from Lassiter, an' it hit Dyer's right arm, an' his gun went off as it dropped. He looked at Lassiter like a cornered sage-wolf, an' sort of howled, an' reached down fer his gun. He'd jest picked it off the floor an' was raisin' it when another thunderin' shot almost tore thet arm off—so it seemed to me. The gun dropped again an' he went down on his knees, kind of flounderin' after it. It was some strange an' terrible to see his awful earnestness. Why would such a man cling so to life? Anyway, he got the gun with left hand an' was raisin' it, pullin' trigger in his madness, when the third thunderin' shot hit his left arm, an' he dropped the gun again. But thet left arm wasn't useless yet, fer he grabbed up the gun, an' with a shakin' aim thet would hev been pitiful to me—in any other man—he began to shoot. One wild bullet struck a man twenty feet from Lassiter. An' it killed thet man, as I seen afterward. Then come a bunch of thunderin' shots—nine I calkilated after, fer they come so quick I couldn't count them—an' I knew Lassiter hed turned the black guns loose on Dyer.

"I'm tellin' you straight, Miss Withersteen, fer I want you to know. Afterward you'll git over it. I've seen some soul-rackin' scenes on this Utah border, but this was the awfulest. I remember I closed my eyes, an' fer a minute I thought of the strangest things, out of place there, such as you'd never dream would come to mind. I saw the sage, an' runnin' hosses— an' thet's the beautfulest sight to me—an' I saw dim things in the dark, an' there was a kind of hummin' in my ears. An' I remember distinctly—fer it was what made all these things whirl out of my mind an' opened my eyes—I remember distinctly it was the smell of gunpowder.

"The court had about adjourned fer thet judge. He was on his knees, en' he wasn't prayin'. He was gaspin' an' tryin' to press his big, floppin', crippled hands over his body. Lassiter had sent all those last thunderin' shots through his body. Thet was Lassiter's way.

"An' Lassiter spoke, en' if I ever forgit his words I'll never forgit the sound of his voice.

"'Proselyter, I reckon you'd better call quick on thet God who reveals Hisself to you on earth, because He won't be visitin' the place you're goin' to!'

"An' then I seen Dyer look at his big, hangin' hands thet wasn't big enough fer the last work he set them to. An' he looked up at Lassiter. An' then he stared horrible at somethin' thet wasn't Lassiter, nor anyone there, nor the room, nor the branches of purple sage peepin' into the winder. Whatever he seen, it was with the look of a man who discovers somethin' too late. Thet's a terrible look!... An' with a horrible understandin' cry he slid forrard on his face."

Judkins paused in his narrative, breathing heavily while he wiped his perspiring brow.

"Thet's about all," he concluded. "Lassiter left the meetin'-house an' I hurried to catch up with him. He was bleedin' from three gunshots, none of them much to bother him. An' we come right up here. I found you layin' in the hall, an' I hed to work some over you."

Jane Withersteen offered up no prayer for Dyer's soul.

Lassiter's step sounded in the hall—the familiar soft, silver-clinking step—and she heard it with thrilling new emotions in which was a vague joy in her very fear of him. The door opened, and she saw him, the old Lassiter, slow, easy, gentle, cool, yet not exactly the same Lassiter. She rose, and for a moment her eyes blurred and swam in tears.

"Are you—all—all right?" she asked, tremulously.

"I reckon."

"Lassiter, I'll ride away with you. Hide me till danger is past—till we are forgotten—then take me where you will. Your people shall be my people, and your God my God!"

He kissed her hand with the quaint grace and courtesy that came to him in rare moments.

"Black Star an' Night are ready," he said, simply.

His quiet mention of the black racers spurred Jane to action. Hurrying to her room, she changed to her rider's suit, packed her jewelry, and the gold that was left, and all the woman's apparel for which there was space in the saddle-bags, and then returned to the hall. Black Star stamped his iron-shod hoofs and tossed his beautiful head, and eyed her with knowing eyes.

"Judkins, I give Bells to you," said Jane. "I hope you will always keep him and be good to him."

Judkins mumbled thanks that he could not speak fluently, and his eyes flashed.

Lassiter strapped Jane's saddle-bags upon Black Star, and led the racers out into the court.

"Judkins, you ride with Jane out into the sage. If you see any riders comin' shout quick twice. An', Jane, don't look back! I'll catch up soon. We'll get to the break into the Pass before midnight, an' then wait until mornin' to go down."

Black Star bent his graceful neck and bowed his noble head, and his broad shoulders yielded as he knelt for Jane to mount.

She rode out of the court beside Judkins, through the grove, across the wide lane into the sage, and she realized that she was leaving Withersteen House forever, and she did not look back. A strange, dreamy, calm peace pervaded her soul. Her doom had fallen upon her, but, instead of finding life no longer worth living she found it doubly significant, full of sweetness as the western breeze, beautiful and unknown as the sage-slope stretching its purple sunset shadows before her. She became aware of Judkins's hand touching hers; she heard him speak a husky good-by; then into the place of Bells shot the dead-black, keen, racy nose of Night, and she knew Lassiter rode beside her.

"Don't—look—back!" he said, and his voice, too, was not clear.

Facing straight ahead, seeing only the waving, shadowy sage, Jane held out her gauntleted hand, to feel it enclosed in strong clasp. So she rode on without a backward glance at the beautiful grove of Cottonwoods. She did not seem to think of the past of what she left forever, but of the color and mystery and wildness of the sage-slope leading down to Deception Pass, and of the future. She watched the shadows lengthen down the slope; she felt the cool west wind sweeping by from the rear; and she wondered at low, yellow clouds sailing swiftly over her and beyond.

"Don't look—back!" said Lassiter.

Thick-driving belts of smoke traveled by on the wind, and with it came a strong, pungent odor of burning wood.

Lassiter had fired Withersteen House! But Jane did not look back.

A misty veil obscured the clear, searching gaze she had kept steadfastly upon the purple slope and the dim lines of canyons. It passed, as passed the rolling clouds of smoke, and she saw the valley deepening into the shades of twilight. Night came on, swift as the fleet racers, and stars peeped out to brighten and grow, and the huge, windy, eastern heave of sage-level paled under a rising moon and turned to silver. Blanched in moonlight, the sage yet seemed to hold its hue of purple and was infinitely more wild and lonely. So the night hours wore on, and Jane Withersteen never once looked back.

21

BLACK STAR AND NIGHT

THE TIME HAD COME for Venters and Bess to leave their retreat. They were at great pains to choose the few things they would be able to carry with them on the journey out of Utah.

"Bern, whatever kind of a pack's this, anyhow?" questioned Bess, rising from her work with reddened face.

Venters, absorbed in his own task, did not look up at all, and in reply said he had brought so much from Cottonwoods that he did not recollect the half of it.

"A woman packed this!" Bess exclaimed.

He scarcely caught her meaning, but the peculiar tone of her voice caused him instantly to rise, and he saw Bess on her knees before an open pack which he recognized as the one given him by Jane.

"By George!" he ejaculated, guiltily, and then at sight of Bess's face he laughed outright.

"A woman packed this," she repeated, fixing woeful, tragic eyes on him.

"Well, is that a crime?'

"There—there is a woman, after all!"

"Now Bess—"

"You've lied to me!"

Then and there Venters found it imperative to postpone work for the present. All her life Bess had been isolated, but she had inherited certain elements of the eternal feminine.

"But there was a woman and you did lie to me," she kept repeating, after he had explained.

"What of that? Bess, I'll get angry at you in a moment. Remember you've been pent up all your life. I venture to say that if you'd been out in the world you'd have had a dozen sweethearts and have told many a lie before this."

"I wouldn't anything of the kind," declared Bess, indignantly.

"Well—perhaps not lie. But you'd have had the sweethearts—You couldn't have helped that—being so pretty."

This remark appeared to be a very clever and fortunate one; and the work of selecting and then of stowing all the packs in the cave went on without further interruption.

Venters closed up the opening of the cave with a thatch of willows and aspens, so that not even a bird or a rat could get in to the sacks of grain. And this work was in order with the precaution habitually observed by him. He might not be able to get out of Utah, and have to return to the valley. But he owed it to Bess to make the attempt, and in case they were compelled to turn back he wanted to find that fine store of food and grain intact. The outfit of implements and utensils he packed away in another cave.

"Bess, we have enough to live here all our lives," he said once, dreamily.

"Shall I go roll Balancing Rock?" she asked, in light speech, but with deep-blue fire in her eyes.

"No—no."

"Ah, you don't forget the gold and the world," she sighed.

"Child, you forget the beautiful dresses and the travel—and everything."

"Oh, I want to go. But I want to stay!"

"I feel the same way."

They let the eight calves out of the corral, and kept only two of the burros Venters had brought from Cottonwoods. These they intended to ride. Bess freed all her pets—the quail and rabbits and foxes.

The last sunset and twilight and night were both the sweetest and saddest they had ever spent in Surprise Valley. Morning brought keen exhilaration and excitement. When Venters had saddled the two burros, strapped on the light packs and the two canteens, the sunlight was dispersing the lazy shadows from the valley. Taking a last look at the caves and the silver spruces, Venters and Bess made a reluctant start, leading the burros. Ring and Whitie looked keen and knowing. Something seemed to drag at Venters's feet and he noticed Bess lagged behind. Never had the climb from terrace to bridge appeared so long.

Not till they reached the opening of the gorge did they stop to rest and take one last look at the valley. The tremendous arch of stone curved clear and sharp in outline against the morning sky. And through it streaked the golden shaft. The valley seemed an enchanted circle of glorious veils of gold and wraiths of white and silver haze and dim, blue, moving shade—beautiful and wild and unreal as a dream.

"We—we can—th—think of it—always—re—remember," sobbed Bess.

"Hush! Don't cry. Our valley has only fitted us for a better life somewhere. Come!"

They entered the gorge and he closed the willow gate. From rosy, golden morning light they passed into cool, dense gloom. The burros pattered up the trail with little hollow-cracking steps. And the gorge widened to narrow outlet and the gloom lightened to gray. At the divide they halted for another rest. Venters's keen, remembering gaze searched Balancing Rock, and the long incline, and the cracked toppling walls, but failed to note the slightest change.

The dogs led the descent; then came Bess leading her burro; then Venters leading his. Bess kept her eyes bent downward. Venters, however, had an irresistible desire to look upward at Balancing Rock. It had always haunted him, and now he wondered if he were really to get through the outlet before the huge stone thundered down. He fancied that would be a miracle. Every few steps he answered to the strange, nervous fear and turned to make sure the rock still stood like a giant statue. And, as he descended, it grew dimmer in his sight. It changed form; it swayed it nodded darkly; and at last, in his heightened fancy, he saw it heave and roll. As in a dream when he felt himself falling yet knew he would never fall, so he saw this long-standing thunderbolt of the little stone-men plunge down to close forever the outlet to Deception Pass.

And while he was giving way to unaccountable dread imaginations the descent was accomplished without mishap.

"I'm glad that's over," he said, breathing more freely. "I hope I'm by that hanging rock for good and all. Since almost the moment I first saw it I've had an idea that it was waiting for me. Now, when it does fall, if I'm thousands of miles away, I'll hear it."

With the first glimpses of the smooth slope leading down to the grotesque cedars and out to the Pass, Venters's cool nerve returned. One long survey to the left, then one to the right, satisfied his caution. Leading the burros down to the spur of rock, he halted at the steep incline.

"Bess, here's the bad place, the place I told you about, with the cut steps. You start down, leading your burro. Take your time and hold on to him if you slip. I've got a rope on him and a half-hitch on this point of rock, so I can let him down safely. Coming up here was a killing job. But it'll be easy going down."

Both burros passed down the difficult stairs cut by the cliff-dwellers, and did it without a misstep. After that the descent down the slope and over the mile of scrawled, ripped, and ridged rock required only careful guidance, and Venters got the burros to level ground in a condition that caused him to congratulate himself.

"Oh, if we only had Wrangle!" exclaimed Venters. "But we're lucky. That's the worst of our trail passed. We've only men to fear now. If we get up in the sage we can hide and slip along like coyotes."

They mounted and rode west through the valley and entered the canyon. From time to time Venters walked, leading his burro. When they got by all the canyons and gullies opening into the Pass they went faster and with fewer halts. Venters did not confide in Bess the alarming fact that he had seen horses and smoke less than a mile up one of the intersecting canyons. He did not talk at all. And long after he had passed this canyon and felt secure once more in the certainty that they had been unobserved he never relaxed his watchfulness. But he did not walk any more, and he kept the burros at a steady trot. Night fell before they reached the last water in the Pass and they made camp by starlight. Venters did not want the burros to stray, so he tied them with long halters in the grass near the spring. Bess, tired out and silent, laid her head in a saddle and went to sleep between the two dogs. Venters did not close his eyes. The canyon silence appeared full of the low, continuous hum of insects. He listened until the hum grew into a roar, and then, breaking the spell, once more he heard it low and clear. He watched the stars and the moving shadows, and always his glance returned to the girl's dimly pale face. And he remembered how white and still it had once looked in the starlight. And again stern thought fought his strange fancies. Would all his labor and his love be for naught? Would he lose her, after all? What did the dark shadow around her portend? Did calamity lurk on that long upland trail through the sage? Why should his heart swell and throb with nameless fear? He listened to the silence and told himself that in the broad light of day he could dispel this leaden-weighted dread.

At the first hint of gray over the eastern rim he awoke Bess, saddled the burros, and began the day's travel. He wanted to get out of the Pass before there was any chance of riders coming down. They gained the break as the first red rays of the rising sun colored the rim.

For once, so eager was he to get up to level ground, he did not send Ring or Whitie in advance. Encouraging Bess to hurry pulling at his patient, plodding burro, he climbed the soft, steep trail.

Brighter and brighter grew the light. He mounted the last broken edge of rim to have the sun-fired, purple sage-slope burst upon him as a glory. Bess panted up to his side, tugging on the halter of her burro.

"We're up!" he cried, joyously. "There's not a dot on the sage. We're safe. We'll not be seen! Oh, Bess—"

Ring growled and sniffed the keen air and bristled. Venters clutched at his rifle. Whitie sometimes made a mistake, but Ring never. The dull thud of hoofs almost deprived Venters of power to turn and see from where disaster threatened. He felt his eyes dilate as he stared at Lassiter leading Black Star and Night out of the sage, with Jane Withersteen, in rider's costume, close beside them.

For an instant Venters felt himself whirl dizzily in the center of vast circles of sage. He recovered partially, enough to see Lassiter standing with a glad smile and Jane riveted in astonishment.

"Why, Bern!" she exclaimed. "How good it is to see you! We're riding away, you see. The storm burst—and I'm a ruined woman!... I thought you were alone."

Venters, unable to speak for consternation, and bewildered out of all sense of what he ought or ought not to do, simply stared at Jane.

"Son, where are you bound for?" asked Lassiter.

"Not safe—where I was. I'm—we're going out of Utah—back East," he found tongue to say.

"I reckon this meetin's the luckiest thing that ever happened to you an' to me—an' to Jane —an' to Bess," said Lassiter, coolly.

"Bess!" cried Jane, with a sudden leap of blood to her pale cheek.

It was entirely beyond Venters to see any luck in that meeting.

Jane Withersteen took one flashing, woman's glance at Bess's scarlet face, at her slender, shapely form.

"Venters! is this a girl—a woman?" she questioned, in a voice that stung.

"Yes."

"Did you have her in that wonderful valley?"

"Yes, but Jane—"

"All the time you were gone?"

"Yes, but I couldn't tell—"

"Was it for her you asked me to give you supplies? Was it for her that you wanted to make your valley a paradise?"

"Oh—Jane—"

"Answer me."

"Yes."

"Oh, you liar!" And with these passionate words Jane Withersteen succumbed to fury. For the second time in her life she fell into the ungovernable rage that had been her father's weakness. And it was worse than his, for she was a jealous woman—jealous even of her friends.

As best he could, he bore the brunt of her anger. It was not only his deceit to her that she visited upon him, but her betrayal by religion, by life itself.

Her passion, like fire at white heat, consumed itself in little time. Her physical strength failed, and still her spirit attempted to go on in magnificent denunciation of those who had wronged her. Like a tree cut deep into its roots, she began to quiver and shake, and her anger weakened into despair. And her ringing voice sank into a broken, husky whisper. Then, spent and pitiable, upheld by Lassiter's arm, she turned and hid her face in Black Star's mane.

Numb as Venters was when at length Jane Withersteen lifted her head and looked at him, he yet suffered a pang.

"Jane, the girl is innocent!" he cried.

"Can you expect me to believe that?" she asked, with weary, bitter eyes.

"I'm not that kind of a liar. And you know it. If I lied—if I kept silent when honor should have made me speak, it was to spare you. I came to Cottonwoods to tell you. But I couldn't add to your pain. I intended to tell you I had come to love this girl. But, Jane I hadn't forgotten how good you were to me. I haven't changed at all toward you. I prize your friendship as I always have. But, however it may look to you—don't be unjust. The girl is innocent. Ask Lassiter."

"Jane, she's jest as sweet an' innocent as little Fay," said Lassiter. There was a faint smile upon his face and a beautiful light.

Venters saw, and knew that Lassiter saw, how Jane Withersteen's tortured soul wrestled with hate and threw it—with scorn doubt, suspicion, and overcame all.

"Bern, if in my misery I accused you unjustly, I crave forgiveness," she said. "I'm not what I once was. Tell me—who is this girl?"

"Jane, she is Oldring's daughter, and his Masked Rider. Lassiter will tell you how I shot her for a rustler, saved her life—all the story. It's a strange story, Jane, as wild as the sage. But it's true—true as her innocence. That you must believe."

"Oldring's Masked Rider! Oldring's daughter!" exclaimed Jane "And she's innocent! You ask me to believe much. If this girl is—is what you say, how could she be going away with the man who killed her father?"

"Why did you tell that?" cried Venters, passionately.

Jane's question had roused Bess out of stupefaction. Her eyes suddenly darkened and dilated. She stepped toward Venters and held up both hands as if to ward off a blow.

"Did—did you kill Oldring?"

"I did, Bess, and I hate myself for it. But you know I never dreamed he was your father. I thought he'd wronged you. I killed him when I was madly jealous."

For a moment Bess was shocked into silence.

"But he was my father!" she broke out, at last. "And now I must go back—I can't go with you. It's all over—that beautiful dream. Oh, I knew it couldn't come true. You can't take me now."

"If you forgive me, Bess, it'll all come right in the end!" implored Venters.

"It can't be right. I'll go back. After all, I loved him. He was good to me. I can't forget that."

"If you go back to Oldring's men I'll follow you, and then they'll kill me," said Venters, hoarsely.

"Oh no, Bern, you'll not come. Let me go. It's best for you to forget me. I've brought you only pain and dishonor."

She did not weep. But the sweet bloom and life died out of her face. She looked haggard and sad, all at once stunted; and her hands dropped listlessly; and her head drooped in slow, final acceptance of a hopeless fate.

"Jane, look there!" cried Venters, in despairing grief. "Need you have told her? Where was all your kindness of heart? This girl has had a wretched, lonely life. And I'd found a way to make her happy. You've killed it. You've killed something sweet and pure and hopeful, just as sure as you breathe."

"Oh, Bern! It was a slip. I never thought—I never thought!" replied Jane. "How could I tell she didn't know?"

Lassiter suddenly moved forward, and with the beautiful light on his face now strangely luminous, he looked at Jane and Venters and then let his soft, bright gaze rest on Bess.

"Well, I reckon you've all had your say, an' now it's Lassiter's turn. Why, I was jest praying for this meetin'. Bess, jest look here."

Gently he touched her arm and turned her to face the others, and then outspread his great hand to disclose a shiny, battered gold locket.

"Open it," he said, with a singularly rich voice.

Bess complied, but listlessly.

"Jane—Venters—come closer," went on Lassiter. "Take a look at the picture. Don't you know the woman?"

Jane, after one glance, drew back.

"Milly Erne!" she cried, wonderingly.

Venters, with tingling pulse, with something growing on him, recognized in the faded miniature portrait the eyes of Milly Erne.

"Yes, that's Milly," said Lassiter, softly. "Bess, did you ever see her face—look hard—with all your heart an' soul?"

"The eyes seem to haunt me," whispered Bess. "Oh, I can't remember—they're eyes of my dreams—but—but—"

Lassiter's strong arm went round her and he bent his head.

"Child, I thought you'd remember her eyes. They're the same beautiful eyes you'd see if you looked in a mirror or a clear spring. They're your mother's eyes. You are Milly Erne's child. Your name is Elizabeth Erne. You're not Oldring's daughter. You're the daughter of Frank Erne, a man once my best friend. Look! Here's his picture beside Milly's. He was handsome, an' as fine an' gallant a Southern gentleman as I ever seen. Frank came of an old family. You come of the best of blood, lass, and blood tells."

Bess slipped through his arm to her knees and hugged the locket to her bosom, and lifted wonderful, yearning eyes.

"It—can't—be—true!"

"Thank God, lass, it is true," replied Lassiter. "Jane an' Bern here—they both recognize Milly. They see Milly in you. They're so knocked out they can't tell you, that's all."

"Who are you?" whispered Bess.

"I reckon I'm Milly's brother an' your uncle!... Uncle Jim! Ain't that fine?"

"Oh, I can't believe—Don't raise me! Bern, let me kneel. I see truth in your face—in Miss Withersteen's. But let me hear it all—all on my knees. Tell me how it's true!"

"Well, Elizabeth, listen," said Lassiter. "Before you was born your father made a mortal enemy of a Mormon named Dyer. They was both ministers an' come to be rivals. Dyer stole your mother away from her home. She gave birth to you in Texas eighteen years ago. Then she was taken to Utah, from place to place, an' finally to the last border settlement— Cottonwoods. You was about three years old when you was taken away from Milly. She never knew what had become of you. But she lived a good while hopin' and prayin' to have you again. Then she gave up an' died. An' I may as well put in here your father died ten years ago. Well, I spent my time tracin' Milly, an' some months back I landed in Cottonwoods. An' jest lately I learned all about you. I had a talk with Oldrin' an' told him you was dead, an' he told me what I had so long been wantin' to know. It was Dyer, of course, who stole you from Milly. Part reason he was sore because Milly refused to give you Mormon teachin', but mostly he still hated Frank Erne so infernally that he made a deal with Oldrin' to take you an' bring you up as an infamous rustler an' rustler's girl. The idea was to break Frank Erne's heart if he ever came to Utah—to show him his daughter with a band of low rustlers. Well—Oldrin' took you, brought you up from childhood, an' then made you his Masked Rider. He made you infamous. He kept that part of the contract, but he learned to love you as a daughter an' never let any but his own men know you was a girl. I heard him say that with my own ears, an' I saw his big eyes grow dim. He told me how he had guarded you always, kept you locked up in his absence, was always at your side or near you on those rides that made you famous on the sage. He said he an' an old rustler whom he trusted had taught you how to read an' write. They selected the books for you. Dyer had wanted you brought up the vilest of the vile! An' Oldrin' brought you up the innocentest of the innocent. He said you didn't know what vileness was. I can hear his big voice tremble now as he said it. He told me how the men—rustlers an' outlaws—who from time to time tried to approach you familiarly—he told me how he shot them dead. I'm tellin' you this 'specially because you've showed such shame—sayin' you was nameless an' all that. Nothin' on earth can be wronger than that idea of yours. An' the truth of it is here. Oldrin' swore to me that if Dyer died, releasin' the contract, he intended to hunt up your father an' give you back to him. It seems Oldrin' wasn't all bad, en' he sure loved you."

Venters leaned forward in passionate remorse.

"Oh, Bess! I know Lassiter speaks the truth. For when I shot Oldring he dropped to his knees and fought with unearthly power to speak. And he said: 'Man—why—didn't—you—wait? Bess was—' Then he fell dead. And I've been haunted by his look and words. Oh, Bess, what a strange, splendid thing for Oldring to do! It all seems impossible. But, dear, you really are not what you thought."

"Elizabeth Erne!" cried Jane Withersteen. "I loved your mother and I see her in you!"

What had been incredible from the lips of men became, in the tone, look, and gesture of a woman, a wonderful truth for Bess. With little tremblings of all her slender body she rocked to and fro on her knees. The yearning wistfulness of her eyes changed to solemn splendor of joy. She believed. She was realizing happiness. And as the process of thought was slow, so were the variations of her expression. Her eyes reflected the transformation of her soul. Dark, brooding, hopeless belief—clouds of gloom—drifted, paled, vanished in glorious light. An exquisite rose flush—a glow—shone from her face as she slowly began to rise from her knees. A spirit uplifted her. All that she had held as base dropped from her.

Venters watched her in joy too deep for words. By it he divined something of what Lassiter's revelation meant to Bess, but he knew he could only faintly understand. That moment when she seemed to be lifted by some spiritual transfiguration was the most beautiful moment of his life. She stood with parted, quivering lips, with hands tightly clasping the locket to her heaving breast. A new conscious pride of worth dignified the old wild, free grace and poise.

"Uncle Jim!" she said, tremulously, with a different smile from any Venters had ever seen on her face.

Lassiter took her into his arms.

"I reckon. It's powerful fine to hear that," replied Lassiter, unsteadily.

Venters, feeling his eyes grow hot and wet, turned away, and found himself looking at Jane Withersteen. He had almost forgotten her presence. Tenderness and sympathy were fast hiding traces of her agitation. Venters read her mind—felt the reaction of her noble heart—saw the joy she was beginning to feel at the happiness of others. And suddenly blinded, choked by his emotions, he turned from her also. He knew what she would do presently; she would make some magnificent amend for her anger; she would give some manifestation of her love; probably all in a moment, as she had loved Milly Erne, so would she love Elizabeth Erne.

"'Pears to me, folks, that we'd better talk a little serious now," remarked Lassiter, at length. "Time flies."

"You're right," replied Venters, instantly. "I'd forgotten time—place—danger. Lassiter, you're riding away. Jane's leaving Withersteen House?"

"Forever," replied Jane.

"I fired Withersteen House," said Lassiter.

"Dyer?" questioned Venters, sharply.

"I reckon where Dyer's gone there won't be any kidnappin' of girls."

"Ah! I knew it. I told Judkins—And Tull?" went on Venters, passionately.

"Tull wasn't around when I broke loose. By now he's likely on our trail with his riders."

"Lassiter, you're going into the Pass to hide till all this storm blows over?"

"I reckon that's Jane's idea. I'm thinkin' the storm'll be a powerful long time blowin' over. I was comin' to join you in Surprise Valley. You'll go back now with me?"

"No. I want to take Bess out of Utah. Lassiter, Bess found gold in the valley. We've a saddle-bag full of gold. If we can reach Sterling—"

"Man! how're you ever goin' to do that? Sterlin' is a hundred miles."

"My plan is to ride on, keeping sharp lookout. Somewhere up the trail we'll take to the sage and go round Cottonwoods and then hit the trail again."

"It's a bad plan. You'll kill the burros in two days."

"Then we'll walk."

"That's more bad an' worse. Better go back down the Pass with me."

"Lassiter, this girl has been hidden all her life in that lonely place," went on Venters. "Oldring's men are hunting me. We'd not be safe there any longer. Even if we would be I'd take this chance to get her out. I want to marry her. She shall have some of the pleasures of life—see cities and people. We've gold—we'll be rich. Why, life opens sweet for both of us. And, by Heaven! I'll get her out or lose my life in the attempt!"

"I reckon if you go on with them burros you'll lose your life all right. Tull will have riders all over this sage. You can't get out on them burros. It's a fool idea. That's not doin' best by the girl. Come with me en' take chances on the rustlers."

Lassiter's cool argument made Venters waver, not in determination to go, but in hope of success.

"Bess, I want you to know. Lassiter says the trip's almost useless now. I'm afraid he's right. We've got about one chance in a hundred to go through. Shall we take it? Shall we go on?"

"We'll go on," replied Bess.

"That settles it, Lassiter."

Lassiter spread wide his hands, as if to signify he could do no more, and his face clouded.

Venters felt a touch on his elbow. Jane stood beside him with a hand on his arm. She was smiling. Something radiated from her, and like an electric current accelerated the motion of his blood.

"Bern, you'd be right to die rather than not take Elizabeth out of Utah—out of this wild country. You must do it. You'll show her the great world, with all its wonders. Think how little she has seen! Think what delight is in store for her! You have gold, You will be free; you will make her happy. What a glorious prospect! I share it with you. I'll think of you—dream of you—pray for you."

"Thank you, Jane," replied Venters, trying to steady his voice. "It does look bright. Oh, if we were only across that wide, open waste of sage!"

"Bern, the trip's as good as made. It'll be safe—easy. It'll be a glorious ride," she said, softly.

Venters stared. Had Jane's troubles made her insane? Lassiter, too, acted queerly, all at once beginning to turn his sombrero round in hands that actually shook.

"You are a rider. She is a rider. This will be the ride of your lives," added Jane, in that same soft undertone, almost as if she were musing to herself.

"Jane!" he cried.

"I give you Black Star and Night!"

"Black Star and Night!" he echoed.

"It's done. Lassiter, put our saddle-bags on the burros."

Only when Lassiter moved swiftly to execute her bidding did Venters's clogged brain grasp at literal meanings. He leaped to catch Lassiter's busy hands.

"No, no! What are you doing?" he demanded, in a kind of fury. "I won't take her racers. What do you think I am? It'd be monstrous. Lassiter! stop it, I say!... You've got her to save. You've miles and miles to go. Tull is trailing you. There are rustlers in the Pass. Give me back that saddle-bag!"

"Son—cool down," returned Lassiter, in a voice he might have used to a child. But the grip with which he tore away Venters's grasping hands was that of a giant. "Listen—you fool boy! Jane's sized up the situation. The burros'll do for us. We'll sneak along an' hide. I'll take your dogs an' your rifle. Why, it's the trick. The blacks are yours, an' sure as I can throw a gun you're goin' to ride safe out of the sage."

"Jane—stop him—please stop him," gasped Venters. "I've lost my strength. I can't do—anything. This is hell for me! Can't you see that? I've ruined you—it was through me you lost all. You've only Black Star and Night left. You love these horses. Oh! I know how you must love them now! And—you're trying to give them to me. To help me out of Utah! To save the girl I love!"

"That will be my glory."

Then in the white, rapt face, in the unfathomable eyes, Venters saw Jane Withersteen in a supreme moment. This moment was one wherein she reached up to the height for which her noble soul had ever yearned. He, after disrupting the calm tenor of her peace, after bringing down on her head the implacable hostility of her churchmen, after teaching her a bitter lesson of life—he was to be her salvation. And he turned away again, this time shaken to the core of his soul. Jane Withersteen was the incarnation of selflessness. He experienced wonder and terror, exquisite pain and rapture. What were all the shocks life had dealt him compared to the thought of such loyal and generous friendship?

And instantly, as if by some divine insight, he knew himself in the remaking—tried, found wanting; but stronger, better, surer—and he wheeled to Jane Withersteen, eager, joyous, passionate, wild, exalted. He bent to her; he left tears and kisses on her hands.

"Jane, I—I can't find words—now," he said. "I'm beyond words. Only—I understand. And I'll take the blacks."

"Don't be losin' no more time," cut in Lassiter. "I ain't certain, but I think I seen a speck up the sage-slope. Mebbe I was mistaken. But, anyway, we must all be movin'. I've shortened the stirrups on Black Star. Put Bess on him."

Jane Withersteen held out her arms.

"Elizabeth Erne!" she cried, and Bess flew to her.

How inconceivably strange and beautiful it was for Venters to see Bess clasped to Jane Withersteen's breast!

Then he leaped astride Night.

"Venters, ride straight on up the slope," Lassiter was saying, "'an if you don't meet any riders keep on till you're a few miles from the village, then cut off in the sage an' go round to the trail. But you'll most likely meet riders with Tull. Jest keep right on till you're jest out of gunshot an' then make your cut-off into the sage. They'll ride after you, but it won't be no use. You can ride, an' Bess can ride. When you're out of reach turn on round to the west, an' hit the trail somewhere. Save the hosses all you can, but don't be afraid. Black Star and Night are good for a hundred miles before sundown, if you have to push them. You can get to Sterlin' by night if you want. But better make it along about to-morrow mornin'. When you get through the notch on the Glaze trail, swing to the right. You'll be able to see both Glaze an' Stone Bridge. Keep away from them villages. You won't run no risk of meetin' any of Oldrin's rustlers from Sterlin' on. You'll find water in them deep hollows north of the Notch. There's an old trail there, not much used, en' it leads to Sterlin'. That's your trail. An' one thing more. If Tull pushes you—or keeps on persistent-like, for a few miles—jest let the blacks out an' lose him an' his riders."

"Lassiter, may we meet again!" said Venters, in a deep voice.

"Son, it ain't likely—it ain't likely. Well, Bess Oldrin'—Masked Rider—Elizabeth Erne—now you climb on Black Star. I've heard you could ride. Well, every rider loves a good horse. An', lass, there never was but one that could beat Black Star."

"Ah, Lassiter, there never was any horse that could beat Black Star," said Jane, with the old pride.

"I often wondered—mebbe Venters rode out that race when he brought back the blacks. Son, was Wrangle the best hoss?"

"No, Lassiter," replied Venters. For this lie he had his reward in Jane's quick smile.

"Well, well, my hoss-sense ain't always right. An' here I'm talkin' a lot, wastin' time. It ain't so easy to find an' lose a pretty niece all in one hour! Elizabeth—good-by!"

"Oh, Uncle Jim!... Good-by!"

"Elizabeth Erne, be happy! Good-by," said Jane.

"Good-by—oh—good-by!" In lithe, supple action Bess swung up to Black Star's saddle.

"Jane Withersteen!... Good-by!" called Venters hoarsely.

"Bern—Bess—riders of the purple sage—good-by!"

22

RIDERS OF THE PURPLE SAGE

BLACK STAR AND NIGHT, answering to spur, swept swiftly westward along the white, slow-rising, sage-bordered trail. Venters heard a mournful howl from Ring, but Whitie was silent. The blacks settled into their fleet, long-striding gallop. The wind sweetly fanned Venters's hot face. From the summit of the first low-swelling ridge he looked back. Lassiter waved his hand; Jane waved her scarf. Venters replied by standing in his stirrups and holding high his sombrero. Then the dip of the ridge hid them. From the height of the next he turned once more. Lassiter, Jane, and the burros had disappeared. They had gone down into the Pass. Venters felt a sensation of irreparable loss.

"Bern—look!" called Bess, pointing up the long slope.

A small, dark, moving dot split the line where purple sage met blue sky. That dot was a band of riders.

"Pull the black, Bess."

They slowed from gallop to canter, then to trot. The fresh and eager horses did not like the check.

"Bern, Black Star has great eyesight."

"I wonder if they're Tull's riders. They might be rustlers. But it's all the same to us."

The black dot grew to a dark patch moving under low dust clouds. It grew all the time, though very slowly. There were long periods when it was in plain sight, and intervals when it dropped behind the sage. The blacks trotted for half an hour, for another half-hour, and still the moving patch appeared to stay on the horizon line. Gradually, however, as time passed, it began to enlarge, to creep down the slope, to encroach upon the intervening distance.

"Bess, what do you make them out?" asked Venters. "I don't think they're rustlers."

"They're sage-riders," replied Bess. "I see a white horse and several grays. Rustlers seldom ride any horses but bays and blacks."

"That white horse is Tull's. Pull the black, Bess. I'll get down and cinch up. We're in for some riding. Are you afraid?"

"Not now," answered the girl, smiling.

"You needn't be. Bess, you don't weigh enough to make Black Star know you're on him. I won't be able to stay with you. You'll leave Tull and his riders as if they were standing still."

"How about you?"

"Never fear. If I can't stay with you I can still laugh at Tull."

"Look, Bern! They've stopped on that ridge. They see us."

"Yes. But we're too far yet for them to make out who we are. They'll recognize the blacks first. We've passed most of the ridges and the thickest sage. Now, when I give the word, let Black Star go and ride!"

Venters calculated that a mile or more still intervened between them and the riders. They were approaching at a swift canter. Soon Venters recognized Tull's white horse, and concluded that the riders had likewise recognized Black Star and Night. But it would be impossible for Tull yet to see that the blacks were not ridden by Lassiter and Jane. Venters noted that Tull and the line of horsemen, perhaps ten or twelve in number, stopped several times and evidently looked hard down the slope. It must have been a puzzling circumstance for Tull. Venters laughed grimly at the thought of what Tull's rage would be when he finally discovered the trick. Venters meant to sheer out into the sage before Tull could possibly be sure who rode the blacks.

The gap closed to a distance of half a mile. Tull halted. His riders came up and formed a dark group around him. Venters thought he saw him wave his arms and was certain of it when the riders dashed into the sage, to right and left of the trail. Tull had anticipated just the move held in mind by Venters.

"Now Bess!" shouted Venters. "Strike north. Go round those riders and turn west."

Black Star sailed over the low sage, and in a few leaps got into his stride and was running. Venters spurred Night after him. It was hard going in the sage. The horses could run as well there, but keen eyesight and judgment must constantly be used by the riders in choosing ground. And continuous swerving from aisle to aisle between the brush, and leaping little washes and mounds of the pack-rats, and breaking through sage, made rough riding. When Venters had turned into a long aisle he had time to look up at Tull's riders. They were now strung out into an extended line riding northeast. And, as Venters and Bess were holding due north, this meant, if the horses of Tull and his riders had the speed and the staying power, they would head the blacks and turn them back down the slope. Tull's men were not saving their mounts; they were driving them desperately. Venters feared only an accident to Black Star or Night, and skilful riding would mitigate possibility of that. One glance ahead served to show him that Bess could pick a course through the sage as well as he. She looked neither back nor at the running riders, and bent forward over Black Star's neck and studied the ground ahead.

It struck Venters, presently, after he had glanced up from time to time, that Bess was drawing away from him as he had expected. He had, however, only thought of the light weight Black Star was carrying and of his superior speed; he saw now that the black was being ridden as never before, except when Jerry Card lost the race to Wrangle. How easily, gracefully, naturally, Bess sat her saddle! She could ride! Suddenly Venters remembered she had said she could ride. But he had not dreamed she was capable of such superb horsemanship. Then all at once, flashing over him, thrilling him, came the recollection that Bess was Oldring's Masked Rider.

He forgot Tull—the running riders—the race. He let Night have a free rein and felt him lengthen out to suit himself, knowing he would keep to Black Star's course, knowing that he had been chosen by the best rider now on the upland sage. For Jerry Card was dead. And fame had rivaled him with only one rider, and that was the slender girl who now swung so easily with Black Star's stride. Venters had abhorred her notoriety, but now he took passionate pride in her skill, her daring, her power over a horse. And he delved into his memory, recalling famous rides which he had heard related in the villages and round the camp-fires. Oldring's Masked Rider! Many times this strange rider, at once well known and unknown, had escaped pursuers by matchless riding. He had to run the gantlet of vigilantes down the main street of Stone Bridge, leaving dead horses and dead rustlers behind. He had jumped his horse over the Gerber Wash, a deep, wide ravine separating the fields of Glaze from the wild sage. He had been surrounded north of Sterling; and he had broken through the line. How often had been told the story of day stampedes, of night raids, of pursuit, and then how the Masked Rider, swift as the wind, was gone in the sage! A fleet, dark horse—a slender, dark form—a black mask—a driving run down the slope—a dot on the purple sage —a shadowy, muffled steed disappearing in the night!

And this Masked Rider of the uplands had been Elizabeth Erne!

The sweet sage wind rushed in Venters's face and sang a song in his ears. He heard the dull, rapid beat of Night's hoofs; he saw Black Star drawing away, farther and farther. He realized both horses were swinging to the west. Then gunshots in the rear reminded him of Tull. Venters looked back. Far to the side, dropping behind, trooped the riders. They were shooting. Venters saw no puffs or dust, heard no whistling bullets. He was out of range. When he looked back again Tull's riders had given up pursuit. The best they could do, no doubt, had been to get near enough to recognize who really rode the blacks. Venters saw Tull drooping in his saddle.

Then Venters pulled Night out of his running stride. Those few miles had scarcely warmed the black, but Venters wished to save him. Bess turned, and, though she was far away, Venters caught the white glint of her waving hand. He held Night to a trot and rode on, seeing Bess and Black Star, and the sloping upward stretch of sage, and from time to time the receding black riders behind. Soon they disappeared behind a ridge, and he turned no more. They would go back to Lassiter's trail and follow it, and follow in vain. So Venters rode on, with the wind growing sweeter to taste and smell, and the purple sage richer and the sky bluer in his sight; and the song in his ears ringing. By and by Bess halted to wait for him, and he knew she had come to the trail. When he reached her it was to smile at sight of her standing with arms round Black Star's neck.

"Oh, Bern! I love him!" she cried. "He's beautiful; he knows; and how he can run! I've had fast horses. But Black Star!... Wrangle never beat him!"

"I'm wondering if I didn't dream that. Bess, the blacks are grand. What it must have cost Jane—ah!—well, when we get out of this wild country with Star and Night, back to my old home in Illinois, we'll buy a beautiful farm with meadows and springs and cool shade. There we'll turn the horses free—free to roam and browse and drink—never to feel a spur again— never to be ridden!"

"I would like that," said Bess.

They rested. Then, mounting, they rode side by side up the white trail. The sun rose higher behind them. Far to the left a low line of green marked the site of Cottonwoods. Venters looked once and looked no more. Bess gazed only straight ahead. They put the blacks to the long, swinging rider's canter, and at times pulled them to a trot, and occasionally to a walk. The hours passed, the miles slipped behind, and the wall of rock loomed in the fore. The Notch opened wide. It was a rugged, stony pass, but with level and open trail, and Venters and Bess ran the blacks through it. An old trail led off to the right, taking the line of the wall, and this Venters knew to be the trail mentioned by Lassiter.

The little hamlet, Glaze, a white and green patch in the vast waste of purple, lay miles down a slope much like the Cottonwoods slope, only this descended to the west. And miles farther west a faint green spot marked the location of Stone Bridge. All the rest of that world was seemingly smooth, undulating sage, with no ragged lines of canyons to accentuate its wildness.

"Bess, we're safe—we're free!" said Venters. "We're alone on the sage. We're half way to Sterling."

"Ah! I wonder how it is with Lassiter and Miss Withersteen."

"Never fear, Bess. He'll outwit Tull. He'll get away and hide her safely. He might climb into Surprise Valley, but I don't think he'll go so far."

"Bern, will we ever find any place like our beautiful valley?"

"No. But, dear, listen. Well go back some day, after years—ten years. Then we'll be forgotten. And our valley will be just as we left it."

"What if Balancing Rock falls and closes the outlet to the Pass?"

"I've thought of that. I'll pack in ropes and ropes. And if the outlet's closed we'll climb up the cliffs and over them to the valley and go down on rope ladders. It could be done. I know just where to make the climb, and I'll never forget."

"Oh yes, let us go back!"

"It's something sweet to look forward to. Bess, it's like all the future looks to me."

"Call me—Elizabeth," she said, shyly.

"Elizabeth Erne! It's a beautiful name. But I'll never forget Bess. Do you know—have you thought that very soon—by this time to-morrow—you will be Elizabeth Venters?"

So they rode on down the old trail. And the sun sloped to the west, and a golden sheen lay on the sage. The hours sped now; the afternoon waned. Often they rested the horses. The glisten of a pool of water in a hollow caught Venters's eye, and here he unsaddled the blacks and let them roll and drink and browse. When he and Bess rode up out of the hollow the sun was low, a crimson ball, and the valley seemed veiled in purple fire and smoke. It was that short time when the sun appeared to rest before setting, and silence, like a cloak of invisible life, lay heavy on all that shimmering world of sage.

They watched the sun begin to bury its red curve under the dark horizon.

"We'll ride on till late," he said. "Then you can sleep a little, while I watch and graze the horses. And we'll ride into Sterling early to-morrow. We'll be married!... We'll be in time to catch the stage. We'll tie Black Star and Night behind—and then—for a country not wild and terrible like this!"

"Oh, Bern!... But look! The sun is setting on the sage—the last time for us till we dare come again to the Utah border. Ten years! Oh, Bern, look, so you will never forget!"

Slumbering, fading purple fire burned over the undulating sage ridges. Long streaks and bars and shafts and spears fringed the far western slope. Drifting, golden veils mingled with low, purple shadows. Colors and shades changed in slow, wondrous transformation.

Suddenly Venters was startled by a low, rumbling roar—so low that it was like the roar in a sea-shell.

"Bess, did you hear anything?" he whispered.

"No."

"Listen!... Maybe I only imagined—Ah!"

Out of the east or north from remote distance, breathed an infinitely low, continuously long sound—deep, weird, detonating, thundering, deadening—dying.

23

THE FALL OF BALANCING ROCK

THROUGH TEAR-BLURRED sight Jane Withersteen watched Venters and Elizabeth Erne and the black racers disappear over the ridge of sage.

"They're gone!" said Lassiter. "An' they're safe now. An' there'll never be a day of their comin' happy lives but what they'll remember Jane Withersteen an'—an' Uncle Jim!... I reckon, Jane, we'd better be on our way."

The burros obediently wheeled and started down the break with little cautious steps, but Lassiter had to leash the whining dogs and lead them. Jane felt herself bound in a feeling that was neither listlessness nor indifference, yet which rendered her incapable of interest. She was still strong in body, but emotionally tired. That hour at the entrance to Deception Pass had been the climax of her suffering—the flood of her wrath—the last of her sacrifice—the supremacy of her love—and the attainment of peace. She thought that if she had little Fay she would not ask any more of life.

Like an automaton she followed Lassiter down the steep trail of dust and bits of weathered stone; and when the little slides moved with her or piled around her knees she experienced no alarm. Vague relief came to her in the sense of being enclosed between dark stone walls, deep hidden from the glare of sun, from the glistening sage. Lassiter lengthened the stirrup straps on one of the burros and bade her mount and ride close to him. She was to keep the burro from cracking his little hard hoofs on stones. Then she was riding on between dark, gleaming walls. There were quiet and rest and coolness in this canyon. She noted indifferently that they passed close under shady, bulging shelves of cliff, through patches of grass and sage and thicket and groves of slender trees, and over white, pebbly washes, and around masses of broken rock. The burros trotted tirelessly; the dogs, once more free, pattered tirelessly; and Lassiter led on with never a stop, and at every open place he looked back. The shade under the walls gave place to sunlight. And presently they came to a dense thicket of slender trees, through which they passed to rich, green grass and water. Here Lassiter rested the burros for a little while, but he was restless, uneasy, silent, always listening, peering under the trees. She dully reflected that enemies were behind them—before them; still the thought awakened no dread or concern or interest.

At his bidding she mounted and rode on close to the heels of his burro. The canyon narrowed; the walls lifted their rugged rims higher; and the sun shone down hot from the center of the blue stream of sky above. Lassiter traveled slower, with more exceeding care as to the ground he chose, and he kept speaking low to the dogs. They were now hunting-dogs —keen, alert, suspicious, sniffing the warm breeze. The monotony of the yellow walls broke in change of color and smooth surface, and the rugged outline of rims grew craggy. Splits appeared in deep breaks, and gorges running at right angles, and then the Pass opened wide at a junction of intersecting canyons.

Lassiter dismounted, led his burro, called the dogs close, and proceeded at snail pace through dark masses of rock and dense thickets under the left wall. Long he watched and listened before venturing to cross the mouths of side canyons. At length he halted, fled his burro, lifted a warning hand to Jane, and then slipped away among the boulders, and, followed by the stealthy dogs, disappeared from sight. The time he remained absent was neither short nor long to Jane Withersteen.

When he reached her side again he was pale, and his lips were set in a hard line, and his gray eyes glittered coldly. Bidding her dismount, he led the burros into a covert of stones and cedars, and tied them.

"Jane, I've run into the fellers I've been lookin' for, an' I'm goin' after them," he said.

"Why?" she asked.

"I reckon I won't take time to tell you."

"Couldn't we slip by without being seen?"

"Likely enough. But that ain't my game. An' I'd like to know, in case I don't come back, what you'll do."

"What can I do?"

"I reckon you can go back to Tull. Or stay in the Pass an' be taken off by rustlers. Which'll you do?"

"I don't know. I can't think very well. But I believe I'd rather be taken off by rustlers."

Lassiter sat down, put his head in his hands, and remained for a few moments in what appeared to be deep and painful thought. When he lifted his face it was haggard, lined, cold as sculptured marble.

"I'll go. I only mentioned that chance of my not comin' back. I'm pretty sure to come."

"Need you risk so much? Must you fight more? Haven't you shed enough blood?"

"I'd like to tell you why I'm goin'," he continued, in coldness he had seldom used to her. She remarked it, but it was the same to her as if he had spoken with his old gentle warmth. "But I reckon I won't. Only, I'll say that mercy an' goodness, such as is in you, though they're the grand things in human nature, can't be lived up to on this Utah border. Life's hell out here. You think—or you used to think—that your religion made this life heaven. Mebbe them scales on your eyes has dropped now. Jane, I wouldn't have you no different, an' that's why I'm going to try to hide you somewhere in this Pass. I'd like to hide many more women, for I've come to see there are more like you among your people. An' I'd like you to see jest how hard an' cruel this border life is. It's bloody. You'd think churches an' churchmen would make it better. They make it worse. You give names to things—bishops, elders, ministers, Mormonism, duty, faith, glory. You dream—or you're driven mad. I'm a man, an' I know. I name fanatics, followers, blind women, oppressors, thieves, ranchers, rustlers, riders. An' we have—what you've lived through these last months. It can't be helped. But it can't last always. An' remember this—some day the border'll be better, cleaner, for the ways of men like Lassiter!"

She saw him shake his tall form erect, look at her strangely and steadfastly, and then, noiselessly, stealthily slip away amid the rocks and trees. Ring and Whitie, not being bidden to follow, remained with Jane. She felt extreme weariness, yet somehow it did not seem to be of her body. And she sat down in the shade and tried to think. She saw a creeping lizard, cactus flowers, the drooping burros, the resting dogs, an eagle high over a yellow crag. Once the meanest flower, a color, the flight of the bee, or any living thing had given her deepest joy. Lassiter had gone off, yielding to his incurable blood lust, probably to his own death; and she was sorry, but there was no feeling in her sorrow.

Suddenly from the mouth of the canyon just beyond her rang out a clear, sharp report of a rifle. Echoes clapped. Then followed a piercingly high yell of anguish, quickly breaking. Again echoes clapped, in grim imitation. Dull revolver shots—hoarse yells— pound of hoofs—shrill neighs of horses—commingling of echoes—and again silence! Lassiter must be busily engaged, thought Jane, and no chill trembled over her, no blanching tightened her skin. Yes, the border was a bloody place. But life had always been bloody. Men were blood-spillers. Phases of the history of the world flashed through her mind—Greek and Roman wars, dark, mediaeval times, the crimes in the name of religion. On sea, on land, everywhere—shooting, stabbing, cursing, clashing, fighting men! Greed, power, oppression, fanaticism, love, hate, revenge, justice, freedom—for these, men killed one another.

She lay there under the cedars, gazing up through the delicate lacelike foliage at the blue sky, and she thought and wondered and did not care.

More rattling shots disturbed the noonday quiet. She heard a sliding of weathered rock, a hoarse shout of warning, a yell of alarm, again the clear, sharp crack of the rifle, and another cry that was a cry of death. Then rifle reports pierced a dull volley of revolver shots. Bullets whizzed over Jane's hiding-place; one struck a stone and whined away in the air. After that, for a time, succeeded desultory shots; and then they ceased under long, thundering fire from heavier guns.

Sooner or later, then, Jane heard the cracking of horses' hoofs on the stones, and the sound came nearer and nearer. Silence intervened until Lassiter's soft, jingling step assured her of his approach. When he appeared he was covered with blood.

"All right, Jane," he said. "I come back. An' don't worry."

With water from a canteen he washed the blood from his face and hands.

"Jane, hurry now. Tear my scarf in two, en' tie up these places. That hole through my hand is some inconvenient, worse 'n this at over my ear. There—you're doin' fine! Not a bit nervous—no tremblin'. I reckon I ain't done your courage justice. I'm glad you're brave jest now—you'll need to be. Well, I was hid pretty good, enough to keep them from shootin' me deep, but they was slingin' lead close all the time. I used up all the rifle shells, an' en I went after them. Mebbe you heard. It was then I got hit. Had to use up every shell in my own gun, an' they did, too, as I seen. Rustlers an' Mormons, Jane! An' now I'm packin' five bullet holes in my carcass, an' guns without shells. Hurry, now."

He unstrapped the saddle-bags from the burros, slipped the saddles and let them lie, turned the burros loose, and, calling the dogs, led the way through stones and cedars to an open where two horses stood.

"Jane, are you strong?" he asked.

"I think so. I'm not tired," Jane replied.

"I don't mean that way. Can you bear up?"

"I think I can bear anything."

"I reckon you look a little cold an' thick. So I'm preparin' you."

"For what?"

"I didn't tell you why I jest had to go after them fellers. I couldn't tell you. I believe you'd have died. But I can tell you now—if you'll bear up under a shock?"

"Go on, my friend."

"I've got little Fay! Alive—bad hurt—but she'll live!"

Jane Withersteen's dead-locked feeling, rent by Lassiter's deep, quivering voice, leaped into an agony of sensitive life.

"Here," he added, and showed her where little Fay lay on the grass.

Unable to speak, unable to stand, Jane dropped on her knees. By that long, beautiful golden hair Jane recognized the beloved Fay. But Fay's loveliness was gone. Her face was drawn and looked old with grief. But she was not dead—her heart beat—and Jane Withersteen gathered strength and lived again.

"You see I jest had to go after Fay," Lassiter was saying, as he knelt to bathe her little pale face. "But I reckon I don't want no more choices like the one I had to make. There was a crippled feller in that bunch, Jane. Mebbe Venters crippled him. Anyway, that's why they were holding up here. I seen little Fay first thing, en' was hard put to it to figure out a way to get her. An' I wanted hosses, too. I had to take chances. So I crawled close to their camp. One feller jumped a hoss with little Fay, an' when I shot him, of course she dropped. She's stunned an' bruised—she fell right on her head. Jane, she's comin' to! She ain't bad hurt!"

Fay's long lashes fluttered; her eyes opened. At first they seemed glazed over. They looked dazed by pain. Then they quickened, darkened, to shine with intelligence—bewilderment—memory—and sudden wonderful joy.

"Muvver—Jane!" she whispered.

"Oh, little Fay, little Fay!" cried Jane, lifting, clasping the child to her.

"Now, we've got to rustle!" said Lassiter, in grim coolness. "Jane, look down the Pass!"

Across the mounds of rock and sage Jane caught sight of a band of riders filing out of the narrow neck of the Pass; and in the lead was a white horse, which, even at a distance of a mile or more, she knew.

"Tull!" she almost screamed.

"I reckon. But, Jane, we've still got the game in our hands. They're ridin' tired hosses. Venters likely give them a chase. He wouldn't forget that. An' we've fresh hosses."

Hurriedly he strapped on the saddle-bags, gave quick glance to girths and cinches and stirrups, then leaped astride.

"Lift little Fay up," he said.

With shaking arms Jane complied.

"Get back your nerve, woman! This's life or death now. Mind that. Climb up! Keep your wits. Stick close to me. Watch where your hoss's goin' en' ride!"

Somehow Jane mounted; somehow found strength to hold the reins, to spur, to cling on, to ride. A horrible quaking, craven fear possessed her soul. Lassiter led the swift flight across the wide space, over washes, through sage, into a narrow canyon where the rapid clatter of hoofs rapped sharply from the walls. The wind roared in her ears; the gleaming cliffs swept by; trail and sage and grass moved under her. Lassiter's bandaged, blood-stained face turned to her; he shouted encouragement; he looked back down the Pass; he spurred his horse. Jane clung on, spurring likewise. And the horses settled from hard, furious gallop into a long-striding, driving run. She had never ridden at anything like that pace; desperately she tried to get the swing of the horse, to be of some help to him in that race, to see the best of the ground and guide him into it. But she failed of everything except to keep her seat the saddle, and to spur and spur. At times she closed her eyes unable to bear sight of Fay's golden curls streaming in the wind. She could not pray; she could not rail; she no longer cared for herself.

All of life, of good, of use in the world, of hope in heaven entered in Lassiter's ride with little Fay to safety. She would have tried to turn the iron-jawed brute she rode, she would have given herself to that relentless, dark-browed Tull. But she knew Lassiter would turn with her, so she rode on and on.

Whether that run was of moments or hours Jane Withersteen could not tell. Lassiter's horse covered her with froth that blew back in white streams. Both horses ran their limit, were allowed slow down in time to save them, and went on dripping, heaving, staggering.

"Oh, Lassiter, we must run—we must run!"

He looked back, saying nothing. The bandage had blown from his head, and blood trickled down his face. He was bowing under the strain of injuries, of the ride, of his burden. Yet how cool and gay he looked—how intrepid!

The horses walked, trotted, galloped, ran, to fall again to walk. Hours sped or dragged. Time was an instant—an eternity. Jane Withersteen felt hell pursuing her, and dared not look back for fear she would fall from her horse.

"Oh, Lassiter! Is he coming?"

The grim rider looked over his shoulder, but said no word. Fay's golden hair floated on the breeze. The sun shone; the walls gleamed; the sage glistened. And then it seemed the sun vanished, the walls shaded, the sage paled. The horses walked—trotted—galloped—ran—to fall again to walk. Shadows gathered under shelving cliffs. The canyon turned, brightened, opened into a long, wide, wall-enclosed valley. Again the sun, lowering in the west, reddened the sage. Far ahead round, scrawled stone appeared to block the Pass.

"Bear up, Jane, bear up!" called Lassiter. "It's our game, if you don't weaken."

"Lassiter! Go on—alone! Save little Fay!"

"Only with you!"

"Oh!—I'm a coward—a miserable coward! I can't fight or think or hope or pray! I'm lost! Oh, Lassiter, look back! Is he coming? I'll not—hold out—"

"Keep your breath, woman, an' ride not for yourself or for me, but for Fay!"

A last breaking run across the sage brought Lassiter's horse to a walk.

"He's done," said the rider.

"Oh, no—no!" moaned Jane.

"Look back, Jane, look back. Three—four miles we've come across this valley, en' no Tull yet in sight. Only a few more miles!"

Jane looked back over the long stretch of sage, and found the narrow gap in the wall, out of which came a file of dark horses with a white horse in the lead. Sight of the riders acted upon Jane as a stimulant. The weight of cold, horrible terror lessened. And, gazing forward at the dogs, at Lassiter's limping horse, at the blood on his face, at the rocks growing nearer, last at Fay's golden hair, the ice left her veins, and slowly, strangely, she gained hold of strength that she believed would see her to the safety Lassiter promised. And, as she gazed, Lassiter's horse stumbled and fell.

He swung his leg and slipped from the saddle.

"Jane, take the child," he said, and lifted Fay up. Jane clasped her arms suddenly strong. "They're gainin'," went on Lassiter, as he watched the pursuing riders. "But we'll beat 'em yet."

Turning with Jane's bridle in his hand, he was about to start when he saw the saddle-bag on the fallen horse.

"I've jest about got time," he muttered, and with swift fingers that did not blunder or fumble he loosened the bag and threw it over his shoulder. Then he started to run, leading Jane's horse, and he ran, and trotted, and walked, and ran again. Close ahead now Jane saw a rise of bare rock. Lassiter reached it, searched along the base, and, finding a low place, dragged the weary horse up and over round, smooth stone. Looking backward, Jane saw Tull's white horse not a mile distant, with riders strung out in a long line behind him. Looking forward, she saw more valley to the right, and to the left a towering cliff. Lassiter pulled the horse and kept on.

Little Fay lay in her arms with wide-open eyes—eyes which were still shadowed by pain, but no longer fixed, glazed in terror. The golden curls blew across Jane's lips; the little hands feebly clasped her arm; a ghost of a troubled, trustful smile hovered round the sweet lips. And Jane Withersteen awoke to the spirit of a lioness.

Lassiter was leading the horse up a smooth slope toward cedar trees of twisted and bleached appearance. Among these he halted.

"Jane, give me the girl en' get down," he said. As if it wrenched him he unbuckled the empty black guns with a strange air of finality. He then received Fay in his arms and stood a moment looking backward. Tull's white horse mounted the ridge of round stone, and several bays or blacks followed. "I wonder what he'll think when he sees them empty guns. Jane, bring your saddle-bag and climb after me."

A glistening, wonderful bare slope, with little holes, swelled up and up to lose itself in a frowning yellow cliff. Jane closely watched her steps and climbed behind Lassiter. He moved slowly. Perhaps he was only husbanding his strength. But she saw drops of blood on the stone, and then she knew. They climbed and climbed without looking back. Her breast labored; she began to feel as if little points of fiery steel were penetrating her side into her lungs. She heard the panting of Lassiter and the quicker panting of the dogs.

"Wait—here," he said.

Before her rose a bulge of stone, nicked with little cut steps, and above that a corner of yellow wall, and overhanging that a vast, ponderous cliff.

The dogs pattered up, disappeared round the corner. Lassiter mounted the steps with Fay, and he swayed like a drunken man, and he too disappeared. But instantly he returned alone, and half ran, half slipped down to her.

Then from below pealed up hoarse shouts of angry men. Tull and several of his riders had reached the spot where Lassiter had parted with his guns.

"You'll need that breath—mebbe!" said Lassiter, facing downward, with glittering eyes.

"Now, Jane, the last pull," he went on. "Walk up them little steps. I'll follow an' steady you. Don't think. Jest go. Little Fay's above. Her eyes are open. She jest said to me, 'Where's muvver Jane?'"

Without a fear or a tremor or a slip or a touch of Lassiter's hand Jane Withersteen walked up that ladder of cut steps.

He pushed her round the corner of the wall. Fay lay, with wide staring eyes, in the shade of a gloomy wall. The dogs waited. Lassiter picked up the child and turned into a dark cleft. It zigzagged. It widened. It opened. Jane was amazed at a wonderfully smooth and steep incline leading up between ruined, splintered, toppling walls. A red haze from the setting sun filled this passage. Lassiter climbed with slow, measured steps, and blood dripped from him to make splotches on the white stone. Jane tried not to step in his blood, but was compelled, for she found no other footing. The saddle-bag began to drag her down; she gasped for breath, she thought her heart was bursting. Slower, slower yet the rider climbed, whistling as he breathed. The incline widened. Huge pinnacles and monuments of stone stood alone, leaning fearfully. Red sunset haze shone through cracks where the wall had split. Jane did not look high, but she felt the overshadowing of broken rims above. She felt that it was a fearful, menacing place. And she climbed on in heartrending effort. And she fell beside Lassiter and Fay at the top of the incline in a narrow, smooth divide.

He staggered to his feet—staggered to a huge, leaning rock that rested on a small pedestal. He put his hand on it—the hand that had been shot through—and Jane saw blood drip from the ragged hole. Then he fell.

"Jane—I—can't—do—it!" he whispered.

"What?"

"Roll the—stone!... All my—life I've loved—to roll stones—en' now I—can't!"

"What of it? You talk strangely. Why roll that stone?"

"I planned to—fetch you here—to roll this stone. See! It'll smash the crags—loosen the walls—close the outlet!"

As Jane Withersteen gazed down that long incline, walled in by crumbling cliffs, awaiting only the slightest jar to make them fall asunder, she saw Tull appear at the bottom and begin to climb. A rider followed him—another—and another.

"See! Tull! The riders!"

"Yes—they'll get us—now."

"Why? Haven't you strength left to roll the stone?"

"Jane—it ain't that—I've lost my nerve!"

"You!... Lassiter!"

"I wanted to roll it—meant to—but I—can't. Venters's valley is down behind here. We could—live there. But if I roll the stone—we're shut in for always. I don't dare. I'm thinkin' of you!"

"Lassiter! Roll the stone!" she cried.

He arose, tottering, but with set face, and again he placed the bloody hand on the Balancing Rock. Jane Withersteen gazed from him down the passageway. Tull was climbing. Almost, she thought, she saw his dark, relentless face. Behind him more riders climbed. What did they mean for Fay—for Lassiter—for herself?

"Roll the stone!... Lassiter, I love you!"

Under all his deathly pallor, and the blood, and the iron of seared cheek and lined brow, worked a great change. He placed both hands on the rock and then leaned his shoulder there and braced his powerful body.

ROLL THE STONE!

It stirred, it groaned, it grated, it moved, and with a slow grinding, as of wrathful relief, began to lean. It had waited ages to fall, and now was slow in starting. Then, as if suddenly instinct with life, it leaped hurtlingly down to alight on the steep incline, to bound more swiftly into the air, to gather momentum, to plunge into the lofty leaning crag below. The crag thundered into atoms. A wave of air—a splitting shock! Dust shrouded the sunset red of shaking rims; dust shrouded Tull as he fell on his knees with uplifted arms. Shafts and monuments and sections of wall fell majestically.

From the depths there rose a long-drawn rumbling roar. The outlet to Deception Pass closed forever.

THE LIGHT OF WESTERN STARS

❧ I ❧

A GENTLEMAN OF THE RANGE

WHEN MADELINE HAMMOND stepped from the train at El Cajon, New Mexico, it was nearly midnight, and her first impression was of a huge dark space of cool, windy emptiness, strange and silent, stretching away under great blinking white stars.

"Miss, there's no one to meet you," said the conductor, rather anxiously.

"I wired my brother," she replied. "The train being so late—perhaps he grew tired of waiting. He will be here presently. But, if he should not come—surely I can find a hotel?"

"There's lodgings to be had. Get the station agent to show you. If you'll excuse me—this is no place for a lady like you to be alone at night. It's a rough little town—mostly Mexicans, miners, cowboys. And they carouse a lot. Besides, the revolution across the border has stirred up some excitement along the line. Miss, I guess it's safe enough, if you—"

"Thank you. I am not in the least afraid."

As the train started to glide away Miss Hammond walked towards the dimly lighted station. As she was about to enter she encountered a Mexican with sombrero hiding his features and a blanket mantling his shoulders.

"Is there any one here to meet Miss Hammond?" she asked.

"No sabe, Senora," he replied from under the muffling blanket, and he shuffled away into the shadow.

She entered the empty waiting-room. An oil-lamp gave out a thick yellow light. The ticket window was open, and through it she saw there was neither agent nor operator in the little compartment. A telegraph instrument clicked faintly.

Madeline Hammond stood tapping a shapely foot on the floor, and with some amusement contrasted her reception in El Cajon with what it was when she left a train at the Grand Central. The only time she could remember ever having been alone like this was once when she had missed her maid and her train at a place outside of Versailles—an adventure that had been a novel and delightful break in the prescribed routine of her much-chaperoned life. She crossed the waiting-room to a window and, holding aside her veil, looked out. At first she could descry only a few dim lights, and these blurred in her sight. As her eyes grew accustomed to the darkness she saw a superbly built horse standing near the window.

Beyond was a bare square. Or, if it was a street, it was the widest one Madeline had ever seen. The dim lights shone from low, flat buildings. She made out the dark shapes of many horses, all standing motionless with drooping heads. Through a hole in the window-glass came a cool breeze, and on it breathed a sound that struck coarsely upon her ear—a discordant mingling of laughter and shout, and the tramp of boots to the hard music of a phonograph.

"Western revelry," mused Miss Hammond, as she left the window. "Now, what to do? I'll wait here. Perhaps the station agent will return soon, or Alfred will come for me."

As she sat down to wait she reviewed the causes which accounted for the remarkable situation in which she found herself. That Madeline Hammond should be alone, at a late hour, in a dingy little Western railroad station, was indeed extraordinary.

The close of her debutante year had been marred by the only unhappy experience of her life—the disgrace of her brother and his leaving home. She dated the beginning of a certain thoughtful habit of mind from that time, and a dissatisfaction with the brilliant life society offered her. The change had been so gradual that it was permanent before she realized it. For a while an active outdoor life—golf, tennis, yachting—kept this realization from becoming morbid introspection. There came a time when even these lost charm for her, and then she believed she was indeed ill in mind. Travel did not help her.

There had been months of unrest, of curiously painful wonderment that her position, her wealth, her popularity no longer sufficed. She believed she had lived through the dreams and fancies of a girl to become a woman of the world. And she had gone on as before, a part of the glittering show, but no longer blind to the truth—that there was nothing in her luxurious life to make it significant.

Sometimes from the depths of her there flashed up at odd moments intimations of a future revolt. She remembered one evening at the opera when the curtain had risen upon a particularly well-done piece of stage scenery—a broad space of deep desolateness, reaching away under an infinitude of night sky, illumined by stars. The suggestion it brought of vast wastes of lonely, rugged earth, of a great, blue-arched vault of starry sky, pervaded her soul with a strange, sweet peace.

When the scene was changed she lost this vague new sense of peace, and she turned away from the stage in irritation. She looked at the long, curved tier of glittering boxes that represented her world. It was a distinguished and splendid world—the wealth, fashion, culture, beauty, and blood of a nation. She, Madeline Hammond, was a part of it. She smiled, she listened, she talked to the men who from time to time strolled into the Hammond box, and she felt that there was not a moment when she was natural, true to herself. She wondered why these people could not somehow, some way be different; but she could not tell what she wanted them to be. If they had been different they would not have fitted the place; indeed, they would not have been there at all. Yet she thought wistfully that they lacked something for her.

And suddenly realizing she would marry one of these men if she did not revolt, she had been assailed by a great weariness, an icy-sickening sense that life had palled upon her. She was tired of fashionable society. She was tired of polished, imperturbable men who sought only to please her. She was tired of being feted, admired, loved, followed, and importuned; tired of people; tired of houses, noise, ostentation, luxury. She was so tired of herself!

In the lonely distances and the passionless stars of boldly painted stage scenery she had caught a glimpse of something that stirred her soul. The feeling did not last. She could not call it back. She imagined that the very boldness of the scene had appealed to her; she divined that the man who painted it had found inspiration, joy, strength, serenity in rugged nature. And at last she knew what she needed—to be alone, to brood for long hours, to gaze out on lonely, silent, darkening stretches, to watch the stars, to face her soul, to find her real self.

Then it was she had first thought of visiting the brother who had gone West to cast his fortune with the cattlemen. As it happened, she had friends who were on the eve of starting for California, and she made a quick decision to travel with them. When she calmly announced her intention of going out West her mother had exclaimed in consternation; and her father, surprised into pathetic memory of the black sheep of the family, had stared at her with glistening eyes. "Why, Madeline! You want to see that wild boy!" Then he had reverted to the anger he still felt for his wayward son, and he had forbidden Madeline to go. Her mother forgot her haughty poise and dignity. Madeline, however, had exhibited a will she had never before been known to possess. She stood her ground even to reminding them that she was twenty-four and her own mistress. In the end she had prevailed, and that without betraying the real state of her mind.

Her decision to visit her brother had been too hurriedly made and acted upon for her to write him about it, and so she had telegraphed him from New York, and also, a day later, from Chicago, where her traveling friends had been delayed by illness. Nothing could have turned her back then. Madeline had planned to arrive in El Cajon on October 3d, her brother's birthday, and she had succeeded, though her arrival occurred at the twenty-fourth hour. Her train had been several hours late. Whether or not the message had reached Alfred's hands she had no means of telling, and the thing which concerned her now was the fact that she had arrived and he was not there to meet her.

It did not take long for thought of the past to give way wholly to the reality of the present.

"I hope nothing has happened to Alfred," she said to herself. "He was well, doing splendidly, the last time he wrote. To be sure, that was a good while ago; but, then, he never wrote often. He's all right. Pretty soon he'll come, and how glad I'll be! I wonder if he has changed."

As Madeline sat waiting in the yellow gloom she heard the faint, intermittent click of the telegraph instrument, the low hum of wires, the occasional stamp of an iron-shod hoof, and a distant vacant laugh rising above the sounds of the dance. These commonplace things were new to her. She became conscious of a slight quickening of her pulse. Madeline had only a limited knowledge of the West. Like all of her class, she had traveled Europe and had neglected America. A few letters from her brother had confused her already vague ideas of plains and mountains, as well as of cowboys and cattle. She had been astounded at the interminable distance she had traveled, and if there had been anything attractive to look at in all that journey she had passed it in the night. And here she sat in a dingy little station, with telegraph wires moaning a lonely song in the wind.

A faint sound like the rattling of thin chains diverted Madeline's attention. At first she imagined it was made by the telegraph wires. Then she heard a step. The door swung wide; a tall man entered, and with him came the clinking rattle. She realized then that the sound came from his spurs. The man was a cowboy, and his entrance recalled vividly to her that of Dustin Farnum in the first act of "The Virginian."

"Will you please direct me to a hotel?" asked Madeline, rising.

The cowboy removed his sombrero, and the sweep he made with it and the accompanying bow, despite their exaggeration, had a kind of rude grace. He took two long strides toward her.

"Lady, are you married?"

In the past Miss Hammond's sense of humor had often helped her to overlook critical exactions natural to her breeding. She kept silence, and she imagined it was just as well that her veil hid her face at the moment. She had been prepared to find cowboys rather striking, and she had been warned not to laugh at them.

This gentleman of the range deliberately reached down and took up her left hand. Before she recovered from her start of amaze he had stripped off her glove.

"Fine spark, but no wedding-ring," he drawled. "Lady, I'm glad to see you're not married."

He released her hand and returned the glove.

"You see, the only ho-tel in this here town is against boarding married women."

"Indeed?" said Madeline, trying to adjust her wits to the situation.

"It sure is," he went on. "Bad business for ho-tels to have married women. Keeps the boys away. You see, this isn't Reno."

Then he laughed rather boyishly, and from that, and the way he slouched on his sombrero, Madeline realized he was half drunk. As she instinctively recoiled she not only gave him a keener glance, but stepped into a position where a better light shone on his face. It was like red bronze, bold, raw, sharp. He laughed again, as if good-naturedly amused with himself, and the laugh scarcely changed the hard set of his features. Like that of all women whose beauty and charm had brought them much before the world, Miss Hammond's intuition had been developed until she had a delicate and exquisitely sensitive perception of the nature of men and of her effect upon them. This crude cowboy, under the influence of drink, had affronted her; nevertheless, whatever was in his mind, he meant no insult.

"I shall be greatly obliged if you will show me to the hotel," she said.

"Lady, you wait here," he replied, slowly, as if his thought did not come swiftly. "I'll go fetch the porter."

She thanked him, and as he went out, closing the door, she sat down in considerable relief. It occurred to her that she should have mentioned her brother's name. Then she fell to wondering what living with such uncouth cowboys had done to Alfred. He had been wild enough in college, and she doubted that any cowboy could have taught him much. She alone of her family had ever believed in any latent good in Alfred Hammond, and her faith had scarcely survived the two years of silence.

Waiting there, she again found herself listening to the moan of the wind through the wires. The horse outside began to pound with heavy hoofs, and once he whinnied. Then Madeline heard a rapid pattering, low at first and growing louder, which presently she recognized as the galloping of horses. She went to the window, thinking, hoping her brother had arrived. But as the clatter increased to a roar, shadows sped by—lean horses, flying manes and tails, sombreroed riders, all strange and wild in her sight. Recalling what the conductor had said, she was at some pains to quell her uneasiness. Dust-clouds shrouded the dim lights in the windows. Then out of the gloom two figures appeared, one tall, the other slight. The cowboy was returning with a porter.

Heavy footsteps sounded without, and lighter ones dragging along, and then suddenly the door rasped open, jarring the whole room. The cowboy entered, pulling a disheveled figure—that of a priest, a padre, whose mantle had manifestly been disarranged by the rude grasp of his captor. Plain it was that the padre was extremely terrified.

Madeline Hammond gazed in bewilderment at the little man, so pale and shaken, and a protest trembled upon her lips; but it was never uttered, for this half-drunken cowboy now appeared to be a cool, grim-smiling devil; and stretching out a long arm, he grasped her and swung her back to the bench.

"You stay there!" he ordered.

His voice, though neither brutal nor harsh nor cruel, had the unaccountable effect of making her feel powerless to move. No man had ever before addressed her in such a tone. It was the woman in her that obeyed—not the personality of proud Madeline Hammond.

The padre lifted his clasped hands as if supplicating for his life, and began to speak hurriedly in Spanish. Madeline did not understand the language. The cowboy pulled out a huge gun and brandished it in the priest's face. Then he lowered it, apparently to point it at the priest's feet. There was a red flash, and then a thundering report that stunned Madeline. The room filled with smoke and the smell of powder. Madeline did not faint or even shut her eyes, but she felt as if she were fast in a cold vise. When she could see distinctly through the smoke she experienced a sensation of immeasurable relief that the cowboy had not shot the padre. But he was still waving the gun, and now appeared to be dragging his victim toward her. What possibly could be the drunken fool's intention? This must be, this surely was a cowboy trick. She had a vague, swiftly flashing recollection of Alfred's first letters descriptive of the extravagant fun of cowboys. Then she vividly remembered a moving picture she had seen—cowboys playing a monstrous joke on a lone school-teacher. Madeline no sooner thought of it than she made certain her brother was introducing her to a little wild West amusement. She could scarcely believe it, yet it must be true. Alfred's old love of teasing her might have extended even to this outrage. Probably he stood just outside the door or window laughing at her embarrassment.

Anger checked her panic. She straightened up with what composure this surprise had left her and started for the door. But the cowboy barred her passage—grasped her arms. Then Madeline divined that her brother could not have any knowledge of this indignity. It was no trick. It was something that was happening, that was real, that threatened she knew not what. She tried to wrench free, feeling hot all over at being handled by this drunken brute. Poise, dignity, culture—all the acquired habits of character—fled before the instinct to fight. She was athletic. She fought. She struggled desperately. But he forced her back with hands of iron. She had never known a man could be so strong. And then it was the man's coolly smiling face, the paralyzing strangeness of his manner, more than his strength, that weakened Madeline until she sank trembling against the bench.

"What—do you—mean?" she panted.

"Dearie, ease up a little on the bridle," he replied, gaily.

Madeline thought she must be dreaming. She could not think clearly. It had all been too swift, too terrible for her to grasp. Yet she not only saw this man, but also felt his powerful presence. And the shaking priest, the haze of blue smoke, the smell of powder—these were not unreal.

Then close before her eyes burst another blinding red flash, and close at her ears bellowed another report. Unable to stand, Madeline slipped down onto the bench. Her drifting faculties refused clearly to record what transpired during the next few moments; presently, however, as her mind steadied somewhat, she heard, though as in a dream, the voice of the padre hurrying over strange words. It ceased, and then the cowboy's voice stirred her.

"Lady, say Si—Si. Say it—quick! Say it—Si!"

From sheer suggestion, a force irresistible at this moment when her will was clamped by panic, she spoke the word.

"And now, lady—so we can finish this properly—what's your name?"

Still obeying mechanically, she told him.

He stared for a while, as if the name had awakened associations in a mind somewhat befogged. He leaned back unsteadily. Madeline heard the expulsion of his breath, a kind of hard puff, not unusual in drunken men.

"What name?" he demanded.

"Madeline Hammond. I am Alfred Hammond's sister."

He put his hand up and brushed at an imaginary something before his eyes. Then he loomed over her, and that hand, now shaking a little, reached out for her veil. Before he could touch it, however, she swept it back, revealing her face.

"You're—not—Majesty Hammond?"

How strange—stranger than anything that had ever happened to her before—was it to hear that name on the lips of this cowboy! It was a name by which she was familiarly known, though only those nearest and dearest to her had the privilege of using it. And now it revived her dulled faculties, and by an effort she regained control of herself.

"You are Majesty Hammond," he replied; and this time he affirmed wonderingly rather than questioned.

Madeline rose and faced him.

"Yes, I am."

He slammed his gun back into its holster.

"Well, I reckon we won't go on with it, then."

"With what, sir? And why did you force me to say Si to this priest?"

"I reckon that was a way I took to show him you'd be willing to get married."

"Oh!... You—you!..." Words failed her.

This appeared to galvanize the cowboy into action. He grasped the padre and led him toward the door, cursing and threatening, no doubt enjoining secrecy. Then he pushed him across the threshold and stood there breathing hard and wrestling with himself.

"Here—wait—wait a minute, Miss—Miss Hammond," he said, huskily. "You could fall into worse company than mine—though I reckon you sure think not. I'm pretty drunk, but I'm—all right otherwise. Just wait—a minute."

She stood quivering and blazing with wrath, and watched this savage fight his drunkenness. He acted like a man who had been suddenly shocked into a rational state of mind, and he was now battling with himself to hold on to it. Madeline saw the dark, damp hair lift from his brows as he held it up to the cool wind. Above him she saw the white stars in the deep-blue sky, and they seemed as unreal to her as any other thing in this strange night. They were cold, brilliant, aloof, distant; and looking at them, she felt her wrath lessen and die and leave her calm.

The cowboy turned and began to talk.

"You see—I was pretty drunk," he labored. "There was a fiesta—and a wedding. I do fool things when I'm drunk. I made a fool bet I'd marry the first girl who came to town.... If you hadn't worn that veil—the fellows were joshing me—and Ed Linton was getting married— and everybody always wants to gamble.... I must have been pretty drunk."

After the one look at her when she had first put aside her veil he had not raised his eyes to her face. The cool audacity had vanished in what was either excessive emotion or the maudlin condition peculiar to some men when drunk. He could not stand still; perspiration collected in beads upon his forehead; he kept wiping his face with his scarf, and he breathed like a man after violent exertions.

"You see—I was pretty—" he began.

"Explanations are not necessary," she interrupted. "I am very tired—distressed. The hour is late. Have you the slightest idea what it means to be a gentleman?"

His bronzed face burned to a flaming crimson.

"Is my brother here—in town to-night?" Madeline went on.

"No. He's at his ranch."

"But I wired him."

"Like as not the message is over in his box at the P.O. He'll be in town to-morrow. He's shipping cattle for Stillwell."

"Meanwhile I must go to a hotel. Will you please—"

If he heard her last words he showed no evidence of it. A noise outside had attracted his attention. Madeline listened. Low voices of men, the softer liquid tones of a woman, drifted in through the open door. They spoke in Spanish, and the voices grew louder. Evidently the speakers were approaching the station. Footsteps crunching on gravel attested to this, and quicker steps, coming with deep tones of men in anger, told of a quarrel. Then the woman's voice, hurried and broken, rising higher, was eloquent of vain appeal.

The cowboy's demeanor startled Madeline into anticipation of something dreadful. She was not deceived. From outside came the sound of a scuffle—a muffled shot, a groan, the thud of a falling body, a woman's low cry, and footsteps padding away in rapid retreat.

Madeline Hammond leaned weakly back in her seat, cold and sick, and for a moment her ears throbbed to the tramp of the dancers across the way and the rhythm of the cheap music. Then into the open door-place flashed a girl's tragic face, lighted by dark eyes and framed by dusky hair. The girl reached a slim brown hand round the side of the door and held on as if to support herself. A long black scarf accentuated her gaudy attire.

"Senor—Gene!" she exclaimed; and breathless glad recognition made a sudden break in her terror.

"Bonita!" The cowboy leaped to her. "Girl! Are you hurt?"

"No, Senor."

He took hold of her. "I heard—somebody got shot. Was it Danny?"

"No, Senor."

"Did Danny do the shooting? Tell me, girl."

"No, Senor."

"I'm sure glad. I thought Danny was mixed up in that. He had Stillwell's money for the boys—I was afraid.... Say, Bonita, but you'll get in trouble. Who was with you? What did you do?"

"Senor Gene—they Don Carlos vaqueros—they quarrel over me. I only dance a leetle, smile a leetle, and they quarrel. I beg they be good—watch out for Sheriff Hawe... and now Sheriff Hawe put me in jail. I so frighten; he try make leetle love to Bonita once, and now he hate me like he hate Senor Gene."

"Pat Hawe won't put you in jail. Take my horse and hit the Peloncillo trail. Bonita, promise to stay away from El Cajon."

"Si, Senor."

He led her outside. Madeline heard the horse snort and champ his bit. The cowboy spoke low; only a few words were intelligible—"stirrups... wait... out of town... mountain... trail ... now ride!"

A moment's silence ensued, and was broken by a pounding of hoofs, a pattering of gravel. Then Madeline saw a big, dark horse run into the wide space. She caught a glimpse of wind-swept scarf and hair, a little form low down in the saddle. The horse was outlined in black against the line of dim lights. There was something wild and splendid in his flight.

Directly the cowboy appeared again in the doorway.

"Miss Hammond, I reckon we want to rustle out of here. Been bad goings-on. And there's a train due."

She hurried into the open air, not daring to look back or to either side. Her guide strode swiftly. She had almost to run to keep up with him. Many conflicting emotions confused her.

She had a strange sense of this stalking giant beside her, silent except for his jangling spurs. She had a strange feeling of the cool, sweet wind and the white stars. Was it only her disordered fancy, or did these wonderful stars open and shut? She had a queer, disembodied thought that somewhere in ages back, in another life, she had seen these stars. The night seemed dark, yet there was a pale, luminous light—a light from the stars—and she fancied it would always haunt her.

Suddenly aware that she had been led beyond the line of houses, she spoke:

"Where are you taking me?"

"To Florence Kingsley," he replied.

"Who is she?"

"I reckon she's your brother's best friend out here." Madeline kept pace with the cowboy for a few moments longer, and then she stopped. It was as much from necessity to catch her breath as it was from recurring fear. All at once she realized what little use her training had been for such an experience as this. The cowboy, missing her, came back the few intervening steps. Then he waited, still silent, looming beside her.

"It's so dark, so lonely," she faltered. "How do I know... what warrant can you give me that you—that no harm will befall me if I go farther?"

"None, Miss Hammond, except that I've seen your face."

✣ 2 ✣
A SECRET KEPT

BECAUSE OF THAT singular reply Madeline found faith to go farther with the cowboy. But at the moment she really did not think about what he had said. Any answer to her would have served if it had been kind. His silence had augmented her nervousness, compelling her to voice her fear. Still, even if he had not replied at all she would have gone on with him. She shuddered at the idea of returning to the station, where she believed there had been murder; she could hardly have forced herself to go back to those dim lights in the street; she did not want to wander around alone in the dark.

And as she walked on into the windy darkness, much relieved that he had answered as he had, reflecting that he had yet to prove his words true, she began to grasp the deeper significance of them. There was a revival of pride that made her feel that she ought to scorn to think at all about such a man. But Madeline Hammond discovered that thought was involuntary, that there were feelings in her never dreamed of before this night.

Presently Madeline's guide turned off the walk and rapped at a door of a low-roofed house.

"Hullo—who's there?" a deep voice answered.

"Gene Stewart," said the cowboy. "Call Florence—quick!"

Thump of footsteps followed, a tap on a door, and voices. Madeline heard a woman exclaim: "Gene! here when there's a dance in town! Something wrong out on the range." A light flared up and shone bright through a window. In another moment there came a patter of soft steps, and the door opened to disclose a woman holding a lamp.

"Gene! Al's not—"

"Al is all right," interrupted the cowboy.

Madeline had two sensations then—one of wonder at the note of alarm and love in the woman's voice, and the other of unutterable relief to be safe with a friend of her brother's.

"It's Al's sister—came on to-night's train," the cowboy was saying. "I happened to be at the station, and I've fetched her up to you."

Madeline came forward out of the shadow.

"Not—not really Majesty Hammond!" exclaimed Florence Kingsley. She nearly dropped the lamp, and she looked and looked, astounded beyond belief.

"Yes, I am really she," replied Madeline. "My train was late, and for some reason Alfred did not meet me. Mr.—Mr. Stewart saw fit to bring me to you instead of taking me to a hotel."

"Oh, I'm so glad to meet you," replied Florence, warmly. "Do come in. I'm so surprised, I forget my manners. Why, Al never mentioned your coming."

"He surely could not have received my messages," said Madeline, as she entered.

The cowboy, who came in with her satchel, had to stoop to enter the door, and, once in, he seemed to fill the room. Florence set the lamp down upon the table. Madeline saw a young woman with a smiling, friendly face, and a profusion of fair hair hanging down over her dressing-gown.

"Oh, but Al will be glad!" cried Florence. "Why, you are white as a sheet. You must be tired. What a long wait you had at the station! I heard the train come in hours ago as I was going to bed. That station is lonely at night. If I had known you were coming! Indeed, you are very pale. Are you ill?"

"No. Only I am very tired. Traveling so far by rail is harder than I imagined. I did have rather a long wait after arriving at the station, but I can't say that it was lonely."

Florence Kingsley searched Madeline's face with keen eyes, and then took a long, significant look at the silent Stewart. With that she deliberately and quietly closed a door leading into another room.

"Miss Hammond, what has happened?" She had lowered her voice.

"I do not wish to recall all that has happened," replied Madeline. "I shall tell Alfred, however, that I would rather have met a hostile Apache than a cowboy."

"Please don't tell Al that!" cried Florence. Then she grasped Stewart and pulled him close to the light. "Gene, you're drunk!"

"I was pretty drunk," he replied, hanging his head.

"Oh, what have you done?"

"Now, see here, Flo, I only—"

"I don't want to know. I'd tell it. Gene, aren't you ever going to learn decency? Aren't you ever going to stop drinking? You'll lose all your friends. Stillwell has stuck to you. Al's been your best friend. Molly and I have pleaded with you, and now you've gone and done—God knows what!"

"What do women want to wear veils for?" he growled. "I'd have known her but for that veil."

"And you wouldn't have insulted her. But you would the next girl who came along. Gene, you are hopeless. Now, you get out of here and don't ever come back."

"Flo!" he entreated.

"I mean it."

"I reckon then I'll come back to-morrow and take my medicine," he replied.

"Don't you dare!" she cried.

Stewart went out and closed the door.

"Miss Hammond, you—you don't know how this hurts me," said Florence. "What you must think of us! It's so unlucky that you should have had this happen right at first. Now, maybe you won't have the heart to stay. Oh, I've known more than one Eastern girl to go home without ever learning what we really are cut here. Miss Hammond, Gene Stewart is a fiend when he's drunk. All the same I know, whatever he did, he meant no shame to you. Come now, don't think about it again to-night." She took up the lamp and led Madeline into a little room. "This is out West," she went on, smiling, as she indicated the few furnishings; "but you can rest. You're perfectly safe. Won't you let me help you undress—can't I do anything for you?"

"You are very kind, thank you, but I can manage," replied Madeline.

"Well, then, good night. The sooner I go the sooner you'll rest. Just forget what happened and think how fine a surprise you're to give your brother to-morrow."

With that she slipped out and softly shut the door.

As Madeline laid her watch on the bureau she noticed that the time was past two o'clock. It seemed long since she had gotten off the train. When she had turned out the lamp and crept wearily into bed she knew what it was to be utterly spent. She was too tired to move a finger. But her brain whirled.

She had at first no control over it, and a thousand thronging sensations came and went and recurred with little logical relation. There were the roar of the train; the feeling of being lost; the sound of pounding hoofs; a picture of her brother's face as she had last seen it five years before; a long, dim line of lights; the jingle of silver spurs; night, wind, darkness, stars. Then the gloomy station, the shadowy blanketed Mexican, the empty room, the dim lights across the square, the tramp of the dancers and vacant laughs and discordant music, the door flung wide and the entrance of the cowboy. She did not recall how he had looked or what he had done. And the next instant she saw him cool, smiling, devilish—saw him in violence; the next his bigness, his apparel, his physical being were vague as outlines in a dream. The white face of the padre flashed along in the train of thought, and it brought the same dull, half-blind, indefinable state of mind subsequent to that last nerve-breaking pistol-shot. That passed, and then clear and vivid rose memories of the rest that had happened—strange voices betraying fury of men, a deadened report, a moan of mortal pain, a woman's poignant cry. And Madeline saw the girl's great tragic eyes and the wild flight of the big horse into the blackness, and the dark, stalking figure of the silent cowboy, and the white stars that seemed to look down remorselessly.

This tide of memory rolled over Madeline again and again, and gradually lost its power and faded. All distress left her, and she felt herself drifting. How black the room was—as black with her eyes open as it was when they were shut! And the silence—it was like a cloak. There was absolutely no sound. She was in another world from that which she knew. She thought of this fair-haired Florence and of Alfred; and, wondering about them, she dropped to sleep.

When she awakened the room was bright with sunlight. A cool wind blowing across the bed caused her to put her hands under the blanket. She was lazily and dreamily contemplating the mud walls of this little room when she remembered where she was and how she had come there.

How great a shock she had been subjected to was manifest in a sensation of disgust that overwhelmed her. She even shut her eyes to try and blot out the recollection. She felt that she had been contaminated.

Presently Madeline Hammond again awoke to the fact she had learned the preceding night—that there were emotions to which she had heretofore been a stranger. She did not try to analyze them, but she exercised her self-control to such good purpose that by the time she had dressed she was outwardly her usual self. She scarcely remembered when she had found it necessary to control her emotions. There had been no trouble, no excitement, no unpleasantness in her life. It had been ordered for her—tranquil, luxurious, brilliant, varied, yet always the same.

She was not surprised to find the hour late, and was going to make inquiry about her brother when a voice arrested her. She recognized Miss Kingsley's voice addressing some one outside, and it had a sharpness she had not noted before.

"So you came back, did you? Well, you don't look very proud of yourself this mawnin'. Gene Stewart, you look like a coyote."

"Say, Flo if I am a coyote I'm not going to sneak," he said.

"What 'd you come for?" she demanded.

"I said I was coming round to take my medicine."

"Meaning you'll not run from Al Hammond? Gene, your skull is as thick as an old cow's. Al will never know anything about what you did to his sister unless you tell him. And if you do that he'll shoot you. She won't give you away. She's a thoroughbred. Why, she was so white last night I thought she'd drop at my feet, but she never blinked an eyelash. I'm a woman, Gene Stewart and if I couldn't feel like Miss Hammond I know how awful an ordeal she must have had. Why, she's one of the most beautiful, the most sought after, the most exclusive women in New York City. There's a crowd of millionaires and lords and dukes after her. How terrible it'd be for a woman like her to be kissed by a drunken cowpuncher! I say it—"

"Flo, I never insulted her that way," broke out Stewart.

"It was worse, then?" she queried, sharply.

"I made a bet that I'd marry the first girl who came to town. I was on the watch and pretty drunk. When she came—well, I got Padre Marcos and tried to bully her into marrying me."

"Oh, Lord!" Florence gasped. "It's worse than I feared.... Gene, Al will kill you."

"That'll be a good thing," replied the cowboy, dejectedly.

"Gene Stewart, it certainly would, unless you turn over a new leaf," retorted Florence. "But don't be a fool." And here she became earnest and appealing. "Go away, Gene. Go join the rebels across the border—you're always threatening that. Anyhow, don't stay here and run any chance of stirring Al up. He'd kill you just the same as you would kill another man for insulting your sister. Don't make trouble for Al. That'd only make sorrow for her, Gene."

The subtle import was not lost upon Madeline. She was distressed because she could not avoid hearing what was not meant for her ears. She made an effort not to listen, and it was futile.

"Flo, you can't see this a man's way," he replied, quietly. "I'll stay and take my medicine."

"Gene, I could sure swear at you or any other pig-head of a cowboy. Listen. My brother-in-law, Jack, heard something of what I said to you last night. He doesn't like you. I'm afraid he'll tell Al. For Heaven's sake, man, go down-town and shut him up and yourself, too."

Then Madeline heard her come into the house and presently rap on the door and call softly:

"Miss Hammond. Are you awake?"

"Awake and dressed, Miss Kingsley. Come in."

"Oh! You've rested. You look so—so different. I'm sure glad. Come out now. We'll have breakfast, and then you may expect to meet your brother any moment."

"Wait, please. I heard you speaking to Mr. Stewart. It was unavoidable. But I am glad. I must see him. Will you please ask him to come into the parlor a moment?"

"Yes," replied Florence, quickly; and as she turned at the door she flashed at Madeline a woman's meaning glance. "Make him keep his mouth shut!"

Presently there were slow, reluctant steps outside the front door, then a pause, and the door opened. Stewart stood bareheaded in the sunlight. Madeline remembered with a kind of shudder the tall form, the embroidered buckskin vest, the red scarf, the bright leather wristbands, the wide silver-buckled belt and chaps. Her glance seemed to run over him swift as lightning. But as she saw his face now she did not recognize it. The man's presence roused in her a revolt. Yet something in her, the incomprehensible side of her nature, thrilled in the look of this splendid dark-faced barbarian.

"Mr. Stewart, will you please come in?" she asked, after that long pause.

"I reckon not," he said. The hopelessness of his tone meant that he knew he was not fit to enter a room with her, and did not care or cared too much.

Madeline went to the door. The man's face was hard, yet it was sad, too. And it touched her.

"I shall not tell my brother of your—your rudeness to me," she began. It was impossible for her to keep the chill out of her voice, to speak with other than the pride and aloofness of her class. Nevertheless, despite her loathing, when she had spoken so far it seemed that kindness and pity followed involuntarily. "I choose to overlook what you did because you were not wholly accountable, and because there must be no trouble between Alfred and you. May I rely on you to keep silence and to seal the lips of that priest? And you know there was a man killed or injured there last night. I want to forget that dreadful thing. I don't want it known that I heard—"

"The Greaser didn't die," interrupted Stewart.

"Ah! then that's not so bad, after all. I am glad for the sake of your friend—the little Mexican girl."

A slow scarlet wave overspread his face, and his shame was painful to see. That fixed in Madeline's mind a conviction that if he was a heathen he was not wholly bad. And it made so much difference that she smiled down at him.

"You will spare me further distress, will you not, please?" His hoarse reply was incoherent, but she needed only to see his working face to know his remorse and gratitude.

Madeline went back to her room; and presently Florence came for her, and directly they were sitting at breakfast. Madeline Hammond's impression of her brother's friend had to be reconstructed in the morning light. She felt a wholesome, frank, sweet nature. She liked the slow Southern drawl. And she was puzzled to know whether Florence Kingsley was pretty or striking or unusual. She had a youthful glow and flush, the clear tan of outdoors, a face that lacked the soft curves and lines of Eastern women, and her eyes were light gray, like crystal, steady, almost piercing, and her hair was a beautiful bright, waving mass.

Florence's sister was the elder of the two, a stout woman with a strong face and quiet eyes. It was a simple fare and service they gave to their guest; but they made no apologies for that. Indeed, Madeline felt their simplicity to be restful. She was sated with respect, sick of admiration, tired of adulation; and it was good to see that these Western women treated her as very likely they would have treated any other visitor. They were sweet, kind; and what Madeline had at first thought was a lack of expression or vitality she soon discovered to be the natural reserve of women who did not live superficial lives. Florence was breezy and frank, her sister quaint and not given much to speech. Madeline thought she would like to have these women near her if she were ill or in trouble. And she reproached herself for a fastidiousness, a hypercritical sense of refinement that could not help distinguishing what these women lacked.

"Can you ride?" Florence was asking. "That's what a Westerner always asks any one from the East. Can you ride like a man—astride, I mean? Oh, that's fine. You look strong enough to hold a horse. We have some fine horses out here. I reckon when Al comes we'll go out to Bill Stillwell's ranch. We'll have to go, whether we want to or not, for when Bill learns you are here he'll just pack us all off. You'll love old Bill. His ranch is run down, but the range and the rides up in the mountains—they are beautiful. We'll hunt and climb, and most of all we'll ride. I love a horse—I love the wind in my face, and a wide stretch with the mountains beckoning. You must have the best horse on the ranges. And that means a scrap between Al and Bill and all the cowboys. We don't all agree about horses, except in case of Gene Stewart's iron-gray."

"Does Mr. Stewart own the best horse in the country?" asked Madeline. Again she had an inexplicable thrill as she remembered the wild flight of Stewart's big dark steed and rider.

"Yes, and that's all he does own," replied Florence. "Gene can't keep even a quirt. But he sure loves that horse and calls him—"

At this juncture a sharp knock on the parlor door interrupted the conversation. Florence's sister went to open it. She returned presently and said:

"It's Gene. He's been dawdlin' out there on the front porch, and he knocked to let us know Miss Hammond's brother is comin'."

Florence hurried into the parlor, followed by Madeline. The door stood open, and disclosed Stewart sitting on the porch steps. From down the road came a clatter of hoofs. Madeline looked out over Florence's shoulder and saw a cloud of dust approaching, and in it she distinguished outlines of horses and riders. A warmth spread over her, a little tingle of gladness, and the feeling recalled her girlish love for her brother. What would he be like after long years?

"Gene, has Jack kept his mouth shut?" queried Florence; and again Madeline was aware of a sharp ring in the girl's voice.

"No," replied Stewart.

"Gene! You won't let it come to a fight? Al can be managed. But Jack hates you and he'll have his friends with him."

"There won't be any fight."

"Use your brains now," added Florence; and then she turned to push Madeline gently back into the parlor.

Madeline's glow of warmth changed to a blank dismay. Was she to see her brother act with the violence she now associated with cowboys? The clatter of hoofs stopped before the door. Looking out, Madeline saw a bunch of dusty, wiry horses pawing the gravel and tossing lean heads. Her swift glance ran over the lithe horsemen, trying to pick out the one who was her brother. But she could not. Her glance, however, caught the same rough dress and hard aspect that characterized the cowboy Stewart. Then one rider threw his bridle, leaped from the saddle, and came bounding up the porch steps. Florence met him at the door.

"Hello, Flo. Where is she?" he called, eagerly. With that he looked over her shoulder to espy Madeline. He actually jumped at her. She hardly knew the tall form and the bronzed face, but the warm flash of blue eyes was familiar. As for him, he had no doubt of his sister, it appeared, for with broken welcome he threw his arms around her, then held her off and looked searchingly at her.

"Well, sister," he began, when Florence turned hurriedly from the door and interrupted him.

"Al, I think you'd better stop the wrangling out there." He stared at her, appeared suddenly to hear the loud voices from the street, and then, releasing Madeline, he said:

"By George! I forgot, Flo. There is a little business to see to. Keep my sister in here, please, and don't be fussed up now."

He went out on the porch and called to his men:

"Shut off your wind, Jack! And you, too, Blaze! I didn't want you fellows to come here. But as you would come, you've got to shut up. This is my business."

Whereupon he turned to Stewart, who was sitting on the fence.

"Hello, Stewart!" he said.

It was a greeting; but there was that in the voice which alarmed Madeline.

Stewart leisurely got up and leisurely advanced to the porch.

"Hello, Hammond!" he drawled.

"Drunk again last night?"

"Well, if you want to know, and if it's any of your mix, yes, I was-pretty drunk," replied Stewart.

It was a kind of cool speech that showed the cowboy in control of himself and master of the situation—not an easy speech to follow up with undue inquisitiveness. There was a short silence.

"Damn it, Stewart," said the speaker, presently, "here's the situation: It's all over town that you met my sister last night at the station and—and insulted her. Jack's got it in for you, so have these other boys. But it's my affair. Understand, I didn't fetch them here. They can see you square yourself, or else—Gene, you've been on the wrong trail for some time, drinking and all that. You're going to the bad. But Bill thinks, and I think, you're still a man. We never knew you to lie. Now what have you to say for yourself?"

"Nobody is insinuating that I am a liar?" drawled Stewart.

"No."

"Well, I'm glad to hear that. You see, Al, I was pretty drunk last night, but not drunk enough to forget the least thing I did. I told Pat Hawe so this morning when he was curious. And that's polite for me to be to Pat. Well, I found Miss Hammond waiting alone at the station. She wore a veil, but I knew she was a lady, of course. I imagine, now that I think of it, that Miss Hammond found my gallantry rather startling, and—"

At this point Madeline, answering to unconsidered impulse, eluded Florence and walked out upon the porch.

Sombreros flashed down and the lean horses jumped.

"Gentlemen," said Madeline, rather breathlessly; and it did not add to her calmness to feel a hot flush in her cheeks, "I am very new to Western ways, but I think you are laboring under a mistake, which, in justice to Mr. Stewart, I want to correct. Indeed, he was rather— rather abrupt and strange when he came up to me last night; but as I understand him now, I can attribute that to his gallantry. He was somewhat wild and sudden and—sentimental in his demand to protect me—and it was not clear whether he meant his protection for last night or forever; but I am happy to say be offered me no word that was not honorable. And he saw me safely here to Miss Kingsley's home."

SISTER AND BROTHER

THEN MADELINE RETURNED to the little parlor with the brother whom she had hardly recognized.

"Majesty!" he exclaimed. "To think of your being here!"

The warmth stole back along her veins. She remembered how that pet name had sounded from the lips of this brother who had given it to her.

"Alfred!"

Then his words of gladness at sight of her, his chagrin at not being at the train to welcome her, were not so memorable of him as the way he clasped her, for he had held her that way the day he left home, and she had not forgotten. But now he was so much taller and bigger, so dusty and strange and different and forceful, that she could scarcely think him the same man. She even had a humorous thought that here was another cowboy bullying her, and this time it was her brother.

"Dear old girl," he said, more calmly, as he let her go, "you haven't changed at all, except to grow lovelier. Only you're a woman now, and you've fulfilled the name I gave you. God! how sight of you brings back home! It seems a hundred years since I left. I missed you more than all the rest."

Madeline seemed to feel with his every word that she was remembering him. She was so amazed at the change in him that she could not believe her eyes. She saw a bronzed, strong-jawed, eagle-eyed man, stalwart, superb of height, and, like the cowboys, belted, booted, spurred. And there was something hard as iron in his face that quivered with his words. It seemed that only in those moments when the hard lines broke and softened could she see resemblance to the face she remembered. It was his manner, the tone of his voice, and the tricks of speech that proved to her he was really Alfred. She had bidden good-by to a disgraced, disinherited, dissolute boy. Well she remembered the handsome pale face with its weakness and shadows and careless smile, with the ever-present cigarette hanging between the lips. The years had passed, and now she saw him a man—the West had made him a man. And Madeline Hammond felt a strong, passionate gladness and gratefulness, and a direct check to her suddenly inspired hatred of the West.

198

"Majesty, it was good of you to come. I'm all broken up. How did you ever do it? But never mind that now. Tell me about that brother of mine."

And Madeline told him, and then about their sister Helen. Question after question he fired at her; and she told him of her mother; of Aunt Grace, who had died a year ago; of his old friends, married, scattered, vanished. But she did not tell him of his father, for he did not ask.

Quite suddenly the rapid-fire questioning ceased; he choked, was silent a moment, and then burst into tears. It seemed to her that a long, stored-up bitterness was flooding away. It hurt her to see him—hurt her more to hear him. And in the succeeding few moments she grew closer to him than she had ever been in the past. Had her father and mother done right by him? Her pulse stirred with unwonted quickness. She did not speak, but she kissed him, which, for her, was an indication of unusual feeling. And when he recovered command over his emotions he made no reference to his breakdown, nor did she. But that scene struck deep into Madeline Hammond's heart. Through it she saw what he had lost and gained.

"Alfred, why did you not answer my last letters?" asked Madeline. "I had not heard from you for two years."

"So long? How time flies! Well, things went bad with me about the last time I heard from you. I always intended to write some day, but I never did."

"Things went wrong? Tell me."

"Majesty, you mustn't worry yourself with my troubles. I want you to enjoy your stay and not be bothered with my difficulties."

"Please tell me. I suspected something had gone wrong. That is partly why I decided to come out."

"All right; if you must know," he began; and it seemed to Madeline that there was a gladness in his decision to unburden himself. "You remember all about my little ranch, and that for a while I did well raising stock? I wrote you all that. Majesty, a man makes enemies anywhere. Perhaps an Eastern man in the West can make, if not so many, certainly more bitter ones. At any rate, I made several. There was a cattleman, Ward by name—he's gone now—and he and I had trouble over cattle. That gave me a back-set. Pat Hawe, the sheriff here, has been instrumental in hurting my business. He's not so much of a rancher, but he has influence at Santa Fe and El Paso and Douglas. I made an enemy of him. I never did anything to him. He hates Gene Stewart, and upon one occasion I spoiled a little plot of his to get Gene in his clutches. The real reason for his animosity toward me is that he loves Florence, and Florence is going to marry me."

"Alfred!"

"What's the matter, Majesty? Didn't Florence impress you favorably?" he asked, with a keen glance.

"Why—yes, indeed. I like her. But I did not think of her in relation to you—that way. I am greatly surprised. Alfred, is she well born? What connections?"

"Florence is just a girl of ordinary people. She was born in Kentucky, was brought up in Texas. My aristocratic and wealthy family would scorn—"

"Alfred, you are still a Hammond," said Madeline, with uplifted head.

Alfred laughed. "We won't quarrel, Majesty. I remember you, and in spite of your pride you've got a heart. If you stay here a month you'll love Florence Kingsley. I want you to know she's had a great deal to do with straightening me up.... Well, to go on with my story. There's Don Carlos, a Mexican rancher, and he's my worst enemy. For that matter, he's as bad an enemy of Bill Stillwell and other ranchers. Stillwell, by the way, is my friend and one of the finest men on earth. I got in debt to Don Carlos before I knew he was so mean. In the first place I lost money at faro—I gambled some when I came West—and then I made unwise cattle deals. Don Carlos is a wily Greaser, he knows the ranges, he has the water, and he is dishonest. So he outfigured me. And now I am practically ruined. He has not gotten possession of my ranch, but that's only a matter of time, pending lawsuits at Santa Fe. At present I have a few hundred cattle running on Stillwell's range, and I am his foreman."

"Foreman?" queried Madeline.

"I am simply boss of Stillwell's cowboys, and right glad of my job."

Madeline was conscious of an inward burning. It required an effort for her to retain her outward tranquillity. Annoying consciousness she had also of the returning sense of new disturbing emotions. She began to see just how walled in from unusual thought-provoking incident and sensation had been her exclusive life.

"Cannot your property be reclaimed?" she asked. "How much do you owe?"

"Ten thousand dollars would clear me and give me another start. But, Majesty, in this country that's a good deal of money, and I haven't been able to raise it. Stillwell's in worse shape than I am."

Madeline went over to Alfred and put her hands on his shoulders.

"We must not be in debt."

He stared at her as if her words had recalled something long forgotten. Then he smiled.

"How imperious you are! I'd forgotten just who my beautiful sister really is. Majesty, you're not going to ask me to take money from you?"

"I am."

"Well, I'll not do it. I never did, even when I was in college, and then there wasn't much beyond me."

"Listen, Alfred," she went on, earnestly, "this is entirely different. I had only an allowance then. You had no way to know that since I last wrote you I had come into my inheritance from Aunt Grace. It was—well, that doesn't matter. Only, I haven't been able to spend half the income. It's mine. It's not father's money. You will make me very happy if you'll consent. Alfred, I'm so—so amazed at the change in you. I'm so happy. You must never take a backward step from now on. What is ten thousand dollars to me? Sometimes I spend that in a month. I throw money away. If you let me help you it will be doing me good as well as you. Please, Alfred."

He kissed her, evidently surprised at her earnestness. And indeed Madeline was surprised herself. Once started, her speech had flowed.

"You always were the best of fellows, Majesty. And if you really care—if you really want to help me I'll be only too glad to accept. It will be fine. Florence will go wild. And that Greaser won't harass me any more. Majesty, pretty soon some titled fellow will be spending your money; I may as well take a little before he gets it all," he finished, jokingly.

"What do you know about me?" she asked, lightly.

"More than you think. Even if we are lost out here in the woolly West we get news. Everybody knows about Anglesbury. And that Dago duke who chased you all over Europe, that Lord Castleton has the running now and seems about to win. How about it, Majesty?"

Madeline detected a hint that suggested scorn in his gay speech. And deep in his searching glance she saw a flame. She became thoughtful. She had forgotten Castleton, New York, society.

"Alfred," she began, seriously, "I don't believe any titled gentleman will ever spend my money, as you elegantly express it."

"I don't care for that. It's you!" he cried, passionately, and he grasped her with a violence that startled her. He was white; his eyes were now like fire. "You are so splendid—so wonderful. People called you the American Beauty, but you're more than that. You're the American Girl! Majesty, marry no man unless you love him, and love an American. Stay away from Europe long enough to learn to know the men—the real men of your own country."

"Alfred, I'm afraid there are not always real men and real love for American girls in international marriages. But Helen knows this. It'll be her choice. She'll be miserable if she marries Anglesbury."

"It'll serve her just right," declared her brother. "Helen was always crazy for glitter, adulation, fame. I'll gamble she never saw more of Anglesbury than the gold and ribbons on his breast."

"I am sorry. Anglesbury is a gentleman; but it is the money he wanted, I think. Alfred, tell me how you came to know about me, 'way out here? You may be assured I was astonished to find that Miss Kingsley knew me as Majesty Hammond."

"I imagine it was a surprise," he replied, with a laugh, "I told Florence about you—gave her a picture of you. And, of course, being a woman, she showed the picture and talked. She's in love with you. Then, my dear sister, we do get New York papers out here occasionally, and we can see and read. You may not be aware that you and your society friends are objects of intense interest in the U. S. in general, and the West in particular. The papers are full of you, and perhaps a lot of things you never did."

"That Mr. Stewart knew, too. He said, 'You're not Majesty Hammond?'"

"Never mind his impudence!" exclaimed Alfred; and then again he laughed. "Gene is all right, only you've got to know him. I'll tell you what he did. He got hold of one of those newspaper pictures of you—the one in the Times; he took it away from here, and in spite of Florence he wouldn't fetch it back. It was a picture of you in riding-habit with your blue-ribbon horse, White Stockings—remember? It was taken at Newport. Well, Stewart tacked the picture up in his bunk-house and named his beautiful horse Majesty. All the cowboys knew it. They would see the picture and tease him unmercifully. But he didn't care. One day I happened to drop in on him and found him just recovering from a carouse. I saw the picture, too, and I said to him, 'Gene, if my sister knew you were a drunkard she'd not be proud of having her picture stuck up in your room.' Majesty, he did not touch a drop for a month, and when he did drink again he took the picture down, and he has never put it back."

Madeline smiled at her brother's amusement, but she did not reply. She simply could not adjust herself to these queer free Western' ways. Her brother had eloquently pleaded for her to keep herself above a sordid and brilliant marriage, yet he not only allowed a cowboy to keep her picture in his room, but actually spoke of her and used her name in a temperance lecture. Madeline just escaped feeling disgust. She was saved from this, however, by nothing less than her brother's naive gladness that through subtle suggestion Stewart had been persuaded to be good for a month. Something made up of Stewart's effrontery to her; of Florence Kingsley meeting her, frankly as it were, as an equal; of the elder sister's slow, quiet, easy acceptance of this visitor who had been honored at the courts of royalty; of that faint hint of scorn in Alfred's voice, and his amused statement in regard to her picture and the name Majesty—something made up of all these stung Madeline Hammond's pride, alienated her for an instant, and then stimulated her intelligence, excited her interest, and made her resolve to learn a little about this incomprehensible West.

"Majesty, I must run down to the siding," he said, consulting his watch. "We're loading a shipment of cattle. I'll be back by supper-time and bring Stillwell with me. You'll like him. Give me the check for your trunk."

She went into the little bedroom and, taking up her bag, she got out a number of checks.

"Six! Six trunks!" he exclaimed. "Well, I'm very glad you intend to stay awhile. Say, Majesty, it will take me as long to realize who you really are as it'll take to break you of being a tenderfoot. I hope you packed a riding-suit. If not you'll have to wear trousers! You'll have to do that, anyway, when we go up in the mountains."

"No!"

"You sure will, as Florence says."

"We shall see about that. I don't know what's in the trunks. I never pack anything. My dear brother, what do I have maids for?"

"How did it come that you didn't travel with a maid?"

"I wanted to be alone. But don't you worry. I shall be able to look after myself. I dare say it will be good for me."

She went to the gate with him.

"What a shaggy, dusty horse! He's wild, too. Do you let him stand that way without being haltered? I should think he would run off."

"Tenderfoot! You'll be great fun, Majesty, especially for the cowboys."

"Oh, will I?" she asked, constrainedly.

"Yes, and in three days they will be fighting one another over you. That's going to worry me. Cowboys fall in love with a plain woman, an ugly woman, any woman, so long as she's young. And you! Good Lord! They'll go out of their heads."

"You are pleased to be facetious, Alfred. I think I have had quite enough of cowboys, and I haven't been here twenty-four hours."

"Don't think too much of first impressions. That was my mistake when I arrived here. Good-by. I'll go now. Better rest awhile. You look tired."

The horse started as Alfred put his foot in the stirrup and was running when the rider slipped his leg over the saddle. Madeline watched him in admiration. He seemed to be loosely fitted to the saddle, moving with the horse.

"I suppose that's a cowboy's style. It pleases me," she said. "How different from the seat of Eastern riders!"

Then Madeline sat upon the porch and fell to interested observation of her surrounding. Near at hand it was decidedly not prepossessing. The street was deep in dust, and the cool wind whipped up little puffs. The houses along this street were all low, square, flat-roofed structures made of some kind of red cement. It occurred to her suddenly that this building-material must be the adobe she had read about. There was no person in sight. The long street appeared to have no end, though the line of houses did not extend far. Once she heard a horse trotting at some distance, and several times the ringing of a locomotive bell. Where were the mountains, wondered Madeline. Soon low over the house-roofs she saw a dim, dark-blue, rugged outline. It seemed to charm her eyes and fix her gaze. She knew the Adirondacks, she had seen the Alps from the summit of Mont Blanc, and had stood under the great black, white-tipped shadow of the Himalayas. But they had not drawn her as these remote Rockies. This dim horizon line boldly cutting the blue sky fascinated her. Florence Kingsley's expression "beckoning mountains" returned to Madeline. She could not see or feel so much as that. Her impression was rather that these mountains were aloof, unattainable, that if approached they would recede or vanish like the desert mirage.

Madeline went to her room, intending to rest awhile, and she fell asleep. She was aroused by Florence's knock and call.

"Miss Hammond, your brother has come back with Stillwell."

"Why, how I have slept!" exclaimed Madeline. "It's nearly six o'clock."

"I'm sure glad. You were tired. And the air here makes strangers sleepy. Come, we want you to meet old Bill. He calls himself the last of the cattlemen. He has lived in Texas and here all his life."

Madeline accompanied Florence to the porch. Her brother, who was sitting near the door, jumped up and said:

"Hello, Majesty!" And as he put his arm around her he turned toward a massive man whose broad, craggy face began to ripple and wrinkle. "I want to introduce my friend Stillwell to you. Bill, this is my sister, the sister I've so often told you about—Majesty."

"Wal, wal, Al, this's the proudest meetin' of my life," replied Stillwell, in a booming voice. He extended a huge hand. "Miss—Miss Majesty, sight of you is as welcome as the rain an' the flowers to an old desert cattleman."

Madeline greeted him, and it was all she could do to repress a cry at the way he crunched her hand in a grasp of iron. He was old, white-haired, weather-beaten, with long furrows down his checks and with gray eyes almost hidden in wrinkles. If he was smiling she fancied it a most extraordinary smile. The next instant she realized that it had been a smile, for his face appeared to stop rippling, the light died, and suddenly it was like rudely chiseled stone. The quality of hardness she had seen in Stewart was immeasurably intensified in this old man's face.

"Miss Majesty, it's plumb humiliatin' to all of us thet we wasn't on hand to meet you," Stillwell said. "Me an' Al stepped into the P. O. an' said a few mild an' cheerful things. Them messages ought to hev been sent out to the ranch. I'm sure afraid it was a bit unpleasant fer you last night at the station."

"I was rather anxious at first and perhaps frightened," replied Madeline.

"Wal, I'm some glad to tell you thet there's no man in these parts except your brother thet I'd as lief hev met you as Gene Stewart."

"Indeed?"

"Yes, an' thet's takin' into consideration Gene's weakness, too. I'm allus fond of sayin' of myself thet I'm the last of the old cattlemen. Wal, Stewart's not a native Westerner, but he's my pick of the last of the cowboys. Sure, he's young, but he's the last of the old style—the picturesque—an' chivalrous, too, I make bold to say, Miss Majesty, as well as the old hard-ridin' kind. Folks are down on Stewart. An' I'm only sayin' a good word for him because he is down, an' mebbe last night he might hev scared you, you bein' fresh from the East."

Madeline liked the old fellow for his loyalty to the cowboy he evidently cared for; but as there did not seem anything for her to say, she remained silent.

"Miss Majesty, the day of the cattleman is about over. An' the day of the cowboy, such as Gene Stewart, is over. There's no place for Gene. If these weren't modern days he'd come near bein' a gun-man, same as we had in Texas, when I ranched there in the 'seventies. But he can't fit nowhere now; he can't hold a job, an' he's goin' down."

"I am sorry to hear it," murmured Madeline. "But, Mr. Stillwell, aren't these modern days out here just a little wild—yet? The conductor on my train told me of rebels, bandits, raiders. Then I have had other impressions of—well, that were wild enough for me."

"Wal, it's some more pleasant an' excitin' these days than for many years," replied Stillwell. "The boys hev took to packin' guns again. But thet's owin' to the revolution in Mexico. There's goin' to be trouble along the border. I reckon people in the East don't know there is a revolution. Wal, Madero will oust Diaz, an' then some other rebel will oust Madero. It means trouble on the border an' across the border, too. I wouldn't wonder if Uncle Sam hed to get a hand in the game. There's already been holdups on the railroads an' raids along the Rio Grande Valley. An' these little towns are full of Greasers, all disturbed by the fightin' down in Mexico. We've been hevin' shootin'-scrapes an' knifin'-scrapes, an' some cattle-raidin'. I hev been losin' a few cattle right along. Reminds me of old times; an' pretty soon if it doesn't stop, I'll take the old-time way to stop it."

"Yes, indeed, Majesty," put in Alfred, "you have hit upon an interesting time to visit us."

"Wal, thet sure 'pears to be so," rejoined Stillwell. "Stewart got in trouble down heah to-day, an' I'm more than sorry to hev to tell you thet your name figgered in it. But I couldn't blame him, fer I sure would hev done the same myself."

"That so?" queried Alfred, laughing. "Well, tell us about it."

Madeline simply gazed at her brother, and, though he seemed amused at her consternation, there was mortification in his face.

It required no great perspicuity, Madeline thought, to see that Stillwell loved to talk, and the way he squared himself and spread his huge hands over his knees suggested that he meant to do this opportunity justice.

"Miss Majesty, I reckon, bein' as you're in the West now, thet you must take things as they come, an' mind each thing a little less than the one before. If we old fellers hedn't been thet way we'd never hev lasted.

"Last night wasn't particular bad, ratin' with some other nights lately. There wasn't much doin'. But, I had a hard knock. Yesterday when we started in with a bunch of cattle I sent one of my cowboys, Danny Mains, along ahead, carryin' money I hed to pay off hands an' my bills, an' I wanted thet money to get in town before dark. Wal, Danny was held up. I don't distrust the lad. There's been strange Greasers in town lately, an' mebbe they knew about the money comin'.

"Wal, when I arrived with the cattle I was some put to it to make ends meet. An' to-day I wasn't in no angelic humor. When I hed my business all done I went around pokin' my nose beak an' there, tryin' to get scent of thet money. An' I happened in at a hall we hev thet does duty fer' jail an' hospital an' election-post an' what not. Wal, just then it was doin' duty as a hospital. Last night was fiesta night—these Greasers hev a fiesta every week or so—an' one Greaser who hed been bad hurt was layin' in the hall, where he hed been fetched from the station. Somebody hed sent off to Douglas fer a doctor, but he hedn't come yet. I've hed some experience with gunshot wounds, an' I looked this feller over. He wasn't shot up much, but I thought there was danger of blood-poison-in'. Anyway, I did all I could.

"The hall was full of cowboys, ranchers, Greasers, miners, an' town folks, along with some strangers. I was about to get started up this way when Pat Hawe come in.

"Pat he's the sheriff. I reckon, Miss Majesty, thet sheriffs are new to you, an' fer sake of the West I'll explain to you thet we don't hev many of the real thing any more. Garrett, who killed Billy the Kid an' was killed himself near a year or so ago—he was the kind of sheriff thet helps to make a self-respectin' country. But this Pat Hawe—wal, I reckon there's no good in me sayin' what I think of him. He come into the hall, an' he was roarin' about things. He was goin' to arrest Danny Mains on sight. Wal, I jest polite-like told Pat thet the money was mine an' he needn't get riled about it. An' if I wanted to trail the thief I reckon I could do it as well as anybody. Pat howled thet law was law, an' he was goin' to lay down the law. Sure it 'peared to me thet Pat was daid set to arrest the first man he could find excuse to.

"Then he cooled down a bit an' was askin' questions about the wounded Greaser when Gene Stewart come in. Whenever Pat an' Gene come together it reminds me of the early days back in the 'seventies. Jest naturally everybody shut up. Fer Pat hates Gene, an' I reckon Gene ain't very sweet on Pat. They're jest natural foes in the first place, an' then the course of events here in El Cajon has been aggravatin'.

"'Hello, Stewart! You're the feller I'm lookin' fer,' said Pat.

204

"Stewart eyed him an' said, mighty cool an' sarcastic, 'Hawe, you look a good deal fer me when I'm hittin' up the dust the other way.'

"Pat went red at thet, but he held in. 'Say, Stewart, you-all think a lot of thet roan horse of yourn, with the aristocratic name?'

"'I reckon I do,' replied Gene, shortly.

"'Wal, where is he?'

"'Thet's none of your business, Hawe.'

"'Oho! it ain't, hey? Wal, I guess I can make it my business. Stewart, there was some queer goings-on last night thet you know somethin' about. Danny Mains robbed—Stillwell's money gone—your roan horse gone—thet little hussy Bonita gone—an' this Greaser near gone, too. Now, seein' thet you was up late an' prowlin' round the station where this Greaser was found, it ain't onreasonable to think you might know how he got plugged—is it?'

"Stewart laughed kind of cold, an' he rolled a cigarette, all the time eyin' Pat, an' then he said if he'd plugged the Greaser it 'd never hev been sich a bunglin' job.

"'I can arrest you on suspicion, Stewart, but before I go thet far I want some evidence. I want to round up Danny Mains an' thet little Greaser girl. I want to find out what's become of your hoss. You've never lent him since you hed him, an' there ain't enough raiders across the border to steal him from you. It's got a queer look—thet hoss bein' gone.'

"'You sure are a swell detective, Hawe, an' I wish you a heap of luck,' replied Stewart.

"Thet 'peared to nettle Pat beyond bounds, an' he stamped around an' swore. Then he had an idea. It jest stuck out all over him, an' he shook his finger in Stewart's face.

"'You was drunk last night?'

"Stewart never batted an eye.

"'You met some woman on Number Eight, didn't you?' shouted Hawe.

"'I met a lady,' replied Stewart, quiet an' menacin' like.

"'You met Al Hammond's sister, an' you took her up to Kingsley's. An' cinch this, my cowboy cavalier, I'm goin' up there an' ask this grand dame some questions, an' if she's as close-mouthed as you are I'll arrest her!'

"Gene Stewart turned white. I fer one expected to see him jump like lightnin', as he does when he's riled sudden. But he was calm an' he was thinkin' hard. Presently he said:

"'Pat, thet's a fool idee, an' if you do the trick it'll hurt you all the rest of your life. There's absolutely no reason to frighten Miss Hammond. An' tryin' to arrest her would be such a damned outrage as won't be stood fer in El Cajon. If you're sore on me send me to jail. I'll go. If you want to hurt Al Hammond, go an' do it some man kind of way. Don't take your spite out on us by insultin' a lady who has come hyar to hev a little visit. We're bad enough without bein' low-down as Greasers.'

"It was a long talk for Gene, an' I was as surprised as the rest of the fellers. Think of Gene Stewart talkin' soft an' sweet to thet red-eyed coyote of a sheriff! An' Pat, he looked so devilishly gleeful thet if somethin' about Gene hedn't held me tight I'd hev got in the game myself. It was plain to me an' others who spoke of it afterwards thet Pat Hawe hed forgotten the law an' the officer in the man an' his hate.

"'I'm a-goin', an' I'm a-goin' right now!' he shouted. "An' after thet any one could hev heerd a clock tick a mile off. Stewart seemed kind of chokin', an' he seemed to hev been bewildered by the idee of Hawe's confrontin' you.

"An' finally he burst out: 'But, man, think who it is! It's Miss Hammond! If you seen her, even if you was locoed or drunk, you—you couldn't do it.'

"'Couldn't I? Wal, I'll show you damn quick. What do I care who she is? Them swell Eastern women—I've heerd of them. They're not so much. This Hammond woman—'

"Suddenly Hawe shut up, an' with his red mug turnin' green he went for his gun."

Stillwell paused in his narrative to get breath, and he wiped his moist brow. And now his face began to lose its cragginess. It changed, it softened, it rippled and wrinkled, and all that strange mobility focused and shone in a wonderful smile.

"An' then, Miss Majesty, then there was somethin' happened. Stewart took Pat's gun away from him and throwed it on the floor. An' what followed was beautiful. Sure it was the beautifulest sight I ever seen. Only it was over so soon! A little while after, when the doctor came, he hed another patient besides the wounded Greaser, an' he said thet this new one would require about four months to be up an' around cheerful-like again. An' Gene Stewart hed hit the trail for the border."

❧ 4 ❧

A RIDE FROM SUNRISE TO SUNSET

NEXT MORNING, when Madeline was aroused by her brother, it was not yet daybreak; the air chilled her, and in the gray gloom she had to feel around for matches and lamp. Her usual languid manner vanished at a touch of the cold water. Presently, when Alfred knocked on her door and said he was leaving a pitcher of hot water outside, she replied, with chattering teeth, "Th-thank y-you, b-but I d-don't ne-need any now." She found it necessary, however, to warm her numb fingers before she could fasten hooks and buttons. And when she was dressed she marked in the dim mirror that there were tinges of red in her cheeks.

"Well, if I haven't some color!" she exclaimed.

Breakfast waited for her in the dining-room. The sisters ate with her. Madeline quickly caught the feeling of brisk action that seemed to be in the air. From the back of the house sounded the tramp of boots and voices of men, and from outside came a dull thump of hoofs, the rattle of harness, and creak of wheels. Then Alfred came stamping in.

"Majesty, here's where you get the real thing," he announced, merrily. "We're rushing you off, I'm sorry to say; but we must hustle back to the ranch. The fall round-up begins to-morrow. You will ride in the buck-board with Florence and Stillwell. I'll ride on ahead with the boys and fix up a little for you at the ranch. Your baggage will follow, but won't get there till to-morrow sometime. It's a long ride out—nearly fifty miles by wagon-road. Flo, don't forget a couple of robes. Wrap her up well. And hustle getting ready. We're waiting."

A little later, when Madeline went out with Florence, the gray gloom was lightening. Horses were champing bits and pounding gravel.

"Mawnin', Miss Majesty," said Stillwell, gruffly, from the front seat of a high vehicle.

Alfred bundled her up into the back seat, and Florence after her, and wrapped them with robes. Then he mounted his horse and started off. "Gid-eb!" growled Stillwell, and with a crack of his whip the team jumped into a trot. Florence whispered into Madeline's ear:

"Bill's grouchy early in the mawnin'. He'll thaw out soon as it gets warm."

It was still so gray that Madeline could not distinguish objects at any considerable distance, and she left El Cajon without knowing what the town really looked like. She did

207

know that she was glad to get out of it, and found an easier task of dispelling persistent haunting memory.

"Here come the cowboys," said Florence.

A line of horsemen appeared coming from the right and fell in behind Alfred, and gradually they drew ahead, to disappear from sight. While Madeline watched them the gray gloom lightened into dawn. All about her was bare and dark; the horizon seemed close; not a hill nor a tree broke the monotony. The ground appeared to be flat, but the road went up and down over little ridges. Madeline glanced backward in the direction of El Cajon and the mountains she had seen the day before, and she saw only bare and dark ground, like that which rolled before.

A puff of cold wind struck her face and she shivered. Florence noticed her and pulled up the second robe and tucked it closely round her up to her chin.

"If we have a little wind you'll sure feel it," said the Western girl.

Madeline replied that she already felt it. The wind appeared to penetrate the robes. It was cold, pure, nipping. It was so thin she had to breathe as fast as if she were under ordinary exertion. It hurt her nose and made her lungs ache.

"Aren't you co-cold?" asked Madeline.

"I?" Florence laughed. "I'm used to it. I never get cold."

The Western girl sat with ungloved hands on the outside of the robe she evidently did not need to draw up around her. Madeline thought she had never seen such a clear-eyed, healthy, splendid girl.

"Do you like to see the sun rise?" asked Florence.

"Yes, I think I do," replied Madeline, thoughtfully. "Frankly, I have not seen it for years."

"We have beautiful sunrises, and sunsets from the ranch are glorious."

Long lines of pink fire ran level with the eastern horizon, which appeared to recede as day brightened. A bank of thin, fleecy clouds was turning rose. To the south and west the sky was dark; but every moment it changed, the blue turning bluer. The eastern sky was opalescent. Then in one place gathered a golden light, and slowly concentrated till it was like fire. The rosy bank of cloud turned to silver and pearl, and behind it shot up a great circle of gold. Above the dark horizon gleamed an intensely bright disk. It was the sun. It rose swiftly, blazing out the darkness between the ridges and giving color and distance to the sweep of land.

"Wal, wal," drawled Stillwell, and stretched his huge arms as if he had just awakened, "thet's somethin' like."

Florence nudged Madeline and winked at her.

"Fine mawnin', girls," went on old Bill, cracking his whip. "Miss Majesty, it'll be some oninterestin' ride all mawnin'. But when we get up a bit you'll sure like it. There! Look to the southwest, jest over thet farthest ridge."

Madeline swept her gaze along the gray, sloping horizon-line to where dark-blue spires rose far beyond the ridge.

"Peloncillo Mountains," said Stillwell. "Thet's home, when we get there. We won't see no more of them till afternoon, when they rise up sudden-like."

Peloncillo! Madeline murmured the melodious name. Where had she heard it? Then she remembered. The cowboy Stewart had told the little Mexican girl Bonita to "hit the Peloncillo trail." Probably the girl had ridden the big, dark horse over this very road at night, alone. Madeline had a little shiver that was not occasioned by the cold wind.

"There's a jack!" cried Florence, suddenly.

Madeline saw her first jack-rabbit. It was as large as a dog, and its ears were enormous. It appeared to be impudently tame, and the horses kicked dust over it as they trotted by. From then on old Bill and Florence vied with each other in calling Madeline's attention to many things along the way. Coyotes stealing away into the brush; buzzards flapping over the carcass of a cow that had been mired in a wash; queer little lizards running swiftly across the road; cattle grazing in the hollows; adobe huts of Mexican herders; wild, shaggy horses, with heads high, watching from the gray ridges—all these things Madeline looked at, indifferently at first, because indifference had become habitual with her, and then with an interest that flourished up and insensibly grew as she rode on. It grew until sight of a little ragged Mexican boy astride the most diminutive burro she had ever seen awakened her to the truth. She became conscious of faint, unmistakable awakening of long-dead feelings—enthusiasm and delight. When she realized that, she breathed deep of the cold, sharp air and experienced an inward joy. And she divined then, though she did not know why, that henceforth there was to be something new in her life, something she had never felt before, something good for her soul in the homely, the commonplace, the natural, and the wild.

Meanwhile, as Madeline gazed about her and listened to her companions, the sun rose higher and grew warm and soared and grew hot; the horses held tirelessly to their steady trot, and mile after mile of rolling land slipped by.

From the top of a ridge Madeline saw down into a hollow where a few of the cowboys had stopped and were sitting round a fire, evidently busy at the noonday meal. Their horses were feeding on the long, gray grass.

"Wal, smell of thet burnin' greasewood makes my mouth water," said Stillwell. "I'm sure hungry. We'll noon hyar an' let the hosses rest. It's a long pull to the ranch."

He halted near the camp-fire, and, clambering down, began to unharness the team. Florence leaped out and turned to help Madeline.

"Walk round a little," she said. "You must be cramped from sitting still so long. I'll get lunch ready."

Madeline got down, glad to stretch her limbs, and began to stroll about. She heard Stillwell throw the harness on the ground and slap his horses. "Roll, you sons-of-guns!" he said. Both horses bent their fore legs, heaved down on their sides, and tried to roll over. One horse succeeded on the fourth try, and then heaved up with a satisfied snort and shook off the dust and gravel. The other one failed to roll over, and gave it up, half rose to his feet, and then lay down on the other side.

"He's sure going to feel the ground," said Florence, smiling at Madeline. "Miss Hammond, I suppose that prize horse of yours—White Stockings—would spoil his coat if he were heah to roll in this greasewood and cactus."

During lunch-time Madeline observed that she was an object of manifestly great interest to the three cowboys. She returned the compliment, and was amused to see that a glance their way caused them painful embarrassment. They were grown men—one of whom had white hair—yet they acted like boys caught in the act of stealing a forbidden look at a pretty girl.

"Cowboys are sure all flirts," said Florence, as if stating an uninteresting fact. But Madeline detected a merry twinkle in her clear eyes. The cowboys heard, and the effect upon them was magical. They fell to shamed confusion and to hurried useless tasks. Madeline found it difficult to see where they had been bold, though evidently they were stricken with conscious guilt. She recalled appraising looks of critical English eyes, impudent French stares, burning Spanish glances—gantlets which any American girl had to run abroad. Compared with foreign eyes the eyes of these cowboys were those of smiling, eager babies.

"Haw, haw!" roared Stillwell. "Florence, you jest hit the nail on the haid. Cowboys are all plumb flirts. I was wonderin' why them boys nooned hyar. This ain't no place to noon. Ain't no grazin' or wood wuth burnin' or nuthin'. Them boys jest held up, throwed the packs, an' waited fer us. It ain't so surprisin' fer Booly an' Ned—they're young an' coltish— but Nels there, why, he's old enough to be the paw of both you girls. It sure is amazin' strange."

A silence ensued. The white-haired cowboy, Nels, fussed aimlessly over the camp-fire, and then straightened up with a very red face.

"Bill, you're a dog-gone liar," he said. "I reckon I won't stand to be classed with Booly an' Ned. There ain't no cowboy on this range thet's more appreciatin' of the ladies than me, but I shore ain't ridin' out of my way. I reckon I hev enough ridin' to do. Now, Bill, if you've sich dog-gone good eyes mebbe you seen somethin' on the way out?"

"Nels, I hevn't seen nothin'," he replied, bluntly. His levity disappeared, and the red wrinkles narrowed round his searching eyes.

"Jest take a squint at these hoss tracks," said Nels, and he drew Stillwell a few paces aside and pointed to large hoofprints in the dust. "I reckon you know the hoss thet made them?"

"Gene Stewart's roan, or I'm a son-of-a-gun!" exclaimed Stillwell, and he dropped heavily to his knees and began to scrutinize the tracks. "My eyes are sure pore; but, Nels, they ain't fresh."

"I reckon them tracks was made early yesterday mornin'."

"Wal, what if they was?" Stillwell looked at his cowboy. "It's sure as thet red nose of yourn Gene wasn't ridin' the roan."

"Who's sayin' he was? Bill, its more 'n your eyes thet's gettin' old. Jest foller them tracks. Come on."

Stillwell walked slowly, with his head bent, muttering to himself. Some thirty paces or more from the camp-fire he stopped short and again flopped to his knees. Then he crawled about, evidently examining horse tracks.

"Nels, whoever was straddlin' Stewart's hoss met somebody. An' they hauled up a bit, but didn't git down."

"Tolerable good for you, Bill, thet reasonin'," replied the cowboy.

Stillwell presently got up and walked swiftly to the left for some rods, halted, and faced toward the southwest, then retraced his steps. He looked at the imperturbable cowboy.

"Nels, I don't like this a little," he growled. "Them tracks make straight fer the Peloncillo trail."

"Shore," replied Nels.

"Wal?" went on Stillwell, impatiently.

"I reckon you know what hoss made the other tracks?"

"I'm thinkin' hard, but I ain't sure."

"It was Danny Mains's bronc."

"How do you know thet?" demanded Stillwell, sharply. "Bill, the left front foot of thet little hoss always wears a shoe thet sets crooked. Any of the boys can tell you. I'd know thet track if I was blind."

Stillwell's ruddy face clouded and he kicked at a cactus plant.

"Was Danny comin' or goin'?" he asked.

"I reckon he was hittin' across country fer the Peloncillo trail. But I ain't shore of thet without back-trailin' him a ways. I was jest waitin' fer you to come up."

"Nels, you don't think the boy's sloped with thet little hussy, Bonita?"

"Bill, he shore was sweet on Bonita, same as Gene was, an' Ed Linton before he got engaged, an' all the boys. She's shore chain-lightnin', that little black-eyed devil. Danny might hev sloped with her all right. Danny was held up on the way to town, an' then in the shame of it he got drunk. But he'll shew up soon."

"Wal, mebbe you an' the boys are right. I believe you are. Nels, there ain't no doubt on earth about who was ridin' Stewart's hoss?"

"Thet's as plain as the hoss's tracks."

"Wal, it's all amazin' strange. It beats me. I wish the boys would ease up on drinkin'. I was pretty fond of Danny an' Gene. I'm afraid Gene's done fer, sure. If he crosses the border where he can fight it won't take long fer him to get plugged. I guess I'm gettin' old. I don't stand things like I used to."

"Bill, I reckon I'd better hit the Peloncillo trail. Mebbe I can find Danny."

"I reckon you had, Nels," replied Stillwell. "But don't take more 'n a couple of days. We can't do much on the round-up without you. I'm short of boys."

That ended the conversation. Stillwell immediately began to hitch up his team, and the cowboys went out to fetch their strayed horses. Madeline had been curiously interested, and she saw that Florence knew it.

"Things happen, Miss Hammond," she said, soberly, almost sadly.

Madeline thought. And then straightway Florence began brightly to hum a tune and to busy herself repacking what was left of the lunch. Madeline conceived a strong liking and respect for this Western girl. She admired the consideration or delicacy or wisdom—whatever it was—which kept Florence from asking her what she knew or thought or felt about the events that had taken place.

Soon they were once more bowling along the road down a gradual incline, and then they began to climb a long ridge that had for hours hidden what lay beyond. That climb was rather tiresome, owing to the sun and the dust and the restricted view.

When they reached the summit Madeline gave a little gasp of pleasure. A deep, gray, smooth valley opened below and sloped up on the other side in little ridges like waves, and these led to the foothills, dotted with clumps of brush or trees, and beyond rose dark mountains, pine-fringed and crag-spired.

"Wal, Miss Majesty, now we're gettin' somewhere," said Stillwell, cracking his whip. "Ten miles across this valley an' we'll be in the foothills where the Apaches used to run."

"Ten miles!" exclaimed Madeline. "It looks no more than half a mile to me."

"Wal, young woman, before you go to ridin' off alone you want to get your eyes corrected to Western distance. Now, what'd you call them black things off there on the slope?"

"Horsemen. No, cattle," replied Madeline, doubtfully.

"Nope. Jest plain, every-day cactus. An' over hyar—look down the valley. Somethin' of a pretty forest, ain't thet?" he asked, pointing.

Madeline saw a beautiful forest in the center of the valley toward the south.

"Wal, Miss Majesty, thet's jest this deceivin' air. There's no forest. It's a mirage."

"Indeed! How beautiful it is!" Madeline strained her gaze on the dark blot, and it seemed to float in the atmosphere, to have no clearly defined margins, to waver and shimmer, and then it faded and vanished.

The mountains dropped down again behind the horizon, and presently the road began once more to slope up. The horses slowed to a walk. There was a mile of rolling ridge, and then came the foothills. The road ascended through winding valleys. Trees and brush and rocks began to appear in the dry ravines. There was no water, yet all along the sandy washes were indications of floods at some periods. The heat and the dust stifled Madeline, and she had already become tired. Still she looked with all her eyes and saw birds, and beautiful quail with crests, and rabbits, and once she saw a deer.

"Miss Majesty," said Stillwell, "in the early days the Indians made this country a bad one to live in. I reckon you never heerd much about them times. Surely you was hardly born then. I'll hev to tell you some day how I fought Comanches in the Panhandle—thet was northern Texas—an' I had some mighty hair-raisin' scares in this country with Apaches."

He told her about Cochise, chief of the Chiricahua Apaches, the most savage and bloodthirsty tribe that ever made life a horror for the pioneer. Cochise befriended the whites once; but he was the victim of that friendliness, and he became the most implacable of foes. Then, Geronimo, another Apache chief, had, as late as 1885, gone on the war-path, and had left a bloody trail down the New Mexico and Arizona line almost to the border. Lone ranchmen and cowboys had been killed, and mothers had shot their children and then themselves at the approach of the Apache. The name Apache curdled the blood of any woman of the Southwest in those days.

Madeline shuddered, and was glad when the old frontiersman changed the subject and began to talk of the settling of that country by the Spaniards, the legends of lost gold-mines handed down to the Mexicans, and strange stories of heroism and mystery and religion. The Mexicans had not advanced much in spite of the spread of civilization to the Southwest. They were still superstitious, and believed the legends of treasures hidden in the walls of their missions, and that unseen hands rolled rocks down the gullies upon the heads of prospectors who dared to hunt for the lost mines of the padres.

"Up in the mountains back of my ranch there's a lost mine," said Stillwell. "Mebbe it's only a legend. But somehow I believe it's there. Other lost mines hev been found. An' as fer' the rollin' stones, I sure know thet's true, as any one can find out if he goes trailin' up the gulch. Mebbe thet's only the weatherin' of the cliffs. It's a sleepy, strange country, this Southwest, an', Miss Majesty, you're a-goin' to love it. You'll call it ro-mantic, Wal, I reckon ro-mantic is correct. A feller gets lazy out hyar an' dreamy, an' he wants to put off work till to-morrow. Some folks say it's a land of manana—a land of to-morrow. Thet's the Mexican of it.

"But I like best to think of what a lady said to me onct—an eddicated lady like you, Miss Majesty. Wal, she said it's a land where it's always afternoon. I liked thet. I always get up sore in the mawnin's, an' don't feel good till noon. But in the afternoon I get sorta warm an' like things. An' sunset is my time. I reckon I don't want nothin' any finer than sunset from my ranch. You look out over a valley that spreads wide between Guadalupe Mountains an' the Chiricahuas, down across the red Arizona desert clear to the Sierra Madres in Mexico. Two hundred miles, Miss Majesty! An' all as clear as print! An' the sun sets behind all thet! When my time comes to die I'd like it to be on my porch smokin' my pipe an' facin' the west."

So the old cattleman talked on while Madeline listened, and Florence dozed in her seat, and the sun began to wane, and the horses climbed steadily. Presently, at the foot of the steep ascent, Stillwell got out and walked, leading the team. During this long climb fatigue claimed Madeline, and she drowsily closed her eyes, to find when she opened them again that the glaring white sky had changed to a steel-blue. The sun had sunk behind the foothills and the air was growing chilly. Stillwell had returned to the driving-seat and was chuckling to the horses. Shadows crept up out of the hollows.

"Wal, Flo," said Stillwell, "I reckon we'd better hev the rest of thet there lunch before dark."

"You didn't leave much of it," laughed Florence, as she produced the basket from under the seat.

While they ate, the short twilight shaded and gloom filled the hollows. Madeline saw the first star, a faint, winking point of light. The sky had now changed to a hazy gray. Madeline saw it gradually clear and darken, to show other faint stars. After that there was perceptible deepening of the gray and an enlarging of the stars and a brightening of new-born ones. Night seemed to come on the cold wind. Madeline was glad to have the robes close around her and to lean against Florence. The hollows were now black, but the tops of the foothills gleamed pale in a soft light. The steady tramp of the horses went on, and the creak of wheels and crunching of gravel. Madeline grew so sleepy that she could not keep her weary eyelids from falling. There were drowsier spells in which she lost a feeling of where she was, and these were disturbed by the jolt of wheels over a rough place. Then came a blank interval, short or long, which ended in a more violent lurch of the buckboard. Madeline awoke to find her head on Florence's shoulder. She sat up laughing and apologizing for her laziness. Florence assured her they would soon reach the ranch.

Madeline observed then that the horses were once more trotting. The wind was colder, the night darker, the foot-hills flatter. And the sky was now a wonderful deep velvet-blue blazing with millions of stars. Some of them were magnificent. How strangely white and alive! Again Madeline felt the insistence of familiar yet baffling associations. These white stars called strangely to her or haunted her.

5

THE ROUND-UP

IT WAS A CRACKLING and roaring of fire that awakened Madeline next morning, and the first thing she saw was a huge stone fireplace in which lay a bundle of blazing sticks. Some one had kindled a fire while she slept. For a moment the curious sensation of being lost returned to her. She just dimly remembered reaching the ranch and being taken into a huge house and a huge, dimly lighted room. And it seemed to her that she had gone to sleep at once, and had awakened without remembering how she had gotten to bed.

But she was wide awake in an instant. The bed stood near one end of an enormous chamber. The adobe walls resembled a hall in an ancient feudal castle, stone-floored, stone-walled, with great darkened rafters running across the ceiling. The few articles of furniture were worn out and sadly dilapidated. Light flooded into the room from two windows on the right of the fireplace and two on the left, and another large window near the bedstead. Looking out from where she lay, Madeline saw a dark, slow up-sweep of mountain. Her eyes returned to the cheery, snapping fire, and she watched it while gathering courage to get up. The room was cold. When she did slip her bare feet out upon the stone floor she very quickly put them back under the warm blankets. And she was still in bed trying to pluck up her courage when, with a knock on the door and a cheerful greeting, Florence entered, carrying steaming hot water.

"Good mawnin', Miss Hammond. Hope you slept well. You sure were tired last night. I imagine you'll find this old rancho house as cold as a barn. It'll warm up directly. Al's gone with the boys and Bill. We're to ride down on the range after a while when your baggage comes."

Florence wore a woolen blouse with a scarf round her neck, a short corduroy divided skirt, and boots; and while she talked she energetically heaped up the burning wood in the fireplace, and laid Madeline's clothes at the foot of the bed, and heated a rug and put that on the floor by the bedside. And lastly, with a sweet, direct smile, she said:

"Al told me—and I sure saw myself—that you weren't used to being without your maid. Will you let me help you?"

"Thank you, I am going to be my own maid for a while. I expect I do appear a very helpless individual, but really I do not feel so. Perhaps I have had just a little too much waiting on."

"All right. Breakfast will be ready soon, and after that we'll look about the place."

Madeline was charmed with the old Spanish house, and the more she saw of it the more she thought what a delightful home it could be made. All the doors opened into a courtyard, or patio, as Florence called it. The house was low, in the shape of a rectangle, and so immense in size that Madeline wondered if it had been a Spanish barracks. Many of the rooms were dark, without windows, and they were empty. Others were full of ranchers' implements and sacks of grain and bales of hay. Florence called these last alfalfa. The house itself appeared strong and well preserved, and it was very picturesque. But in the living-rooms were only the barest necessities, and these were worn out and comfortless.

However, when Madeline went outdoors she forgot the cheerless, bare interior. Florence led the way out on a porch and waved a hand at a vast, colored void. "That's what Bill likes," she said.

At first Madeline could not tell what was sky and what was land. The immensity of the scene stunned her faculties of conception. She sat down in one of the old rocking-chairs and looked and looked, and knew that she was not grasping the reality of what stretched wondrously before her.

"We're up at the edge of the foothills," Florence said. "You remember we rode around the northern end of the mountain range? Well, that's behind us now, and you look down across the line into Arizona and Mexico. That long slope of gray is the head of the San Bernardino Valley. Straight across you see the black Chiricahua Mountains, and away down to the south the Guadalupe Mountains. That awful red gulf between is the desert, and far, far beyond the dim, blue peaks are the Sierra Madres in Mexico."

Madeline listened and gazed with straining eyes, and wondered if this was only a stupendous mirage, and why it seemed so different from all else that she had seen, and so endless, so baffling, so grand.

"It'll sure take you a little while to get used to being up high and seeing so much," explained Florence. "That's the secret—we're up high, the air is clear, and there's the whole bare world beneath us. Don't it somehow rest you? Well, it will. Now see those specks in the valley. They are stations, little towns. The railroad goes down that way. The largest speck is Chiricahua. It's over forty miles by trail. Here round to the north you can see Don Carlos's rancho. He's fifteen miles off, and I sure wish he were a thousand. That little green square about half-way between here and Don Carlos—that's Al's ranch. Just below us are the adobe houses of the Mexicans. There's a church, too. And here to the left you see Stillwell's corrals and bunk-houses and his stables all falling to pieces. The ranch has gone to ruin. All the ranches are going to ruin. But most of them are little one-horse affairs. And here—see that cloud of dust down in the valley? It's the round-up. The boys are there, and the cattle. Wait, I'll get the glasses."

By their aid Madeline saw in the foreground a great, dense herd of cattle with dark, thick streams and dotted lines of cattle leading in every direction. She saw streaks and clouds of dust, running horses, and a band of horses grazing; and she descried horsemen standing still like sentinels, and others in action.

"The round-up! I want to know all about it—to see it," declared Madeline. "Please tell me what it means, what it's for, and then take me down there."

"It's sure a sight, Miss Hammond. I'll be glad to take you down, but I fancy you'll not want to go close. Few Eastern people who regularly eat their choice cuts of roast beef and porterhouse have any idea of the open range and the struggle cattle have to live and the hard life of cowboys. It'll sure open your eyes, Miss Hammond. I'm glad you care to know. Your brother would have made a big success in this cattle business if it hadn't been for crooked work by rival ranchers. He'll make it yet, in spite of them."

"Indeed he shall," replied Madeline. "But tell me, please, all about the round-up."

"Well, in the first place, every cattleman has to have a brand to identify his stock. Without it no cattleman, nor half a hundred cowboys, if he had so many, could ever recognize all the cattle in a big herd. There are no fences on our ranges. They are all open to everybody. Some day I hope we'll be rich enough to fence a range. The different herds graze together. Every calf has to be caught, if possible, and branded with the mark of its mother. That's no easy job. A maverick is an unbranded calf that has been weaned and shifts for itself. The maverick then belongs to the man who finds it and brands it. These little calves that lose their mothers sure have a cruel time of it. Many of them die. Then the coyotes and wolves and lions prey on them. Every year we have two big round-ups, but the boys do some branding all the year. A calf should be branded as soon as it's found. This is a safeguard against cattle-thieves. We don't have the rustling of herds and bunches of cattle like we used to. But there's always the calf-thief, and always will be as long as there's cattle-raising. The thieves have a good many cunning tricks. They kill the calf's mother or slit the calf's tongue so it can't suck and so loses its mother. They steal and hide a calf and watch it till it's big enough to fare for itself, and then brand it. They make imperfect brands and finish them at a later time.

"We have our big round-up in the fall, when there's plenty of grass and water, and all the riding-stock as well as the cattle are in fine shape. The cattlemen in the valley meet with their cowboys and drive in all the cattle they can find. Then they brand and cut out each man's herd and drive it toward home. Then they go on up or down the valley, make another camp, and drive in more cattle. It takes weeks. There are so many Greasers with little bands of stock, and they are crafty and greedy. Bill says he knows Greaser cowboys, vaqueros, who never owned a steer or a cow, and now they've got growing herds. The same might be said of more than one white cowboy. But there's not as much of that as there used to be."

"And the horses? I want to know about them," said Madeline, when Florence paused.

"Oh, the cow-ponies! Well, they sure are interesting. Broncos, the boys call them. Wild! they're wilder than the steers they have to chase. Bill's got broncos heah that never have been broken and never will be. And not every boy can ride them, either. The vaqueros have the finest horses. Don Carlos has a black that I'd give anything to own. And he has other fine stock. Gene Stewart's big roan is a Mexican horse, the swiftest and proudest I ever saw. I was up on him once and—oh, he can run! He likes a woman, too, and that's sure something I want in a horse. I heard Al and Bill talking at breakfast about a horse for you. They were wrangling. Bill wanted you to have one, and Al another. It was funny to hear them. Finally they left the choice to me, until the round-up is over. Then I suppose every cowboy on the range will offer you his best mount. Come, let's go out to the corrals and look over the few horses left."

For Madeline the morning hours flew by, with a goodly part of the time spent on the porch gazing out over that ever-changing vista. At noon a teamster drove up with her trunks. Then while Florence helped the Mexican woman get lunch Madeline unpacked part of her effects and got out things for which she would have immediate need. After lunch she changed her dress for a riding-habit and, going outside, found Florence waiting with the horses.

The Western girl's clear eyes seemed to take stock of Madeline's appearance in one swift, inquisitive glance and then shone with pleasure.

"You sure look—you're a picture, Miss Hammond. That riding-outfit is a new one. What it 'd look like on me or another woman I can't imagine, but on you it's—it's stunning. Bill won't let you go within a mile of the cowboys. If they see you that'll be the finish of the round-up."

While they rode down the slope Florence talked about the open ranges of New Mexico and Arizona.

"Water is scarce," she said. "If Bill could afford to pipe water down from the mountains he'd have the finest ranch in the valley."

She went on to tell that the climate was mild in winter and hot in summer. Warm, sunshiny days prevailed nearly all the year round. Some summers it rained, and occasionally there would be a dry year, the dreaded ano seco of the Mexicans. Rain was always expected and prayed for in the midsummer months, and when it came the grama-grass sprang up, making the valleys green from mountain to mountain. The intersecting valleys, ranging between the long slope of foothills, afforded the best pasture for cattle, and these were jealously sought by the Mexicans who had only small herds to look after. Stillwell's cowboys were always chasing these vaqueros off land that belonged to Stillwell. He owned twenty thousand acres of unfenced land adjoining the open range. Don Carlos possessed more acreage than that, and his cattle were always mingling with Stillwell's. And in turn Don Carlos's vaqueros were always chasing Stillwell's cattle away from the Mexican's watering-place. Bad feeling had been manifested for years, and now relations were strained to the breaking-point.

As Madeline rode along she made good use of her eyes. The soil was sandy and porous, and she understood why the rain and water from the few springs disappeared so quickly. At a little distance the grama-grass appeared thick, but near at hand it was seen to be sparse. Bunches of greasewood and cactus plants were interspersed here and there in the grass. What surprised Madeline was the fact that, though she and Florence had seemed to be riding quite awhile, they had apparently not drawn any closer to the round-up. The slope of the valley was noticeable only after some miles had been traversed. Looking forward, Madeline imagined the valley only a few miles wide. She would have been sure she could walk her horse across it in an hour. Yet that black, bold range of Chiricahua Mountains was distant a long day's journey for even a hard-riding cowboy. It was only by looking back that Madeline could grasp the true relation of things; she could not be deceived by distance she had covered.

Gradually the black dots enlarged and assumed shape of cattle and horses moving round a great dusty patch. In another half-hour Madeline rode behind Florence to the outskirts of the scene of action. They drew rein near a huge wagon in the neighborhood of which were more than a hundred horses grazing and whistling and trotting about and lifting heads to watch the new-comers. Four cowboys stood mounted guard over this drove of horses. Perhaps a quarter of a mile farther out was a dusty melee. A roar of tramping hoofs filled Madeline's ears. The lines of marching cattle had merged into a great, moving herd half obscured by dust.

"I can make little of what is going on," said Madeline. "I want to go closer."

They trotted across half the intervening distance, and when Florence halted again Madeline was still not satisfied and asked to be taken nearer. This time, before they reined in again, Al Hammond saw them and wheeled his horse in their direction. He yelled something which Madeline did not understand, and then halted them.

"Close enough," he called; and in the din his voice was not very clear. "It's not safe. Wild steers! I'm glad you came, girls. Majesty, what do you think of that bunch of cattle?"

Madeline could scarcely reply what she thought, for the noise and dust and ceaseless action confused her.

"They're milling, Al," said Florence.

"We just rounded them up. They're milling, and that's bad. The vaqueros are hard drivers. They beat us all hollow, and we drove some, too." He was wet with sweat, black with dust, and out of breath. "I'm off now. Flo, my sister will have enough of this in about two minutes. Take her back to the wagon. I'll tell Bill you're here, and run in whenever I get a minute."

The bawling and bellowing, the crackling of horns and pounding of hoofs, the dusty whirl of cattle, and the flying cowboys disconcerted Madeline and frightened her a little; but she was intensely interested and meant to stay there until she saw for herself what that strife of sound and action meant. When she tried to take in the whole scene she did not make out anything clearly and she determined to see it little by little.

"Will you stay longer?" asked Florence; and, receiving an affirmative reply, she warned Madeline: "If a runaway steer or angry cow comes this way let your horse go. He'll get out of the way."

That lent the situation excitement, and Madeline became absorbed. The great mass of cattle seemed to be eddying like a whirlpool, and from that Madeline understood the significance of the range word "milling." But when Madeline looked at one end of the herd she saw cattle standing still, facing outward, and calves cringing close in fear. The motion of the cattle slowed from the inside of the herd to the outside and gradually ceased. The roar and tramp of hoofs and crack of horns and thump of heads also ceased in degree, but the bawling and bellowing continued. While she watched, the herd spread, grew less dense, and stragglers appeared to be about to bolt through the line of mounted cowboys.

From that moment so many things happened, and so swiftly, that Madeline could not see a tenth of what was going on within eyesight. It seemed horsemen darted into the herd and drove out cattle. Madeline pinned her gaze on one cowboy who rode a white horse and was chasing a steer. He whirled a lasso around his head and threw it; the rope streaked out and the loop caught the leg of the steer. The white horse stopped with wonderful suddenness, and the steer slid in the dust. Quick as a flash the cowboy was out of the saddle, and, grasping the legs of the steer before it could rise, he tied them with a rope. It had all been done almost as quickly as thought. Another man came with what Madeline divined was a branding-iron. He applied it to the flank of the steer. Then it seemed the steer was up with a jump, wildly looking for some way to run, and the cowboy was circling his lasso. Madeline saw fires in the background, with a man in charge, evidently heating the irons. Then this same cowboy roped a heifer which bawled lustily when the hot iron seared its hide. Madeline saw the smoke rising from the touch of the iron, and the sight made her shrink and want to turn away, but she resolutely fought her sensitiveness. She had never been able to bear the sight of any animal suffering. The rough work in men's lives was as a sealed book to her; and now, for some reason beyond her knowledge, she wanted to see and hear and learn some of the every-day duties that made up those lives.

"Look, Miss Hammond, there's Don Carlos!" said Florence. "Look at that black horse!"

Madeleine saw a dark-faced Mexican riding by. He was too far away for her to distinguish his features, but he reminded her of an Italian brigand. He bestrode a magnificent horse.

Stillwell rode up to the girls then and greeted them in his big voice.

"Right in the thick of it, hey? Wal, that's sure fine. I'm glad to see, Miss Majesty, thet you ain't afraid of a little dust or smell of burnin' hide an' hair."

"Couldn't you brand the calves without hurting them?" asked Madeline.

"Haw, haw! Why, they ain't hurt none. They jest bawl for their mammas. Sometimes, though, we hev to hurt one jest to find which is his mamma."

"I want to know how you tell what brand to put on those calves that are separated from their mothers," asked Madeline.

"Thet's decided by the round-up bosses. I've one boss an' Don Carlos has one. They decide everything, an' they hev to be obeyed. There's Nick Steele, my boss. Watch him! He's ridin' a bay in among the cattle there. He orders the calves an' steers to be cut out. Then the cowboys do the cuttin' out an' the brandin'. We try to divide up the mavericks as near as possible."

At this juncture Madeline's brother joined the group, evidently in search of Stillwell.

"Bill, Nels just rode in," he said.

"Good! We sure need him. Any news of Danny Mains?"

"No. Nels said he lost the trail when he got on hard ground."

"Wal, wal. Say, Al, your sister is sure takin' to the round-up. An' the boys are gettin' wise. See thet sun-of-a-gun Ambrose cuttin' capers all around. He'll sure do his prettiest. Ambrose is a ladies' man, he thinks."

The two men and Florence joined in a little pleasant teasing of Madeline, and drew her attention to what appeared to be really unnecessary feats of horsemanship all made in her vicinity. The cowboys evinced their interest in covert glances while recoiling a lasso or while passing to and fro. It was all too serious for Madeline to be amused at that moment. She did not care to talk. She sat her horse and watched.

The lithe, dark vaqueros fascinated her. They were here, there, everywhere, with lariats flying, horses plunging back, jerking calves and yearlings to the grass. They were cruel to their mounts, cruel to their cattle. Madeline winced as the great silver rowels of the spurs went plowing into the flanks of their horses. She saw these spurs stained with blood, choked with hair. She saw the vaqueros break the legs of calves and let them lie till a white cowboy came along and shot them. Calves were jerked down and dragged many yards; steers were pulled by one leg. These vaqueros were the most superb horsemen Madeline had ever seen, and she had seen the Cossacks and Tatars of the Russian steppes. They were swift, graceful, daring; they never failed to catch a running steer, and the lassoes always went true. What sharp dashes the horses made, and wheelings here and there, and sudden stops, and how they braced themselves to withstand the shock!

The cowboys, likewise, showed wonderful horsemanship, and, reckless as they were, Madeline imagined she saw consideration for steed and cattle that was wanting in the vaqueros. They changed mounts oftener than the Mexican riders, and the horses they unsaddled for fresh ones were not so spent, so wet, so covered with lather. It was only after an hour or more of observation that Madeline began to realize the exceedingly toilsome and dangerous work cowboys had to perform. There was little or no rest for them. They were continually among wild and vicious and wide-horned steers. In many instances they owed their lives to their horses. The danger came mostly when the cowboy leaped off to tie and brand a calf he had thrown. Some of the cows charged with lowered, twisting horns. Time and again Madeline's heart leaped to her throat for fear a man would be gored. One cowboy roped a calf that bawled loudly. Its mother dashed in and just missed the kneeling cowboy as he rolled over. Then he had to run, and he could not run very fast. He was bow-legged and appeared awkward. Madeline saw another cowboy thrown and nearly run over by a plunging steer. His horse bolted as if it intended to leave the range. Then close by Madeline a big steer went down at the end of a lasso. The cowboy who had thrown it nimbly jumped down, and at that moment his horse began to rear and prance and suddenly to lower his head close to the ground and kick high. He ran round in a circle, the fallen steer on the taut lasso acting as a pivot. The cowboy loosed the rope from the steer, and then was dragged about on the grass. It was almost frightful for Madeline to see that cowboy go at his horse. But she recognized the mastery and skill. Then two horses came into collision on the run. One horse went down; the rider of the other was unseated and was kicked before he could get up. This fellow limped to his mount and struck at him, while the horse showed his teeth in a vicious attempt to bite.

All the while this ceaseless activity was going on there was a strange uproar—bawl and bellow, the shock of heavy bodies meeting and falling, the shrill jabbering of the vaqueros, and the shouts and banterings of the cowboys. They took sharp orders and replied in jest. They went about this stern toil as if it were a game to be played in good humor. One sang a rollicking song, another whistled, another smoked a cigarette. The sun was hot, and they, like their horses, were dripping with sweat. The characteristic red faces had taken on so much dust that cowboys could not be distinguished from vaqueros except by the difference in dress. Blood was not wanting on tireless hands. The air was thick, oppressive, rank with the smell of cattle and of burning hide.

Madeline began to sicken. She choked with dust, was almost stifled by the odor. But that made her all the more determined to stay there. Florence urged her to come away, or at least move back out of the worst of it. Stillwell seconded Florence. Madeline, however, smilingly refused. Then her brother said: "Here, this is making you sick. You're pale." And she replied that she intended to stay until the day's work ended. Al gave her a strange look, and made no more comment. The kindly Stillwell then began to talk.

"Miss Majesty, you're seein' the life of the cattleman an' cowboy—the real thing—same as it was in the early days. The ranchers in Texas an' some in Arizona hev took on style, new-fangled idees thet are good, an' I wish we could follow them. But we've got to stick to the old-fashioned, open-range round-up. It looks cruel to you, I can see thet. Wal, mebbe so, mebbe so. Them Greasers are cruel, thet's certain. Fer thet matter, I never seen a Greaser who wasn't cruel. But I reckon all the strenuous work you've seen to-day ain't any tougher than most any day of a cowboy's life. Long hours on hossback, poor grub, sleepin' on the ground, lonesome watches, dust an' sun an' wind an' thirst, day in an' day out all the year round—thet's what a cowboy has.

"Look at Nels there. See, what little hair he has is snow-white. He's red an' thin an' hard —burned up. You notice thet hump of his shoulders. An' his hands, when he gets close—jest take a peep at his hands. Nels can't pick up a pin. He can't hardly button his shirt or untie a knot in his rope. He looks sixty years—an old man. Wal, Nels 'ain't seen forty. He's a young man, but he's seen a lifetime fer every year. Miss Majesty, it was Arizona thet made Nels what he is, the Arizona desert an' the work of a cowman. He's seen ridin' at Canyon Diablo an' the Verdi an' Tonto Basin. He knows every mile of Aravaipa Valley an' the Pinaleno country. He's ranged from Tombstone to Douglas. He hed shot bad white men an' bad Greasers before he was twenty-one. He's seen some life, Nels has. My sixty years ain't nothin'; my early days in the Staked Plains an' on the border with Apaches ain't nothin' to what Nels has seen an' lived through. He's just come to be part of the desert; you might say he's stone an' fire an' silence an' cactus an' force. He's a man, Miss Majesty, a wonderful man. Rough he'll seem to you. Wal, I'll show you pieces of quartz from the mountains back of my ranch an' they're thet rough they'd cut your hands. But there's pure gold in them. An' so it is with Nels an' many of these cowboys.

"An' there's Price—Monty Price. Monty stands fer Montana, where he hails from. Take a good look at him, Miss Majesty. He's been hurt, I reckon. Thet accounts fer him bein' without hoss or rope; an' thet limp. Wal, he's been ripped a little. It's sure rare an seldom thet a cowboy gets foul of one of them thousands of sharp horns; but it does happen."

Madeline saw a very short, wizened little man, ludicrously bow-legged, with a face the color and hardness of a burned-out cinder. He was hobbling by toward the wagon, and one of his short, crooked legs dragged.

"Not much to look at, is he?" went on Stillwell. "Wal; I know it's natural thet we're all best pleased by good looks in any one, even a man. It hedn't ought to be thet way. Monty Price looks like hell. But appearances are sure deceivin'. Monty saw years of ridin' along the Missouri bottoms, the big prairies, where there's high grass an' sometimes fires. In Montana they have blizzards that freeze cattle standin' in their tracks. An' hosses freeze to death. They tell me thet a drivin' sleet in the face with the mercury forty below is somethin' to ride against. You can't get Monty to say much about cold. All you hev to do is to watch him, how he hunts the sun. It never gets too hot fer Monty. Wal, I reckon he was a little more prepossessin' once. The story thet come to us about Monty is this: He got caught out in a prairie fire an' could hev saved himself easy, but there was a lone ranch right in the line of fire, an' Monty knowed the rancher was away, an' his wife an' baby was home. He knowed, too, the way the wind was, thet the ranch-house would burn. It was a long chance he was takin'. But he went over, put the woman up behind him, wrapped the baby an' his hoss's haid in a wet blanket, an' rode away. Thet was sure some ride, I've heerd. But the fire ketched Monty at the last. The woman fell an' was lost, an' then his hoss. An' Monty ran an' walked an' crawled through the fire with thet baby, an' he saved it. Monty was never much good as a cowboy after thet. He couldn't hold no jobs. Wal, he'll have one with me as long as I have a steer left."

❧ 6 ❧

A GIFT AND A PURCHASE

FOR A WEEK the scene of the round-up lay within riding-distance of the ranch-house, and Madeline passed most of this time in the saddle, watching the strenuous labors of the vaqueros and cowboys. She overestimated her strength, and more than once had to be lifted from her horse. Stillwell's pleasure in her attendance gave place to concern. He tried to persuade her to stay away from the round-up, and Florence grew even more solicitous.

Madeline, however, was not moved by their entreaties. She grasped only dimly the truth of what it was she was learning—something infinitely more than the rounding up of cattle by cowboys, and she was loath to lose an hour of her opportunity.

Her brother looked out for her as much as his duties permitted; but for several days he never once mentioned her growing fatigue and the strain of excitement, or suggested that she had better go back to the house with Florence. Many times she felt the drawing power of his keen blue eyes on her face. And at these moments she sensed more than brotherly regard. He was watching her, studying her, weighing her, and the conviction was vaguely disturbing. It was disquieting for Madeline to think that Alfred might have guessed her trouble. From time to time he brought cowboys to her and introduced them, and laughed and jested, trying to make the ordeal less embarrassing for these men so little used to women.

Before the week was out, however, Alfred found occasion to tell her that it would be wiser for her to let the round-up go on without gracing it further with her presence. He said it laughingly; nevertheless, he was serious. And when Madeline turned to him in surprise he said, bluntly:

"I don't like the way Don Carlos follows you around. Bill's afraid that Nels or Ambrose or one of the cowboys will take a fall out of the Mexican. They're itching for the chance. Of course, dear, it's absurd to you, but it's true."

Absurd it certainly was, yet it served to show Madeline how intensely occupied she had been with her own feelings, roused by the tumult and toil of the round-up. She recalled that Don Carlos had been presented to her, and that she had not liked his dark, striking face with its bold, prominent, glittering eyes and sinister lines; and she had not liked his suave, sweet, insinuating voice or his subtle manner, with its slow bows and gestures. She had thought he looked handsome and dashing on the magnificent black horse. However, now that Alfred's words made her think, she recalled that wherever she had been in the field the noble horse, with his silver-mounted saddle and his dark rider, had been always in her vicinity.

"Don Carlos has been after Florence for a long time," said Alfred. "He's not a young man by any means. He's fifty, Bill says; but you can seldom tell a Mexican's age from his looks. Don Carlos is well educated and a man we know very little about. Mexicans of his stamp don't regard women as we white men do. Now, my dear, beautiful sister from New York, I haven't much use for Don Carlos; but I don't want Nels or Ambrose to make a wild throw with a rope and pull the Don off his horse. So you had better ride up to the house and stay there."

"Alfred, you are joking, teasing me," said Madeline. "Indeed not," replied Alfred. "How about it, Flo?" Florence replied that the cowboys would upon the slightest provocation treat Don Carlos with less ceremony and gentleness than a roped steer. Old Bill Stillwell came up to be importuned by Alfred regarding the conduct of cowboys on occasion, and he not only corroborated the assertion, but added emphasis and evidence of his own.

"An', Miss Majesty," he concluded, "I reckon if Gene Stewart was ridin' fer me, thet grinnin' Greaser would hev hed a bump in the dust before now."

Madeline had been wavering between sobriety and laughter until Stillwell's mention of his ideal of cowboy chivalry decided in favor of the laughter.

"I am not convinced, but I surrender," she said. "You have only some occult motive for driving me away. I am sure that handsome Don Carlos is being unjustly suspected. But as I have seen a little of cowboys' singular imagination and gallantry, I am rather inclined to fear their possibilities. So good-by."

Then she rode with Florence up the long, gray slope to the ranch-house. That night she suffered from excessive weariness, which she attributed more to the strange working of her mind than to riding and sitting her horse. Morning, however, found her in no disposition to rest. It was not activity that she craved, or excitement, or pleasure. An unerring instinct, rising dear from the thronging sensations of the last few days, told her that she had missed something in life. It could not have been love, for she loved brother, sister, parents, friends; it could not have been consideration for the poor, the unfortunate, the hapless; she had expressed her sympathy for these by giving freely; it could not have been pleasure, culture, travel, society, wealth, position, fame, for these had been hers all her life. Whatever this something was, she had baffling intimations of it, hopes that faded on the verge of realizations, haunting promises that were unfulfilled. Whatever it was, it had remained hidden and unknown at home, and here in the West it began to allure and drive her to discovery. Therefore she could not rest; she wanted to go and see; she was no longer chasing phantoms; it was a hunt for treasure that held aloof, as intangible as the substance of dreams.

That morning she spoke a desire to visit the Mexican quarters lying at the base of the foothills. Florence protested that this was no place to take Madeline. But Madeline insisted, and it required only a few words and a persuading smile to win Florence over.

From the porch the cluster of adobe houses added a picturesque touch of color and contrast to the waste of gray valley. Near at hand they proved the enchantment lent by distance. They were old, crumbling, broken down, squalid. A few goats climbed around upon them; a few mangy dogs barked announcement of visitors; and then a troop of half-naked, dirty, ragged children ran out. They were very shy, and at first retreated in affright. But kind words and smiles gained their confidence, and then they followed in a body, gathering a quota of new children at each house. Madeline at once conceived the idea of doing something to better the condition of these poor Mexicans, and with this in mind she decided to have a look indoors. She fancied she might have been an apparition, judging from the effect her presence had upon the first woman she encountered. While Florence exercised what little Spanish she had command of, trying to get the women to talk, Madeline looked about the miserable little rooms. And there grew upon her a feeling of sickness, which increased as she passed from one house to another. She had not believed such squalor could exist anywhere in America. The huts reeked with filth; vermin crawled over the dirt floors. There was absolutely no evidence of water, and she believed what Florence told her—that these people never bathed. There was little evidence of labor. Idle men and women smoking cigarettes lolled about, some silent, others jabbering. They did not resent the visit of the American women, nor did they show hospitality. They appeared stupid. Disease was rampant in these houses; when the doors were shut there was no ventilation, and even with the doors open Madeline felt choked and stifled. A powerful penetrating odor pervaded the rooms that were less stifling than others, and this odor Florence explained came from a liquor the Mexicans distilled from a cactus plant. Here drunkenness was manifest, a terrible inert drunkenness that made its victims deathlike.

Madeline could not extend her visit to the little mission-house. She saw a padre, a starved, sad-faced man who, she instinctively felt, was good. She managed to mount her horse and ride up to the house; but, once there, she weakened and Florence had almost to carry her in-doors. She fought off a faintness, only to succumb to it when alone in her room. Still, she did not entirely lose consciousness, and soon recovered to the extent that she did not require assistance.

Upon the morning after the end of the round-up, when she went out on the porch, her brother and Stillwell appeared to be arguing about the identity of a horse.

"Wal, I reckon it's my old roan," said Stillwell, shading his eyes with his hand.

"Bill, if that isn't Stewart's horse my eyes are going back on me," replied Al. "It's not the color or shape—the distance is too far to judge by that. It's the motion—the swing."

"Al, mebbe you're right. But they ain't no rider up on thet hoss. Flo, fetch my glass."

Florence went into the house, while Madeline tried to discover the object of attention. Presently far up the gray hollow along a foothill she saw dust, and then the dark, moving figure of a horse. She was watching when Florence returned with the glass. Bill took a long look, adjusted the glasses carefully, and tried again.

"Wal, I hate to admit my eyes are gettin' pore. But I guess I'll hev to. Thet's Gene Stewart's hoss, saddled, an' comin' at a fast clip without a rider. It's amazin' strange, an' some in keepin' with other things concernin' Gene."

"Give me the glass," said Al. "Yes, I was right. Bill, the horse is not frightened. He's coming steadily; he's got something on his mind."

"Thet's a trained hoss, Al. He has more sense than some men I know. Take a look with the glasses up the hollow. See anybody?"

"No."

"Swing up over the foothills—where the trail leads. Higher—along thet ridge where the rocks begin. See anybody?"

"By Jove! Bill—two horses! But I can't make out much for dust. They are climbing fast. One horse gone among the rocks. There—the other's gone. What do you make of that?"

"Wal, I can't make no more 'n you. But I'll bet we know somethin' soon, fer Gene's hoss is comin' faster as he nears the ranch."

The wide hollow sloping up into the foothills lay open to unobstructed view, and less than half a mile distant Madeline saw the riderless horse coming along the white trail at a rapid canter. She watched him, recalling the circumstances under which she had first seen him, and then his wild flight through the dimly lighted streets of El Cajon out into the black night. She thrilled again and believed she would never think of that starry night's adventure without a thrill. She watched the horse and felt more than curiosity. A shrill, piercing whistle pealed in.

"Wal, he's seen us, thet's sure," said Bill.

The horse neared the corrals, disappeared into a lane, and then, breaking his gait again, thundered into the inclosure and pounded to a halt some twenty yards from where Stillwell waited for him.

One look at him at close range in the clear light of day was enough for Madeline to award him a blue ribbon over all horses, even her prize-winner, White Stockings. The cowboy's great steed was no lithe, slender-bodied mustang. He was a charger, almost tremendous of build, with a black coat faintly mottled in gray, and it shone like polished glass in the sun. Evidently he had been carefully dressed down for this occasion, for there was no dust on him, nor a kink in his beautiful mane, nor a mark on his glossy hide.

"Come hyar, you son-of-a-gun," said Stillwell.

The horse dropped his head, snorted, and came obediently up. He was neither shy nor wild. He poked a friendly nose at Stillwell, and then looked at Al and the women. Unhooking the stirrups from the pommel, Stillwell let them fall and began to search the saddle for something which he evidently expected to find. Presently from somewhere among the trappings he produced a folded bit of paper, and after scrutinizing it handed it to Al.

"Addressed to you; an' I'll bet you two bits I know what's in it," he said.

Alfred unfolded the letter, read it, and then looked at Stillwell.

"Bill, you're a pretty good guesser. Gene's made for the border. He sent the horse by somebody, no names mentioned, and wants my sister to have him if she will accept."

"Any mention of Danny Mains?" asked the rancher.

"Not a word."

"Thet's bad. Gene'd know about Danny if anybody did. But he's a close-mouthed cuss. So he's sure hittin' for Mexico. Wonder if Danny's goin', too? Wal, there's two of the best cowmen I ever seen gone to hell an' I'm sorry."

With that he bowed his head and, grumbling to himself, went into the house. Alfred lifted the reins over the head of the horse and, leading him to Madeline, slipped the knot over her arm and placed the letter in her hand.

"Majesty, I'd accept the horse," he said. "Stewart is only a cowboy now, and as tough as any I've known. But he comes of a good family. He was a college man and a gentleman once. He went to the bad out here, like so many fellows go, like I nearly did. Then he had told me about his sister and mother. He cared a good deal for them. I think he has been a source of unhappiness to them. It was mostly when he was reminded of this in some way that he'd get drunk. I have always stuck to him, and I would do so yet if I had the chance. You can see Bill is heartbroken about Danny Mains and Stewart. I think he rather hoped to get good news. There's not much chance of them coming back now, at least not in the case of Stewart. This giving up his horse means he's going to join the rebel forces across the border. What wouldn't I give to see that cowboy break loose on a bunch of Greasers! Oh, damn the luck! I beg your pardon, Majesty. But I'm upset, too. I'm sorry about Stewart. I liked him pretty well before he thrashed that coyote of a sheriff, Pat Hawe, and afterward I guess I liked him more. You read the letter, sister, and accept the horse."

In silence Madeline bent her gaze from her brother's face to the letter:

Friend Al,—I'm sending my horse down to you because I'm going away and haven't the nerve to take him where he'd get hurt or fall into strange hands.

If you think it's all right, why, give him to your sister with my respects. But if you don't like the idea, Al, or if she won't have him, then he's for you. I'm not forgetting your kindness to me, even if I never showed it. And, Al, my horse has never felt a quirt or a spur, and I'd like to think you'd never hurt him. I'm hoping your sister will take him. She'll be good to him, and she can afford to take care of him. And, while I'm waiting to be plugged by a Greaser bullet, if I happen to have a picture in mind of how she'll look upon my horse, why, man, it's not going to make any difference to you. She needn't ever know it. Between you and me, Al, don't let her or Flo ride alone over Don Carlos's way. If I had time I could tell you something about that slick Greaser. And tell your sister, if there's ever any reason for her to run away from anybody when she's up on that roan, just let her lean over and yell in his ear. She'll find herself riding the wind. So long.

Gene Stewart.

Madeline thoughtfully folded the letter and murmured, "How he must love his horse!"

"Well, I should say so," replied Alfred. "Flo will tell you. She's the only person Gene ever let ride that horse, unless, as Bill thinks, the little Mexican girl, Bonita, rode him out of El Cajon the other night. Well, sister mine, how about it—will you accept the horse?"

"Assuredly. And very happy indeed am I to get him. Al, you said, I think, that Mr. Stewart named him after me—saw my nickname in the New York paper?"

"Yes."

"Well, I will not change his name. But, Al, how shall I ever climb up on him? He's taller than I am. What a giant of a horse! Oh, look at him—he's nosing my hand. I really believe he understood what I said. Al, did you ever see such a splendid head and such beautiful eyes? They are so large and dark and soft—and human. Oh, I am a fickle woman, for I am forgetting White Stockings."

"I'll gamble he'll make you forget any other horse," said Alfred. "You'll have to get on him from the porch."

As Madeline was not dressed for the saddle, she did not attempt to mount.

"Come, Majesty—how strange that sounds!—we must get acquainted. You have now a new owner, a very severe young woman who will demand loyalty from you and obedience, and some day, after a decent period, she will expect love."

Madeline led the horse to and fro, and was delighted with his gentleness. She discovered that he did not need to be led. He came at her call, followed her like a pet dog, rubbed his black muzzle against her. Sometimes, at the turns in their walk, he lifted his head and with ears forward looked up the trail by which he had come, and beyond the foothills. He was looking over the range. Some one was calling to him, perhaps, from beyond the mountains. Madeline liked him the better for that memory, and pitied the wayward cowboy who had parted with his only possession for very love of it.

That afternoon when Alfred lifted Madeline to the back of the big roan she felt high in the air.

"We'll have a run out to the mesa," said her brother, as he mounted. "Keep a tight rein on him and ease up when you want him to go faster. But don't yell in his ear unless you want Florence and me to see you disappear on the horizon."

He trotted out of the yard, down by the corrals, to come out on the edge of a gray, open flat that stretched several miles to the slope of a mesa. Florence led, and Madeline saw that she rode like a cowboy. Alfred drew on to her side, leaving Madeline in the rear. Then the leading horses broke into a gallop. They wanted to run, and Madeline felt with a thrill that she would hardly be able to keep Majesty from running, even if she wanted to. He sawed on the tight bridle as the others drew away and broke from pace to gallop. Then Florence put her horse into a run. Alfred turned and called to Madeline to come along.

"This will never do. They are running away from us," said Madeline, and she eased up her hold on the bridle. Something happened beneath her just then; she did not know at first exactly what. As much as she had been on horseback she had never ridden at a running gait. In New York it was not decorous or safe. So when Majesty lowered and stretched and changed the stiff, jolting gallop for a wonderful, smooth, gliding run it required Madeline some moments to realize what was happening. It did not take long for her to see the distance diminishing between her and her companions. Still they had gotten a goodly start and were far advanced. She felt the steady, even rush of the wind. It amazed her to find how easily, comfortably she kept to the saddle. The experience was new. The one fault she had heretofore found with riding was the violent shaking-up. In this instance she experienced nothing of that kind, no strain, no necessity to hold on with a desperate awareness of work. She had never felt the wind in her face, the whip of a horse's mane, the buoyant, level spring of a tanning gait. It thrilled her, exhilarated her, fired her blood. Suddenly she found herself alive, throbbing; and, inspired by she knew not what, she loosened the bridle and, leaning far forward, she cried, "Oh, you splendid fellow, run!"

She heard from under her a sudden quick clattering roar of hoofs, and she swayed back with the wonderfully swift increase in Majesty's speed. The wind stung her face, howled in her ears, tore at her hair. The gray plain swept by on each side, and in front seemed to be waving toward her. In her blurred sight Florence and Alfred appeared to be coming back. But she saw presently, upon nearer view, that Majesty was overhauling the other horses, was going to pass them. Indeed, he did pass them, shooting by so as almost to make them appear standing still. And he ran on, not breaking his gait till he reached the steep side of the mesa, where he slowed down and stopped.

"Glorious!" exclaimed Madeline. She was all in a blaze, and every muscle and nerve of her body tingled and quivered. Her hands, as she endeavored to put up the loosened strands of hair, trembled and failed of their accustomed dexterity. Then she faced about and waited for her companions.

Alfred reached her first, laughing, delighted, yet also a little anxious.

"Holy smoke! But can't he run? Did he bolt on you?"

"No, I called in his ear," replied Madeline.

"So that was it. That's the woman of you, and forbidden fruit. Flo said she'd do it the minute she was on him. Majesty, you can ride. See if Flo doesn't say so."

The Western girl came up then with her pleasure bright in her face.

"It was just great to see you. How your hair burned in the wind! Al, she sure can ride. Oh, I'm so glad! I was a little afraid. And that horse! Isn't he grand? Can't he run?"

Alfred led the way up the steep, zigzag trail to the top of the mesa. Madeline saw a beautiful flat surface of short grass, level as a floor. She uttered a little cry of wonder and enthusiasm.

"Al, what a place for golf! This would be the finest links in the world."

"Well, I've thought of that myself," he replied. "The only trouble would be—could anybody stop looking at the scenery long enough to hit a ball? Majesty, look!"

And then it seemed that Madeline was confronted by a spectacle too sublime and terrible for her gaze. The immensity of this red-ridged, deep-gulfed world descending incalculable distances refused to be grasped, and awed her, shocked her.

"Once, Majesty, when I first came out West, I was down and out—determined to end it all," said Alfred. "And happened to climb up here looking for a lonely place to die. When I saw that I changed my mind."

Madeline was silent. She remained so during the ride around the rim of the mesa and down the steep trail. This time Alfred and Florence failed to tempt her into a race. She had been awe-struck; she had been exalted she had been confounded; and she recovered slowly without divining exactly what had come to her.

She reached the ranch-house far behind her companions, and at supper-time was unusually thoughtful. Later, when they assembled on the porch to watch the sunset, Stillwell's humorous complainings inspired the inception of an idea which flashed up in her mind swift as lightning. And then by listening sympathetically she encouraged him to recite the troubles of a poor cattleman. They were many and long and interesting, and rather numbing to the life of her inspired idea.

"Mr. Stillwell, could ranching here on a large scale, with up-to-date methods, be made—well, not profitable, exactly, but to pay—to run without loss?" she asked, determined to kill her new-born idea at birth or else give it breath and hope of life.

"Wal, I reckon it could," he replied, with a short laugh. "It'd sure be a money-maker. Why, with all my bad luck an' poor equipment I've lived pretty well an' paid my debts an' haven't really lost any money except the original outlay. I reckon thet's sunk fer good."

"Would you sell—if some one would pay your price?"

"Miss Majesty, I'd jump at the chance. Yet somehow I'd hate to leave hyar. I'd jest be fool enough to go sink the money in another ranch."

"Would Don Carlos and these other Mexicans sell?"

"They sure would. The Don has been after me fer years, wantin' to sell thet old rancho of his; an' these herders in the valley with their stray cattle, they'd fall daid at sight of a little money."

"Please tell me, Mr. Stillwell, exactly what you would do here if you had unlimited means?" went on Madeline.

"Good Lud!" ejaculated the rancher, and started so he dropped his pipe. Then with his clumsy huge fingers he refilled it, relighted it, took a few long pulls, puffed great clouds of smoke, and, squaring round, hands on his knees, he looked at Madeline with piercing intentness. His hard face began to relax and soften and wrinkle into a smile.

"Wal, Miss Majesty, it jest makes my old heart warm up to think of sich a thing. I dreamed a lot when I first come hyar. What would I do if I hed unlimited money? Listen. I'd buy out Don Carlos an' the Greasers. I'd give a job to every good cowman in this country. I'd make them prosper as I prospered myself. I'd buy all the good horses on the ranges. I'd fence twenty thousand acres of the best grazin'. I'd drill fer water in the valley. I'd pipe water down from the mountains. I'd dam up that draw out there. A mile-long dam from hill to hill would give me a big lake, an' hevin' an eye fer beauty, I'd plant cottonwoods around it. I'd fill that lake full of fish. I'd put in the biggest field of alfalfa in the South-west. I'd plant fruit-trees an' garden. I'd tear down them old corrals an' barns an' bunk-houses to build new ones. I'd make this old rancho some comfortable an' fine. I'd put in grass an' flowers all around an' bring young pine-trees down from the mountains. An' when all thet was done I'd sit in my chair an' smoke an' watch the cattle stringin' in fer water an' stragglin' back into the valley. An' I see the cowboys ridin' easy an' heah them singin' in their bunks. An' thet red sun out there wouldn't set on a happier man in the world than Bill Stillwell, last of the old cattlemen."

Madeline thanked the rancher, and then rather abruptly retired to her room, where she felt no restraint to hide the force of that wonderful idea, now full-grown and tenacious and alluring.

Upon the next day, late in the afternoon, she asked Alfred if it would be safe for her to ride out to the mesa.

"I'll go with you," he said, gaily.

"Dear fellow, I want to go alone," she replied.

"Ah!" Alfred exclaimed, suddenly serious. He gave her just a quick glance, then turned away. "Go ahead. I think it's safe. I'll make it safe by sitting here with my glass and keeping an eye on you. Be careful coming down the trail. Let the horse pick his way. That's all."

She rode Majesty across the wide flat, up the zigzag trail, across the beautiful grassy level to the far rim of the mesa, and not till then did she lift her eyes to face the southwest.

Madeline looked from the gray valley at her feet to the blue Sierra Madres, gold-tipped in the setting sun. Her vision embraced in that glance distance and depth and glory hitherto unrevealed to her. The gray valley sloped and widened to the black sentinel Chiricahuas, and beyond was lost in a vast corrugated sweep of earth, reddening down to the west, where a golden blaze lifted the dark, rugged mountains into bold relief. The scene had infinite beauty. But after Madeline's first swift, all-embracing flash of enraptured eyes, thought of beauty passed away. In that darkening desert there was something illimitable. Madeline saw the hollow of a stupendous hand; she felt a mighty hold upon her heart. Out of the endless space, out of silence and desolation and mystery and age, came slow-changing colored shadows, phantoms of peace, and they whispered to Madeline. They whispered that it was a great, grim, immutable earth; that time was eternity; that life was fleeting. They whispered for her to be a woman; to love some one before it was too late; to love any one, every one; to realize the need of work, and in doing it to find happiness.

She rode back across the mesa and down the trail, and, once more upon the flat, she called to the horse and made him run. His spirit seemed to race with hers. The wind of his speed blew her hair from its fastenings. When he thundered to a halt at the porch steps Madeline, breathless and disheveled, alighted with the mass of her hair tumbling around her.

Alfred met her, and his exclamation, and Florence's rapt eyes shining on her face, and Stillwell's speechlessness made her self-conscious. Laughing, she tried to put up the mass of hair.

"I must—look a—fright," she panted.

"Wal, you can say what you like," replied the old cattleman, "but I know what I think."

Madeline strove to attain calmness.

"My hat—and my combs—went on the wind. I thought my hair would go, too.... There is the evening star.... I think I am very hungry."

And then she gave up trying to be calm, and likewise to fasten up her hair, which fell again in a golden mass.

"Mr. Stillwell," she began, and paused, strangely aware of a hurried note, a deeper ring in her voice. "Mr. Stillwell, I want to buy your ranch—to engage you as my superintendent. I want to buy Don Carlos's ranch and other property to the extent, say, of fifty thousand acres. I want you to buy horses and cattle—in short, to make all those improvements which you said you had so long dreamed of. Then I have ideas of my own, in the development of which I must have your advice and Alfred's. I intend to better the condition of those poor Mexicans in the valley. I intend to make life a little more worth living for them and for the cowboys of this range. To-morrow we shall talk it all over, plan all the business details."

Madeline turned from the huge, ever-widening smile that beamed down upon her and held out her hands to her brother.

"Alfred, strange, is it not, my coming out to you? Nay, don't smile. I hope I have found myself—my work—my happiness—here under the light of that western star."

❧ 7 ❧

HER MAJESTY'S RANCHO

FIVE MONTHS BROUGHT ALL that Stillwell had dreamed of, and so many more changes and improvements and innovations that it was as if a magic touch had transformed the old ranch. Madeline and Alfred and Florence had talked over a fitting name, and had decided on one chosen by Madeline. But this instance was the only one in the course of developments in which Madeline's wishes were not compiled with. The cowboys named the new ranch "Her Majesty's Rancho." Stillwell said the names cowboys bestowed were felicitous, and as unchangeable as the everlasting hills; Florence went over to the enemy; and Alfred, laughing at Madeline's protest, declared the cowboys had elected her queen of the ranges, and that there was no help for it. So the name stood "Her Majesty's Rancho."

The April sun shone down upon a slow-rising green knoll that nestled in the lee of the foothills, and seemed to center bright rays upon the long ranch-house, which gleamed snow-white from the level summit. The grounds around the house bore no semblance to Eastern lawns or parks; there had been no landscape-gardening; Stillwell had just brought water and grass and flowers and plants to the knoll-top, and there had left them, as it were, to follow nature. His idea may have been crude, but the result was beautiful. Under that hot sun and balmy air, with cool water daily soaking into the rich soil, a green covering sprang into life, and everywhere upon it, as if by magic, many colored flowers rose in the sweet air. Pale wild flowers, lavender daisies, fragile bluebells, white four-petaled lilies like Eastern mayflowers, and golden poppies, deep sunset gold, color of the West, bloomed in happy confusion. California roses, crimson as blood, nodded heavy heads and trembled with the weight of bees. Low down in bare places, isolated, open to the full power of the sun, blazed the vermilion and magenta blossoms of cactus plants.

Green slopes led all the way down to where new adobe barns and sheds had been erected, and wide corrals stretched high-barred fences down to the great squares of alfalfa gently inclining to the gray of the valley. The bottom of a dammed-up hollow shone brightly with its slowly increasing acreage of water, upon which thousands of migratory wildfowl whirred and splashed and squawked, as if reluctant to leave this cool, wet surprise so new in the long desert journey to the northland. Quarters for the cowboys—comfortable, roomy

231

adobe houses that not even the lamest cowboy dared describe as crampy bunks—stood in a row upon a long bench of ground above the lake. And down to the edge of the valley the cluster of Mexican habitations and the little church showed the touch of the same renewing hand.

All that had been left of the old Spanish house which had been Stillwell's home for so long was the bare, massive structure, and some of this had been cut away for new doors and windows. Every modern convenience, even to hot and cold running water and acetylene light, had been installed; and the whole interior painted and carpentered and furnished. The ideal sought had not been luxury, but comfort. Every door into the patio looked out upon dark, rich grass and sweet-faced flowers, and every window looked down the green slopes.

Madeline's rooms occupied the west end of the building and comprised four in number, all opening out upon the long porch. There was a small room for her maid, another which she used as an office, then her sleeping-apartment; and, lastly, the great light chamber which she had liked so well upon first sight, and which now, simply yet beautifully furnished and containing her favorite books and pictures, she had come to love as she had never loved any room at home. In the morning the fragrant, balmy air blew the white curtains of the open windows; at noon the drowsy, sultry quiet seemed to creep in for the siesta that was characteristic of the country; in the afternoon the westering sun peeped under the porch roof and painted the walls with gold bars that slowly changed to red.

Madeline Hammond cherished a fancy that the transformation she had wrought in the old Spanish house and in the people with whom she had surrounded herself, great as that transformation had been, was as nothing compared to the one wrought in herself. She had found an object in life. She was busy, she worked with her hands as well as mind, yet she seemed to have more time to read and think and study and idle and dream than ever before. She had seen her brother through his difficulties, on the road to all the success and prosperity that he cared for. Madeline had been a conscientious student of ranching and an apt pupil of Stillwell. The old cattleman, in his simplicity, gave her the place in his heart that was meant for the daughter he had never had. His pride in her, Madeline thought, was beyond reason or belief or words to tell. Under his guidance, sometimes accompanied by Alfred and Florence, Madeline had ridden the ranges and had studied the life and work of the cowboys. She had camped on the open range, slept under the blinking stars, ridden forty miles a day in the face of dust and wind. She had taken two wonderful trips down into the desert—one trip to Chiricahua, and from there across the waste of sand and rock and alkali and cactus to the Mexican borderline; and the other through the Aravaipa Valley, with its deep, red-walled canyons and wild fastnesses.

This breaking-in, this training into Western ways, though she had been a so-called outdoor girl, had required great effort and severe pain; but the education, now past its grades, had become a labor of love. She had perfect health, abounding spirits. She was so active hat she had to train herself into taking the midday siesta, a custom of the country and imperative during the hot summer months. Sometimes she looked in her mirror and laughed with sheer joy at sight of the lithe, audacious, brown-faced, flashing-eyed creature reflected there. It was not so much joy in her beauty as sheer joy of life. Eastern critics had been wont to call her beautiful in those days when she had been pale and slender and proud and cold. She laughed. If they could only see her now! From the tip of her golden head to her feet she was alive, pulsating, on fire.

Sometimes she thought of her parents, sister, friends, of how they had persistently refused to believe she could or would stay in the West. They were always asking her to come home. And when she wrote, which was dutifully often, the last thing under the sun that she was likely to mention was the change in her. She wrote that she would return to her old home some time, of course, for a visit; and letters such as this brought returns that amused Madeline, sometimes saddened her. She meant to go back East for a while, and after that once or twice every year. But the initiative was a difficult step from which she shrank. Once home, she would have to make explanations, and these would not be understood. Her father's business had been such that he could not leave it for the time required for a Western trip, or else, according to his letter, he would have come for her. Mrs. Hammond could not have been driven to cross the Hudson River; her un-American idea of the wilderness westward was that Indians still chased buffalo on the outskirts of Chicago. Madeline's sister Helen had long been eager to come, as much from curiosity, Madeline thought, as from sisterly regard. And at length Madeline concluded that the proof of her breaking permanent ties might better be seen by visiting relatives and friends before she went back East. With that in mind she invited Helen to visit her during the summer, and bring as many friends as she liked.

No slight task indeed was it to oversee the many business details of Her Majesty's Rancho and to keep a record of them. Madeline found the course of business training upon which her father had insisted to be invaluable to her now. It helped her to assimilate and arrange the practical details of cattle-raising as put forth by the blunt Stillwell. She split up the great stock of cattle into different herds, and when any of these were out running upon the open range she had them closely watched. Part of the time each herd was kept in an inclosed range, fed and watered, and carefully handled by a big force of cowboys. She employed three cowboy scouts whose sole duty was to ride the ranges searching for stray, sick, or crippled cattle or motherless calves, and to bring these in to be treated and nursed. There were two cowboys whose business was to master a pack of Russian stag-hounds and to hunt down the coyotes, wolves, and lions that preyed upon the herds. The better and tamer milch cows were separated from the ranging herds and kept in a pasture adjoining the dairy. All branding was done in corrals, and calves were weaned from mother-cows at the proper time to benefit both. The old method of branding and classing, that had so shocked Madeline, had been abandoned, and one had been inaugurated whereby cattle and cowboys and horses were spared brutality and injury.

Madeline established an extensive vegetable farm, and she planted orchards. The climate was superior to that of California, and, with abundant water, trees and plants and gardens flourished and bloomed in a way wonderful to behold. It was with ever-increasing pleasure that Madeline walked through acres of ground once bare, now green and bright and fragrant. There were poultry-yards and pig-pens and marshy quarters for ducks and geese. Here in the farming section of the ranch Madeline found employment for the little colony of Mexicans. Their lives had been as hard and barren as the dry valley where they had lived. But as the valley had been transformed by the soft, rich touch of water, so their lives had been transformed by help and sympathy and work. The children were wretched no more, and many that had been blind could now see, and Madeline had become to them a new and blessed virgin.

Madeline looked abroad over these lands and likened the change in them and those who lived by them to the change in her heart. It may have been fancy, but the sun seemed to be brighter, the sky bluer, the wind sweeter. Certain it was that the deep green of grass and garden was not fancy, nor the white and pink of blossom, nor the blaze and perfume of flower, nor the sheen of lake and the fluttering of new-born leaves. Where there had been monotonous gray there was now vivid and changing color. Formerly there had been silence both day and night; now during the sunny hours there was music. The whistle of prancing stallions pealed in from the grassy ridges. Innumerable birds had come and, like the northward-journeying ducks, they had tarried to stay. The song of meadow-lark and blackbird and robin, familiar to Madeline from childhood, mingled with the new and strange heart-throbbing song of mocking-bird and the piercing blast of the desert eagle and the melancholy moan of turtle-dove.

One April morning Madeline sat in her office wrestling with a problem. She had problems to solve every day. The majority of these were concerned with the management of twenty-seven incomprehensible cowboys. This particular problem involved Ambrose Mills, who had eloped with her French maid, Christine.

Stillwell faced Madeline with a smile almost as huge as his bulk.

"Wal, Miss Majesty, we ketched them; but not before Padre Marcos had married them. All thet speedin' in the autoomoobile was jest a-scarin' of me to death fer nothin'. I tell you Link Stevens is crazy about runnin' thet car. Link never hed no sense even with a hoss. He ain't afraid of the devil hisself. If my hair hedn't been white it 'd be white now. No more rides in thet thing fer me! Wal, we ketched Ambrose an' the girl too late. But we fetched them back, an' they're out there now, spoonin', sure oblivious to their shameless conduct."

"Stillwell, what shall I say to Ambrose? How shall I punish him? He has done wrong to deceive me. I never was so surprised in my life. Christine did not seem to care any more for Ambrose than for any of the other cowboys. What does my authority amount to? I must do something. Stillwell, you must help me."

Whenever Madeline fell into a quandary she had to call upon the old cattleman. No man ever held a position with greater pride than Stillwell, but he had been put to tests that steeped him in humility. Here he scratched his head in great perplexity.

"Dog-gone the luck! What's this elopin' bizness to do with cattle-raisin'? I don't know nothin' but cattle. Miss Majesty, it's amazin' strange what these cowboys hev come to. I never seen no cowboys like these we've got hyar now. I don't know them any more. They dress swell an' read books, an' some of them hev actooly stopped cussin' an' drinkin'. I ain't sayin' all this is against them. Why, now, they're jest the finest bunch of cow-punchers I ever seen or dreamed of. But managin' them now is beyond me. When cowboys begin to play thet game gol-lof an' run off with French maids I reckon Bill Stillwell has got to resign."

"Stillwell! Oh, you will not leave me? What in the world would I do?" exclaimed Madeline, in great anxiety.

"Wal, I sure won't leave you, Miss Majesty. No, I never'll do thet. I'll run the cattle bizness fer you an' see after the hosses an' other stock. But I've got to hev a foreman who can handle this amazin' strange bunch of cowboys."

"You've tried half a dozen foremen. Try more until you find the man who meets your requirements," said Madeline. "Never mind that now. Tell me how to impress Ambrose—to make him an example, so to speak. I must have another maid. And I do not want a new one carried off in this summary manner."

"Wal, if you fetch pretty maids out hyar you can't expect nothin' else. Why, thet black-eyed little French girl, with her white skin an' pretty airs an' smiles an' shrugs, she had the cowboys crazy. It'll be wuss with the next one."

"Oh dear!" sighed Madeline.

"An' as fer impressin' Ambrose, I reckon I can tell you how to do thet. Jest give it to him good an' say you're goin' to fire him. That'll fix Ambrose, an' mebbe scare the other boys fer a spell."

"Very well, Stillwell, bring Ambrose in to see me, and tell Christine to wait in my room."

It was a handsome debonair, bright-eyed cowboy that came tramping into Madeline's presence. His accustomed shyness and awkwardness had disappeared in an excited manner. He was a happy boy. He looked straight into Madeline's face as if he expected her to wish him joy. And Madeline actually found that expression trembling to her lips. She held it back until she could be severe. But Madeline feared she would fail of much severity. Something warm and sweet, like a fragrance, had entered the room with Ambrose.

"Ambrose, what have you done?" she asked.

"Miss Hammond, I've been and gone and got married," replied Ambrose, his words tumbling over one another. His eyes snapped, and there was a kind of glow upon his clean-shaven brown cheek. "I've stole a march on the other boys. There was Frank Slade pushin' me close, and I was havin' some runnin' to keep Jim Bell back in my dust. Even old man Nels made eyes at Christine! So I wasn't goin' to take any chances. I just packed her off to El Cajon and married her."

"Oh, so I heard," said Madeline, slowly, as she watched him. "Ambrose, do you—love her?"

He reddened under her clear gaze, dropped his head, and fumbled with his new sombrero, and there was a catch in his breath. Madeline saw his powerful brown hand tremble. It affected her strangely that this stalwart cowboy, who could rope and throw and tie a wild steer in less than one minute, should tremble at a mere question. Suddenly he raised his head, and at the beautiful blase of his eyes Madeline turned her own away.

"Yes, Miss Hammond, I love her," he said. "I think I love her in the way you're askin' about. I know the first time I saw her I thought how wonderful it'd be to have a girl like that for my wife. It's all been so strange—her comin' an' how she made me feel. Sure I never knew many girls, and I haven't seen any girls at all for years. But when she came! A girl makes a wonderful difference in a man's feelin's and thoughts. I guess I never had any before. Leastways, none like I have now. My—it—well, I guess I have a little understandin' now of Padre Marcos's blessin'."

"Ambrose, have you nothing to say to me?" asked Madeline.

"I'm sure sorry I didn't have time to tell you. But I was in some hurry."

"What did you intend to do? Where were you going when Stillwell found you?"

"We'd just been married. I hadn't thought of anything after that. Suppose I'd have rustled back to my job. I'll sure have to work now and save my money."

"Oh, well, Ambrose, I am glad you realize your responsibilities. Do you earn enough—is your pay sufficient to keep a wife?"

"Sure it is! Why, Miss Hammond, I never before earned half the salary I'm gettin' now. It's some fine to work for you. I'm goin' to fire the boys out of my bunk-house and fix it up for Christine and me. Say, won't they be jealous?"

"Ambrose, I—I congratulate you. I wish you joy," said Madeline. "I—I shall make Christine a little wedding-present. I want to talk to her for a few moments. You may go now."

It would have been impossible for Madeline to say one severe word to that happy cowboy. She experienced difficulty in hiding her own happiness at the turn of events. Curiosity and interest mingled with her pleasure when she called to Christine.

"Mrs. Ambrose Mills, please come in."

ZANE GREY

No sound came from the other room.

"I should like very much to see the bride," went on Madeline.

Still there was no stir or reply

"Christine!" called Madeline.

Then it was as if a little whirlwind of flying feet and entreating hands and beseeching eyes blew in upon Madeline. Christine was small, graceful, plump, with very white skin and very dark hair. She had been Madeline's favorite maid for years and there was sincere affection between the two. Whatever had been the blissful ignorance of Ambrose, it was manifestly certain that Christine knew how she had transgressed. Her fear and remorse and appeal for forgiveness were poured out in an incoherent storm. Plain it was that the little French maid had been overwhelmed. It was only after Madeline had taken the emotional girl in her arms and had forgiven and soothed her that her part in the elopement became clear. Christine was in a maze. But gradually, as she talked and saw that she was forgiven, calmness came in some degree, and with it a story which amused yet shocked Madeline. The unmistakable, shy, marveling love, scarcely realized by Christine, gave Madeline relief and joy. If Christine loved Ambrose there was no harm done. Watching the girl's eyes, wonderful with their changes of thought, listening to her attempts to explain what it was evident she did not understand, Madeline gathered that if ever a caveman had taken unto himself a wife, if ever a barbarian had carried off a Sabine woman, then Ambrose Mills had acted with the violence of such ancient forebears. Just how it all happened seemed to be beyond Christine.

"He say he love me," repeated the girl, in a kind of rapt awe. "He ask me to marry him— he kees me—he hug me—he lift me on ze horse—he ride with me all night—he marry me."

And she exhibited a ring on the third finger of her left hand. Madeline saw that, whatever had been the state of Christine's feeling for Ambrose before this marriage, she loved him now. She had been taken forcibly, but she was won.

After Christine had gone, comforted and betraying her shy eagerness to get back to Ambrose, Madeline was haunted by the look in the girl's eyes, and her words. Assuredly the spell of romance was on this sunny land. For Madeline there was a nameless charm, a nameless thrill combating her sense of the violence and unfitness of Ambrose's wooing. Something, she knew not what, took arms against her intellectual arraignment of the cowboy's method of getting himself a wife. He had said straight out that he loved the girl— he had asked her to marry him—he kissed her—he hugged her—he lifted her upon his horse —he rode away with her through the night—and he married her. In whatever light Madeline reviewed this thing she always came back to her first natural impression; it thrilled her, charmed her. It went against all the precepts of her training; nevertheless, it was somehow splendid and beautiful. She imagined it stripped another artificial scale from her over-sophisticated eyes.

Scarcely had she settled again to the task on her desk when Stillwell's heavy tread across the porch interrupted her. This time when he entered he wore a look that bordered upon the hysterical; it was difficult to tell whether he was trying to suppress grief or glee.

"Miss Majesty, there's another amazin' strange thing sprung on me. Hyars Jim Bell come to see you, an', when I taxed him, sayin' you was tolerable busy, he up an' says he was hungry an' he ain't a-goin' to eat any more bread made in a wash-basin! Says he'll starve first. Says Nels hed the gang over to big bunk an' feasted them on bread you taught him how to make in some new-fangled bucket-machine with a crank. Jim says thet bread beat any cake he ever eat, an' he wants you to show him how to make some. Now, Miss Majesty, as superintendent of this ranch I ought to know what's goin' on. Mebbe Jim is jest a-joshin' me.

Mebbe he's gone clean dotty. Mebbe I hev. An' beggin' your pardon, I want to know if there's any truth in what Jim says Nels says."

Whereupon it became necessary for Madeline to stifle her mirth and to inform the sadly perplexed old cattleman that she had received from the East a patent bread-mixer, and in view of the fact that her household women had taken fright at the contrivance, she had essayed to operate it herself. This had turned out to be so simple, so saving of time and energy and flour, so much more cleanly than the old method of mixing dough with the hands, and particularly it had resulted in such good bread, that Madeline had been pleased. Immediately she ordered more of the bread-mixers. One day she had happened upon Nels making biscuit dough in his wash-basin, and she had delicately and considerately introduced to him the idea of her new method. Nels, it appeared, had a great reputation as a bread-maker, and he was proud of it. Moreover, he was skeptical of any clap-trap thing with wheels and cranks. He consented, however, to let her show how the thing worked and to sample some of the bread. To that end she had him come up to the house, where she won him over. Stillwell laughed loud and long.

"Wal, wal, wal!" he exclaimed, at length. "Thet's fine, an' it's powerful funny. Mebbe you don't see how funny? Wal, Nels has jest been lordin' it over the boys about how you showed him, an' now you'll hev to show every last cowboy on the place the same thing. Cowboys are the jealousest kind of fellers. They're all crazy about you, anyway. Take Jim out hyar. Why, thet lazy cowpuncher jest never would make bread. He's notorious fer shirkin' his share of the grub deal. I've knowed Jim to trade off washin' the pots an' pans fer a lonely watch on a rainy night. All he wants is to see you show him the same as Nels is crowin' over. Then he'll crow over his bunkie, Frank Slade, an' then Frank'll get lonely to know all about this wonderful bread-machine. Cowboys are amazin' strange critters, Miss Majesty. An' now thet you've begun with them this way, you'll hev to keep it up. I will say I never seen such a bunch to work. You've sure put heart in them."

"Indeed, Stillwell, I am glad to hear that," replied Madeline. "And I shall be pleased to teach them all. But may I not have them all up here at once—at least those off duty?"

"Wal, I reckon you can't onless you want to hev them scrappin'," rejoined Stillwell, dryly. "What you've got on your hands now, Miss Majesty, is to let 'em come one by one, an' make each cowboy think you're takin' more especial pleasure in showin' him than the feller who came before him. Then mebbe we can go on with cattle-raisin'."

Madeline protested, and Stillwell held inexorably to what he said was wisdom. Several times Madeline had gone against his advice, to her utter discomfiture and rout. She dared not risk it again, and resigned herself gracefully and with subdued merriment to her task. Jim Bell was ushered into the great, light, spotless kitchen, where presently Madeline appeared to put on an apron and roll up her sleeves. She explained the use of the several pieces of aluminum that made up the bread-mixer and fastened the bucket to the table-shelf. Jim's life might have depended upon this lesson, judging from his absorbed manner and his desire to have things explained over and over, especially the turning of the crank. When Madeline had to take Jim's hand three times to show him the simple mechanism and then he did not understand she began to have faint misgivings as to his absolute sincerity. She guessed that as long as she touched Jim's hand he never would understand. Then as she began to measure out flour and milk and lard and salt and yeast she saw with despair that Jim was not looking at the ingredients, was not paying the slightest attention to them. His eyes were covertly upon her.

"Jim, I am not sure about you," said Madeline, severely. "How can you learn to make bread if you do not watch me mix it?"

"I am a-watchin' you," replied Jim, innocently.

Finally Madeline sent the cowboy on his way rejoicing with the bread-mixer under his arm. Next morning, true to Stillwell's prophecy, Frank Slade, Jim's bunkmate, presented himself cheerfully to Madeline and unbosomed himself of a long-deferred and persistent desire to relieve his overworked comrade of some of the house-keeping in their bunk.

"Miss Hammond," said Frank, "Jim's orful kind wantin' to do it all hisself. But he ain't very bright, an' I didn't believe him. You see, I'm from Missouri, an' you'll have to show me."

For a whole week Madeline held clinics where she expounded the scientific method of modern bread-making. She got a good deal of enjoyment out of her lectures. What boys these great hulking fellows were! She saw through their simple ruses. Some of them were grave as deacons; others wore expressions important enough to have fitted the faces of statesmen signing government treaties. These cowboys were children; they needed to be governed; but in order to govern them they had to be humored. A more light-hearted, fun-loving crowd of boys could not have been found. And they were grown men. Stillwell explained that the exuberance of spirits lay in the difference in their fortunes. Twenty-seven cowboys, in relays of nine, worked eight hours a day. That had never been heard of before in the West. Stillwell declared that cowboys from all points of the compass would head their horses toward Her Majesty's Rancho.

❦ 8 ❦

EL CAPITAN

Stillwell's interest in the revolution across the Mexican line had manifestly increased with the news that Gene Stewart had achieved distinction with the rebel forces. Thereafter the old cattleman sent for El Paso and Douglas newspapers, wrote to ranchmen he knew on the big bend of the Rio Grande, and he would talk indefinitely to any one who would listen to him. There was not any possibility of Stillwell's friends at the ranch forgetting his favorite cowboy. Stillwell always prefaced his eulogy with an apologetic statement that Stewart had gone to the bad. Madeline liked to listen to him, though she was not always sure which news was authentic and which imagination.

There appeared to be no doubt, however, that the cowboy had performed some daring feats for the rebels. Madeline found his name mentioned in several of the border papers. When the rebels under Madero stormed and captured the city of Juarez, Stewart did fighting that won him the name of El Capitan. This battle apparently ended the revolution. The capitulation of President Diaz followed shortly, and there was a feeling of relief among ranchers on the border from Texas to California. Nothing more was heard of Gene Stewart until April, when a report reached Stillwell that the cowboy had arrived in El Cajon, evidently hunting trouble. The old cattleman saddled a horse and started post-haste for town. In two days he returned, depressed in spirit. Madeline happened to be present when Stillwell talked to Alfred.

"I got there too late, Al," said the cattleman. "Gene was gone. An' what do you think of this? Danny Mains hed jest left with a couple of burros packed. I couldn't find what way he went, but I'm bettin' he hit the Peloncillo trail."

"Danny will show up some day," replied Alfred. "What did you learn about Stewart? Maybe he left with Danny."

"Not much," said Stillwell, shortly. "Gene's hell-bent fer election! No mountains fer him."

"Well tell us about him."

Stillwell wiped his sweaty brow and squared himself to talk.

"Wal, it's sure amazin' strange about Gene. Its got me locoed. He arrived in El Cajon a week or so ago. He was trained down like as if he'd been ridin' the range all winter. He hed

239

plenty of money—Mex, they said. An' all the Greasers was crazy about him. Called him El Capitan. He got drunk an' went roarin' round fer Pat Hawe. You remember that Greaser who was plugged last October—the night Miss Majesty arrived? Wal, he's daid. He's daid, an' people says thet Pat is a-goin' to lay thet killin' onto Gene. I reckon thet's jest talk, though Pat is mean enough to do it, if he hed the nerve. Anyway, if he was in El Cajon he kept mighty much to hisself. Gene walked up an' down, up an' down, all day an' night, lookin' fer Pat. But he didn't find him. An', of course, he kept gettin' drunker. He jest got plumb bad. He made lots of trouble, but there wasn't no gun-play. Mebbe thet made him sore, so he went an' licked Flo's brother-in-law. Thet wasn't so bad. Jack sure needed a good lickin'. Wal, then Gene met Danny an' tried to get Danny drunk. An' he couldn't! What do you think of that? Danny hedn't been drinkin'—wouldn't touch a drop. I'm sure glad of thet, but it's amazin' strange. Why, Danny was a fish fer red liquor. I guess he an' Gene had some pretty hard words, though I'm not sure about thet. Anyway, Gene went down to the railroad an' he got on an engine, an' he was in the engine when it pulled out. Lord, I hope he doesn't hold up the train! If he gets gay over in Arizona he'll go to the pen at Yuma. An' thet pen is a graveyard fer cowboys. I wired to agents along the railroad to look out fer Stewart, an' to wire back to me if he's located."

"Suppose you do find him, Stillwell, what can you do?" inquired Alfred.

The old man nodded gloomily.

"I straightened him up once. Mebbe I can do it again." Then, brightening somewhat, he turned to Madeline. "I jest hed an idee, Miss Majesty. If I can get him, Gene Stewart is the cowboy I want fer my foreman. He can manage this bunch of cow-punchers thet are drivin' me dotty. What's more, since he's fought fer the rebels an' got that name El Capitan, all the Greasers in the country will kneel to him. Now, Miss Majesty, we hevn't got rid of Don Carlos an' his vaqueros yet. To be sure, he sold you his house an' ranch an' stock. But you remember nothin' was put in black and white about when he should get out. An' Don Carlos ain't gettin' out. I don't like the looks of things a little bit. I'll tell you now thet Don Carlos knows somethin' about the cattle I lost, an' thet you've been losin' right along. Thet Greaser is hand an' glove with the rebels. I'm willin' to gamble thet when he does get out he an' his vaqueros will make another one of the bands of guerrillas thet are harassin' the border. This revolution ain't over' yet. It's jest commenced. An' all these gangs of outlaws are goin' to take advantage of it. We'll see some old times, mebbe. Wal, I need Gene Stewart. I need him bad. Will you let me hire him, Miss Majesty, if I can get him straightened up?"

The old cattleman ended huskily.

"Stillwell, by all means find Stewart, and do not wait to straighten him up. Bring him to the ranch," replied Madeline.

Thanking her, Stillwell led his horse away.

"Strange how he loves that cowboy!" murmured Madeline.

"Not so strange, Majesty," replied her brother. "Not when you know. Stewart has been with Stillwell on some hard trips into the desert alone. There's no middle course of feeling between men facing death in the desert. Either they hate each other or love each other. I don't know, but I imagine Stewart did something for Stillwell—saved us life, perhaps. Besides, Stewart's a lovable chap when he's going straight. I hope Stillwell brings him back. We do need him, Majesty. He's a born leader. Once I saw him ride into a bunch of Mexicans whom we suspected of rustling. It was fine to see him. Well, I'm sorry to tell you that we are worried about Don Carlos. Some of his vaqueros came into my yard the other day when I had left Flo alone. She had a bad scare. These vaqueros have been different since Don Carlos sold the ranch. For that matter, I never would have trusted a white woman alone with them.

But they are bolder now. Something's in the wind. They've got assurance. They can ride off any night and cross the border."

During the succeeding week Madeline discovered that a good deal of her sympathy for Stillwell in his hunt for the reckless Stewart had insensibly grown to be sympathy for the cowboy. It was rather a paradox, she thought, that opposed to the continual reports of Stewart's wildness as he caroused from town to town were the continual expressions of good will and faith and hope universally given out by those near her at the ranch. Stillwell loved the cowboy; Florence was fond of him; Alfred liked and admired him, pitied him; the cowboys swore their regard for him the more he disgraced himself. The Mexicans called him El Gran Capitan. Madeline's personal opinion of Stewart had not changed in the least since the night it had been formed. But certain attributes of his, not clearly defined in her mind, and the gift of his beautiful horse, his valor with the fighting rebels, and all this strange regard for him, especially that of her brother, made her exceedingly regret the cowboy's present behavior.

Meanwhile Stillwell was so earnest and zealous that one not familiar with the situation would have believed he was trying to find and reclaim his own son. He made several trips to little stations in the valley, and from these he returned with a gloomy face. Madeline got the details from Alfred. Stewart was going from bad to worse—drunk, disorderly, savage, sure to land in the penitentiary. Then came a report that hurried Stillwell off to Rodeo. He returned on the third day, a crushed man. He had been so bitterly hurt that no one, not even Madeline, could get out of him what had happened. He admitted finding Stewart, failing to influence him; and when the old cattleman got so far he turned purple in the face and talked to himself, as if dazed: "But Gene was drunk. He was drunk, or he couldn't hev treated old Bill like thet!"

Madeline was stirred with an anger toward the brutal cowboy that was as strong as her sorrow for the loyal old cattleman. And it was when Stillwell gave up that she resolved to take a hand. The persistent faith of Stillwell, his pathetic excuses in the face of what must have been Stewart's violence, perhaps baseness, actuated her powerfully, gave her new insight into human nature. She honored a faith that remained unshaken. And the strange thought came to her that Stewart must somehow be worthy of such a faith, or he never could have inspired it. Madeline discovered that she wanted to believe that somewhere deep down in the most depraved and sinful wretch upon earth there was some grain of good. She yearned to have the faith in human nature that Stillwell had in Stewart.

She sent Nels, mounted upon his own horse, and leading Majesty, to Rodeo in search of Stewart. Nels had instructions to bring Stewart back to the ranch. In due time Nels returned, leading the roan without a rider.

"Yep, I shore found him," replied Nels, when questioned. "Found him half sobered up. He'd been in a scrap, an' somebody hed put him to sleep, I guess. Wal, when he seen thet roan hoss he let out a yell an' grabbed him round the neck. The hoss knowed him, all right. Then Gene hugged the hoss an' cried—cried like—I never seen no one who cried like he did. I waited awhile, an' was jest goin' to say somethin' to him when he turned on me red-eyed, mad as fire. 'Nels,' he said, 'I care a hell of a lot fer thet boss, an' I liked you pretty well, but if you don't take him away quick I'll shoot you both.' Wal, I lit out. I didn't even git to say howdy to him."

"Nels, you think it useless—any attempt to see him—persuade him?" asked Madeline.

"I shore do, Miss Hammond," replied Nels, gravely. "I've seen a few sun-blinded an' locoed an' snake-poisoned an' skunk-bitten cow-punchers in my day, but Gene Stewart beats 'em all. He's shore runnin' wild fer the divide."

Madeline dismissed Nels, but before he got out of earshot she heard him speak to Stillwell, who awaited him on the porch.

"Bill, put this in your pipe an' smoke it—none of them scraps Gene has hed was over a woman! It used to be thet when he was drank he'd scrap over every pretty Greaser girl he'd run across. Thet's why Pat Hawe thinks Gene plugged the strange vaquero who was with little Bonita thet night last fall. Wal, Gene's scrappin' now jest to git shot up hisself, for some reason thet only God Almighty knows."

Nels's story of how Stewart wept over his horse influenced Madeline powerfully. Her next move was to persuade Alfred to see if he could not do better with this doggedly bent cowboy. Alfred needed only a word of persuasion, for he said he had considered going to Rodeo of his own accord. He went, and returned alone.

"Majesty, I can't explain Stewart's singular actions," said Alfred. "I saw him, talked with him. He knew me, but nothing I said appeared to get to him. He has changed terribly. I fancy his once magnificent strength is breaking. It—it actually hurt me to look at him. I couldn't have fetched him back here—not as he is now. I heard all about him, and if he isn't downright out of his mind he's hell-bent, as Bill says, on getting killed. Some of his escapades are—are not for your ears. Bill did all any man could do for another. We've all done our best for Stewart. If you'd been given a chance perhaps you could have saved him. But it's too late. Put it out of mind now, dear."

Madeline, however, did not forget nor give it up. If she had forgotten or surrendered, she felt that she would have been relinquishing infinitely more than hope to aid one ruined man. But she was at a loss to know what further steps to take. Days passed, and each one brought additional gossip of Stewart's headlong career toward the Yuma penitentiary. For he had crossed the line into Cochise County, Arizona, where sheriffs kept a stricter observance of law. Finally a letter came from a friend of Nels's in Chiricahua saying that Stewart had been hurt in a brawl there. His hurt was not serious, but it would probably keep him quiet long enough to get sober, and this opportunity, Nels's informant said, would be a good one for Stewart's friends to take him home before he got locked up. This epistle inclosed a letter to Stewart from his sister. Evidently, it had been found upon him. It told a story of illness and made an appeal for aid. Nels's friend forwarded this letter without Stewart's knowledge, thinking Stillwell might care to help Stewart's family. Stewart had no money, he said.

The sister's letter found its way to Madeline. She read it, tears in her eyes. It told Madeline much more than its brief story of illness and poverty and wonder why Gene had not written home for so long. It told of motherly love, sisterly love, brotherly love—dear family ties that had not been broken. It spoke of pride in this El Capitan brother who had become famous. It was signed "your loving sister Letty."

Not improbably, Madeline revolved in mind, this letter was one reason for Stewart's headstrong, long-continued abasement. It had been received too late—after he had squandered the money that would have meant so much to mother and sister. Be that as it might, Madeline immediately sent a bank-draft to Stewart's sister with a letter explaining that the money was drawn in advance on Stewart's salary. This done, she impulsively determined to go to Chiricahua herself.

The horseback-rides Madeline had taken to this little Arizona hamlet had tried her endurance to the utmost; but the journey by automobile, except for some rocky bits of road and sandy stretches, was comfortable, and a matter of only a few hours. The big touring-car was still a kind of seventh wonder to the Mexicans and cowboys; not that automobiles were very new and strange, but because this one was such an enormous machine and capable of greater speed than an express-train. The chauffeur who had arrived with the car found his situation among the jealous cowboys somewhat far removed from a bed of roses. He had been induced to remain long enough to teach the operating and mechanical technique of the car. And choice fell upon Link Stevens, for the simple reason that of all the cowboys he was the only one with any knack for mechanics. Now Link had been a hard riding, hard-driving cowboy, and that winter he had sustained an injury to his leg, caused by a bad fall, and was unable to sit his horse. This had been gall and wormwood to him. But when the big white automobile came and he was elected to drive it, life was once more worth living for him. But all the other cowboys regarded Link and his machine as some correlated species of demon. They were deathly afraid of both.

It was for this reason that Nels, when Madeline asked him to accompany her to Chiricahua, replied, reluctantly, that he would rather follow on his horse. However, she prevailed over his hesitancy, and with Florence also in the car they set out. For miles and miles the valley road was smooth, hard-packed, and slightly downhill. And when speeding was perfectly safe, Madeline was not averse to it. The grassy plain sailed backward in gray sheets, and the little dot in the valley grew larger and larger. From time to time Link glanced round at unhappy Nels, whose eyes were wild and whose hands clutched his seat. While the car was crossing the sandy and rocky places, going slowly, Nels appeared to breathe easier. And when it stopped in the wide, dusty street of Chiricahua Nels gladly tumbled out.

"Nels, we shall wait here in the car while you find Stewart," said Madeline.

"Miss Hammond, I reckon Gene'll run when he sees us, if he's able to run," replied Nels. "Wal, I'll go find him an' make up my mind then what we'd better do."

Nels crossed the railroad track and disappeared behind the low, flat houses. After a little time he reappeared and hurried up to the car. Madeline felt his gray gaze searching her face.

"Miss Hammond, I found him," said Nels. "He was sleepin'. I woke him. He's sober an' not bad hurt; but I don't believe you ought to see him. Mebbe Florence—"

"Nels, I want to see him myself. Why not? What did he say when you told him I was here?"

"Shore I didn't tell him that. I jest says, 'Hullo, Gene!' an' he says, 'My Gawd! Nels! mebbe I ain't glad to see a human bein'.' He asked me who was with me, an' I told him Link an' some friends. I said I'd fetch them in. He hollered at thet. But I went, anyway. Now, if you really will see him, Miss Hammond, it's a good chance. But shore it's a touchy matter, an' you'll be some sick at sight of him. He's layin' in a Greaser hole over here. Likely the Greasers hev been kind to him. But they're shore a poor lot."

Madeline did not hesitate a moment.

"Thank you, Nels. Take me at once. Come, Florence."

They left the car, now surrounded by gaping-eyed Mexican children, and crossed the dusty space to a narrow lane between red adobe walls. Passing by several houses, Nels stopped at the door of what appeared to be an alleyway leading back. It was filthy.

"He's in there, around thet first corner. It's a patio, open an' sunny. An', Miss Hammond, if you don't mind, I'll wait here for you. I reckon Gene wouldn't like any fellers around when he sees you girls."

It was that which made Madeline hesitate then and go forward slowly. She had given no thought at all to what Stewart might feel when suddenly surprised by her presence.

"Florence, you wait also," said Madeline, at the doorway, and turned in alone.

And she had stepped into a broken-down patio littered with alfalfa straw and debris, all clear in the sunlight. Upon a bench, back toward her, sat a man looking out through the rents in the broken wall. He had not heard her. The place was not quite so filthy and stifling as the passages Madeline had come through to get there. Then she saw that it had been used as a corral. A rat ran boldly across the dirt floor. The air swarmed with flies, which the man brushed at with weary hand. Madeline did not recognize Stewart. The side of his face exposed to her gaze was black, bruised, bearded. His clothes were ragged and soiled. There were bits of alfalfa in his hair. His shoulders sagged. He made a wretched and hopeless figure sitting there. Madeline divined something of why Nels shrank from being present.

"Mr. Stewart. It is I, Miss Hammond, come to see you," she said.

He grew suddenly perfectly motionless, as if he had been changed to stone. She repeated her greeting.

His body jerked. He moved violently as if instinctively to turn and face this intruder; but a more violent movement checked him.

Madeline waited. How singular that this ruined cowboy had pride which kept him from showing his face! And was it not shame more than pride?

"Mr. Stewart, I have come to talk with you, if you will let me."

"Go away," he muttered.

"Mr. Stewart!" she began, with involuntary hauteur. But instantly she corrected herself, became deliberate and cool, for she saw that she might fail to be even heard by this man. "I have come to help you. Will you let me?"

"For God's sake! You—you—" he choked over the words. "Go away!"

"Stewart, perhaps it was for God's sake that I came," said Madeline, gently. "Surely it was for yours—and your sister's—" Madeline bit her tongue, for she had not meant to betray her knowledge of Letty.

He groaned, and, staggering up to the broken wall, he leaned there with his face hidden. Madeline reflected that perhaps the slip of speech had been well.

"Stewart, please let me say what I have to say?"

He was silent. And she gathered courage and inspiration.

"Stillwell is deeply hurt, deeply grieved that he could not turn you back from this—this fatal course. My brother is also. They wanted to help you. And so do I. I have come, thinking somehow I might succeed where they have failed. Nels brought your sister's letter. I—I read it. I was only the more determined to try to help you, and indirectly help your mother and Letty. Stewart, we want you to come to the ranch. Stillwell needs you for his foreman. The position is open to you, and you can name your salary. Both Al and Stillwell are worried about Don Carlos, the vaqueros, and the raids down along the border. My cowboys are without a capable leader. Will you come?"

"No," he answered.

"But Stillwell wants you so badly."

"No."

"Stewart, I want you to come."

"No."

His replies had been hoarse, loud, furious. They disconcerted Madeline, and she paused, trying to think of a way to proceed. Stewart staggered away from the wall, and, falling upon the bench, he hid his face in his hands. All his motions, like his speech, had been violent.

"Will you please go away?" he asked.

"Stewart, certainly I cannot remain here longer if you insist upon my going. But why not listen to me when I want so much to help you? Why?"

"I'm a damned blackguard," he burst out. "But I was a gentleman once, and I'm not so low that I can stand for you seeing me here."

"When I made up my mind to help you I made it up to see you wherever you were. Stewart, come away, come back with us to the ranch. You are in a bad condition now.

Everything looks black to you. But that will pass. When you are among friends again you will get well. You will be your old self. The very fact that you were once a gentleman, that you come of good family, makes you owe so much more to yourself. Why, Stewart, think how young you are! It is a shame to waste your life. Come back with me."

"Miss Hammond, this was my last plunge," he replied, despondently. "It's too late."

"Oh no, it is not so bad as that."

"It's too late."

"At least make an effort, Stewart. Try!"

"No. There's no use. I'm done for. Please leave me—thank you for—"

He had been savage, then sullen, and now he was grim. Madeline all but lost power to resist his strange, deadly, cold finality. No doubt he knew he was doomed. Yet something halted her—held her even as she took a backward step. And she became conscious of a subtle change in her own feeling. She had come into that squalid hole, Madeline Hammond, earnest enough, kind enough in her own intentions; but she had been almost imperious—a woman habitually, proudly used to being obeyed. She divined that all the pride, blue blood, wealth, culture, distinction, all the impersonal condescending persuasion, all the fatuous philanthropy on earth would not avail to turn this man a single hair's-breadth from his downward career to destruction. Her coming had terribly augmented his bitter hate of himself. She was going to fail to help him. She experienced a sensation of impotence that amounted almost to distress. The situation assumed a tragic keenness. She had set forth to reverse the tide of a wild cowboy's fortunes; she faced the swift wasting of his life, the damnation of his soul. The subtle consciousness of change in her was the birth of that faith she had revered in Stillwell. And all at once she became merely a woman, brave and sweet and indomitable.

"Stewart, look at me," she said.

He shuddered. She advanced and laid a hand on his bent shoulder. Under the light touch he appeared to sink.

"Look at me," she repeated.

But he could not lift his head. He was abject, crushed. He dared not show his swollen, blackened face. His fierce, cramped posture revealed more than his features might have shown; it betrayed the torturing shame of a man of pride and passion, a man who had been confronted in his degradation by the woman he had dared to enshrine in his heart. It betrayed his love.

"Listen, then," went on Madeline, and her voice was unsteady. "Listen to me, Stewart. The greatest men are those who have fallen deepest into the mire, sinned most, suffered most, and then have fought their evil natures and conquered. I think you can shake off this desperate mood and be a man."

"No!" he cried.

"Listen to me again. Somehow I know you're worthy of Stillwell's love. Will you come back with us—for his sake?"

"No. It's too late, I tell you."

"Stewart, the best thing in life is faith in human nature. I have faith in you. I believe you are worth it."

"You're only kind and good—saying that. You can't mean it."

"I mean it with all my heart," she replied, a sudden rich warmth suffusing her body as she saw the first sign of his softening. "Will you come back—if not for your own sake or Stillwell's—then for mine?"

"What am I to such a woman as you?"

"A man in trouble, Stewart. But I have come to help you, to show my faith in you."

"If I believed that I might try," he said.

"Listen," she began, softly, hurriedly. "My word is not lightly given. Let it prove my faith in you. Look at me now and say you will come."

He heaved up his big frame as if trying to cast off a giant's burden, and then slowly he turned toward her. His face was a blotched and terrible thing. The physical brutalizing marks were there, and at that instant all that appeared human to Madeline was the dawning in dead, furnace-like eyes of a beautiful light.

"I'll come," he whispered, huskily. "Give me a few days to straighten up, then I'll come."

❧ 9 ❧

THE NEW FOREMAN

TOWARD THE END of the week Stillwell informed Madeline that Stewart had arrived at the ranch and had taken up quarters with Nels.

"Gene's sick. He looks bad," said the old cattleman. "He's so weak an' shaky he can't lift a cup. Nels says that Gene has hed some bad spells. A little liquor would straighten him up now. But Nels can't force him to drink a drop, an' has hed to sneak some liquor in his coffee. Wal, I think we'll pull Gene through. He's forgotten a lot. I was goin' to tell him what he did to me up at Rodeo. But I know if he'd believe it he'd be sicker than he is. Gene's losin' his mind, or he's got somethin' powerful strange on it."

From that time Stillwell, who evidently found Madeline his most sympathetic listener, unburdened himself daily of his hopes and fears and conjectures.

Stewart was really ill. It became necessary to send Link Stevens for a physician. Then Stewart began slowly to mend and presently was able to get up and about. Stillwell said the cowboy lacked interest and seemed to be a broken man. This statement, however, the old cattleman modified as Stewart continued to improve. Then presently it was a good augury of Stewart's progress that the cowboys once more took up the teasing relation which had been characteristic of them before his illness. A cowboy was indeed out of sorts when he could not vent his peculiar humor on somebody or something. Stewart had evidently become a broad target for their badinage.

"Wal, the boys are sure after Gene," said Stillwell, with his huge smile. "Joshin' him all the time about how he sits around an' hangs around an' loafs around jest to get a glimpse of you, Miss Majesty. Sure all the boys hev a pretty bad case over their pretty boss, but none of them is a marker to Gene. He's got it so bad, Miss Majesty, thet he actooly don't know they are joshin' him. It's the amazin'est strange thing I ever seen. Why, Gene was always a feller thet you could josh. An' he'd laugh an' get back at you. But he was never before deaf to talk, an' there was a certain limit no feller cared to cross with him. Now he takes every word an' smiles dreamy like, an' jest looks an' looks. Why, he's beginnin' to make me tired. He'll never run thet bunch of cowboys if he doesn't wake up quick."

Madeline smiled her amusement and expressed a belief that Stillwell wanted too much in such short time from a man who had done body and mind a grievous injury.

It had been impossible for Madeline to fail to observe Stewart's singular behavior. She never went out to take her customary walks and rides without seeing him somewhere in the distance. She was aware that he watched for her and avoided meeting her. When she sat on the porch during the afternoon or at sunset Stewart could always be descried at some point near. He idled listlessly in the sun, lounged on the porch of his bunk-house, sat whittling the top bar of the corral fence, and always it seemed to Madeline he was watching her. Once, while going the rounds with her gardener, she encountered Stewart and greeted him kindly. He said little, but he was not embarrassed. She did not recognize in his face any feature that she remembered. In fact, on each of the few occasions when she had met Stewart he had looked so different that she had no consistent idea of his facial appearance. He was now pale, haggard, drawn. His eyes held a shadow through which shone a soft, subdued light; and, once having observed this, Madeline fancied it was like the light in Majesty's eyes, in the dumb, worshiping eyes of her favorite stag-hound. She told Stewart that she hoped he would soon be in the saddle again, and passed on her way.

That Stewart loved her Madeline could not help but see. She endeavored to think of him as one of the many who, she was glad to know, liked her. But she could not regulate her thoughts to fit the order her intelligence prescribed. Thought of Stewart dissociated itself from thought of the other cowboys. When she discovered this she felt a little surprise and annoyance. Then she interrogated herself, and concluded that it was not that Stewart was so different from his comrades, but that circumstances made him stand out from them. She recalled her meeting with him that night when he had tried to force her to marry him. This was unforgettable in itself. She called subsequent mention of him, and found it had been peculiarly memorable. The man and his actions seemed to hinge on events. Lastly, the fact standing clear of all others in its relation to her interest was that he had been almost ruined, almost lost, and she had saved him. That alone was sufficient to explain why she thought of him differently. She had befriended, uplifted the other cowboys; she had saved Stewart's life. To be sure, he had been a ruffian, but a woman could not save the life of even a ruffian without remembering it with gladness. Madeline at length decided her interest in Stewart was natural, and that her deeper feeling was pity. Perhaps the interest had been forced from her; however, she gave the pity as she gave everything.

Stewart recovered his strength, though not in time to ride at the spring round-up; and Stillwell discussed with Madeline the advisability of making the cowboy his foreman.

"Wal, Gene seems to be gettin' along," said Stillwell. "But he ain't like his old self. I think more of him at thet. But where's his spirit? The boys'd ride rough-shod all over him. Mebbe I'd do best to wait longer now, as the slack season is on. All the same, if those vaquero of Don Carlos's don't lay low I'll send Gene over there. Thet'll wake him up."

A few days afterward Stillwell came to Madeline, rubbing his big hands in satisfaction and wearing a grin that was enormous.

"Miss Majesty, I reckon before this I've said things was amazin' strange. But now Gene Stewart has gone an' done it! Listen to me. Them Greasers down on our slope hev been gettin' prosperous. They're growin' like bad weeds. An' they got a new padre—the little old feller from El Cajon, Padre Marcos. Wal, this was all right, all the boys thought, except Gene. An' he got blacker 'n thunder an' roared round like a dehorned bull. I was sure glad to see he could get mad again. Then Gene haids down the slope fer the church. Nels an' me follered him, thinkin' he might hev been took sudden with a crazy spell or somethin'. He hasn't never been jest right yet since he left off drinkin'. Wal, we run into him comin' out of the church. We never was so dumfounded in our lives. Gene was crazy, all right—he sure hed a spell. But it was the kind of a spell he hed thet paralyzed us. He ran past us like a streak, an' we follered. We couldn't ketch him. We heerd him laugh—the strangest laugh I ever heerd! You'd thought the feller was suddenly made a king. He was like thet feller who was tied in a bunyin'-sack an' throwed into the sea, an' cut his way out, an' swam to the island where the treasures was, an' stood up yellin', 'The world is mine.' Wal, when we got up to his bunk-house he was gone. He didn't come back all day an' all night. Frankie Slade, who has a sharp tongue, says Gene hed gone crazy for liquor an' thet was his finish. Nels was some worried. An' I was sick.

"Wal' this mawnin' I went over to Nels's bunk. Some of the fellers was there, all speculatin' about Gene. Then big as life Gene struts round the corner. He wasn't the same Gene. His face was pale an' his eyes burned like fire. He had thet old mockin', cool smile, an' somethin' besides thet I couldn't understand. Frankie Slade up an' made a remark—no wuss than he'd been makin' fer days—an' Gene tumbled him out of his chair, punched him good, walked all over him. Frankie wasn't hurt so much as he was bewildered. 'Gene,' he says, 'what the hell struck you?' An' Gene says, kind of sweet like, 'Frankie, you may be a nice feller when you're alone, but your talk's offensive to a gentleman.'

"After thet what was said to Gene was with a nice smile. Now, Miss Majesty, it's beyond me what to allow for Gene's sudden change. First off, I thought Padre Marcos had converted him. I actooly thought thet. But I reckon it's only Gene Stewart come back—the old Gene Stewart an' some. Thet's all I care about. I'm rememberin' how I once told you thet Gene was the last of the cowboys. Perhaps I should hev said he's the last of my kind of cowboys. Wal, Miss Majesty, you'll be appreciatin' of what I meant from now on."

It was also beyond Madeline to account for Gene Stewart's antics, and, making allowance for the old cattleman's fancy, she did not weigh his remarks very heavily. She guessed why Stewart might have been angry at the presence of Padre Marcos. Madeline supposed that it was rather an unusual circumstance for a cowboy to be converted to religious belief. But it was possible. And she knew that religious fervor often manifested itself in extremes of feeling and action. Most likely, in Stewart's case, his real manner had been both misunderstood and exaggerated. However, Madeline had a curious desire, which she did not wholly admit to herself, to see the cowboy and make her own deductions.

The opportunity did not present itself for nearly two weeks. Stewart had taken up his duties as foreman, and his activities were ceaseless. He was absent most of the time, ranging down toward the Mexican line. When he returned Stillwell sent for him.

This was late in the afternoon of a day in the middle of April. Alfred and Florence were with Madeline on the porch. They saw the cowboy turn his horse over to one of the Mexican boys at the corral and then come with weary step up to the house, beating the dust out of his gauntlets. Little streams of gray sand trickled from his sombrero as he removed it and bowed to the women.

Madeline saw the man she remembered, but with a singularly different aspect. His skin was brown; his eyes were piercing and dark and steady; he carried himself erect; he seemed preoccupied, and there was not a trace of embarrassment in his manner.

"Wal, Gene, I'm sure glad to see you," Stillwell was saying. "Where do you hail from?"

"Guadaloupe Canyon," replied the cowboy.

Stillwell whistled.

"Way down there! You don't mean you follered them hoss tracks thet far?"

"All the way from Don Carlos's rancho across the Mexican line. I took Nick Steele with me. Nick is the best tracker in the outfit. This trail we were on led along the foothill valleys.

First we thought whoever made it was hunting for water. But they passed two ranches without watering. At Seaton's Wash they dug for water. Here they met a pack-train of burros that came down the mountain trail. The burros were heavily loaded. Horse and burro tracks struck south from Seaton's to the old California emigrant road. We followed the trail through Guadelope Canyon and across the border. On the way back we stopped at Slaughter's ranch, where the United States cavalry are camping. There we met foresters from the Peloncillo forest reserve. If these fellows knew anything they kept it to themselves. So we hit the trail home."

"Wal, I reckon you know enough?" inquired Stillwell, slowly.

"I reckon," replied Stewart.

"Wal, out with it, then," said Stillwell, gruffly. "Miss Hammond can't be kept in the dark much longer. Make your report to her."

The cowboy shifted his dark gaze to Madeline. He was cool and slow.

"We're losing a few cattle on the open range. Night-drives by the vaqueros. Some of these cattle are driven across the valley, others up to the foothills. So far as I can find out no cattle are being driven south. So this raiding is a blind to fool the cowboys. Don Carlos is a Mexican rebel. He located his rancho here a few years ago and pretended to raise cattle. All that time he has been smuggling arms and ammunition across the border. He was for Madero against Diaz. Now he is against Madero because he and all the rebels think Madero failed to keep his promises. There will be another revolution. And all the arms go from the States across the border. Those burros I told about were packed with contraband goods."

"That's a matter for the United States cavalry. They are patrolling the border," said Alfred.

"They can't stop the smuggling of arms, not down in that wild corner," replied Stewart.

"What is my—my duty? What has it to do with me?" inquired Madeline, somewhat perturbed.

"Wal, Miss Majesty, I reckon it hasn't nothing to do with you," put in Stillwell. "Thet's my bizness an' Stewart's. But I jest wanted you to know. There might be some trouble follerin' my orders."

"Your orders?"

"I want to send Stewart over to fire Don Carlos an' his vaqueros off the range. They've got to go. Don Carlos is breakin' the law of the United States, an' doin' it on our property an' with our hosses. Hev I your permission, Miss Hammond?"

"Why, assuredly you have! Stillwell, you know what to do. Alfred, what do you think best?"

"It'll make trouble, Majesty, but it's got to be done," replied Alfred. "Here you have a crowd of Eastern friends due next month. We want the range to ourselves then. But, Stillwell, if you drive those vaqueros off, won't they hang around in the foothills? I declare they are a bad lot."

Stillwell's mind was not at ease. He paced the porch with a frown clouding his brow.

"Gene, I reckon you got this Greaser deal figgered better'n me," said Stillwell. "Now what do you say?"

"He'll have to be forced off," replied Stewart, quietly. "The Don's pretty slick, but his vaqueros are bad actors. It's just this way. Nels said the other day to me, 'Gene, I haven't packed a gun for years until lately, and it feels good whenever I meet any of those strange Greasers.' You see, Stillwell, Don Carlos has vaqueros coming and going all the time. They're guerrilla bands, that's all. And they're getting uglier. There have been several shooting-scrapes lately. A rancher named White, who lives up the valley, was badly hurt. It's only a matter of time till something stirs up the boys here. Stillwell, you know Nels and Monty and Nick."

"Sure I know 'em. An' you're not mentionin' one more particular cowboy in my outfit," said Stillwell, with a dry chuckle and a glance at Stewart.

Madeline divined the covert meaning, and a slight chill passed over her, as if a cold wind had blown in from the hills.

"Stewart, I see you carry a gun," she said, pointing to a black handle protruding from a sheath swinging low along his leather chaps.

"Yes, ma'am."

"Why do you carry it?" she asked.

"Well," he said, "it's not a pretty gun—and it's heavy." She caught the inference. The gun was not an ornament. His keen, steady, dark gaze caused her vague alarm. What had once seemed cool and audacious about this cowboy was now cold and powerful and mystical. Both her instinct and her intelligence realized the steel fiber of the man's nature. As she was his employer, she had the right to demand that he should not do what was so chillingly manifest that he might do. But Madeline could not demand. She felt curiously young and weak, and the five months of Western life were as if they had never been. She now had to do with a question involving human life. And the value she placed upon human life and its spiritual significance was a matter far from her cowboy's thoughts. A strange idea flashed up. Did she place too much value upon all human life? She checked that, wondering, almost horrified at herself. And then her intuition told her that she possessed a far stronger power to move these primitive men than any woman's stern rule or order.

"Stewart, I do not fully understand what you hint that Nels and his comrades might do. Please be frank with me. Do you mean Nels would shoot upon little provocation?"

"Miss Hammond, as far as Nels is concerned, shooting is now just a matter of his meeting Don Carlos's vaqueros. It's wonderful what Nels has stood from them, considering the Mexicans he's already killed."

"Already killed! Stewart, you are not in earnest?" cried Madeline, shocked.

"I am. Nels has seen hard life along the Arizona border. He likes peace as well as any man. But a few years of that doesn't change what the early days made of him. As for Nick Steele and Monty, they're just bad men, and looking for trouble."

"How about yourself, Stewart? Stillwell's remark was not lost upon me," said Madeline, prompted by curiosity.

Stewart did not reply. He looked at her in respectful silence. In her keen earnestness Madeline saw beneath his cool exterior and was all the more baffled. Was there a slight, inscrutable, mocking light in his eyes, or was it only her imagination? However, the cowboy's face was as hard as flint.

"Stewart, I have come to love my ranch," said Madeline, slowly, "and I care a great deal for my—my cowboys. It would be dreadful if they were to kill anybody, or especially if one of them should be killed."

"Miss Hammond, you've changed things considerable out here, but you can't change these men. All that's needed to start them is a little trouble. And this Mexican revolution is bound to make rough times along some of the wilder passes across the border. We're in line, that's all. And the boys are getting stirred up."

"Very well, then, I must accept the inevitable. I am facing a rough time. And some of my cowboys cannot be checked much longer. But, Stewart, whatever you have been in the past, you have changed." She smiled at him, and her voice was singularly sweet and rich. "Stillwell has so often referred to you as the last of his kind of cowboy. I have just a faint idea

ZANE GREY

of what a wild life you have led. Perhaps that fits you to be a leader of such rough men. I am no judge of what a leader should do in this crisis. My cowboys are entailing risk in my employ; my property is not safe; perhaps my life even might be endangered. I want to rely upon you, since Stillwell believes, and I, too, that you are the man for this place. I shall give you no orders. But is it too much to ask that you be my kind of a cowboy?"

Madeline remembered Stewart's former brutality and shame and abject worship, and she measured the great change in him by the contrast afforded now in his dark, changeless, intent face.

"Miss Hammond, what kind of a cowboy is that?" he asked.

"I—I don't exactly know. It is that kind which I feel you might be. But I do know that in the problem at hand I want your actions to be governed by reason, not passion. Human life is not for any man to sacrifice unless in self-defense or in protecting those dependent upon him. What Stillwell and you hinted makes me afraid of Nels and Nick Steele and Monty. Cannot they be controlled? I want to feel that they will not go gunning for Don Carlos's men. I want to avoid all violence. And yet when my guests come I want to feel that they will be safe from danger or fright or even annoyance. May I not rely wholly upon you, Stewart? Just trust you to manage these obstreperous cowboys and protect my property and Alfred's, and take care of us—of me, until this revolution is ended? I have never had a day's worry since I bought the ranch. It is not that I want to shirk my responsibilities; it is that I like being happy. May I put so much faith in you?"

"I hope so, Miss Hammond," replied Stewart. It was an instant response, but none the less fraught with consciousness of responsibility. He waited a moment, and then, as neither Stillwell nor Madeline offered further speech, he bowed and turned down the path, his long spurs clinking in the gravel.

"Wal, wal," exclaimed Stillwell, "that's no little job you give him, Miss Majesty."

"It was a woman's cunning, Stillwell," said Alfred. "My sister used to be a wonder at getting her own way when we were kids. Just a smile or two, a few sweet words or turns of thought, and she had what she wanted."

"Al, what a character to give me!" protested Madeline. "Indeed, I was deeply in earnest with Stewart. I do not understand just why, but I trust him. He seems like iron and steel. Then I was a little frightened at the prospect of trouble with the vaqueros. Both you and Stillwell have influenced me to look upon Stewart as invaluable. I thought it best to confess my utter helplessness and to look to him for support."

"Majesty, whatever actuated you, it was a stroke of diplomacy," replied her brother. "Stewart has got good stuff in him. He was down and out. Well, he's made a game fight, and it looks as if he'd win. Trusting him, giving him responsibility, relying upon him, was the surest way to strengthen his hold upon himself. Then that little touch of sentiment about being your kind of cowboy and protecting you—well, if Gene Stewart doesn't develop into an Argus-eyed knight I'll say I don't know cowboys. But, Majesty, remember, he's a composite of tiger breed and forked lightning, and don't imagine he has failed you if he gets into a fight."

"I'll sure tell you what Gene Stewart will do," said Florence. "Don't I know cowboys? Why, they used to take me up on their horses when I was a baby. Gene Stewart will be the kind of cowboy your sister said he might be, whatever that is. She may not know and we may not guess, but he knows."

"Wal, Flo, there you hit plumb center," replied the old cattleman. "An' I couldn't be gladder if he was my own son."

❧ 10 ❧

DON CARLOS'S VAQUEROS

EARLY THE FOLLOWING MORNING STEWART, with a company of cowboys, departed for Don Carlos's rancho. As the day wore on without any report from him, Stillwell appeared to grow more at ease; and at nightfall he told Madeline that he guessed there was now no reason for concern.

"Wal, though it's sure amazin' strange," he continued, "I've been worryin' some about how we was goin' to fire Don Carlos. But Gene has a way of doin' things."

Next day Stillwell and Alfred decided to ride over Don Carlos's place, taking Madeline and Florence with them, and upon the return trip to stop at Alfred's ranch. They started in the cool, gray dawn, and after three hours' riding, as the sun began to get bright, they entered a mesquite grove, surrounding corrals and barns, and a number of low, squat buildings and a huge, rambling structure, all built of adobe and mostly crumbling to ruin. Only one green spot relieved the bald red of grounds and walls; and this evidently was made by the spring which had given both value and fame to Don Carlos's range. The approach to the house was through a wide courtyard, bare, stony, hard packed, with hitching-rails and watering-troughs in front of a long porch. Several dusty, tired horses stood with drooping heads and bridles down, their wet flanks attesting to travel just ended.

"Wal, dog-gone it, Al, if there ain't Pat Hawe's hoss I'll eat it," exclaimed Stillwell.

"What's Pat want here, anyhow?" growled Alfred.

No one was in sight; but Madeline heard loud voices coming from the house. Stillwell dismounted at the porch and stalked in at the door. Alfred leaped off his horse, helped Florence and Madeline down, and, bidding them rest and wait on the porch, he followed Stillwell.

"I hate these Greaser places," said Florence, with a grimace. "They're so mysterious and creepy. Just watch now! They'll be dark-skinned, beady-eyed, soft-footed Greasers slip right up out of the ground! There'll be an ugly face in every door and window and crack."

"It's like a huge barn with its characteristic odor permeated by tobacco smoke," replied Madeline, sitting down beside Florence. "I don't think very much of this end of my purchase. Florence, isn't that Don Carlos's black horse over there in the corral?"

"It sure is. Then the Don's heah yet. I wish we hadn't been in such a hurry to come over. There! that doesn't sound encouraging."

From the corridor came the rattling of spurs, tramping of boots, and loud voices. Madeline detected Alfred's quick notes when he was annoyed: "We'll rustle back home, then," he said. The answer came, "No!" Madeline recognized Stewart's voice, and she quickly straightened up. "I won't have them in here," went on Alfred.

"Outdoors or in, they've got to be with us!" replied Stewart, sharply. "Listen, Al," came the boom of Stillwell's big voice, "now that we've butted in over hyar with the girls, you let Stewart run things."

Then a crowd of men tramped pell-mell out upon the porch. Stewart, dark-browed and somber, was in the lead. Nels hung close to him, and Madeline's quick glance saw that Nels had undergone some indescribable change. The grinning, brilliant-eyed Don Carlos came jostling out beside a gaunt, sharp-featured man wearing a silver shield. This, no doubt, was Pat Hawe. In the background behind Stillwell and Alfred stood Nick Steele, head and shoulders over a number of vaqueros and cowboys.

"Miss Hammond, I'm sorry you came," said Stewart, bluntly. "We're in a muddle here. I've insisted that you and Flo be kept close to us. I'll explain later. If you can't stop your ears I beg you to overlook rough talk."

With that he turned to the men behind him: "Nick, take Booly, go back to Monty and the boys. Fetch out that stuff. All of it. Rustle, now!"

Stillwell and Alfred disengaged themselves from the crowd to take up positions in front of Madeline and Florence. Pat Hawe leaned against a post and insolently ogled Madeline and then Florence. Don Carlos pressed forward. His whole figure filled Madeline's reluctant but fascinated eyes. He wore tight velveteen breeches, with a heavy fold down the outside seam, which was ornamented with silver buttons. Round his waist was a sash, and a belt with fringed holster, from which protruded a pearl-handled gun. A vest or waistcoat, richly embroidered, partly concealed a blouse of silk and wholly revealed a silken scarf round his neck. His swarthy face showed dark lines, like cords, under the surface. His little eyes were exceedingly prominent and glittering. To Madeline his face seemed to be a bold, handsome mask through which his eyes piercingly betrayed the evil nature of the man.

He bowed low with elaborate and sinuous grace. His smile revealed brilliant teeth, enhanced the brilliance of his eyes. He slowly spread deprecatory hands.

"Senoritas, I beg a thousand pardons," he said. How strange it was for Madeline to hear English spoken in a soft, whiningly sweet accent! "The gracious hospitality of Don Carlos has passed with his house."

Stewart stepped forward and, thrusting Don Carlos aside, he called, "Make way, there!"

The crowd fell back to the tramp of heavy boots. Cowboys appeared staggering out of the corridor with long boxes. These they placed side by side upon the floor of the porch.

"Now, Hawe, we'll proceed with our business," said Stewart. "You see these boxes, don't you?"

"I reckon I see a good many things round hyar," replied Hawe, meaningly.

"Well, do you intend to open these boxes upon my say-so?"

"No!" retorted Hawe. "It's not my place to meddle with property as come by express an' all accounted fer regular."

"You call yourself a sheriff!" exclaimed Stewart, scornfully.

"Mebbe you'll think so before long," rejoined Hawe, sullenly.

"I'll open them. Here, one of you boys, knock the tops off these boxes," ordered Stewart. "No, not you, Monty. You use your eyes. Let Booly handle the ax. Rustle, now!"

Monty Price had jumped out of the crowd into the middle of the porch. The manner in which he gave way to Booly and faced the vaqueros was not significant of friendliness or trust.

"Stewart, you're dead wrong to bust open them boxes. Thet's ag'in' the law," protested Hawe, trying to interfere.

Stewart pushed him back. Then Don Carlos, who had been stunned by the appearance of the boxes, suddenly became active in speech and person. Stewart thrust him back also. The Mexican's excitement increased. He wildly gesticulated; he exclaimed shrilly in Spanish. When, however, the lids were wrenched open and an inside packing torn away he grew rigid and silent. Madeline raised herself behind Stillwell to see that the boxes were full of rifles and ammunition.

"There, Hawe! What did I tell you?" demanded Stewart. "I came over here to take charge of this ranch. I found these boxes hidden in an unused room. I suspected what they were. Contraband goods!"

"Wal, supposin' they are? I don't see any call fer sech all-fired fuss as you're makin'. Stewart, I calkilate you're some stuck on your new job an' want to make a big show before—"

"Hawe, stop slinging that kind of talk," interrupted Stewart. "You got too free with your mouth once before! Now here, I'm supposed to be consulting an officer of the law. Will you take charge of these contraband goods?"

"Say, you're holdin' on high an' mighty," replied Hawe, in astonishment that was plainly pretended. "What're you drivin' at?"

Stewart muttered an imprecation. He took several swift strides across the porch; he held out his hands to Stillwell as if to indicate the hopelessness of intelligent and reasonable arbitration; he looked at Madeline with a glance eloquent of his regret that he could not handle the situation to please her. Then as he wheeled he came face to face with Nels, who had slipped forward out of the crowd.

Madeline gathered serious import from the steel-blue meaning flash of eyes whereby Nels communicated something to Stewart. Whatever that something was, it dispelled Stewart's impatience. A slight movement of his hand brought Monty Price forward with a jump. In these sudden jumps of Monty's there was a suggestion of restrained ferocity. Then Nels and Monty lined up behind Stewart. It was a deliberate action, even to Madeline, unmistakably formidable. Pat Hawe's face took on an ugly look; his eyes had a reddish gleam. Don Carlos added a pale face and extreme nervousness to his former expressions of agitation. The cowboys edged away from the vaqueros and the bronzed, bearded horsemen who were evidently Hawe's assistants.

"I'm driving at this," spoke up Stewart, presently; and now he was slow and caustic. "Here's contraband of war! Hawe, do you get that? Arms and ammunition for the rebels across the border! I charge you as an officer to confiscate these goods and to arrest the smuggler—Don Carlos."

These words of Stewart's precipitated a riot among Don Carlos and his followers, and they surged wildly around the sheriff. There was an upflinging of brown, clenching hands, a shrill, jabbering babel of Mexican voices. The crowd around Don Carlos grew louder and denser with the addition of armed vaqueros and barefooted stable-boys and dusty-booted herdsmen and blanketed Mexicans, the last of whom suddenly slipped from doors and windows and round corners. It was a motley assemblage. The laced, fringed, ornamented vaqueros presented a sharp contrast to the bare-legged, sandal-footed boys and the ragged herders. Shrill cries, evidently from Don Carlos, somewhat quieted the commotion. Then

Don Carlos could be heard addressing Sheriff Hawe in an exhortation of mingled English and Spanish. He denied, he avowed, he proclaimed, and all in rapid, passionate utterance. He tossed his black hair in his vehemence; he waved his fists and stamped the floor; he rolled his glittering eyes; he twisted his thin lips into a hundred different shapes, and like a cornered wolf showed snarling white teeth.

It seemed to Madeline that Don Carlos denied knowledge of the boxes of contraband goods, then knowledge of their real contents, then knowledge of their destination, and, finally, everything except that they were there in sight, damning witnesses to somebody's complicity in the breaking of neutrality laws. Passionate as had been his denial of all this, it was as nothing compared to his denunciation of Stewart.

"Senor Stewart, he keel my Vaquero!" shouted Don Carlos, as, sweating and spent, he concluded his arraignment of the cowboy. "Him you must arrest! Senor Stewart a bad man! He keel my vaquero!"

"Do you hear thet?" yelled Hawe. "The Don's got you figgered fer thet little job at El Cajon last fall."

The clamor burst into a roar. Hawe began shaking his finger in Stewart's face and hoarsely shouting. Then a lithe young vaquero, swift as an Indian, glided under Hawe's uplifted arm. Whatever the action he intended, he was too late for its execution. Stewart lunged out, struck the vaquero, and knocked him off the porch. As he fell a dagger glittered in the sunlight and rolled clinking over the stones. The man went down hard and did not move. With the same abrupt violence, and a manner of contempt, Stewart threw Hawe off the porch, then Don Carlos, who, being less supple, fell heavily. Then the mob backed before Stewart's rush until all were down in the courtyard.

The shuffling of feet ceased, the clanking of spurs, and the shouting. Nels and Monty, now reinforced by Nick Steele, were as shadows of Stewart, so closely did they follow him. Stewart waved them back and stepped down into the yard. He was absolutely fearless; but what struck Madeline so keenly was his magnificent disdain. Manifestly, he knew the nature of the men with whom he was dealing. From the look of him it was natural for Madeline to expect them to give way before him, which they did, even Hawe and his attendants sullenly retreating.

Don Carlos got up to confront Stewart. The prostrate vaquero stirred and moaned, but did not rise.

"You needn't jibber Spanish to me," said Stewart. "You can talk American, and you can understand American. If you start a rough-house here you and your Greasers will be cleaned up. You've got to leave this ranch. You can have the stock, the packs and traps in the second corral. There's grub, too. Saddle up and hit the trail. Don Carlos, I'm dealing more than square with you. You're lying about these boxes of guns and cartridges. You're breaking the laws of my country, and you're doing it on property in my charge. If I let smuggling go on here I'd be implicated myself. Now you get off the range. If you don't I'll have the United States cavalry here in six hours, and you can gamble they'll get what my cowboys leave of you."

Don Carlos was either a capital actor and gratefully relieved at Stewart's leniency or else he was thoroughly cowed by references to the troops. "Si, Senor! Gracias, Senor!" he exclaimed; and then, turning away, he called to his men. They hurried after him, while the fallen vaquero got to his feet with Stewart's help and staggered across the courtyard. In a moment they were gone, leaving Hawe and his several comrades behind.

Hawe was spitefully ejecting a wad of tobacco from his mouth and swearing in an undertone about "white-livered Greasers." He cocked his red eye speculatively at Stewart.

"Wal, I reckon as you're so hell-bent on doin' it up brown thet you'll try to fire me off'n the range, too?"

"If I ever do, Pat, you'll need to be carried off," replied Stewart. "Just now I'm politely inviting you and your deputy sheriffs to leave."

"We'll go; but we're comin' back one of these days, an' when we do we'll put you in irons."

"Hawe, if you've got it in that bad for me, come over here in the corral and let's fight it out."

"I'm an officer, an' I don't fight outlaws an' sich except when I hev to make arrests."

"Officer! You're a disgrace to the county. If you ever did get irons on me you'd take me some place out of sight, shoot me, and then swear you killed me in self-defense. It wouldn't be the first time you pulled that trick, Pat Hawe."

"Ho, ho!" laughed Hawe, derisively. Then he started toward the horses.

Stewart's long arm shot out, his hand clapped on Hawe's shoulder, spinning him round like a top.

"You're leaving, Pat, but before you leave you'll come out with your play or you'll crawl," said Stewart. "You've got it in for me, man to man. Speak up now and prove you're not the cowardly skunk I've always thought you. I've called your hand."

Pat Hawe's face turned a blackish-purple hue.

"You can jest bet thet I've got it in fer you," he shouted, hoarsely. "You're only a low-down cow-puncher. You never hed a dollar or a decent job till you was mixed up with thet Hammond woman—"

Stewart's hand flashed out and hit Hawe's face in a ringing slap. The sheriff's head jerked back, his sombrero fell to the ground. As he bent over to reach it his hand shook, his arm shook, his whole body shook.

Monty Price jumped straight forward and crouched down with a strange, low cry.

Stewart seemed all at once rigid, bending a little.

"Say Miss Hammond, if there's occasion to use her name," said Stewart, in a voice that seemed coolly pleasant, yet had a deadly undernote.

Hawe did a moment's battle with strangling fury, which he conquered in some measure.

"I said you was a low-down, drunken cow-puncher, a tough as damn near a desperado as we ever hed on the border," went on Hawe, deliberately. His speech appeared to be addressed to Stewart, although his flame-pointed eyes were riveted upon Monty Price. "I know you plugged that vaquero last fall, an' when I git my proof I'm comin' after you."

"That's all right, Hawe. You can call me what you like, and you can come after me when you like," replied Stewart. "But you're going to get in bad with me. You're in bad now with Monty and Nels. Pretty soon you'll queer yourself with all the cowboys and the ranchers, too. If that don't put sense into you—Here, listen to this. You knew what these boxes contained. You know Don Carlos has been smuggling arms and ammunition across the border. You know he is hand and glove with the rebels. You've been wearing blinders, and it has been to your interest. Take a hunch from me. That's all. Light out now, and the less we see of your handsome mug the better we'll like you."

Muttering, cursing, pallid of face, Hawe climbed astride his horse. His comrades followed suit. Certain it appeared that the sheriff was contending with more than fear and wrath. He must have had an irresistible impulse to fling more invective and threat upon Stewart, but he was speechless. Savagely he spurred his horse, and as it snorted and leaped he turned in his saddle, shaking his fist. His comrades led the way, with their horses clattering into a canter. They disappeared through the gate.

When, later in the day, Madeline and Florence, accompanied by Alfred and Stillwell, left Don Carlos's ranch it was not any too soon for Madeline. The inside of the Mexican's home was more unprepossessing and uncomfortable than the outside. The halls were dark, the rooms huge, empty, and musty; and there was an air of silence and secrecy and mystery about them most fitting to the character Florence had bestowed upon the place.

On the other hand, Alfred's ranch-house, where the party halted to spend the night, was picturesquely located, small and cozy, camplike in its arrangement, and altogether agreeable to Madeline.

The day's long rides and the exciting events had wearied her. She rested while Florence and the two men got supper. During the meal Stillwell expressed satisfaction over the good riddance of the vaqueros, and with his usual optimism trusted he had seen the last of them. Alfred, too, took a decidedly favorable view of the day's proceedings. However, it was not lost upon Madeline that Florence appeared unusually quiet and thoughtful. Madeline wondered a little at the cause. She remembered that Stewart had wanted to come with them, or detail a few cowboys to accompany them, but Alfred had laughed at the idea and would have none of it.

After supper Alfred monopolized the conversation by describing what he wanted to do to improve his home before he and Florence were married.

Then at an early hour they all retired.

Madeline's deep slumbers were disturbed by a pounding upon the wall, and then by Florence's crying out in answer to a call:

"Get up! Throw some clothes on and come out!"

It was Alfred's voice.

"What's the matter?" asked Florence, as she slipped out of bed.

"Alfred, is there anything wrong?" added Madeline, sitting up.

The room was dark as pitch, but a faint glow seemed to mark the position of the window.

"Oh, nothing much," replied Alfred. "Only Don Carlos's rancho going up in smoke."

"Fire!" cried Florence, sharply.

"You'll think so when you see it. Hurry out. Majesty, old girl, now you won't have to tear down that heap of adobe, as you threatened. I don't believe a wall will stand after that fire."

"Well, I'm glad of it," said Madeline. "A good healthy fire will purify the atmosphere over there and save me expense. Ugh! that haunted rancho got on my nerves! Florence, I do believe you've appropriated part of my riding-habit. Doesn't Alfred have lights in this house?"

Florence laughingly helped Madeline to dress. Then they hurriedly stumbled over chairs, and, passing through the dining-room, went out upon the porch.

Away to the westward, low down along the horizon, she saw leaping red flames and wind-swept columns of smoke.

Stillwell appeared greatly perturbed.

"Al, I'm lookin' fer that ammunition to blow up," he said. "There was enough of it to blow the roof off the rancho."

"Bill, surely the cowboys would get that stuff out the first thing," replied Alfred, anxiously.

"I reckon so. But all the same, I'm worryin'. Mebbe there wasn't time. Supposin' thet powder went off as the boys was goin' fer it or carryin' it out! We'll know soon. If the explosion doesn't come quick now we can figger the boys got the boxes out."

For the next few moments there was a silence of sustained and painful suspense. Florence gripped Madeline's arm. Madeline felt a fullness in her throat and a rapid beating of her heart. Presently she was relieved with the others when Stillwell declared the danger of an explosion needed to be feared no longer.

"Sure you can gamble on Gene Stewart," he added.

The night happened to be partly cloudy, with broken rifts showing the moon, and the wind blew unusually strong. The brightness of the fire seemed subdued. It was like a huge bonfire smothered by some great covering, penetrated by different, widely separated points of flame. These corners of flame flew up, curling in the wind, and then died down. Thus the scene was constantly changing from dull light to dark. There came a moment when a blacker shade overspread the wide area of flickering gleams and then obliterated them. Night enfolded the scene. The moon peeped a curved yellow rim from under broken clouds. To all appearances the fire had burned itself out. But suddenly a pinpoint of light showed where all had been dense black. It grew and became long and sharp. It moved. It had life. It leaped up. Its color warmed from white to red. Then from all about it burst flame on flame, to leap into a great changing pillar of fire that climbed high and higher. Huge funnels of smoke, yellow, black, white, all tinged with the color of fire, slanted skyward, drifting away on the wind.

"Wal, I reckon we won't hev the good of them two thousand tons of alfalfa we was figgerin' on," remarked Stillwell.

"Ah! Then that last outbreak of fire was burning hay," said Madeline. "I do not regret the rancho. But it's too bad to lose such a quantity of good feed for the stock."

"It's lost, an' no mistake. The fire's dyin' as quick as she flared up. Wal, I hope none of the boys got risky to save a saddle or blanket. Monty—he's hell on runnin' the gantlet of fire. He's like a hoss that's jest been dragged out of a burnin' stable an' runs back sure locoed. There! She's smolderin' down now. Reckon we-all might jest as well turn in again. It's only three o'clock."

"I wonder how the fire originated?" remarked Alfred. "Some careless cowboy's cigarette, I'll bet."

Stillwell rolled out his laugh.

"Al, you sure are a free-hearted, trustin' feller. I'm some doubtin' the cigarette idee; but you can gamble if it was a cigarette it belonged to a cunnin' vaquero, an' wasn't dropped accident-like."

"Now, Bill, you don't mean Don Carlos burned the rancho?" ejaculated Alfred, in mingled amaze and anger.

Again the old cattleman laughed.

"Powerful strange to say, my friend, ole Bill means jest thet."

"Of course Don Carlos set that fire," put in Florence, with spirit. "Al, if you live out heah a hundred years you'll never learn that Greasers are treacherous. I know Gene Stewart suspected something underhand. That's why he wanted us to hurry away. That's why he put me on the black horse of Don Carlos's. He wants that horse for himself, and feared the Don would steal or shoot him. And you, Bill Stillwell, you're as bad as Al. You never distrust anybody till it's too late. You've been singing ever since Stewart ordered the vaqueros off the range. But you sure haven't been thinking."

"Wal, now, Flo, you needn't pitch into me jest because I hev a natural Christian spirit," replied Stillwell, much aggrieved. "I reckon I've hed enough trouble in my life so's not to go lookin' fer more. Wal, I'm sorry about the hay burnin'. But mebbe the boys saved the stock. An' as fer that ole adobe house of dark holes an' under-ground passages, so long's Miss

Majesty doesn't mind, I'm darn <u>glad</u> it burned. Come, let's all turn in again. Somebody'll ride over early an' tell us what's what."

Madeline awakened early, but not so early as the others, who were up and had breakfast ready when she went into the dining-room. Stillwell was not in an amiable frame of mind. The furrows of worry lined his broad brow and he continually glanced at his watch, and growled because the cowboys were so late in riding over with the news. He gulped his breakfast, and while Madeline and the others ate theirs he tramped up and down the porch. Madeline noted that Alfred grew nervous and restless. Presently he left the table to join Stillwell outside.

"They'll slope off to Don Carlos's rancho and leave us to ride home alone," observed Florence.

"Do you mind?" questioned Madeline.

"No, I don't exactly mind; we've got the fastest horses in this country. I'd like to run that big black devil off his legs. No, I don't mind; but I've no hankering for a situation Gene Stewart thinks—"

Florence began disconnectedly, and she ended evasively. Madeline did not press the point, although she had some sense of misgiving. Stillwell tramped in, shaking the floor with his huge boots; Alfred followed him, carrying a field-glass.

"Not a hoss in sight," complained Stillwell. "Some-thin' wrong over Don Carlos's way. Miss Majesty, it'll be jest as well fer you an' Flo to hit the home trail. We can telephone over an' see that the boys know you're comin'."

Alfred, standing in the door, swept the gray valley with his field-glass.

"Bill, I see running stock-horses or cattle; I can't make out which. I guess we'd better rustle over there."

Both men hurried out, and while the horses were being brought up and saddled Madeline and Florence put away the breakfast-dishes, then speedily donned spurs, sombreros, and gauntlets.

"Here are the horses ready," called Alfred. "Flo, that black Mexican horse is a prince."

The girls went out in time to hear Stillwell's good-by as he mounted and spurred away. Alfred went through the motions of assisting Madeline and Florence to mount, which assistance they always flouted, and then he, too, swung up astride.

"I guess it's all right," he said, rather dubiously. "You really must not go over toward Don Carlos's. It's only a few miles home."

"Sure it's all right. We can ride, can't we?" retorted Florence. "Better have a care for yourself, going off over there to mix in goodness knows what."

Alfred said good-by, spurred his horse, and rode away.

"If Bill didn't forget to telephone!" exclaimed Florence. "I declare he and Al were sure rattled."

Florence dismounted and went into the house. She left the door open. Madeline had some difficulty in holding Majesty. It struck Madeline that Florence stayed rather long indoors. Presently she came out with sober face and rather tight lips.

"I couldn't get anybody on the 'phone. No answer. I tried a dozen times."

"Why, Florence!" Madeline was more concerned by the girl's looks than by the information she imparted.

"The wire's been cut," said Florence. Her gray glance swept swiftly after Alfred, who was now far out of earshot. "I don't like this a little bit. Heah's where I've got to 'figger,' as Bill says."

She pondered a moment, then hurried into the house, to return presently with the field-glass that Alfred had used. With this she took a survey of the valley, particularly in the direction of Madeline's ranch-house. This was hidden by low, rolling ridges which were quite close by.

"Anyway, nobody in that direction can see us leave heah," she mused. "There's mesquite on the ridges. We've got cover long enough to save us till we can see what's ahead."

"Florence, what—what do you expect?" asked Madeline, nervously.

"I don't know. There's never any telling about Greasers. I wish Bill and Al hadn't left us. Still, come to think of that, they couldn't help us much in case of a chase. We'd run right away from them. Besides, they'd shoot. I guess I'm as well as satisfied that we've got the job of getting home on our own hands. We don't dare follow Al toward Don Carlos's ranch. We know there's trouble over there. So all that's left is to hit the trail for home. Come, let's ride. You stick like a Spanish needle to me."

A heavy growth of mesquite covered the top of the first ridge, and the trail went through it. Florence took the lead, proceeding cautiously, and as soon as she could see over the summit she used the field-glass. Then she went on. Madeline, following closely, saw down the slope of the ridge to a bare, wide, grassy hollow, and onward to more rolling land, thick with cactus and mesquite. Florence appeared cautious, deliberate, yet she lost no time. She was ominously silent. Madeline's misgivings took definite shape in the fear of vaqueros in ambush.

Upon the ascent of the third ridge, which Madeline remembered was the last uneven ground between the point she had reached and home, Florence exercised even more guarded care in advancing. Before she reached the top of this ridge she dismounted, looped her bridle round a dead snag, and, motioning Madeline to wait, she slipped ahead through the mesquite out of sight. Madeline waited, anxiously listening and watching. Certain it was that she could not see or hear anything alarming. The sun began to have a touch of heat; the morning breeze rustled the thin mesquite foliage; the deep magenta of a cactus flower caught her eye; a long-tailed, cruel-beaked, brown bird sailed so close to her she could have touched it with her whip. But she was only vaguely aware of these things. She was watching for Florence, listening for some sound fraught with untoward meaning. All of a sudden she saw Majesty's ears were held straight up. Then Florence's face, now strangely white, showed round the turn of the trail.

"'S-s-s-sh!" whispered Florence, holding up a warning finger. She reached the black horse and petted him, evidently to still an uneasiness he manifested. "We're in for it," she went on. "A whole bunch of vaqueros hiding among the mesquite over the ridge! They've not seen or heard us yet. We'd better risk riding ahead, cut off the trail, and beat them to the ranch. Madeline, you're white as death! Don't faint now!"

"I shall not faint. But you frighten me. Is there danger? What shall we do?"

"There's danger. Madeline, I wouldn't deceive you," went on Florence, in an earnest whisper. "Things have turned out just as Gene Stewart hinted. Oh, we should—Al should have listened to Gene! I believe—I'm afraid Gene knew!"

"Knew what?" asked Madeline.

"Never mind now. Listen. We daren't take the back trail. We'll go on. I've a scheme to fool that grinning Don Carlos. Get down, Madeline—hurry."

Madeline dismounted.

"Give me your white sweater. Take it off—And that white hat! Hurry, Madeline."

"Florence, what on earth do you mean?" cried Madeline.

"Not so loud," whispered the other. Her gray eyes snapped. She had divested herself of sombrero and jacket, which she held out to Madeline. "Heah. Take these. Give me yours. Then get up on the black. I'll ride Majesty. Rustle now, Madeline. This is no time to talk."

"But, dear, why—why do you want—? Ah! You're going to make the vaqueros take you for me!"

"You guessed it. Will you—"

"I shall not allow you to do anything of the kind," returned Madeline.

It was then that Florence's face, changing, took on the hard, stern sharpness so typical of a cowboy's. Madeline had caught glimpses of that expression in Alfred's face, and on Stewart's when he was silent, and on Stillwell's always. It was a look of iron and fire—unchangeable, unquenchable will. There was even much of violence in the swift action whereby Florence compelled Madeline to the change of apparel.

"It 'd been my idea, anyhow, if Stewart hadn't told me to do it," said Florence, her words as swift as her hands. "Don Carlos is after you—you, Miss Madeline Hammond! He wouldn't ambush a trail for any one else. He's not killing cowboys these days. He wants you for some reason. So Gene thought, and now I believe him. Well, we'll know for sure in five minutes. You ride the black; I'll ride Majesty. We'll slip round through the brush, out of sight and sound, till we can break out into the open. Then we'll split. You make straight for the ranch. I'll cut loose for the valley where Gene said positively the cowboys were with the cattle. The vaqueros will take me for you. They all know those striking white things you wear. They'll chase me. They'll never get anywhere near me. And you'll be on a fast horse. He can take you home ahead of any vaqueros. But you won't be chased. I'm staking all on that. Trust me, Madeline. If it were only my calculation, maybe I'd—It's because I remember Stewart. That cowboy knows things. Come, this heah's the safest and smartest way to fool Don Carlos." Madeline felt herself more forced than persuaded into acquiescence. She mounted the black and took up the bridle. In another moment she was guiding her horse off the trail in the tracks of Majesty. Florence led off at right angles, threading a slow passage through the mesquite. She favored sandy patches and open aisles between the trees, and was careful not to break a branch. Often she stopped to listen. This detour of perhaps half a mile brought Madeline to where she could see open ground, the ranch-house only a few miles off, and the cattle dotting the valley. She had not lost her courage, but it was certain that these familiar sights somewhat lightened the pressure upon her breast. Excitement gripped her. The shrill whistle of a horse made both the black and Majesty jump. Florence quickened the gait down the slope. Soon Madeline saw the edge of the brush, the gray-bleached grass and level ground.

Florence waited at the opening between the low trees. She gave Madeline a quick, bright glance.

"All over but the ride! That'll sure be easy. Bolt now and keep your nerve!"

When Florence wheeled the fiery roan and screamed in his ear Madeline seemed suddenly to grow lax and helpless. The big horse leaped into thundering action. This was memorable of Bonita of the flying hair and the wild night ride. Florence's hair streamed on the wind and shone gold in the sunlight. Yet Madeline saw her with the same thrill with which she had seen the wild-riding Bonita. Then hoarse shouts unclamped Madeline's power of movement, and she spurred the black into the open.

He wanted to run and he was swift. Madeline loosened the reins—laid them loose upon his neck. His action was strange to her. He was hard to ride. But he was fast, and she cared for nothing else. Madeline knew horses well enough to realize that the black had found he was free and carrying a light weight. A few times she took up the bridle and pulled to right or left, trying to guide him. He kept a straight course, however, and crashed through small patches of mesquite and jumped the cracks and washes. Uneven ground offered no perceptible obstacle to his running. To Madeline there was now a thrilling difference in the lash of wind and the flash of the gray ground underneath. She was running away from something; what that was she did not know. But she remembered Florence, and she wanted to look back, yet hated to do so for fear of the nameless danger Florence had mentioned.

Madeline listened for the pounding of pursuing hoofs in her rear. Involuntarily she glanced back. On the mile or more of gray level between her and the ridge there was not a horse, a man, or anything living. She wheeled to look back on the other side, down the valley slope.

The sight of Florence riding Majesty in zigzag flight before a whole troop of vaqueros blanched Madeline's cheek and made her grip the pommel of her saddle in terror. That strange gait of her roan was not his wonderful stride. Could Majesty be running wild? Madeline saw one vaquero draw closer, whirling his lasso round his head, but he did not get near enough to throw. So it seemed to Madeline. Another vaquero swept across in front of the first one. Then, when Madeline gasped in breathless expectancy, the roan swerved to elude the attack. It flashed over Madeline that Florence was putting the horse to some such awkward flight as might have been expected of an Eastern girl frightened out of her wits. Madeline made sure of this when, after looking again, she saw that Florence, in spite of the horse's breaking gait and the irregular course, was drawing slowly and surely down the valley.

Madeline had not lost her head to the extent of forgetting her own mount and the nature of the ground in front. When, presently, she turned again to watch Florence, uncertainty ceased in her mind. The strange features of that race between girl and vaqueros were no longer in evidence. Majesty was in his beautiful, wonderful stride, low down along the ground, stretching, with his nose level and straight for the valley. Between him and the lean horses in pursuit lay an ever-increasing space. He was running away from the vaqueros. Florence was indeed "riding the wind," as Stewart had aptly expressed his idea of flight upon the fleet roan.

A dimness came over Madeline's eyes, and it was not all owing to the sting of the wind. She rubbed it away, seeing Florence as a flying dot in a strange blur. What a daring, intrepid girl! This kind of strength—and aye, splendid thought for a weaker sister—was what the West inculcated in a woman.

The next time Madeline looked back Florence was far ahead of her pursuers and going out of sight behind a low knoll. Assured of Florence's safety, Madeline put her mind to her own ride and the possibilities awaiting at the ranch. She remembered the failure to get any of her servants or cowboys on the telephone. To be sure, a wind-storm had once broken the wire. But she had little real hope of such being the case in this instance. She rode on, pulling the black as she neared the ranch. Her approach was from the south and off the usual trail, so that she went up the long slope of the knoll toward the back of the house. Under these circumstances she could not consider it out of the ordinary that she did not see any one about the grounds.

It was perhaps fortunate for her, she thought, that the climb up the slope cut the black's speed so she could manage him. He was not very hard to stop. The moment she dismounted, however, he jumped and trotted off. At the edge of the slope, facing the corrals, he halted to lift his head and shoot up his ears. Then he let out a piercing whistle and dashed down the lane.

Madeline, prepared by that warning whistle, tried to fortify herself for a new and unexpected situation; but as she espied an unfamiliar company of horsemen rapidly riding down a hollow leading from the foothills she felt the return of fears gripping at her like cold hands, and she fled precipitously into the house.

❧ II ❧

A BAND OF GUERRILLAS

MADELINE BOLTED THE DOOR, and, flying into the kitchen, she told the scared servants to shut themselves in. Then she ran to her own rooms. It was only a matter of a few moments for her to close and bar the heavy shutters, yet even as she was fastening the last one in the room she used as an office a clattering roar of hoofs seemed to swell up to the front of the house. She caught a glimpse of wild, shaggy horses and ragged, dusty men. She had never seen any vaqueros that resembled these horsemen. Vaqueros had grace and style; they were fond of lace and glitter and fringe; they dressed their horses in silvered trappings. But the riders now trampling into the driveway were uncouth, lean, savage. They were guerrillas, a band of the raiders who had been harassing the border since the beginning of the revolution. A second glimpse assured Madeline that they were not all Mexicans.

The presence of outlaws in that band brought home to Madeline her real danger. She remembered what Stillwell had told her about recent outlaw raids along the Rio Grande. These flying bands, operating under the excitement of the revolution, appeared here and there, everywhere, in remote places, and were gone as quickly as they came. Mostly they wanted money and arms, but they would steal anything, and unprotected women had suffered at their hands.

Madeline, hurriedly collecting her securities and the considerable money she had in her desk, ran out, closed and locked the door, crossed the patio to the opposite side of the house, and, entering again, went down a long corridor, trying to decide which of the many unused rooms would be best to hide in. And before she made up her mind she came to the last room. Just then a battering on door or window in the direction of the kitchen and shrill screams from the servant women increased Madeline's alarm.

She entered the last room. There was no lock or bar upon the door. But the room was large and dark, and it was half full of bales of alfalfa hay. Probably it was the safest place in the house; at least time would be necessary to find any one hidden there. She dropped her valuables in a dark corner and covered them with loose hay. That done, she felt her way down a narrow aisle between the piled-up bales and presently crouched in a niche.

With the necessity of action over for the immediate present, Madeline became conscious that she was quivering and almost breathless. Her skin felt tight and cold. There was a weight on her chest; her mouth was dry, and she had a strange tendency to swallow. Her listening faculty seemed most acute. Dull sounds came from parts of the house remote from her. In the intervals of silence between these sounds she heard the squeaking and rustling of mice in the hay. A mouse ran over her hand.

She listened, waiting, hoping yet dreading to hear the clattering approach of her cowboys. There would be fighting—blood—men injured, perhaps killed. Even the thought of violence of any kind hurt her. But perhaps the guerrillas would run in time to avoid a clash with her men. She hoped for that, prayed for it. Through her mind flitted what she knew of Nels, of Monty, of Nick Steele; and she experienced a sensation that left her somewhat chilled and sick. Then she thought of the dark-browed, fire-eyed Stewart. She felt a thrill drive away the cold nausea. And her excitement augmented.

Waiting, listening increased all her emotions. Nothing appeared to be happening. Yet hours seemed to pass while she crouched there. Had Florence been overtaken? Could any of those lean horses outrun Majesty? She doubted it; she knew it could not be true. Nevertheless, the strain of uncertainty was torturing.

Suddenly the bang of the corridor door pierced her through and through with the dread of uncertainty. Some of the guerrillas had entered the east wing of the house. She heard a babel of jabbering voices, the shuffling of boots and clinking of spurs, the slamming of doors and ransacking of rooms.

Madeline lost faith in her hiding-place. Moreover, she found it impossible to take the chance. The idea of being caught in that dark room by those ruffians filled her with horror. She must get out into the light. Swiftly she rose and went to the window. It was rather more of a door than window, being a large aperture closed by two wooden doors on hinges. The iron hook yielded readily to her grasp, and one door stuck fast, while the other opened a few inches. She looked out upon a green slope covered with flowers and bunches of sage and bushes. Neither man nor horse showed in the narrow field of her vision. She believed she would be safer hidden out there in the shrubbery than in the house. The jump from the window would be easy for her. And with her quick decision came a rush and stir of spirit that warded off her weakness.

She pulled at the door. It did not budge. It had caught at the bottom. Pulling with all her might proved to be in vain. Pausing, with palms hot and bruised, she heard a louder, closer approach of the invaders of her home. Fear, wrath, and impotence contested for supremacy over her and drove her to desperation. She was alone here, and she must rely on herself. And as she strained every muscle to move that obstinate door and heard the quick, harsh voices of men and the sounds of a hurried search she suddenly felt sure that they were hunting for her. She knew it. She did not wonder at it. But she wondered if she were really Madeline Hammond, and if it were possible that brutal men would harm her. Then the tramping of heavy feet on the floor of the adjoining room lent her the last strength of fear. Pushing with hands and shoulders, she moved the door far enough to permit the passage of her body. Then she stepped up on the sill and slipped through the aperture. She saw no one. Lightly she jumped down and ran in among the bushes. But these did not afford her the cover she needed. She stole from one clump to another, finding too late that she had chosen with poor judgment. The position of the bushes had drawn her closer to the front of the house rather than away from it, and just before her were horses, and beyond a group of excited men. With her heart in her throat Madeline crouched down.

A shrill yell, followed by running and mounting guerrillas, roused her hope. They had sighted the cowboys and were in flight. Rapid thumping of boots on the porch told of men hurrying from the house. Several horses dashed past her, not ten feet distant. One rider saw her, for he turned to shout back. This drove Madeline into a panic. Hardly knowing what she did, she began to run away from the house. Her feet seemed leaden. She felt the same horrible powerlessness that sometimes came over her when she dreamed of being pursued. Horses with shouting riders streaked past her in the shrubbery. There was a thunder of hoofs behind her. She turned aside, but the thundering grew nearer. She was being run down.

As Madeline shut her eyes and, staggering, was about to fall, apparently right under pounding hoofs, a rude, powerful hand clapped round her waist, clutched deep and strong, and swung her aloft. She felt a heavy blow when the shoulder of the horse struck her, and then a wrenching of her arm as she was dragged up. A sudden blighting pain made sight and feeling fade from her.

But she did not become unconscious to the extent that she lost the sense of being rapidly borne away. She seemed to hold that for a long time. When her faculties began to return the motion of the horse was no longer violent. For a few moments she could not determine her position. Apparently she was upside down. Then she saw that she was facing the ground, and must be lying across a saddle with her head hanging down. She could not move a hand; she could not tell where her hands were. Then she felt the touch of soft leather. She saw a high-topped Mexican boot, wearing a huge silver spur, and the reeking flank and legs of a horse, and a dusty, narrow trail. Soon a kind of red darkness veiled her eyes, her head swam, and she felt motion and pain only dully.

After what seemed a thousand weary hours some one lifted her from the horse and laid her upon the ground, where, gradually, as the blood left her head and she could see, she began to get the right relation of things.

She lay in a sparse grove of firs, and the shadows told of late afternoon. She smelled wood smoke, and she heard the sharp crunch of horses' teeth nipping grass. Voices caused her to turn her face. A group of men stood and sat round a camp-fire eating like wolves. The looks of her captors made Madeline close her eyes, and the fascination, the fear they roused in her made her open them again. Mostly they were thin-bodied, thin-bearded Mexicans, black and haggard and starved. Whatever they might be, they surely were hunger-stricken and squalid. Not one had a coat. A few had scarfs. Some wore belts in which were scattered cartridges. Only a few had guns, and these were of diverse patterns. Madeline could see no packs, no blankets, and only a few cooking-utensils, all battered and blackened. Her eyes fastened upon men she believed were white men; but it was from their features and not their color that she judged. Once she had seen a band of nomad robbers in the Sahara, and somehow was reminded of them by this motley outlaw troop.

They divided attention between the satisfying of ravenous appetites and a vigilant watching down the forest aisles. They expected some one, Madeline thought, and, manifestly, if it were a pursuing posse, they did not show anxiety. She could not understand more than a word here and there that they uttered. Presently, however, the name of Don Carlos revived keen curiosity in her and realization of her situation, and then once more dread possessed her breast.

A low exclamation and a sweep of arm from one of the guerrillas caused the whole band to wheel and concentrate their attention in the opposite direction. They heard something. They saw some one. Grimy hands sought weapons, and then every man stiffened. Madeline saw what hunted men looked like at the moment of discovery, and the sight was terrible. She closed her eyes, sick with what she saw, fearful of the moment when the guns would leap out.

There were muttered curses, a short period of silence followed by whisperings, and then a clear voice rang out, "El Capitan!"

A strong shock vibrated through Madeline, and her eyelids swept open. Instantly she associated the name El Capitan with Stewart and experienced a sensation of strange regret. It was not pursuit or rescue she thought of then, but death. These men would kill Stewart. But surely he had not come alone. The lean, dark faces, corded and rigid, told her in what direction to look. She heard the slow, heavy thump of hoofs. Soon into the wide aisle between the trees moved the form of a man, arms flung high over his head. Then Madeline saw the horse, and she recognized Majesty, and she knew it was really Stewart who rode the roan. When doubt was no longer possible she felt a suffocating sense of gladness and fear and wonder.

Many of the guerrillas leaped up with drawn weapons. Still Stewart approached with his hands high, and he rode right into the camp-fire circle. Then a guerrilla, evidently the chief, waved down the threatening men and strode up to Stewart. He greeted him. There was amaze and pleasure and respect in the greeting. Madeline could tell that, though she did not know what was said. At the moment Stewart appeared to her as cool and careless as if he were dismounting at her porch steps. But when he got down she saw that his face was white. He shook hands with the guerrilla, and then his glittering eyes roved over the men and around the glade until they rested upon Madeline. Without moving from his tracks he seemed to leap, as if a powerful current had shocked him. Madeline tried to smile to assure him she was alive and well; but the intent in his eyes, the power of his controlled spirit telling her of her peril and his, froze the smile on her lips.

With that he faced the chief and spoke rapidly in the Mexican jargon Madeline had always found so difficult to translate. The chief answered, spreading wide his hands, one of which indicated Madeline as she lay there. Stewart drew the fellow a little aside and said something for his ear alone. The chief's hands swept up in a gesture of surprise and acquiescence. Again Stewart spoke swiftly. His hearer then turned to address the band. Madeline caught the words "Don Carlos" and "pesos." There was a brief muttering protest which the chief thundered down. Madeline guessed her release had been given by this guerrilla and bought from the others of the band.

Stewart strode to her side, leading the roan. Majesty reared and snorted when he saw his mistress prostrate. Stewart knelt, still holding the bridle.

"Are you all right?" he asked.

"I think so," she replied, essaying a laugh that was rather a failure. "My feet are tied."

Dark blood blotted out all the white from his face, and lightning shot from his eyes. She felt his hands, like steel tongs, loosening the bonds round her ankles. Without a word he lifted her upright and then upon Majesty. Madeline reeled a little in the saddle, held hard to the pommel with one hand, and tried to lean on Stewart's shoulder with the other.

"Don't give up," he said.

She saw him gaze furtively into the forest on all sides. And it surprised her to see the guerrillas riding away. Putting the two facts together, Madeline formed an idea that neither Stewart nor the others desired to meet with some one evidently due shortly in the glade. Stewart guided the roan off to the right and walked beside Madeline, steadying her in the saddle. At first Madeline was so weak and dizzy that she could scarcely retain her seat. The dizziness left her presently, and then she made an effort to ride without help. Her weakness, however, and a pain in her wrenched arm made the task laborsome.

Stewart had struck off the trail, if there were one, and was keeping to denser parts of the forest. The sun sank low, and the shafts of gold fell with a long slant among the firs. Majesty's hoofs made no sound on the soft ground, and Stewart strode on without speaking. Neither his hurry nor vigilance relaxed until at least two miles had been covered. Then he held to a straighter course and did not send so many glances into the darkening woods. The level of the forest began to be cut up by little hollows, all of which sloped and widened. Presently the soft ground gave place to bare, rocky soil. The horse snorted and tossed his head. A sound of splashing water broke the silence. The hollow opened into a wider one through which a little brook murmured its way over the stones. Majesty snorted again and stopped and bent his head.

"He wants a drink," said Madeline. "I'm thirsty, too, and very tired."

Stewart lifted her out of the saddle, and as their hands parted she felt something moist and warm. Blood was running down her arm and into the palm of her hand.

"I'm—bleeding," she said, a little unsteadily. "Oh, I remember. My arm was hurt."

She held it out, the blood making her conscious of her weakness. Stewart's fingers felt so firm and sure. Swiftly he ripped the wet sleeve. Her forearm had been cut or scratched. He washed off the blood.

"Why, Stewart, it's nothing. I was only a little nervous. I guess that's the first time I ever saw my own blood."

He made no reply as he tore her handkerchief into strips and bound her arm. His swift motions and his silence gave her a hint of how he might meet a more serious emergency. She felt safe. And because of that impression, when he lifted his head and she saw that he was pale and shaking, she was surprised. He stood before her folding his scarf, which was still wet, and from which he made no effort to remove the red stains.

"Miss Hammond," he said, hoarsely, "it was a man's hands—a Greaser's finger-nails— that cut your arm. I know who he was. I could have killed him. But I mightn't have got your freedom. You understand? I didn't dare."

Madeline gazed at Stewart, astounded more by his speech than his excessive emotion.

"My dear boy!" she exclaimed. And then she paused. She could not find words.

He was making an apology to her for not killing a man who had laid a rough hand upon her person. He was ashamed and seemed to be in a torture that she would not understand why he had not killed the man. There seemed to be something of passionate scorn in him that he had not been able to avenge her as well as free her.

"Stewart, I understand. You were being my kind of cowboy. I thank you."

But she did not understand so much as she implied. She had heard many stories of this man's cool indifference to peril and death. He had always seemed as hard as granite. Why should the sight of a little blood upon her arm pale his cheek and shake his hand and thicken his voice? What was there in his nature to make him implore her to see the only reason he could not kill an outlaw? The answer to the first question was that he loved her. It was beyond her to answer the second. But the secret of it lay in the same strength from which his love sprang—an intensity of feeling which seemed characteristic of these Western men of simple, lonely, elemental lives. All at once over Madeline rushed a tide of realization of how greatly it was possible for such a man as Stewart to love her. The thought came to her in all its singular power. All her Eastern lovers who had the graces that made them her equals in the sight of the world were without the only great essential that a lonely, hard life had given to Stewart. Nature here struck a just balance. Something deep and dim in the future, an unknown voice, called to Madeline and disturbed her. And because it was not a voice to her intelligence she deadened the ears of her warm and throbbing life and decided never to listen.

"Is it safe to rest a little?" she asked. "I am so tired. Perhaps I'll be stronger if I rest."

"We're all right now," he said. "The horse will be better, too. I ran him out. And uphill, at that."

"Where are we?"

"Up in the mountains, ten miles and more from the ranch. There's a trail just below here. I can get you home by midnight. They'll be some worried down there."

"What happened?"

"Nothing much to any one but you. That's the—the hard luck of it. Florence caught us out on the slope. We were returning from the fire. We were dead beat. But we got to the ranch before any damage was done. We sure had trouble in finding a trace of you. Nick spotted the prints of your heels under the window. And then we knew. I had to fight the boys. If they'd come after you we'd never have gotten you without a fight. I didn't want that. Old Bill came out packing a dozen guns. He was crazy. I had to rope Monty. Honest, I tied him to the porch. Nels and Nick promised to stay and hold him till morning. That was the best I could do. I was sure lucky to come up with the band so soon. I had figured right. I knew that guerrilla chief. He's a bandit in Mexico. It's a business with him. But he fought for Madero, and I was with him a good deal. He may be a Greaser, but he's white."

"How did you effect my release?"

"I offered them money. That's what the rebels all want. They need money. They're a lot of poor, hungry devils."

"I gathered that you offered to pay ransom. How much?"

"Two thousand dollars Mex. I gave my word. I'll have to take the money. I told them when and where I'd meet them."

"Certainly. I'm glad I've got the money." Madeline laughed. "What a strange thing to happen to me! I wonder what dad would say to that? Stewart, I'm afraid he'd say two thousand dollars is more than I'm worth. But tell me. That rebel chieftain did not demand money?"

"No. The money is for his men."

"What did you say to him? I saw you whisper in his ear."

Stewart dropped his head, averting her direct gaze.

"We were comrades before Juarez. One day I dragged him out of a ditch. I reminded him. Then I—I told him something I—I thought—"

"Stewart, I know from the way he looked at me that you spoke of me."

Her companion did not offer a reply to this, and Madeline did not press the point.

"I heard Don Carlos's name several times. That interests me. What have Don Carlos and his vaqueros to do with this?"

"That Greaser has all to do with it," replied Stewart, grimly. "He burned his ranch and corrals to keep us from getting them. But he also did it to draw all the boys away from your home. They had a deep plot, all right. I left orders for some one to stay with you. But Al and Stillwell, who're both hot-headed, rode off this morning. Then the guerrillas came down."

"Well, what was the idea—the plot—as you call it?"

"To get you," he said, bluntly.

"Me! Stewart, you do not mean my capture—whatever you call it—was anything more than mere accident?"

"I do mean that. But Stillwell and your brother think the guerrillas wanted money and arms, and they just happened to make off with you because you ran under a horse's nose."

"You do not incline to that point of view?"

"I don't. Neither does Nels nor Nick Steele. And we know Don Carlos and the Greasers. Look how the vaqueros chased Flo for you!"

"What do you think, then?"

"I'd rather not say."

"But, Stewart, I would like to know. If it is about me, surely I ought to know," protested Madeline. "What reason have Nels and Nick to suspect Don Carlos of plotting to abduct me?"

"I suppose they've no reason you'd take. Once I heard Nels say he'd seen the Greaser look at you, and if he ever saw him do it again he'd shoot him."

"Why, Stewart, that is ridiculous. To shoot a man for looking at a woman! This is a civilized country."

"Well, maybe it would be ridiculous in a civilized country. There's some things about civilization I don't care for."

"What, for instance?"

"For one thing, I can't stand for the way men let other men treat women."

"But, Stewart, this is strange talk from you, who, that night I came—"

She broke off, sorry that she had spoken. His shame was not pleasant to see. Suddenly he lifted his head, and she felt scorched by flaming eyes.

"Suppose I was drunk. Suppose I had met some ordinary girl. Suppose I had really made her marry me. Don't you think I would have stopped being a drunkard and have been good to her?"

"Stewart, I do not know what to think about you," replied Madeline.

Then followed a short silence. Madeline saw the last bright rays of the setting sun glide up over a distant crag. Stewart rebridled the horse and looked at the saddle-girths.

"I got off the trail. About Don Carlos I'll say right out, not what Nels and Nick think, but what I know. Don Carlos hoped to make off with you for himself, the same as if you had been a poor peon slave-girl down in Sonora. Maybe he had a deeper plot than my rebel friend told me. Maybe he even went so far as to hope for American troops to chase him. The rebels are trying to stir up the United States. They'd welcome intervention. But, however that may be, the Greaser meant evil to you, and has meant it ever since he saw you first. That's all."

"Stewart, you have done me and my family a service we can never hope to repay."

"I've done the service. Only don't mention pay to me. But there's one thing I'd like you to know, and I find it hard to say. It's prompted, maybe, by what I know you think of me and what I imagine your family and friends would think if they knew. It's not prompted by pride or conceit. And it's this: Such a woman as you should never have come to this God-forsaken country unless she meant to forget herself. But as you did come, and as you were dragged away by those devils, I want you to know that all your wealth and position and influence— all that power behind you—would never have saved you from hell to-night. Only such a man as Nels or Nick Steele or I could have done that."

Madeline Hammond felt the great leveling force of the truth. Whatever the difference between her and Stewart, or whatever the imagined difference set up by false standards of class and culture, the truth was that here on this wild mountain-side she was only a woman and he was simply a man. It was a man that she needed, and if her choice could have been considered in this extremity it would have fallen upon him who had just faced her in quiet, bitter speech. Here was food for thought.

"I reckon we'd better start now," he said, and drew the horse close to a large rock. "Come."

Madeline's will greatly exceeded her strength. For the first time she acknowledged to herself that she had been hurt. Still, she did not feel much pain except when she moved her shoulder. Once in the saddle, where Stewart lifted her, she drooped weakly. The way was rough; every step the horse took hurt her; and the slope of the ground threw her forward on the pommel. Presently, as the slope grew rockier and her discomfort increased, she forgot everything except that she was suffering.

"Here is the trail," said Stewart, at length.

Not far from that point Madeline swayed, and but for Stewart's support would have fallen from the saddle. She heard him swear under his breath.

"Here, this won't do," he said. "Throw your leg over the pommel. The other one—there."

Then, mounting, he slipped behind her and lifted and turned her, and then held her with his left arm so that she lay across the saddle and his knees, her head against his shoulder.

As the horse started into a rapid walk Madeline gradually lost all pain and discomfort when she relaxed her muscles. Presently she let herself go and lay inert, greatly to her relief. For a little while she seemed to be half drunk with the gentle swaying of a hammock. Her mind became at once dreamy and active, as if it thoughtfully recorded the slow, soft impressions pouring in from all her senses.

A red glow faded in the west. She could see out over the foothills, where twilight was settling gray on the crests, dark in the hollows. Cedar and pinyon trees lined the trail, and there were no more firs. At intervals huge drab-colored rocks loomed over her. The sky was clear and steely. A faint star twinkled. And lastly, close to her, she saw Stewart's face, once more dark and impassive, with the inscrutable eyes fixed on the trail.

His arm, like a band of iron, held her, yet it was flexible and yielded her to the motion of the horse. One instant she felt the brawn, the bone, heavy and powerful; the next the stretch and ripple, the elasticity of muscles. He held her as easily as if she were a child. The roughness of his flannel shirt rubbed her cheek, and beneath that she felt the dampness of the scarf he had used to bathe her arm, and deeper still the regular pound of his heart. Against her ear, filling it with strong, vibrant beat, his heart seemed a mighty engine deep within a great cavern. Her head had never before rested on a man's breast, and she had no liking for it there; but she felt more than the physical contact. The position was mysterious and fascinating, and something natural in it made her think of life. Then as the cool wind blew down from the heights, loosening her tumbled hair, she was compelled to see strands of it curl softly into Stewart's face, before his eyes, across his lips. She was unable to reach it with her free hand, and therefore could not refasten it. And when she shut her eyes she felt those loosened strands playing against his cheeks.

In the keener press of such sensations she caught the smell of dust and a faint, wild, sweet tang on the air. There was a low, rustling sigh of wind in the brush along the trail. Suddenly the silence ripped apart to the sharp bark of a coyote, and then, from far away, came a long wail. And then Majesty's metal-rimmed hoof rang on a stone.

These later things lent probability to that ride for Madeline. Otherwise it would have seemed like a dream. Even so it was hard to believe. Again she wondered if this woman who had begun to think and feel so much was Madeline Hammond. Nothing had ever happened to her. And here, playing about her like her hair played about Stewart's face, was adventure, perhaps death, and surely life. She could not believe the evidence of the day's happenings. Would any of her people, her friends, ever believe it? Could she tell it? How impossible to think that a cunning Mexican might have used her to further the interests of a forlorn revolution. She remembered the ghoulish visages of those starved rebels, and marveled at her blessed fortune in escaping them. She was safe, and now self-preservation had some meaning for her. Stewart's arrival in the glade, the courage with which he had faced the outlawed men, grew as real to her now as the iron arm that clasped her. Had it been an instinct which had importuned her to save this man when he lay ill and hopeless in the shack at Chiricahua? In helping him had she hedged round her forces that had just operated to save her life, or if not that, more than life was to her? She believed so.

Madeline opened her eyes after a while and found that night had fallen. The sky was a dark, velvety blue blazing with white stars. The cool wind tugged at her hair, and through waving strands she saw Stewart's profile, bold and sharp against the sky.

Then, as her mind succumbed to her bodily fatigue, again her situation became unreal and wild. A heavy languor, like a blanket, began to steal upon her. She wavered and drifted. With the last half-conscious sense of a muffled throb at her ear, a something intangibly sweet, deep-toned, and strange, like a distant calling bell, she fell asleep with her head on Stewart's breast.

12

FRIENDS FROM THE EAST

THREE DAYS after her return to the ranch Madeline could not discover any physical discomfort as a reminder of her adventurous experiences. This surprised her, but not nearly so much as the fact that after a few weeks she found she scarcely remembered the adventures at all. If it had not been for the quiet and persistent guardianship of her cowboys she might almost have forgotten Don Carlos and the raiders. Madeline was assured of the splendid physical fitness to which this ranch life had developed her, and that she was assimilating something of the Western disregard of danger. A hard ride, an accident, a day in the sun and dust, an adventure with outlaws—these might once have been matters of large import, but now for Madeline they were in order with all the rest of her changed life.

There was never a day that something interesting was not brought to her notice. Stillwell, who had ceaselessly reproached himself for riding away the morning Madeline was captured, grew more like an anxious parent than a faithful superintendent. He was never at ease regarding her unless he was near the ranch or had left Stewart there, or else Nels and Nick Steele. Naturally, he trusted more to Stewart than to any one else.

"Miss Majesty, it's sure amazin' strange about Gene," said the old cattleman, as he tramped into Madeline's office.

"What's the matter now?" she inquired.

"Wal, Gene has rustled off into the mountains again."

"Again? I did not know he had gone. I gave him money for that band of guerrillas. Perhaps he went to take it to them."

"No. He took that a day or so after he fetched you back home. Then in about a week he went a second time. An' he packed some stuff with him. Now he's sneaked off, an' Nels, who was down to the lower trail, saw him meet somebody that looked like Padre Marcos. Wal, I went down to the church, and, sure enough, Padre Marcos is gone. What do you think of that, Miss Majesty?"

"Maybe Stewart is getting religious," laughed Madeline. You told me so once.

Stillwell puffed and wiped his red face.

"If you'd heerd him cuss Monty this mawnin' you'd never guess it was religion. Monty

274

an' Nels hev been givin' Gene a lot of trouble lately. They're both sore an' in fightin' mood ever since Don Carlos hed you kidnapped. Sure they're goin' to break soon, an' then we'll hev a couple of wild Texas steers ridin' the range. I've a heap to worry me."

"Let Stewart take his mysterious trips into the mountains. Here, Stillwell, I have news for you that may give you reason for worry. I have letters from home. And my sister, with a party of friends, is coming out to visit me. They are society folk, and one of them is an English lord."

"Wal, Miss Majesty, I reckon we'll all be glad to see them," said Stillwell. "Onless they pack you off back East."

"That isn't likely," replied Madeline, thoughtfully. "I must go back some time, though. Well, let me read you a few extracts from my mail."

Madeline took up her sister's letter with a strange sensation of how easily sight of a crested monogram and scent of delicately perfumed paper could recall the brilliant life she had given up. She scanned the pages of beautiful handwriting. Helen's letter was in turn gay and brilliant and lazy, just as she was herself; but Madeline detected more of curiosity in it than of real longing to see the sister and brother in the Far West. Much of what Helen wrote was enthusiastic anticipation of the fun she expected to have with bashful cowboys. Helen seldom wrote letters, and she never read anything, not even popular novels of the day. She was as absolutely ignorant of the West as the Englishman, who, she said, expected to hunt buffalo and fight Indians. Moreover, there was a satiric note in the letter that Madeline did not like, and which roused her spirit. Manifestly, Helen was reveling in the prospect of new sensation.

When she finished reading aloud a few paragraphs the old cattleman snorted and his face grew redder.

"Did your sister write that?" he asked.

"Yes."

"Wal, I—I beg pawdin, Miss Majesty. But it doesn't seem like you. Does she think we're a lot of wild men from Borneo?"

"Evidently she does. I rather think she is in for a surprise. Now, Stillwell, you are clever and you can see the situation. I want my guests to enjoy their stay here, but I do not want that to be at the expense of the feelings of all of us, or even any one. Helen will bring a lively crowd. They'll crave excitement—the unusual. Let us see that they are not disappointed. You take the boys into your confidence. Tell them what to expect, and tell them how to meet it. I shall help you in that. I want the boys to be on dress-parade when they are off duty. I want them to be on their most elegant behavior. I do not care what they do, what measures they take to protect themselves, what tricks they contrive, so long as they do not overstep the limit of kindness and courtesy. I want them to play their parts seriously, naturally, as if they had lived no other way. My guests expect to have fun. Let us meet them with fun. Now what do you say?"

Stillwell rose, his great bulk towering, his huge face beaming.

"Wal, I say it's the most amazin' fine idee I ever heerd in my life."

"Indeed, I am glad you like it," went on Madeline.

"Come to me again, Stillwell, after you have spoken to the boys. But, now that I have suggested it, I am a little afraid. You know what cowboy fun is. Perhaps—"

"Don't you go back on that idee," interrupted Stillwell. He was assuring and bland, but his hurry to convince Madeline betrayed him. "Leave the boys to me. Why, don't they all swear by you, same as the Mexicans do to the Virgin? They won't disgrace you, Miss Majesty. They'll be simply immense. It'll beat any show you ever seen."

"I believe it will," replied Madeline. She was still doubtful of her plan, but the enthusiasm of the old cattleman was infectious and irresistible. "Very well, we will consider it settled. My guests will arrive on May ninth. Meanwhile let us get Her Majesty's Rancho in shape for this invasion."

⚜

On the afternoon of the ninth of May, perhaps half an hour after Madeline had received a telephone message from Link Stevens announcing the arrival of her guests at El Cajon, Florence called her out upon the porch. Stillwell was there with his face wrinkled by his wonderful smile and his eagle eyes riveted upon the distant valley. Far away, perhaps twenty miles, a thin streak of white dust rose from the valley floor and slanted skyward.

"Look!" said Florence, excitedly.

"What is that?" asked Madeline.

"Link Stevens and the automobile!"

"Oh no! Why, it's only a few minutes since he telephoned saying the party had just arrived."

"Take a look with the glasses," said Florence.

One glance through the powerful binoculars convinced Madeline that Florence was right. And another glance at Stillwell told her that he was speechless with delight. She remembered a little conversation she had had with Link Stevens a short while previous.

"Stevens, I hope the car is in good shape," she had said. "Now, Miss Hammond, she's as right as the best-trained hoss I ever rode," he had replied.

"The valley road is perfect," she had gone on, musingly. "I never saw such a beautiful road, even in France. No fences, no ditches, no rocks, no vehicles. Just a lonely road on the desert."

"Shore, it's lonely," Stevens had answered, with slowly brightening eyes. "An' safe, Miss Hammond."

"My sister used to like fast riding. If I remember correctly, all of my guests were a little afflicted with the speed mania. It is a common disease with New-Yorkers. I hope, Stevens, that you will not give them reason to think we are altogether steeped in the slow, dreamy manana languor of the Southwest."

Link doubtfully eyed her, and then his bronze face changed its dark aspect and seemed to shine.

"Beggin' your pardon, Miss Hammond, thet's shore tall talk fer Link Stevens to savvy. You mean—as long as I drive careful an' safe I can run away from my dust, so to say, an' get here in somethin' less than the Greaser's to-morrow?"

Madeline had laughed her assent. And now, as she watched the thin streak of dust, at that distance moving with snail pace, she reproached herself. She trusted Stevens; she had never known so skilful, daring, and iron-nerved a driver as he was. If she had been in the car herself she would have had no anxiety. But, imagining what Stevens would do on forty miles and more of that desert road, Madeline suffered a prick of conscience.

"Oh, Stillwell!" she exclaimed. "I am afraid I will go back on my wonderful idea. What made me do it?"

"Your sister wanted the real thing, didn't she? Said they all wanted it. Wal, I reckon they've begun gettin' it," replied Stillwell.

That statement from the cattleman allayed Madeline's pangs of conscience. She understood just what she felt, though she could not have put it in words. She was hungry for

276

a sight of well-remembered faces; she longed to hear the soft laughter and gay repartee of old friends; she was eager for gossipy first-hand news of her old world. Nevertheless, something in her sister's letter, in messages from the others who were coming, had touched Madeline's pride. In one sense the expected guests were hostile, inasmuch as they were scornful and curious about the West that had claimed her. She imagined what they would expect in a Western ranch. They would surely get the real thing, too, as Stillwell said; and in that certainty was satisfaction for a small grain of something within Madeline which approached resentment. She wistfully wondered, however, if her sister or friends would come to see the West even a little as she saw it. That, perhaps, would he hoping too much. She resolved once for all to do her best to give them the sensation their senses craved, and equally to show them the sweetness and beauty and wholesomeness and strength of life in the Southwest.

"Wal, as Nels says, I wouldn't be in that there ottomobile right now for a million pesos," remarked Stillwell.

"Why? Is Stevens driving fast?"

"Good Lord! Fast? Miss Majesty, there hain't ever been anythin' except a streak of lightnin' run so fast in this country. I'll bet Link for once is in heaven. I can jest see him now, the grim, crooked-legged little devil, hunchin' down over that wheel as if it was a hoss's neck."

"I told him not to let the ride be hot or dusty," remarked Madeline.

"Haw, haw!" roared Stillwell. "Wal, I'll be goin'. I reckon I'd like to be hyar when Link drives up, but I want to be with the boys down by the bunks. It'll be some fun to see Nels an' Monty when Link comes flyin' along."

"I wish Al had stayed to meet them," said Madeline.

Her brother had rather hurried a shipment of cattle to California: and it was Madeline's supposition that he had welcomed the opportunity to absent himself from the ranch.

"I am sorry he wouldn't stay," replied Florence. "But Al's all business now. And he's doing finely. It's just as well, perhaps."

"Surely. That was my pride speaking. I would like to have all my family and all my old friends see what a man Al has become. Well, Link Stevens is running like the wind. The car will be here before we know it. Florence, we've only a few moments to dress. But first I want to order many and various and exceedingly cold refreshments for that approaching party."

Less than a half-hour later Madeline went again to the porch and found Florence there.

"Oh, you look just lovely!" exclaimed Florence, impulsively, as she gazed wide-eyed up at Madeline. "And somehow so different!"

Madeline smiled a little sadly. Perhaps when she had put on that exquisite white gown something had come to her of the manner which befitted the wearing of it. She could not resist the desire to look fair once more in the eyes of these hypercritical friends. The sad smile had been for the days that were gone. For she knew that what society had once been pleased to call her beauty had trebled since it had last been seen in a drawing-room. Madeline wore no jewels, but at her waist she had pinned two great crimson roses. Against the dead white they had the life and fire and redness of the desert.

"Link's hit the old round-up trail," said Florence, "and oh, isn't he riding that car!"

With Florence, as with most of the cowboys, the car was never driven, but ridden.

A white spot with a long trail of dust showed low down in the valley. It was now headed almost straight for the ranch. Madeline watched it growing larger moment by moment, and her pleasurable emotion grew accordingly. Then the rapid beat of a horse's hoofs caused her to turn.

Stewart was riding in on his black horse. He had been absent on an important mission, and his duty had taken him to the international boundary-line. His presence home long before he was expected was particularly gratifying to Madeline, for it meant that his mission had been brought to a successful issue. Once more, for the hundredth time, the man's reliability struck Madeline. He was a doer of things. The black horse halted wearily without the usual pound of hoofs on the gravel, and the dusty rider dismounted wearily. Both horse and rider showed the heat and dust and wind of many miles.

Madeline advanced to the porch steps. And Stewart, after taking a parcel of papers from a saddle-bag, turned toward her.

"Stewart, you are the best of couriers," she said. "I am pleased."

Dust streamed from his sombrero as he doffed it. His dark face seemed to rise as he straightened weary shoulders.

"Here are the reports, Miss Hammond," he replied.

As he looked up to see her standing there, dressed to receive her Eastern guests, he checked his advance with a violent action which recalled to Madeline the one he had made on the night she had met him, when she disclosed her identity. It was not fear nor embarrassment nor awkwardness. And it was only momentary. Yet, slight as had been his pause, Madeline received from it an impression of some strong halting force. A man struck by a bullet might have had an instant jerk of muscular control such as convulsed Stewart. In that instant, as her keen gaze searched his dust-caked face, she met the full, free look of his eyes. Her own did not fall, though she felt a warmth steal to her cheeks. Madeline very seldom blushed. And now, conscious of her sudden color a genuine blush flamed on her face. It was irritating because it was incomprehensible. She received the papers from Stewart and thanked him. He bowed, then led the black down the path toward the corrals.

"When Stewart looks like that he's been riding," said Florence. "But when his horse looks like that he's sure been burning the wind."

Madeline watched the weary horse and rider limp down the path. What had made her thoughtful? Mostly it was something new or sudden or inexplicable that stirred her mind to quick analysis. In this instance the thing that had struck Madeline was Stewart's glance. He had looked at her, and the old burning, inscrutable fire, the darkness, had left his eyes. Suddenly they had been beautiful. The look had not been one of surprise or admiration; nor had it been one of love. She was familiar, too familiar with all three. It had not been a gaze of passion, for there was nothing beautiful in that. Madeline pondered. And presently she realized that Stewart's eyes had expressed a strange joy of pride. That expression Madeline had never before encountered in the look of any man. Probably its strangeness had made her notice it and accounted for her blushing. The longer she lived among these outdoor men the more they surprised her. Particularly, how incomprehensible was this cowboy Stewart! Why should he have pride or joy at sight of her?

Florence's exclamation made Madeline once more attend to the approaching automobile. It was on the slope now, some miles down the long gradual slant. Two yellow funnel-shaped clouds of dust seemed to shoot out from behind the car and roll aloft to join the column that stretched down the valley.

"I wonder what riding a mile a minute would be like," said Florence. "I'll sure make Link take me. Oh, but look at him come!"

The giant car resembled a white demon, and but for the dust would have appeared to be sailing in the air. Its motion was steadily forward, holding to the road as if on rails. And its velocity was astounding. Long, gray veils, like pennants, streamed in the wind. A low rushing sound became perceptible, and it grew louder, became a roar. The car shot like an arrow past the alfalfa-field, by the bunk-houses, where the cowboys waved and cheered. The horses and burros in the corrals began to snort and tramp and race in fright. At the base of the long slope of the foothill Link cut the speed more than half. Yet the car roared up, rolling the dust, flying capes and veils and ulsters, and crashed and cracked to a halt in the yard before the porch.

Madeline descried a gray, disheveled mass of humanity packed inside the car. Besides the driver there were seven occupants, and for a moment they appeared to be coming to life, moving and exclaiming under the veils and wraps and dust-shields.

Link Stevens stepped out and, removing helmet and goggles, coolly looked at his watch.

"An hour an' a quarter, Miss Hammond," he said. "It's sixty-three miles by the valley road, an' you know there's a couple of bad hills. I reckon we made fair time, considerin' you wanted me to drive slow an' safe."

From the mass of dusty-veiled humanity in the car came low exclamations and plaintive feminine wails.

Madeline stepped to the front of the porch. Then the deep voices of men and softer voices of women united in one glad outburst, as much a thanksgiving as a greeting, "MAJESTY!"

Helen Hammond was three years younger than Madeline, and a slender, pretty girl. She did not resemble her sister, except in whiteness and fineness of skin, being more of a brown-eyed, brown-haired type. Having recovered her breath soon after Madeline took her to her room, she began to talk.

"Majesty, old girl, I'm here; but you can bet I would never have gotten here if I had known about that ride from the railroad. You never wrote that you had a car. I thought this was out West—stage-coach, and all that sort of thing. Such a tremendous car! And the road! And that terrible little man with the leather trousers! What kind of a chauffeur is he?"

"He's a cowboy. He was crippled by falling under his horse, so I had him instructed to run the car. He can drive, don't you think?"

"Drive? Good gracious! He scared us to death, except Castleton. Nothing could scare that cold-blooded little Englishman. I am dizzy yet. Do you know, Majesty, I was delighted when I saw the car. Then your cowboy driver met us at the platform. What a queer-looking individual! He had a big pistol strapped to those leather trousers. That made me nervous. When he piled us all in with our grips, he put me in the seat beside him, whether I liked it or not. I was fool enough to tell him I loved to travel fast. What do you think he said? Well, he eyed me in a rather cool and speculative way and said, with a smile, 'Miss, I reckon anything you love an' want bad will be coming to you out here!' I didn't know whether it was delightful candor or impudence. Then he said to all of us: 'Shore you had better wrap up in the veils an' dusters. It's a long, slow, hot, dusty ride to the ranch, an' Miss Hammond's order was to drive safe.' He got our baggage checks and gave them to a man with a huge wagon and a four-horse team. Then he cranked the car, jumped in, wrapped his arms round the wheel, and sank down low in his seat. There was a crack, a jerk, a kind of flash around us, and that dirty little town was somewhere on the map behind. For about five minutes I had a lovely time. Then the wind began to tear me to pieces. I couldn't hear anything but the rush of wind and roar of the car. I could see only straight ahead. What a road! I never saw a road in my life till to-day. Miles and miles and miles ahead, with not even a post or tree. That big car seemed to leap at the miles. It hummed and sang. I was fascinated, then terrified. We went so fast I couldn't catch my breath. The wind went through me, and I expected to be disrobed by it any minute. I was afraid I couldn't hold any clothes on. Presently all I could see was a flashing gray wall with a white line in the middle. Then my eyes blurred. My face burned. My ears grew full of a hundred thousand howling devils. I was about ready to die when the car stopped. I looked and looked, and when I could see, there you stood!"

"Helen, I thought you were fond of speeding," said Madeline, with a laugh.

"I was. But I assure you I never before was in a fast car; I never saw a road; I never met a driver."

"Perhaps I may have a few surprises for you out here in the wild and woolly West."

Helen's dark eyes showed a sister's memory of possibilities.

"You've started well," she said. "I am simply stunned. I expected to find you old and dowdy. Majesty, you're the handsomest thing I ever laid eyes on. You're so splendid and strong, and your skin is like white gold. What's happened to you? What's changed you? This beautiful room, those glorious roses out there, the cool, dark sweetness of this wonderful house! I know you, Majesty, and, though you never wrote it, I believe you have made a home out here. That's the most stunning surprise of all. Come, confess. I know I've always been selfish and not much of a sister; but if you are happy out here I am glad. You were not happy at home. Tell me about yourself and about Alfred. Then I shall give you all the messages and news from the East."

It afforded Madeline exceeding pleasure to have from one and all of her guests varied encomiums of her beautiful home, and a real and warm interest in what promised to be a delightful and memorable visit.

Of them all Castleton was the only one who failed to show surprise. He greeted her precisely as he had when he had last seen her in London. Madeline, rather to her astonishment, found meeting him again pleasurable. She discovered she liked this imperturbable Englishman. Manifestly her capacity for liking any one had immeasurably enlarged. Quite unexpectedly her old girlish love for her younger sister sprang into life, and with it interest in these half-forgotten friends, and a warm regard for Edith Wayne, a chum of college days.

Helen's party was smaller than Madeline had expected it to be. Helen had been careful to select a company of good friends, all of whom were well known to Madeline. Edith Wayne was a patrician brunette, a serious, soft-voiced woman, sweet and kindly, despite a rather bitter experience that had left her worldly wise. Mrs. Carrollton Beck, a plain, lively person, had chaperoned the party. The fourth and last of the feminine contingent was Miss Dorothy Coombs—Dot, as they called her—a young woman of attractive blond prettiness.

For a man Castleton was of very small stature. He had a pink-and-white complexion, a small golden mustache, and his heavy eyelids, always drooping, made him look dull. His attire, cut to what appeared to be an exaggerated English style, attracted attention to his diminutive size. He was immaculate and fastidious. Robert Weede was a rather large florid young man, remarkable only for his good nature. Counting Boyd Harvey, a handsome, pale-faced fellow, with the careless smile of the man for whom life had been easy and pleasant, the party was complete.

Dinner was a happy hour, especially for the Mexican women who served it and who could not fail to note its success. The mingling of low voices and laughter, the old, gay, superficial talk, the graciousness of a class which lived for the pleasure of things and to make time pass pleasurably for others—all took Madeline far back into the past. She did not care to return to it, but she saw that it was well she had not wholly cut herself off from her people and friends.

When the party adjourned to the porch the heat had markedly decreased and the red sun was sinking over the red desert. An absence of spoken praise, a gradually deepening silence, attested to the impression on the visitors of that noble sunset. Just as the last curve of red rim vanished beyond the dim Sierra Madres and the golden lightning began to flare brighter Helen broke the silence with an exclamation.

"It wants only life. Ah, there's a horse climbing the hill! See, he's up! He has a rider!"

Madeline knew before she looked the identity of the man riding up the mesa. But she did not know until that moment how the habit of watching for him at this hour had grown upon her. He rode along the rim of the mesa and out to the point, where, against the golden background, horse and rider stood silhouetted in bold relief.

"What's he doing there? Who is he?" inquired the curious Helen.

"That is Stewart, my right-hand man," replied Madeline. "Every day when he is at the ranch he rides up there at sunset. I think he likes the ride and the scene; but he goes to take a look at the cattle in the valley."

"Is he a cowboy?" asked Helen.

"Indeed yes!" replied Madeline, with a little laugh. "You will think so when Stillwell gets hold of you and begins to talk."

Madeline found it necessary to explain who Stillwell was, and what he thought of Stewart, and, while she was about it, of her own accord she added a few details of Stewart's fame.

"El Capitan. How interesting!" mused Helen. "What does he look like?"

"He is superb."

Florence handed the field-glass to Helen and bade her look.

"Oh, thank you!" said Helen, as she complied. "There. I see him. Indeed, he is superb. What a magnificent horse! How still he stands! Why, he seems carved in stone."

"Let me look?" said Dorothy Coombs, eagerly.

Helen gave her the glass.

"You can look, Dot, but that's all. He's mine. I saw him first."

Whereupon Madeline's feminine guests held a spirited contest over the field-glass, and three of them made gay, bantering boasts not to consider Helen's self-asserted rights. Madeline laughed with the others while she watched the dark figure of Stewart and his black outline against the sky. There came over her a thought not by any means new or strange— she wondered what was in Stewart's mind as he stood there in the solitude and faced the desert and the darkening west. Some day she meant to ask him. Presently he turned the horse and rode down into the shadow creeping up the mesa.

"Majesty, have you planned any fun, any excitement for us?" asked Helen. She was restless, nervous, and did not seem to be able to sit still a moment.

"You will think so when I get through with you," replied Madeline.

"What, for instance?" inquired Helen and Dot and Mrs. Beck, in unison. Edith Wayne smiled her interest.

"Well, I am not counting rides and climbs and golf; but these are necessary to train you for trips over into Arizona. I want to show you the desert and the Aravaipa Canyon. We have to go on horseback and pack our outfit. If any of you are alive after those trips and want more we shall go up into the mountains. I should like very much to know what you each want particularly."

"I'll tell you," replied Helen, promptly. "Dot will be the same out here as she was in the East. She wants to look bashfully down at her hand—a hand imprisoned in another, by the way—and listen to a man talk poetry about her eyes. If cowboys don't make love that way Dot's visit will be a failure. Now Elsie Beck wants solely to be revenged upon us for dragging her out here. She wants some dreadful thing to happen to us. I don't know what's in Edith's head, but it isn't fun. Bobby wants to be near Elsie, and no more. Boyd wants what he has always wanted—the only thing he ever wanted that he didn't get. Castleton has a horrible bloodthirsty desire to kill something."

"I declare now, I want to ride and camp out, also," protested Castleton.

"As for myself," went on Helen, "I want—Oh, if I only knew what it is that I want! Well, I know I want to be outdoors, to get into the open, to feel sun and wind, to burn some color into my white face. I want some flesh and blood and life. I am tired out. Beyond all that I don't know very well. I'll try to keep Dot from attaching all the cowboys to her train."

"What a diversity of wants!" said Madeline.

"Above all, Majesty, we want something to happen," concluded Helen, with passionate finality.

"My dear sister, maybe you will have your wish fulfilled," replied Madeline, soberly. "Edith, Helen has made me curious about your especial yearning."

"Majesty, it is only that I wanted to be with you for a while," replied this old friend.

There was in the wistful reply, accompanied by a dark and eloquent glance of eyes, what told Madeline of Edith's understanding, of her sympathy, and perhaps a betrayal of her own unquiet soul. It saddened Madeline. How many women might there not be who had the longing to break down the bars of their cage, but had not the spirit!

❦ 13 ❦

COWBOY GOLF

IN THE WHIRL of the succeeding days it was a mooted question whether Madeline's guests or her cowboys or herself got the keenest enjoyment out of the flying time. Considering the sameness of the cowboys' ordinary life, she was inclined to think they made the most of the present. Stillwell and Stewart, however, had found the situation trying. The work of the ranch had to go on, and some of it got sadly neglected. Stillwell could not resist the ladies any more than he could resist the fun in the extraordinary goings-on of the cowboys. Stewart alone kept the business of cattle-raising from a serious setback. Early and late he was in the saddle, driving the lazy Mexicans whom he had hired to relieve the cowboys.

One morning in June Madeline was sitting on the porch with her merry friends when Stillwell appeared on the corral path. He had not come to consult Madeline for several days —an omission so unusual as to be remarked.

"Here comes Bill—in trouble," laughed Florence.

Indeed, he bore some faint resemblance to a thundercloud as he approached the porch; but the greetings he got from Madeline's party, especially from Helen and Dorothy, chased away the blackness from his face and brought the wonderful wrinkling smile.

"Miss Majesty, sure I'm a sad demoralized old cattleman," he said, presently. "An' I'm in need of a heap of help."

"What's wrong now?" asked Madeline, with her encouraging smile.

"Wal, it's so amazin' strange what cowboys will do. I jest am about to give up. Why, you might say my cowboys were all on strike for vacations. What do you think of that? We've changed the shifts, shortened hours, let one an' another off duty, hired Greasers, an', in fact, done everythin' that could be thought of. But this vacation idee growed worse. When Stewart set his foot down, then the boys begin to get sick. Never in my born days as a cattleman have I heerd of so many diseases. An' you ought to see how lame an' crippled an' weak many of the boys have got all of a sudden. The idee of a cowboy comin' to me with a sore finger an' askin' to be let off for a day! There's Booly. Now I've knowed a hoss to fall all over him, an' onct he rolled down a canyon. Never bothered him at all. He's got a blister on his heel, a ridin' blister, an' he says it's goin' to blood-poisonin' if he doesn't rest. There's Jim

Bell. He's developed what he says is spinal mengalootis, or some such like. There's Frankie Slade. He swore he had scarlet fever because his face burnt so red, I guess, an' when I hollered that scarlet fever was contagious an' he must be put away somewhere, he up an' says he guessed it wasn't that. But he was sure awful sick an' needed to loaf around an' be amused. Why, even Nels doesn't want to work these days. If it wasn't for Stewart, who's had Greasers with the cattle, I don't know what I'd do."

"Why all this sudden illness and idleness?" asked Madeline.

"Wal, you see, the truth is every blamed cowboy on the range except Stewart thinks it's his bounden duty to entertain the ladies."

"I think that is just fine!" exclaimed Dorothy Coombs; and she joined in the general laugh.

"Stewart, then, doesn't care to help entertain us?" inquired Helen, in curious interest.

"Wal, Miss Helen, Stewart is sure different from the other cowboys," replied Stillwell. "Yet he used to be like them. There never was a cowboy fuller of the devil than Gene. But he's changed. He's foreman here, an' that must be it. All the responsibility rests on him. He sure has no time for amusin' the ladies."

"I imagine that is our loss," said Edith Wayne, in her earnest way. "I admire him."

"Stillwell, you need not be so distressed with what is only gallantry in the boys, even if it does make a temporary confusion in the work," said Madeline.

"Miss Majesty, all I said is not the half, nor the quarter, nor nuthin' of what's troublin' me," answered he, sadly.

"Very well; unburden yourself."

"Wal, the cowboys, exceptin' Gene, have gone plumb batty, jest plain crazy over this heah game of gol-lof."

A merry peal of mirth greeted Stillwell's solemn assertion.

"Oh, Stillwell, you are in fun," replied Madeline.

"I hope to die if I'm not in daid earnest," declared the cattleman. "It's an amazin' strange fact. Ask Flo. She'll tell you. She knows cowboys, an' how if they ever start on somethin' they ride it as they ride a hoss."

Florence being appealed to, and evidently feeling all eyes upon her, modestly replied that Stillwell had scarcely misstated the situation.

"Cowboys play like they work or fight," she added. "They give their whole souls to it. They are great big simple boys."

"Indeed they are," said Madeline. "Oh, I'm glad if they like the game of golf. They have so little play."

"Wal, somethin's got to be did if we're to go on raisin' cattle at Her Majesty's Rancho," replied Stillwell. He appeared both deliberate and resigned.

Madeline remembered that despite Stillwell's simplicity he was as deep as any of his cowboys, and there was absolutely no gaging him where possibilities of fun were concerned. Madeline fancied that his exaggerated talk about the cowboys' sudden craze for golf was in line with certain other remarkable tales that had lately emanated from him. Some very strange things had occurred of late, and it was impossible to tell whether or not they were accidents, mere coincidents, or deep-laid, skilfully worked-out designs of the fun-loving cowboys. Certainly there had been great fun, and at the expense of her guests, particularly Castleton. So Madeline was at a loss to know what to think about Stillwell's latest elaboration. From mere force of habit she sympathized with him and found difficulty in doubting his apparent sincerity.

"To go back a ways," went on Stillwell, as Madeline looked up expectantly, "you recollect what pride the boys took in fixin' up that gol-lof course out on the mesa? Wal, they worked on that job, an' though I never seen any other course, I'll gamble yours can't be beat. The boys was sure curious about that game. You recollect also how they all wanted to see you an' your brother play, an' be caddies for you? Wal, whenever you'd quit they'd go to work tryin' to play the game. Monty Price, he was the leadin' spirit. Old as I am, Miss Majesty, an' used as I am to cowboy excentrikities, I nearly dropped daid when I heered that little hobble-footed, burned-up Montana cow-puncher say there wasn't any game too swell for him, an' gol-lof was just his speed. Serious as a preacher, mind you, he was. An' he was always practisin'. When Stewart gave him charge of the course an' the club-house an' all them funny sticks, why, Monty was tickled to death. You see, Monty is sensitive that he ain't much good any more for cowboy work. He was glad to have a job that he didn't feel he was hangin' to by kindness. Wal, he practised the game, an' he read the books in the club-house, an' he got the boys to doin' the same. That wasn't very hard, I reckon. They played early an' late an' in the moonlight. For a while Monty was coach, an' the boys stood it. But pretty soon Frankie Slade got puffed on his game, an' he had to have it out with Monty. Wal, Monty beat him bad. Then one after another the other boys tackled Monty. He beat them all. After that they split up an' begin to play matches, two on a side. For a spell this worked fine. But cowboys can't never be satisfied long onless they win all the time. Monty an' Link Stevens, both cripples, you might say, joined forces an' elected to beat all comers. Wal, they did, an' that's the trouble. Long an' patient the other cowboys tried to beat them two game legs, an' hevn't done it. Mebbe if Monty an' Link was perfectly sound in their legs like the other cowboys there wouldn't hev been such a holler. But no sound cowboys'll ever stand for a disgrace like that. Why, down at the bunks in the evenin's it's some mortifyin' the way Monty an' Link crow over the rest of the outfit. They've taken on superior airs. You couldn't reach up to Monty with a trimmed spruce pole. An' Link—wal, he's just amazin' scornful.

"'It's a swell game, ain't it?' says Link, powerful sarcastic. 'Wal, what's hurtin' you low-down common cowmen? You keep harpin' on Monty's game leg an' on my game leg. If we hed good legs we'd beat you all the wuss. It's brains that wins in gol-lof. Brains an' airstoocratik blood, which of the same you fellers sure hev little.'

"An' then Monty he blows smoke powerful careless an' superior, an' he says:

"'Sure it's a swell game. You cow-headed gents think beef an' brawn ought to hev the call over skill an' gray matter. You'll all hev to back up an' get down. Go out an' learn the game. You don't know a baffy from a Chinee sandwich. All you can do is waggle with a club an' fozzle the ball.'

"Whenever Monty gets to usin' them queer names the boys go round kind of dotty. Monty an' Link hev got the books an' directions of the game, an' they won't let the other boys see them. They show the rules, but that's all. An', of course, every game ends in a row almost before it's started. The boys are all turrible in earnest about this gol-lof. An' I want to say, for the good of ranchin', not to mention a possible fight, that Monty an' Link hev got to be beat. There'll be no peace round this ranch till that's done."

Madeline's guests were much amused. As for herself, in spite of her scarcely considered doubt, Stillwell's tale of woe occasioned her anxiety. However, she could hardly control her mirth.

"What in the world can I do?"

"Wal, I reckon I couldn't say. I only come to you for advice. It seems that a queer kind of game has locoed my cowboys, an' for the time bein' ranchin' is at a standstill. Sounds ridiculous, I know, but cowboys are as strange as wild cattle. All I'm sure of is that the conceit has got to be taken out of Monty an' Link. Onct, just onct, will square it, an' then we can resoome our work."

"Stillwell, listen," said Madeline, brightly. "We'll arrange a match game, a foursome, between Monty and Link and your best picked team. Castleton, who is an expert golfer, will umpire. My sister, and friends, and I will take turns as caddies for your team. That will be fair, considering yours is the weaker. Caddies may coach, and perhaps expert advice is all that is necessary for your team to defeat Monty's."

"A grand idee," declared Stillwell, with instant decision. "When can we have this match game?"

"Why, to-day—this afternoon. We'll all ride out to the links."

"Wal, I reckon I'll be some indebted to you, Miss Majesty, an' all your guests," replied Stillwell, warmly. He rose with sombrero in hand, and a twinkle in his eye that again prompted Madeline to wonder. "An' now I'll be goin' to fix up for the game of cowboy gol-lof. Adios."

The idea was as enthusiastically received by Madeline's guests as it had been by Stillwell. They were highly amused and speculative to the point of taking sides and making wagers on their choice. Moreover, this situation so frankly revealed by Stillwell had completed their deep mystification. They were now absolutely nonplussed by the singular character of American cowboys. Madeline was pleased to note how seriously they had taken the old cattleman's story. She had a little throb of wild expectancy that made her both fear and delight in the afternoon's prospect.

The June days had set in warm; in fact, hot during the noon hours: and this had inculcated in her insatiable visitors a tendency to profit by the experience of those used to the Southwest. They indulged in the restful siesta during the heated term of the day.

Madeline was awakened by Majesty's well-known whistle and pounding on the gravel. Then she heard the other horses. When she went out she found her party assembled in gala golf attire, and with spirits to match their costumes. Castleton, especially, appeared resplendent in a golf coat that beggared description. Madeline had faint misgivings when she reflected on what Monty and Nels and Nick might do under the influence of that blazing garment.

"Oh. Majesty," cried Helen, as Madeline went up to her horse, "don't make him kneel! Try that flying mount. We all want to see it. It's so stunning."

"But that way, too, I must have him kneel," said Madeline, "or I can't reach the stirrup. He's so tremendously high."

Madeline had to yield to the laughing insistence of her friends, and after all of them except Florence were up she made Majesty go down on one knee. Then she stood on his left side, facing back, and took a good firm grip on the bridle and pommel and his mane. After she had slipped the toe of her boot firmly into the stirrup she called to Majesty. He jumped and swung her up into the saddle.

"Now just to see how it ought to be done watch Florence," said Madeline.

The Western girl was at her best in riding-habit and with her horse. It was beautiful to see the ease and grace with which she accomplished the cowboys' flying mount. Then she led the party down the slope and across the flat to climb the mesa.

Madeline never saw a group of her cowboys without looking them over, almost unconsciously, for her foreman, Gene Stewart. This afternoon, as usual, he was not present. However, she now had a sense—of which she was wholly conscious—that she was both disappointed and irritated. He had really not been attentive to her guests, and he, of all her cowboys, was the one of whom they wanted most to see something. Helen, particularly, had asked to have him attend the match. But Stewart was with the cattle. Madeline thought of his faithfulness, and was ashamed of her momentary lapse into that old imperious habit of desiring things irrespective of reason.

Stewart, however, immediately slipped out of her mind as she surveyed the group of cowboys on the links. By actual count there were sixteen, not including Stillwell. And the same number of splendid horses, all shiny and clean, grazed on the rim in the care of Mexican lads. The cowboys were on dress-parade, looking very different in Madeline's eyes, at least, from the way cowboys usually appeared. But they were real and natural to her guests; and they were so picturesque that they might have been stage cowboys instead of real ones. Sombreros with silver buckles and horsehair bands were in evidence; and bright silk scarfs, embroidered vests, fringed and ornamented chaps, huge swinging guns, and clinking silver spurs lent a festive appearance.

Madeline and her party were at once eagerly surrounded by the cowboys, and she found it difficult to repress a smile. If these cowboys were still remarkable to her, what must they be to her guests?

"Wal, you-all raced over, I seen," said Stillwell, taking Madeline's bridle. "Get down—get down. We're sure amazin' glad an' proud. An', Miss Majesty, I'm offerin' to beg pawdin for the way the boys are packin' guns. Mebbe it ain't polite. But it's Stewart's orders."

"Stewart's orders!" echoed Madeline. Her friends were suddenly silent.

"I reckon he won't take no chances on the boys bein' surprised sudden by raiders. An' there's raiders operatin' in from the Guadalupes. That's all. Nothin' to worry over. I was just explainin'."

Madeline, with several of her party, expressed relief, but Helen showed excitement and then disappointment.

"Oh, I want something to happen!" she cried.

Sixteen pairs of keen cowboy eyes fastened intently upon her pretty, petulant face; and Madeline divined, if Helen did not, that the desired consummation was not far off.

"So do I," said Dot Coombs. "It would be perfectly lovely to have a real adventure."

The gaze of the sixteen cowboys shifted and sought the demure face of this other discontented girl. Madeline laughed, and Stillwell wore his strange, moving smile.

"Wal, I reckon you ladies sure won't have to go home unhappy," he said. "Why, as boss of this heah outfit I'd feel myself disgraced forever if you didn't have your wish. Just wait. An' now, ladies, the matter on hand may not be amusin' or excitin' to you; but to this heah cowboy outfit it's powerful important. An' all the help you can give us will sure be thankfully received. Take a look across the links. Do you-all see them two apologies for human bein's prancin' like a couple of hobbled broncs? Wal, you're gazin' at Monty Price an' Link Stevens, who have of a sudden got too swell to associate with their old bunkies. They're practisin' for the toornament. They don't want my boys to see how they handle them crooked clubs."

"Have you picked your team?" inquired Madeline.

Stillwell mopped his red face with an immense bandana, and showed something of confusion and perplexity.

"I've sixteen boys, an' they all want to play," he replied. "Pickin' the team ain't goin' to be an easy job. Mebbe it won't be healthy, either. There's Nels and Nick. They just stated cheerful-like that if they didn't play we won't have any game at all. Nick never tried before, an' Nels, all he wants is to get a crack at Monty with one of them crooked clubs."

"I suggest you let all your boys drive from the tee and choose the two who drive the farthest," said Madeline.

Stillwell's perplexed face lighted up.

"Wal, that's a plumb good idee. The boys'll stand for that."

Wherewith he broke up the admiring circle of cowboys round the ladies.

"Grap a rope—I mean a club—all you cow-punchers, an' march over hyar an' take a swipe at this little white bean."

The cowboys obeyed with alacrity. There was considerable difficulty over the choice of clubs and who should try first. The latter question had to be adjusted by lot. However, after Frankie Slade made several ineffectual attempts to hit the ball from the teeing-ground, at last to send it only a few yards, the other players were not so eager to follow. Stillwell had to push Booly forward, and Booly executed a most miserable shot and retired to the laughing comments of his comrades. The efforts of several succeeding cowboys attested to the extreme difficulty of making a good drive.

"Wal, Nick, it's your turn," said Stillwell.

"Bill, I ain't so all-fired particular about playin'," replied Nick.

"Why? You was roarin' about it a little while ago. Afraid to show how bad you'll play?"

"Nope, jest plain consideration for my feller cow-punchers," answered Nick, with spirit. "I'm appreciatin' how bad they play, an' I'm not mean enough to show them up."

"Wal, you've got to show me," said Stillwell. "I know you never seen a gol-lof stick in your life. What's more, I'll bet you can't hit that little ball square—not in a dozen cracks at it."

"Bill, I'm also too much of a gent to take your money. But you know I'm from Missouri. Gimme a club."

Nick's angry confidence seemed to evaporate as one after another he took up and handled the clubs. It was plain that he had never before wielded one. But, also, it was plain that he was not the kind of a man to give in. Finally he selected a driver, looked doubtfully at the small knob, and then stepped into position on the teeing-ground.

Nick Steele stood six feet four inches in height. He had the rider's wiry slenderness, yet he was broad of shoulder. His arms were long. Manifestly he was an exceedingly powerful man. He swung the driver aloft and whirled it down with a tremendous swing. Crack! The white ball disappeared, and from where it had been rose a tiny cloud of dust.

Madeline's quick sight caught the ball as it lined somewhat to the right. It was shooting low and level with the speed of a bullet. It went up and up in swift, beautiful flight, then lost its speed and began to sail, to curve, to drop; and it fell out of sight beyond the rim of the mesa. Madeline had never seen a drive that approached this one. It was magnificent, beyond belief except for actual evidence of her own eyes.

The yelling of the cowboys probably brought Nick Steele out of the astounding spell with which he beheld his shot. Then Nick, suddenly alive to the situation, recovered from his trance and, resting nonchalantly upon his club, he surveyed Stillwell and the boys. After their first surprised outburst they were dumb.

"You-all seen thet?" Nick grandly waved his hand. "Thought I was joshin', didn't you? Why, I used to go to St. Louis an' Kansas City to play this here game. There was some talk of the golf clubs takin' me down East to play the champions. But I never cared fer the game. Too easy fer me! Them fellers back in Missouri were a lot of cheap dubs, anyhow, always kickin' because whenever I hit a ball hard I always lost it. Why, I hed to hit sort of left-handed to let 'em stay in my class. Now you-all can go ahead an' play Monty an' Link. I could beat 'em both, playin' with one hand, if I wanted to. But I ain't interested. I jest hit thet ball off the mesa to show you. I sure wouldn't be seen playin' on your team."

With that Nick sauntered away toward the horses. Stillwell appeared crushed. And not a scornful word was hurled after Nick, which fact proved the nature of his victory. Then Nels strode into the limelight. As far as it was possible for this iron-faced cowboy to be so, he was bland and suave. He remarked to Stillwell and the other cowboys that sometimes it was painful for them to judge of the gifts of superior cowboys such as belonged to Nick and himself. He picked up the club Nick had used and called for a new ball. Stillwell carefully built up a little mound of sand and, placing the ball upon it, squared away to watch. He looked grim and expectant.

Nels was not so large a man as Nick, and did not look so formidable as he waved his club at the gaping cowboys. Still he was lithe, tough, strong. Briskly, with a debonair manner, he stepped up and then delivered a mighty swing at the ball. He missed. The power and momentum of his swing flung him off his feet, and he actually turned upside down and spun round on his head. The cowboys howled. Stillwell's stentorian laugh rolled across the mesa. Madeline and her guests found it impossible to restrain their mirth. And when Nels got up he cast a reproachful glance at Madeline. His feelings were hurt.

His second attempt, not by any means so violent, resulted in as clean a miss as the first, and brought jeers from the cowboys. Nels's red face flamed redder. Angrily he swung again. The mound of sand spread over the teeing-ground and the exasperating little ball rolled a few inches. This time he had to build up the sand mound and replace the ball himself. Stillwell stood scornfully by, and the boys addressed remarks to Nels.

"Take off them blinders," said one.

"Nels, your eyes are shore bad," said another.

"You don't hit where you look."

"Nels, your left eye has sprung a limp."

"Why, you dog-goned old fule, you cain't hit thet bawl."

Nels essayed again, only to meet ignominious failure. Then carefully he gathered himself together, gaged distance, balanced the club, swung cautiously. And the head of the club made a beautiful curve round the ball.

"Shore it's jest thet crooked club," he declared.

He changed clubs and made another signal failure. Rage suddenly possessing him, he began to swing wildly. Always, it appeared, the illusive little ball was not where he aimed. Stillwell hunched his huge bulk, leaned hands on knees, and roared his riotous mirth. The cowboys leaped up and down in glee.

"You cain't hit thet bawl," sang out one of the noisiest. A few more whirling, desperate lunges on the part of Nels, all as futile as if the ball had been thin air, finally brought to the dogged cowboy a realization that golf was beyond him.

Stillwell bawled: "Oh, haw, haw, haw! Nels, you're—too old—eyes no good!"

Nels slammed down the club, and when he straightened up with the red leaving his face, then the real pride and fire of the man showed. Deliberately he stepped off ten paces and turned toward the little mound upon which rested the ball. His arm shot down, elbow crooked, hand like a claw.

"Aw, Nels, this is fun!" yelled Stillwell.

But swift as a gleam of light Nels flashed his gun, and the report came with the action. Chips flew from the golf-ball as it tumbled from the mound. Nels had hit it without raising the dust. Then he dropped the gun back in its sheath and faced the cowboys.

"Mebbe my eyes ain't so orful bad," he said, coolly, and started to walk off.

"But look ah-heah, Nels," yelled Stillwell, "we come out to play gol-lof! We can't let you knock the ball around with your gun. What'd you want to get mad for? It's only fun. Now you an' Nick hang round heah an' be sociable. We ain't depreciatin' your company none, nor your usefulness on occasions. An' if you just hain't got inborn politeness sufficient to do the gallant before the ladies, why, remember Stewart's orders."

"Stewart's orders?" queried Nels, coming to a sudden halt.

"That's what I said," replied Stillwell, with asperity. "His orders. Are you forgettin' orders? Wal, you're a fine cowboy. You an' Nick an' Monty, 'specially, are to obey orders."

Nels took off his sombrero and scratched his head. "Bill, I reckon I'm some forgetful. But I was mad. I'd 'a' remembered pretty soon, an' mebbe my manners."

"Sure you would," replied Stillwell. "Wal, now, we don't seem to be proceedin' much with my gol-lof team. Next ambitious player step up."

In Ambrose, who showed some skill in driving, Stillwell found one of his team. The succeeding players, however, were so poor and so evenly matched that the earnest Stillwell was in despair. He lost his temper just as speedily as Nels had. Finally Ed Linton's wife appeared riding up with Ambrose's wife, and perhaps this helped, for Ed suddenly disclosed ability that made Stillwell single him out.

"Let me coach you a little," said Bill.

"Sure, if you like," replied Ed. "But I know more about this game than you do."

"Wal, then, let's see you hit a ball straight. Seems to me you got good all-fired quick. It's amazin' strange." ere Bill looked around to discover the two young wives modestly casting eyes of admiration upon their husbands. "Haw, haw! It ain't so darned strange. Mebbe that'll help some. Now, Ed, stand up and don't sling your club as if you was ropin' a steer. Come round easy-like an' hit straight."

Ed made several attempts which, although better than those of his predecessors, were rather discouraging to the exacting coach. Presently, after a particularly atrocious shot, Stillwell strode in distress here and there, and finally stopped a dozen paces or more in front of the teeing-ground. Ed, who for a cowboy was somewhat phlegmatic, calmly made ready for another attempt.

"Fore!" he called.

Stillwell stared.

"Fore!" yelled Ed.

"Why're you hollerin' that way at me?" demanded Bill.

"I mean for you to lope off the horizon. Get back from in front."

"Oh, that was one of them durned crazy words Monty is always hollerin'. Wal, I reckon I'm safe enough hyar. You couldn't hit me in a million years."

"Bill, ooze away," urged Ed.

"Didn't I say you couldn't hit me? What am I coachin' you for? It's because you hit crooked, ain't it? Wal, go ahaid an' break your back."

Ed Linton was a short, heavy man, and his stocky build gave evidence of considerable strength. His former strokes had not been made at the expense of exertion, but now he got ready for a supreme effort. A sudden silence clamped down upon the exuberant cowboys. It was one of those fateful moments when the air was charged with disaster. As Ed swung the club it fairly whistled.

Crack! Instantly came a thump. But no one saw the ball until it dropped from Stillwell's shrinking body. His big hands went spasmodically to the place that hurt, and a terrible groan rumbled from him.

Then the cowboys broke into a frenzy of mirth that seemed to find adequate expression only in dancing and rolling accompaniment to their howls. Stillwell recovered his dignity as soon as he caught his breath, and he advanced with a rueful face.

"Wal, boys, it's on Bill," he said. "I'm a livin' proof of the pig-headedness of mankind. Ed, you win. You're captain of the team. You hit straight, an' if I hadn't been obstructin' the general atmosphere that ball would sure have gone clear to the Chiricahuas."

Then making a megaphone of his huge hands, he yelled a loud blast of defiance at Monty and Link.

"Hey, you swell gol-lofers! We're waitin'. Come on if you ain't scared."

Instantly Monty and Link quit practising, and like two emperors came stalking across the links.

"Guess my bluff didn't work much," said Stillwell. Then he turned to Madeline and her friends. "Sure I hope, Miss Majesty, that you-all won't weaken an' go over to the enemy. Monty is some eloquent, an', besides, he has a way of gettin' people to agree with him. He'll be plumb wild when he heahs what he an' Link are up against. But it's a square deal, because he wouldn't help us or lend the book that shows how to play. An', besides, it's policy for us to beat him. Now, if you'll elect who's to be caddies an' umpire I'll be powerful obliged."

Madeline's friends were hugely amused over the prospective match; but, except for Dorothy and Castleton, they disclaimed any ambition for active participation. Accordingly, Madeline appointed Castleton to judge the play, Dorothy to act as caddie for Ed Linton, and she herself to be caddie for Ambrose. While Stillwell beamingly announced this momentous news to his team and supporters Monty and Link were striding up.

Both were diminutive in size, bow-legged, lame in one foot, and altogether unprepossessing. Link was young, and Monty's years, more than twice Link's, had left their mark. But it would have been impossible to tell Monty's age. As Stillwell said, Monty was burned to the color and hardness of a cinder. He never minded the heat, and always wore heavy sheepskin chaps with the wool outside. This made him look broader than he was long. Link, partial to leather, had, since he became Madeline's chauffeur, taken to leather altogether. He carried no weapon, but Monty wore a huge gun-sheath and gun. Link smoked a cigarette and looked coolly impudent. Monty was dark-faced, swaggering, for all the world like a barbarian chief.

"That Monty makes my flesh creep," said Helen, low-voiced. "Really, Mr. Stillwell, is he so bad—desperate—as I've heard? Did he ever kill anybody?"

"Sure. 'Most as many as Nels," replied Stillwell, cheerfully.

"Oh! And is that nice Mr. Nels a desperado, too? I wouldn't have thought so. He's so kind and old-fashioned and soft-voiced."

"Nels is sure an example of the dooplicity of men, Miss Helen. Don't you listen to his soft voice. He's really as bad as a side-winder rattlesnake."

At this juncture Monty and Link reached the teeing-ground, and Stillwell went out to meet them. The other cowboys pressed forward to surround the trio. Madeline heard Stillwell's voice, and evidently he was explaining that his team was to have skilled advice during the play. Suddenly there came from the center of the group a loud, angry roar that broke off as suddenly. Then followed excited voices all mingled together. Presently Monty appeared, breaking away from restraining hands, and he strode toward Madeline.

Monty Price was a type of cowboy who had never been known to speak to a woman unless he was first addressed, and then he answered in blunt, awkward shyness. Upon this great occasion, however, it appeared that he meant to protest or plead with Madeline, for he showed stress of emotion. Madeline had never gotten acquainted with Monty. She was a little in awe, if not in fear, of him, and now she found it imperative for her to keep in mind that more than any other of the wild fellows on her ranch this one should be dealt with as if he were a big boy.

Monty removed his sombrero—something he had never done before—and the single instant when it was off was long enough to show his head entirely bald. This was one of the hall-marks of that terrible Montana prairie fire through which he had fought to save the life of a child. Madeline did not forget it, and all at once she wanted to take Monty's side. Remembering Stillwell's wisdom, however, she forebore yielding to sentiment, and called upon her wits.

"Miss—Miss Hammond," began Monty, stammering, "I'm extendin' admirin' greetin's to you an' your friends. Link an' me are right down proud to play the match game with you watchin'. But Bill says you're goin' to caddie for his team an' coach 'em on the fine points. An' I want to ask, all respectful, if thet's fair an' square?"

"Monty, that is for you to say," replied Madeline. "It was my suggestion. But if you object in the least, of course we shall withdraw. It seems fair to me, because you have learned the game; you are expert, and I understand the other boys have no chance with you. Then you have coached Link. I think it would be sportsmanlike of you to accept the handicap."

"Aw, a handicap! Thet was what Bill was drivin' at. Why didn't he say so? Every time Bill comes to a word thet's pie to us old golfers he jest stumbles. Miss Majesty, you've made it all clear as print. An' I may say with becomin' modesty thet you wasn't mistaken none about me bein' sportsmanlike. Me an' Link was born thet way. An' we accept the handicap. Lackin' thet handicap, I reckon Link an' me would have no ambish to play our most be-ootiful game. An' thankin' you, Miss Majesty, an' all your friends, I want to add thet if Bill's outfit couldn't beat us before, they've got a swell chanct now, with you ladies a-watchin' me an' Link."

Monty had seemed to expand with pride as he delivered this speech, and at the end he bowed low and turned away. He joined the group round Stillwell. Once more there was animated discussion and argument and expostulation. One of the cowboys came for Castleton and led him away to exploit upon ground rules.

It seemed to Madeline that the game never would begin. She strolled on the rim of the mesa, arm in arm with Edith Wayne, and while Edith talked she looked out over the gray valley leading to the rugged black mountains and the vast red wastes. In the foreground on the gray slope she saw cattle in movement and cowboys riding to and fro. She thought of Stewart. Then Boyd Harvey came for them, saying all details had been arranged. Stillwell met them half-way, and this cool, dry, old cattleman, whose face and manner scarcely changed at the announcement of a cattle-raid, now showed extreme agitation.

"Wal, Miss Majesty, we've gone an' made a foozle right at the start," he said, dejectedly.

"A foozle? But the game has not yet begun," replied Madeline.

"A bad start, I mean. It's amazin' bad, an' we're licked already."

"What in the world is wrong?"

She wanted to laugh, but Stillwell's distress restrained her.

"Wal, it's this way. That darn Monty is as cute an' slick as a fox. After he got done declaimin' about the handicap he an' Link was so happy to take, he got Castleton over hyar an' drove us all dotty with his crazy gol-lof names. Then he borrowed Castleton's gol-lof coat. I reckon borrowed is some kind word. He just about took that blazin' coat off the Englishman. Though I ain't sayin' but that Casleton was agreeable when he tumbled to Monty's meanin'. Which was nothin' more 'n to break Ambrose's heart. That coat dazzles Ambrose. You know how vain Ambrose is. Why, he'd die to get to wear that Englishman's gol-lof coat. An' Monty forestalled him. It's plumb pitiful to see the look in Ambrose's eyes. He won't be able to play much. Then what do you think? Monty fixed Ed Linton, all right. Usually Ed is easy-goin' an' cool. But now he's on the rampage. Wal, mebbe it's news to you to learn that Ed's wife is powerful, turrible jealous of him. Ed was somethin' of a devil with the wimmen. Monty goes over an' tells Beulah—that's Ed's wife—that Ed is goin' to have for caddie the lovely Miss Dorothy with the goo-goo eyes. I reckon this was some disrespectful, but with all doo respect to Miss Dorothy she has got a pair of unbridled eyes. Mebbe it's just natural for her to look at a feller like that. Oh, it's all right; I'm not sayin' any-thin'! I know it's all proper an' regular for girls back East to use their eyes. But out hyar it's bound to result disastrous. All the boys talk about among themselves is Miss Dot's eyes, an' all they brag about is which feller is the luckiest. Anyway, sure Ed's wife knows it. An' Monty up an' told her that it was fine for her to come out an' see how swell Ed was prancin' round under the light of Miss Dot's brown eyes. Beulah calls over Ed, figgertively speakin', ropes him for a minnit. Ed comes back huggin' a grouch as big as a hill. Oh, it was funny! He was goin' to punch Monty's haid off. An' Monty stands there an' laughs. Says Monty, sarcastic as alkali water: 'Ed, we-all knowed you was a heap married man, but you're some locoed to give yourself away.' That settled Ed. He's some touchy about the way Beulah henpecks him. He lost his spirit. An' now he couldn't play marbles, let alone gol-lof. Nope, Monty was too smart. An' I reckon he was right about brains bein' what wins."

The game began. At first Madeline and Dorothy essayed to direct the endeavors of their respective players. But all they said and did only made their team play the worse. At the third hole they were far behind and hopelessly bewildered. What with Monty's borrowed coat, with its dazzling effect upon Ambrose, and Link's oft-repeated allusion to Ed's matrimonial state, and Stillwell's vociferated disgust, and the clamoring good intention and pursuit of the cowboy supporters, and the embarrassing presence of the ladies, Ambrose and Ed wore through all manner of strange play until it became ridiculous.

"Hey, Link," came Monty's voice booming over the links, "our esteemed rivals are playin' shinny."

Madeline and Dorothy gave up, presently, when the game became a rout, and they sat down with their followers to watch the fun. Whether by hook or crook, Ed and Ambrose forged ahead to come close upon Monty and Link. Castleton disappeared in a mass of gesticulating, shouting cowboys. When that compact mass disintegrated Castleton came forth rather hurriedly, it appeared, to stalk back toward his hostess and friends.

"Look!" exclaimed Helen, in delight. "Castleton is actually excited. Whatever did they do to him? Oh, this is immense!"

Castleton was excited, indeed, and also somewhat disheveled.

"By Jove! that was a rum go," he said, as he came up. "Never saw such blooming golf! I resigned my office as umpire."

Only upon considerable pressure did he reveal the reason. "It was like this, don't you know. They were all together over there, watching each other. Monty Price's ball dropped into a hazard, and he moved it to improve the lie. By Jove! they've all been doing that. But over there the game was waxing hot. Stillwell and his cowboys saw Monty move the ball, and there was a row. They appealed to me. I corrected the play, showed the rules. Monty agreed he was in the wrong. However, when it came to moving his ball back to its former lie in the hazard there was more blooming trouble. Monty placed the ball to suit him, and then he transfixed me with an evil eye.

"'Dook,' he said. I wish the bloody cowboy would not call me that. 'Dook, mebbe this game ain't as important as international politics or some other things relatin', but there's some health an' peace dependin' on it. Savvy? For some space our opponents have been dead to honor an' sportsmanlike conduct. I calculate the game depends on my next drive. I'm placin' my ball as near to where it was as human eyesight could. You seen where it was same as I seen it. You're the umpire, an', Dook, I take you as a honorable man. Moreover, never in my born days has my word been doubted without sorrow. So I'm askin' you, wasn't my ball layin' just about here?'

"The bloody little desperado smiled cheerfully, and he dropped his right hand down to the butt of his gun. By Jove, he did! Then I had to tell a blooming lie!"

Castleton even caught the tone of Monty's voice, but it was plain that he had not the least conception that Monty had been fooling. Madeline and her friends divined it, however; and, there being no need of reserve, they let loose the fountains of mirth.

❧ 14 ❧

BANDITS

WHEN MADELINE and her party recovered composure they sat up to watch the finish of the match. It came with spectacular suddenness. A sharp yell pealed out, and all the cowboys turned attentively in its direction. A big black horse had surmounted the rim of the mesa and was just breaking into a run. His rider yelled sharply to the cowboys. They wheeled to dash toward their grazing horses.

"That's Stewart. There is something wrong," said Madeline, in alarm.

Castleton stared. The other men exclaimed uneasily. The women sought Madeline's face with anxious eyes.

The black got into his stride and bore swiftly down upon them.

"Oh, look at that horse run!" cried Helen. "Look at that fellow ride!"

Helen was not alone in her admiration, for Madeline divided her emotions between growing alarm of some danger menacing and a thrill and quickening of pulse-beat that tingled over her whenever she saw Stewart in violent action. No action of his was any longer insignificant, but violent action meant so much. It might mean anything. For one moment she remembered Stillwell and all his talk about fun, and plots, and tricks to amuse her guest. Then she discountenanced the thought. Stewart might lend himself to a little fun, but he cared too much for a horse to run him at that speed unless there was imperious need. That alone sufficed to answer Madeline's questioning curiosity. And her alarm mounted to fear not so much for herself as for her guests. But what danger could there be? She could think of nothing except the guerrillas.

Whatever threatened, it would be met and checked by this man Stewart, who was thundering up on his fleet horse; and as he neared her, so that she could see the dark gleam of face and eyes, she had a strange feeling of trust in her dependence upon him.

The big black was so close to Madeline and her friends that when Stewart pulled him the dust and sand kicked up by his pounding hoofs flew in their faces.

"Oh, Stewart, what is it?" cried Madeline.

"Guess I scared you, Miss Hammond," he replied. "But I'm pressed for time. There's a gang of bandits hiding on the ranch, most likely in a deserted hut. They held up a train near

Agua Prieta. Pat Hawe is with the posse that's trailing them, and you know Pat has no use for us. I'm afraid it wouldn't be pleasant for you or your guests to meet either the posse or the bandits."

"I fancy not," said Madeline, considerably relieved. "We'll hurry back to the house."

They exchanged no more speech at the moment, and Madeline's guests were silent. Perhaps Stewart's actions and looks belied his calm words. His piercing eyes roved round the rim of the mesa, and his face was as hard and stern as chiseled bronze.

Monty and Nick came galloping up, each leading several horses by the bridles. Nels appeared behind them with Majesty, and he was having trouble with the roan. Madeline observed that all the other cowboys had disappeared.

One sharp word from Stewart calmed Madeline's horse; the other horses, however, were frightened and not inclined to stand. The men mounted without trouble, and likewise Madeline and Florence. But Edith Wayne and Mrs. Beck, being nervous and almost helpless, were with difficulty gotten into the saddle.

"Beg pardon, but I'm pressed for time," said Stewart, coolly, as with iron arm he forced Dorothy's horse almost to its knees. Dorothy, who was active and plucky, climbed astride; and when Stewart loosed his hold on bit and mane the horse doubled up and began to buck. Dorothy screamed as she shot into the air. Stewart, as quick as the horse, leaped forward and caught Dorothy in his arms. She had slipped head downward and, had he not caught her, would have had a serious fall. Stewart, handling her as if she were a child, turned her right side up to set her upon her feet. Dorothy evidently thought only of the spectacle she presented, and made startled motions to readjust her riding-habit. It was no time to laugh, though Madeline felt as if she wanted to. Besides, it was impossible to be anything but sober with Stewart in violent mood. For he had jumped at Dorothy's stubborn mount. All cowboys were masters of horses. It was wonderful to see him conquer the vicious animal. He was cruel, perhaps, yet it was from necessity. When, presently, he led the horse back to Dorothy she mounted without further trouble. Meanwhile, Nels and Nick had lifted Helen into her saddle.

"We'll take the side trail," said Stewart, shortly, as he swung upon the big black. Then he led the way, and the other cowboys trotted in the rear.

It was only a short distance to the rim of the mesa, and when Madeline saw the steep trail, narrow and choked with weathered stone, she felt that her guests would certainly flinch.

"That's a jolly bad course," observed Castleton.

The women appeared to be speechless.

Stewart checked his horse at the deep cut where the trail started down.

"Boys, drop over, and go slow," he said, dismounting. "Flo, you follow. Now, ladies, let your horses loose and hold on. Lean forward and hang to the pommel. It looks bad. But the horses are used to such trails."

Helen followed closely after Florence; Mrs. Beck went next, and then Edith Wayne. Dorothy's horse balked.

"I'm not so—so frightened," said Dorothy. "If only he would behave!"

She began to urge him into the trail, making him rear, when Stewart grasped the bit and jerked the horse down.

"Put your foot in my stirrup," said Stewart. "We can't waste time."

He lifted her upon his horse and started him down over the rim.

"Go on, Miss Hammond. I'll have to lead this nag down. It'll save time."

Then Madeline attended to the business of getting down herself. It was a loose trail. The weathered slopes seemed to slide under the feet of the horses. Dust-clouds formed; rocks rolled and rattled down; cactus spikes tore at horse and rider. Mrs. Beck broke into laughter, and there was a note in it that suggested hysteria. Once or twice Dorothy murmured plaintively. Half the time Madeline could not distinguish those ahead through the yellow dust. It was dry and made her cough. The horses snorted. She heared Stewart close behind, starting little avalanches that kept rolling on Majesty's fetlocks. She feared his legs might be cut or bruised, for some of the stones cracked by and went rattling down the slope. At length the clouds of dust thinned and Madeline saw the others before her ride out upon a level. Soon she was down, and Stewart also.

Here there was a delay, occasioned by Stewart changing Dorothy from his horse to her own. This struck Madeline as being singular, and made her thoughtful. In fact, the alert, quiet manner of all the cowboys was not reassuring. As they resumed the ride it was noticeable that Nels and Nick were far in advance, Monty stayed far in the rear, and Stewart rode with the party. Madeline heard Boyd Harvey ask Stewart if lawlessness such as he had mentioned was not unusual. Stewart replied that, except for occasional deeds of outlawry such as might break out in any isolated section of the country, there had been peace and quiet along the border for years. It was the Mexican revolution that had revived wild times, with all the attendant raids and holdups and gun-packing. Madeline knew that they were really being escorted home under armed guard.

When they rounded the head of the mesa, bringing into view the ranch-house and the valley, Madeline saw dust or smoke hovering over a hut upon the outskirts of the Mexican quarters. As the sun had set and the light was fading, she could not distinguish which it was. Then Stewart set a fast pace for the house. In a few minutes the party was in the yard, ready and willing to dismount.

Stillwell appeared, ostensibly cheerful, too cheerful to deceive Madeline. She noted also that a number of armed cowboys were walking with their horses just below the house.

"Wal, you-all had a nice little run," Stillwell said, speaking generally. "I reckon there wasn't much need of it. Pat Hawe thinks he's got some outlaws corralled on the ranch. Nothin' at all to be fussed up about. Stewart's that particular he won't have you meetin' with any rowdies."

Many and fervent were the expressions of relief from Madeline's feminine guests as they dismounted and went into the house. Madeline lingered behind to speak with Stillwell and Stewart.

"Now, Stillwell, out with it," she said, briefly.

The cattleman stared, and then he laughed, evidently pleased with her keenness.

"Wal, Miss Majesty, there's goin' to be a fight somewhere, an' Stewart wanted to get you-all in before it come off. He says the valley's overrun by vaqueros an' guerrillas an' robbers, an' Lord knows what else."

He stamped off the porch, his huge spurs rattling, and started down the path toward the waiting men.

Stewart stood in his familiar attentive position, erect, silent, with a hand on pommel and bridle.

"Stewart, you are exceedingly—thoughtful of my interests," she said, wanting to thank him, and not readily finding words. "I would not know what to do without you. Is there danger?"

"I'm not sure. But I want to be on the safe side."

She hesitated. It was no longer easy for her to talk to him, and she did not know why.

"May I know the special orders you gave Nels and Nick and Monty?" she asked.

"Who said I gave those boys special orders?"

"I heard Stillwell tell them so."

"Of course I'll tell you if you insist. But why should you worry over something that'll likely never happen?"

"I insist, Stewart," she replied, quietly.

"My orders were that at least one of them must be on guard near you day and night—never to be out of hearing of your voice."

"I thought as much. But why Nels or Monty or Nick? That seems rather hard on them. For that matter, why put any one to keep guard over me? Do you not trust any other of my cowboys?"

"I'd trust their honesty, but not their ability."

"Ability? Of what nature?"

"With guns."

"Stewart!" she exclaimed.

"Miss Hammond, you have been having such a good time entertaining your guests that you forget. I'm glad of that. I wish you had not questioned me."

"Forget what?"

"Don Carlos and his guerrillas."

"Indeed I have not forgotten. Stewart, you still think Don Carlos tried to make off with me—may try it again?"

"I don't think. I know."

"And besides all your other duties you have shared the watch with these three cowboys?"

"Yes."

"It has been going on without my knowledge?"

"Yes."

"Since when?"

"Since I brought you down from the mountains last month."

"How long is it to continue?"

"That's hard to say. Till the revolution is over, anyhow."

She mused a moment, looking away to the west, where the great void was filling with red haze. She believed implicitly in him, and the menace hovering near her fell like a shadow upon her present happiness.

"What must I do?" she asked.

"I think you ought to send your friends back East—and go with them, until this guerrilla war is over."

"Why, Stewart, they would be broken-hearted, and so would I."

He had no reply for that.

"If I do not take your advice it will be the first time since I have come to look to you for so much," she went on. "Cannot you suggest something else? My friends are having such a splendid visit. Helen is getting well. Oh, I should be sorry to see them go before they want to."

"We might take them up into the mountains and camp out for a while," he said, presently. "I know a wild place up among the crags. It's a hard climb, but worth the work. I never saw a more beautiful spot. Fine water, and it will be cool. Pretty soon it'll be too hot here for your party to go out-of-doors."

"You mean to hide me away among the crags and clouds?" replied Madeline, with a laugh.

"Well, it'd amount to that. Your friends need not know. Perhaps in a few weeks this spell of trouble on the border will be over till fall."

"You say it's a hard climb up to this place?"

"It surely is. Your friends will get the real thing if they make that trip."

"That suits me. Helen especially wants something to happen. And they are all crazy for excitement."

"They'd get it up there. Bad trails, canyons to head, steep climbs, wind-storms, thunder and lightning, rain, mountain-lions and wildcats."

"Very well, I am decided. Stewart, of course you will take charge? I don't believe I— Stewart, isn't there something more you could tell me—why you think, why you know my own personal liberty is in peril?"

"Yes. But do not ask me what it is. If I hadn't been a rebel soldier I would never have known."

"If you had not been a rebel soldier, where would Madeline Hammond be now?" she asked, earnestly.

He made no reply.

"Stewart," she continued, with warm impulse, "you once mentioned a debt you owed me —" And seeing his dark face pale, she wavered, then went on. "It is paid."

"No, no," he answered, huskily.

"Yes. I will not have it otherwise."

"No. That never can be paid."

Madeline held out her hand.

"It is paid, I tell you," she repeated.

Suddenly he drew back from the outstretched white hand that seemed to fascinate him.

"I'd kill a man to touch your hand. But I won't touch it on the terms you offer."

His unexpected passion disconcerted her.

"Stewart, no man ever before refused to shake hands with me, for any reason. It—it is scarcely flattering," she said, with a little laugh. "Why won't you? Because you think I offer it as mistress to servant—rancher to cowboy?"

"No."

"Then why? The debt you owed me is paid. I cancel it. So why not shake hands upon it, as men do?"

"I won't. That's all."

"I fear you are ungracious, whatever your reason," she replied. "Still, I may offer it again some day. Good night."

He said good night and turned. Madeline wonderingly watched him go down the path with his hand on the black horse's neck.

She went in to rest a little before dressing for dinner, and, being fatigued from the day's riding and excitement, she fell asleep. When she awoke it was twilight. She wondered why her Mexican maid had not come to her, and she rang the bell. The maid did not put in an appearance, nor was there any answer to the ring. The house seemed unusually quiet. It was a brooding silence, which presently broke to the sound of footsteps on the porch. Madeline recognized Stillwell's tread, though it appeared to be light for him. Then she heard him call softly in at the open door of her office. The suggestion of caution in his voice suited the strangeness of his walk. With a boding sense of trouble she hurried through the rooms. He was standing outside her office door.

"Stillwell!" she exclaimed.

"Anybody with you?" he asked, in a low tone.

"No."

"Please come out on the porch," he added.

She complied, and, once out, was enabled to see him. His grave face, paler than she had ever beheld it, caused her to stretch an appealing hand toward him. Stillwell intercepted it and held it in his own.

"Miss Majesty, I'm amazin' sorry to tell worrisome news." He spoke almost in a whisper, cautiously looked about him, and seemed both hurried and mysterious. "If you'd heerd Stewart cuss you'd sure know how we hate to hev to tell you this. But it can't be avoided. The fact is we're in a bad fix. If your guests ain't scared out of their skins it'll be owin' to your nerve an' how you carry out Stewart's orders."

"You can rely upon me," replied Madeline, firmly, though she trembled.

"Wal, what we're up against is this: that gang of bandits Pat Hawe was chasin'—they're hidin' in the house!"

"In the house?" echoed Madeline, aghast.

"Miss Majesty, it's the amazin' truth, an' shamed indeed am I to admit it. Stewart—why, he's wild with rage to think it could hev happened. You see, it couldn't hev happened if I hedn't sloped the boys off to the gol-lof-links, an' if Stewart hedn't rid out on the mesa after us. It's my fault. I've hed too much femininity around fer my old haid. Gene cussed me—he cussed me sure scandalous. But now we've got to face it—to figger."

"Do you mean that a gang of hunted outlaws—bandits—have actually taken refuge somewhere in my house?" demanded Madeline.

"I sure do. Seems powerful strange to me why you didn't find somethin' was wrong, seem' all your servants hev sloped."

"Gone? Ah, I missed my maid! I wondered why no lights were lit. Where did my servants go?"

"Down to the Mexican quarters, an' scared half to death. Now listen. When Stewart left you an hour or so ago he follered me direct to where me an' the boys was tryin' to keep Pat Hawe from tearin' the ranch to pieces. At that we was helpin' Pat all we could to find them bandits. But when Stewart got there he made a difference. Pat was nasty before, but seein' Stewart made him wuss. I reckon Gene to Pat is the same as red to a Greaser bull. Anyway, when the sheriff set fire to an old adobe hut Stewart called him an' called him hard. Pat Hawe hed six fellers with him, an' from all appearances bandit-huntin' was some fiesta. There was a row, an 'it looked bad fer a little. But Gene was cool, an' he controlled the boys. Then Pat an' his tough de-pooties went on huntin'. That huntin', Miss Majesty, petered out into what was only a farce. I reckon Pat could hev kept on foolin' me an' the boys, but as soon as Stewart showed up on the scene—wal, either Pat got to blunderin' or else we-all shed our blinders. Anyway, the facts stood plain. Pat Hawe wasn't lookin' hard fer any bandits; he wasn't daid set huntin' anythin', unless it was trouble fer Stewart. Finally, when Pat's men made fer our storehouse, where we keep ammunition, grub, liquors, an' sich, then Gene called a halt. An' he ordered Pat Hawe off the ranch. It was hyar Hawe an' Stewart locked horns.

"An' hyar the truth come out. There was a gang of bandits hid somewheres, an' at fust Pat Hawe hed been powerful active an' earnest in his huntin'. But sudden-like he'd fetched a pecooliar change of heart. He had been some flustered with Stewart's eyes a-pryin' into his moves, an' then, mebbe to hide somethin', mebbe jest nat'rul, he got mad. He hollered law. He pulled down off the shelf his old stock grudge on Stewart, accusin' him over again of that Greaser murder last fall. Stewart made him look like a fool—showed him up as bein' scared of the bandits or hevin' some reason fer slopin' off the trail. Anyway, the row started all right, an' but fer Nels it might hev amounted to a fight. In the thick of it, when Stewart was drivin' Pat an' his crowd off the place, one of them de-pooties lost his head an' went fer his gun. Nels throwed his gun an' crippled the feller's arm. Monty jumped then an' throwed two forty-fives, an' fer a second or so it looked ticklish. But the bandit-hunters crawled, an' then lit out."

Stillwell paused in the rapid delivery of his narrative; he still retained Madeline's hand, as if by that he might comfort her.

"After Pat left we put our haids together," began the old cattleman, with a long respiration. "We rounded up a lad who hed seen a dozen or so fellers—he wouldn't to they was Greasers—breakin' through the shrubbery to the back of the house. That was while Stewart was ridin' out to the mesa. Then this lad seen your servants all runnin' down the hill toward the village. Now, heah's the way Gene figgers. There sure was some deviltry down along the railroad, an' Pat Hawe trailed bandits up to the ranch. He hunts hard an' then all to onct he quits. Stewart says Pat Hawe wasn't scared, but he discovered signs or somethin', or got wind in some strange way that there was in the gang of bandits some fellers he didn't want to ketch. Sabe? Then Gene, quicker 'n a flash, springs his plan on me. He'd go down to Padre Marcos an' hev him help to find out all possible from your Mexican servants. I was to hurry up hyar an' tell you—give you orders, Miss Majesty. Ain't that amazin' strange? Wal, you're to assemble all your guests in the kitchen. Make a grand bluff an' pretend, as your help has left, that it'll be great fun fer your guests to cook dinner. The kitchen is the safest room in the house. While you're joshin' your party along, makin' a kind of picnic out of it, I'll place cowboys in the long corridor, an' also outside in the corner where the kitchen joins on to the main house. It's pretty sure the bandits think no one's wise to where they're hid. Stewart says they're in that end room where the alfalfa is, an' they'll slope in the night. Of course, with me an' the boys watchin', you-all will be safe to go to bed. An' we're to rouse your guests early before daylight, to hit the trail up into the mountains. Tell them to pack outfits before goin' to bed. Say as your servants hev sloped, you might as well go campin' with the cowboys. That's all. If we hev any luck your' friends'll never know they've been sittin' on a powder-mine."

"Stillwell, do you advise that trip up into the mountains?" asked Madeline.

"I reckon I do, considerin' everythin'. Now, Miss Majesty, I've used up a lot of time explainin'. You'll sure keep your nerve?"

"Yes," Madeline replied, and was surprised at herself. "Better tell Florence. She'll be a power of comfort to you. I'm goin' now to fetch up the boys."

Instead of returning to her room Madeline went through the office into the long corridor. It was almost as dark as night. She fancied she saw a slow-gliding figure darker than the surrounding gloom; and she entered upon the fulfilment of her part of the plan in something like trepidation. Her footsteps were noiseless. Finding the door to the kitchen, and going in, she struck lights. Upon passing out again she made certain she discerned a dark shape, now motionless, crouching along the wall. But she mistrusted her vivid imagination. It took all her boldness to enable her unconcernedly and naturally to strike the corridor light. Then she went on through her own rooms and thence into the patio.

Her guests laughingly and gladly entered into the spirit of the occasion. Madeline fancied her deceit must have been perfect, seeing that it deceived even Florence. They trooped merrily into the kitchen. Madeline, delaying at the door, took a sharp but unobtrusive glance down the great, barnlike hall. She saw nothing but blank dark space. Suddenly from one side, not a rod distant, protruded a pale, gleaming face breaking the even blackness. Instantly it flashed back out of sight. Yet that time was long enough for Madeline to see a pair of glittering eyes, and to recognize them as Don Carlos's.

Without betraying either hurry or alarm, she closed the door. It had a heavy bolt which she slowly, noiselessly shot. Then the cold amaze that had all but stunned her into inaction throbbed into wrath. How dared that Mexican steal into her home! What did he mean? Was he one of the bandits supposed to be hidden in her house? She was thinking herself into greater anger and excitement, and probably would have betrayed herself had not Florence, who had evidently seen her bolt the door and now read her thoughts, come toward her with a bright, intent, questioning look. Madeline caught herself in time.

Thereupon she gave each of her guests a duty to perform. Leading Florence into the pantry, she unburdened herself of the secret in one brief whisper. Florence's reply was to point out of the little open window, passing which was a file of stealthily moving cowboys. Then Madeline lost both anger and fear, retaining only the glow of excitement.

Madeline could be gay, and she initiated the abandonment of dignity by calling Castleton into the pantry, and, while interesting him in some pretext or other, imprinting the outlines of her flour-covered hands upon the back of his black coat. Castleton innocently returned to the kitchen to be greeted with a roar. That surprising act of the hostess set the pace, and there followed a merry, noisy time. Everybody helped. The miscellaneous collection of dishes so confusingly contrived made up a dinner which they all heartily enjoyed. Madeline enjoyed it herself, even with the feeling of a sword hanging suspended over her.

The hour was late when she rose from the table and told her guests to go to their rooms, don their riding-clothes, pack what they needed for the long and adventurous camping trip that she hoped would be the climax of their Western experience, and to snatch a little sleep before the cowboys roused them for the early start.

Madeline went immediately to her room, and was getting out her camping apparel when a knock interrupted her. She thought Florence had come to help her pack. But this knock was upon the door opening out in the porch. It was repeated.

"Who's there?" she questioned.

"Stewart," came the reply.

She opened the door. He stood on the threshold. Beyond him, indistinct in the gloom, were several cowboys.

"May I speak to you?" he asked.

"Certainly." She hesitated a moment, then asked him in and closed the door. "Is—is everything all right?"

"No. These bandits stick to cover pretty close. They must have found out we're on the watch. But I'm sure we'll get you and your friends away before anything starts. I wanted to tell you that I've talked with your servants. They were just scared. They'll come back to-morrow, soon as Bill gets rid of this gang. You need not worry about them or your property."

"Do you have any idea who is hiding in the house?"

"I was worried some at first. Pat Hawe acted queer. I imagined he'd discovered he was trailing bandits who might turn out to be his smuggling guerrilla cronies. But talking with your servants, finding a bunch of horses upon hidden down in the mesquite behind the pond —several things have changed my mind. My idea is that a cowardly handful of riffraff outcasts from the border have hidden in your house, more by accident than design. We'll let them go—get rid of them without even a shot. If I didn't think so—well, I'd be considerably worried. It would make a different state of affairs."

"Stewart, you are wrong," she said.

He started, but his reply did not follow swiftly. The expression of his eyes altered.

Presently he spoke:

"How so?"

"I saw one of these bandits. I distinctly recognized him."

One long step brought him close to her.

"Who was he?" demanded Stewart.

"Don Carlos."

He muttered low and deep, then said, "Are you sure?"

"Absolutely. I saw his figure twice in the hall, then his face in the light. I could never mistake his eyes."

"Did he know you saw him?"

"I am not positive, but I think so. Oh, he must have known! I was standing full in the light. I had entered the door, then purposely stepped out. His face showed from around a corner, and swiftly flashed out of sight."

Madeline was tremblingly conscious that Stewart underwent a transformation. She saw as well as felt the leaping passion that changed him.

"Call your friends—get them in here!" he ordered, tersely, and wheeled toward the door.

"Stewart, wait!" she said.

He turned. His white face, his burning eyes, his presence now charged with definite, fearful meaning, influenced her strangely, weakened her.

"What will you do?" she asked.

"That needn't concern you. Get your party in here. Bar the windows and lock the doors. You'll be safe."

"Stewart! Tell me what you intend to do."

"I won't tell you," he replied, and turned away again.

"But I will know," she said. With a hand on his arm she detained him. She saw how he halted—felt the shock in him as she touched him. "Oh, I do know. You mean to fight!"

"Well, Miss Hammond, isn't it about time?" he asked. Evidently he overcame a violent passion for instant action. There was weariness, dignity, even reproof in his question. "The fact of that Mexican's presence here in your house ought to prove to you the nature of the case. These vaqueros, these guerrillas, have found out you won't stand for any fighting on the part of your men. Don Carlos is a sneak, a coward, yet he's not afraid to hide in your own house. He has learned you won't let your cowboys hurt anybody. He's taking advantage of it. He'll rob, burn, and make off with you. He'll murder, too, if it falls his way. These Greasers use knives in the dark. So I ask—isn't it about time we stop him?"

"Stewart, I forbid you to fight, unless in self-defense. I forbid you."

"What I mean to do is self-defense. Haven't I tried to explain to you that just now we've wild times along this stretch of border? Must I tell you again that Don Carlos is hand and glove with the revolution? The rebels are crazy to stir up the United States. You are a woman of prominence. Don Carlos would make off with you. If he got you, what little matter to cross the border with you! Well, where would the hue and cry go? Through the troops along the border! To New York! To Washington! Why, it would mean what the rebels are working for— United States intervention. In other words, war!"

"Oh, surely you exaggerate!" she cried.

"Maybe so. But I'm beginning to see the Don's game. And, Miss Hammond, I—It's awful for me to think what you'd suffer if Don Carlos got you over the line. I know these low-caste Mexicans. I've been among the peons—the slaves."

"Stewart, don't let Don Carlos get me," replied Madeline, in sweet directness.

She saw him shake, saw his throat swell as he swallowed hard, saw the hard fierceness return to his face.

"I won't. That's why I'm going after him."

"But I forbade you to start a fight deliberately."

"Then I'll go ahead and start one without your permission," he replied shortly, and again he wheeled.

This time, when Madeline caught his arm she held to it, even after he stopped.

"No," she said, imperiously.

He shook off her hand and strode forward.

"Please don't go!" she called, beseechingly. But he kept on. "Stewart!"

She ran ahead of him, intercepted him, faced him with her back against the door. He swept out a long arm as if to brush her aside. But it wavered and fell. Haggard, troubled, with working face, he stood before her.

"It's for your sake," he expostulated.

"If it is for my sake, then do what pleases me."

"These guerrillas will knife somebody. They'll burn the house. They'll make off with you. They'll do something bad unless we stop them."

"Let us risk all that," she importuned.

"But it's a terrible risk, and it oughtn't be run," he exclaimed, passionately. "I know best here. Stillwell upholds me. Let me out, Miss Hammond. I'm going to take the boys and go after these guerrillas."

"No!"

"Good Heavens!" exclaimed Stewart. "Why not let me go? It's the thing to do. I'm sorry to distress you and your guests. Why not put an end to Don Carlos's badgering? Is it because you're afraid a rumpus will spoil your friends' visit?"

"It isn't—not this time."

"Then it's the idea of a little shooting at these Greasers?"

"No."

"You're sick to think of a little Greaser blood staining the halls of your home?"

"No!"

"Well, then, why keep me from doing what I know is best?"

"Stewart, I—I—" she faltered, in growing agitation. "I'm frightened—confused. All this is too—too much for me. I'm not a coward. If you have to fight you'll see I'm not a coward. But your way seems so reckless—that hall is so dark—the guerrillas would shoot from behind doors. You're so wild, so daring, you'd rush right into peril. Is that necessary? I think—I mean—I don't know just why I feel so—so about you doing it. But I believe it's because I'm afraid you—you might be hurt."

"You're afraid I—I might be hurt?" he echoed, wonderingly, the hard whiteness of his face warming, flushing, glowing.

"Yes."

The single word, with all it might mean, with all it might not mean, softened him as if by magic, made him gentle, amazed, shy as a boy, stifling under a torrent of emotions.

Madeline thought she had persuaded him—worked her will with him. Then another of his startlingly sudden moves told her that she had reckoned too quickly. This move was to put her firmly aside so he could pass; and Madeline, seeing he would not hesitate to lift her out of the way, surrendered the door. He turned on the threshold. His face was still working, but the flame-pointed gleam of his eyes indicated the return of that cowboy ruthlessness.

"I'm going to drive Don Carlos and his gang out of the house," declared Stewart. "I think I may promise you to do it without a fight. But if it takes a fight, off he goes!"

❧ 15 ❧

THE MOUNTAIN TRAIL

As Stewart departed from one door Florence knocked upon another; and Madeline, far shaken out of her usual serenity, admitted the cool Western girl with more than gladness. Just to have her near helped Madeline to get back her balance. She was conscious of Florence's sharp scrutiny, then of a sweet, deliberate change of manner. Florence might have been burning with curiosity to know more about the bandits hidden in the house, the plans of the cowboys, the reason for Madeline's suppressed emotion; but instead of asking Madeline questions she introduced the important subject of what to take on the camping trip. For an hour they discussed the need of this and that article, selected those things most needful, and then packed them in Madeline's duffle-bags.

That done, they decided to lie down, fully dressed as they were in riding-costume, and sleep, or at least rest, the little remaining time left before the call to saddle. Madeline turned out the light and, peeping through her window, saw dark forms standing sentinel-like in the gloom. When she lay down she heard soft steps on the path. This fidelity to her swelled her heart, while the need of it presaged that fearful something which, since Stewart's passionate appeal to her, haunted her as inevitable.

Madeline did not expect to sleep, yet she did sleep, and it seemed to have been only a moment until Florence called her. She followed Florence outside. It was the dark hour before dawn. She could discern saddled horses being held by cowboys. There was an air of hurry and mystery about the departure. Helen, who came tip-toeing out with Madeline's other guests, whispered that it was like an escape. She was delighted. The others were amused. To Madeline it was indeed an escape.

In the darkness Madeline could not see how many escorts her party was to have. She heard low voices, the champing of bits and thumping of hoofs, and she recognized Stewart when he led up Majesty for her to mount. Then came a pattering of soft feet and the whining of dogs. Cold noses touched her hands, and she saw the long, gray, shaggy shapes of her pack of Russian wolf-hounds. That Stewart meant to let them go with her was indicative of how he studied her pleasure. She loved to be out with the hounds and her horse.

Stewart led Majesty out into the darkness past a line of mounted horses.

305

"Guess we're ready?" he said. "I'll make the count." He went back along the line, and on the return Madeline heard him say several times, "Now, everybody ride close to the horse in front, and keep quiet till daylight." Then the snorting and pounding of the big black horse in front of her told Madeline that Stewart had mounted.

"All right, we're off," he called.

Madeline lifted Majesty's bridle and let the roan go. There was a crack and crunch of gravel, fire struck from stone, a low whinny, a snort, and then steady, short, clip-clop of iron hoofs on hard ground. Madeline could just discern Stewart and his black outlined in shadowy gray before her. Yet they were almost within touching distance. Once or twice one of the huge stag-hounds leaped up at her and whined joyously. A thick belt of darkness lay low, and seemed to thin out above to a gray fog, through which a few wan stars showed. It was altogether an unusual departure from the ranch; and Madeline, always susceptible even to ordinary incident that promised well, now found herself thrillingly sensitive to the soft beat of hoofs, the feel of cool, moist air, the dim sight of Stewart's dark figure. The caution, the early start before dawn, the enforced silence—these lent the occasion all that was needful to make it stirring.

Majesty plunged into a gully, where sand and rough going made Madeline stop romancing to attend to riding. In the darkness Stewart was not so easy to keep close to even on smooth trails, and now she had to be watchfully attentive to do it. Then followed a long march through dragging sand. Meantime the blackness gradually changed to gray. At length Majesty climbed out of the wash, and once more his iron shoes rang on stone. He began to climb. The figure of Stewart and his horse loomed more distinctly in Madeline's sight. Bending over, she tried to see the trail, but could not. She wondered how Stewart could follow a trail in the dark. His eyes must be as piercing as they sometimes looked. Over her shoulder Madeline could not see the horse behind her, but she heard him.

As Majesty climbed steadily Madeline saw the gray darkness grow opaque, change and lighten, lose its substance, and yield the grotesque shapes of yucca and ocotillo. Dawn was about to break. Madeline imagined she was facing east, still she saw no brightening of sky. All at once, to her surprise, Stewart and his powerful horse stood clear in her sight. She saw the characteristic rock and cactus and brush that covered the foothills. The trail was old and seldom used, and it zigzagged and turned and twisted. Looking back, she saw the short, squat figure of Monty Price humped over his saddle. Monty's face was hidden under his sombrero. Behind him rode Dorothy Coombs, and next loomed up the lofty form of Nick Steele. Madeline and the members of her party were riding between cowboy escorts.

Bright daylight came, and Madeline saw the trail was leading up through foothills. It led in a round-about way through shallow gullies full of stone and brush washed down by floods. At every turn now Madeline expected to come upon water and the waiting pack-train. But time passed, and miles of climbing, and no water or horses were met. Expectation in Madeline gave place to desire; she was hungry.

Presently Stewart's horse went splashing into a shallow pool. Beyond that damp places in the sand showed here and there, and again more water in rocky pockets. Stewart kept on. It was eight o'clock by Madeline's watch when, upon turning into a wide hollow, she saw horses grazing on spare grass, a great pile of canvas-covered bundles, and a fire round which cowboys and two Mexican women were busy.

Madeline sat her horse and reviewed her followers as they rode up single file. Her guests were in merry mood, and they all talked at once.

"Breakfast—and rustle," called out Stewart, without ceremony.

"No need to tell me to rustle," said Helen. "I am simply ravenous. This air makes me hungry."

For that matter, Madeline observed Helen did not show any marked contrast to the others. The hurry order, however, did not interfere with the meal being somewhat in the nature of a picnic. While they ate and talked and laughed the cowboys were packing horses and burros and throwing the diamond-hitch, a procedure so interesting to Castleton that he got up with coffee-cup in hand and tramped from one place to another.

"Heard of that diamond-hitch-up," he observed to a cowboy. "Bally nice little job!"

As soon as the pack-train was in readiness Stewart started it off in the lead to break trail. A heavy growth of shrub interspersed with rock and cactus covered the slopes; and now all the trail appeared to be uphill. It was not a question of comfort for Madeline and her party, for comfort was impossible; it was a matter of making the travel possible for him. Florence wore corduroy breeches and high-top boots, and the advantage of this masculine garb was at once in evidence. The riding-habits of the other ladies suffered considerably from the sharp spikes. It took all Madeline's watchfulness to save her horse's legs, to pick the best bits of open ground, to make cut-offs from the trail, and to protect herself from outreaching thorny branches, so that the time sped by without her knowing it. The pack-train forged ahead, and the trailing couples grew farther apart. At noon they got out of the foothills to face the real ascent of the mountains. The sun beat down hot. There was little breeze, and the dust rose thick and hung in a pall. The view was restricted, and what scenery lay open to the eye was dreary and drab, a barren monotony of slow-mounting slopes ridged by rocky canyons.

Once Stewart waited for Madeline, and as she came up he said:

"We're going to have a storm."

"That will be a relief. It's so hot and dusty," replied Madeline.

"Shall I call a halt and make camp?"

"Here? Oh no! What do you think best?"

"Well, if we have a good healthy thunder-storm it will be something new for your friends. I think we'd be wise to keep on the go. There's no place to make a good camp. The wind would blow us off this slope if the rain didn't wash us off. It'll take all-day travel to reach a good camp-site, and I don't promise that. We're making slow time. If it rains, let it rain. The pack outfit is well covered. We will have to get wet."

"Surely," replied Madeline; and she smiled at his inference. She knew what a storm was in that country, and her guests had yet to experience one. "If it rains, let it rain."

Stewart rode on, and Madeline followed. Up the slope toiled and nodded the pack-animals, the little burros going easily where the horses labored. Their packs, like the humps of camels, bobbed from side to side. Stones rattled down; the heat-waves wavered black; the dust puffed up and sailed. The sky was a pale blue, like heated steel, except where dark clouds peeped over the mountain crests. A heavy, sultry atmosphere made breathing difficult. Down the slope the trailing party stretched out in twos and threes, and it was easy to distinguish the weary riders.

Half a mile farther up Madeline could see over the foothills to the north and west and a little south, and she forgot the heat and weariness and discomfort for her guests in wide, unlimited prospects of sun-scorched earth. She marked the gray valley and the black mountains and the wide, red gateway of the desert, and the dim, shadowy peaks, blue as the sky they pierced. She was sorry when the bleak, gnarled cedar-trees shut off her view.

Then there came a respite from the steep climb, and the way led in a winding course through a matted, storm-wrenched forest of stunted trees. Even up to this elevation the desert reached with its gaunt hand. The clouds overspreading the sky, hiding the sun, made a welcome change. The pack-train rested, and Stewart and Madeline waited for the party to come up. Here he briefly explained to her that Don Carlos and his bandits had left the ranch some time in the night. Thunder rumbled in the distance, and a faint wind rustled the scant foliage of the cedars. The air grew oppressive; the horses panted.

"Sure it'll be a hummer," said Stewart. "The first storm almost always is bad. I can feel it in the air."

The air, indeed, seemed to be charged with a heavy force that was waiting to be liberated.

One by one the couples mounted to the cedar forest, and the feminine contingent declaimed eloquently for rest. But there was to be no permanent rest until night and then that depended upon reaching the crags. The pack-train wagged onward, and Stewart fell in behind. The storm-center gathered slowly around the peaks; low rumble and howl of thunder increased in frequence; slowly the light shaded as smoky clouds rolled up; the air grew sultrier, and the exasperating breeze puffed a few times and then failed.

An hour later the party had climbed high and was rounding the side of a great bare ridge that long had hidden the crags. The last burro of the pack-train plodded over the ridge out of Madeline's sight. She looked backward down the slope, amused to see her guests change wearily from side to side in their saddles. Far below lay the cedar flat and the foothills. Far to the west the sky was still clear, with shafts of sunlight shooting down from behind the encroaching clouds.

Stewart reached the summit of the ridge and, though only a few rods ahead, he waved to her, sweeping his hand round to what he saw beyond. It was an impressive gesture, and Madeline, never having climbed as high as this, anticipated much.

Majesty surmounted the last few steps and, snorting, halted beside Stewart's black. To Madeline the scene was as if the world had changed. The ridge was a mountain-top. It dropped before her into a black, stone-ridged, shrub-patched, many-canyoned gulf. Eastward, beyond the gulf, round, bare mountain-heads loomed up. Upward, on the right, led giant steps of cliff and bench and weathered slope to the fir-bordered and pine-fringed crags standing dark and bare against the stormy sky. Massed inky clouds were piling across the peaks, obscuring the highest ones. A fork of white lightning flashed, and, like the booming of an avalanche, thunder followed.

That bold world of broken rock under the slow mustering of storm-clouds was a grim, awe-inspiring spectacle. It had beauty, but beauty of the sublime and majestic kind. The fierce desert had reached up to meet the magnetic heights where heat and wind and frost and lightning and flood contended in everlasting strife. And before their onslaught this mighty upflung world of rugged stone was crumbling, splitting, wearing to ruin.

Madeline glanced at Stewart. He had forgotten her presence. Immovable as stone, he sat his horse, dark-faced, dark-eyed, and, like an Indian unconscious of thought, he watched and watched. To see him thus, to divine the strange affinity between the soul of this man, become primitive, and the savage environment that had developed him, were powerful helps to Madeline Hammond in her strange desire to understand his nature.

A cracking of iron-shod hoofs behind her broke the spell. Monty had reached the summit.

"Gene, what it won't all be doin' in a minnut Moses hisself couldn't tell," observed Monty.

Then Dorothy climbed to his side and looked.

"Oh, isn't it just perfectly lovely!" she exclaimed. "But I wish it wouldn't storm. We'll all get wet."

Once more Stewart faced the ascent, keeping to the slow heave of the ridge as it rose southward toward the looming spires of rock. Soon he was off smooth ground, and

Madeline, some rods behind him, looked back with concern at her friends. Here the real toil, the real climb began, and a mountain storm was about to burst in all its fury.

The slope that Stewart entered upon was a magnificent monument to the ruined crags above. It was a southerly slope, and therefore semi-arid, covered with cercocarpus and yucca and some shrub that Madeline believed was manzanita. Every foot of the trail seemed to slide under Majesty. What hard ground there was could not be traveled upon, owing to the spiny covering or masses of shattered rocks. Gullies lined the slope.

Then the sky grew blacker; the slow-gathering clouds appeared to be suddenly agitated; they piled and rolled and mushroomed and obscured the crags. The air moved heavily and seemed to be laden with sulphurous smoke, and sharp lightning flashes began to play. A distant roar of wind could be heard between the peals of thunder.

Stewart waited for Madeline under the lee of a shelving cliff, where the cowboys had halted the pack-train. Majesty was sensitive to the flashes of lightning. Madeline patted his neck and softly called to him. The weary burros nodded; the Mexican women covered their heads with their mantles. Stewart untied the slicker at the back of Madeline's saddle and helped her on with it. Then he put on his own. The other cowboys followed suit. Presently Madeline saw Monty and Dorothy rounding the cliff, and hoped the others would come soon.

A blue-white, knotted rope of lightning burned down out of the clouds, and instantly a thunder-clap crashed, seeming to shake the foundations of the earth. Then it rolled, as if banging from cloud to cloud, and boomed along the peaks, and reverberated from deep to low, at last to rumble away into silence. Madeline felt the electricity in Majesty's mane, and it seemed to tingle through her nerves. The air had a weird, bright cast. The ponderous clouds swallowed more and more of the eastern domes. This moment of the breaking of the storm, with the strange growing roar of wind, like a moaning monster, was pregnant with a heart-disturbing emotion for Madeline Hammond. Glorious it was to be free, healthy, out in the open, under the shadow of the mountain and cloud, in the teeth of the wind and rain and storm.

Another dazzling blue blaze showed the bold mountain-side and the storm-driven clouds. In the flare of light Madeline saw Stewart's face.

"Are you afraid?" she asked.

"Yes," he replied, simply.

Then the thunderbolt racked the heavens, and as it boomed away in lessening power Madeline reflected with surprise upon Stewart's answer. Something in his face had made her ask him what she considered a foolish question. His reply amazed her. She loved a storm. Why should he fear it—he, with whom she could not associate fear?

"How strange! Have you not been out in many storms?"

A smile that was only a gleam flitted over his dark face.

"In hundreds of them. By day, with the cattle stampeding. At night, alone on the mountain, with the pines crashing and the rocks rolling—in flood on the desert."

"It's not only the lightning, then?" she asked.

"No. All the storm."

Madeline felt that henceforth she would have less faith in what she had imagined was her love of the elements. What little she knew! If this iron-nerved man feared a storm, then there was something about a storm to fear.

And suddenly, as the ground quaked under her horse's feet, and all the sky grew black and crisscrossed by flaming streaks, and between thunderous reports there was a strange hollow roar sweeping down upon her, she realized how small was her knowledge and experience of the mighty forces of nature. Then, with that perversity of character of which she was wholly conscious, she was humble, submissive, reverent, and fearful even while she gloried in the grandeur of the dark, cloud-shadowed crags and canyons, the stupendous strife of sound, the wonderful driving lances of white fire.

With blacker gloom and deafening roar came the torrent of rain. It was a cloud-burst. It was like solid water tumbling down. For long Madeline sat her horse, head bent to the pelting rain. When its force lessened and she heard Stewart call for all to follow, she looked up to see that he was starting once more. She shot a glimpse at Dorothy and as quickly glanced away. Dorothy, who would not wear a hat suitable for inclement weather, nor one of the horrid yellow, sticky slickers, was a drenched and disheveled spectacle. Madeline did not trust herself to look at the other girls. It was enough to hear their lament. So she turned her horse into Stewart's trail.

Rain fell steadily. The fury of the storm, however, had passed, and the roll of thunder diminished in volume. The air had wonderfully cleared and was growing cool. Madeline began to feel uncomfortably cold and wet. Stewart was climbing faster than formerly, and she noted that Monty kept at her heels, pressing her on. Time had been lost, and the camp-site was a long way off. The stag-hounds began to lag and get footsore. The sharp rocks of the trail were cruel to their feet. Then, as Madeline began to tire, she noticed less and less around her. The ascent grew rougher and steeper—slow toil for panting horses. The thinning rain grew colder, and sometimes a stronger whip of wind lashed stingingly in Madeline's face. Her horse climbed and climbed, and brush and sharp corners of stone everlastingly pulled and tore at her wet garments. A gray gloom settled down around her. Night was approaching. Majesty heaved upward with a snort, the wet saddle creaked, and an even motion told Madeline she was on level ground. She looked up to see looming crags and spires, like huge pipe-organs, dark at the base and growing light upward. The rain had ceased, but the branches of fir-trees and juniper were water-soaked arms reaching out for her. Through an opening between crags Madeline caught a momentary glimpse of the west. Red sun-shafts shone through the murky, broken clouds. The sun had set.

Stewart's horse was on a jog-trot now, and Madeline left the trail more to Majesty than to her own choosing. The shadows deepened, and the crags grew gloomy and spectral. A cool wind moaned through the dark trees. Coyotes, scenting the hounds, kept apace of them, and barked and howled off in the gloom. But the tired hounds did not appear to notice.

As black night began to envelop her surroundings, Madeline marked that the fir-trees had given place to pine forest. Suddenly a pin-point of light pierced the ebony blackness. Like a solitary star in dark sky it twinkled and blinked. She lost sight of it—found it again. It grew larger. Black tree-trunks crossed her line of vision. The light was a fire. She heard a cowboy song and the wild chorus of a pack of coyotes. Drops of rain on the branches of trees glittered in the rays of the fire. Stewart's tall figure, with sombrero slouched down, was now and then outlined against a growing circle of light. And by the aid of that light she saw him turn every moment or so to look back, probably to assure himself that she was close behind.

With a prospect of fire and warmth, and food and rest, Madeline's enthusiasm revived. What a climb! There was promise in this wild ride and lonely trail and hidden craggy height, not only in the adventure her friends yearned for, but in some nameless joy and spirit for herself.

🦋 16 🦋

THE CRAGS

GLAD INDEED WAS MADELINE to be lifted off her horse beside a roaring fire—to see steaming pots upon red-hot coals. Except about her shoulders, which had been protected by the slicker, she was wringing wet. The Mexican women came quickly to help her change in a tent near by; but Madeline preferred for the moment to warm her numb feet and hands and to watch the spectacle of her arriving friends.

Dorothy plumped off her saddle into the arms of several waiting cowboys. She could scarcely walk. Far removed in appearance was she from her usual stylish self. Her face was hidden by a limp and lopsided hat. From under the disheveled brim came a plaintive moan: "O-h-h! what a-an a-awful ride!" Mrs. Beck was in worse condition; she had to be taken off her horse. "I'm paralyzed—I'm a wreck. Bobby, get a roller-chair." Bobby was solicitous and willing, but there were no roller-chairs. Florence dismounted easily, and but for her mass of hair, wet and tumbling, would have been taken for a handsome cowboy. Edith Wayne had stood the physical strain of the ride better than Dorothy; however, as her mount was rather small, she had been more at the mercy of cactus and brush. Her habit hung in tatters. Helen had preserved a remnant of style, as well as of pride, and perhaps a little strength. But her face was white, her eyes were big, and she limped. "Majesty!" she exclaimed. "What did you want to do to us? Kill us outright or make us homesick?" Of all of them, however, Ambrose's wife, Christine, the little French maid, had suffered the most in that long ride. She was unaccustomed to horses. Ambrose had to carry her into the big tent. Florence persuaded Madeline to leave the fire, and when they went in with the others Dorothy was wailing because her wet boots would not come off, Mrs. Beck was weeping and trying to direct a Mexican woman to unfasten her bedraggled dress, and there was general pandemonium.

"Warm clothes—hot drinks and grub—warm blankets," rang out Stewart's sharp order.

Then, with Florence helping the Mexican women, it was not long until Madeline and the feminine side of the party were comfortable, except for the weariness and aches that only rest and sleep could alleviate.

Neither fatigue nor pains, however, nor the strangeness of being packed sardine-like under canvas, nor the howls of coyotes, kept Madeline's guests from stretching out with

311

long, grateful sighs, and one by one dropping into deep slumber. Madeline whispered a little to Florence, and laughed with her once or twice, and then the light flickering on the canvas faded and her eyelids closed. Darkness and roar of camp life, low voices of men, thump of horses' hoofs, coyote serenade, the sense of warmth and sweet rest—all drifted away.

When she awakened shadows of swaying branches moved on the sunlit canvas above her. She heard the ringing strokes of an ax, but no other sound from outside. Slow, regular breathing attested to the deep slumbers of her tent comrades. She observed presently that Florence was missing from the number. Madeline rose and peeped out between the flaps.

An exquisitely beautiful scene surprised and enthralled her gaze. She saw a level space, green with long grass, bright with flowers, dotted with groves of graceful firs and pines and spruces, reaching to superb crags, rosy and golden in the sunlight. Eager to get out where she could enjoy an unrestricted view, she searched for her pack, found it in a corner, and then hurriedly and quietly dressed.

Her favorite stag-hounds, Russ and Tartar, were asleep before the door, where they had been chained. She awakened them and loosened them, thinking the while that it must have been Stewart who had chained them near her. Close at hand also was a cowboy's bed rolled up in a tarpaulin.

The cool air, fragrant with pine and spruce and some subtle nameless tang, sweet and tonic, made Madeline stand erect and breathe slowly and deeply. It was like drinking of a magic draught. She felt it in her blood, that it quickened its flow. Turning to look in the other direction, beyond the tent, she saw the remnants of last night's temporary camp, and farther on a grove of beautiful pines from which came the sharp ring of the ax. Wider gaze took in a wonderful park, not only surrounded by lofty crags, but full of crags of lesser height, many lifting their heads from dark-green groves of trees. The morning sun, not yet above the eastern elevations, sent its rosy and golden shafts in between the towering rocks, to tip the pines.

Madeline, with the hounds beside her, walked through the nearest grove. The ground was soft and springy and brown with pine-needles. Then she saw that a clump of trees had prevented her from seeing the most striking part of this natural park. The cowboys had selected a campsite where they would have the morning sun and afternoon shade. Several tents and flies were already up; there was a huge lean-to made of spruce boughs; cowboys were busy round several camp-fires; piles of packs lay covered with tarpaulins, and beds were rolled up under the trees. This space was a kind of rolling meadow, with isolated trees here and there, and other trees in aisles and circles; and it mounted up in low, grassy banks to great towers of stone five hundred feet high. Other crags rose behind these. From under a mossy cliff, huge and green and cool, bubbled a full, clear spring. Wild flowers fringed its banks. Out in the meadow the horses were knee-deep in grass that waved in the morning breeze.

Florence espied Madeline under the trees and came running. She was like a young girl, with life and color and joy. She wore a flannel blouse, corduroy skirt, and moccasins. And her hair was fastened under a band like an Indian's.

"Castleton's gone with a gun, for hours, it seems," said Florence. "Gene just went to hunt him up. The other gentlemen are still asleep. I imagine they sure will sleep up heah in this air."

Then, business-like, Florence fell to questioning Madeline about details of camp arrangement which Stewart, and Florence herself, could hardly see to without suggestion.

Before any of Madeline's sleepy guests awakened the camp was completed. Madeline and Florence had a tent under a pine-tree, but they did not intend to sleep in it except during stormy weather. They spread a tarpaulin, made their bed on it, and elected to sleep under the light of the stars. After that, taking the hounds with them, they explored. To Madeline's surprise, the park was not a little half-mile nook nestling among the crags, but extended farther than they cared to walk, and was rather a series of parks. They were no more than small valleys between gray-toothed peaks. As the day advanced the charm of the place grew upon Madeline. Even at noon, with the sun beating down, there was comfortable warmth rather than heat. It was the kind of warmth that Madeline liked to feel in the spring. And the sweet, thin, rare atmosphere began to affect her strangely. She breathed deeply of it until she felt light-headed, as if her body lacked substance and might drift away like a thistledown. All at once she grew uncomfortably sleepy. A dreamy languor possessed her, and, lying under a pine with her head against Florence, she went to sleep. When she opened her eyes the shadows of the crags stretched from the west, and between them streamed a red-gold light. It was hazy, smoky sunshine losing its fire. The afternoon had far advanced. Madeline sat up. Florence was lazily reading. The two Mexican women were at work under the fly where the big stone fireplace had been erected. No one else was in sight.

Florence, upon being questioned, informed Madeline that incident about camp had been delightfully absent. Castleton had returned and was profoundly sleeping with the other men. Presently a chorus of merry calls attracted Madeline's attention, and she turned to see Helen limping along with Dorothy, and Mrs. Beck and Edith supporting each other. They were all rested, but lame, and delighted with the place, and as hungry as bears awakened from a winter's sleep. Madeline forthwith escorted them round the camp, and through the many aisles between the trees, and to the mossy, pine-matted nooks under the crags.

Then they had dinner, sitting on the ground after the manner of Indians; and it was a dinner that lacked merriment only because everybody was too busily appeasing appetite.

Later Stewart led them across a neck of the park, up a rather steep climb between towering crags, to take them out upon a grassy promontory that faced the great open west— a vast, ridged, streaked, and reddened sweep of earth rolling down, as it seemed, to the golden sunset end of the world. Castleton said it was a jolly fine view; Dorothy voiced her usual languid enthusiasm; Helen was on fire with pleasure and wonder; Mrs. Beck appealed to Bobby to see how he liked it before she ventured, and she then reiterated his praise; and Edith Wayne, like Madeline and Florence, was silent. Boyd was politely interested; he was the kind of man who appeared to care for things as other people cared for them.

Madeline watched the slow transformation of the changing west, with its haze of desert dust, through which mountain and cloud and sun slowly darkened. She watched until her eyes ached, and scarcely had a thought of what she was watching. When her eyes shifted to encounter the tall form of Stewart standing motionless on the rim, her mind became active again. As usual, he stood apart from the others, and now he seemed aloof and unconscious. He made a dark, powerful figure, and he fitted that wild promontory.

She experienced a strange, annoying surprise when she discovered both Helen and Dorothy watching Stewart with peculiar interest. Edith, too, was alive to the splendid picture the cowboy made. But when Edith smiled and whispered in her ear, "It's so good to look at a man like that," Madeline again felt the surprise, only this time the accompaniment was a vague pleasure rather than annoyance. Helen and Dorothy were flirts, one deliberate and skilled, the other unconscious and natural. Edith Wayne, occasionally—and Madeline reflected that the occasions were infrequent—admired a man sincerely. Just here Madeline might have fallen into a somewhat revealing state of mind if it had not been for the fact that she believed Stewart was only an object of deep interest to her, not as a man, but as a part of this wild and wonderful West which was claiming her. So she did not inquire of herself why Helen's coquetry and Dorothy's languishing allurement annoyed her, or why Edith's eloquent smile and words had pleased her. She got as far, however, as to think scornfully how Helen and Dorothy would welcome and meet a flirtation with this cowboy and then go back home and forget him as utterly as if he had never existed. She wondered, too, with a curious twist of feeling that was almost eagerness, how the cowboy would meet their advances. Obviously the situation was unfair to him; and if by some strange accident he escaped unscathed by Dorothy's beautiful eyes he would never be able to withstand Helen's subtle and fascinating and imperious personality.

They returned to camp in the cool of the evening and made merry round a blazing camp-fire. But Madeline's guests soon succumbed to the persistent and irresistible desire to sleep.

Then Madeline went to bed with Florence under the pine-tree. Russ lay upon one side and Tartar upon the other. The cool night breeze swept over her, fanning her face, waving her hair. It was not strong enough to make any sound through the branches, but it stirred a faint, silken rustle in the long grass. The coyotes began their weird bark and howl. Russ raised his head to growl at their impudence.

Madeline faced upward, and it seemed to her that under those wonderful white stars she would never be able to go to sleep. They blinked down through the black-barred, delicate crisscross of pine foliage, and they looked so big and so close. Then she gazed away to open space, where an expanse of sky glittered with stars, and the longer she gazed the larger they grew and the more she saw.

It was her belief that she had come to love all the physical things from which sensations of beauty and mystery and strength poured into her responsive mind; but best of all she loved these Western stars, for they were to have something to do with her life, were somehow to influence her destiny.

For a few days the prevailing features of camp life for Madeline's guests were sleep and rest. Dorothy Coombs slept through twenty-four hours, and then was so difficult to awaken that for a while her friends were alarmed. Helen almost fell asleep while eating and talking. The men were more visibly affected by the mountain air than the women. Castleton, however, would not succumb to the strange drowsiness while he had a chance to prowl around with a gun.

This languorous spell disappeared presently, and then the days were full of life and action. Mrs. Beck and Bobby and Boyd, however, did not go in for anything very strenuous. Edith Wayne, too, preferred to walk through the groves or sit upon the grassy promontory. It was Helen and Dorothy who wanted to explore the crags and canyons, and when they could not get the others to accompany them they went alone, giving the cowboy guides many a long climb.

Necessarily, of course, Madeline and her guests were now thrown much in company with the cowboys. And the party grew to be like one big family. Her friends not only adapted themselves admirably to the situation, but came to revel in it. As for Madeline, she saw that outside of a certain proclivity of the cowboys to be gallant and on dress-parade and alive to possibilities of fun and excitement, they were not greatly different from what they were at all times. If there were a leveling process here it was made by her friends coming down to meet the Westerners. Besides, any class of people would tend to grow natural in such circumstances and environment.

Madeline found the situation one of keen and double interest for her. If before she had cared to study her cowboys, particularly Stewart, now, with the contrasts afforded by her guests, she felt by turns she was amused and mystified and perplexed and saddened, and then again subtly pleased.

Monty, once he had overcome his shyness, became a source of delight to Madeline, and, for that matter, to everybody. Monty had suddenly discovered that he was a success among the ladies. Either he was exalted to heroic heights by this knowledge or he made it appear so. Dorothy had been his undoing, and in justice to her Madeline believed her innocent. Dorothy thought Monty hideous to look at, and, accordingly, if he had been a hero a hundred times and had saved a hundred poor little babies' lives, he could not have interested her. Monty followed her around, reminding her, she told Madeline, of a little adoring dog one moment and the next of a huge, devouring gorilla.

Nels and Nick stalked at Helen's heels like grenadiers on duty, and if she as much as dropped her glove they almost came to blows to see who should pick it up.

In a way Castleton was the best feature of the camping party. He was such an absurd-looking little man, and his abilities were at such tremendous odds with what might have been expected of him from his looks. He could ride, tramp, climb, shoot. He liked to help around the camp, and the cowboys could not keep him from it. He had an insatiable desire to do things that were new to him. The cowboys played innumerable tricks upon him, not one of which he ever discovered. He was serious, slow in speech and action, and absolutely imperturbable. If imperturbability could ever be good humor, then he was always good-humored. Presently the cowboys began to understand him, and then to like him. When they liked a man it meant something. Madeline had been sorry more than once to see how little the cowboys chose to speak to Boyd Harvey. With Castleton, however, they actually became friends. They did not know it, and certainly such a thing never occurred to him; all the same, it was a fact. And it grew solely out of the truth that the Englishman was manly in the only way cowboys could have interpreted manliness. When, after innumerable attempts, he succeeded in throwing the diamond-hitch on a pack-horse the cowboys began to respect him. Castleton needed only one more accomplishment to claim their hearts, and he kept trying that—to ride a bucking bronco. One of the cowboys had a bronco that they called Devil. Every day for a week Devil threw the Englishman all over the park, ruined his clothes, bruised him, and finally kicked him. Then the cowboys solicitously tried to make Castleton give up; and this was remarkable enough, for the spectacle of an English lord on a bucking bronco was one that any Westerner would have ridden a thousand miles to see. Whenever Devil threw Castleton the cowboys went into spasms. But Castleton did not know the meaning of the word fail, and there came a day when Devil could not throw him. Then it was a singular sight to see the men line up to shake hands with the cool Englishman. Even Stewart, who had watched from the background, came forward with a warm and pleasant smile on his dark face. When Castleton went to his tent there was much characteristic cowboy talk, and this time vastly different from the former persiflage.

"By Gawd!" ejaculated Monty Price, who seemed to be the most amazed and elated of them all. "Thet's the fust Englishman I ever seen! He's orful deceivin' to look at, but I know now why England rules the wurrld. Jest take a peek at thet bronco. His spirit is broke. Rid by a leetle English dook no bigger 'n a grasshopper! Fellers, if it hain't dawned on you yit, let Monty Price give you a hunch. There's no flies on Castleton. An' I'll bet a million steers to a rawhide rope thet next he'll be throwin' a gun as good as Nels."

It was a distinct pleasure for Madeline to realize that she liked Castleton all the better for the traits brought out so forcibly by his association with the cowboys. On the other hand, she liked the cowboys better for something in them that contact with Easterners brought out. This was especially true in Stewart's case. She had been wholly wrong when she had imagined he would fall an easy victim to Dorothy's eyes and Helen's lures. He was kind, helpful, courteous, and watchful. But he had no sentiment. He did not see Dorothy's charms or feel Helen's fascination. And their efforts to captivate him were now so obvious that Mrs. Beck taunted them, and Edith smiled knowingly, and Bobby and Boyd made playful remarks. All of which cut Helen's pride and hurt Dorothy's vanity. They essayed open conquest of Stewart.

So it came about that Madeline unconsciously admitted the cowboy to a place in her mind never occupied by any other. The instant it occurred to her why he was proof against the wiles of the other women she drove that amazing and strangely disturbing thought from her. Nevertheless, as she was human, she could not help thinking and being pleased and enjoying a little the discomfiture of the two coquettes.

Moreover, from this thought of Stewart, and the watchfulness growing out of it she discovered more about him. He was not happy; he often paced up and down the grove at night; he absented himself from camp sometimes during the afternoon when Nels and Nick and Monty were there; he was always watching the trails, as if he expected to see some one come riding up. He alone of the cowboys did not indulge in the fun and talk around the camp-fire. He remained preoccupied and sad, and was always looking away into distance. Madeline had a strange sense of his guardianship over her; and, remembering Don Carlos, she imagined he worried a good deal over his charge, and, indeed, over the safety of all the party.

But if he did worry about possible visits from wandering guerrillas, why did he absent himself from camp? Suddenly into Madeline's inquisitive mind flashed a remembrance of the dark-eyed Mexican girl, Bonita, who had never been heard of since that night she rode Stewart's big horse out of El Cajon. The remembrance of her brought an idea. Perhaps Stewart had a rendezvous in the mountains, and these lonely trips of his were to meet Bonita. With the idea hot blood flamed into Madeline's cheek. Then she was amazed at her own feelings—amazed because her swiftest succeeding thought was to deny the idea—amazed that its conception had fired her cheek with shame. Then her old self, the one aloof from this red-blooded new self, gained control over her emotions.

But Madeline found that new-born self a creature of strange power to return and govern at any moment. She found it fighting loyally for what intelligence and wisdom told her was only her romantic conception of a cowboy. She reasoned: If Stewart were the kind of man her feminine skepticism wanted to make him, he would not have been so blind to the coquettish advances of Helen and Dorothy. He had once been—she did not want to recall what he had once been. But he had been uplifted. Madeline Hammond declared that. She was swayed by a strong, beating pride, and her instinctive woman's faith told her that he could not stoop to such dishonor. She reproached herself for having momentarily thought of it.

One afternoon a huge storm-cloud swooped out of the sky and enveloped the crags. It obscured the westering sun and laid a mantle of darkness over the park. Madeline was uneasy because several of her party, including Helen and Dorothy, had ridden off with the cowboys that afternoon and had not returned. Florence assured her that even if they did not get back before the storm broke there was no reason for apprehension. Nevertheless, Madeline sent for Stewart and asked him to go or send some one in search of them.

Perhaps half an hour later Madeline heard the welcome pattering of hoofs on the trail.

The big tent was brightly lighted by several lanterns. Edith and Florence were with her. It was so black outside that Madeline could not see a rod before her face. The wind was moaning in the trees, and big drops of rain were pelting upon the canvas.

Presently, just outside the door, the horses halted, and there was a sharp bustle of sound, such as would naturally result from a hurried dismounting and confusion in the dark. Mrs. Beck came running into the tent out of breath and radiant because they had beaten the storm. Helen entered next, and a little later came Dorothy, but long enough to make her entrance more noticeable. The instant Madeline saw Dorothy's blazing eyes she knew something unusual had happened. Whatever it was might have escaped comment had not Helen caught sight of Dorothy.

"Heavens, Dot, but you're handsome occasionally!" remarked Helen. "When you get some life in your face and eyes!"

Dorothy turned her face away from the others, and perhaps it was only accident that she looked into a mirror hanging on the tent wall. Swiftly she put her hand up to feel a wide red welt on her cheek. Dorothy had been assiduously careful of her soft, white skin, and here was an ugly mark marring its beauty.

"Look at that!" she cried, in distress. "My complexion's ruined!"

"How did you get such a splotch?" inquired Helen, going closer.

"I've been kissed!" exclaimed Dorothy, dramatically.

"What?" queried Helen, more curiously, while the others laughed.

"I've been kissed—hugged and kissed by one of those shameless cowboys! It was so pitch-dark outside I couldn't see a thing. And so noisy I couldn't hear. But somebody was trying to help me off my horse. My foot caught in the stirrup, and away I went—right into somebody's arms. Then he did it, the wretch! He hugged and kissed me in a most awful bearish manner. I couldn't budge a finger. I'm simply boiling with rage!"

When the outburst of mirth subsided Dorothy turned her big, dilated eyes upon Florence.

"Do these cowboys really take advantage of a girl when she's helpless and in the dark?"

"Of course they do," replied Florence, with her frank smile.

"Dot, what in the world could you expect?" asked Helen. "Haven't you been dying to be kissed?"

"No."

"Well, you acted like it, then. I never before saw you in a rage over being kissed."

"I—I wouldn't care so much if the brute hadn't scoured the skin off my face. He had whiskers as sharp and stiff as sandpaper. And when I jerked away he rubbed my cheek with them."

This revelation as to the cause of her outraged dignity almost prostrated her friends with glee.

"Dot, I agree with you; it's one thing to be kissed, and quite another to have your beauty spoiled," replied Helen, presently. "Who was this particular savage?"

"I don't know!" burst out Dorothy. "If I did I'd—I'd—"

Her eyes expressed the direful punishment she could not speak.

"Honestly now, Dot, haven't you the least idea who did it?" questioned Helen.

"I hope—I think it was Stewart," replied Dorothy.

"Ah! Dot, your hope is father to the thought. My dear, I'm sorry to riddle your little romance. Stewart did not—could not have been the offender or hero."

"How do you know he couldn't?" demanded Dorothy, flushing.

"Because he was clean-shaven to-day at noon, before we rode out. I remember perfectly how nice and smooth and brown his face looked."

"Oh, do you? Well, if your memory for faces is so good, maybe you can tell me which one of these cowboys wasn't clean-shaven."

"Merely a matter of elimination," replied Helen, merrily. "It was not Nick; it was not Nels; it was not Frankie. There was only one other cowboy with us, and he had a short, stubby growth of black beard, much like that cactus we passed on the trail."

"Oh, I was afraid of it," moaned Dorothy. "I knew he was going to do it. That horrible little smiling demon, Monty Price!"

A favorite lounging-spot of Madeline's was a shaded niche under the lee of crags facing the east. Here the outlook was entirely different from that on the western side. It was not red and white and glaring, nor so changeable that it taxed attention. This eastern view was one of the mountains and valleys, where, to be sure, there were arid patches; but the restful green of pine and fir was there, and the cool gray of crags. Bold and rugged indeed were these mountain features, yet they were companionably close, not immeasurably distant and unattainable like the desert. Here in the shade of afternoon Madeline and Edith would often lounge under a low-branched tree. Seldom they talked much, for it was afternoon and dreamy with the strange spell of this mountain fastness. There was smoky haze in the valleys, a fleecy cloud resting over the peaks, a sailing eagle in the blue sky, silence that was the unbroken silence of the wild heights, and a soft wind laden with incense of pine.

One afternoon, however, Edith appeared prone to talk seriously.

"Majesty, I must go home soon. I cannot stay out here forever. Are you going back with me?"

"Well, maybe," replied Madeline, thoughtfully. "I have considered it. I shall have to visit home some time. But this summer mother and father are going to Europe."

"See here, Majesty Hammond, do you intend to spend the rest of your life in this wilderness?" asked Edith, bluntly.

Madeline was silent.

"Oh, it is glorious! Don't misunderstand me, dear," went on Edith, earnestly, as she laid her hand on Madeline's. "This trip has been a revelation to me. I did not tell you, Majesty, that I was ill when I arrived. Now I'm well. So well! Look at Helen, too. Why, she was a ghost when we got here. Now she is brown and strong and beautiful. If it were for nothing else than this wonderful gift of health I would love the West. But I have come to love it for other things—even spiritual things. Majesty, I have been studying you. I see and feel what this life has made of you. When I came I wondered at your strength, your virility, your serenity, your happiness. And I was stunned. I wondered at the causes of your change. Now I know. You were sick of idleness, sick of uselessness, if not of society—sick of the horrible noises and smells and contacts one can no longer escape in the cities. I am sick of all that, too, and I could tell you many women of our kind who suffer in a like manner. You have done what many of us want to do, but have not the courage. You have left it. I am not blind to the splendid difference you have made in your life. I think I would have discovered, even if your brother had not told me, what good you have done to the Mexicans and cattlemen of your range. Then you have work to do. That is much the secret of your happiness, is it not? Tell me. Tell me something of what it means to you?"

"Work, of course, has much to do with any one's happiness," replied Madeline. "No one can be happy who has no work. As regards myself—for the rest I can hardly tell you. I have never tried to put it in words. Frankly, I believe, if I had not had money that I could not have found such contentment here. That is not in any sense a judgment against the West. But if I had been poor I could not have bought and maintained my ranch. Stillwell tells me there are many larger ranches than mine, but none just like it. Then I am almost paying my expenses out of my business. Think of that! My income, instead of being wasted, is mostly saved. I think—I hope I am useful. I have been of some little good to the Mexicans—eased the hardships of a few cowboys. For the rest, I think my life is a kind of dream. Of course my ranch and range are real, my cowboys are typical. If I were to tell you how I feel about them it would simply be a story of how Madeline Hammond sees the West. They are true to the West. It is I who am strange, and what I feel for them may be strange, too. Edith, hold to your own impressions."

"But, Majesty, my impressions have changed. At first I did not like the wind, the dust, the sun, the endless open stretches. But now I do like them. Where once I saw only terrible wastes of barren ground now I see beauty and something noble. Then, at first, your cowboys struck me as dirty, rough, loud, crude, savage—all that was primitive. I did not want them near me. I imagined them callous, hard men, their only joy a carouse with their kind. But I was wrong. I have changed. The dirt was only dust, and this desert dust is clean. They are still rough, loud, crude, and savage in my eyes, but with a difference. They are natural men. They are little children. Monty Price is one of nature's noblemen. The hard thing is to discover it. All his hideous person, all his actions and speech, are masks of his real nature. Nels is a joy, a simple, sweet, kindly, quiet man whom some woman should have loved. What would love have meant to him! He told me that no woman ever loved him except his mother, and he lost her when he was ten. Every man ought to be loved—especially such a man as Nels. Somehow his gun record does not impress me. I never could believe he killed a man. Then take your foreman, Stewart. He is a cowboy, his work and life the same as the others. But he has education and most of the graces we are in the habit of saying make a gentleman. Stewart is a strange fellow, just like this strange country. He's a man, Majesty, and I admire him. So, you see, my impressions are developing with my stay out here."

"Edith, I am so glad you told me that," replied Madeline, warmly.

"I like the country, and I like the men," went on Edith. "One reason I want to go home soon is because I am discontented enough at home now, without falling in love with the West. For, of course, Majesty, I would. I could not live out here. And that brings me to my point. Admitting all the beauty and charm and wholesomeness and good of this wonderful country, still it is no place for you, Madeline Hammond. You have your position, your wealth, your name, your family. You must marry. You must have children. You must not give up all that for a quixotic life in a wilderness."

"I am convinced, Edith, that I shall live here all the rest of my life."

"Oh, Majesty! I hate to preach this way. But I promised your mother I would talk to you. And the truth is I hate—I hate what I'm saying. I envy you your courage and wisdom. I know you have refused to marry Boyd Harvey. I could see that in his face. I believe you will refuse Castleton. Whom will you marry? What chance is there for a woman of your position to marry out here? What in the world will become of you?"

"Quien sabe?" replied Madeline, with a smile that was almost sad.

Not so many hours after this conversation with Edith, Madeline sat with Boyd Harvey upon the grassy promontory overlooking the west, and she listened once again to his suave courtship.

Suddenly she turned to him and said, "Boyd, if I married you would you be willing—glad to spend the rest of your life here in the West?"

"Majesty!" he exclaimed. There was amaze in the voice usually so even and well modulated—amaze in the handsome face usually so indifferent. Her question had startled him. She saw him look down the iron-gray cliffs, over the barren slopes and cedared ridges, beyond the cactus-covered foothills to the grim and ghastly desert. Just then, with its red veils of sunlit dust-clouds, its illimitable waste of ruined and upheaved earth, it was a sinister spectacle.

"No," he replied, with a tinge of shame in his cheek. Madeline said no more, nor did he speak. She was spared the pain of refusing him, and she imagined he would never ask her again. There was both relief and regret in the conviction. Humiliated lovers seldom made good friends.

It was impossible not to like Boyd Harvey. The thought of that, and why she could not marry him, concentrated her never-satisfied mind upon the man. She looked at him, and she thought of him.

He was handsome, young, rich, well born, pleasant, cultivated—he was all that made a gentleman of his class. If he had any vices she had not heard of them. She knew he had no thirst for drink or craze for gambling. He was considered a very desirable and eligible young man. Madeline admitted all this.

Then she thought of things that were perhaps exclusively her own strange ideas. Boyd Harvey's white skin did not tan even in this southwestern sun and wind. His hands were whiter than her own, and as soft. They were really beautiful, and she remembered what care he took of them. They were a proof that he never worked. His frame was tall, graceful, elegant. It did not bear evidence of ruggedness. He had never indulged in a sport more strenuous than yachting. He hated effort and activity. He rode horseback very little, disliked any but moderate motoring, spent much time in Newport and Europe, never walked when he could help it, and had no ambition unless it were to pass the days pleasantly. If he ever had any sons they would be like him, only a generation more toward the inevitable extinction of his race.

Madeline returned to camp in just the mood to make a sharp, deciding contrast. It happened—fatefully, perhaps—that the first man she saw was Stewart. He had just ridden into camp, and as she came up he explained that he had gone down to the ranch for the important mail about which she had expressed anxiety.

"Down and back in one day!" she exclaimed.

"Yes," he replied. "It wasn't so bad."

"But why did you not send one of the boys, and let him make the regular two-day trip?"

"You were worried about your mail," he answered, briefly, as he delivered it. Then he bent to examine the fetlocks of his weary horse.

It was midsummer now, Madeline reflected and exceedingly hot and dusty on the lower trail. Stewart had ridden down the mountain and back again in twelve hours. Probably no horse in the outfit, except his big black or Majesty, could have stood that trip. And his horse showed the effects of a grueling day. He was caked with dust and lame and weary.

Stewart looked as if he had spared the horse his weight on many a mile of that rough ascent. His boots were evidence of it. His heavy flannel shirt, wet through with perspiration, adhered closely to his shoulders and arms, so that every ripple of muscle plainly showed. His face was black, except round the temples and forehead, where it was bright red. Drops of sweat, running off his blackened hands dripped to the ground. He got up from examining the lame foot, and then threw off the saddle. The black horse snorted and lunged for the watering-pool. Stewart let him drink a little, then with iron arms dragged him away. In this action the man's lithe, powerful form impressed Madeline with a wonderful sense of muscular force. His brawny wrist was bare; his big, strong hand, first clutching the horse's mane, then patting his neck, had a bruised knuckle, and one finger was bound up. That hand expressed as much gentleness and thoughtfulness for the horse as it had strength to drag him back from too much drinking at a dangerous moment.

Stewart was a combination of fire, strength, and action. These attributes seemed to cling about him. There was something vital and compelling in his presence. Worn and spent and drawn as he was from the long ride, he thrilled Madeline with his potential youth and unused vitality and promise of things to be, red-blooded deeds, both of flesh and spirit. In him she saw the strength of his forefathers unimpaired. The life in him was marvelously significant. The dust, the dirt, the sweat, the soiled clothes, the bruised and bandaged hand, the brawn and bone—these had not been despised by the knights of ancient days, nor by modern women whose eyes shed soft light upon coarse and bloody toilers.

Madeline Hammond compared the man of the East with the man of the West; and that comparison was the last parting regret for her old standards.

❧ 17 ❧

THE LOST MINE OF THE PADRES

In the cool, starry evenings the campers sat around a blazing fire and told and listened to stories thrillingly fitted to the dark crags and the wild solitude.

Monty Price had come to shine brilliantly as a storyteller. He was an atrocious liar, but this fact would not have been evident to his enthralled listeners if his cowboy comrades, in base jealousy, had not betrayed him. The truth about his remarkable fabrications, however, had not become known to Castleton, solely because of the Englishman's obtuseness. And there was another thing much stranger than this and quite as amusing. Dorothy Coombs knew Monty was a liar; but she was so fascinated by the glittering, basilisk eyes he riveted upon her, so taken in by his horrible tales of blood, that despite her knowledge she could not help believing them.

Manifestly Monty was very proud of his suddenly acquired gift. Formerly he had hardly been known to open his lips in the presence of strangers. Monty had developed more than one singular and hitherto unknown trait since his supremacy at golf had revealed his possibilities. He was as sober and vain and pompous about his capacity for lying as about anything else. Some of the cowboys were jealous of him because he held the attention and, apparently, the admiration of the ladies; and Nels was jealous, not because Monty made himself out to be a wonderful gun-man, but because Monty could tell a story. Nels really had been the hero of a hundred fights; he had never been known to talk about them; but Dorothy's eyes and Helen's smile had somehow upset his modesty. Whenever Monty would begin to talk Nels would growl and knock his pipe on a log, and make it appear he could not stay and listen, though he never really left the charmed circle of the camp-fire. Wild horses could not have dragged him away.

One evening at twilight, as Madeline was leaving her tent, she encountered Monty. Evidently, he had way-laid her. With the most mysterious of signs and whispers he led her a little aside.

"Miss Hammond, I'm makin' bold to ask a favor of you," he said.

Madeline smiled her willingness.

322

"To-night, when they've all shot off their chins an' it's quiet-like, I want you to ask me, jest this way, 'Monty, seein' as you've hed more adventures than all them cow-punchers put together, tell us about the most turrible time you ever hed.' Will you ask me, Miss Hammond, jest kinda sincere like?"

"Certainly I will, Monty," she replied.

His dark, seared face had no more warmth than a piece of cold, volcanic rock, which it resembled. Madeline appreciated how monstrous Dorothy found this burned and distorted visage, how deformed the little man looked to a woman of refined sensibilities. It was difficult for Madeline to look into his face. But she saw behind the blackened mask. And now she saw in Monty's deep eyes a spirit of pure fun.

So, true to her word, Madeline remembered at an opportune moment, when conversation had hushed and only the long, dismal wail of coyotes broke the silence, to turn toward the little cowboy.

"Monty," she said, and paused for effect—"Monty, seeing that you have had more adventures than all the cowboys together, tell us about the most terrible time you ever had."

Monty appeared startled at the question that fastened all eyes upon him. He waved a deprecatory hand.

"Aw, Miss Hammond, thankin' you all modest-like fer the compliment, I'll hev to refuse," replied Monty, laboring in distress. "It's too harrowin' fer tender-hearted gurls to listen to."

"Go on?" cried everybody except the cowboys. Nels began to nod his head as if he, as well as Monty, understood human nature. Dorothy hugged her knees with a kind of shudder. Monty had fastened the hypnotic eyes upon her. Castleton ceased smoking, adjusted his eyeglass, and prepared to listen in great earnestness.

Monty changed his seat to one where the light from the blazing logs fell upon his face; and he appeared plunged into melancholy and profound thought.

"Now I tax myself, I can't jest decide which was the orfulest time I ever hed," he said, reflectively.

Here Nels blew forth an immense cloud of smoke, as if he desired to hide himself from sight. Monty pondered, and then when the smoke rolled away he turned to Nels.

"See hyar, old pard, me an' you seen somethin' of each other in the Panhandle, more 'n thirty years ago—"

"Which we didn't," interrupted Nels, bluntly. "Shore you can't make me out an ole man."

"Mebbe it wasn't so darn long. Anyhow, Nels, you recollect them three hoss-thieves I hung all on one cottonwood-tree, an' likewise thet boo-tiful blond gurl I rescooed from a band of cutthroats who murdered her paw, ole Bill Warren, the buffalo-hunter? Now, which of them two scraps was the turriblest, in your idee?"

"Monty, my memory's shore bad," replied the unimpeachable Nels.

"Tell us about the beautiful blonde," cried at least three of the ladies. Dorothy, who had suffered from nightmare because of a former story of hanging men on trees, had voicelessly appealed to Monty to spare her more of that.

"All right, we'll hev the blond gurl," said Monty, settling back, "though I ain't thinkin' her story is most turrible of the two, an' it'll rake over tender affections long slumberin' in my breast."

As he paused there came a sharp, rapping sound. This appeared to be Nels knocking the ashes out of his pipe on a stump—a true indication of the passing of content from that jealous cowboy.

"It was down in the Panhandle, 'way over in the west end of thet Comanche huntin'-

ground, an' all the redskins an' outlaws in thet country were hidin' in the river-bottoms, an' chasin' some of the last buffalo herds thet hed wintered in there. I was a young buck them days, an' purty much of a desperado, I'm thinkin'. Though of all the seventeen notches on my gun—an' each notch meant a man killed face to face—there was only one thet I was ashamed of. Thet one was fer an express messenger who I hit on the head most unprofessional like, jest because he wouldn't hand over a leetle package. I hed the kind of a reputashun thet made all the fellers in saloons smile an' buy drinks.

"Well, I dropped into a place named Taylor's Bend, an' was peaceful standin' to the bar when three cow-punchers come in, an', me bein' with my back turned, they didn't recognize me an' got playful. I didn't stop drinkin', an' I didn't turn square round; but when I stopped shootin' under my arm the saloon-keeper hed to go over to the sawmill an' fetch a heap of sawdust to cover up what was left of them three cow-punchers, after they was hauled out. You see, I was rough them days, an' would shoot ears off an' noses off an' hands off; when in later days I'd jest kill a man quick, same as Wild Bill.

"News drifts into town thet night thet a gang of cut-throats hed murdered ole Bill Warren an' carried off his gurl. I gathers up a few good gun-men, an' we rid out an' down the river-bottom, to an ole log cabin, where the outlaws hed a rondevoo. We rid up boldlike, an' made a hell of a racket. Then the gang began to throw lead from the cabin, an' we all hunted cover. Fightin' went on all night. In the mornin' all my outfit was killed but two, an' they was shot up bad. We fought all day without eatin' or drinkin', except some whisky I hed, an' at night I was on the job by my lonesome.

"Bein' bunged up some myself, I laid off an' went down to the river to wash the blood off, tie up my wounds, an' drink a leetle. While I was down there along comes one of the cutthroats with a bucket. Instead of gettin' water he got lead, an' as he was about to croak he tells me a whole bunch of outlaws was headin' in there, doo to-morrer. An' if I wanted to rescoo the gurl I hed to be hurryin'. There was five fellers left in the cabin.

"I went back to the thicket where I hed left my hoss, an' loaded up with two more guns an' another belt, an' busted a fresh box of shells. If I recollect proper, I got some cigarettes, too. Well, I mozied back to the cabin. It was a boo-tiful moonshiny night, an' I wondered if ole Bill's gun was as purty as I'd heerd. The grass growed long round the cabin, an' I crawled up to the door without startin' anythin'. Then I figgered. There was only one door in thet cabin, an' it was black dark inside. I jest grabbed open the door an' slipped in quick. It worked all right. They heerd me, but hedn't been quick enough to ketch me in the light of the door. Of course there was some shots, but I ducked too quick, an' changed my position.

"Ladies an' gentlemen, thet there was some dool by night. An' I wasn't often in the place where they shot. I was most wonderful patient, an' jest waited until one of them darned ruffians would get so nervous he'd hev to hunt me up. When mornin' come there they was all piled up on the floor, all shot to pieces. I found the gurl. Purty! Say, she was boo-tiful. We went down to the river, where she begun to bathe my wounds. I'd collected a dozen more or so, an' the sight of tears in her lovely eyes, an' my blood a-stainin' of her little hands, jest nat'rally wakened a trembly spell in my heart. I seen she was took the same way, an' thet settled it.

"We was comin' up from the river, an' I hed jest straddled my hoss, with the gurl behind, when we run right into thet cutthroat gang thet was doo about then. Bein' some handicapped, I couldn't drop more 'n one gun-round of them, an' then I hed to slope. The whole gang follered me, an' some miles out chased me over a ridge right into a big herd of buffalo. Before I knowed what was what thet herd broke into a stampede, with me in the middle. Purty soon the buffalo closed in tight. I knowed I was in some peril then. But the gurl trusted me somethin' pitiful. I seen again thet she hed fell in love with me. I could tell from the way she hugged me an' yelled. Before long I was some put to it to keep my hoss on his feet. Far as I could see was dusty, black, bobbin', shaggy humps. A huge cloud of dust went along over our heads. The roar of tramplin' hoofs was turrible. My hoss weakened, went down, an' was carried along a leetle while I slipped off with the gurl on to the backs of the buffalo.

"Ladies, I ain't denyin' that then Monty Price was some scairt. Fust time in my life! But the trustin' face of thet boo-tiful gurl, as she lay in my arms an' hugged me an' yelled, made my spirit leap like a shootin' star. I just began to jump from buffalo to buffalo. I must hev jumped a mile of them bobbin' backs before I come to open places. An' here's where I performed the greatest stunts of my life. I hed on my big spurs, an' I jest sit down an' rid an' spurred till thet pertickler buffalo I was on got near another, an' then I'd flop over. Thusly I got to the edge of the herd, tumbled off'n the last one, an' rescooed the gurl.

"Well, as my memory takes me back, thet was a most affectin' walk home to the little town where she lived. But she wasn't troo to me, an' married another feller. I was too much a sport to kill him. But thet low-down trick rankled in my breast. Gurls is strange. I've never stopped wonderin' how any gurl who has been hugged an' kissed by one man could marry another. But matoor experience teaches me thet sich is the case."

The cowboys roared; Helen and Mrs. Beck and Edith laughed till they cried; Madeline found repression absolutely impossible; Dorothy sat hugging her knees, her horror at the story no greater than at Monty's unmistakable reference to her and to the fickleness of women; and Castleton for the first time appeared to be moved out of his imperturbability, though not in any sense by humor. Indeed, when he came to notice it, he was dumfounded by the mirth.

"By Jove! you Americans are an extraordinary people," he said. "I don't see anything blooming funny in Mr. Price's story of his adventure. By Jove! that was a bally warm occasion. Mr. Price, when you speak of being frightened for the only time in your life, I appreciate what you mean. I have experienced that. I was frightened once."

"Dook, I wouldn't hev thought it of you," replied Monty. "I'm sure tolerable curious to hear about it."

Madeline and her friends dared not break the spell, for fear that the Englishman might hold to his usual modest reticence. He had explored in Brazil, seen service in the Boer War, hunted in India and Africa—matters of experience of which he never spoke. Upon this occasion, however, evidently taking Monty's recital word for word as literal truth, and excited by it into a Homeric mood, he might tell a story. The cowboys almost fell upon their knees in their importunity. There was a suppressed eagerness in their solicitations, a hint of something that meant more than desire, great as it was, to hear a story told by an English lord. Madeline divined instantly that the cowboys had suddenly fancied that Castleton was not the dense and easily fooled person they had made such game of; that he had played his part well; that he was having fun at their expense; that he meant to tell a story, a lie which would simply dwarf Monty's. Nels's keen, bright expectation suggested how he would welcome the joke turned upon Monty. The slow closing of Monty's cavernous smile, the gradual sinking of his proud bearing, the doubt with which he began to regard Castleton— these were proofs of his fears.

"I have faced charging tigers and elephants in India, and charging rhinos and lions in Africa," began Castleton, his quick and fluent speech so different from the drawl of his ordinary conversation; "but I never was frightened but once. It will not do to hunt those wild beasts if you are easily balled up. This adventure I have in mind happened in British East

Africa, in Uganda. I was out with safari, and we were in a native district much infested by man-eating lions. Perhaps I may as well state that man-eaters are very different from ordinary lions. They are always matured beasts, and sometimes—indeed, mostly—are old. They become man-eaters most likely by accident or necessity. When old they find it more difficult to make a kill, being slower, probably, and with poorer teeth. Driven by hunger, they stalk and kill a native, and, once having tasted human blood, they want no other. They become absolutely fearless and terrible in their attacks.

"The natives of this village near where we camped were in a terrorized state owing to depredations of two or more man-eaters. The night of our arrival a lion leaped a stockade fence, seized a native from among others sitting round a fire, and leaped out again, carrying the screaming fellow away into the darkness. I determined to kill these lions, and made a permanent camp in the village for that purpose. By day I sent beaters into the brush and rocks of the river-valley, and by night I watched. Every night the lions visited us, but I did not see one. I discovered that when they roared around the camp they were not so liable to attack as when they were silent. It was indeed remarkable how silently they could stalk a man. They could creep through a thicket so dense you would not believe a rabbit could get through, and do it without the slightest sound. Then, when ready to charge, they did so with terrible onslaught and roar. They leaped right into a circle of fires, tore down huts, even dragged natives from the low trees. There was no way to tell at which point they would make an attack.

"After ten days or more of this I was worn out by loss of sleep. And one night, when tired out with watching, I fell asleep. My gun-bearer was alone in the tent with me. A terrible roar awakened me, then an unearthly scream pierced right into my ears. I always slept with my rifle in my hands, and, grasping it, I tried to rise. But I could not for the reason that a lion was standing over me. Then I lay still. The screams of my gun-bearer told me that the lion had him. I was fond of this fellow and wanted to save him. I thought it best, however, not to move while the lion stood over me. Suddenly he stepped, and I felt poor Luki's feet dragging across me. He screamed, 'Save me, master!' And instinctively I grasped at him and caught his foot. The lion walked out of the tent dragging me as I held to Luki's foot. The night was bright moonlight. I could see the lion distinctly. He was a huge, black-maned brute, and he held Luki by the shoulder. The poor lad kept screaming frightfully. The man-eater must have dragged me forty yards before he became aware of a double incumbrance to his progress. Then he halted and turned. By Jove! he made a devilish fierce object with his shaggy, massive head, his green-fire eyes, and his huge jaws holding Luki. I let go of Luki's foot and bethought myself of the gun. But as I lay there on my side, before attempting to rise, I made a horrible discovery. I did not have my rifle at all. I had Luki's iron spear, which he always had near him. My rifle had slipped out of the hollow of my arm, and when the lion awakened me, in my confusion I picked up Luki's spear instead. The bloody brute dropped Luki and uttered a roar that shook the ground. It was then I felt frightened. For an instant I was almost paralyzed. The lion meant to charge, and in one spring he could reach me. Under circumstances like those a man can think many things in little time. I knew to try to run would be fatal. I remembered how strangely lions had been known to act upon occasion. One had been frightened by an umbrella; one had been frightened by a blast from a cow-horn; another had been frightened by a native who in running from one lion ran right at the other which he had not seen. Accordingly, I wondered if I could frighten the lion that meant to leap at me. Acting upon wild impulse, I prodded him in the hind quarters with the spear. Ladies and gentlemen, I am a blooming idiot if that lion did not cower like a whipped dog, put his tail down, and begin to slink away. Quick to see my chance, I jumped up yelling, and made after him, prodding him again. He let out a bellow such as you could imagine would come from an outraged king of beasts. I prodded again, and then he loped off. I found Luki not badly hurt. In fact, he got well. But I've never forgotten that scare."

When Castleton finished his narrative there was a trenchant silence. All eyes were upon Monty. He looked beaten, disgraced, a disgusted man. Yet there shone from his face a wonderful admiration for Castleton.

"Dook, you win!" he said; and, dropping his head, he left the camp-fire circle with the manner of a deposed emperor.

Then the cowboys exploded. The quiet, serene, low-voiced Nels yelled like a madman and he stood upon his head. All the other cowboys went through marvelous contortions. Mere noise was insufficient to relieve their joy at what they considered the fall and humiliation of the tyrant Monty.

The Englishman stood there and watched them in amused consternation. They baffled his understanding. Plain it was to Madeline and her friends that Castleton had told the simple truth. But never on the earth, or anywhere else, could Nels and his comrades have been persuaded that Castleton had not lied deliberately to humble their great exponent of Ananias.

Everybody seemed reluctant to break the camp-fire spell. The logs had burned out to a great heap of opal and gold and red coals, in the heart of which quivered a glow alluring to the spirit of dreams. As the blaze subsided the shadows of the pines encroached darker and darker upon the circle of fading light. A cool wind fanned the embers, whipped up flakes of white ashes, and moaned through the trees. The wild yelps of coyotes were dying in the distance, and the sky was a wonderful dark-blue dome spangled with white stars.

"What a perfect night!" said Madeline. "This is a night to understand the dream, the mystery, the wonder of the Southwest. Florence, for long you have promised to tell us the story of the lost mine of the padres. It will give us all pleasure, make us understand something of the thrall in which this land held the Spaniards who discovered it so many years ago. It will be especially interesting now, because this mountain hides somewhere under its crags the treasures of the lost mine of the padres."

"In the sixteenth century," Florence began, in her soft, slow voice so suited to the nature of the legend, "a poor young padre of New Spain was shepherding his goats upon a hill when the Virgin appeared before him. He prostrated himself at her feet, and when he looked up she was gone. But upon the maguey plant near where she had stood there were golden ashes of a strange and wonderful substance. He took the incident as a good omen and went again to the hilltop. Under the maguey had sprung up slender stalks of white, bearing delicate gold flowers, and as these flowers waved in the wind a fine golden dust, as fine as powdered ashes, blew away toward the north. Padre Juan was mystified, but believed that great fortune attended upon him and his poor people. So he went again and again to the hilltop in hope that the Virgin would appear to him.

"One morning, as the sun rose gloriously, he looked across the windy hill toward the waving grass and golden flowers under the maguey, and he saw the Virgin beckoning to him. Again he fell upon his knees; but she lifted him and gave him of the golden flowers, and bade him leave his home and people to follow where these blowing golden ashes led. There he would find gold—pure gold—wonderful fortune to bring back to his poor people to build a church for them, and a city.

"Padre Juan took the flowers and left his home, promising to return, and he traveled northward over the hot and dusty desert, through the mountain passes, to a new country where fierce and warlike Indians menaced his life. He was gentle and good, and of a persuasive speech. Moreover, he was young and handsome of person. The Indians were Apaches, and among them he became a missionary, while always he was searching for the flowers of gold. He heard of gold lying in pebbles upon the mountain slopes, but he never found any. A few of the Apaches he converted; the most of them, however, were prone to be hostile to him and his religion. But Padre Juan prayed and worked on.

"There came a time when the old Apache chief, imagining the padre had designs upon his influence with the tribe, sought to put him to death by fire. The chief's daughter, a beautiful, dark-eyed maiden, secretly loved Juan and believed in his mission, and she interceded for his life and saved him. Juan fell in love with her. One day she came to him wearing golden flowers in her dark hair, and as the wind blew the flowers a golden dust blew upon it. Juan asked her where to find such flowers, and she told him that upon a certain day she would take him to the mountain to look for them. And upon the day she led up to the mountain-top from which they could see beautiful valleys and great trees and cool waters. There at the top of a wonderful slope that looked down upon the world, she showed Juan the flowers. And Juan found gold in such abundance that he thought he would go out of his mind. Dust of gold! Grains of gold! Pebbles of gold! Rocks of gold! He was rich beyond all dreams. He remembered the Virgin and her words. He must return to his people and build their church, and the great city that would bear his name.

"But Juan tarried. Always he was going manana. He loved the dark-eyed Apache girl so well that he could not leave her. He hated himself for his infidelity to his Virgin, to his people. He was weak and false, a sinner. But he could not go, and he gave himself up to love of the Indian maiden.

"The old Apache chief discovered the secret love of his daughter and the padre. And, fierce in his anger, he took her up into the mountains and burned her alive and cast her ashes upon the wind. He did not kill Padre Juan. He was too wise, and perhaps too cruel, for he saw the strength of Juan's love. Besides, many of his tribe had learned much from the Spaniard.

"Padre Juan fell into despair. He had no desire to live. He faded and wasted away. But before he died he went to the old Indians who had burned the maiden, and he begged them, when he was dead, to burn his body and to cast his ashes to the wind from that wonderful slope, where they would blow away to mingle forever with those of his Indian sweetheart.

"The Indians promised, and when Padre Juan died they burned his body and took his ashes to the mountain heights and cast them to the wind, where they drifted and fell to mix with the ashes of the Indian girl he had loved.

"Years passed. More padres traveled across the desert to the home of the Apaches, and they heard the story of Juan. Among their number was a padre who in his youth had been one of Juan's people. He set forth to find Juan's grave, where he believed he would also find the gold. And he came back with pebbles of gold and flowers that shed a golden dust, and he told a wonderful story. He had climbed and climbed into the mountains, and he had come to a wonderful slope under the crags. That slope was yellow with golden flowers. When he touched them golden ashes drifted from them and blew down among the rocks. There the padre found dust of gold, grains of gold, pebbles of gold, rocks of gold.

"Then all the padres went into the mountains. But the discoverer of the mine lost his way. They searched and searched until they were old and gray, but never found the wonderful slope and flowers that marked the grave and the mine of Padre Juan.

"In the succeeding years the story was handed down from father to son. But of the many who hunted for the lost mine of the padres there was never a Mexican or an Apache. For the Apache the mountain slopes were haunted by the spirit of an Indian maiden who had been false to her tribe and forever accursed. For the Mexican the mountain slopes were haunted by the spirit of the false padre who rolled stones upon the heads of those adventurers who sought to find his grave and his accursed gold."

18

BONITA

FLORENCE'S STORY of the lost mine fired Madeline's guests with the fever for gold-hunting. But after they had tried it a few times and the glamour of the thing wore off they gave up and remained in camp. Having exhausted all the resources of the mountain, such that had interest for them, they settled quietly down for a rest, which Madeline knew would soon end in a desire for civilized comforts. They were almost tired of roughing it. Helen's discontent manifested itself in her remark, "I guess nothing is going to happen, after all."

Madeline awaited their pleasure in regard to the breaking of camp; and meanwhile, as none of them cared for more exertion, she took her walks without them, sometimes accompanied by one of the cowboys, always by the stag-hounds. These walks furnished her exceeding pleasure. And, now that the cowboys would talk to her without reserve, she grew fonder of listening to their simple stories. The more she knew of them the more she doubted the wisdom of shut-in lives. Companionship with Nels and most of the cowboys was in its effect like that of the rugged pines and crags and the untainted wind. Humor, their predominant trait when a person grew to know them, saved Madeline from finding their hardness trying. They were dreamers, as all men who lived lonely lives in the wilds were dreamers.

The cowboys all had secrets. Madeline learned some of them. She marveled most at the strange way in which they hid emotions, except of violence of mirth and temper so easily aroused. It was all the more remarkable in view of the fact that they felt intensely over little things to which men of the world were blind and dead. Madeline had to believe that a hard and perilous life in a barren and wild country developed great principles in men. Living close to earth, under the cold, bleak peaks, on the dust-veiled desert, men grew like the nature that developed them—hard, fierce, terrible, perhaps, but big—big with elemental force.

But one day, while out walking alone, before she realized it she had gone a long way down a dim trail winding among the rocks. It was the middle of a summer afternoon, and all about her were shadows of the crags crossing the sunlit patches. The quiet was undisturbed. She went on and on, not blind to the fact that she was perhaps going too far from camp, but risking it because she was sure of her way back, and enjoying the wild, craggy recesses that were new to her. Finally she came out upon a bank that broke abruptly into a beautiful little glade. Here she sat down to rest before undertaking the return trip.

Suddenly Russ, the keener of the stag-hounds, raised his head and growled. Madeline feared he might have scented a mountain-lion or wildcat. She quieted him and carefully looked around. To each side was an irregular line of massive blocks of stone that had weathered from the crags. The little glade was open and grassy, with here a pine-tree, there a boulder. The outlet seemed to go down into a wilderness of canyons and ridges. Looking in this direction, Madeline saw the slight, dark figure of a woman coming stealthily along under the pines. Madeline was amazed, then a little frightened, for that stealthy walk from tree to tree was suggestive of secrecy, if nothing worse.

Presently the woman was joined by a tall man who carried a package, which he gave to her. They came on up the glade and appeared to be talking earnestly. In another moment Madeline recognized Stewart. She had no greater feeling of surprise than had at first been hers. But for the next moment she scarcely thought at all—merely watched the couple approaching. In a flash came back her former curiosity as to Stewart's strange absences from camp, and then with the return of her doubt of him the recognition of the woman. The small, dark head, the brown face, the big eyes—Madeline now saw distinctly—belonged to the Mexican girl Bonita. Stewart had met her there. This was the secret of his lonely trips, taken ever since he had come to work for Madeline. This secluded glade was a rendezvous. He had her hidden there.

Quietly Madeline arose, with a gesture to the dogs, and went back along the trail toward camp. Succeeding her surprise was a feeling of sorrow that Stewart's regeneration had not been complete. Sorrow gave place to insufferable distrust that while she had been romancing about this cowboy, dreaming of her good influence over him, he had been merely base. Somehow it stung her. Stewart had been nothing to her, she thought, yet she had been proud of him. She tried to revolve the thing, to be fair to him, when every instinctive tendency was to expel him, and all pertaining to him, from her thoughts. And her effort at sympathy, at extenuation, failed utterly before her pride. Exerting her will-power, she dismissed Stewart from her mind.

Madeline did not think of him again till late that afternoon, when, as she was leaving her tent to join several of her guests, Stewart appeared suddenly in her path.

"Miss Hammond, I saw your tracks down the trail," he began, eagerly, but his tone was easy and natural. "I'm thinking—well, maybe you sure got the idea—"

"I do not wish for an explanation," interrupted Madeline.

Stewart gave a slight start. His manner had a semblance of the old, cool audacity. As he looked down at her it subtly changed.

What effrontery, Madeline thought, to face her before her guests with an explanation of his conduct! Suddenly she felt an inward flash of fire that was pain, so strange, so incomprehensible, that her mind whirled. Then anger possessed her, not at Stewart, but at herself, that anything could rouse in her a raw emotion. She stood there, outwardly cold, serene, with level, haughty eyes upon Stewart; but inwardly she was burning with rage and shame.

"I'm sure not going to have you think—" He began passionately, but he broke off, and a slow, dull crimson blotted over the healthy red-brown of his neck and cheeks.

"What you do or think, Stewart, is no concern of mine."

"Miss—Miss Hammond! You don't believe—" faltered Stewart.

The crimson receded from his face, leaving it pale. His eyes were appealing. They had a kind of timid look that struck Madeline even in her anger. There was something boyish about him then. He took a step forward and reached out with his hand open-palmed in a gesture that was humble, yet held a certain dignity.

"But listen. Never mind now what you—you think about me. There's a good reason—"

"I have no wish to hear your reason."

"But you ought to," he persisted.

"Sir!"

Stewart underwent another swift change. He started violently. A dark tide shaded his face and a glitter leaped to his eyes. He took two long strides—loomed over her.

"I'm not thinking about myself," he thundered. "Will you listen?"

"No," she replied; and there was freezing hauteur in her voice. With a slight gesture of dismissal, unmistakable in its finality, she turned her back upon him. Then she joined her guests.

Stewart stood perfectly motionless. Then slowly he began to lift his right hand in which he held his sombrero. He swept it up and up high over his head. His tall form towered. With fierce suddenness he flung his sombrero down. He leaped at his black horse and dragged him to where his saddle lay. With one pitch he tossed the saddle upon the horse's back. His strong hands flashed at girths and straps. Every action was swift, decisive, fierce. Bounding for his bridle, which hung over a bush, he ran against a cowboy who awkwardly tried to avoid the onslaught.

"Get out of my way!" he yelled.

Then with the same savage haste he adjusted the bridle on his horse.

"Mebbe you better hold on a minnit, Gene, ole feller," said Monty Price.

"Monty, do you want me to brain you?" said Stewart, with the short, hard ring in his voice.

"Now, considerin' the high class of my brains, I oughter be real careful to keep 'em," replied Monty. "You can betcher life, Gene, I ain't goin' to git in front of you. But I jest says —Listen!"

Stewart raised his dark face. Everybody listened. And everybody heard the rapid beat of a horse's hoofs. The sun had set, but the park was light. Nels appeared down the trail, and his horse was running. In another moment he was in the circle, pulling his bay back to a sliding halt. He leaped off abreast of Stewart.

Madeline saw and felt a difference in Nels's presence.

"What's up, Gene?" he queried, sharply.

"I'm leaving camp," replied Stewart, thickly. His black horse began to stamp as Stewart grasped bridle and mane and kicked the stirrup round.

Nels's long arm shot out, and his hand fell upon Stewart, holding him down.

"Shore I'm sorry," said Nels, slowly. "Then you was goin' to hit the trail?"

"I am going to. Let go, Nels."

"Shore you ain't goin', Gene?"

"Let go, damn you!" cried Stewart, as he wrestled free.

"What's wrong?" asked Nels, lifting his hand again.

"Man! Don't touch me!"

Nels stepped back instantly. He seemed to become aware of Stewart's white, wild passion. Again Stewart moved to mount.

"Nels, don't make me forget we've been friends," he said.

"Shore I ain't fergettin'," replied Nels. "An' I resign my job right here an' now!"

His strange speech checked the mounting cowboy. Stewart stepped down from the stirrup. Then their hard faces were still and cold while their eyes locked glances.

Madeline was as much startled by Nels's speech as Stewart. Quick to note a change in these men, she now sensed one that was unfathomable.

"Resign?" questioned Stewart.

"Shore. What 'd you think I'd do under circumstances sich as has come up?"

"But see here, Nels, I won't stand for it."

"You're not my boss no more, an' I ain't beholdin' to Miss Hammond, neither. I'm my own boss, an' I'll do as I please. Sabe, senor?"

Nels's words were at variance with the meaning in his face.

"Gene, you sent me on a little scout down in the mountains, didn't you?" he continued.

"Yes, I did," replied Stewart, with a new sharpness in his voice.

"Wal, shore you was so good an' right in your figgerin', as opposed to mine, that I'm sick with admirin' of you. If you hedn't sent me—wal, I'm reckonin' somethin' might hev happened. As it is we're shore up against a hell of a proposition!"

How significant was the effect of his words upon all the cowboys! Stewart made a fierce and violent motion, terrible where his other motions had been but passionate. Monty leaped straight up into the air in a singular action as suggestive of surprise as it was of wild acceptance of menace. Like a stalking giant Nick Steele strode over to Nels and Stewart. The other cowboys rose silently, without a word.

Madeline and her guests, in a little group, watched and listened, unable to divine what all this strange talk and action meant.

"Hold on, Nels, they don't need to hear it," said Stewart, hoarsely, as he waved a hand toward Madeline's silent group.

"Wal, I'm sorry, but I reckon they'd as well know fust as last. Mebbe thet yearnin' wish of Miss Helen's fer somethin' to happen will come true. Shore I—"

"Cut out the joshin'," rang out Monty's strident voice.

It had as decided an effect as any preceding words or action. Perhaps it was the last thing needed to transform these men, doing unaccustomed duty as escorts of beautiful women, to their natural state as men of the wild.

"Tell us what's what," said Stewart, cool and grim.

"Don Carlos an' his guerrillas are campin' on the trails thet lead up here. They've got them trails blocked. By to-morrer they'd hed us corralled. Mebbe they meant to surprise us. He's got a lot of Greasers an' outlaws. They're well armed. Now what do they mean? You-all can figger it out to suit yourselves. Mebbe the Don wants to pay a sociable call on our ladies. Mebbe his gang is some hungry, as usual. Mebbe they want to steal a few hosses, or anythin' they can lay hands on. Mebbe they mean wuss, too. Now my idee is this, an' mebbe it's wrong. I long since separated from love with Greasers. Thet black-faced Don Carlos has got a deep game. Thet two-bit of a revolution is hevin' hard times. The rebels want American intervention. They'd stretch any point to make trouble. We're only ten miles from the border. Suppose them guerrillas got our crowd across thet border? The U. S. cavalry would foller. You-all know what thet'd mean. Mebbe Don Carlos's mind works thet way. Mebbe it don't. I reckon we'll know soon. An' now, Stewart, whatever the Don's game is, shore you're the man to outfigger him. Mebbe it's just as well you're good an' mad about somethin'. An' I resign my job because I want to feel unbeholdin' to anybody. Shore it struck me long since thet the old days hed come back fer a little spell, an' there I was trailin' a promise not to hurt any Greaser."

✣ 19 ✣

DON CARLOS

Stewart took Nels, Monty, and Nick Steele aside out of earshot, and they evidently entered upon an earnest colloquy. Presently the other cowboys were called. They all talked more or less, but the deep voice of Stewart predominated over the others. Then the consultation broke up, and the cowboys scattered.

"Rustle, you Indians!" ordered Stewart.

The ensuing scene of action was not reassuring to Madeline and her friends. They were quiet, awaiting some one to tell them what to do. At the offset the cowboys appeared to have forgotten Madeline. Some of them ran off into the woods, others into the open, grassy places, where they rounded up the horses and burros. Several cowboys spread tarpaulins upon the ground and began to select and roll small packs, evidently for hurried travel. Nels mounted his horse to ride down the trail. Monty and Nick Steele went off into the grove, leading their horses. Stewart climbed up a steep jumble of stone between two sections of low, cracked cliff back of the camp.

Castleton offered to help the packers, and was curtly told he would be in the way. Madeline's friends all importuned her: Was there real danger? Were the guerrillas coming? Would a start be made at once for the ranch? Why had the cowboys suddenly become so different? Madeline answered as best she could; but her replies were only conjecture, and modified to allay the fears of her guests. Helen was in a white glow of excitement.

Soon cowboys appeared riding barebacked horses, driving in others and the burros. Some of these horses were taken away and evidently hidden in deep recesses between the crags. The string of burros were packed and sent off down the trail in charge of a cowboy. Nick Steele and Monty returned. Then Stewart appeared, clambering down the break between the cliffs.

His next move was to order all the baggage belonging to Madeline and her guests taken up the cliff. This was strenuous toil, requiring the need of lassoes to haul up the effects.

"Get ready to climb," said Stewart, turning to Madelines party.

"Where?" asked Helen.

He waved his hand at the ascent to be made. Exclamations of dismay followed his gesture.

"Mr. Stewart, is there danger?" asked Dorothy; and her voice trembled.

This was the question Madeline had upon her lips to ask Stewart, but she could not speak it.

"No, there's no danger," replied Stewart, "but we're taking precautions we all agreed on as best."

Dorothy whispered that she believed Stewart lied. Castleton asked another question, and then Harvey followed suit. Mrs. Beck made a timid query.

"Please keep quiet and do as you're told," said Stewart, bluntly.

At this juncture, when the last of the baggage was being hauled up the cliff, Monty approached Madeline and removed his sombrero. His black face seemed the same, yet this was a vastly changed Monty.

"Miss Hammond, I'm givin' notice I resign my job," he said.

"Monty! What do you mean? What does Nels mean now, when danger threatens?"

"We jest quit. Thet's all," replied Monty, tersely. He was stern and somber; he could not stand still; his eyes roved everywhere.

Castleton jumped up from the log where he had been sitting, and his face was very red.

"Mr. Price, does all this blooming fuss mean we are to be robbed or attacked or abducted by a lot of ragamuffin guerrillas?"

"You've called the bet."

Dorothy turned a very pale face toward Monty.

"Mr. Price, you wouldn't—you couldn't desert us now? You and Mr. Nels—"

"Desert you?" asked Monty, blankly.

"Yes, desert us. Leave us when we may need you so much, with something dreadful coming."

Monty uttered a short, hard laugh as he bent a strange look upon the girl.

"Me an' Nels is purty much scared, an' we're goin' to slope. Miss Dorothy, bein' as we've rustled round so much; it sorta hurts us to see nice young girls dragged off by the hair."

Dorothy uttered a little cry and then became hysterical. Castleton for once was fully aroused.

"By Gad! You and your partner are a couple of blooming cowards. Where now is that courage you boasted of?"

Monty's dark face expressed extreme sarcasm.

"Dook, in my time I've seen some bright fellers, but you take the cake. It's most marvelous how bright you are. Figger'n' me an' Nels so correct. Say, Dook, if you don't git rustled off to Mexico an' roped to a cactus-bush you'll hev a swell story fer your English chums. Bah Jove! You'll tell 'em how you seen two old-time gun-men run like scared jack-rabbits from a lot of Greasers. Like hell you will! Unless you lie like the time you told about proddin' the lion. That there story allus—"

"Monty, shut up!" yelled Stewart, as he came hurriedly up. Then Monty slouched away, cursing to himself.

Madeline and Helen, assisted by Castleton, worked over Dorothy, and with some difficulty quieted her. Stewart passed several times without noticing them, and Monty, who had been so ridiculously eager to pay every little attention to Dorothy, did not see her at all. Rude it seemed; in Monty's case more than that. Madeline hardly knew what to make of it.

Stewart directed cowboys to go to the head of the open place in the cliff and let down lassoes. Then, with little waste of words, he urged the women toward this rough ladder of stones.

"We want to hide you," he said, when they demurred. "If the guerrillas come we'll tell them you've all gone down to the ranch. If we have to fight you'll be safe up there."

Helen stepped boldly forward and let Stewart put the loop of a lasso round her and tighten it. He waved his hand to the cowboys above.

"Just walk up, now," he directed Helen.

It proved to the watchers to be an easy, safe, and rapid means of scaling the steep passage. The men climbed up without assistance. Mrs. Beck, as usual, had hysteria; she half walked and was half dragged up. Stewart supported Dorothy with one arm, while with the other he held to the lasso. Ambrose had to carry Christine. The Mexican women required no assistance. Edith Wayne and Madeline climbed last; and, once up, Madeline saw a narrow bench, thick with shrubs, and overshadowed by huge, leaning crags. There were holes in the rock, and dark fissures leading back. It was a rough, wild place. Tarpaulins and bedding were then hauled up, and food and water. The cowboys spread comfortable beds in several of the caves, and told Madeline and her friends to be as quiet as possible, not to make a light, and to sleep dressed, ready for travel at a moment's notice.

After the cowboys had gone down it was not a cheerful group left there in the darkening twilight. Castleton prevailed upon them to eat.

"This is simply great," whispered Helen.

"Oh, it's awful!" moaned Dorothy. "It's your fault, Helen. You prayed for something to happen."

"I believe it's a horrid trick those cowboys are playing," said Mrs. Beck.

Madeline assured her friends that no trick was being played upon them, and that she deplored the discomfort and distress, but felt no real alarm. She was more inclined to evasive kindness here than to sincerity, for she had a decided uneasiness. The swift change in the manner and looks of her cowboys had been a shock to her. The last glance she had of Stewart's face, then stern, almost sad, and haggard with worry, remained to augment her foreboding.

Darkness appeared to drop swiftly down; the coyotes began their haunting, mournful howls; the stars showed and grew brighter; the wind moaned through the tips of the pines. Castleton was restless. He walked to and fro before the overhanging shelf of rock, where his companions sat lamenting, and presently he went out to the ledge of the bench. The cowboys below had built a fire, and the light from it rose in a huge, fan-shaped glow. Castleton's little figure stood out black against this light. Curious and anxious also, Madeline joined him and peered down from the cliff. The distance was short, and occasionally she could distinguish a word spoken by the cowboys. They were unconcernedly cooking and eating. She marked the absence of Stewart, and mentioned it to Castleton. Silently Castleton pointed almost straight down, and there in the gloom stood Stewart, with the two stag-hounds at his feet.

Presently Nick Steele silenced the camp-fire circle by raising a warning hand. The cowboys bent their heads, listening. Madeline listened with all her might. She heard one of the hounds whine, then the faint beat of horse's hoofs. Nick spoke again and turned to his supper, and the other men seemed to slacken in attention. The beat of hoofs grew louder, entered the grove, then the circle of light. The rider was Nels. He dismounted, and the sound of his low voice just reached Madeline.

"Gene, it's Nels. Somethin' doin'," Madeline heard one of the cowboys call, softly.

"Send him over," replied Stewart.

Nels stalked away from the fire.

"See here, Nels, the boys are all right, but I don't want them to know everything about this mix-up," said Stewart, as Nels came up. "Did you find the girl?"

Madeline guessed that Stewart referred to the Mexican girl Bonita.

"No. But I met"—Madeline did not catch the name—"an' he was wild. He was with a forest ranger. An' they said Pat Hawe had trailed her an' was takin' her down under arrest."

Stewart muttered deep under his breath, evidently cursing.

"Wonder why he didn't come on up here?" he queried, presently. "He can see a trail."

"Wal, Gene, Pat knowed you was here all right, fer thet ranger said Pat hed wind of the guerrillas, an' Pat said if Don Carlos didn't kill you—which he hoped he'd do—then it 'd be time enough to put you in jail when you come down."

"He's dead set to arrest me, Nels."

"An' he'll do it, like the old lady who kept tavern out West. Gene, the reason thet red-faced coyote didn't trail you up here is because he's scared. He allus was scared of you. But I reckon he's shore scared to death of me an' Monty."

"Well, we'll take Pat in his turn. The thing now is, when will that Greaser stalk us, and what'll we do when he comes?"

"My boy, there's only one way to handle a Greaser. I shore told you thet. He means rough toward us. He'll come smilin' up, all soci'ble like, insinuatin' an' sweeter 'n a woman. But he's treacherous; he's wuss than an Indian. An', Gene, we know for a positive fact how his gang hev been operatin' between these hills an' Agua Prieta. They're no nervy gang of outlaws like we used to hev. But they're plumb bad. They've raided and murdered through the San Luis Pass an' Guadalupe Canyon. They've murdered women, an' wuss than thet, both north an' south of Agua Prieta. Mebbe the U. S. cavalry don't know it, an' the good old States; but we, you an' me an' Monty an' Nick, we know it. We know jest about what thet rebel war down there amounts to. It's guerrilla war, an' shore some harvest-time fer a lot of cheap thieves an' outcasts."

"Oh, you're right, Nels. I'm not disputing that," replied Stewart. "If it wasn't for Miss Hammond and the other women, I'd rather enjoy seeing you and Monty open up on that bunch. I'm thinking I'd be glad to meet Don Carlos. But Miss Hammond! Why, Nels, such a woman as she is would never recover from the sight of real gun-play, let alone any stunts with a rope. These Eastern women are different. I'm not belittling our Western women. It's in the blood. Miss Hammond is—is—"

"Shore she is," interrupted Nels; "but she's got a damn sight more spunk than you think she has, Gene Stewart. I'm no thick-skulled cow. I'd hate somethin' powerful to hev Miss Hammond see any rough work, let alone me an' Monty startin' somethin'. An' me an' Monty'll stick to you, Gene, as long as seems reasonable. Mind, ole feller, beggin' your pardon, you're shore stuck on Miss Hammond, an' over-tender not to hurt her feelin's or make her sick by lettin' some blood. We're in bad here, an' mebbe we'll hev to fight. Sabe, senor? Wal, we do you can jest gamble thet Miss Hammond'll be game. An' I'll bet you a million pesos thet if you got goin' onct, an' she seen you as I've seen you—wal, I know what she'd think of you. This old world ain't changed much. Some women may be white-skinned an' soft-eyed an' sweet-voiced an' high-souled, but they all like to see a man! Gene, here's your game. Let Don Carlos come along. Be civil. If he an' his gang are hungry, feed 'em. Take even a little overbearin' Greaser talk. Be blind if he wants his gang to steal somethin'. Let him think the women hev mosied down to the ranch. But if he says you're lyin'—if he as much as looks round to see the women—jest jump him same as you jumped Pat Hawe. Me an' Monty'll hang back fer thet, an' if your strong bluff don't go through, if the Don's gang even

337

thinks of flashin' guns, then we'll open up. An' all I got to say is if them Greasers stand fer real gun-play they'll be the fust I ever seen."

"Nels, there are white men in that gang," said Stewart.

"Shore. But me an' Monty'll be thinkin' of thet. If they start anythin' it'll hev to be shore quick."

"All right, Nels, old friend, and thanks," replied Stewart. Nels returned to the camp-fire, and Stewart resumed his silent guard.

Madeline led Castleton away from the brink of the wall.

"By Jove! Cowboys are blooming strange folk!" he exclaimed. "They are not what they pretend to be."

"Indeed, you are right," replied Madeline. "I cannot understand them. Come, let us tell the others that Nels and Monty were only talking and do not intend to leave us. Dorothy, at least, will be less frightened if she knows."

Dorothy was somewhat comforted. The others, however, complained of the cowboys' singular behavior. More than once the idea was advanced that an elaborate trick had been concocted. Upon general discussion this idea gained ground. Madeline did not combat it, because she saw it tended to a less perturbed condition of mind among her guests. Castleton for once proved that he was not absolutely obtuse, and helped along the idea.

They sat talking in low voices until a late hour. The incident now began to take on the nature of Helen's long-yearned-for adventure. Some of the party even grew merry in a subdued way. Then, gradually, one by one they tired and went to bed. Helen vowed she could not sleep in a place where there were bats and crawling things. Madeline fancied, however, that they all went to sleep while she lay wide-eyed, staring up at the black bulge of overhanging rock and beyond the starry sky.

To keep from thinking of Stewart and the burning anger he had caused her to feel for herself, Madeline tried to keep her mind on other things. But thought of him recurred, and each time there was a hot commotion in her breast hard to stifle. Intelligent reasoning seemed out of her power. In the daylight it had been possible for her to be oblivious to Stewart's deceit after the moment of its realization. At night, however, in the strange silence and hovering shadows of gloom, with the speaking stars seeming to call to her, with the moan of the wind in the pines, and the melancholy mourn of coyotes in the distance, she was not able to govern her thought and emotion. The day was practical, cold; the night was strange and tense. In the darkness she had fancies wholly unknown to her in the bright light of the sun. She battled with a haunting thought. She had inadvertently heard Nels's conversation with Stewart; she had listened, hoping to hear some good news or to hear the worst; she had learned both, and, moreover, enlightenment on one point of Stewart's complex motives. He wished to spare her any sight that might offend, frighten, or disgust her. Yet this Stewart, who showed a fineness of feeling that might have been wanting even in Boyd Harvey, maintained a secret rendezvous with that pretty, abandoned Bonita. Here always the hot shame, like a live, stinging, internal fire, abruptly ended Madeline's thought. It was intolerable, and it was the more so because she could neither control nor understand it. The hours wore on, and at length, as the stars began to pale and there was no sound whatever, she fell asleep.

She was called out of her slumber. Day had broken bright and cool. The sun was still below the eastern crags. Ambrose, with several other cowboys, had brought up buckets of spring-water, and hot coffee and cakes. Madeline's party appeared to be none the worse for the night's experience. Indeed, the meager breakfast might have been as merrily partaken of as it was hungrily had not Ambrose enjoined silence.

"They're expectin' company down below," he said.

This information and the summary manner in which the cowboys soon led the party higher up among the ruined shelves of rock caused a recurrence of anxiety. Madeline insisted on not going beyond a projection of cliff from which she could see directly down into the camp. As the vantage-point was one affording concealment, Ambrose consented, but he placed the frightened Christine near Madeline and remained there himself.

"Ambrose, do you really think the guerrillas will come?" asked Madeline.

"Sure. We know. Nels just rode in and said they were on their way up. Miss Hammond, can I trust you? You won't let out a squeal if there's a fight down there? Stewart told me to hide you out of sight or keep you from lookin'."

"I promise not to make any noise," replied Madeline. Madeline arranged her coat so that she could lie upon it, and settled down to wait developments. There came a slight rattling of stones in the rear. She turned to see Helen sliding down a bank with a perplexed and troubled cowboy. Helen came stooping low to where Madeline lay and said: "I am going to see what happens, if I die in the attempt! I can stand it if you can." She was pale and big-eyed. Ambrose promptly swore at the cowboy who had let her get away from him. "Take a half-hitch on her yourself an' see where you end up," replied the fellow, and disappeared in the jumble of rocks. Ambrose, finding words useless, sternly and heroically prepared to carry Helen back to the others. He laid hold of her. In a fury, with eyes blazing, Helen whispered:

"Let go of me! Majesty, what does this fool mean?"

Madeline laughed. She knew Helen, and had marked the whisper, when ordinarily Helen would have spoken imperiously, and not low. Madeline explained to her the exigency of the situation. "I might run, but I'll never scream," said Helen. With that Ambrose had to be content to let her stay. However, he found her a place somewhat farther back from Madeline's position, where he said there was less danger of her being seen. Then he sternly bound her to silence, tarried a moment to comfort Christine, and returned to where Madeline lay concealed. He had been there scarcely a moment when he whispered:

"I hear hosses. The guerrillas are comin'."

Madeline's hiding-place was well protected from possible discovery from below. She could peep over a kind of parapet, through an opening in the tips of the pines that reached up to the cliff, and obtain a commanding view of the camp circle and its immediate surroundings. She could not, however, see far either to right or left of the camp, owing to the obstructing foliage. Presently the sound of horses' hoofs quickened the beat of her pulse and caused her to turn keener gaze upon the cowboys below.

Although she had some inkling of the course Stewart and his men were to pursue, she was not by any means prepared for the indifference she saw. Frank was asleep, or pretended to be. Three cowboys were lazily and unconcernedly attending to camp-fire duties, such as baking biscuits, watching the ovens, and washing tins and pots. The elaborate set of aluminum plates, cups, etc., together with the other camp fixtures that had done service for Madeline's party, had disappeared. Nick Steele sat with his back to a log, smoking his pipe. Another cowboy had just brought the horses closer into camp, where they stood waiting to be saddled. Nels appeared to be fussing over a pack. Stewart was rolling a cigarette. Monty had apparently nothing to do for the present except whistle, which he was doing much more loudly than melodiously. The whole ensemble gave an impression of careless indifference.

The sound of horses' hoofs grew louder and slowed its beat. One of the cowboys pointed down the trail, toward which several of his comrades turned their heads for a moment, then went on with their occupations.

Presently a shaggy, dusty horse bearing a lean, ragged, dark rider rode into camp and halted. Another followed, and another. Horses with Mexican riders came in single file and stopped behind the leader.

The cowboys looked up, and the guerrillas looked down. "Buenos dias, senor," ceremoniously said the foremost guerrilla.

By straining her ears Madeline heard that voice, and she recognized it as belonging to Don Carlos. His graceful bow to Stewart was also familiar. Otherwise she would never have recognized the former elegant vaquero in this uncouth, roughly dressed Mexican.

Stewart answered the greeting in Spanish, and, waving his hand toward the camp-fire, added in English, "Get down and eat."

The guerrillas were anything but slow in complying. They crowded to the fire, then spread in a little circle and squatted upon the ground, laying their weapons beside them. In appearance they tallied with the band of guerrillas that had carried Madeline up into the foothills, only this band was larger and better armed. The men, moreover, were just as hungry and as wild and beggarly. The cowboys were not cordial in their reception of this visit, but they were hospitable. The law of the desert had always been to give food and drink to wayfaring men, whether lost or hunted or hunting.

"There's twenty-three in that outfit," whispered Ambrose, "includin' four white men. Pretty rummy outfit."

"They appear to be friendly enough," whispered Madeline.

"Things down there ain't what they seem," replied Ambrose.

"Ambrose, tell me—explain to me. This is my opportunity. As long as you will let me watch them, please let me know the—the real thing."

"Sure. But recollect, Miss Hammond, that Gene'll give it to me good if he ever knows I let you look and told you what's what. Well, decent-like Gene is seen' them poor devils get a square meal. They're only a lot of calf-thieves in this country. Across the border they're bandits, some of them, the others just riffraff outlaws. That rebel bluff doesn't go down with us. I'd have to see first before I'd believe them Greasers would fight. They're a lot of hard-ridin' thieves, and they'd steal a fellow's blanket or tobacco. Gene thinks they're after you ladies—to carry you off. But Gene—Oh, Gene's some highfalutin in his ideas lately. Most of us boys think the guerrillas are out to rob—that's all."

Whatever might have been the secret motive of Don Carlos and his men, they did not allow it to interfere with a hearty appreciation of a generous amount of food. Plainly, each individual ate all that he was able to eat at the time. They jabbered like a flock of parrots; some were even merry, in a kind of wild way. Then, as each and every one began to roll and smoke the inevitable cigarette of the Mexican, there was a subtle change in manner. They smoked and looked about the camp, off into the woods, up at the crags, and back at the leisurely cowboys. They had the air of men waiting for something.

"Senor," began Don Carlos, addressing Stewart. As he spoke he swept his sombrero to indicate the camp circle.

Madeline could not distinguish his words, but his gesture plainly indicated a question in regard to the rest of the camping party. Stewart's reply and the wave of his hand down the trail meant that his party had gone home. Stewart turned to some task, and the guerrilla leader quietly smoked. He looked cunning and thoughtful. His men gradually began to manifest a restlessness, noticeable in the absence of former languor and slow puffing of cigarette smoke. Presently a big-boned man with a bullet head and a blistered red face of evil coarseness got up and threw away his cigarette. He was an American.

"Hey, cull," he called in loud voice, "ain't ye goin' to cough up a drink?"

"My boys don't carry liquor on the trail," replied Stewart. He turned now to face the guerrillas.

"Haw, haw! I heerd over in Rodeo thet ye was gittin' to be shore some fer temperance," said this fellow. "I hate to drink water, but I guess I've gotter do it."

He went to the spring, sprawled down to drink, and all of a sudden he thrust his arm down in the water to bring forth a basket. The cowboys in the hurry of packing had neglected to remove this basket; and it contained bottles of wine and liquors for Madeline's guests. They had been submerged in the spring to keep them cold. The guerrilla fumbled with the lid, opened it, and then got up, uttering a loud roar of delight.

Stewart made an almost imperceptible motion, as if to leap forward; but he checked the impulse, and after a quick glance at Nels he said to the guerrilla:

"Guess my party forgot that. You're welcome to it." Like bees the guerrillas swarmed around the lucky finder of the bottles. There was a babel of voices. The drink did not last long, and it served only to liberate the spirit of recklessness. The several white outlaws began to prowl around the camp; some of the Mexicans did likewise; others waited, showing by their ill-concealed expectancy the nature of their thoughts.

It was the demeanor of Stewart and his comrades that puzzled Madeline. Apparently they felt no anxiety or even particular interest. Don Carlos, who had been covertly watching them, now made his scrutiny open, even aggressive. He looked from Stewart to Nels and Monty, and then to the other cowboys. While some of his men prowled around the others watched him, and the waiting attitude had taken on something sinister. The guerrilla leader seemed undecided, but not in any sense puzzled. When he turned his cunning face upon Nels and Monty he had the manner of a man in whom decision was lacking.

In her growing excitement Madeline had not clearly heard Ambrose's low whispers and she made an effort to distract some of her attention from those below to the cowboy crouching beside her.

The quality, the note of Ambrose's whisper had changed. It had a slight sibilant sound.

"Don't be mad if sudden-like I clap my hands over your eyes, Miss Hammond," he was saying. "Somethin's brewin' below. I never seen Gene so cool. That's a dangerous sign in him. And look, see how the boys are workin' together! Oh, it's slow and accident-like, but I know it's sure not accident. That foxy Greaser knows, too. But maybe his men don't. If they are wise they haven't sense enough to care. The Don, though—he's worried. He's not payin' so much attention to Gene, either. It's Nels and Monty he's watchin'. And well he need do it! There, Nick and Frank have settled down on that log with Booly. They don't seem to be packin' guns. But look how heavy their vests hang. A gun in each side! Those boys can pull a gun and flop over that log quicker than you can think. Do you notice how Nels and Monty and Gene are square between them guerrillas and the trail up here? It doesn't seem on purpose, but it is. Look at Nels and Monty. How quiet they are confabbin' together, payin' no attention to the guerrillas. I see Monty look at Gene, then I see Nels look at Gene. Well, it's up to Gene. And they're goin' to back him. I reckon, Miss Hammond, there'd be dead Greasers round that camp long ago if Nels and Monty were foot-loose. They're beholdin' to Gene. That's plain. And, Lord! how it tickles me to watch them! Both packin' two forty-fives, butts swingin' clear. There's twenty-four shots in them four guns. And there's twenty-three guerrillas. If Nels and Monty ever throw guns at that close range, why, before you'd know what was up there'd be a pile of Greasers. There! Stewart said something to the Don. I wonder what. I'll gamble it was something to get the Don's outfit all close together. Sure! Greasers have no sense. But them white guerrillas, they're lookin' some dubious. Whatever's comin' off will come soon, you can bet. I wish I was down there. But maybe it won't come to a scrap. Stewart's set on avoidin' that. He's a wonderful chap to get his way. Lord, though, I'd like to see him go after that overbearin' Greaser! See! the Don can't stand prosperity. All this strange behavior of cowboys is beyond his pulque-soaked brains. Then he's a Greaser. If Gene doesn't knock him on the head presently he'll begin to get over his scare, even of Nels and Monty. But Gene'll pick out the right time. And I'm gettin' nervous. I want somethin' to start. Never saw Nels in but one fight, then he just shot a Greaser's arm off for tryin' to draw on him. But I've heard all about him. And Monty! Monty's the real old-fashioned gun-man. Why, none of them stories, them lies he told to entertain the Englishman, was a marker to what Monty has done. What I don't understand is how Monty keeps so quiet and easy and peaceful-like. That's not his way, with such an outfit lookin' for trouble. O-ha! Now for the grand bluff. Looks like no fight at all!"

The guerrilla leader had ceased his restless steps and glances, and turned to Stewart with something of bold resolution in his aspect.

"Gracias, senor," he said. "Adios." He swept his sombrero in the direction of the trail leading down the mountain to the ranch; and as he completed the gesture a smile, crafty and jeering, crossed his swarthy face.

Ambrose whispered so low that Madeline scarcely heard him. "If the Greaser goes that way he'll find our horses and get wise to the trick. Oh, he's wise now! But I'll gamble he never even starts on that trail."

Neither hurriedly nor guardedly Stewart rose out of his leaning posture and took a couple of long strides toward Don Carlos.

"Go back the way you came," he fairly yelled; and his voice had the ring of a bugle.

Ambrose nudged Madeline; his whisper was tense and rapid: "Don't miss nothin'. Gene's called him. Whatever's comin' off will be here quick as lightnin'. See! I guess maybe that Greaser don't savvy good U. S. lingo. Look at that dirty yaller face turn green. Put one eye on Nels and Monty! That's great—just to see 'em. Just as quiet and easy. But oh, the difference! Bent and stiff—that means every muscle is like a rawhide riata. They're watchin' with eyes that can see the workin's of them Greasers' minds. Now there ain't a hoss-hair between them Greasers and hell!"

Don Carlos gave Stewart one long malignant stare; then he threw back his head, swept up the sombrero, and his evil smile showed gleaming teeth.

"Senor—" he began.

With magnificent bound Stewart was upon him. The guerrilla's cry was throttled in his throat. A fierce wrestling ensued, too swift to see clearly; then heavy, sodden blows, and Don Carlos was beaten to the ground. Stewart leaped back. Then, crouching with his hands on the butts of guns at his hips, he yelled, he thundered at the guerrillas. He had been quicker than a panther, and now his voice was so terrible that it curdled Madeline's blood, and the menace of deadly violence in his crouching position made her shut her eyes. But she had to open them. In that single instant Nels and Monty had leaped to Stewart's side. Both were bent down, with hands on the butts of guns at their hips. Nels's piercing yell seemed to divide Monty's roar of rage. Then they ceased, and echoes clapped from the crags. The silence of those three men crouching like tigers about to leap was more menacing than the nerve-racking yells.

Then the guerrillas wavered and broke and ran for their horses. Don Carlos rolled over, rose, and staggered away, to be helped upon his mount. He looked back, his pale and bloody face that of a thwarted demon. The whole band got into action and were gone in a moment.

"I knew it," declared Ambrose. "Never seen a Greaser who could face gun-play. That was some warm. And Monty Price never flashed a gun! He'll never get over that. I reckon, Miss

Harnmond, we're some lucky to avoid trouble. Gene had his way, as you seen. We'll be makin' tracks for the ranch in about two shakes."

"Why?" whispered Madeline, breathlessly. She became conscious that she was weak and shaken.

"Because the guerrillas sure will get their nerve back, and come sneakin' on our trail or try to head us off by ambushin'," replied Ambrose. "That's their way. Otherwise three cowboys couldn't bluff a whole gang like that. Gene knows the nature of Greasers. They're white-livered. But I reckon we're in more danger now than before, unless we get a good start down the mountain. There! Gene's callin'. Come! Hurry!"

Helen had slipped down from her vantage-point, and therefore had not seen the last act in that little camp-fire drama. It seemed, however, that her desire for excitement was satisfied, for her face was pale and she trembled when she asked if the guerrillas were gone.

"I didn't see the finish, but those horrible yells were enough for me."

Ambrose hurried the three women over the rough rocks, down the cliff. The cowboys below were saddling horses in haste. Evidently all the horses had been brought out of hiding. Swiftly, with regard only for life and limb, Madeline, Helen, and Christine were lowered by lassoes and half carried down to the level. By the time they were safely down the other members of the party appeared on the cliff above. They were in excellent spirits, appearing to treat the matter as a huge joke.

Ambrose put Christine on a horse and rode away through the pines; Frankie Slade did likewise with Helen. Stewart led Madeline's horse up to her, helped her to mount, and spoke one stern word, "Wait!" Then as fast as one of the women reached the level she was put upon a horse and taken away by a cowboy escort. Few words were spoken. Haste seemed to be the great essential. The horses were urged, and, once in the trail, spurred and led into a swift trot. One cowboy drove up four pack-horses, and these were hurriedly loaded with the party's baggage. Castleton and his companions mounted, and galloped off to catch the others in the lead. This left Madeline behind with Stewart and Nels and Monty.

"They're goin' to switch off at the holler thet heads near the trail a few miles down," Nels was saying, as he tightened his saddle-girth. "Thet holler heads into a big canyon. Once in thet, it'll be every man fer hisself. I reckon there won't be anythin' wuss than a rough ride."

Nels smiled reassuringly at Madeline, but he did not speak to her. Monty took her canteen and filled it at the spring and hung it over the pommel of her saddle. He put a couple of biscuits in the saddle-bag.

"Don't fergit to take a drink an' a bite as you're ridin' along," he said. "An' don't worry, Miss Majesty. Stewart'll be with you, an' me an' Nels hangin' on the back-trail."

His somber and sullen face did not change in its strange intensity, but the look in his eyes Madeline felt she would never forget. Left alone with these three men, now stripped of all pretense, she realized how fortune had favored her and what peril still hung in the balance. Stewart swung astride his big black, spurred him, and whistled. At the whistle Majesty jumped, and with swift canter followed Stewart. Madeline looked back to see Nels already up and Monty handing him a rifle. Then the pines hid her view.

Once in the trail, Stewart's horse broke into a gallop. Majesty changed his gait and kept at the black's heels. Stewart called back a warning. The low, wide-spreading branches of trees might brush Madeline out of the saddle. Fast riding through the forest along a crooked, obstructed trail called forth all her alertness. Likewise the stirring of her blood, always susceptible to the spirit and motion of a ride, let alone one of peril, now began to throb and burn away the worry, the dread, the coldness that had weighted her down.

Before long Stewart wheeled at right angles off the trail and entered a hollow between two low bluffs. Madeline saw tracks in the open patches of ground. Here Stewart's horse took to a brisk walk. The hollow deepened, narrowed, became rocky, full of logs and brush. Madeline exerted all her keenness, and needed it, to keep close to Stewart. She did not think of him, nor her own safety, but of keeping Majesty close in the tracks of the black, of eluding the sharp spikes in the dead brush, of avoiding the treacherous loose stones.

At last Madeline was brought to a dead halt by Stewart and his horse blocking the trail. Looking up, she saw they were at the head of a canyon that yawned beneath and widened its gray-walled, green-patched slopes down to a black forest of fir. The drab monotony of the foothills made contrast below the forest, and away in the distance, rosy and smoky, lay the desert. Retracting her gaze, Madeline saw pack-horses cross an open space a mile below, and she thought she saw the stag-hounds. Stewart's dark eyes searched the slopes high up along the craggy escarpments. Then he put the black to the descent.

If there had been a trail left by the leading cowboys, Stewart did not follow it. He led off to the right, zigzagging an intricate course through the roughest ground Madeline had ever ridden over. He crashed through cedars, threaded a tortuous way among boulders, made his horse slide down slanting banks of soft earth, picked a slow and cautious progress across weathered slopes of loose rock. Madeline followed, finding in this ride a tax on strength and judgment. On an ordinary horse she never could have kept in Stewart's trail. It was dust and heat, a parching throat, that caused Madeline to think of time; and she was amazed to see the sun sloping to the west. Stewart never stopped; he never looked back; he never spoke. He must have heard the horse close behind him. Madeline remembered Monty's advice about drinking and eating as she rode along. The worst of that rough travel came at the bottom of the canyon. Dead cedars and brush and logs were easy to pass compared with the miles, it seemed, of loose boulders. The horses slipped and stumbled. Stewart proceeded here with exceeding care. At last, when the canyon opened into a level forest of firs, the sun was setting red in the west.

Stewart quickened the gait of his horse. After a mile or so of easy travel the ground again began to fall decidedly, sloping in numerous ridges, with draws between. Soon night shadowed the deeper gullies. Madeline was refreshed by the cooling of the air.

Stewart traveled slowly now. The barks of coyotes seemed to startle him. Often he stopped to listen. And during one of those intervals the silence was broken by sharp rifle-shots. Madeline could not tell whether they were near or far, to right or left, behind or before. Evidently Stewart was both alarmed and baffled. He dismounted. He went cautiously forward to listen. Madeline fancied she heard a cry, low and far away. It was only that of a coyote, she convinced herself, yet it was so wailing, so human, that she shuddered. Stewart came back. He slipped the bridles of both horses, and he led them. Every few paces he stopped to listen. He changed his direction several times, and the last time he got among rough, rocky ridges. The iron shoes of the horses cracked on the rocks. That sound must have penetrated far into the forest. It perturbed Stewart, for he searched for softer ground. Meanwhile the shadows merged into darkness. The stars shone. The wind rose. Madeline believed hours passed.

Stewart halted again. In the gloom Madeline discerned a log cabin, and beyond it pear-pointed dark trees piercing the sky-line. She could just make out Stewart's tall form as he leaned against his horse. Either he was listening or debating what to do—perhaps both. Presently he went inside the cabin. Madeline heard the scratching of a match; then she saw a faint light. The cabin appeared to be deserted. Probably it was one of the many habitations belonging to prospectors and foresters who lived in the mountains. Stewart came out again. He walked around the horses, out into the gloom, then back to Madeline. For a long moment he stood as still as a statue and listened. Then she heard him mutter, "If we have to start quick I can ride bareback." With that he took the saddle and blanket off his horse and carried them into the cabin.

"Get off," he said, in a low voice, as he stepped out of the door.

He helped her down and led her inside, where again he struck a match. Madeline caught a glimpse of a rude fireplace and rough-hewn logs. Stewart's blanket and saddle lay on the hard-packed earthen floor.

"Rest a little," he said. "I'm going into the woods a piece to listen. Gone only a minute or so."

Madeline had to feel round in the dark to locate the saddle and blanket. When she lay down it was with a grateful sense of ease and relief. As her body rested, however, her mind became the old thronging maze for sensation and thought. All day she had attended to the alert business of helping her horse. Now, what had already happened, the night, the silence, the proximity of Stewart and his strange, stern caution, the possible happenings to her friends—all claimed their due share of her feeling. She went over them all with lightning swiftness of thought. She believed, and she was sure Stewart believed, that her friends, owing to their quicker start down the mountain, had not been headed off in their travel by any of the things which had delayed Stewart. This conviction lifted the suddenly returning dread from her breast; and as for herself, somehow she had no fear. But she could not sleep; she did not try to.

Stewart's soft steps sounded outside. His dark form loomed in the door. As he sat down Madeline heard the thump of a gun that he laid beside him on the sill; then the thump of another as he put that down, too. The sounds thrilled her. Stewart's wide shoulders filled the door; his finely shaped head and strong, stern profile showed clearly in outline against the sky; the wind waved his hair. He turned his ear to that wind and listened. Motionless he sat for what to her seemed hours.

Then the stirring memory of the day's adventure, the feeling of the beauty of the night, and a strange, deep-seated, sweetly vague consciousness of happiness portending, were all burned out in hot, pressing pain at the remembrance of Stewart's disgrace in her eyes. Something had changed within her so that what had been anger at herself was sorrow for him. He was such a splendid man. She could not feel the same; she knew her debt to him, yet she could not thank him, could not speak to him. She fought an unintelligible bitterness.

Then she rested with closed eyes, and time seemed neither short nor long. When Stewart called her she opened her eyes to see the gray of dawn. She rose and stepped outside. The horses whinnied. In a moment she was in the saddle, aware of cramped muscles and a weariness of limbs. Stewart led off at a sharp trot into the fir forest. They came to a trail into which he turned. The horses traveled steadily; the descent grew less steep; the firs thinned out; the gray gloom brightened.

When Madeline rode out of the firs the sun had arisen and the foothills rolled beneath her; and at their edge, where the gray of valley began, she saw a dark patch that she knew was the ranch-house.

❧ 20 ❧

THE SHERIFF OF EL CAJON

ABOUT THE MIDDLE of the forenoon of that day Madeline reached the ranch. Her guests had all arrived there late the night before, and wanted only her presence and the assurance of her well-being to consider the last of the camping trip a rare adventure. Likewise, they voted it the cowboys' masterpiece of a trick. Madeline's delay, they averred, had been only a clever coup to give a final effect. She did not correct their impression, nor think it needful to state that she had been escorted home by only one cowboy.

Her guests reported an arduous ride down the mountain, with only one incident to lend excitement. On the descent they had fallen in with Sheriff Hawe and several of his deputies, who were considerably under the influence of drink and very greatly enraged by the escape of the Mexican girl Bonita. Hawe had used insulting language to the ladies and, according to Ambrose, would have inconvenienced the party on some pretext or other if he had not been sharply silenced by the cowboys.

Madeline's guests were two days in recovering from the hard ride. On the third day they leisurely began to prepare for departure. This period was doubly trying for Madeline. She had her own physical need of rest, and, moreover, had to face a mental conflict that could scarcely be postponed further. Her sister and friends were kindly and earnestly persistent in their entreaties that she go back East with them. She desired to go. It was not going that mattered; it was how and when and under what circumstances she was to return that roused in her disturbing emotion. Before she went East she wanted to have fixed in mind her future relation to the ranch and the West. When the crucial hour arrived she found that the West had not claimed her yet. These old friends had warmed cold ties.

It turned out, however, that there need be no hurry about making the decision. Madeline would have welcomed any excuse to procrastinate; but, as it happened, a letter from Alfred made her departure out of the question for the present. He wrote that his trip to California had been very profitable, that he had a proposition for Madeline from a large cattle company, and, particularly, that he wanted to marry Florence soon after his arrival home and would bring a minister from Douglas for that purpose.

Madeline went so far, however, as to promise Helen and her friends that she would go

346

East soon, at the very latest by Thanksgiving. With that promise they were reluctantly content to say good-by to the ranch and to her. At the last moment there seemed a great likelihood of a hitch in plans for the first stage of that homeward journey. All of Madeline's guests held up their hands, Western fashion, when Link Stevens appeared with the big white car. Link protested innocently, solemnly, that he would drive slowly and safely; but it was necessary for Madeline to guarantee Link's word and to accompany them before they would enter the car. At the station good-bys were spoken and repeated, and Madeline's promise was exacted for the hundredth time.

Dorothy Coombs's last words were: "Give my love to Monty Price. Tell him I'm—I'm glad he kissed me!"

Helen's eyes had a sweet, grave, yet mocking light as she said:

"Majesty, bring Stewart with you when you come. He'll be the rage."

Madeline treated the remark with the same merry lightness with which it was received by the others; but after the train had pulled out and she was on her way home she remembered Helen's words and looks with something almost amounting to a shock. Any mention of Stewart, any thought of him, displeased her.

"What did Helen mean?" mused Madeline. And she pondered. That mocking light in Helen's eyes had been simply an ironical glint, a cynical gleam from that worldly experience so suspicious and tolerant in its wisdom. The sweet gravity of Helen's look had been a deeper and more subtle thing. Madeline wanted to understand it, to divine in it a new relation between Helen and herself, something fine and sisterly that might lead to love. The thought, however, revolving around a strange suggestion of Stewart, was poisoned at its inception, and she dismissed it.

Upon the drive in to the ranch, as she was passing the lower lake, she saw Stewart walking listlessly along the shore. When he became aware of the approach of the car he suddenly awakened from his aimless sauntering and disappeared quickly in the shade of the shrubbery. This was not by any means the first time Madeline had seen him avoid a possible meeting with her. Somehow the act had pained her, though affording her a relief. She did not want to meet him face to face.

It was annoying for her to guess that Stillwell had something to say in Stewart's defense. The old cattleman was evidently distressed. Several times he had tried to open a conversation with Madeline relating to Stewart; she had evaded him until the last time, when his persistence had brought a cold and final refusal to hear another word about the foreman. Stillwell had been crushed.

As days passed Stewart remained at the ranch without his old faithfulness to his work. Madeline was not moved to a kinder frame of mind to see him wandering dejectedly around. It hurt her, and because it hurt her she grew all the harder. Then she could not help hearing snatches of conversation which strengthened her suspicions that Stewart was losing his grip on himself, that he would soon take the downward course again. Verification of her own suspicion made it a belief, and belief brought about a sharp conflict between her generosity and some feeling that she could not name. It was not a question of justice or mercy or sympathy. If a single word could have saved Stewart from sinking his splendid manhood into the brute she had recoiled from at Chiricahua, she would not have spoken it. She could not restore him to his former place in her regard; she really did not want him at the ranch at all. Once, considering in wonder her knowledge of men, she interrogated herself to see just why she could not overlook Stewart's transgression. She never wanted to speak to him again, or see him, or think of him. In some way, through her interest in Stewart, she had come to feel for herself an inexplicable thing close to scorn.

347

ZANE GREY

A telegram from Douglas, heralding the coming of Alfred and a minister, put an end to Madeline's brooding, and she shared something of Florence Kingsley's excitement. The cowboys were as eager and gossipy as girls. It was arranged to have the wedding ceremony performed in Madeline's great hall-chamber, and the dinner in the cool, flower-scented patio.

Alfred and his minister arrived at the ranch in the big white car. They appeared considerably wind-blown. In fact, the minister was breathless, almost sightless, and certainly hatless. Alfred, used as he was to wind and speed, remarked that he did not wonder at Nels's aversion to riding a fleeting cannon-ball. The imperturbable Link took off his cap and goggles and, consulting his watch, made his usual apologetic report to Madeline, deploring the fact that a teamster and a few stray cattle on the road had held him down to the manana time of only a mile a minute.

Arrangements for the wedding brought Alfred's delighted approval. When he had learned all Florence and Madeline would tell him he expressed a desire to have the cowboys attend; and then he went on to talk about California, where he was going take Florence on a short trip. He was curiously interested to find out all about Madeline's guests and what had happened to them. His keen glance at Madeline grew softer as she talked.

"I breathe again," he said, and laughed. "I was afraid. Well, I must have missed some sport. I can just fancy what Monty and Nels did to that Englishman. So you went up to the crags. That's a wild place. I'm not surprised at guerrillas falling in with you up there. The crags were a famous rendezvous for Apaches—it's near the border—almost inaccessible—good water and grass. I wonder what the U. S. cavalry would think if they knew these guerrillas crossed the border right under their noses. Well, it's practically impossible to patrol some of that border-line. It's desert, mountain, and canyon, exceedingly wild and broken. I'm sorry to say that there seems to be more trouble in sight with these guerrillas than at any time heretofore. Orozco, the rebel leader, has failed to withstand Madero's army. The Federals are occupying Chihuahua now, and are driving the rebels north. Orozco has broken up his army into guerrilla bands. They are moving north and west, intending to carry on guerrilla warfare in Sonora. I can't say just how this will affect us here. But we're too close to the border for comfort. These guerrillas are night-riding hawks; they can cross the border, raid us here, and get back the same night. Fighting, I imagine, will not be restricted to northern Mexico. With the revolution a failure the guerrillas will be more numerous, bolder, and hungrier. Unfortunately, we happen to be favorably situated for them down here in this wilderness corner of the state."

On the following day Alfred and Florence were married. Florence's sister and several friends from El Cajon were present, besides Madeline, Stillwell, and his men. It was Alfred's express wish that Stewart attend the ceremony. Madeline was amused when she noticed the painfully suppressed excitement of the cowboys. For them a wedding must have been an unusual and impressive event. She began to have a better understanding of the nature of it when they cast off restraint and pressed forward to kiss the bride. In all her life Madeline had never seen a bride kissed so much and so heartily, nor one so flushed and disheveled and happy. This indeed was a joyful occasion. There was nothing of the "effete East" about Alfred Hammond; he might have been a Westerner all his days. When Madeline managed to get through the press of cowboys to offer her congratulations Alfred gave her a bear hug and a kiss. This appeared to fascinate the cowboys. With shining eyes and faces aglow, with smiling, boyish boldness, they made a rush at Madeline. For one instant her heart leaped to her throat. They looked as if they could most shamelessly kiss and maul her. That little, ugly-faced, soft-eyed, rude, tender-hearted ruffian, Monty Price, was in the lead. He resembled a dragon actuated by sentiment. All at once Madeline's instinctive antagonism to being touched by strange hands or lips battled with a real, warm, and fun-loving desire to let the cowboys work their will with her. But she saw Stewart hanging at the back of the crowd, and something—some fierce, dark expression of pain—amazed her, while it froze her desire to be kind. Then she did not know what change must have come to her face and bearing; but she saw Monty fall back sheepishly and the other cowboys draw aside to let her lead the way into the patio.

The dinner began quietly enough with the cowboys divided between embarrassment and voracious appetites that they evidently feared to indulge. Wine, however, loosened their tongues, and when Stillwell got up to make the speech everybody seemed to expect of him they greeted him with a roar.

Stillwell was now one huge, mountainous smile. He was so happy that he appeared on the verge of tears. He rambled on ecstatically till he came to raise his glass.

"An' now, girls an' boys, let's all drink to the bride an' groom; to their sincere an' lastin' love; to their happiness an' prosperity; to their good health an' long life. Let's drink to the unitin' of the East with the West. No man full of red blood an' the real breath of life could resist a Western girl an' a good hoss an' God's free hand—that open country out there. So we claim Al Hammond, an' may we be true to him. An', friends, I think it fittin' that we drink to his sister an' to our hopes. Heah's to the lady we hope to make our Majesty! Heah's to the man who'll come ridin' out of the West, a fine, big-hearted man with a fast hoss an' a strong rope, an' may he win an' hold her! Come, friends, drink."

A heavy pound of horses' hoofs and a yell outside arrested Stillwell's voice and halted his hand in midair.

The patio became as silent as an unoccupied room.

Through the open doors and windows of Madeline's chamber burst the sounds of horses stamping to a halt, then harsh speech of men, and a low cry of a woman in pain.

Rapid steps crossed the porch, entered Madeline's room. Nels appeared in the doorway. Madeline was surprised to see that he had not been at the dinner-table. She was disturbed at sight of his face.

"Stewart, you're wanted outdoors," called Nels, bluntly. "Monty, you slope out here with me. You, Nick, an' Stillwell—I reckon the rest of you hed better shut the doors an' stay inside."

Nels disappeared. Quick as a cat Monty glided out. Madeline heard his soft, swift steps pass from her room into her office. He had left his guns there. Madeline trembled. She saw Stewart get up quietly and without any change of expression on his dark, sad face leave the patio. Nick Steele followed him. Stillwell dropped his wine-glass. As it broke, shivering the silence, his huge smile vanished. His face set into the old cragginess and the red slowly thickened into black. Stillwell went out and closed the door behind him.

Then there was a blank silence. The enjoyment of the moment had been rudely disrupted. Madeline glanced down the lines of brown faces to see the pleasure fade into the old familiar hardness.

"What's wrong?" asked Alfred, rather stupidly. The change of mood had been too rapid for him. Suddenly he awakened, thoroughly aroused at the interruption. "I'm going to see who's butted in here to spoil our dinner," he said, and strode out.

He returned before any one at the table had spoken or moved, and now the dull red of anger mottled his forehead.

"It's the sheriff of El Cajon!" he exclaimed, contemptuously. "Pat Hawe with some of his tough deputies come to arrest Gene Stewart. They've got that poor little Mexican girl out there tied on a horse. Confound that sheriff!"

Madeline calmly rose from the table, eluding Florence's entreating hand, and started for the door. The cowboys jumped up. Alfred barred her progress.

"Alfred, I am going out," she said.

"No, I guess not," he replied. "That's no place for you."

"I am going." She looked straight at him.

"Madeline! Why, what is it? You look—Dear, there's pretty sure to be trouble outside. Maybe there'll be a fight. You can do nothing. You must not go."

"Perhaps I can prevent trouble," she replied.

As she left the patio she was aware that Alfred, with Florence at his side and the cowboys behind, were starting to follow her. When she got out of her room upon the porch she heard several men in loud, angry discussion. Then, at sight of Bonita helplessly and cruelly bound upon a horse, pale and disheveled and suffering, Madeline experienced the thrill that sight or mention of this girl always gave her. It yielded to a hot pang in her breast—that live pain which so shamed her. But almost instantly, as a second glance showed an agony in Bonita's face, her bruised arms where the rope bit deep into the flesh, her little brown hands stained with blood, Madeline was overcome by pity for the unfortunate girl and a woman's righteous passion at such barbarous treatment of one of her own sex.

The man holding the bridle of the horse on which Bonita had been bound was at once recognized by Madeline as the big-bodied, bullet-headed guerrilla who had found the basket of wine in the spring at camp. Redder of face, blacker of beard, coarser of aspect, evidently under the influence of liquor, he was as fierce-looking as a gorilla and as repulsive. Besides him there were three other men present, all mounted on weary horses. The one in the foreground, gaunt, sharp-featured, red-eyed, with a pointed beard, she recognized as the sheriff of El Cajon.

Madeline hesitated, then stopped in the middle of the porch. Alfred, Florence, and several others followed her out; the rest of the cowboys and guests crowded the windows and doors. Stillwell saw Madeline, and, throwing up his hands, roared to be heard. This quieted the gesticulating, quarreling men.

"Wal now, Pat Hawe, what's drivin' you like a locoed steer on the rampage?" demanded Stillwell.

"Keep in the traces, Bill," replied Hawe. "You savvy what I come fer. I've been bidin' my time. But I'm ready now. I'm hyar to arrest a criminal."

The huge frame of the old cattleman jerked as if he had been stabbed. His face turned purple.

"What criminal?" he shouted, hoarsely.

The sheriff flicked his quirt against his dirty boot, and he twisted his thin lips into a leer. The situation was agreeable to him.

"Why, Bill, I knowed you hed a no-good outfit ridin' this range; but I wasn't wise thet you hed more 'n one criminal."

"Cut that talk! Which cowboy are you wantin' to arrest?"

Hawe's manner altered.

"Gene Stewart," he replied, curtly.

"On what charge?"

"Fer killin' a Greaser one night last fall."

"So you're still harpin' on that? Pat, you're on the wrong trail. You can't lay that killin' onto Stewart. The thing's ancient by now. But if you insist on bringin' him to court, let the arrest go to-day—we're hevin' some fiesta hyar—an' I'll fetch Gene in to El Cajon."

"Nope. I reckon I'll take him when I got the chance, before he slopes."

"I'm givin' you my word," thundered Stillwell.

"I reckon I don't hev to take your word, Bill, or anybody else's."

Stillwell's great bulk quivered with his rage, yet he made a successful effort to control it.

"See hyar, Pat Hawe, I know what's reasonable. Law is law. But in this country there always has been an' is now a safe an' sane way to proceed with the law. Mebbe you've forgot that. The law as invested in one man in a wild country is liable, owin' to that man's weaknesses an' onlimited authority, to be disputed even by a decent ole cattleman like myself. I'm a-goin' to give you a hunch. Pat, you're not overliked in these parts. You've rid too much with a high hand. Some of your deals hev been shady, an' don't you overlook what I'm sayin'. But you're the sheriff, an' I'm respectin' your office. I'm respectin' it this much. If the milk of human decency is so soured in your breast that you can't hev a kind feelin', then try to avoid the onpleasantness that'll result from any contrary move on your part to-day. Do you get that hunch?"

"Stillwell, you're threatenin' an officer," replied Hawe, angrily.

"Will you hit the trail quick out of hyar?" queried Stillwell, in strained voice. "I guarantee Stewart's appearance in El Cajon any day you say."

"No. I come to arrest him, an' I'm goin' to."

"So that's your game!" shouted Stillwell. "We-all are glad to get you straight, Pat. Now listen, you cheap, red-eyed coyote of a sheriff! You don't care how many enemies you make. You know you'll never get office again in this county. What do you care now? It's amazin' strange how earnest you are to hunt down the man who killed that particular Greaser. I reckon there's been some dozen or more killin's of Greasers in the last year. Why don't you take to trailin' some of them killin's? I'll tell you why. You're afraid to go near the border. An' your hate of Gene Stewart makes you want to hound him an' put him where he's never been yet—in jail. You want to spite his friends. Wal, listen, you lean-jawed, skunk-bitten coyote! Go ahead an' try to arrest him!"

Stillwell took one mighty stride off the porch. His last words had been cold. His rage appeared to have been transferred to Hawe. The sheriff had begun to stutter and shake a lanky red hand at the cattleman when Stewart stepped out.

"Here, you fellows, give me a chance to say a word."

As Stewart appeared the Mexican girl suddenly seemed vitalized out of her stupor. She strained at her bonds, as if to lift her hands beseechingly. A flush animated her haggard face, and her big dark eyes lighted.

"Senor Gene!" she moaned. "Help me! I so seek. They beat me, rope me, 'mos' keel me. Oh, help me, Senor Gene!"

"Shut up, er I'll gag you," said the man who held Bonita's horse.

"Muzzle her, Sneed, if she blabs again," called Hawe. Madeline felt something tense and strained working in the short silence. Was it only a phase of her thrilling excitement? Her swift glance showed the faces of Nels and Monty and Nick to be brooding, cold, watchful. She wondered why Stewart did not look toward Bonita. He, too, was now dark-faced, cool, quiet, with something ominous about him.

"Hawe, I'll submit to arrest without any fuss," he said, slowly, "if you'll take the ropes off that girl."

"Nope," replied the sheriff. "She got away from me onct. She's hawg-tied now, an' she'll stay hawg-tied."

Madeline thought she saw Stewart give a slight start. But an unaccountable dimness came over her eyes, at brief intervals obscuring her keen sight. Vaguely she was conscious of a clogged and beating tumult in her breast.

"All right, let's hurry out of here," said Stewart. "You've made annoyance enough. Ride down to the corral with me. I'll get my horse and go with you."

"Hold on!" yelled Hawe, as Stewart turned away. "Not so fast. Who's doin' this? You don't come no El Capitan stunts on me. You'll ride one of my pack-horses, an' you'll go in irons."

"You want to handcuff me?" queried Stewart, with sudden swift start of passion.

"Want to? Haw, haw! Nope, Stewart, thet's jest my way with hoss-thieves, raiders, Greasers, murderers, an' sich. See hyar, you Sneed, git off an' put the irons on this man."

The guerrilla called Sneed slid off his horse and began to fumble in his saddle-bags.

"You see, Bill," went on Hawe, "I swore in a new depooty fer this particular job. Sneed is some handy. He rounded up thet little Mexican cat fer me."

Stillwell did not hear the sheriff; he was gazing at Stewart in a kind of imploring amaze.

"Gene, you ain't goin' to stand fer them handcuffs?" he pleaded.

"Yes," replied the cowboy. "Bill, old friend, I'm an outsider here. There's no call for Miss Hammond and—and her brother and Florence to be worried further about me. Their happy day has already been spoiled on my account. I want to get out quick."

"Wal, you might be too damn considerate of Miss Hammond's sensitive feelin's." There was now no trace of the courteous, kindly old rancher. He looked harder than stone. "How about my feelin's? I want to know if you're goin' to let this sneakin' coyote, this last gasp of the old rum-guzzlin' frontier sheriffs, put you in irons an' hawg-tie you an' drive you off to jail?"

"Yes," replied Stewart, steadily.

"Wal, by Gawd! You, Gene Stewart! What's come over you? Why, man, go in the house, an' I'll 'tend to this feller. Then to-morrow you can ride in an' give yourself up like a gentleman."

"No. I'll go. Thanks, Bill, for the way you and the boys would stick to me. Hurry, Hawe, before my mind changes."

His voice broke at the last, betraying the wonderful control he had kept over his passions. As he ceased speaking he seemed suddenly to become spiritless. He dropped his head.

Madeline saw in him then a semblance to the hopeless, shamed Stewart of earlier days. The vague riot in her breast leaped into conscious fury—a woman's passionate repudiation of Stewart's broken spirit. It was not that she would have him be a lawbreaker; it was that she could not bear to see him deny his manhood. Once she had entreated him to become her kind of a cowboy—a man in whom reason tempered passion. She had let him see how painful and shocking any violence was to her. And the idea had obsessed him, softened him, had grown like a stultifying lichen upon his will, had shorn him of a wild, bold spirit she now strangely longed to see him feel. When the man Sneed came forward, jingling the iron fetters, Madeline's blood turned to fire. She would have forgiven Stewart then for lapsing into the kind of cowboy it had been her blind and sickly sentiment to abhor. This was a man's West—a man's game. What right had a woman reared in a softer mold to use her beauty and her influence to change a man who was bold and free and strong? At that moment, with her blood hot and racing, she would have gloried in the violence which she had so deplored: she would have welcomed the action that had characterized Stewart's treatment of Don Carlos; she had in her the sudden dawning temper of a woman who had been assimilating the life and nature around her and who would not have turned her eyes away from a harsh and bloody deed.

But Stewart held forth his hands to be manacled. Then Madeline heard her own voice burst out in a ringing, imperious "Wait!"

In the time it took her to make the few steps to the edge of the porch, facing the men, she not only felt her anger and justice and pride summoning forces to her command, but there was something else calling—a deep, passionate, mysterious thing not born of the moment.

Sneed dropped the manacles. Stewart's face took on a chalky whiteness. Hawe, in a slow, stupid embarrassment beyond his control, removed his sombrero in a respect that seemed wrenched from him.

"Mr. Hawe, I can prove to you that Stewart was not concerned in any way whatever with the crime for which you want to arrest him."

The sheriff's stare underwent a blinking change. He coughed, stammered, and tried to speak. Manifestly, he had been thrown completely off his balance. Astonishment slowly merged into discomfiture.

"It was absolutely impossible for Stewart to have been connected with that assault," went on Madeline, swiftly, "for he was with me in the waiting-room of the station at the moment the assault was made outside. I assure you I have a distinct and vivid recollection. The door was open. I heard the voices of quarreling men. They grew louder. The language was Spanish. Evidently these men had left the dance-hall opposite and were approaching the station. I heard a woman's voice mingling with the others. It, too, was Spanish, and I could not understand. But the tone was beseeching. Then I heard footsteps on the gravel. I knew Stewart heard them. I could see from his face that something dreadful was about to happen. Just outside the door then there were hoarse, furious voices, a scuffle, a muffled shot, a woman's cry, the thud of a falling body, and rapid footsteps of a man running away. Next, the girl Bonita staggered into the door. She was white, trembling, terror-stricken. She recognized Stewart, appealed to him. Stewart supported her and endeavored to calm her. He was excited. He asked her if Danny Mains had been shot, or if he had done the shooting. The girl said no. She told Stewart that she had danced a little, flirted a little with vaqueros, and they had quarreled over her. Then Stewart took her outside and put her upon his horse. I saw the girl ride that horse down the street to disappear in the darkness."

While Madeline spoke another change appeared to be working in the man Hawe. He was not long disconcerted, but his discomfiture wore to a sullen fury, and his sharp features fixed in an expression of craft.

"Thet's mighty interestin', Miss Hammond, 'most as interestin' as a story-book," he said. "Now, since you're so obligin' a witness, I'd sure like to put a question or two. What time did you arrive at El Cajon thet night?"

"It was after eleven o'clock," replied Madeline.

"Nobody there to meet you?"

"No."

"The station agent an' operator both gone?"

"Yes."

"Wal, how soon did this feller Stewart show up?" Hawe continued, with a wry smile.

"Very soon after my arrival. I think—perhaps fifteen minutes, possibly a little more."

"Some dark an' lonesome around thet station, wasn't it?"

"Indeed yes."

"An' what time was the Greaser shot?" queried Hawe, with his little eyes gleaming like coals.

"Probably close to half past one. It was two o'clock when I looked at my watch at Florence Kingsley's house. Directly after Stewart sent Bonita away he took me to Miss Kingsley's. So, allowing for the walk and a few minutes' conversation with her, I can pretty definitely say the shooting took place at about half past one."

Stillwell heaved his big frame a step closer to the sheriff. "What 're you drivin' at?" he roared, his face black again.

"Evidence," snapped Hawe.

Madeline marveled at this interruption; and as Stewart irresistibly drew her glance she saw him gray-faced as ashes, shaking, utterly unnerved.

"I thank you, Miss Hammond," he said, huskily. "But you needn't answer any more of Hawe's questions. He's—he's—It's not necessary. I'll go with him now, under arrest. Bonita will corroborate your testimony in court, and that will save me from this—this man's spite."

Madeline, looking at Stewart, seeing a humility she at first took for cowardice, suddenly divined that it was not fear for himself which made him dread further disclosures of that night, but fear for her—fear of shame she might suffer through him.

Pat Hawe cocked his head to one side, like a vulture about to strike with his beak, and cunningly eyed Madeline.

"Considered as testimony, what you've said is sure important an' conclusive. But I'm calculatin' thet the court will want to hev explained why you stayed from eleven-thirty till one-thirty in thet waitin'-room alone with Stewart."

His deliberate speech met with what Madeline imagined a remarkable reception from Stewart, who gave a tigerish start; from Stillwell, whose big hands tore at the neck of his shirt, as if he was choking; from Alfred, who now strode hotly forward, to be stopped by the cold and silent Nels; from Monty Price, who uttered a violent "Aw!" which was both a hiss and a roar.

In the rush of her thought Madeline could not interpret the meaning of these things which seemed so strange at that moment. But they were portentous. Even as she was forming a reply to Hawe's speech she felt a chill creep over her.

"Stewart detained me in the waiting-room," she said, clear-voiced as a bell. "But we were not alone—all the time."

For a moment the only sound following her words was a gasp from Stewart. Hawe's face became transformed with a hideous amaze and joy.

"Detained?" he whispered, craning his lean and corded neck. "How's thet?"

"Stewart was drunk. He—"

With sudden passionate gesture of despair Stewart appealed to her:

"Oh, Miss Hammond, don't! don't! DON'T!..."

Then he seemed to sink down, head lowered upon his breast, in utter shame. Stillwell's great hand swept to the bowed shoulder, and he turned to Madeline.

"Miss Majesty, I reckon you'd be wise to tell all," said the old cattleman, gravely. "There ain't one of us who could misunderstand any motive or act of yours. Mebbe a stroke of lightnin' might clear this murky air. Whatever Gene Stewart did that onlucky night—you tell it."

Madeline's dignity and self-possession had been disturbed by Stewart's importunity. She broke into swift, disconnected speech:

"He came into the station—a few minutes after I got there. I asked-to be shown to a hotel. He said there wasn't any that would accommodate married women. He grasped my hand—looked for a wedding-ring. Then I saw he was—he was intoxicated. He told me he would go for a hotel porter. But he came back with a padre—Padre Marcos. The poor priest was—terribly frightened. So was I. Stewart had turned into a devil. He fired his gun at the padre's feet. He pushed me into a bench. Again he shot—right before my face. I—I nearly fainted. But I heard him cursing the padre—heard the padre praying or chanting—I didn't know what. Stewart tried to make me say things in Spanish. All at once he asked my name. I told him. He jerked at my veil. I took it off. Then he threw his gun down—pushed the padre out of the door. That was just before the vaqueros approached with Bonita. Padre Marcos must have seen them—must have heard them. After that Stewart grew quickly sober. He was mortified—distressed—stricken with shame. He told me he had been drinking at a wedding —I remember, it was Ed Linton's wedding. Then he explained—the boys were always gambling—he wagered he would marry the first girl who arrived at El Cajon. I happened to be the first one. He tried to force me to marry him. The rest—relating to the assault on the vaquero—I have already told you."

Madeline ended, out of breath and panting, with her hands pressed upon her heaving bosom. Revelation of that secret liberated emotion; those hurried outspoken words had made her throb and tremble and burn. Strangely then she thought of Alfred and his wrath. But he stood motionless, as if dazed. Stillwell was trying to holster up the crushed Stewart.

Hawe rolled his red eyes and threw back his head.

"Ho, ho, ho! Ho, ho, ho! Say, Sneed, you didn't miss any of it, did ye? Haw, haw! Best I ever heerd in all my born days. Ho, ho!"

Then he ceased laughing, and with glinting gaze upon Madeline, insolent and vicious and savage, he began to drawl:

"Wal now, my lady, I reckon your story, if it tallies with Bonita's an' Padre Marcos's, will clear Gene Stewart in the eyes of the court." Here he grew slower, more biting, sharper and harder of face. "But you needn't expect Pat Hawe or the court to swaller thet part of your story—about bein' detained unwillin'!"

Madeline had not time to grasp the sense of his last words. Stewart had convulsively sprung upward, white as chalk. As he leaped at Hawe Stillwell interposed his huge bulk and wrapped his arms around Stewart. There was a brief, whirling, wrestling struggle. Stewart appeared to be besting the old cattleman.

"Help, boys, help!" yelled Stillwell. "I can't hold him. Hurry, or there's goin' to be blood spilled!"

Nick Steele and several cowboys leaped to Stillwell's assistance. Stewart, getting free, tossed one aside and then another. They closed in on him. For an instant a furious straining wrestle of powerful bodies made rasp and shock and blow. Once Stewart heaved them from him. But they plunged back upon him—conquered him.

"Gene! Why, Gene!" panted the old cattleman. "Sure you're locoed—to act this way. Cool down! Cool down! Why, boy, it's all right. Jest stand still—give us a chance to talk to you. It's only ole Bill, you know—your ole pal who's tried to be a daddy to you. He's only wantin' you to hev sense—to be cool—to wait."

"Let me go! Let me go!" cried Stewart; and the poignancy of that cry pierced Madeline's heart. "Let me go, Bill, if you're my friend. I saved your life once—over in the desert. You swore you'd never forget. Boys, make him let me go! Oh, I don't care what Hawe's said or done to me! It was that about her! Are you all a lot of Greasers? How can you stand it? Damn you for a lot of cowards! There's a limit, I tell you." Then his voice broke, fell to a whisper. "Bill, dear old Bill, let me go. I'll kill him! You know I'll kill him!"

"Gene, I know you'd kill him if you hed an even break," replied Stillwell, soothingly. "But, Gene, why, you ain't even packin' a gun! An' there's Pat lookin' nasty, with his hand nervous-like. He seen you hed no gun. He'd jump at the chance to plug you now, an' then holler about opposition to the law. Cool down, son; it'll all come right."

Suddenly Madeline was transfixed by a terrible sound.

Her startled glance shifted from the anxious group round Stewart to see that Monty Price had leaped off the porch. He crouched down with his bands below his hips, where the big guns swung. From his distorted lips issued that which was combined roar and bellow and Indian war-whoop, and, more than all, a horrible warning cry. He resembled a hunchback about to make the leap of a demon. He was quivering, vibrating. His eyes, black and hot, were fastened with most piercing intentness upon Hawe and Sneed.

"Git back, Bill, git back!" he roared. "Git 'em back!" With one lunge Stillwell shoved Stewart and Nick and the other cowboys up on the porch. Then he crowded Madeline and Alfred and Florence to the wall, tried to force them farther. His motions were rapid and stern. But failing to get them through door and windows, he planted his wide person between the women and danger. Madeline grasped his arm, held on, and peered fearfully from behind his broad shoulder.

"You, Hawe! You, Sneed!" called Monty, in that same wild voice. "Don't you move a finger or an eyelash!"

Madeline's faculties nerved to keen, thrilling divination. She grasped the relation between Monty's terrible cry and the strange hunched posture he had assumed. Stillwell's haste and silence, too, were pregnant of catastrophe.

"Nels, git in this!" yelled Monty; and all the time he never shifted his intent gaze as much as a hair's-breadth from Hawe and his deputy. "Nels, chase away them two fellers hangin' back there. Chase 'em, quick!"

These men, the two deputies who had remained in the background with the pack-horses, did not wait for Nels. They spurred their mounts, wheeled, and galloped away.

"Now, Nels, cut the gurl loose," ordered Monty.

Nels ran forward, jerked the halter out of Sneed's hand, and pulled Bonita's horse in close to the porch. As he slit the rope which bound her she fell into his arms.

"Hawe, git down!" went on Monty. "Face front an' stiff!"

The sheriff swung his leg, and, never moving his hands, with his face now a deathly, sickening white, he slid to the ground.

"Line up there beside your guerrilla pard. There! You two make a damn fine pictoor, a damn fine team of pizened coyote an' a cross between a wild mule an' a Greaser. Now listen!"

Monty made a long pause, in which his breathing was plainly audible.

Madeline's eyes were riveted upon Monty. Her mind, swift as lightning, had gathered the subtleties in action and word succeeding his domination of the men. Violence, terrible violence, the thing she had felt, the thing she had feared, the thing she had sought to eliminate from among her cowboys, was, after many months, about to be enacted before her eyes. It had come at last. She had softened Stillwell, she had influenced Nels, she had changed Stewart; but this little black-faced, terrible Monty Price now rose, as it were, out of his past wild years, and no power on earth or in heaven could stay his hand. It was the hard life of wild men in a wild country that was about to strike this blow at her. She did not shudder; she did not wish to blot out from sight this little man, terrible in his mood of wild justice. She suffered a flash of horror that Monty, blind and dead to her authority, cold as steel toward her presence, understood the deeps of a woman's soul. For in this moment of strife, of insult to her, of torture to the man she had uplifted and then broken, the passion of her reached deep toward primitive hate. With eyes slowly hazing red, she watched Monty Price; she listened with thrumming ears; she waited, slowly sagging against Stillwell.

"Hawe, if you an' your dirty pard hev loved the sound of human voice, then listen an' listen hard," said Monty. "Fer I've been goin' contrary to my ole style jest to hev a talk with you. You all but got away on your nerve, didn't you? 'Cause why? You roll in here like a mad steer an' flash yer badge an' talk mean, then almost bluff away with it. You heerd all about

Miss Hammond's cowboy outfit stoppin' drinkin' an' cussin' an' packin' guns. They've took on religion an' decent livin', an' sure they'll be easy to hobble an' drive to jail. Hawe, listen. There was a good an' noble an be-ootiful woman come out of the East somewheres, an' she brought a lot of sunshine an' happiness an' new ideas into the tough lives of cowboys. I reckon it's beyond you to know what she come to mean to them. Wal, I'll tell you. They-all went clean out of their heads. They-all got soft an' easy an' sweet-tempered. They got so they couldn't kill a coyote, a crippled calf in a mud-hole. They took to books, an' writin' home to mother an' sister, an' to savin' money, an' to gittin' married. Onct they was only a lot of poor cowboys, an' then sudden-like they was human bein's, livin' in a big world thet hed somethin' sweet even fer them. Even fer me—an ole, worn-out, hobble-legged, burned-up cowman like me! Do you git thet? An' you, Mister Hawe, you come along, not satisfied with ropin' an' beatin', an' Gaw knows what else, of thet friendless little Bonita; you come along an' face the lady we fellers honor an' love an' reverence, an' you—you—Hell's fire!"

With whistling breath, foaming at the mouth, Monty Price crouched lower, hands at his hips, and he edged inch by inch farther out from the porch, closer to Hawe and Sneed. Madeline saw them only in the blurred fringe of her sight. They resembled specters. She heard the shrill whistle of a horse and recognized Majesty calling her from the corral.

"Thet's all!" roared Monty, in a voice now strangling. Lower and lower he bent, a terrible figure of ferocity. "Now, both you armed ocifers of the law, come on! Flash your guns! Throw 'em, an' be quick! Monty Price is done! There'll be daylight through you both before you fan a hammer! But I'm givin' you a chanst to sting me. You holler law, an' my way is the ole law."

His breath came quicker, his voice grew hoarser, and he crouched lower. All his body except his rigid arms quivered with a wonderful muscular convulsion.

"Dogs! Skunks! Buzzards! Flash them guns, er I'll flash mine! Aha!"

To Madeline it seemed the three stiff, crouching men leaped into instant and united action. She saw streaks of fire—streaks of smoke. Then a crashing volley deafened her. It ceased as quickly. Smoke veiled the scene. Slowly it drifted away to disclose three fallen men, one of whom, Monty, leaned on his left hand, a smoking gun in his right. He watched for a movement from the other two. It did not come. Then, with a terrible smile, he slid back and stretched out.

❧ 21 ❧

UNBRIDLED

In waking and sleeping hours Madeline Hammond could not release herself from the thralling memory of that tragedy. She was haunted by Monty Price's terrible smile. Only in action of some kind could she escape; and to that end she worked, she walked and rode. She even overcame a strong feeling, which she feared was unreasonable disgust, for the Mexican girl Bonita, who lay ill at the ranch, bruised and feverish, in need of skilful nursing.

Madeline felt there was something inscrutable changing her soul. That strife—the struggle to decide her destiny for East or West—held still further aloof. She was never spiritually alone. There was a step on her trail. Indoors she was oppressed. She required the open—the light and wind, the sight of endless slope, the sounds of corral and pond and field, physical things, natural things.

One afternoon she rode down to the alfalfa-fields, round them, and back up to the spillway of the lower lake, where a group of mesquite-trees, owing to the water that seeped through the sand to their roots, had taken on bloom and beauty of renewed life. Under these trees there was shade enough to make a pleasant place to linger. Madeline dismounted, desiring to rest a little. She liked this quiet, lonely spot. It was really the only secluded nook near the house. If she rode down into the valley or out to the mesa or up on the foothills she could not go alone. Probably now Stillwell or Nels knew her whereabouts. But as she was comparatively hidden here, she imagined a solitude that was not actually hers.

Her horse, Majesty, tossed his head and flung his mane and switched his tail at the flies. He would rather have been cutting the wind down the valley slope. Madeline sat with her back against a tree, and took off her sombrero. The soft breeze, fanning her hot face, blowing strands of her hair, was refreshingly cool. She heard the slow tramp of cattle going in to drink. That sound ceased, and the grove of mesquites appeared to be lifeless, except for her and her horse. It was, however, only after moments of attention that she found the place was far from being dead. Keen eyes and ears brought reward. Desert quail, as gray as the bare earth, were dusting themselves in a shady spot. A bee, swift as light, hummed by. She saw a horned toad, the color of stone, squatting low, hiding fearfully in the sand within reach of her whip. She extended the point of the whip, and the toad quivered and swelled and hissed. It was instinct with fight. The wind faintly stirred the thin foliage of the mesquites, making a mournful sigh. From far up in the foothills, barely distinguishable, came the scream of an eagle. The bray of a burro brought a brief, discordant break. Then a brown bird darted down from an unseen perch and made a swift, irregular flight after a fluttering winged insect. Madeline heard the sharp snapping of a merciless beak. Indeed, there was more than life in the shade of the mesquites.

Suddenly Majesty picked up his long ears and snorted. Then Madeline heard a slow pad of hoofs. A horse was approaching from the direction of the lake. Madeline had learned to be wary, and, mounting Majesty, she turned him toward the open. A moment later she felt glad of her caution, for, looking back between the trees, she saw Stewart leading a horse into the grove. She would as lief have met a guerrilla as this cowboy.

Majesty had broken into a trot when a shrill whistle rent the air. The horse leaped and, wheeling so swiftly that he nearly unseated Madeline, he charged back straight for the mesquites. Madeline spoke to him, cried angrily at him, pulled with all her strength upon the bridle, but was helplessly unable to stop him. He whistled a piercing blast. Madeline realized then that Stewart, his old master, had called him and that nothing could turn him. She gave up trying, and attended to the urgent need of intercepting mesquite boughs that Majesty thrashed into motion. The horse thumped into an aisle between the trees and, stopping before Stewart, whinnied eagerly.

Madeline, not knowing what to expect, had not time for any feeling but amaze. A quick glance showed her Stewart in rough garb, dressed for the trail, and leading a wiry horse, saddled and packed. When Stewart, without looking at her, put his arm around Majesty's neck and laid his face against the flowing mane Madeline's heart suddenly began to beat with unwonted quickness. Stewart seemed oblivious to her presence. His eyes were closed. His dark face softened, lost its hardness and fierceness and sadness, and for an instant became beautiful.

Madeline instantly divined what his action meant. He was leaving the ranch; this was his good-by to his horse. How strange, sad, fine was this love between man and beast! A dimness confused Madeline's eyes; she hurriedly brushed it away, and it came back wet and blurring. She averted her face, ashamed of the tears Stewart might see. She was sorry for him. He was going away, and this time, judging from the nature of his farewell to his horse, it was to be forever. Like a stab from a cold blade a pain shot through Madeline's heart. The wonder of it, the incomprehensibility of it, the utter newness and strangeness of this sharp pain that now left behind a dull pang, made her forget Stewart, her surroundings, everything except to search her heart. Maybe here was the secret that had eluded her. She trembled on the brink of something unknown. In some strange way the emotion brought back her girlhood. Her mind revolved swift queries and replies; she was living, feeling, learning; happiness mocked at her from behind a barred door, and the bar of that door seemed to be an inexplicable pain. Then like lightning strokes shot the questions: Why should pain hide her happiness? What was her happiness? What relation had it to this man? Why should she feel strangely about his departure? And the voices within her were silenced, stunned, unanswered.

"I want to talk to you," said Stewart.

Madeline started, turned to him, and now she saw the earlier Stewart, the man who reminded her of their first meeting at El Cajon, of that memorable meeting at Chiricahua.

"I want to ask you something," he went on. "I've been wanting to know something. That's why I've hung on here. You never spoke to me, never noticed me, never gave me a chance to ask you. But now I'm going over—over the border. And I want to know. Why did you refuse to listen to me?"

At his last words that hot shame, tenfold more stifling than when it had before humiliated Madeline, rushed over her, sending the scarlet in a wave to her temples. It seemed that his words made her realize she was actually face to face with him, that somehow a shame she would rather have died than revealed was being liberated. Biting her lips to hold back speech, she jerked on Majesty's bridle, struck him with her whip, spurred him. Stewart's iron arm held the horse. Then Madeline, in a flash of passion, struck at Stewart's face, missed it, struck again, and hit. With one pull, almost drawing her from the saddle, he tore the whip from her hands. It was not that action on his part, or the sudden strong masterfulness of his look, so much as the livid mark on his face where the whip had lashed that quieted, if it did not check, her fury.

"That's nothing," he said, with something of his old audacity. "That's nothing to how you've hurt me."

Madeline battled with herself for control. This man would not be denied. Never before had the hardness of his face, the flinty hardness of these desert-bred men, so struck her with its revelation of the unbridled spirit. He looked stern, haggard, bitter. The dark shade was changing to gray—the gray to ash-color of passion. About him now there was only the ghost of that finer, gentler man she had helped to bring into being. The piercing dark eyes he bent upon her burned her, went through her as if he were looking into her soul. Then Madeline's quick sight caught a fleeting doubt, a wistfulness, a surprised and saddened certainty in his eyes, saw it shade and pass away. Her woman's intuition, as keen as her sight, told her Stewart in that moment had sustained a shock of bitter, final truth.

For the third time he repeated his question to her. Madeline did not answer; she could not speak.

"You don't know I love you, do you?" he continued, passionately. "That ever since you stood before me in that hole at Chiricahua I've loved you? You can't see I've been another man, loving you, working for you, living for you? You won't believe I've turned my back on the old wild life, that I've been decent and honorable and happy and useful—your kind of a cowboy? You couldn't tell, though I loved you, that I never wanted you to know it, that I never dared to think of you except as my angel, my holy Virgin? What do you know of a man's heart and soul? How could you tell of the love, the salvation of a man who's lived his life in the silence and loneliness? Who could teach you the actual truth—that a wild cowboy, faithless to mother and sister, except in memory, riding a hard, drunken trail straight to hell; had looked into the face, the eyes of a beautiful woman infinitely beyond him, above him, and had so loved her that he was saved—that he became faithful again—that he saw her face in every flower and her eyes in the blue heaven? Who could tell you, when at night I stood alone under these Western stars, how deep in my soul I was glad just to be alive, to be able to do something for you, to be near you, to stand between you and worry, trouble, danger, to feel somehow that I was a part, just a little part of the West you had come to love?"

Madeline was mute. She heard her heart thundering in her ears.

Stewart leaped at her. His powerful hand closed on her arm. She trembled. His action presaged the old instinctive violence.

"No; but you think I kept Bonita up in the mountains, that I went secretly to meet her, that all the while I served you I was—Oh, I know what you think! I know now. I never knew till I made you look at me. Now, say it! Speak!"

White-hot, blinded, utterly in the fiery grasp of passion, powerless to stem the rush of a word both shameful and revealing and fatal, Madeline cried:

"YES!"

He had wrenched that word from her, but he was not subtle enough, not versed in the mystery of woman's motive enough, to divine the deep significance of her reply.

For him the word had only literal meaning confirming the dishonor in which she held him. Dropping her arm, he shrank back, a strange action for the savage and crude man she judged him to be.

"But that day at Chiricahua you spoke of faith," he burst out. "You said the greatest thing in the world was faith in human nature. You said the finest men had been those who had fallen low and had risen. You said you had faith in me! You made me have faith in myself!"

His reproach, without bitterness or scorn, was a lash to her old egoistic belief in her fairness. She had preached a beautiful principle that she had failed to live up to. She understood his rebuke, she wondered and wavered, but the affront to her pride had been too great, the tumult within her breast had been too startlingly fierce; she could not speak, the moment passed, and with it his brief, rugged splendor of simplicity.

"You think I am vile," he said. "You think that about Bonita! And all the time I've been... I could make you ashamed—I could tell you—"

His passionate utterance ceased with a snap of his teeth. His lips set in a thin, bitter line. The agitation of his face preceded a convulsive wrestling of his shoulders. All this swift action denoted an inner combat, and it nearly overwhelmed him.

"No, no!" he panted. Was it his answer to some mighty temptation? Then, like a bent sapling released, he sprang erect. "But I'll be the man—the dog—you think me!"

He laid hold of her arm with rude, powerful clutch. One pull drew her sliding half out of the saddle into his arms. She fell with her breast against his, not wholly free of stirrups or horse, and there she hung, utterly powerless. Maddened, writhing, she tore to release herself. All she could accomplish was to twist herself, raise herself high enough to see his face. That almost paralyzed her. Did he mean to kill her? Then he wrapped his arms around her and crushed her tighter, closer to him. She felt the pound of his heart; her own seemed to have frozen. Then he pressed his burning lips to hers. It was a long, terrible kiss. She felt him shake.

"Oh, Stewart! I—implore—you—let—me—go!" she whispered.

His white face loomed over hers. She closed her eyes. He rained kisses upon her face, but no more upon her mouth. On her closed eyes, her hair, her cheeks, her neck he pressed swift lips—lips that lost their fire and grew cold. Then he released her, and, lifting and righting her in the saddle, he still held her arm to keep her from falling.

For a moment Madeline sat on her horse with shut eyes. She dreaded the light.

"Now you can't say you've never been kissed," Stewart said. His voice seemed a long way off. "But that was coming to you, so be game. Here!"

She felt something hard and cold and metallic thrust into her hand. He made her fingers close over it, hold it. The feel of the thing revived her. She opened her eyes. Stewart had given her his gun. He stood with his broad breast against her knee, and she looked up to see that old mocking smile on his face.

"Go ahead! Throw my gun on me! Be a thoroughbred!"

Madeline did not yet grasp his meaning.

"You can put me down in that quiet place on the hill—beside Monty Price."

Madeline dropped the gun with a shuddering cry of horror. The sense of his words, the memory of Monty, the certainty that she would kill Stewart if she held the gun an instant longer, tortured the self-accusing cry from her.

Stewart stooped to pick up the weapon.

"You might have saved me a hell of a lot of trouble," he said, with another flash of the mocking smile. "You're beautiful and sweet and proud, but you're no thoroughbred! Majesty Hammond, adios!"

Stewart leaped for the saddle of his horse, and with the flying mount crashed through the mesquites to disappear.

❧ 22 ❧

THE SECRET TOLD

IN THE SHADED seclusion of her room, buried face down deep among the soft cushions on her couch, Madeline Hammond lay prostrate and quivering under the outrage she had suffered.

The afternoon wore away; twilight fell; night came; and then Madeline rose to sit by the window to let the cool wind blow upon her hot face. She passed through hours of unintelligible shame and impotent rage and futile striving to reason away her defilement.

The train of brightening stars seemed to mock her with their unattainable passionless serenity. She had loved them, and now she imagined she hated them and everything connected with this wild, fateful, and abrupt West.

She would go home.

Edith Wayne had been right; the West was no place for Madeline Hammond. The decision to go home came easily, naturally, she thought, as the result of events. It caused her no mental strife. Indeed, she fancied she felt relief. The great stars, blinking white and cold over the dark crags, looked down upon her, and, as always, after she had watched them for a while they enthralled her. "Under Western stars," she mused, thinking a little scornfully of the romantic destiny they had blazed for her idle sentiment. But they were beautiful; they were speaking; they were mocking; they drew her. "Ah!" she sighed. "It will not be so very easy to leave them, after all."

Madeline closed and darkened the window. She struck a light. It was necessary to tell the anxious servants who knocked that she was well and required nothing. A soft step on the walk outside arrested her. Who was there—Nels or Nick Steele or Stillwell? Who shared the guardianship over her, now that Monty Price was dead and that other—that savage—? It was monstrous and unfathomable that she regretted him.

The light annoyed her. Complete darkness fitted her strange mood. She retired and tried to compose herself to sleep. Sleep for her was not a matter of will. Her cheeks burned so hotly that she rose to bathe them. Cold water would not alleviate this burn, and then, despairing of forgetfulness, she lay down again with a shameful gratitude for the cloak of night. Stewart's kisses were there, scorching her lips, her closed eyes, her swelling neck. They

363

penetrated deeper and deeper into her blood, into her heart, into her soul—the terrible farewell kisses of a passionate, hardened man. Despite his baseness, he had loved her.

Late in the night Madeline fell asleep. In the morning she was pale and languid, but in a mental condition that promised composure.

It was considerably after her regular hour that Madeline repaired to her office. The door was open, and just outside, tipped back in a chair, sat Stillwell.

"Mawnin', Miss Majesty," he said, as he rose to greet her with his usual courtesy. There were signs of trouble in his lined face. Madeline shrank inwardly, fearing his old lamentations about Stewart. Then she saw a dusty, ragged pony in the yard and a little burro drooping under a heavy pack. Both animals bore evidence of long, arduous travel.

"To whom do they belong?" asked Madeline.

"Them critters? Why, Danny Mains," replied Stillwell, with a cough that betrayed embarrassment.

"Danny Mains?" echoed Madeline, wonderingly.

"Wal, I said so."

Stillwell was indeed not himself.

"Is Danny Mains here?" she asked, in sudden curiosity.

The old cattleman nodded gloomily.

"Yep, he's hyar, all right. Sloped in from the hills, an' he hollered to see Bonita. He's locoed, too, about that little black-eyed hussy. Why, he hardly said, 'Howdy, Bill,' before he begun to ask wild an' eager questions. I took him in to see Bonita. He's been there more 'n a half-hour now."

Evidently Stillwell's sensitive feelings had been ruffled. Madeline's curiosity changed to blank astonishment, which left her with a thrilling premonition. She caught her breath. A thousand thoughts seemed thronging for clear conception in her mind.

Rapid footsteps with an accompaniment of clinking spurs sounded in the hallway. Then a young man ran out upon the porch. He resembled a cowboy in his lithe build, his garb and action, in the way he wore his gun, but his face, instead of being red, was clear brown tan. His eyes were blue; his hair was light and curly. He was a handsome, frank-faced boy. At sight of Madeline he slammed down his sombrero and, leaping at her, he possessed himself of her hands. His swift violence not only alarmed her, but painfully reminded her of something she wished to forget.

This cowboy bent his head and kissed her hands and wrung them, and when he straightened up he was crying.

"Miss Hammond, she's safe an' almost well, an' what I feared most ain't so, thank God," he cried. "Sure I'll never be able to pay you for all you've done for her. She's told me how she was dragged down here, how Gene tried to save her, how you spoke up for Gene an' her, too, how Monty at the last throwed his guns. Poor Monty! We were good friends, Monty an' I. But it wasn't friendship for me that made Monty stand in there. He would have saved her, anyway. Monty Price was the whitest man I ever knew. There's Nels an' Nick an' Gene, he's been some friend to me; but Monty Price was—he was grand. He never knew, any more than you or Bill, here, or the boys, what Bonita was to me."

Stillwell's kind and heavy hand fell upon the cowboy's shoulder.

"Danny, what's all this queer gab?" he asked. "An' you're takin' some liberty with Miss Hammond, who never seen you before. Sure I'm makin' allowance fer amazin' strange talk. I see you're not drinkin'. Mebbe you're plumb locoed. Come, ease up now an' talk sense."

The cowboy's fine, frank face broke into a smile. He dashed the tears from his eyes. Then he laughed. His laugh had a pleasant, boyish ring—a happy ring.

"Bill, old pal, stand bridle down a minute, will you?" Then he bowed to Madeline. "I beg your pardon, Miss Hammond, for seemin' rudeness. I'm Danny Mains. An' Bonita is my wife. I'm so crazy glad she's safe an' unharmed—so grateful to you that—why, sure it's a wonder I didn't kiss you outright."

"Bonita's your wife!" ejaculated Stillwell.

"Sure. We've been married for months," replied Danny, happily. "Gene Stewart did it. Good old Gene, he's hell on marryin'. I guess maybe I haven't come to pay him up for all he's done for me! You see, I've been in love with Bonita for two years. An' Gene—you know, Bill, what a way Gene has with girls—he was—well, he was tryin' to get Bonita to have me."

Madeline's quick, varying emotions were swallowed up in a boundless gladness. Something dark, deep, heavy, and somber was flooded from her heart. She had a sudden rich sense of gratitude toward this smiling, clean-faced cowboy whose blue eyes flashed through tears.

"Danny Mains!" she said, tremulously and smilingly. "If you are as glad as your news has made me—if you really think I merit such a reward—you may kiss me outright."

With a bashful wonder, but with right hearty will, Danny Mains availed himself of this gracious privilege. Stillwell snorted. The signs of his phenomenal smile were manifest, otherwise Madeline would have thought that snort an indication of furious disapproval.

"Bill, straddle a chair," said Danny. "You've gone back a heap these last few months, frettin' over your bad boys, Danny an' Gene. You'll need support under you while I'm throwin' my yarn. Story of my life, Bill." He placed a chair for Madeline. "Miss Hammond, beggin' your pardon again, I want you to listen, also. You've the face an' eyes of a woman who loves to hear of other people's happiness. Besides, somehow, it's easy for me to talk lookin' at you."

His manner subtly changed then. Possibly it took on a little swagger; certainly he lost the dignity that he had shown under stress of feeling; he was now more like a cowboy about to boast or affect some stunning maneuver. Walking off the porch, he stood before the weary horse and burro.

"Played out!" he exclaimed.

Then with the swift violence so characteristic of men of his class he slipped the pack from the burro and threw saddle and bridle from the horse.

"There! See 'em! Take a look at the last dog-gone weight you ever packed! You've been some faithful to Danny Mains. An' Danny Mains pays! Never a saddle again or a strap or a halter or a hobble so long as you live! So long as you live nothin' but grass an' clover, an' cool water in shady places, an' dusty swales to roll in an' rest an' sleep!"

Then he untied the pack and, taking a small, heavy sack from it, he came back upon the porch. Deliberately he dumped the contents of the sack at Stillwell's feet. Piece after piece of rock thumped upon the floor. The pieces were sharp, ragged, evidently broken from a ledge; the body of them was white in color, with yellow veins and bars and streaks. Stillwell grasped up one rock after another, stared and stuttered, put the rocks to his lips, dug into them with his shaking fingers; then he lay back in his chair, head against the wall, and as he gaped at Danny the old smile began to transform his face.

"Lord, Danny if you hevn't been an' gone an' struck it rich!"

Danny regarded Stillwell with lofty condescension.

"Some rich," he said. "Now, Bill, what've we got here, say, offhand?"

"Oh, Lord, Danny! I'm afraid to say. Look, Miss Majesty, jest look at the gold. I've lived among prospectors an' gold-mines fer thirty years, an' I never seen the beat of this."

"The Lost Mine of the Padres!" cried Danny, in stentorian voice. "An' it belongs to me!"

Stillwell made some incoherent sound as he sat up fascinated, quite beside himself.

"Bill, it was some long time ago since you saw me," said Danny. "Fact is, I know how you felt, because Gene kept me posted. I happened to run across Bonita, an' I wasn't goin' to let her ride away alone, when she told me she was in trouble. We hit the trail for the Peloncillos. Bonita had Gene's horse, an' she was to meet him up on the trail. We got to the mountains all right, an' nearly starved for a few days till Gene found us. He had got in trouble himself an' couldn't fetch much with him.

"We made for the crags an' built a cabin. I come down that day Gene sent his horse Majesty to you. Never saw Gene so broken-hearted. Well, after he sloped for the border Bonita an' I were hard put to it to keep alive. But we got along, an' I think it was then she began to care a little for me. Because I was decent. I killed cougars an' went down to Rodeo to get bounties for the skins, an' bought grub an' supplies I needed. Once I went to El Cajon an' run plumb into Gene. He was back from the revolution an' cuttin' up some. But I got away from him after doin' all I could to drag him out of town. A long time after that Gene trailed up to the crags an' found us. Gene had stopped drinkin', he'd changed wonderful, was fine an' dandy. It was then he began to pester the life out of me to make me marry Bonita. I was happy, so was she, an' I was some scared of spoilin' it. Bonita had been a little flirt, an' I was afraid she'd get shy of a halter, so I bucked against Gene. But I was all locoed, as it turned out. Gene would come up occasionally, packin' supplies for us, an' always he'd get after me to do the right thing by Bonita. Gene's so dog-gone hard to buck against! I had to give in, an' I asked Bonita to marry me. Well, she wouldn't at first—said she wasn't good enough for me. But I saw the marriage idea was workin' deep, an' I just kept on bein' as decent as I knew how. So it was my wantin' to marry Bonita—my bein' glad to marry her—that made her grow soft an' sweet an' pretty as—as a mountain quail. Gene fetched up Padre Marcos, an' he married us."

Danny paused in his narrative, breathing hard, as if the memory of the incident described had stirred strong and thrilling feeling in him. Stillwell's smile was rapturous. Madeline leaned toward Danny with her eyes shining.

"Miss Hammond, an' you, Bill Stillwell, now listen, for this is strange I've got to tell you. The afternoon Bonita an' I were married, when Gene an' the padre had gone, I was happy one minute an' low-hearted the next. I was miserable because I had a bad name. I couldn't buy even a decent dress for my pretty wife. Bonita heard me, an' she was some mysterious. She told me the story of the lost mine of the padres, an' she kissed me an made joyful over me in the strangest way. I knew marriage went to women's heads, an' I thought even Bonita had a spell.

"Well, she left me for a little, an' when she came back she wore some pretty yellow flowers in her hair. Her eyes were big an' black an' beautiful. She said some queer things about spirits rollin' rocks down the canyon. Then she said she wanted to show me where she always sat an' waited an' watched for me when I was away.

"She led me around under the crags to a long slope. It was some pretty there—clear an' open, with a long sweep, an' the desert yawnin' deep an' red. There were yellow flowers on that slope, the same kind she had in her hair—the same kind that Apache girl wore hundreds of years ago when she led the padre to the gold-mine.

"When I thought of that, an' saw Bonita's eyes, an' then heard the strange crack of rollin' rocks—heard them rattle down an' roll an' grow faint—I was some out of my head. But not for long. Them rocks were rollin' all right, only it was the weatherin' of the cliffs.

"An' there under the crags was a gold pocket.

"Then I was worse than locoed. I went gold-crazy. I worked like seventeen burros. Bill, I dug a lot of goldbearin' quartz. Bonita watched the trails for me, brought me water. That was how she come to get caught by Pat Hawe an' his guerrillas. Sure! Pat Hawe was so set on doin' Gene dirt that he mixed up with Don Carlos. Bonita will tell you some staggerin' news about that outfit. Just now my story is all gold."

Danny Mains got up and kicked back his chair. Blue lightning gleamed from his eyes as he thrust a hand toward Stillwell.

"Bill, old pal, put her there—give me your hand," he said. "You were always my friend. You had faith in me. Well, Danny Mains owes you, an' he owes Gene Stewart a good deal, an' Danny Mains pays. I want two pardners to help me work my gold-mine. You an' Gene. If there's any ranch hereabouts that takes your fancy I'll buy it. If Miss Hammond ever gets tired of her range an stock an' home I'll buy them for Gene. If there's any railroad or town round here that she likes I'll buy it. If I see anythin' myself that I like I'll buy it. Go out; find Gene for me. I'm achin' to see him, to tell him. Go fetch him; an' right here in this house, with my wife an' Miss Hammond as witnesses, we'll draw up a pardnership. Go find him, Bill. I want to show him this gold, show him how Danny Mains pays! An' the only bitter drop in my cup to-day is that I can't ever pay Monty Price."

Madeline's lips tremblingly formed to tell Danny Mains and Stillwell that the cowboy they wanted so much had left the ranch; but the flame of fine loyalty that burned in Danny's eyes, the happiness that made the old cattleman's face at once amazing and beautiful, stiffened her lips. She watched the huge Stillwell and the little cowboy, both talking wildly, as they walked off arm in arm to find Stewart. She imagined something of what Danny's disappointment would be, of the elder man's consternation and grief, when he learned Stewart had left for the border. At this juncture she looked up to see a strange, yet familiar figure approaching. Padre Marcos! Certain it was that Madeline felt herself trembling. What did his presence mean on this day? He had always avoided meeting her whenever possible. He had been exceedingly grateful for all she had done for his people, his church, and himself; but he had never thanked her in person. Perhaps he had come for that purpose now. But Madeline did not believe so.

Mention of Padre Marcos, sight of him, had always occasioned Madeline a little indefinable shock; and now, as he stepped to the porch, a shrunken, stooped, and sad-faced man, she was startled.

The padre bowed low to her.

"Senora, will you grant me audience?" he asked, in perfect English, and his voice was low-toned and grave.

"Certainly, Padre Marcos," replied Madeline; and she led him into her office.

"May I beg to close the doors?" he asked. "It is a matter of great moment, which you might not care to have any one hear."

Wonderingly Madeline inclined her head. The padre gently closed one door and then the others.

"Senora, I have come to disclose a secret—my own sinfulness in keeping it—and to implore your pardon. Do you remember that night Senor Stewart dragged me before you in the waiting-room at El Cajon?"

"Yes," replied Madeline.

"Senora, since that night you have been Senor Stewart's wife!"

Madeline became as motionless as stone. She seemed to feel nothing, only to hear.

"You are Senor Stewart's wife. I have kept the secret under fear of death. But I could keep it no longer. Senor Stewart may kill me now. Ah, Senora, it is very strange to you. You were so frightened that night, you knew not what happened. Senor Stewart threatened me. He forced you. He made me speak the service. He made you speak the Spanish yes. And I, Senora, knowing the deeds of these sinful cowboys, fearing worse than disgrace to one so beautiful and so good as you, I could not do less than marry you truly. At least you should be his wife. So I married you, truly, in the service of my church."

"My God!" cried Madeline, rising.

"Hear me! I implore you, Senora, hear me out! Do not leave me! Do not look so—so—Ah, Senora, let me speak a word for Senor Stewart. He was drunk that night. He did not know what he was about. In the morning he came to me, made me swear by my cross that I would not reveal the disgrace he had put upon you. If I did he would kill me. Life is nothing to the American vaquero, Senora. I promised to respect his command. But I did not tell him you were his wife. He did not dream I had truly married you. He went to fight for the freedom of my country—Senora, he is one splendid soldier—and I brooded over the sin of my secret. If he were killed I need never tell you. But if he lived I knew that I must some day.

"Strange indeed that Senor Stewart and Padre Marcos should both come to this ranch together. The great change your goodness wrought in my beloved people was no greater than the change in Senor Stewart. Senora, I feared you would go away one day, go back to your Eastern home, ignorant of the truth. The time came when I confessed to Stewart—said I must tell you. Senor, the man went mad with joy. I have never seen so supreme a joy. He threatened no more to kill me. That strong, cruel vaquero begged me not to tell the secret— never to reveal it. He confessed his love for you—a love something like the desert storm. He swore by all that was once sacred to him, and by my cross and my church, that he would be a good man, that he would be worthy to have you secretly his wife for the little time life left him to worship at your shrine. You needed never to know. So I held my tongue, half pitying him, half fearing him, and praying for some God-sent light.

"Senora, it was a fool's paradise that Stewart lived in. I saw him, often. When he took me up into the mountains to have me marry that wayward Bonita and her lover I came to have respect for a man whose ideas about nature and life and God were at a variance with mine. But the man is a worshiper of God in all material things. He is a part of the wind and sun and desert and mountain that have made him. I have never heard more beautiful words than those in which he persuaded Bonita to accept Senor Mains, to forget her old lovers, and henceforth to be happy. He is their friend. I wish I could tell you what that means. It sounds so simple. It is really simple. All great things are so. For Senor Stewart it was natural to be loyal to his friend, to have a fine sense of the honor due to a woman who had loved and given, to bring about their marriage, to succor them in their need and loneliness. It was natural for him never to speak of them. It would have been natural for him to give his life in their defense if peril menaced them. Senora, I want you to understand that to me the man has the same stability, the same strength, the same elements which I am in the habit of attributing to the physical life around me in this wild and rugged desert."

Madeline listened as one under a spell. It was not only that this soft-voiced, eloquent priest knew how to move the heart, stir the soul; but his defense, his praise of Stewart, if they had been couched in the crude speech of cowboys, would have been a glory to her.

"Senora, I pray you, do not misunderstand my mission. Beyond my confession to you I have only a duty to tell you of the man whose wife you are. But I am a priest and I can read the soul. The ways of God are inscrutable. I am only a humble instrument. You are a noble woman, and Senor Stewart is a man of desert iron forged anew in the crucible of love. Quien sabe? Senor Stewart swore he would kill me if I betrayed him. But he will not lift his hand against me. For the man bears you a very great and pure love, and it has changed him. I no longer fear his threat, but I do fear his anger, should he ever know I spoke of his love, of his fool's paradise. I have watched his dark face turned to the sun setting over the desert. I have watched him lift it to the light of the stars. Think, my gracious and noble lady, think what is his paradise? To love you above the spirit of the flesh; to know you are his wife, his, never to be another's except by his sacrifice; to watch you with a secret glory of joy and pride; to stand, while he might, between you and evil; to find his happiness in service; to wait, with never a dream of telling you, for the hour to come when to leave you free he must go out and get himself shot! Senora, that is beautiful, it is sublime, it is terrible. It has brought me to you with my confession. I repeat, Senora, the ways of God are inscrutable. What is the meaning of your influence upon Senor Stewart? Once he was merely an animal, brutal, unquickened; now he is a man—I have not seen his like! So I beseech you in my humble office as priest, as a lover of mankind, before you send Stewart to his death, to be sure there is here no mysterious dispensation of God. Love, that mighty and blessed and unknown thing, might be at work. Senora, I have heard that somewhere in the rich Eastern cities you are a very great lady. I know you are good and noble. That is all I want to know. To me you are only a woman, the same as Senor Stewart is only a man. So I pray you, Senora, before you let Stewart give you freedom at such cost be sure you do not want his love, lest you cast away something sweet and ennobling which you yourself have created."

❧ 23 ❧

THE LIGHT OF WESTERN STARS

BLINDED, like a wild creature, Madeline Hammond ran to her room. She felt as if a stroke of lightning had shattered the shadowy substance of the dream she had made of real life. The wonder of Danny Mains's story, the strange regret with which she had realized her injustice to Stewart, the astounding secret as revealed by Padre Marcos—these were forgotten in the sudden consciousness of her own love.

Madeline fled as if pursued. With trembling hands she locked the doors, drew the blinds of the windows that opened on the porch, pushed chairs aside so that she could pace the length of her room. She was now alone, and she walked with soft, hurried, uneven steps. She could be herself here; she needed no mask; the long habit of serenely hiding the truth from the world and from herself could be broken. The seclusion of her darkened chamber made possible that betrayal of herself to which she was impelled.

She paused in her swift pacing to and fro. She liberated the thought that knocked at the gates of her mind. With quivering lips she whispered it. Then she spoke aloud:

"I will say it—hear it. I—I love him!"

"I love him!" she repeated the astounding truth, but she doubted her identity.

"Am I still Madeline Hammond? What has happened? Who am I?" She stood where the light from one unclosed window fell upon her image in the mirror. "Who is this woman?"

She expected to see a familiar, dignified person, a quiet, unruffled figure, a tranquil face with dark, proud eyes and calm, proud lips. No, she did not see Madeline Hammond. She did not see any one she knew. Were her eyes, like her heart, playing her false? The figure before her was instinct with pulsating life. The hands she saw, clasped together, pressed deep into a swelling bosom that heaved with each panting breath. The face she saw—white, rapt, strangely glowing, with parted, quivering lips, with great, staring, tragic eyes—this could not be Madeline Hammond's face.

Yet as she looked she knew no fancy could really deceive her, that she was only Madeline Hammond come at last to the end of brooding dreams. She swiftly realized the change in her, divined its cause and meaning, accepted it as inevitable, and straightway fell back again into the mood of bewildering amaze.

Calmness was unattainable. The surprise absorbed her. She could not go back to count the innumerable, imperceptible steps of her undoing. Her old power of reflecting, analyzing, even thinking at all, seemed to have vanished in a pulse-stirring sense of one new emotion. She only felt all her instinctive outward action that was a physical relief, all her involuntary inner strife that was maddening, yet unutterably sweet; and they seemed to be just one bewildering effect of surprise.

In a nature like hers, where strength of feeling had long been inhibited as a matter of training, such a transforming surprise as sudden consciousness of passionate love required time for its awakening, time for its sway.

By and by that last enlightening moment came, and Madeline Hammond faced not only the love in her heart, but the thought of the man she loved.

Suddenly, as she raged, something in her—this dauntless new personality—took arms against indictment of Gene Stewart. Her mind whirled about him and his life. She saw him drunk, brutal; she saw him abandoned, lost. Then out of the picture she had of him thus slowly grew one of a different man—weak, sick, changed by shock, growing strong, strangely, spiritually altered, silent, lonely like an eagle, secretive, tireless, faithful, soft as a woman, hard as iron to endure, and at the last noble.

She softened. In a flash her complex mood changed to one wherein she thought of the truth, the beauty, the wonder of Stewart's uplifting. Humbly she trusted that she had helped him to climb. That influence had been the best she had ever exerted. It had wrought magic in her own character. By it she had reached some higher, nobler plane of trust in man. She had received infinitely more than she had given.

Her swiftly flying memory seemed to assort a vast mine of treasures of the past. Of that letter Stewart had written to her brother she saw vivid words. But ah! she had known, and if it had not made any difference then, now it made all in the world. She recalled how her loosened hair had blown across his lips that night he had ridden down from the mountains carrying her in his arms. She recalled the strange joy of pride in Stewart's eyes when he had suddenly come upon her dressed to receive her Eastern guests in the white gown with the red roses at her breast.

Swiftly as they had come these dreamful memories departed. There was to be no rest for her mind. All she had thought and felt seemed only to presage a tumult.

Heedless, desperate, she cast off the last remnant of self-control, turned from the old proud, pale, cold, self-contained ghost of herself to face this strange, strong, passionate woman. Then, with hands pressed to her beating heart, with eyes shut, she listened to the ringing trip-hammer voice of circumstance, of truth, of fatality. The whole story was revealed, simple enough in the sum of its complicated details, strange and beautiful in part, remorseless in its proof of great love on Stewart's side, in dreaming blindness on her own, and, from the first fatal moment to the last, prophetic of tragedy.

Madeline, like a prisoner in a cell, began again to pace to and fro.

"Oh, it is all terrible!" she cried. "I am his wife. His wife! That meeting with him—the marriage—then his fall, his love, his rise, his silence, his pride! And I can never be anything to him. Could I be anything to him? I, Madeline Hammond? But I am his wife, and I love him! His wife! I am the wife of a cowboy! That might be undone. Can my love be undone? Ah, do I want anything undone? He is gone. Gone! Could he have meant—I will not, dare not think of that. He will come back. No, he never will come back. Oh, what shall I do?"

For Madeline Hammond the days following that storm of feeling were leaden-footed, endless, hopeless—a long succession of weary hours, sleepless hours, passionate hours, all haunted by a fear slowly growing into torture, a fear that Stewart had crossed the border to invite the bullet which would give her freedom. The day came when she knew this to be true. The spiritual tidings reached her, not subtly as so many divinations had come, but in a clear, vital flash of certainty. Then she suffered. She burned inwardly, and the nature of that deep fire showed through her eyes. She kept to herself, waiting, waiting for her fears to be confirmed.

At times she broke out in wrath at the circumstances she had failed to control, at herself, at Stewart.

"He might have learned from Ambrose!" she exclaimed, sick with a bitterness she knew was not consistent with her pride. She recalled Christine's trenchant exposition of Ambrose's wooing: "He tell me he love me; he kees me; he hug me; he put me on his horse; he ride away with me; he marry me."

Then in the next breath Madeline denied this insistent clamoring of a love that was gradually breaking her spirit. Like a somber shadow remorse followed her, shading blacker. She had been blind to a man's honesty, manliness, uprightness, faith, and striving. She had been dead to love, to nobility that she had herself created. Padre Marcos's grave, wise words returned to haunt her. She fought her bitterness, scorned her intelligence, hated her pride, and, weakening, gave up more and more to a yearning, hopeless hope.

She had shunned the light of the stars as she had violently dismissed every hinting suggestive memory of Stewart's kisses. But one night she went deliberately to her window. There they shone. Her stars! Beautiful, passionless as always, but strangely closer, warmer, speaking a kinder language, helpful as they had never been, teaching her now that regret was futile, revealing to her in their one grand, blazing task the supreme duty of life—to be true.

Those shining stars made her yield. She whispered to them that they had claimed her— the West claimed her—Stewart claimed her forever, whether he lived or died. She gave up to her love. And it was as if he was there in person, dark-faced, fire-eyed, violent in his action, crushing her to his breast in that farewell moment, kissing her with one burning kiss of passion, then with cold, terrible lips of renunciation.

"I am your wife!" she whispered to him. In that moment, throbbing, exalted, quivering in her first sweet, tumultuous surrender to love, she would have given her all, her life, to be in his arms again, to meet his lips, to put forever out of his power any thought of wild sacrifice.

And on the morning of the next day, when Madeline went out upon the porch, Stillwell, haggard and stern, with a husky, incoherent word, handed her a message from El Cajon. She read:

El Capitan Stewart captured by rebel soldiers in fight at Agua Prieta yesterday. He was a sharpshooter in the Federal ranks. Sentenced to death Thursday at sunset.

❦ 24 ❦

THE RIDE

"STILLWELL!"

MADELINE'S CRY was more than the utterance of a breaking heart. It was full of agony. But also it uttered the shattering of a structure built of false pride, of old beliefs, of bloodless standards, of ignorance of self. It betrayed the final conquest of her doubts, and out of their darkness blazed the unquenchable spirit of a woman who had found herself, her love, her salvation, her duty to a man, and who would not be cheated.

The old cattleman stood mute before her, staring at her white face, at her eyes of flame.

"Stillwell! I am Stewart's wife!"

"My Gawd, Miss Majesty!" he burst out. "I knowed somethin' turrible was wrong. Aw, sure it's a pity—"

"Do you think I'll let him be shot when I know him now, when I'm no longer blind, when I love him?" she asked, with passionate swiftness. "I will save him. This is Wednesday morning. I have thirty-six hours to save his life. Stillwell, send for Link and the car!"

She went into her office. Her mind worked with extraordinary rapidity and clearness. Her plan, born in one lightning-like flash of thought, necessitated the careful wording of telegrams to Washington, to New York, to San Antonio. These were to Senators, Representatives, men high in public and private life, men who would remember her and who would serve her to their utmost. Never before had her position meant anything to her comparable with what it meant now. Never in all her life had money seemed the power that it was then. If she had been poor! A shuddering chill froze the thought at its inception. She dispelled heartbreaking thoughts. She had power. She had wealth. She would set into operation all the unlimited means these gave her—the wires and pulleys and strings underneath the surface of political and international life, the open, free, purchasing value of money or the deep, underground, mysterious, incalculably powerful influence moved by gold. She could save Stewart. She must await results—deadlocked in feeling, strained perhaps almost beyond endurance, because the suspense would be great; but she would allow no possibility of failure to enter her mind.

When she went outside the car was there with Link, helmet in hand, a cool, bright gleam

373

in his eyes, and with Stillwell, losing his haggard misery, beginning to respond to Madeline's spirit.

"Link, drive Stillwell to El Cajon in time for him to catch the El Paso train," she said. "Wait there for his return, and if any message comes from him, telephone it at once to me."

Then she gave Stillwell the telegrams to send from El Cajon and drafts to cash in El Paso. She instructed him to go before the rebel junta, then stationed at Juarez, to explain the situation, to bid them expect communications from Washington officials requesting and advising Stewart's exchange as a prisoner of war, to offer to buy his release from the rebel authorities.

When Stillwell had heard her through his huge, bowed form straightened, a ghost of his old smile just moved his lips. He was no longer young, and hope could not at once drive away stern and grim realities. As he bent over her hand his manner appeared courtly and reverent. But either he was speechless or felt the moment not one for him to break silence.

He climbed to a seat beside Link, who pocketed the watch he had been studying and leaned over the wheel. There was a crack, a muffled sound bursting into a roar, and the big car jerked forward to bound over the edge of the slope, to leap down the long incline, to shoot out upon the level valley floor and disappear in moving dust.

For the first time in days Madeline visited the gardens, the corrals, the lakes, the quarters of the cowboys. Though imagining she was calm, she feared she looked strange to Nels, to Nick, to Frankie Slade, to those boys best known to her. The situation for them must have been one of tormenting pain and bewilderment. They acted as if they wanted to say something to her, but found themselves spellbound. She wondered—did they know she was Stewart's wife? Stillwell had not had time to tell them; besides, he would not have mentioned the fact. These cowboys only knew that Stewart was sentenced to be shot; they knew if Madeline had not been angry with him he would not have gone in desperate fighting mood across the border. She spoke of the weather, of the horses and cattle, asked Nels when he was to go on duty, and turned away from the wide, sunlit, adobe-arched porch where the cowboys stood silent and bareheaded. Then one of her subtle impulses checked her.

"Nels, you and Nick need not go on duty to-day," she said. "I may want you. I—I—"

She hesitated, paused, and stood lingering there. Her glance had fallen upon Stewart's big black horse prancing in a near-by corral.

"I have sent Stillwell to El Paso," she went on, in a low voice she failed to hold steady. "He will save Stewart. I have to tell you—I am Stewart's wife!"

She felt the stricken amaze that made these men silent and immovable. With level gaze averted she left them. Returning to the house and her room, she prepared for something—for what? To wait!

Then a great invisible shadow seemed to hover behind her. She essayed many tasks, to fail of attention, to find that her mind held only Stewart and his fortunes. Why had he become a Federal? She reflected that he had won his title, El Capitan, fighting for Madero, the rebel. But Madero was now a Federal, and Stewart was true to him. In crossing the border had Stewart any other motive than the one he had implied to Madeline in his mocking smile and scornful words, "You might have saved me a hell of a lot of trouble!" What trouble? She felt again the cold shock of contact with the gun she had dropped in horror. He meant the trouble of getting himself shot in the only way a man could seek death without cowardice. But had he any other motive? She recalled Don Carlos and his guerrillas. Then the thought leaped up in her mind with gripping power that Stewart meant to hunt Don Carlos, to meet him, to kill him. It would be the deed of a silent, vengeful, implacable man driven by wild justice such as had been the deadly leaven in Monty Price. It was a deed to expect of Nels or

THE LIGHT OF WESTERN STARS

Nick Steel—and, aye, of Gene Stewart. Madeline felt regret that Stewart, as he had climbed so high, had not risen above deliberate seeking to kill his enemy, however evil that enemy.

The local newspapers, which came regularly a day late from El Paso and Douglas, had never won any particular interest from Madeline; now, however, she took up any copies she could find and read all the information pertaining to the revolution. Every word seemed vital to her, of moving significant force.

AMERICANS ROBBED BY MEXICAN REBELS

MADERA, STATE OF CHIHUAHUA, MEXICO, July 17.—Having looted the Madera Lumber Company's storehouses of $25,000 worth of goods and robbed scores of foreigners of horses and saddles, the rebel command of Gen. Antonio Rojas, comprising a thousand men, started westward to-day through the state of Sonora for Agnaymas and Pacific coast points.

The troops are headed for Dolores, where a mountain pass leads into the state of Sonora. Their entrance will be opposed by 1,000 Maderista volunteers, who are reported to be waiting the rebel invasion.

The railroad south of Madera is being destroyed and many Americans who were traveling to Chihuahua from Juarez are marooned here.

General Rojas executed five men while here for alleged offenses of a trivial character. Gen. Rosalio y Hernandez, Lieut. Cipriano Amador, and three soldiers were the unfortunates.

WASHINGTON, July 17.—Somewhere in Mexico Patrick Dunne, an American citizen, is in prison under sentence of death. This much and no more the State Department learned through Representative Kinkaid of Nebraska. Consular officers in various sections of Mexico have been directed to make every effort to locate Dunne and save his life.

JUAREZ, MEXICO, July 31.—General Orozco, chief of the rebels, declared to-day:

"If the United States will throw down the barriers and let us have all the ammunition we can buy, I promise in sixty days to have peace restored in Mexico and a stable government in charge."

CASAS GRANDES, CHIHUAHUA, July 31.—Rebel soldiers looted many homes of Mormons near here yesterday. All the Mormon families have fled to El Paso. Although General Salazar had two of his soldiers executed yesterday for robbing Mormons, he has not made any attempt to stop his men looting the unprotected homes of Americans.

Last night's and to-day's trains carried many Americans from Pearson, Madera, and other localities outside the Mormon settlements. Refugees from Mexico continued to pour into El Paso. About one hundred came last night, the majority of whom were men. Heretofore few men came.

Madeline read on in feverish absorption. It was not a real war, but a starving, robbing, burning, hopeless revolution. Five men executed for alleged offenses of a trivial nature! What chance had, then, a Federal prisoner, an enemy to be feared, an American cowboy in the clutches of those crazed rebels?

Madeline endured patiently, endured for long interminable hours while holding to her hope with indomitable will.

No message came. At sunset she went outdoors, suffering a torment of accumulating suspense. She faced the desert, hoping, praying for strength. The desert did not influence her as did the passionless, unchangeable stars that had soothed her spirit. It was red, mutable, shrouded in shadows, terrible like her mood. A dust-veiled sunset colored the vast, brooding, naked waste of rock and sand. The grim Chiricahua frowned black and sinister. The dim blue domes of the Guadalupes seemed to whisper, to beckon to her. Beyond them somewhere was Stewart, awaiting the end of a few brief hours—hours that to her were boundless, endless, insupportable.

37557575

Night fell. But now the white, pitiless stars failed her. Then she sought the seclusion and darkness of her room, there to lie with wide eyes, waiting, waiting. She had always been susceptible to the somber, mystic unrealities of the night, and now her mind slowly revolved round a vague and monstrous gloom. Nevertheless, she was acutely sensitive to outside impressions. She heard the measured tread of a guard, the rustle of wind stirring the window-curtain, the remote, mournful wail of a coyote. By and by the dead silence of the night insulated her with leaden oppression. There was silent darkness for so long that when the window casements showed gray she believed it was only fancy and that dawn would never come. She prayed for the sun not to rise, not to begin its short twelve-hour journey toward what might be a fatal setting for Stewart. But the dawn did lighten, swiftly she thought, remorselessly. Daylight had broken, and this was Thursday!

Sharp ringing of the telephone bell startled her, roused her into action. She ran to answer the call.

"Hello—hello—Miss Majesty!" came the hurried reply. "This is Link talkin'. Messages for you. Favorable, the operator said. I'm to ride out with them. I'll come a-hummin'."

That was all. Madeline heard the bang of the receiver as Stevens threw it down. She passionately wanted to know more, but was immeasurably grateful for so much! Favorable! Then Stillwell had been successful. Her heart leaped. Suddenly she became weak and her hands failed of their accustomed morning deftness. It took her what seemed a thousand years to dress. Breakfast meant nothing to her except that it helped her to pass dragging minutes.

Finally a low hum, mounting swiftly to a roar and ending with a sharp report, announced the arrival of the car. If her feet had kept pace with her heart she would have raced out to meet Link. She saw him, helmet thrown back, watch in hand, and he looked up at her with his cool, bright smile, with his familiar apologetic manner.

"Fifty-three minutes, Miss Majesty," he said, "but I hed to ride round a herd of steers an' bump a couple off the trail."

He gave her a packet of telegrams. Madeline tore them open with shaking fingers, began to read with swift, dim eyes. Some were from Washington, assuring her of every possible service; some were from New York; others written in Spanish were from El Paso, and these she could not wholly translate in a brief glance. Would she never find Stillwell's message? It was the last. It was lengthy. It read:

Bought Stewart's release. Also arranged for his transfer as prisoner of war. Both matters official. He's safe if we can get notice to his captors. Not sure I've reached them by wire. Afraid to trust it. You go with Link to Agua Prieta. Take the messages sent you in Spanish. They will protect you and secure Stewart's freedom. Take Nels with you. Stop for nothing. Tell Link all—trust him—let him drive that car.

STILLWELL.

The first few lines of Stillwell's message lifted Madeline to the heights of thanksgiving and happiness. Then, reading on, she experienced a check, a numb, icy, sickening pang. At the last line she flung off doubt and dread, and in white, cold passion faced the issue.

"Read," she said, briefly, handing the telegram to Link. He scanned it and then looked blankly up at her.

"Link, do you know the roads, the trails—the desert between here and Agua Prieta?" she asked.

"Thet's sure my old stampin'-ground. An' I know Sonora, too."

"We must reach Agua Prieta before sunset—long before, so if Stewart is in some near-by camp we can get to it in—in time."

"Miss Majesty, it ain't possible!" he exclaimed. "Stillwell's crazy to say thet."

"Link, can an automobile be driven from here into northern Mexico?"

"Sure. But it 'd take time."

"We must do it in little time," she went on, in swift eagerness. "Otherwise Stewart may be —probably will be—be shot."

Link Stevens appeared suddenly to grow lax, shriveled, to lose all his peculiar pert brightness, to weaken and age.

"I'm only a—a cowboy, Miss Majesty." He almost faltered. It was a singular change in him. "Thet's an awful ride—down over the border. If by some luck I didn't smash the car I'd turn your hair gray. You'd never be no good after thet ride!"

"I am Stewart's wife," she answered him and she looked at him, not conscious of any motive to persuade or allure, but just to let him know the greatness of her dependence upon him.

He started violently—the old action of Stewart, the memorable action of Monty Price. This man was of the same wild breed.

Then Madeline's words flowed in a torrent. "I am Stewart's wife. I love him; I have been unjust to him; I must save him. Link, I have faith in you. I beseech you to do your best for Stewart's sake—for my sake. I'll risk the ride gladly—bravely. I'll not care where or how you drive. I'd far rather plunge into a canyon—go to my death on the rocks—than not try to save Stewart."

How beautiful the response of this rude cowboy—to realize his absolute unconsciousness of self, to see the haggard shade burn out of his face, the old, cool, devil-may-care spirit return to his eyes, and to feel something wonderful about him then! It was more than will or daring or sacrifice. A blood-tie might have existed between him and Madeline. She sensed again that indefinable brother-like quality, so fine, so almost invisible, which seemed to be an inalienable trait in these wild cowboys.

"Miss Majesty, thet ride figgers impossible, but I'll do it!" he replied. His cool, bright glance thrilled her. "I'll need mebbe half an hour to go over the car an' to pack on what I'll want."

She could not thank him, and her reply was merely a request that he tell Nels and other cowboys off duty to come up to the house. When Link had gone Madeline gave a moment's thought to preparations for the ride. She placed what money she had and the telegrams in a satchel. The gown she had on was thin and white, not suitable for travel, but she would not risk the losing of one moment in changing it. She put on a long coat and wound veils round her head and neck, arranging them in a hood so she could cover her face when necessary. She remembered to take an extra pair of goggles for Nels's use, and then, drawing on her gloves, she went out ready for the ride.

A number of cowboys were waiting. She explained the situation and left them in charge of her home. With that she asked Nels to accompany her down into the desert. He turned white to his lips, and this occasioned Madeline to remember his mortal dread of the car and Link's driving.

"Nels, I'm sorry to ask you," she added. "I know you hate the car. But I need you—may need you, oh! so much."

"Why, Miss Majesty, thet's shore all a mistaken idee of yours about me hatin' the car," he said, in his slow, soft drawl. "I was only jealous of Link; an' the boys, they made thet joke up on me about bein' scared of ridin' fast. Shore I'm powerful proud to go. An' I reckon if you hedn't asked me my feelin's might hev been some hurt. Because if you're goin' down among the Greasers you want me."

His cool, easy speech, his familiar swagger, the smile with which he regarded her did not in the least deceive Madeline. The gray was still in his face. Incomprehensible as it seemed, Nels had a dread, an uncanny fear, and it was of that huge white automobile. But he lied about it. Here again was that strange quality of faithfulness.

Madeline heard the buzz of the car. Link appeared driving up the slope. He made a short, sliding turn and stopped before the porch. Link had tied two long, heavy planks upon the car, one on each side, and in every available space he had strapped extra tires. A huge cask occupied one back seat, and another seat was full of tools and ropes. There was just room in this rear part of the car for Nels to squeeze in. Link put Madeline in front beside him, then bent over the wheel. Madeline waved her hand at the silent cowboys on the porch. Not an audible good-by was spoken.

The car glided out of the yard, leaped from level to slope, and started swiftly down the road, out into the open valley. Each stronger rush of dry wind in Madeline's face marked the increase of speed. She took one glance at the winding cattle-road, smooth, unobstructed, disappearing in the gray of distance. She took another at the leather-garbed, leather-helmeted driver beside her, and then she drew the hood of veils over her face and fastened it round her neck so there was no possibility of its blowing loose.

Harder and stronger pressed the wind till it was like sheeted lead forcing her back in her seat. There was a ceaseless, intense, inconceivably rapid vibration under her; occasionally she felt a long swing, as if she were to be propelled aloft; but no jars disturbed the easy celerity of the car. The buzz, the roar of wheels, of heavy body in flight, increased to a continuous droning hum. The wind became an insupportable body moving toward her, crushing her breast, making the task of breathing most difficult. To Madeline the time seemed to fly with the speed of miles. A moment came when she detected a faint difference in hum and rush and vibration, in the ceaseless sweeping of the invisible weight against her. This difference became marked. Link was reducing speed. Then came swift change of all sensation, and she realized the car had slowed to normal travel.

Madeline removed her hood and goggles. It was a relief to breathe freely, to be able to use her eyes. To her right, not far distant, lay the little town of Chiricahua. Sight of it made her remember Stewart in a way strange to her constant thought of him. To the left inclined the gray valley. The red desert was hidden from view, but the Guadalupe Mountains loomed close in the southwest.

Opposite Chiricahua, where the road forked, Link Stevens headed the car straight south and gradually increased speed. Madeline faced another endless gray incline. It was the San Bernardino Valley. The singing of the car, the stinging of the wind warned her to draw the hood securely down over her face again, and then it was as if she was riding at night. The car lurched ahead, settled into that driving speed which wedged Madeline back as in a vise. Again the moments went by fleet as the miles. Seemingly, there was an acceleration of the car till it reached a certain swiftness—a period of time in which it held that pace, and then a diminishing of all motion and sound which contributed to Madeline's acute sensation. Uncovering her face, she saw Link was passing another village. Could it be Bernardino? She asked Link—repeated the question.

"Sure," he replied. "Eighty miles."

Link did not this time apologize for the work of his machine. Madeline marked the omission with her first thrill of the ride. Leaning over, she glanced at Link's watch, which he had fastened upon the wheel in front of his eyes. A quarter to ten! Link had indeed made short work of the valley miles.

Beyond Bernardino Link sheered off the road and put the car to a long, low-rising slope. Here the valley appeared to run south under the dark brows of the Guadalupes. Link was heading southwest. Madeline observed that the grass began to fail as they climbed the ridge; bare, white, dusty spots appeared; there were patches of mesquite and cactus and scattering areas of broken rock.

She might have been prepared for what she saw from the ridge-top. Beneath them the desert blazed. Seen from afar, it was striking enough, but riding down into its red jaws gave Madeline the first affront to her imperious confidence. All about her ranch had been desert, the valleys were desert; but this was different. Here began the red desert, extending far into Mexico, far across Arizona and California to the Pacific. She saw a bare, hummocky ridge, down which the car was gliding, bounding, swinging, and this long slant seemed to merge into a corrugated world of rock and sand, patched by flats and basins, streaked with canyons and ranges of ragged, saw-toothed stone. The distant Sierra Madres were clearer, bluer, less smoky and suggestive of mirage than she had ever seen them. Madeline's sustaining faith upheld her in the face of this appalling obstacle. Then the desert that had rolled its immensity beneath her gradually began to rise, to lose its distant margins, to condense its varying lights and shades, at last to hide its yawning depths and looming heights behind red ridges, which were only little steps, little outposts, little landmarks at its gates.

The bouncing of the huge car, throwing Madeline up, directed her attention and fastened it upon the way Link Stevens was driving and upon the immediate foreground. Then she discovered that he was following an old wagon-road. At the foot of that long slope they struck into rougher ground, and here Link took to a cautious zigzag course. The wagon-road disappeared and then presently reappeared. But Link did not always hold to it. He made cuts, detours, crosses, and all the time seemed to be getting deeper into a maze of low, red dunes, of flat canyon-beds lined by banks of gravel, of ridges mounting higher. Yet Link Stevens kept on and never turned back. He never headed into a place that he could not pass. Up to this point of travel he had not been compelled to back the car, and Madeline began to realize that it was the cowboy's wonderful judgment of ground that made advance possible. He knew the country; he was never at a loss; after making a choice of direction, he never hesitated.

Then at the bottom of a wide canyon he entered a wash where the wheels just barely turned in dragging sand. The sun beat down white-hot, the dust arose, there was not a breath of wind; and no sound save the slide of a rock now and then down the weathered slopes and the labored chugging of the machine. The snail pace, like the sand at the wheels, began to drag at Madeline's faith. Link gave over the wheel to Madeline, and, leaping out, he called Nels. When they untied the long planks and laid them straight in front for the wheels to pass over Madeline saw how wise had been Link's forethought. With the aid of those planks they worked the car through sand and gravel otherwise impossible to pass.

This canyon widened and opened into space affording an unobstructed view for miles. The desert sloped up in steps, and in the morning light, with the sun bright on the mesas and escarpments, it was gray, drab, stone, slate, yellow, pink, and, dominating all, a dull rust-red. There was level ground ahead, a wind-swept floor as hard as rock. Link rushed the car over this free distance. Madeline's ears filled with a droning hum like the sound of a monstrous, hungry bee and with a strange, incessant crinkle which she at length guessed to be the spreading of sheets of gravel from under the wheels. The giant car attained such a speed that

Madeline could only distinguish the colored landmarks to the fore, and these faded as the wind stung her eyes.

Then Link began the ascent of the first step, a long, sweeping, barren waste with dunes of wonderful violet and heliotrope hues. Here were well-defined marks of an old wagon-road lately traversed by cattle. The car climbed steadily, surmounted the height, faced another long bench that had been cleaned smooth by desert winds. The sky was an intense, light, steely blue, hard on the eyes. Madeline veiled her face, and did not uncover it until Link had reduced the racing speed. From the summit of the next ridge she saw more red ruin of desert.

A deep wash crossing the road caused Link Stevens to turn due south. There was a narrow space along the wash just wide enough for the car. Link seemed oblivious to the fact that the outside wheels were perilously close to the edge. Madeline heard the rattle of loosened gravel and earth sliding into the gully. The wash widened and opened out into a sandy flat. Link crossed this and turned up on the opposite side. Rocks impeded the progress of the car, and these had to be rolled out of the way. The shelves of silt, apparently ready to slide with the slightest weight, the little tributary washes, the boulder-strewn stretches of slope, the narrow spaces allowing no more than a foot for the outside wheels, the spear-pointed cactus that had to be avoided—all these obstacles were as nothing to the cowboy driver. He kept on, and when he came to the road again he made up for the lost time by speed.

Another height was reached, and here Madeline fancied that Link had driven the car to the summit of a high pass between two mountain ranges. The western slope of that pass appeared to be exceedingly rough and broken. Below it spread out another gray valley, at the extreme end of which glistened a white spot that Link grimly called Douglas. Part of that white spot was Agua Prieta, the sister town across the line. Madeline looked with eyes that would fain have pierced the intervening distance.

The descent of the pass began under difficulties. Sharp stones and cactus spikes penetrated the front tires, bursting them with ripping reports. It took time to replace them. The planks were called into requisition to cross soft places. A jagged point of projecting rock had to be broken with a sledge. At length a huge stone appeared to hinder any further advance. Madeline caught her breath. There was no room to turn the car. But Link Stevens had no intention of such a thing. He backed the car to a considerable distance, then walked forward. He appeared to be busy around the boulder for a moment and returned down the road on the run. A heavy explosion, a cloud of dust, and a rattle of falling fragments told Madeline that her indomitable driver had cleared a passage with dynamite. He seemed to be prepared for every emergency. Madeline looked to see what effect the discovery of Link carrying dynamite would have upon the silent Nels.

"Shore, now, Miss Majesty, there ain't nothin' goin' to stop Link," said Nels, with a reassuring smile. The significance of the incident had not dawned upon Nels, or else he was heedless of it. After all, he was afraid only of the car and Link, and that fear was an idiosyncrasy. Madeline began to see her cowboy driver with clearer eyes and his spirit awoke something in her that made danger of no moment. Nels likewise subtly responded, and, though he was gray-faced, tight-lipped, his eyes took on the cool, bright gleam of Link's.

Cactus barred the way, rocks barred the way, gullies barred the way, and these Nels addressed in the grim humor with which he was wont to view tragic things. A mistake on Link's part, a slip of a wheel, a bursting of a tire at a critical moment, an instant of the bad luck which might happen a hundred times on a less perilous ride—any one of these might spell disaster for the car, perhaps death to the occupants. Again and again Link used the planks to cross washes in sand. Sometimes the wheels ran all the length of the planks, sometimes slipped off. Presently Link came to a ditch where water had worn deep into the road. Without hesitation he placed them, measuring distance carefully, and then started across. The danger was in ditching the machine. One of the planks split, sagged a little, but Link made the crossing without a slip.

The road led round under an overhanging cliff and was narrow, rocky, and slightly downhill. Bidding Madeline and Nels walk round this hazardous corner, Link drove the car. Madeline expected to hear it crash down into the canyon, but presently she saw Link waiting to take them aboard again. Then came steeper parts of the road, places that Link could run down if he had space below to control the car, and on the other hand places where the little inclines ended in abrupt ledges upon one side or a declivity upon the other. Here the cowboy, with ropes on the wheels and half-hitches upon the spurs of rock, let the car slide down.

Once at a particularly bad spot Madeline exclaimed involuntarily, "Oh, time is flying!" Link Stevens looked up at her as if he had been reproved for his care. His eyes shone like the glint of steel on ice. Perhaps that utterance of Madeline's was needed to liberate his recklessness to its utmost. Certainly he put the car to seemingly impossible feats. He rimmed gullies, he hurdled rising ground, he leaped little breaks in the even road. He made his machine cling like a goat to steep inclines; he rounded corners with the inside wheels higher than the outside; he passed over banks of soft earth that caved in the instant he crossed weak places. He kept on and on, threading tortuous passages through rock-strewn patches, keeping to the old road where it was clear, abandoning it for open spaces, and always going down.

At length a mile of clean, brown slope, ridged and grooved like a washboard, led gently down to meet the floor of the valley, where the scant grama-grass struggled to give a tinge of gray. The road appeared to become more clearly defined, and could be seen striking straight across the valley.

To Madeline's dismay, that road led down to a deep, narrow wash. It plunged on one side, ascended on the other at a still steeper angle. The crossing would have been laborsome for a horse; for an automobile it was unpassable. Link turned the car to the right along the rim and drove as far along the wash as the ground permitted. The gully widened, deepened all the way. Then he took the other direction. When he made this turn Madeline observed that the sun had perceptibly begun its slant westward. It shone in her face, glaring and wrathful. Link drove back to the road, crossed it, and kept on down the line of the wash. It was a deep cut in red earth, worn straight down by swift water in the rainy seasons. It narrowed. In some places it was only five feet wide. Link studied these points and looked up the slope, and seemed to be making deductions. The valley was level now, and there were nothing but little breaks in the rim of the wash. Link drove mile after mile, looking for a place to cross, and there was none. Finally progress to the south was obstructed by impassable gullies where the wash plunged into the head of a canyon. It was necessary to back the car a distance before there was room to turn. Madeline looked at the imperturbable driver. His face revealed no more than the same old hard, immutable character. When he reached the narrowest points, which had so interested him, he got out of the car and walked from place to place. Once with a little jump he cleared the wash. Then Madeline noted that the farther rim was somewhat lower. In a flash she divined Link's intention. He was hunting a place to jump the car over the crack in the ground.

Soon he found one that seemed to suit him, for he tied his red scarf upon a greasewood-bush. Then, returning to the car, he clambered in, and, muttering, broke his long silence: "This ain't no air-ship, but I've outfiggered thet damn wash." He backed up the gentle slope and halted just short of steeper ground. His red scarf waved in the wind. Hunching low over the wheel, he started, slowly at first, then faster, and then faster. The great car gave a spring like a huge tiger. The impact of suddenly formed wind almost tore Madeline out of her seat. She felt Nels's powerful hands on her shoulders. She closed her eyes. The jolting headway of the car gave place to a gliding rush. This was broken by a slight jar, and then above the hum and roar rose a cowboy yell. Madeline waited with strained nerves for the expected crash. It did not come. Opening her eyes, she saw the level valley floor without a break. She had not even noticed the instant when the car had shot over the wash.

A strange breathlessness attacked her, and she attributed it to the celerity with which she was being carried along. Pulling the hood down over her face, she sank low in the seat. The whir of the car now seemed to be a world-filling sound. Again the feeling of excitement, the poignancy of emotional heights, the ever-present impending sense of catastrophe became held in abeyance to the sheer intensity of physical sensations. There came a time when all her strength seemed to unite in an effort to lift her breast against the terrific force of the wind—to draw air into her flattened lungs. She became partly dazed. The darkness before her eyes was not all occasioned by the blood that pressed like a stone mask on her face. She had a sense that she was floating, sailing, drifting, reeling, even while being borne swiftly as a thunderbolt. Her hands and arms were immovable under the weight of mountains. There was a long, blank period from which she awakened to feel an arm supporting her. Then she rallied. The velocity of the car had been cut to the speed to which she was accustomed. Throwing back the hood, she breathed freely again, recovered fully.

The car was bowling along a wide road upon the outskirts of a city. Madeline asked what place it could be.

"Douglas," replied Link. "An' jest around is Agua Prieta!"

That last name seemed to stun Madeline. She heard no more, and saw little until the car stopped. Nels spoke to some one. Then sight of khaki-clad soldiers quickened Madeline's faculties. She was on the boundary-line between the United States and Mexico, and Agua Prieta, with its white and blue walled houses, its brown-tiled roofs, lay before her. A soldier, evidently despatched by Nels, returned and said an officer would come at once. Madeline's attention was centered in the foreground, upon the guard over the road, upon the dry, dusty town beyond; but she was aware of noise and people in the rear. A cavalry officer approached the car, stared, and removed his sombrero.

"Can you tell me anything about Stewart, the American cowboy who was captured by rebels a few days ago?" asked Madeline.

"Yes," replied the officer. "There was a skirmish over the line between a company of Federals and a large force of guerrillas and rebels. The Federals were driven west along the line. Stewart is reported to have done reckless fighting and was captured. He got a Mexican sentence. He is known here along the border, and the news of his capture stirred up excitement. We did all we could to get his release. The guerrillas feared to execute him here, and believed he might be aided to escape. So a detachment departed with him for Mezquital."

"He was sentenced to be shot Thursday at sunset—to-night?"

"Yes. It was rumored there was a personal resentment against Stewart. I regret that I can't give you definite information. If you are friends of Stewart—relatives—I might find—"

"I am his wife," interrupted Madeline. "Will you please read these." She handed him the telegrams. "Advise me—help me, if you can?"

With a wondering glance at her the officer received the telegrams. He read several, and whistled low in amaze. His manner became quick, alert, serious.

"I can't read these written in Spanish, but I know the names signed." Swiftly he ran through the others.

"Why, these mean Stewart's release has been authorized. They explain mysterious rumors we have heard here. Greaser treachery! For some strange reason messages from the rebel junta have failed to reach their destination. We heard reports of an exchange for Stewart, but nothing came of it. No one departed for Mezquital with authority. What an outrage! Come, I'll go with you to General Salazar, the rebel chief in command. I know him. Perhaps we can find out something."

Nels made room for the officer. Link sent the car whirring across the line into Mexican territory. Madeline's sensibilities were now exquisitely alive. The white road led into Agua Prieta, a town of colored walls and roofs. Goats and pigs and buzzards scattered before the roar of the machine. Native women wearing black mantles peeped through iron-barred windows. Men wearing huge sombreros, cotton shirts and trousers, bright sashes round their waists, and sandals, stood motionless, watching the car go by. The road ended in an immense plaza, in the center of which was a circular structure that in some measure resembled a corral. It was a bull-ring, where the national sport of bull-fighting was carried on. Just now it appeared to be quarters for a considerable army. Ragged, unkempt rebels were everywhere, and the whole square was littered with tents, packs, wagons, arms. There were horses, mules, burros, and oxen.

The place was so crowded that Link was compelled to drive slowly up to the entrance to the bull-ring. Madeline caught a glimpse of tents inside, then her view was obstructed by a curious, pressing throng. The cavalry officer leaped from the car and pushed his way into the entrance.

"Link, do you know the road to this Mezquital?" asked Madeline.

"Yes. I've been there."

"How far is it?"

"Aw, not so very far," he mumbled.

"Link! How many miles?" she implored.

"I reckon only a few."

Madeline knew that he lied. She asked him no more; nor looked at him, nor at Nels. How stifling was this crowded, ill-smelling plaza! The sun, red and lowering, had sloped far down in the west, but still burned with furnace heat. A swarm of flies whirled over the car. The shadows of low-sailing buzzards crossed Madeline's sight. Then she saw a row of the huge, uncanny black birds sitting upon the tiled roof of a house. They had neither an air of sleeping nor resting. They were waiting. She fought off a horrible ghastly idea before its full realization. These rebels and guerrillas—what lean, yellow, bearded wretches! They curiously watched Link as he went working over the car. No two were alike, and all were ragged. They had glittering eyes sunk deep in their heads. They wore huge sombreros of brown and black felt, of straw, of cloth. Every man wore a belt or sash into which was thrust some kind of weapon. Some wore boots, some shoes, some moccasins, some sandals, and many were barefooted. They were an excited, jabbering, gesticulating mob. Madeline shuddered to think how a frenzy to spill blood could run through these poor revolutionists. If it was liberty they fought for, they did not show the intelligence in their faces. They were like wolves upon a scent. They affronted her, shocked her. She wondered if their officers were men of the same class. What struck her at last and stirred pity in her was the fact that every man of the horde her swift glance roamed over, however dirty and bedraggled he was, wore upon him some ornament, some tassel or fringe or lace, some ensign, some band, bracelet, badge, or belt, some twist of scarf, something that betrayed the vanity which was the poor jewel of their souls. It was in the race.

Suddenly the crowd parted to let the cavalry officer and a rebel of striking presence get to the car.

"Madam, it is as I suspected," said the officer, quickly. "The messages directing Stewart's release never reached Salazar. They were intercepted. But even without them we might have secured Stewart's exchange if it had not been for the fact that one of his captors wanted him shot. This guerrilla intercepted the orders, and then was instrumental in taking Stewart to Mezquital. It is exceedingly sad. Why, he should be a free man this instant. I regret—"

"Who did this—this thing?" cried Madeline, cold and sick. "Who is the guerrilla?"

"Senor Don Carlos Martinez. He has been a bandit, a man of influence in Sonora. He is more of a secret agent in the affairs of the revolution than an active participator. But he has seen guerrilla service."

"Don Carlos! Stewart in his power! O God!" Madeline sank down, almost overcome. Then two great hands, powerful, thrilling, clasped her shoulders, and Nels bent over her.

"Miss Majesty, shore we're wastin' time here," he said. His voice, like his hands, was uplifting. She wheeled to him in trembling importunity. How cold, bright, blue the flash of his eyes! They told Madeline she must not weaken. But she could not speak her thought to Nels—could only look at Link.

"It figgers impossible, but I'll do it!" said Link Stevens, in answer to her voiceless query. The cold, grim, wild something about her cowboys blanched Madeline's face, steeled her nerve, called to the depths of her for that last supreme courage of a woman. The spirit of the moment was nature with Link and Nels; with her it must be passion.

"Can I get a permit to go into the interior—to Mezquital?" asked Madeline of the officer.

"You are going on? Madam, it's a forlorn hope. Mezquital is a hundred miles away. But there's a chance—the barest chance if your man can drive this car. The Mexicans are either murderous or ceremonious in their executions. The arrangements for Stewart's will be elaborate. But, barring unusual circumstances, it will take place precisely at the hour designated. You need no permit. Your messages are official papers. But to save time, perhaps delay, I suggest you take this Mexican, Senor Montes, with you. He outranks Don Carlos and knows the captain of the Mezquital detachment."

"Ah! Then Don Carlos is not in command of the forces holding Stewart?"

"No."

"I thank you, sir. I shall not forget your kindness," concluded Madeline.

She bowed to Senor Montes, and requested him to enter the car. Nels stowed some of the paraphernalia away, making room in the rear seat. Link bent over the wheel. The start was so sudden, with such crack and roar, that the crowd split in wild disorder. Out of the plaza the car ran, gathering headway; down a street lined by white and blue walls; across a square where rebels were building barricades; along a railroad track full of iron flat-cars that carried mounted pieces of artillery; through the outlying guards, who waved to the officer, Montes.

Madeline bound her glasses tightly over her eyes, and wound veils round the lower part of her face. She was all in a strange glow, she had begun to burn, to throb, to thrill, to expand, and she meant to see all that was possible. The sullen sun, red as fire, hung over the mountain range in the west. How low it had sunk! Before her stretched a narrow, white road, dusty, hard as stone—a highway that had been used for centuries. If it had been wide enough to permit passing a vehicle it would have been a magnificent course for automobiles. But the weeds and the dusty flowers and the mesquite boughs and arms of cactus brushed the car as it sped by.

Faster, faster, faster! That old resistless weight began to press Madeline back; the old incessant bellow of wind filled her ears. Link Stevens hunched low over the wheel. His eyes were hidden under leather helmet and goggles, but the lower part of his face was unprotected. He resembled a demon, so dark and stone-hard and strangely grinning was he. All at once Madeline realized how matchless, how wonderful a driver was this cowboy. She divined that weakening could not have been possible to Link Stevens. He was a cowboy, and he really was riding that car, making it answer to his will, as it had been born in him to master a horse. He had never driven to suit himself, had never reached an all-satisfying speed until now. Beyond that his motive was to save Stewart—to make Madeline happy. Life was nothing to him. That fact gave him the superhuman nerve to face the peril of this ride. Because of his disregard of self he was able to operate the machine, to choose the power, the speed, the guidance, the going with the best judgment and highest efficiency possible. Madeline knew he would get her to Mezquital in time to save Stewart or he would kill her in the attempt.

The white, narrow road flashed out of the foreground, slipped with inconceivable rapidity under the car. When she marked a clump of cactus far ahead it seemed to shoot at her, to speed behind her even the instant she noticed it. Nevertheless, Madeline knew Link was not putting the car to its limit. Swiftly as he was flying, he held something in reserve. But he took the turns of the road as if he knew the way was cleared before him. He trusted to a cowboy's luck. A wagon in one of those curves, a herd of cattle, even a frightened steer, meant a wreck. Madeline never closed her eyes at these fateful moments. If Link could stake himself, the others, and her upon such chance, what could not she stake with her motive? So while the great car hummed and thrummed, and darted round the curves on two wheels, and sped on like a bullet, Madeline lived that ride, meant to feel it to the uttermost.

But it was not all swift going. A stretch of softer ground delayed Link, made the car labor and pant and pound and grind through gravel. Moreover, the cactus plants assumed an alarming ability to impede progress. Long, slender arms of the ocotillo encroached upon the road; broad, round leaves did likewise; fluted columns, fallen like timbers in a forest, lay along the narrow margins; the bayonet cactus and the bisnagi leaned threateningly; clusters of maguey, shadowed by the huge, looming saguaro, infringed upon the highway to Mezquital. And every leaf and blade and branch of cactus bore wicked thorns, any one of which would be fatal to a tire.

It came at length, the bursting report. The car lurched, went on like a crippled thing, and halted, obedient to the master hand at the wheel. Swift as Link was in replacing the tire, he lost time. The red sun, more sullen, duskier as it neared the black, bold horizon, appeared to mock Madeline, to eye her in derision.

Link leaped in, and the car sprang ahead. The road-bed changed, the trees changed—all the surroundings changed except the cactus. There were miles of rolling ridges, rough in the hollows, and short rocky bits of road, and washes to cross, and a low, sandy swale where mesquites grouped a forest along a trickling inch-deep sheet of water. Green things softened the hard, dry aspect of the desert. There were birds and parrots and deer and wild boars. All these Madeline remarked with clear eyes, with remarkable susceptibility of attention; but what she strained to see, what she yearned for, prayed for, was straight, unobstructed road.

But the road began to wind up; it turned and twisted in tantalizing lazy curves; it was in no hurry to surmount a hill that began to assume proportions of a mountain; it was leisurely, as were all things in Mexico except strife. That was quick, fierce, bloody—it was Spanish.

The descent from that elevation was difficult, extremely hazardous, yet Link Stevens drove fast. At the base of the hill rocks and sand all but halted him for good. Then in taking an abrupt curve a grasping spear ruined another tire. This time the car rasped across the road into the cactus, bursting the second front-wheel tire. Like demons indeed Link and Nels worked. Shuddering, Madeline felt the declining heat of the sun, saw with gloomy eyes the shading of the red light over the desert. She did not look back to see how near the sun was to the horizon. She wanted to ask Nels. Strange as anything on this terrible ride was the absence of speech. As yet no word had been spoken. Madeline wanted to shriek to Link to hurry. But he was more than humanly swift in all his actions. So with mute lips, with the fire in her beginning to chill, with a lifelessness menacing her spirit, she watched, hoped against hope, prayed for a long, straight, smooth road.

Quite suddenly she saw it, seemingly miles of clear, narrow lane disappearing like a thin, white streak in distant green. Perhaps Link Stevens's heart leaped like Madeline's. The huge car with a roar and a jerk seemed to answer Madeline's call, a cry no less poignant because it was silent.

Faster, faster, faster! The roar became a whining hum. Then for Madeline sound ceased to be anything—she could not hear. The wind was now heavy, imponderable, no longer a swift, plastic thing, but solid, like an on-rushing wall. It bore down upon Madeline with such resistless weight that she could not move. The green of desert plants along the road merged in two shapeless fences, sliding at her from the distance. Objects ahead began to blur the white road, to grow streaky, like rays of light, the sky to take on more of a reddening haze.

Madeline, realizing her sight was failing her, turned for one more look at Link Stevens. It had come to be his ride almost as much as it was hers. He hunched lower than ever, rigid, strained to the last degree, a terrible, implacable driver. This was his hour, and he was great. If he so much as brushed a flying tire against one of the millions of spikes clutching out, striking out from the cactus, there would be a shock, a splitting wave of air—an end. Madeline thought she saw that Link's bulging cheek and jaw were gray, that his tight-shut lips were white, that the smile was gone. Then he really was human—not a demon. She felt a strange sense of brotherhood. He understood a woman's soul as Monty Price had understood it. Link was the lightning-forged automaton, the driving, relentless, unconquerable instrument of a woman's will. He was a man whose force was directed by a woman's passion. He reached up to her height, felt her love, understood the nature of her agony. These made him heroic. But it was the hard life, the wild years of danger on the desert, the companionship of ruthless men, the elemental, that made possible his physical achievement. Madeline loved his spirit then and gloried in the man.

She had pictured upon her heart, never to be forgotten, this little hunched, deformed figure of Link's hanging with dauntless, with deathless grip over the wheel, his gray face like a marble mask.

That was Madeline's last clear sensation upon the ride. Blinded, dazed, she succumbed to the demands upon her strength. She reeled, fell back, only vaguely aware of a helping hand. Confusion seized her senses. All about her was a dark chaos through which she was rushing, rushing, rushing under the wrathful red eye of a setting sun. Then, as there was no more sound or sight for her, she felt there was no color. But the rush never slackened—a rush through opaque, limitless space. For moments, hours, ages she was propelled with the velocity of a shooting-star. The earth seemed a huge automobile. And it sped with her down an endless white track through the universe. Looming, ghostly, ghastly, spectral forms of cacti plants, large as pine-trees, stabbed her with giant spikes. She became an unstable being in a shapeless, colorless, soundless cosmos of unrelated things, but always rushing, even to meet the darkness that haunted her and never reached her.

But at an end of infinite time that rush ceased. Madeline lost the queer feeling of being disembodied by a frightfully swift careening through boundless distance. She distinguished voices, low at first, apparently far away. Then she opened her eyes to blurred but conscious sight.

The car had come to a stop. Link was lying face down over the wheel. Nels was rubbing her hands, calling to her. She saw a house with clean whitewashed wall and brown-tiled roof. Beyond, over a dark mountain range, peeped the last red curve, the last beautiful ray of the setting sun.

☙ 25 ❧

AT THE END OF THE ROAD

MADELINE SAW that the car was surrounded by armed Mexicans. They presented a contrast to the others she had seen that day; she wondered a little at their silence, at their respectful front.

Suddenly a sharp spoken order opened up the ranks next to the house. Senor Montes appeared in the break, coming swiftly. His dark face wore a smile; his manner was courteous, important, authoritative.

"Senora, it is not too late!"

He spoke her language with an accent strange to her, so that it seemed to hinder understanding.

"Senora, you got here in time," he went on. "El Capitan Stewart will be free."

"Free!" she whispered.

She rose, reeling.

"Come," replied Montes, taking her arm. "Perdoneme, Senora."

Without his assistance she would have fallen wholly upon Nels, who supported her on the other side. They helped her alight from the car. For a moment the white walls, the hazy red sky, the dark figures of the rebels, whirled before Madeline's eyes. She took a few steps, swaying between her escorts; then the confusion of her sight and mind passed away. It was as if she quickened with a thousand vivifying currents, as if she could see and hear and feel everything in the world, as if nothing could be overlooked, forgotten, neglected.

She turned back, remembering Link. He was lurching from the car, helmet and goggles thrust back, the gray shade gone from his face, the cool, bright gleam of his eyes disappearing for something warmer.

Senor Montes led Madeline and her cowboys through a hall to a patio, and on through a large room with flooring of rough, bare boards that rattled, into a smaller room full of armed quiet rebels facing an open window.

Madeline scanned the faces of these men, expecting to see Don Carlos. But he was not present. A soldier addressed her in Spanish too swiftly uttered, too voluble for her to translate. But, like Senor Montes, he was gracious and, despite his ragged garb and uncouth appearance, he bore the unmistakable stamp of authority.

Montes directed Madeline's attention to a man by the window. A loose scarf of vivid red hung from his hand.

"Senora, they were waiting for the sun to set when we arrived," said Montes. "The signal was about to be given for Senor Stewart's walk to death."

"Stewart's walk!" echoed Madeline.

"Ah, Senora, let me tell you his sentence—the sentence I have had the honor and happiness to revoke for you."

Stewart had been court-martialed and sentenced according to a Mexican custom observed in cases of brave soldiers to whom honorable and fitting executions were due. His hour had been set for Thursday when the sun had sunk. Upon signal he was to be liberated and was free to walk out into the road, to take any direction he pleased. He knew his sentence; knew that death awaited him, that every possible avenue of escape was blocked by men with rifles ready. But he had not the slightest idea at what moment or from what direction the bullets were to come.

"Senora, we have sent messengers to every squad of waiting soldiers—an order that El Capitan is not to be shot. He is ignorant of his release. I shall give the signal for his freedom."

Montes was ceremonious, gallant, emotional. Madeline saw his pride, and divined that the situation was one which brought out the vanity, the ostentation, as well as the cruelty of his race. He would keep her in an agony of suspense, let Stewart start upon that terrible walk in ignorance of his freedom. It was the motive of a Spaniard. Suddenly Madeline had a horrible quaking fear that Montes lied, that he meant her to be a witness of Stewart's execution. But no, the man was honest; he was only barbarous. He would satisfy certain instincts of his nature—sentiment, romance, cruelty—by starting Stewart upon that walk, by watching Stewart's actions in the face of seeming death, by seeing Madeline's agony of doubt, fear, pity, love. Almost Madeline felt that she could not endure the situation. She was weak and tottering.

"Senora! Ah, it will be one beautiful thing!" Montes caught the scarf from the rebel's hand. He was glowing, passionate; his eyes had a strange, soft, cold flash; his voice was low, intense. He was living something splendid to him. "I'll wave the scarf, Senora. That will be the signal. It will be seen down at the other end of the road. Senor Stewart's jailer will see the signal, take off Stewart's irons, release him, open the door for his walk. Stewart will be free. But he will not know. He will expect death. As he is a brave man, he will face it. He will walk this way. Every step of that walk he will expect to be shot from some unknown quarter. But he will not be afraid. Senora, I have seen El Captain fighting in the field. What is death to him? Ah, will it not be magnificent to see him come forth—to walk down? Senora, you will see what a man he is. All the way he will expect cold, swift death. Here at this end of the road he will meet his beautiful lady!"

"Is there no—no possibility of a mistake?" faltered Madeline.

"None. My order included unloading of rifles."

"Don Carlos?"

"He is in irons, and must answer to General Salazar," replied Montes.

Madeline looked down the deserted road. How strange to see the last ruddy glow of the sun over the brow of the mountain range! The thought of that sunset had been torture for her. Yet it had passed, and now the afterlights were luminous, beautiful, prophetic.

With a heart stricken by both joy and agony, she saw Montes wave the scarf.

Then she waited. No change manifested itself down the length of that lonely road. There was absolute silence in the room behind her. How terribly, infinitely long seemed the waiting! Never in all her future life would she forget the quaint pink, blue, and white walled houses with their colored roofs. That dusty bare road resembled one of the uncovered streets of Pompeii with its look of centuries of solitude.

Suddenly a door opened and a tall man stepped out.

Madeline recognized Stewart. She had to place both hands on the window-sill for support, while a storm of emotion swayed her. Like a retreating wave it rushed away. Stewart lived. He was free. He had stepped out into the light. She had saved him. Life changed for her in that instant of realization and became sweet, full, strange.

Stewart shook hands with some one in the doorway. Then he looked up and down the road. The door closed behind him. Leisurely he rolled a cigarette, stood close to the wall while he scratched a match. Even at that distance Madeline's keen eyes caught the small flame, the first little puff of smoke.

Stewart then took to the middle of the road and leisurely began his walk.

To Madeline he appeared natural, walked as unconcernedly as if he were strolling for pleasure; but the absence of any other living thing, the silence, the red haze, the surcharged atmosphere—these were all unnatural. From time to time Stewart stopped to turn face forward toward houses and corners. Only silence greeted these significant moves of his. Once he halted to roll and light another cigarette. After that his step quickened.

Madeline watched him, with pride, love, pain, glory combating for a mastery over her. This walk of his seemingly took longer than all her hours of awakening, of strife, of remorse, longer than the ride to find him. She felt that it would be impossible for her to wait till he reached the end of the road. Yet in the hurry and riot of her feelings she had fleeting panics. What could she say to him? How meet him? Well she remembered the tall, powerful form now growing close enough to distinguish its dress. Stewart's face was yet only a dark gleam. Soon she would see it—long before he could know she was there. She wanted to run to meet him. Nevertheless, she stood rooted to her covert behind the window, living that terrible walk with him to the uttermost thought of home, sister, mother, sweetheart, wife, life itself— every thought that could come to a man stalking to meet his executioners. With all that tumult in her mind and heart Madeline still fell prey to the incomprehensible variations of emotion possible to a woman. Every step Stewart took thrilled her. She had some strange, subtle intuition that he was not unhappy, and that he believed beyond shadow of doubt that he was walking to his death. His steps dragged a little, though they had begun to be swift. The old, hard, physical, wild nerve of the cowboy was perhaps in conflict with spiritual growth of the finer man, realizing too late that life ought not to be sacrificed.

Then the dark gleam that was his face took shape, grew sharper and clearer. He was stalking now, and there was a suggestion of impatience in his stride. It took these hidden Mexicans a long time to kill him! At a point in the middle of the road, even with the corner of a house and opposite to Madeline's position, Stewart halted stock-still. He presented a fair, bold mark to his executioners, and he stood there motionless a full moment.

Only silence greeted him. Plain it was to Madeline, and she thought to all who had eyes to see, that to Stewart, since for some reason he had been spared all along his walk, this was the moment when he ought to be mercifully shot. But as no shots came a rugged dignity left him for a reckless scorn manifest in the way he strolled, across to the corner of the house, rolled yet another cigarette, and, presenting a broad breast to the window, smoked and waited.

That wait was almost unendurable for Madeline. Perhaps it was only a moment, several moments at the longest, but the time seemed a year. Stewart's face was scornful, hard. Did he suspect treachery on the part of his captors, that they meant to play with him as a cat with a mouse, to murder him at leisure? Madeline was sure she caught the old, inscrutable, mocking smile fleeting across his lips. He held that position for what must have been a reasonable time to his mind, then with a laugh and a shrug he threw the cigarette into the road. He shook his head as if at the incomprehensible motives of men who could have no fair reasons now for delay.

He made a sudden violent action that was more than a straightening of his powerful frame. It was the old instinctive violence. Then he faced north. Madeline read his thought, knew he was thinking of her, calling her a last silent farewell. He would serve her to his last breath, leave her free, keep his secret. That picture of him, dark-browed, fire-eyed, strangely sad and strong, sank indelibly into Madeline's heart of hearts.

The next instant he was striding forward, to force by bold and scornful presence a speedy fulfilment of his sentence.

Madeline stepped into the door, crossed the threshold. Stewart staggered as if indeed the bullets he expected had pierced him in mortal wound. His dark face turned white. His eyes had the rapt stare, the wild fear of a man who saw an apparition, yet who doubted his sight. Perhaps he had called to her as the Mexicans called to their Virgin; perhaps he imagined sudden death had come unawares, and this was her image appearing to him in some other life.

"Who—are—you?" he whispered, hoarsely.

She tried to lift her hands, failed, tried again, and held them out, trembling.

"It is I. Majesty. Your wife!"

THE RAINBOW TRAIL

RED LAKE

SHEFFORD HALTED his tired horse and gazed with slowly realizing eyes.

A league-long slope of sage rolled and billowed down to Red Lake, a dry red basin, denuded and glistening, a hollow in the desert, a lonely and desolate door to the vast, wild, and broken upland beyond.

All day Shefford had plodded onward with the clear horizon-line a thing unattainable; and for days before that he had ridden the wild bare flats and climbed the rocky desert benches. The great colored reaches and steps had led endlessly onward and upward through dim and deceiving distance.

A hundred miles of desert travel, with its mistakes and lessons and intimations, had not prepared him for what he now saw. He beheld what seemed a world that knew only magnitude. Wonder and awe fixed his gaze, and thought remained aloof. Then that dark and unknown northland flung a menace at him. An irresistible call had drawn him to this seamed and peaked border of Arizona, this broken battlemented wilderness of Utah upland; and at first sight they frowned upon him, as if to warn him not to search for what lay hidden beyond the ranges. But Shefford thrilled with both fear and exultation. That was the country which had been described to him. Far across the red valley, far beyond the ragged line of black mesa and yellow range, lay the wild canyon with its haunting secret.

Red Lake must be his Rubicon. Either he must enter the unknown to seek, to strive, to find, or turn back and fail and never know and be always haunted. A friend's strange story had prompted his singular journey; a beautiful rainbow with its mystery and promise had decided him. Once in his life he had answered a wild call to the kingdom of adventure within him, and once in his life he had been happy. But here in the horizon-wide face of that up-flung and cloven desert he grew cold; he faltered even while he felt more fatally drawn.

As if impelled Shefford started his horse down the sandy trail, but he checked his former far-reaching gaze. It was the month of April, and the waning sun lost heat and brightness. Long shadows crept down the slope ahead of him and the scant sage deepened its gray. He watched the lizards shoot like brown streaks across the sand, leaving their slender tracks; he heard the rustle of pack-rats as they darted into their brushy homes; the whir of a low-sailing hawk startled his horse.

Like ocean waves the slope rose and fell, its hollows choked with sand, its ridge-tops showing scantier growth of sage and grass and weed. The last ridge was a sand-dune, beautifully ribbed and scalloped and lined by the wind, and from its knife-sharp crest a thin wavering sheet of sand blew, almost like smoke. Shefford wondered why the sand looked red at a distance, for here it seemed almost white. It rippled everywhere, clean and glistening, always leading down.

Suddenly Shefford became aware of a house looming out of the bareness of the slope. It dominated that long white incline. Grim, lonely, forbidding, how strangely it harmonized with the surroundings! The structure was octagon-shaped, built of uncut stone, and resembled a fort. There was no door on the sides exposed to Shefford's gaze, but small apertures two-thirds the way up probably served as windows and port-holes. The roof appeared to be made of poles covered with red earth.

Like a huge cold rock on a wide plain this house stood there on the windy slope. It was an outpost of the trader Presbrey, of whom Shefford had heard at Flagstaff and Tuba. No living thing appeared in the limit of Shefford's vision. He gazed shudderingly at the unwelcoming habitation, at the dark eyelike windows, at the sweep of barren slope merging into the vast red valley, at the bold, bleak bluffs. Could any one live here? The nature of that sinister valley forbade a home there, and the spirit of the place hovered in the silence and space. Shefford thought irresistibly of how his enemies would have consigned him to just such a hell. He thought bitterly and mockingly of the narrow congregation that had proved him a failure in the ministry, that had repudiated his ideas of religion and immortality and God, that had driven him, at the age of twenty-four, from the calling forced upon him by his people. As a boy he had yearned to make himself an artist; his family had made him a clergyman; fate had made him a failure. A failure only so far in his life, something urged him to add—for in the lonely days and silent nights of the desert he had experienced a strange birth of hope. Adventure had called him, but it was a vague and spiritual hope, a dream of promise, a nameless attainment that fortified his wilder impulse.

As he rode around a corner of the stone house his horse snorted and stopped. A lean, shaggy pony jumped at sight of him, almost displacing a red long-haired blanket that covered an Indian saddle. Quick thuds of hoofs in sand drew Shefford's attention to a corral made of peeled poles, and here he saw another pony.

Shefford heard subdued voices. He dismounted and walked to an open door. In the dark interior he dimly descried a high counter, a stairway, a pile of bags of flour, blankets, and silver-ornamented objects, but the persons he had heard were not in that part of the house. Around another corner of the octagon-shaped wall he found another open door, and through it saw goat-skins and a mound of dirty sheep-wool, black and brown and white. It was light in this part of the building. When he crossed the threshold he was astounded to see a man struggling with a girl—an Indian girl. She was straining back from him, panting, and uttering low guttural sounds. The man's face was corded and dark with passion. This scene affected Shefford strangely. Primitive emotions were new to him.

Before Shefford could speak the girl broke loose and turned to flee. She was an Indian and this place was the uncivilized desert, but Shefford knew terror when he saw it. Like a dog the man rushed after her. It was instinct that made Shefford strike, and his blow laid the man flat. He lay stunned a moment, then raised himself to a sitting posture, his hand to his face, and the gaze he fixed upon Shefford seemed to combine astonishment and rage.

"I hope you're not Presbrey," said Shefford, slowly. He felt awkward, not sure of himself.

The man appeared about to burst into speech, but repressed it. There was blood on his mouth and his hand. Hastily he scrambled to his feet. Shefford saw this man's amaze and rage change to shame. He was tall and rather stout; he had a smooth tanned face, soft of outline, with a weak chin; his eyes were dark. The look of him and his corduroys and his soft shoes gave Shefford an impression that he was not a man who worked hard. By contrast with the few other worn and rugged desert men Shefford had met this stranger stood out strikingly. He stooped to pick up a soft felt hat and, jamming it on his head, he hurried out. Shefford followed him and watched him from the door. He went directly to the corral, mounted the pony, and rode out, to turn down the slope toward the south. When he reached the level of the basin, where evidently the sand was hard, he put the pony to a lope and gradually drew away.

"Well!" ejaculated Shefford. He did not know what to make of this adventure. Presently he became aware that the Indian girl was sitting on a roll of blankets near the wall. With curious interest Shefford studied her appearance. She had long, raven-black hair, tangled and disheveled, and she wore a soiled white band of cord above her brow. The color of her face struck him; it was dark, but not red nor bronzed; it almost had a tinge of gold. Her profile was clear-cut, bold, almost stern. Long black eyelashes hid her eyes. She wore a tight-fitting waist garment of material resembling velveteen. It was ripped along her side, exposing a skin still more richly gold than that of her face. A string of silver ornaments and turquoise-and-white beads encircled her neck, and it moved gently up and down with the heaving of her full bosom. Her skirt was some gaudy print goods, torn and stained and dusty. She had little feet, incased in brown moccasins, fitting like gloves and buttoning over the ankles with silver coins.

"Who was that man? Did he hurt you?" inquired Shefford, turning to gaze down the valley where a moving black object showed on the bare sand.

"No savvy," replied the Indian girl.

"Where's the trader Presbrey?" asked Shefford.

She pointed straight down into the red valley.

"Toh," she said.

In the center of the basin lay a small pool of water shining brightly in the sunset glow. Small objects moved around it, so small that Shefford thought he saw several dogs led by a child. But it was the distance that deceived him. There was a man down there watering his horses. That reminded Shefford of the duty owing to his own tired and thirsty beast. Whereupon he untied his pack, took off the saddle, and was about ready to start down when the Indian girl grasped the bridle from his hand.

"Me go," she said.

He saw her eyes then, and they made her look different. They were as black as her hair. He was puzzled to decide whether or not he thought her handsome.

"Thanks, but I'll go," he replied, and, taking the bridle again, he started down the slope. At every step he sank into the deep, soft sand. Down a little way he came upon a pile of tin cans; they were everywhere, buried, half buried, and lying loose; and these gave evidence of how the trader lived. Presently Shefford discovered that the Indian girl was following him with her own pony. Looking upward at her against the light, he thought her slender, lithe, picturesque. At a distance he liked her.

He plodded on, at length glad to get out of the drifts of sand to the hard level floor of the valley. This, too, was sand, but dried and baked hard, and red in color. At some season of the year this immense flat must be covered with water. How wide it was, and empty! Shefford experienced again a feeling that had been novel to him—and it was that he was loose, free, unanchored, ready to veer with the wind. From the foot of the slope the water hole had appeared to be a few hundred rods out in the valley. But the small size of the figures made Shefford doubt; and he had to travel many times a few hundred rods before those figures began to grow. Then Shefford made out that they were approaching him.

Thereafter they rapidly increased to normal proportions of man and beast. When Shefford met them he saw a powerful, heavily built young man leading two ponies.

"You're Mr. Presbrey, the trader?" inquired Shefford.

"Yes, I'm Presbrey, without the Mister," he replied.

"My name's Shefford. I'm knocking about on the desert. Rode from beyond Tuba to-day."

"Glad to see you," said Presbrey. He offered his hand. He was a stalwart man, clad in gray shirt, overalls, and boots. A shock of tumbled light hair covered his massive head; he was tanned, but not darkly, and there was red in his cheeks; under his shaggy eyebrows were deep, keen eyes; his lips were hard and set, as if occasion for smiles or words was rare; and his big, strong jaw seemed locked.

"Wish more travelers came knocking around Red Lake," he added. "Reckon here's the jumping-off place."

"It's pretty—lonesome," said Shefford, hesitating as if at a loss for words.

Then the Indian girl came up. Presbrey addressed her in her own language, which Shefford did not understand. She seemed shy and would not answer; she stood with downcast face and eyes. Presbrey spoke again, at which she pointed down the valley, and then moved on with her pony toward the water-hole.

Presbrey's keen eyes fixed on the receding black dot far down that oval expanse.

"That fellow left—rather abruptly," said Shefford, constrainedly. "Who was he?"

"His name's Willetts. He's a missionary. He rode in to-day with this Navajo girl. He was taking her to Blue canyon, where he lives and teaches the Indians. I've met him only a few times. You see, not many white men ride in here. He's the first white man I've seen in six months, and you're the second. Both the same day!... Red Lake's getting popular! It's queer, though, his leaving. He expected to stay all night. There's no other place to stay. Blue canyon is fifty miles away."

"I'm sorry to say—no, I'm not sorry, either—but I must tell you I was the cause of Mr. Willetts leaving," replied Shefford.

"How so?" inquired the other.

Then Shefford related the incident following his arrival.

"Perhaps my action was hasty," he concluded, apologetically. "I didn't think. Indeed, I'm surprised at myself."

Presbrey made no comment and his face was as hard to read as one of the distant bluffs.

"But what did the man mean?" asked Shefford, conscious of a little heat. "I'm a stranger out here. I'm ignorant of Indians—how they're controlled. Still I'm no fool.... If Willetts didn't mean evil, at least he was brutal."

"He was teaching her religion," replied Presbrey. His tone held faint scorn and implied a joke, but his face did not change in the slightest.

Without understanding just why, Shefford felt his conviction justified and his action approved. Then he was sensible of a slight shock of wonder and disgust.

"I am—I was a minister of the Gospel," he said to Presbrey. "What you hint seems impossible. I can't believe it."

"I didn't hint," replied Presbrey, bluntly, and it was evident that he was a sincere, but close-mouthed, man. "Shefford, so you're a preacher?... Did you come out here to try to convert the Indians?"

"No. I said I WAS a minister. I am no longer. I'm just a—a wanderer."

"I see. Well, the desert's no place for missionaries, but it's good for wanderers.... Go water your horse and take him up to the corral. You'll find some hay for him. I'll get grub ready."

Shefford went on with his horse to the pool. The water appeared thick, green, murky, and there was a line of salty crust extending around the margin of the pool. The thirsty horse splashed in and eagerly bent his head. But he did not like the taste. Many times he refused to drink, yet always lowered his nose again. Finally he drank, though not his fill. Shefford saw the Indian girl drink from her hand. He scooped up a handful and found it too sour to swallow. When he turned to retrace his steps she mounted her pony and followed him.

A golden flare lit up the western sky, and silhouetted dark and lonely against it stood the trading-post. Upon his return Shefford found the wind rising, and it chilled him. When he reached the slope thin gray sheets of sand were blowing low, rising, whipping, falling, sweeping along with soft silken rustle. Sometimes the gray veils hid his boots. It was a long, toilsome climb up that yielding, dragging ascent, and he had already been lame and tired. By the time he had put his horse away twilight was everywhere except in the west. The Indian girl left her pony in the corral and came like a shadow toward the house.

Shefford had difficulty in finding the foot of the stairway. He climbed to enter a large loft, lighted by two lamps. Presbrey was there, kneading biscuit dough in a pan.

"Make yourself comfortable," he said.

The huge loft was the shape of a half-octagon. A door opened upon the valley side, and here, too, there were windows. How attractive the place was in comparison with the impressions gained from the outside! The furnishings consisted of Indian blankets on the floor, two beds, a desk and table, several chairs and a couch, a gun-rack full of rifles, innumerable silver-ornamented belts, bridles, and other Indian articles upon the walls, and in one corner a wood-burning stove with teakettle steaming, and a great cupboard with shelves packed full of canned foods.

Shefford leaned in the doorway and looked out. Beneath him on a roll of blankets sat the Indian girl, silent and motionless. He wondered what was in her mind, what she would do, how the trader would treat her. The slope now was a long slant of sheeted moving shadows of sand. Dusk had gathered in the valley. The bluffs loomed beyond. A pale star twinkled above. Shefford suddenly became aware of the intense nature of the stillness about him. Yet, as he listened to this silence, he heard an intermittent and immeasurably low moan, a fitful, mournful murmur. Assuredly it was only the wind. Nevertheless, it made his blood run cold. It was a different wind from that which had made music under the eaves of his Illinois home. This was a lonely, haunting wind, with desert hunger in it, and more which he could not name. Shefford listened to this spirit-brooding sound while he watched night envelop the valley. How black, how thick the mantle! Yet it brought no comforting sense of close-folded protection, of walls of soft sleep, of a home. Instead there was the feeling of space, of emptiness, of an infinite hall down which a mournful wind swept streams of murmuring sand.

"Well, grub's about ready," said Presbrey.

"Got any water?" asked Shefford.

"Sure. There in the bucket. It's rain-water. I have a tank here."

Shefford's sore and blistered face felt better after he had washed off the sand and alkali dust.

"Better not wash your face often while you're in the desert. Bad plan," went on Presbrey, noting how gingerly his visitor had gone about his ablutions. "Well, come and eat."

Shefford marked that if the trader did live a lonely life he fared well. There was more on the table than twice two men could have eaten. It was the first time in four days that Shefford had sat at a table, and he made up for lost opportunity.

His host's actions indicated pleasure, yet the strange, hard face never relaxed, never changed. When the meal was finished Presbrey declined assistance, had a generous thought of the Indian girl, who, he said, could have a place to eat and sleep down-stairs, and then with the skill and despatch of an accomplished housewife cleared the table, after which work he filled a pipe and evidently prepared to listen.

It took only one question for Shefford to find that the trader was starved for news of the outside world; and for an hour Shefford fed that appetite, even as he had been done by. But when he had talked himself out there seemed indication of Presbrey being more than a good listener.

"How'd you come in?" he asked, presently.

"By Flagstaff—across the Little Colorado—and through Moencopie."

"Did you stop at Moen Ave?"

"No. What place is that?"

"A missionary lives there. Did you stop at Tuba?"

"Only long enough to drink and water my horse. That was a wonderful spring for the desert."

"You said you were a wanderer.... Do you want a job? I'll give you one."

"No, thank you, Presbrey."

"I saw your pack. That's no pack to travel with in this country. Your horse won't last, either. Have you any money?"

"Yes, plenty of money."

"Well, that's good. Not that a white man out here would ever take a dollar from you. But you can buy from the Indians as you go. Where are you making for, anyhow?"

Shefford hesitated, debating in mind whether to tell his purpose or not. His host did not press the question.

"I see. Just foot-loose and wandering around," went on Presbrey. "I can understand how the desert appeals to you. Preachers lead easy, safe, crowded, bound lives. They're shut up in a church with a Bible and good people. When once in a lifetime they get loose—they break out."

"Yes, I've broken out—beyond all bounds," replied Shefford, sadly. He seemed retrospective for a moment, unaware of the trader's keen and sympathetic glance, and then he caught himself. "I want to see some wild life. Do you know the country north of here?"

"Only what the Navajos tell me. And they're not much to talk. There's a trail goes north, but I've never traveled it. It's a new trail every time an Indian goes that way, for here the sand blows and covers old tracks. But few Navajos ride in from the north. My trade is mostly with Indians up and down the valley."

"How about water and grass?"

"We've had rain and snow. There's sure to be, water. Can't say about grass, though the sheep and ponies from the north are always fat.... But, say, Shefford, if you'll excuse me for advising you—don't go north."

"Why?" asked Shefford, and it was certain that he thrilled.

"It's unknown country, terribly broken, as you can see from here, and there are bad Indians biding in the canyon. I've never met a man who had been over the pass between here and Kayenta. The trip's been made, so there must be a trail. But it's a dangerous trip for any man, let alone a tenderfoot. You're not even packing a gun."

"What's this place Kayenta?" asked Shefford.

"It's a spring. Kayenta means Bottomless Spring. There's a little trading-post, the last and the wildest in northern Arizona. Withers, the trader who keeps it, hauls his supplies in from Colorado and New Mexico. He's never come down this way. I never saw him. Know nothing of him except hearsay. Reckon he's a nervy and strong man to hold that post. If you want to go there, better go by way of Keams canyon, and then around the foot of Black Mesa. It'll be a long ride—maybe two hundred miles."

"How far straight north over the pass?"

"Can't say. Upward of seventy-five miles over rough trails, if there are trails at all.... I've heard rumors of a fine tribe of Navajos living in there, rich in sheep and horses. It may be true and it may not. But I do know there are bad Indians, half-breeds and outcasts, hiding in there. Some of them have visited me here. Bad customers! More than that, you'll be going close to the Utah line, and the Mormons over there are unfriendly these days."

"Why?" queried Shefford, again with that curious thrill.

"They are being persecuted by the government."

Shefford asked no more questions and his host vouchsafed no more information on that score. The conversation lagged. Then Shefford inquired about the Indian girl and learned that she lived up the valley somewhere. Presbrey had never seen her before Willetts came with her to Red Lake. And this query brought out the fact that Presbrey was comparatively new to Red Lake and vicinity. Shefford wondered why a lonely six months there had not made the trader old in experience. Probably the desert did not readily give up its secrets. Moreover, this Red Lake house was only an occasionally used branch of Presbrey's main trading-post, which was situated at Willow Springs, fifty miles westward over the mesa.

"I'm closing up here soon for a spell," said Presbrey, and now his face lost its set hardness and seemed singularly changed. It was a difference, of light and softness. "Won't be so lonesome over at Willow Springs.... I'm being married soon."

"That's fine," replied Shefford, warmly. He was glad for the sake of this lonely desert man. What good a wife would bring into a trader's life!

Presbrey's naive admission, however, appeared to detach him from his present surroundings, and with his massive head enveloped by a cloud of smoke he lived in dreams.

Shefford respected his host's serene abstraction. Indeed, he was grateful for silence. Not for many nights had the past impinged so closely upon the present. The wound in his soul had not healed, and to speak of himself made it bleed anew. Memory was too poignant; the past was too close; he wanted to forget until he had toiled into the heart of this forbidding wilderness—until time had gone by and he dared to face his unquiet soul. Then he listened to the steadily rising roar of the wind. How strange and hollow! That wind was freighted with heavy sand, and he heard it sweep, sweep, sweep by in gusts, and then blow with dull, steady blast against the walls. The sound was provocative of thought. This moan and rush of wind was no dream—this presence of his in a night-enshrouded and sand-besieged house of the lonely desert was reality—this adventure was not one of fancy. True indeed, then, must be the wild, strange story that had led him hither. He was going on to seek, to strive, to find. Somewhere northward in the broken fastnesses lay hidden a valley walled in from the world. Would they be there, those lost fugitives whose story had thrilled him? After twelve years would she be alive, a child grown to womanhood in the solitude of a beautiful canyon? Incredible! Yet he believed his friend's story and he indeed knew how strange and tragic life was. He fancied he heard her voice on the sweeping wind. She called to him, haunted him.

He admitted the improbability of her existence, but lost nothing of the persistent intangible hope that drove him. He believed himself a man stricken in soul, unworthy, through doubt of God, to minister to the people who had banished him. Perhaps a labor of Hercules, a mighty and perilous work of rescue, the saving of this lost and imprisoned girl, would help him in his trouble. She might be his salvation. Who could tell? Always as a boy and as a man he had fared forth to find the treasure at the foot of the rainbow.

❧ 2 ❧
THE SAGI

NEXT MORNING the Indian girl was gone and the tracks of her pony led north. Shefford's first thought was to wonder if he would overtake her on the trail; and this surprised him with the proof of how unconsciously his resolve to go on had formed.

Presbrey made no further attempt to turn Shefford back. But he insisted on replenishing the pack, and that Shefford take weapons. Finally Shefford was persuaded to accept a revolver. The trader bade him good-by and stood in the door while Shefford led his horse down the slope toward the water-hole. Perhaps the trader believed he was watching the departure of a man who would never return. He was still standing at the door of the post when Shefford halted at the pool.

Upon the level floor of the valley lay thin patches of snow which had fallen during the night. The air was biting cold, yet stimulated Shefford while it stung him. His horse drank rather slowly and disgustedly. Then Shefford mounted and reluctantly turned his back upon the trading-post.

As he rode away from the pool he saw a large flock of sheep approaching. They were very closely, even densely, packed, in a solid slow-moving mass and coming with a precision almost like a march. This fact surprised Shefford, for there was not an Indian in sight. Presently he saw that a dog was leading the flock, and a little later he discovered another dog in the rear of the sheep. They were splendid, long-haired dogs, of a wild-looking shepherd breed. He halted his horse to watch the procession pass by. The flock covered fully an acre of ground and the sheep were black, white, and brown. They passed him, making a little pattering roar on the hard-caked sand. The dogs were taking the sheep in to water.

Shefford went on and was drawing close to the other side of the basin, where the flat red level was broken by rising dunes and ridges, when he espied a bunch of ponies. A shrill whistle told him that they had seen him. They were wild, shaggy, with long manes and tails. They stopped, threw up their heads, and watched him. Shefford certainly returned the attention. There was no Indian with them. Presently, with a snort, the leader, which appeared to be a stallion, trotted behind the others, seemed to be driving them, and went clear round

403

the band to get in the lead again. He was taking them in to water, the same as the dogs had taken the sheep.

These incidents were new and pleasing to Shefford. How ignorant he had been of life in the wilderness! Once more he received subtle intimations of what he might learn out in the open; and it was with a less weighted heart that he faced the gateway between the huge yellow bluffs on his left and the slow rise of ground to the black mesa on his right. He looked back in time to see the trading-post, bleak and lonely on the bare slope, pass out of sight behind the bluffs. Shefford felt no fear—he really had little experience of physical fear—but it was certain that he gritted his teeth and welcomed whatever was to come to him. He had lived a narrow, insulated life with his mind on spiritual things; his family and his congregation and his friends—except that one new friend whose story had enthralled him— were people of quiet religious habit; the man deep down in him had never had a chance. He breathed hard as he tried to imagine the world opening to him, and almost dared to be glad for the doubt that had sent him adrift.

The tracks of the Indian girl's pony were plain in the sand. Also there were other tracks, not so plain, and these Shefford decided had been made by Willetts and the girl the day before. He climbed a ridge, half soft sand and half hard, and saw right before him, rising in striking form, two great yellow buttes, like elephant legs. He rode between them, amazed at their height. Then before him stretched a slowly ascending valley, walled on one side by the black mesa and on the other by low bluffs. For miles a dark-green growth of greasewood covered the valley, and Shefford could see where the green thinned and failed, to give place to sand. He trotted his horse and made good time on this stretch.

The day contrasted greatly with any he had yet experienced. Gray clouds obscured the walls of rock a few miles to the west, and Shefford saw squalls of snow like huge veils dropping down and spreading out. The wind cut with the keenness of a knife. Soon he was chilled to the bone. A squall swooped and roared down upon him, and the wind that bore the driving white pellets of snow, almost like hail, was so freezing bitter cold that the former wind seemed warm in comparison. The squall passed as swiftly as it had come, and it left Shefford so benumbed he could not hold the bridle. He tumbled off his horse and walked. By and by the sun came out and soon warmed him and melted the thin layer of snow on the sand. He was still on the trail of the Indian girl, but hers were now the only tracks he could see.

All morning he gradually climbed, with limited view, until at last he mounted to a point where the country lay open to his sight on all sides except where the endless black mesa ranged on into the north. A rugged yellow peak dominated the landscape to the fore, but it was far away. Red and jagged country extended westward to a huge flat-topped wall of gray rock. Lowering swift clouds swept across the sky, like drooping mantles, and darkened the sun. Shefford built a little fire out of dead greasewood sticks, and with his blanket round his shoulders he hung over the blaze, scorching his clothes and hands. He had been cold before in his life but he had never before appreciated fire. This desert blast pierced him. The squall enveloped him, thicker and colder and windier than the other, but, being better fortified, he did not suffer so much. It howled away, hiding the mesa and leaving a white desert behind. Shefford walked on, leading his horse, until the exercise and the sun had once more warmed him.

This last squall had rendered the Indian girl's trail difficult to follow. The snow did not quickly melt, and, besides, sheep tracks and the tracks of horses gave him trouble, until at last he was compelled to admit that he could not follow her any longer. A faint path or trail led north, however, and, following that, he soon forgot the girl. Every surmounted ridge held a surprise for him. The desert seemed never to change in the vast whole that encompassed him, yet near him it was always changing. From Red Lake he had seen a peaked, walled, and canyoned country, as rough as a stormy sea; but when he rode into that country the sharp and broken features held to the distance.

He was glad to get out of the sand. Long narrow flats, gray with grass and dotted with patches of greasewood, and lined by low bare ridges of yellow rock, stretched away from him, leading toward the yellow peak that seemed never to be gained upon.

Shefford had pictures in his mind, pictures of stone walls and wild valleys and domed buttes, all of which had been painted in colorful and vivid words by his friend Venters. He believed he would recognize the distinctive and remarkable landmarks Venters had portrayed, and he was certain that he had not yet come upon one of them. This was his second lonely day of travel and he had grown more and more susceptible to the influence of horizon and the different prominent points. He attributed a gradual change in his feelings to the loneliness and the increasing wildness. Between Tuba and Flagstaff he had met Indians and an occasional prospector and teamster. Here he was alone, and though he felt some strange gladness, he could not help but see the difference.

He rode on during the gray, lowering, chilly day, and toward evening the clouds broke in the west, and a setting sun shone through the rift, burnishing the desert to red and gold. Shefford's instinctive but deadened love of the beautiful in nature stirred into life, and the moment of its rebirth was a melancholy and sweet one. Too late for the artist's work, but not too late for his soul!

For a place to make camp he halted near a low area of rock that lay like an island in a sea of grass. There was an abundance of dead greasewood for a camp-fire, and, after searching over the rock, he found little pools of melted snow in the depressions. He took off the saddle and pack, watered his horse, and, hobbling him as well as his inexperience permitted, he turned him loose on the grass.

Then while he built a fire and prepared a meal the night came down upon him. In the lee of the rock he was well sheltered from the wind, but the air, was bitter cold. He gathered all the dead greasewood in the vicinity, replenished the fire, and rolled in his blanket, back to the blaze. The loneliness and the coyotes did not bother him this night. He was too tired and cold. He went to sleep at once and did not awaken until the fire died out. Then he rebuilt it and went to sleep again. Every half-hour all night long he repeated this, and was glad indeed when the dawn broke.

The day began with misfortune. His horse was gone; it had been stolen, or had worked out of sight, or had broken the hobbles and made off. From a high stone ridge Shefford searched the grassy flats and slopes, all to no purpose. Then he tried to track the horse, but this was equally futile. He had expected disasters, and the first one did not daunt him. He tied most of his pack in the blanket, threw the canteen across his shoulder, and set forth, sure at least of one thing—that he was a very much better traveler on foot than on horseback.

Walking did not afford him the leisure to study the surrounding country; however, from time to time, when he surmounted a bench he scanned the different landmarks that had grown familiar. It took hours of steady walking to reach and pass the yellow peak that had been a kind of goal. He saw many sheep trails and horse tracks in the vicinity of this mountain, and once he was sure he espied an Indian watching him from a bold ridge-top.

The day was bright and warm, with air so clear it magnified objects he knew to be far away. The ascent was gradual; there were many narrow flats connected by steps; and the grass grew thicker and longer. At noon Shefford halted under the first cedar-tree, a lonely, dwarfed shrub that seemed to have had a hard life. From this point the rise of ground was more perceptible, and straggling cedars led the eye on to a purple slope that merged into green of pinon and pine. Could that purple be the sage Venters had so feelingly described, or was it merely the purple of deceiving distance? Whatever it might be, it gave Shefford a thrill and made him think of the strange, shy, and lovely woman Venters had won out here in this purple-sage country.

He calculated that he had ridden thirty miles the day before and had already traveled ten miles today, and therefore could hope to be in the pass before night. Shefford resumed his journey with too much energy and enthusiasm to think of being tired. And he discovered presently that the straggling cedars and the slope beyond were much closer than he had judged them to be. He reached the sage to find it gray instead of purple. Yet it was always purple a little way ahead, and if he half shut his eyes it was purple near at hand. He was surprised to find that he could not breathe freely, or it seemed so, and soon made the discovery that the sweet, pungent, penetrating fragrance of sage and cedar had this strange effect upon him. This was an exceedingly dry and odorous forest, where every open space between the clumps of cedars was choked with luxuriant sage. The pinyons were higher up on the mesa, and the pines still higher. Shefford appeared to lose himself. There were no trails; the black mesa on the right and the wall of stone on the left could not be seen; but he pushed on with what was either singular confidence or rash impulse. And he did not know whether that slope was long or short. Once at the summit he saw with surprise that it broke abruptly and the descent was very steep and short on that side. Through the trees he once more saw the black mesa, rising to the dignity of a mountain; and he had glimpses of another flat, narrow valley, this time with a red wall running parallel with the mesa. He could not help but hurry down to get an unobstructed view. His eagerness was rewarded by a splendid scene, yet to his regret he could not force himself to believe it had any relation to the pictured scenes in his mind. The valley was half a mile wide, perhaps several miles long, and it extended in a curve between the cedar-sloped mesa and a looming wall of red stone. There was not a bird or a beast in sight. He found a well-defined trail, but it had not been recently used. He passed a low structure made of peeled logs and mud, with a dark opening like a door. It did not take him many minutes to learn that the valley was longer than he had calculated. He walked swiftly and steadily, in spite of the fact that the pack had become burdensome. What lay beyond the jutting corner of the mesa had increasing fascination for him and acted as a spur. At last he turned the corner, only to be disappointed at sight of another cedar slope. He had a glimpse of a single black shaft of rock rising far in the distance, and it disappeared as his striding forward made the crest of the slope rise toward the sky.

Again his view became restricted, and he lost the sense of a slow and gradual uplift of rock and an increase in the scale of proportion. Half-way up this ascent he was compelled to rest; and again the sun was slanting low when he entered the cedar forest. Soon he was descending, and he suddenly came into the open to face a scene that made his heart beat thick and fast.

He saw lofty crags and cathedral spires, and a wonderful canyon winding between huge beetling red walls. He heard the murmur of flowing water. The trail led down to the canyon floor, which appeared to be level and green and cut by deep washes in red earth. Could this canyon be the mouth of Deception Pass? It bore no resemblance to any place Shefford had heard described, yet somehow he felt rather than saw that it was the portal to the wild vastness he had traveled so far to enter.

Not till he had descended the trail and had dropped his pack did he realize how weary and footsore he was. Then he rested. But his eyes roved to and fro, and his mind was active. What a wild and lonesome spot! The low murmur of shallow water came up to him from a deep, narrow cleft. Shadows were already making the canyon seem full of blue haze. He saw a bare slope of stone out of which cedar-trees were growing. And as he looked about him he became aware of a singular and very perceptible change in the lights and shades. The sun was setting; the crags were gold-tipped; the shadows crept upward; the sky seemed to darken swiftly; then the gold changed to red, slowly dulled, and the grays and purples stood out. Shefford was entranced with the beautiful changing effects, and watched till the walls turned black and the sky grew steely and a faint star peeped out. Then he set about the necessary camp tasks.

Dead cedars right at hand assured him a comfortable night with steady fire; and when he had satisfied his hunger he arranged an easy seat before the blazing logs, and gave his mind over to thought of his weird, lonely environment.

The murmur of running water mingled in harmonious accompaniment with the moan of the wind in the cedars—wild, sweet sounds that were balm to his wounded spirit! They seemed a part of the silence, rather than a break in it or a hindrance to the feeling of it. But suddenly that silence did break to the rattle of a rock. Shefford listened, thinking some wild animal was prowling around. He felt no alarm. Presently he heard the sound again, and again. Then he recognized the crack of unshod hoofs upon rock. A horse was coming down the trail. Shefford rather resented the interruption, though he still had no alarm. He believed he was perfectly safe. As a matter of fact, he had never in his life been anything but safe and padded around with wool, hence, never having experienced peril, he did not know what fear was.

Presently he saw a horse and rider come into dark prominence on the ridge just above his camp. They were silhouetted against the starry sky. The horseman stopped and he and his steed made a magnificent black statue, somehow wild and strange, in Shefford's sight. Then he came on, vanished in the darkness under the ridge, presently to emerge into the circle of camp-fire light.

He rode to within twenty feet of Shefford and the fire. The horse was dark, wild-looking, and seemed ready to run. The rider appeared to be an Indian, and yet had something about him suggesting the cowboy. At once Shefford remembered what Presbrey had said about half-breeds. A little shock, inexplicable to Shefford, rippled over him.

He greeted his visitor, but received no answer. Shefford saw a dark, squat figure bending forward in the saddle. The man was tense. All about him was dark except the glint of a rifle across the saddle. The face under the sombrero was only a shadow. Shefford kicked the fire-logs and a brighter blaze lightened the scene. Then he saw this stranger a little more clearly, and made out an unusually large head, broad dark face, a sinister tight-shut mouth, and gleaming black eyes.

Those eyes were unmistakably hostile. They roved searchingly over Shefford's pack and then over his person. Shefford felt for the gun that Presbrey had given him. But it was gone. He had left it back where he had lost his horse, and had not thought of it since. Then a strange, slow-coming cold agitation possessed Shefford. Something gripped his throat.

Suddenly Shefford was stricken at a menacing movement on the part of the horseman. He had drawn a gun. Shefford saw it shine darkly in the firelight. The Indian meant to murder him. Shefford saw the grim, dark face in a kind of horrible amaze. He felt the meaning of that drawn weapon as he had never felt anything before in his life. And he collapsed back into his seat with an icy, sickening terror. In a second he was dripping wet with cold sweat. Lightning-swift thoughts flashed through his mind. It had been one of his platitudes that he was not afraid of death. Yet here he was a shaking, helpless coward. What had he learned about either life or death? Would this dark savage plunge him into the unknown? It was then that Shefford realized his hollow philosophy and the bitter-sweetness of life. He had a brain and a soul, and between them he might have worked out his salvation. But what were they to this ruthless night-wanderer, this raw and horrible wildness of the desert?

Incapable of voluntary movement, with tongue cleaving to the roof of his mouth, Shefford watched the horseman and the half-poised gun. It was not yet leveled. Then it dawned upon Shefford that the stranger's head was turned a little, his ear to the wind. He was listening. His horse was listening. Suddenly he straightened up, wheeled his horse, and trotted away into the darkness. But he did not climb the ridge down which he had come.

Shefford heard the click of hoofs upon the stony trail. Other horses and riders were descending into the canyon. They had been the cause of his deliverance, and in the relaxation of feeling he almost fainted. Then he sat there, slowly recovering, slowly ceasing to tremble, divining that this situation was somehow to change his attitude toward life.

Three horses, two with riders, moved in dark shapes across the skyline above the ridge, disappeared as had Shefford's first visitor, and then rode into the light. Shefford saw two Indians—a man and a woman; then with surprise recognized the latter to be the Indian girl he had met at Red Lake. He was still more surprised to recognize in the third horse the one he had lost at the last camp. Shefford rose, a little shaky on his legs, to thank these Indians for a double service. The man slipped from his saddle and his moccasined feet thudded lightly. He was tall, lithe, erect, a singularly graceful figure, and as he advanced Shefford saw a dark face and sharp, dark eyes. The Indian was bareheaded, with his hair bound in a band. He resembled the girl, but appeared to have a finer face.

"How do?" he said, in a voice low and distinct. He extended his hand, and Shefford felt a grip of steel. He returned the greeting. Then the Indian gave Shefford the bridle of the horse, and made signs that appeared to indicate the horse had broken his hobbles and strayed. Shefford thanked him. Thereupon the Indian unsaddled and led the horses away, evidently to water them. The girl remained behind. Shefford addressed her, but she was shy and did not respond. He set about cooking a meal for his visitors, and was busily engaged at this when the Indian returned without the horses. Presently Shefford resumed his seat by the fire and watched the two eat what he had prepared. They certainly were hungry and soon had the pans and cups empty. Then the girl drew back a little into the shadow, while the man sat with his legs crossed and his feet tucked under him.

His dark face was smooth, yet it seemed to have lines under the surface. Shefford was impressed. He had never seen an Indian who interested him as this one. Looked at superficially, he appeared young, wild, silent, locked in his primeval apathy, just a healthy savage; but looked at more attentively, he appeared matured, even old, a strange, sad, brooding figure, with a burden on his shoulders. Shefford found himself growing curious.

"What place?" asked Shefford, waving his hand toward the dark opening between the black cliffs.

"Sagi," replied the Indian.

That did not mean anything to Shefford, and he asked if the Sagi was the pass, but the Indian shook his head.

"Wife?" asked Shefford, pointing to the girl.

The Indian shook his head again. "*Bi-la*," he said.

"What you mean?" asked Shefford. "What *bi-la*?"

"Sister," replied the Indian. He spoke the word reluctantly, as if the white man's language did not please him, but the clearness and correct pronunciation surprised Shefford.

"What name—what call her?" he went on.

"Glen Naspa."

"What your name?" inquired Shefford, indicating the Indian.

"Nas Ta Bega," answered the Indian.

"Navajo?"

The Indian bowed with what seemed pride and stately dignity.

"My name John Shefford. Come far way back toward rising sun. Come stay here long."

Nas Ta Bega's dark eyes were fixed steadily upon Shefford. He reflected that he could not remember having felt so penetrating a gaze. But neither the Indian's eyes nor face gave any clue to his thoughts.

"Navajo no savvy Jesus Christ," said the Indian, and his voice rolled out low and deep.

Shefford felt both amaze and pain. The Indian had taken him for a missionary.

"No!... Me no missionary," cried Shefford, and he flung up a passionately repudiating hand.

A singular flash shot from the Indian's dark eyes. It struck Shefford even at this stinging moment when the past came back.

"Trade—buy wool—blanket?" queried Nas Ta Bega.

"No," replied Shefford. "Me want ride—walk far." He waved his hand to indicate a wide sweep of territory. "Me sick."

Nas Ta Bega laid a significant finger upon his lungs.

"No," replied Shefford. "Me strong. Sick here." And with motions of his hands he tried to show that his was a trouble of the heart.

Shefford received instant impression of this Indian's intelligent comprehension, but he could not tell just what had given him the feeling. Nas Ta Bega rose then and walked away into the shadow. Shefford heard him working around the dead cedar-tree, where he had probably gone to get fire-wood. Then Shefford heard a splintering crash, which was followed by a crunching, bumping sound. Presently he was astounded to see the Indian enter the lighted circle dragging the whole cedar-tree, trunk first. Shefford would have doubted the ability of two men to drag that tree, and here came Nas Ta Bega, managing it easily. He laid the trunk on the fire, and then proceeded to break off small branches, to place them advantageously where the red coals kindled them into a blaze.

The Indian's next move was to place his saddle, which he evidently meant to use for a pillow. Then he spread a goat-skin on the ground, lay down upon it, with his back to the fire, and, pulling a long-haired saddle-blanket over his shoulders, he relaxed and became motionless. His sister, Glen Naspa, did likewise, except that she stayed farther away from the fire, and she had a larger blanket, which covered her well. It appeared to Shefford that they went to sleep at once.

Shefford felt as tired as he had ever been, but he did not think he could soon drop into slumber, and in fact he did not want to.

There was something in the companionship of these Indians that he had not experienced before. He still had a strange and weak feeling—the aftermath of that fear which had sickened him with its horrible icy grip. Nas Ta Bega's arrival had frightened away that dark and silent prowler of the night; and Shefford was convinced the Indian had saved his life. The measure of his gratitude was a source of wonder to him. Had he cared so much for life? Yes—he had, when face to face with death. That was something to know. It helped him. And he gathered from his strange feeling that the romantic quest which had brought him into the wilderness might turn out to be an antidote for the morbid bitterness of heart.

With new sensations had come new thoughts. Right then it was very pleasant to sit in the warmth and light of the roaring cedar fire. There was a deep-seated ache of fatigue in his bones. What joy it was to rest! He had felt the dry scorch of desert thirst and the pang of hunger. How wonderful to learn the real meaning of water and food! He had just finished the longest, hardest day's work of his life! Had that anything to do with a something almost like peace which seemed to hover near in the shadows, trying to come to him? He had befriended an Indian girl, and now her brother had paid back the service. Both the giving and receiving were somehow sweet to Shefford. They opened up hitherto vague channels of thought. For years he had imagined he was serving people, when he had never lifted a hand. A blow given in the defense of an Indian girl had somehow operated to make a change in John Shefford's existence. It had liberated a spirit in him. Moreover, it had worked its influence outside his mind. The Indian girl and her brother had followed his trail to return his horse, perhaps to guide him safely, but, unknowingly perhaps, they had done infinitely more than that for him. As Shefford's eye wandered over the dark, still figures of the sleepers he had a strange, dreamy premonition, or perhaps only a fancy, that there was to be more come of this fortunate meeting.

For the rest, it was good to be there in the speaking silence, to feel the heat on his outstretched palms and the cold wind on his cheek, to see the black wall lifting its bold outline and the crags reaching for the white stars.

✵ 3 ✵

KAYENTA

THE STAMPING of horses awoke Shefford. He saw a towering crag, rosy in the morning light, like a huge red spear splitting the clear blue of sky. He got up, feeling cramped and sore, yet with unfamiliar exhilaration. The whipping air made him stretch his hands to the fire. An odor of coffee and broiled meat mingled with the fragrance of wood smoke. Glen Naspa was on her knees broiling a rabbit on a stick over the red coals. Nas Ta Bega was saddling the ponies. The canyon appeared to be full of purple shadows under one side of dark cliffs and golden streaks of mist on the other where the sun struck high up on the walls.

"Good morning," said Shefford.

Glen Naspa shyly replied in Navajo.

"How," was Nas Ta Bega's greeting.

In daylight the Indian lost some of the dark somberness of face that had impressed Shefford. He had a noble head, in poise like that of an eagle, a bold, clean-cut profile, and stern, close-shut lips. His eyes were the most striking and attractive feature about him; they were coal-black and piercing; the intent look out of them seemed to come from a keen and inquisitive mind.

Shefford ate breakfast with the Indians, and then helped with the few preparations for departure. Before they mounted, Nas Ta Bega pointed to horse tracks in the dust. They were those that had been made by Shefford's threatening visitor of the night before. Shefford explained by word and sign, and succeeded at least in showing that he had been in danger. Nas Ta Bega followed the tracks a little way and presently returned.

"Shadd," he said, with an ominous shake of his head. Shefford did not understand whether he meant the name of his visitor or something else, but the menace connected with the word was clear enough.

Glen Naspa mounted her pony, and it was a graceful action that pleased Shefford. He climbed a little stiffly into his own saddle. Then Nas Ta Bega got up and pointed northward.

"Kayenta?" he inquired.

Shefford nodded and then they were off, with Glen Naspa in the lead. They did not climb the trail which they had descended, but took one leading to the right along the base of the

411

slope. Shefford saw down into the red wash that bisected the canyon floor. It was a sheer wall of red clay or loam, a hundred feet high, and at the bottom ran a swift, shallow stream of reddish water. Then for a time a high growth of greasewood hid the surroundings from Shefford's sight. Presently the trail led out into the open, and Shefford saw that he was at the neck of a wonderful valley that gradually widened with great jagged red peaks on the left and the black mesa, now a mountain, running away to the right. He turned to find that the opening of the Sagi could no longer be seen, and he was conscious of a strong desire to return and explore that canyon.

Soon Glen Naspa put her pony to a long, easy, swinging canter and her followers did likewise. As they got outward into the valley Shefford lost the sense of being overshadowed and crowded by the nearness of the huge walls and crags. The trail appeared level underfoot, but at a distance it was seen to climb. Shefford found where it disappeared over the foot of a slope that formed a graceful rising line up to the cedared flank of the mesa. The valley floor, widening away to the north, remained level and green. Beyond rose the jagged range of red peaks, all strangely cut and slanting. These distant deceiving features of the country held Shefford's gaze until the Indian drew his attention to things near at hand. Then Shefford saw flocks of sheep dotting the gray-green valley, and bands of beautiful long-maned, long-tailed ponies.

For several miles the scene did not change except that Shefford imagined he came to see where the upland plain ended or at least broke its level. He was right, for presently the Indian pointed, and Shefford went on to halt upon the edge of a steep slope leading down into a valley vast in its barren gray reaches.

"Kayenta," said Nas Ta Bega.

Shefford at first saw nothing except the monotonous gray valley reaching far to the strange, grotesque monuments of yellow cliff. Then close under the foot of the slope he espied two squat stone houses with red roofs, and a corral with a pool of water shining in the sun.

The trail leading down was steep and sandy, but it was not long. Shefford's sweeping eyes appeared to take in everything at once—the crude stone structures with their earthen roofs, the piles of dirty wool, the Indians lolling around, the tents, and wagons, and horses, little lazy burros and dogs, and scattered everywhere saddles, blankets, guns, and packs.

Then a white man came out of the door. He waved a hand and shouted. Dust and wool and flour were thick upon him. He was muscular and weather-beaten, and appeared young in activity rather than face. A gun swung at his hip and a row of brass-tipped cartridges showed in his belt. Shefford looked into a face that he thought he had seen before, until he realized the similarity was only the bronze and hard line and rugged cast common to desert men. The gray searching eyes went right through him.

"Glad to see you. Get down and come in. Just heard from an Indian that you were coming. I'm the trader Withers," he said to Shefford. His voice was welcoming and the grip of his hand made Shefford's ache.

Shefford told his name and said he was as glad as he was lucky to arrive at Kayenta.

"Hello! Nas Ta Bega!" exclaimed Withers. His tone expressed a surprise his face did not show. "Did this Indian bring you in?"

Withers shook hands with the Navajo while Shefford briefly related what he owed to him. Then Withers looked at Nas Ta Bega and spoke to him in the Indian tongue.

"Shadd," said Nas Ta Bega. Withers let out a dry little laugh and his strong hand tugged at his mustache.

"Who's Shadd?" asked Shefford.

"He's a half-breed Ute—bad Indian, outlaw, murderer. He's in with a gang of outlaws who hide in the San Juan country.... Reckon you're lucky. How'd you come to be there in the Sagi alone?"

"I traveled from Red Lake. Presbrey, the trader there, advised against it, but I came anyway."

"Well." Withers's gray glance was kind, if it did express the foolhardiness of Shefford's act. "Come into the house.... Never mind the horse. My wife will sure be glad to see you."

Withers led Shefford by the first stone house, which evidently was the trading-store, into the second. The room Shefford entered was large, with logs smoldering in a huge open fireplace, blankets covering every foot of floor space, and Indian baskets and silver ornaments everywhere, and strange Indian designs painted upon the whitewashed walls. Withers called his wife and made her acquainted with Shefford. She was a slight, comely little woman, with keen, earnest, dark eyes. She seemed to be serious and quiet, but she made Shefford feel at home immediately. He refused, however, to accept the room offered him, saying that he me meant to sleep out under the open sky. Withers laughed at this and said he understood. Shefford, remembering Presbrey's hunger for news of the outside world, told this trader and his wife all he could think of; and he was listened to with that close attention a traveler always gained in the remote places.

"Sure am glad you rode in," said Withers, for the fourth time. "Now you make yourself at home. Stay here—come over to the store—do what you like. I've got to work. To-night we'll talk."

Shefford went out with his host. The store was as interesting as Presbrey's, though much smaller and more primitive. It was full of everything, and smelled strongly of sheep and goats. There was a narrow aisle between sacks of flour and blankets on one side and a high counter on the other. Behind this counter Withers stood to wait upon the buying Indians. They sold blankets and skins and bags of wool, and in exchange took silver money. Then they lingered and with slow, staid reluctance bought one thing and then another—flour, sugar, canned goods, coffee, tobacco, ammunition. The counter was never without two or three Indians leaning on their dark, silver-braceleted arms. But as they were slow to sell and buy and go, so were others slow to come in. Their voices were soft and low and it seemed to Shefford they were whispering. He liked to hear them and to look at the banded heads, the long, twisted rolls of black hair tied with white cords, the still dark faces and watchful eyes, the silver ear-rings, the slender, shapely brown hands, the lean and sinewy shapes, the corduroys with a belt and gun, and the small, close-fitting buckskin moccasins buttoned with coins. These Indians all appeared young, and under the quiet, slow demeanor there was fierce blood and fire.

By and by two women came in, evidently squaw and daughter. The former was a huge, stout Indian with a face that was certainly pleasant if not jolly.

She had the corners of a blanket tied under her chin, and in the folds behind on her broad back was a naked Indian baby, round and black of head, brown-skinned, with eyes as bright as beads. When the youngster caught sight of Shefford he made a startled dive into the sack of the blanket. Manifestly, however, curiosity got the better of fear, for presently Shefford caught a pair of wondering dark eyes peeping at him.

"They're good spenders, but slow," said Withers. "The Navajos are careful and cautious. That's why they're rich. This squaw, Yan As Pa, has flocks of sheep and more mustangs than she knows about."

"Mustangs. So that's what you call the ponies?" replied Shefford.

"Yep. They're mustangs, and mostly wild as jack-rabbits."

Shefford strolled outside and made the acquaintance of Withers's helper, a Mormon named Whisner. He was a stockily built man past maturity, and his sun-blistered face and watery eyes told of the open desert. He was engaged in weighing sacks of wool brought in by the Indians. Near by stood a framework of poles from which an immense bag was suspended. From the top of this bag protruded the head and shoulders of an Indian who appeared to be stamping and packing wool with his feet. He grinned at the curious Shefford. But Shefford was more interested in the Mormon. So far as he knew, Whisner was the first man of that creed he had ever met, and he could scarcely hide his eagerness. Venters's stories had been of a long-past generation of Mormons, fanatical, ruthless, and unchangeable. Shefford did not expect to meet Mormons of this kind. But any man of that religion would have interested him. Besides this, Whisner seemed to bring him closer to that wild secret canyon he had come West to find. Shefford was somewhat amazed and discomfited to have his polite and friendly overtures repulsed. Whisner might have been an Indian. He was cold, incommunicative, aloof; and there was something about him that made the sensitive Shefford feel his presence was resented.

Presently Shefford strolled on to the corral, which was full of shaggy mustangs. They snorted and kicked at him. He had a half-formed wish that he would never be called upon to ride one of those wild brutes, and then he found himself thinking that he would ride one of them, and after a while any of them. Shefford did not understand himself, but he fought his natural instinctive reluctance to meet obstacles, peril, suffering.

He traced the white-bordered little stream that made the pool in the corral, and when he came to where it oozed out of the sand under the bluff he decided that was not the spring which had made Kayenta famous. Presently down below the trading-post he saw a trough from which burros were drinking. Here he found the spring, a deep well of eddying water walled in by stones, and the overflow made a shallow stream meandering away between its borders of alkali, like a crust of salt. Shefford tasted the water. It bit, but it was good.

Shefford had no trouble in making friends with the lazy sleepy-eyed burros. They let him pull their long ears and rub their noses, but the mustangs standing around were unapproachable. They had wild eyes; they raised long ears and looked vicious. He let them alone.

Evidently this trading-post was a great deal busier than Red Lake. Shefford counted a dozen Indians lounging outside, and there were others riding away. Big wagons told how the bags of wool were transported out of the wilds and how supplies were brought in. A wide, hard-packed road led off to the east, and another, not so clearly defined, wound away to the north. And Indian trails streaked off in all directions.

Shefford discovered, however, when he had walked off a mile or so across the valley to lose sight of the post, that the feeling of wildness and loneliness returned to him. It was a wonderful country. It held something for him besides the possible rescue of an imprisoned girl from a wild canyon.

That night after supper, when Withers and Shefford sat alone before the blazing logs in the huge fireplace, the trader laid his hand on Shefford's and said, with directness and force:

"I've lived my life in the desert. I've met many men and have been a friend to most.... You're no prospector or trader or missionary?"

"No," replied Shefford.

"You've had trouble?"

"Yes."

"Have you come in here to hide? Don't be afraid to tell me. I won't give you away."

"I didn't come to hide."

"Then no one is after you? You've done no wrong?"

"Perhaps I wronged myself, but no one else," replied Shefford, steadily.

"I reckoned so. Well, tell me, or keep your secret—it's all one to me."

Shefford felt a desire to unburden himself. This man was strong, persuasive, kindly. He drew Shefford.

"You're welcome in Kayenta," went on Withers. "Stay as long as you like. I take no pay from a white man. If you want work I have it aplenty."

"Thank you. That is good. I need to work. We'll talk of it later. ... But just yet I can't tell you why I came to Kayenta, what I want to do, how long I shall stay. My thoughts put in words would seem so like dreams. Maybe they are dreams. Perhaps I'm only chasing a phantom—perhaps I'm only hunting the treasure at the foot of the rainbow."

"Well, this is the country for rainbows," laughed Withers. "In summer from June to August when it storms we have rainbows that'll make you think you're in another world. The Navajos have rainbow mountains, rainbow canyons, rainbow bridges of stone, rainbow trails. It sure is rainbow country."

That deep and mystic chord in Shefford thrilled. Here it was again—something tangible at the bottom of his dream.

Withers did not wait for Shefford to say any more, and almost as if he read his visitor's mind he began to talk about the wild country he called home.

He had lived at Kayenta for several years—hard and profitless years by reason of marauding outlaws. He could not have lived there at all but for the protection of the Indians. His father-in-law had been friendly with the Navajos and Piutes for many years, and his wife had been brought up among them. She was held in peculiar reverence and affection by both tribes in that part of the country. Probably she knew more of the Indians' habits, religion, and life than any white person in the West. Both tribes were friendly and peaceable, but there were bad Indians, half-breeds, and outlaws that made the trading-post a venture Withers had long considered precarious, and he wanted to move and intended to some day. His nearest neighbors in New Mexico and Colorado were a hundred miles distant and at some seasons the roads were impassable. To the north, however, twenty miles or so, was situated a Mormon village named Stonebridge. It lay across the Utah line. Withers did some business with this village, but scarcely enough to warrant the risks he had to run. During the last year he had lost several pack-trains, one of which he had never heard of after it left Stonebridge.

"Stonebridge!" exclaimed Shefford, and he trembled. He had heard that name. In his memory it had a place beside the name of another village Shefford longed to speak of to this trader.

"Yes—Stonebridge," replied Withers. "Ever heard the name?"

"I think so. Are there other villages in—in that part of the country?"

"A few, but not close. Glaze is now only a water-hole. Bluff and Monticello are far north across the San Juan.... There used to be another village—but that wouldn't interest you."

"Maybe it would," replied Shefford, quietly.

But his hint was not taken by the trader. Withers suddenly showed a semblance of the aloofness Shefford had observed in Whisner.

"Withers, pardon an impertinence—I am deeply serious.... Are you a Mormon?"

"Indeed I'm not," replied the trader, instantly.

"Are you for the Mormons or against them?"

"Neither. I get along with them. I know them. I believe they are a misunderstood people."

"That's for them."

"No. I'm only fair-minded."

Shefford paused, trying to curb his thrilling impulse, but it was too strong.

"You said there used to be another village.... Was the name of it—Cottonwoods?"

Withers gave a start and faced round to stare at Shefford in blank astonishment.

"Say, did you give me a straight story about yourself?" he queried, sharply.

"So far as I went," replied Shefford.

"You're no spy on the lookout for sealed wives?"

"Absolutely not. I don't even know what you mean by sealed wives."

"Well, it's damn strange that you'd know the name Cottonwoods.... Yes, that's the name of the village I meant—the one that used to be. It's gone now, all except a few stone walls."

"What became of it?"

"Torn down by Mormons years ago. They destroyed it and moved away. I've heard Indians talk about a grand spring that was there once. It's gone, too. Its name was—let me see—"

"Amber Spring," interrupted Shefford.

"By George, you're right!" rejoined the trader, again amazed. "Shefford, this beats me. I haven't heard that name for ten years. I can't help seeing what a tenderfoot—stranger—you are to the desert. Yet, here you are—speaking of what you should know nothing of.... And there's more behind this."

Shefford rose, unable to conceal his agitation.

"Did you ever hear of a rider named Venters?"

"Rider? You mean a cowboy? Venters. No, I never heard that name."

"Did you ever hear of a gunman named Lassiter?" queried Shefford, with increasing emotion.

"No."

"Did you ever hear of a Mormon woman named—Jane Withersteen?"

"No."

Shefford drew his breath sharply. He had followed a gleam—he had caught a fleeting glimpse of it.

"Did you ever hear of a child—a girl—a woman—called Fay Larkin?"

Withers rose slowly with a paling face.

"If you're a spy it'll go hard with you—though I'm no Mormon," he said, grimly.

Shefford lifted a shaking hand.

"I WAS a clergyman. Now I'm nothing—a wanderer—least of all a spy."

Withers leaned closer to see into the other man's eyes; he looked long and then appeared satisfied.

"I've heard the name Fay Larkin," he said, slowly. "I reckon that's all I'll say till you tell your story."

Shefford stood with his back to the fire and he turned the palms of his hands to catch the warmth. He felt cold. Withers had affected him strangely. What was the meaning of the trader's somber gravity? Why was the very mention of Mormons attended by something austere and secret?

"My name is John Shefford. I am twenty-four," began Shefford. "My family—"

Here a knock on the door interrupted Shefford.

"Come in," called Withers.

The door opened and like a shadow Nas Ta Bega slipped in. He said something in Navajo to the trader.

"How," he said to Shefford, and extended his hand. He was stately, but there was no mistaking his friendliness. Then he sat down before the fire, doubled his legs under him after the Indian fashion, and with dark eyes on the blazing logs seemed to lose himself in meditation.

"He likes the fire," explained Withers. "Whenever he comes to Kayenta he always visits me like this.... Don't mind him. Go on with your story."

"My family were plain people, well-to-do, and very religious," went on Shefford. "When I was a boy we moved from the country to a town called Beaumont, Illinois. There was a college in Beaumont and eventually I was sent to it to study for the ministry. I wanted to be —— But never mind that.... By the time I was twenty-two I was ready for my career as a clergyman. I preached for a year around at different places and then got a church in my home town of Beaumont. I became exceedingly good friends with a man named Venters, who had recently come to Beaumont. He was a singular man. His wife was a strange, beautiful woman, very reserved, and she had wonderful dark eyes. They had money and were devoted to each other, and perfectly happy. They owned the finest horses ever seen in Illinois, and their particular enjoyment seemed to be riding. They were always taking long rides. It was something worth going far for to see Mrs. Venters on a horse.

"It was through my own love of horses that I became friendly with Venters. He and his wife attended my church, and as I got to see more of them, gradually we grew intimate. And it was not until I did get intimate with them that I realized that both seemed to be haunted by the past. They were sometimes sad even in their happiness. They drifted off into dreams. They lived back in another world. They seemed to be listening. Indeed, they were a singularly interesting couple, and I grew genuinely fond of them. By and by they had a little girl whom they named Jane. The coming of the baby made a change in my friends. They were happier, and I observed that the haunting shadow did not so often return.

"Venters had spoken of a journey west that he and his wife meant to take some time. But after the baby came he never mentioned his wife in connection with the trip. I gathered that he felt compelled to go to clear up a mystery or to find something—I did not make out just what. But eventually, and it was about a year ago, he told me his story—the strangest, wildest, and most tragic I ever heard. I can't tell it all now. It is enough to say that fifteen years before he had been a rider for a rich Mormon woman named Jane Withersteen, of this village Cottonwoods. She had adopted a beautiful Gentile child named Fay Larkin. Her interest in Gentiles earned the displeasure of her churchmen, and as she was proud there came a breach. Venters and a gunman named Lassiter became involved in her quarrel. Finally Venters took to the canyon. Here in the wilds he found the strange girl he eventually married. For a long time they lived in a wonderful hidden valley, the entrance to which was guarded by a huge balancing rock. Venters got away with the girl. But Lassiter and Jane Withersteen and the child Fay Larkin were driven into the canyon. They escaped to the valley where Venters had lived. Lassiter rolled the balancing rock, and, crashing down the narrow trail, it loosened the weathered walls and closed the narrow outlet for ever."

❧ 4 ❧

NEW FRIENDS

SHEFFORD ENDED his narrative out of breath, pale, and dripping with sweat. Withers sat leaning forward with an expression of intense interest. Nas Ta Bega's easy, graceful pose had succeeded to one of strained rigidity. He seemed a statue of bronze. Could a few intelligible words, Shefford wondered, have created that strange, listening posture?

"Venters got out of Utah, of course, as you know," went on Shefford. "He got out, knowing—as I feel I would have known—that Jane, Lassiter, and little Fay Larkin were shut up, walled up in Surprise Valley. For years Venters considered it would not have been safe for him to venture to rescue them. He had no fears for their lives. They could live in Surprise Valley. But Venters always intended to come back with Bess and find the valley and his friends. No wonder he and Bess were haunted. However, when his wife had the baby that made a difference. It meant he had to go alone. And he was thinking seriously of starting when—when there were developments that made it desirable for me to leave Beaumont. Venters's story haunted me as he had been haunted. I dreamed of that wild valley—of little Fay Larkin grown to womanhood—such a woman as Bess Venters was. And the longing to come was great.... And, Withers—here I am."

The trader reached out and gave Shefford the grip of a man in whom emotion was powerful, but deep and difficult to express.

"Listen to this.... I wish I could help you. Life is a queer deal. ... Shefford, I've got to trust you. Over here in the wild canyon country there's a village of Mormons' sealed wives. It's in Arizona, perhaps twenty miles from here, and near the Utah line. When the United States government began to persecute, or prosecute, the Mormons for polygamy, the Mormons over here in Stonebridge took their sealed wives and moved them out of Utah, just across the line. They built houses, established a village there. I'm the only Gentile who knows about it. And I pack supplies every few weeks in to these women. There are perhaps fifty women, mostly young—second or third or fourth wives of Mormons—sealed wives. And I want you to understand that sealed means SEALED in all that religion or loyalty can get out of the word. There are also some old women and old men in the village, but they hardly count. And there's a flock of the finest children you ever saw in your life.

"The idea of the Mormons must have been to escape prosecution. The law of the government is one wife for each man—no more. All over Utah polygamists have been arrested. The Mormons are deeply concerned. I believe they are a good, law-abiding people. But this law is a direct blow at their religion. In my opinion they can't obey both. And therefore they have not altogether given up plural wives. Perhaps they will some day. I have no proof, but I believe the Mormons of Stonebridge pay secret night visits to their sealed wives across the line in the lonely, hidden village.

"Now once over in Stonebridge I overheard some Mormons talking about a girl who was named Fay Larkin. I never forgot the name. Later I heard the name in this sealed-wife village. But, as I told you, I never heard of Lassiter or Jane Withersteen. Still, if Mormons had found them I would never have heard of it. And Deception Pass—that might be the Sagi.... I'm not surprised at your rainbow-chasing adventure. It's a great story.... This Fay Larkin I've heard of MIGHT be your Fay Larkin—I almost believe so. Shefford, I'll help you find out."

"Yes, yes—I must know," replied Shefford. "Oh, I hope, I pray we can find her! But—I'd rather she was dead—if she's not still hidden in the valley."

"Naturally. You've dreamed yourself into rescuing this lost Fay Larkin.... But, Shefford, you're old enough to know life doesn't work out as you want it to. One way or another I fear you're in for a bitter disappointment."

"Withers, take me to the village."

"Shefford, you're liable to get in bad out here," said the trader, gravely.

"I couldn't be any more ruined than I am now," replied Shefford, passionately.

"But there's risk in this—risk such as you never had," persisted Withers.

"I'll risk anything."

"Reckon this is a funny deal for a sheep-trader to have on his hands," continued Withers. "Shefford, I like you. I've a mind to see you through this. It's a damn strange story.... I'll tell you what—I will help you. I'll give you a job packing supplies in to the village. I meant to turn that over to a Mormon cowboy—Joe Lake. The job shall be yours, and I'll go with you first trip. Here's my hand on it.... Now, Shefford, I'm more curious about you than I was before you told your story. What ruined you? As we're to be partners, you can tell me now. I'll keep your secret. Maybe I can do you good."

Shefford wanted to confess, yet it was hard. Perhaps, had he not been so agitated, he would not have answered to impulse. But this trader was a man—a man of the desert—he would understand.

"I told you I was a clergyman," said Shefford in low voice. "I didn't want to be one, but they made me one. I did my best. I failed.... I had doubts of religion—of the Bible—of God, as my Church believed in them. As I grew older thought and study convinced me of the narrowness of religion as my congregation lived it. I preached what I believed. I alienated them. They put me out, took my calling from me, disgraced me, ruined me."

"So that's all!" exclaimed Withers, slowly. "You didn't believe in the God of the Bible.... Well, I've been in the desert long enough to know there IS a God, but probably not the one your Church worships. ... Shefford, go to the Navajo for a faith!"

Shefford had forgotten the presence of Nas Ta Bega, and perhaps Withers had likewise. At this juncture the Indian rose to his full height, and he folded his arms to stand with the somber pride of a chieftain while his dark, inscrutable eyes were riveted upon Shefford. At that moment he seemed magnificent. How infinitely more he seemed than just a common Indian who had chanced to befriend a white man! The difference was obscure to Shefford. But he felt that it was there in the Navajo's mind. Nas Ta Bega's strange look was not to be interpreted. Presently he turned and passed from the room.

"By George!" cried Withers, suddenly, and he pounded his knee with his fist. "I'd forgotten."

"What?" ejaculated Shefford.

"Why, that Indian understood every word we said. He knows English. He's educated. Well, if this doesn't beat me.... Let me tell you about Nas Ta Bega."

Withers appeared to be recalling something half forgotten.

"Years ago, in fifty-seven, I think, Kit Carson with his soldiers chased the Navajo tribes and rounded them up to be put on reservations. But he failed to catch all the members of one tribe. They escaped up into wild canyon like the Sagi. The descendants of these fugitives live there now and are the finest Indians on earth—the finest because unspoiled by the white man. Well, as I got the story, years after Carson's round-up one of his soldiers guided some interested travelers in here. When they left they took an Indian boy with them to educate. From what I know of Navajos I'm inclined to think the boy was taken against his parents' wish. Anyway, he was taken. That boy was Nas Ta Bega. The story goes that he was educated somewhere. Years afterward, and perhaps not long before I came in here, he returned to his people. There have been missionaries and other interested fools who have given Indians a white man's education. In all the instances I know of, these educated Indians returned to their tribes, repudiating the white man's knowledge, habits, life, and religion. I have heard that Nas Ta Bega came back, laid down the white man's clothes along with the education, and never again showed that he had known either.

"You have just seen how strangely he acted. It's almost certain he heard our conversation. Well, it doesn't matter. He won't tell. He can hardly be made to use an English word. Besides, he's a noble red man, if there ever was one. He has been a friend in need to me. If you stay long out here you'll learn something from the Indians. Nas Ta Bega has befriended you, too, it seems. I thought he showed unusual interest in you."

"Perhaps that was because I saved his sister—well, to be charitable, from the rather rude advances of a white man," said Shefford, and he proceeded to tell of the incident that occurred at Red Lake.

"Willetts!" exclaimed Withers, with much the same expression that Presbrey had used. "I never met him. But I know about him. He's—well, the Indians don't like him much. Most of the missionaries are good men—good for the Indians, in a way, but sometimes one drifts out here who is bad. A bad missionary teaching religion to savages! Queer, isn't it? The queerest part is the white people's blindness—the blindness of those who send the missionaries. Well, I dare say Willetts isn't very good. When Presbrey said that was Willetts's way of teaching religion he meant just what he said. If Willetts drifts over here he'll be risking much.... This you told me explains Nas Ta Bega's friendliness toward you, and also his bringing his sister Glen Naspa to live with relatives up in the pass. She had been living near Red Lake."

"Do you mean Nas Ta Bega wants to keep his sister far removed from Willetts?" inquired Shefford.

"I mean that," replied Withers, "and I hope he's not too late."

Later Shefford went outdoors to walk and think. There was no moon, but the stars made light enough to cast his shadow on the ground. The dark, illimitable expanse of blue sky seemed to be glittering with numberless points of fire. The air was cold and still. A dreaming silence lay over the land. Shefford saw and felt all these things, and their effect was continuous and remained with him and helped calm him. He was conscious of a burden removed from his mind. Confession of his secret had been like tearing a thorn from his flesh, but, once done, it afforded him relief and a singular realization that out here it did not matter much. In a crowd of men all looking at him and judging him by their standards he had been made to suffer. Here, if he were judged at all, it would be by what he could do, how he sustained himself and helped others.

He walked far across the valley toward the low bluffs, but they did not seem to get any closer. And, finally, he stopped beside a stone and looked around at the strange horizon and up at the heavens. He did not feel utterly aloof from them, nor alone in a waste, nor a useless atom amid incomprehensible forces. Something like a loosened mantle fell from about him, dropping down at his feet; and all at once he was conscious of freedom. He did not understand in the least why abasement left him, but it was so. He had come a long way, in bitterness, in despair, believing himself to be what men had called him. The desert and the stars and the wind, the silence of the night, the loneliness of this vast country where there was room for a thousand cities—these somehow vaguely, yet surely, bade him lift his head. They withheld their secret, but they made a promise. The thing which he had been feeling every day and every night was a strange enveloping comfort. And it was at this moment that Shefford, divining whence his help was to come, embraced all that wild and speaking nature around and above him and surrendered himself utterly.

"I am young. I am free. I have my life to live," he said. "I'll be a man. I'll take what comes. Let me learn here!"

When he had spoken out, settled once and for ever his attitude toward his future, he seemed to be born again, wonderfully alive to the influences around him, ready to trust what yet remained a mystery.

Then his thoughts reverted to Fay Larkin. Could this girl be known to the Mormons? It was possible. Fay Larkin was an unusual name. Deep into Shefford's heart had sunk the story Venters had told. Shefford found that he had unconsciously created a like romance—he had been loving a wild and strange and lonely girl, like beautiful Bess Venters. It was a shock to learn the truth, but, as it had been only a dream, it could hardly be vital.

Shefford retraced his steps toward the post. Halfway back he espied a tall, dark figure moving toward him, and presently the shape and the step seemed familiar. Then he recognized Nas Ta Bega. Soon they were face to face. Shefford felt that the Indian had been trailing him over the sand, and that this was to be a significant meeting. Remembering Withers's revelation about the Navajo, Shefford scarcely knew how to approach him now. There was no difference to be made out in Nas Ta Bega's dark face and inscrutable eyes, yet there was a difference to be felt in his presence. But the Indian did not speak, and turned to walk by Shefford's side. Shefford could not long be silent.

"Nas Ta Bega, were you looking for me?" he asked.

"You had no gun," replied the Indian.

But for his very low voice, his slow speaking of the words, Shefford would have thought him a white man. For Shefford there was indeed an instinct in this meeting, and he turned to face the Navajo.

"Withers told me you had been educated, that you came back to the desert, that you never showed your training.... Nas Ta Bega, did you understand all I told Withers?"

"Yes," replied the Indian.

"You won't betray me?"

"I am a Navajo."

"Nas Ta Bega, you trail me—you say I had no gun." Shefford wanted to ask this Indian if he cared to be the white man's friend, but the question was not easy to put, and, besides, seemed unnecessary. "I am alone and strange in this wild country. I must learn."

"Nas Ta Bega will show you the trails and the water-holes and how to hide from Shadd."

"For money—for silver you will do this?" inquired Shefford.

Shefford felt that the Indian's silence was a rebuke. He remembered Withers's singular praise of this red man. He realized he must change his idea of Indians.

"Nas Ta Bega, I know nothing. I feel like a child in the wilderness. When I speak it is out of the mouths of those who have taught me. I must find a new voice and a new life.... You heard my story to Withers. I am an outcast from my own people. If you will be my friend —be so."

The Indian clasped Shefford's hand and held it in a response that was more beautiful for its silence. So they stood for a moment in the starlight.

"Nas Ta Bega, what did Withers mean when he said go to the Navajo for a faith?" asked Shefford.

"He meant the desert is my mother.... Will you go with Nas Ta Bega into the canyon and the mountains?"

"Indeed I will."

They unclasped hands and turned toward the trading-post.

"Nas Ta Bega, have you spoken my tongue to any other white man since you returned to your home?" asked Shefford.

"No."

"Why do you—why are you different for me?"

The Indian maintained silence.

"Is it because of—of Glen Naspa?" inquired Shefford.

Nas Ta Bega stalked on, still silent, but Shefford divined that, although his service to Glen Naspa would never be forgotten, still it was not wholly responsible for the Indian's subtle sympathy.

"Bi Nai! The Navajo will call his white friend Bi Nai—brother," said Nas Ta Bega, and he spoke haltingly, not as if words were hard to find, but strange to speak. "I was stolen from my mother's hogan and taken to California. They kept me ten years in a mission at San Bernardino and four years in a school. They said my color and my hair were all that was left of the Indian in me. But they could not see my heart. They took fourteen years of my life. They wanted to make me a missionary among my own people. But the white man's ways and his life and his God are not the Indian's. They never can be."

How strangely productive of thought for Shefford to hear the Indian talk! What fatality in this meeting and friendship! Upon Nas Ta Bega had been forced education, training, religion, that had made him something more and something less than an Indian. It was something assimilated from the white man which made the Indian unhappy and alien in his own home —something meant to be good for him and his kind that had ruined him. For Shefford felt the passion and the tragedy of this Navajo.

"Bi Nai, the Indian is dying!" Nas Ta Bega's low voice was deep and wonderful with its intensity of feeling. "The white man robbed the Indian of lands and homes, drove him into the deserts, made him a gaunt and sleepless spiller of blood.... The blood is all spilled now, for the Indian is broken. But the white man sells him rum and seduces his daughters.... He will not leave the Indian in peace with his own God!... Bi Nai, the Indian is dying!"

That night Shefford lay in his blankets out under the open sky and the stars. The earth had never meant much to him, and now it was a bed. He had preached of the heavens, but until now had never studied them. An Indian slept beside him. And not until the gray of morning had blotted out the starlight did Shefford close his eyes.

. . .

422

With break of the next day came full, varied, and stirring incidents to Shefford. He was strong, though unskilled at most kinds of outdoor tasks. Withers had work for ten men, if they could have been found. Shefford dug and packed and lifted till he was so sore and tired that rest was a blessing.

He never succeeded in getting on a friendly footing with the Mormon Whisner, though he kept up his agreeable and kindly advances. He listened to the trader's wife as she told him about the Indians, and what he learned he did not forget. And his wonder and respect increased in proportion to his knowledge.

One day there rode into Kayenta the Mormon for whom Withers had been waiting. His name was Joe Lake. He appeared young, and slipped off his superb bay with a grace and activity that were astounding in one of his huge bulk. He had a still, smooth face, with the color of red bronze and the expression of a cherub; big, soft, dark eyes; and a winning smile. He was surprisingly different from Whisner or any Mormon character that Shefford had naturally conceived. His costume was that of the cowboy on active service; and he packed a gun at his hip. The hand-shake he gave Shefford was an ordeal for that young man and left him with his whole right side momentarily benumbed.

"I sure am glad to meet you," he said in a lazy, mild voice. And he was taking friendly stock of Shefford when the bay mustang reached with vicious muzzle to bite at him. Lake gave a jerk on the bridle that almost brought the mustang to his knees. He reared then, snorted, and came down to plant his forefeet wide apart, and watched his master with defiant eyes. This mustang was the finest horse Shefford had ever seen. He appeared quite large for his species, was almost red in color, had a racy and powerful build, and a fine thoroughbred head with dark, fiery eyes. He did not look mean, but he had spirit.

"Navvy, you've sure got bad manners," said Lake, shaking the mustang's bridle. He spoke as if he were chiding a refractory little boy. "Didn't I break you better'n that? What's this gentleman goin' to think of you? Tryin' to bite my ear off!"

Lake had arrived about the middle of the forenoon, and Withers announced his intention of packing at once for the trip. Indians were sent out on the ranges to drive in burros and mustangs. Shefford had his thrilling expectancy somewhat chilled by what he considered must have been Lake's reception of the trader's plan. Lake seemed to oppose him, and evidently it took vehemence and argument on Withers's part to make the Mormon tractable. But Withers won him over, and then he called Shefford to his side.

"You fellows got to be good friends," he said. "You'll have charge of my pack-trains. Nas Ta Bega wants to go with you. I'll feel safer about my supplies and stock than I've ever been.... Joe, I'll back this stranger for all I'm worth. He's square.... And, Shefford, Joe Lake is a Mormon of the younger generation. I want to start you right. You can trust him as you trust me. He's white clean through. And he's the best horse-wrangler in Utah."

It was Lake who first offered his hand, and Shefford made haste to meet it with his own. Neither of them spoke. Shefford intuitively felt an alteration in Lake's regard, or at least a singular increase of interest. Lake had been told that Shefford had been a clergyman, was now a wanderer, without any religion. Again it seemed to Shefford that he owed a forming of friendship to this singular fact. And it hurt him. But strangely it came to him that he had taken a liking to a Mormon.

About one o'clock the pack-train left Kayenta. Nas Ta Bega led the way up the slope. Following him climbed half a dozen patient, plodding, heavily laden burros. Withers came next, and he turned in his saddle to wave good-by to his wife. Joe Lake appeared to be busy keeping a red mule and a wild gray mustang and a couple of restive blacks in the trail. Shefford brought up in the rear.

His mount was a beautiful black mustang with three white feet, a white spot on his nose, and a mane that swept to his knees. "His name's Nack-yal," Withers had said. "It means two bits, or twenty-five cents. He ain't worth more." To look at Nack-yal had pleased Shefford very much indeed, but, once upon his back, he grew dubious. The mustang acted queer. He actually looked back at Shefford, and it was a look of speculation and disdain. Shefford took exception to Nack-yal's manner and to his reluctance to go, and especially to a habit the mustang had of turning off the trail to the left. Shefford had managed some rather spirited horses back in Illinois; and though he was willing and eager to learn all over again, he did not enjoy the prospect of Lake and Withers seeing this black mustang make a novice of him. And he guessed that was just what Nack-yal intended to do. However, once up over the hill, with Kayenta out of sight, Nack-yal trotted along fairly well, needing only now and then to be pulled back from his strange swinging to the left off the trail.

The pack-train traveled steadily and soon crossed the upland plain to descend into the valley again. Shefford saw the jagged red peaks with an emotion he could not name. The canyon between them were purple in the shadows, the great walls and slopes brightened to red, and the tips were gold in the sun. Shefford forgot all about his mustang and the trail.

Suddenly with a pound of hoofs Nack-yal seemed to rise. He leaped sidewise out of the trail, came down stiff-legged. Then Shefford shot out of the saddle. He landed so hard that he was stunned for an instant. Sitting up, he saw the mustang bent down, eyes and ears showing fight, and his forefeet spread. He appeared to be looking at something in the trail. Shefford got up and soon saw what had been the trouble. A long, crooked stick, rather thick and black and yellow, lay in the trail, and any mustang looking for an excuse to jump might have mistaken it for a rattlesnake. Nack-yal appeared disposed to be satisfied, and gave Shefford no trouble in mounting. The incident increased Shefford's dubiousness. These Arizona mustangs were unknown quantities.

Thereafter Shefford had an eye for the trail rather than the scenery, and this continued till the pack-train entered the mouth of the Sagi. Then those wonderful lofty cliffs, with their peaks and towers and spires, loomed so close and so beautiful that he did not care if Nack-yal did throw him. Along here, however, the mustang behaved well, and presently Shefford decided that if it had been otherwise he would have walked. The trail suddenly stood on end and led down into the deep wash, where some days before he had seen the stream of reddish water. This day there appeared to be less water and it was not so red. Nack-yal sank deep as he took short and careful steps down. The burros and other mustangs were drinking, and Nack-yal followed suit. The Indian, with a hand clutching his mustang's mane, rode up a steep, sandy slope on the other side that Shefford would not have believed any horse could climb. The burros plodded up and over the rim, with Withers calling to them. Joe Lake swung his rope and cracked the flanks of the gray mare and the red mule; and the way the two kicked was a revelation and a warning to Shefford. When his turn came to climb the trail he got off and walked, an action that Nack-yal appeared fully to appreciate.

From the head of this wash the trail wound away up the widening canyon, through greasewood flats and over grassy levels and across sandy stretches. The looming walls made the valley look narrow, yet it must have been half a mile wide. The slopes under the cliffs were dotted with huge stones and cedar-trees. There were deep indentations in the walls, running back to form box canyon, choked with green of cedar and spruce and pinon. These notches haunted Shefford, and he was ever on the lookout for more of them.

Withers came back to ride just in advance and began to talk.

"Reckon this Sagi canyon is your Deception Pass," he said. "It's sure a queer hole. I've been lost more than once, hunting mustangs in here. I've an idea Nas Ta Bega knows all this country. He just pointed out a cliff-dwelling to me. See it?... There 'way up in that cave of the wall."

Shefford saw a steep, rough slope leading up to a bulge of the cliff, and finally he made out strange little houses with dark, eyelike windows. He wanted to climb up there. Withers called his attention to more caves with what he believed were the ruins of cliff-dwellings. And as they rode along the trader showed him remarkable formations of rock where the elements were slowly hollowing out a bridge. They came presently to a region of intersecting canyon, and here the breaking of the trail up and down the deep washes took Withers back to his task with the burros and gave Shefford more concern than he liked with Nack-yal. The mustang grew unruly and was continually turning to the left. Sometimes he tried to climb the steep slope. He had to be pulled hard away from the opening canyon on the left. It seemed strange to Shefford that the mustang never swerved to the right. This habit of Nack-yal's and the increasing caution needed on the trail took all of Shefford's attention. When he dismounted, however, he had a chance to look around, and more and more he was amazed at the increasing proportions and wildness of the Sagi.

He came at length to a place where a fallen tree blocked the trail. All of the rest of the pack-train had jumped the log. But Nack-yal balked. Shefford dismounted, pulled the bridle over the mustang's head, and tried to lead him. Nack-yal, however, refused to budge. Whereupon Shefford got a stick and, remounting, he gave the balky mustang a cut across the flank. Then something violent happened. Shefford received a sudden propelling jolt, and then he was rising into the air, and then falling. Before he alighted he had a clear image of Nack-yal in the air above him, bent double, and seemingly possessed of devils. Then Shefford hit the ground with no light thud. He was thoroughly angry when he got dizzily upon his feet, but he was not quick enough to catch the mustang. Nack-yal leaped easily over the log and went on ahead, dragging his bridle. Shefford hurried after him, and the faster he went just by so much the cunning Nack-yal accelerated his gait. As the pack-train was out of sight somewhere ahead, Shefford could not call to his companions to halt his mount, so he gave up trying, and walked on now with free and growing appreciation of his surroundings.

The afternoon had waned. The sun blazed low in the west in a notch of the canyon ramparts, and one wall was darkening into purple shadow while the other shone through a golden haze. It was a weird, wild world to Shefford, and every few strides he caught his breath and tried to realize actuality was not a dream.

Nack-yal kept about a hundred paces to the fore and ever and anon he looked back to see how his new master was progressing. He varied these occasions by reaching down and nipping a tuft of grass. Evidently he was too intelligent to go on fast enough to be caught by Withers. Also he kept continually looking up the slope to the left as if seeking a way to climb out of the valley in that direction. Shefford thought it was well the trail lay at the foot of a steep slope that ran up to unbroken bluffs.

The sun set and the canyon lost its red and its gold and deepened its purple. Shefford calculated he had walked five miles, and though he did not mind the effort, he would rather have ridden Nack-yal into camp. He mounted a cedar ridge, crossed some sandy washes, turned a corner of bold wall to enter a wide, green level. The mustangs were rolling and snorting. He heard the bray of a burro. A bright blaze of camp-fire greeted him, and the dark figure of the Indian approached to intercept and catch Nack-yal. When he stalked into camp Withers wore a beaming smile, and Joe Lake, who was on his knees making biscuit dough in a pan, stopped proceedings and drawled:

"Reckon Nack-yal bucked you off."

"Bucked! Was that it? Well, he separated himself from me in a new and somewhat painful manner—to me."

"Sure, I saw that in his eye," replied Lake; and Withers laughed with him.

"Nack-yal never was well broke," he said. "But he's a good mustang, nothing like Joe's Navvy or that gray mare Dynamite. All this Indian stock will buck on a man once in a while."

"I'll take the bucking along with the rest," said Shefford. Both men liked his reply, and the Indian smiled for the first time.

Soon they all sat round a spread tarpaulin and ate like wolves. After supper came the rest and talk before the camp-fire. Joe Lake was droll; he said the most serious things in a way to make Shefford wonder if he was not joking. Withers talked about the canyon, the Indians, the mustangs, the scorpions running out of the heated sand; and to Shefford it was all like a fascinating book. Nas Ta Bega smoked in silence, his brooding eyes upon the fire.

❧ 5 ❧

ON THE TRAIL

SHEFFORD WAS AWAKENED next morning by a sound he had never heard before—the plunging of hobbled horses on soft turf. It was clear daylight, with a ruddy color in the sky and a tinge of red along the canyon rim. He saw Withers, Lake, and the Indian driving the mustangs toward camp.

The burros appeared lazy, yet willing. But the mustangs and the mule Withers called Red and the gray mare Dynamite were determined not to be driven into camp. It was astonishing how much action they had, how much ground they could cover with their forefeet hobbled together. They were exceedingly skilful; they lifted both forefeet at once, and then plunged. And they all went in different directions. Nas Ta Bega darted in here and there to head off escape.

Shefford pulled on his boots and went out to help. He got too close to the gray mare and, warned by a yell from Withers, he jumped back just in time to avoid her vicious heels. Then Shefford turned his attention to Nack-yal and chased him all over the flat in a futile effort to catch him. Nas Ta Bega came to Shefford's assistance and put a rope over Nack-yal's head.

"Don't ever get behind one of these mustangs," said Withers, warningly, as Shefford came up. "You might be killed.... Eat your bite now. We'll soon be out of here."

Shefford had been late in awakening. The others had breakfasted. He found eating somewhat difficult in the excitement that ensued. Nas Ta Bega held ropes which were round the necks of Red and Dynamite. The mule showed his cunning and always appeared to present his heels to Withers, who tried to approach him with a pack-saddle. The patience of the trader was a revelation to Shefford. And at length Red was cornered by the three men, the pack-saddle was strapped on, and then the packs. Red promptly bucked the packs off, and the work had to be done over again. Then Red dropped his long ears and seemed ready to be tractable.

When Shefford turned his attention to Dynamite he decided that this was his first sight of a wild horse. The gray mare had fiery eyes that rolled and showed the white. She jumped straight up, screamed, pawed, bit, and then plunged down to shoot her hind hoofs into the air as high as her head had been. She was amazingly agile and she seemed mad to kill

427

something. She dragged the Indian about, and when Joe Lake got a rope on her hind foot he dragged them both. They lashed her with the ends of the lassoes, which action only made her kick harder. She plunged into camp, drove Shefford flying for his life, knocked down two of the burros, and played havoc with the unstrapped packs. Withers ran to the assistance of Lake, and the two of them hauled back with all their strength and weight. They were both powerful and heavy men. Dynamite circled round and finally, after kicking the camp-fire to bits, fell down on her haunches in the hot embers. "Let—her—set—there!" panted Withers. And Joe Lake shouted, "Burn up, you durn coyote!" Both men appeared delighted that she had brought upon herself just punishment. Dynamite sat in the remains of the fire long enough to get burnt, and then she got up and meekly allowed Withers to throw a tarpaulin and a roll of blankets over her and tie them fast.

Lake and Withers were sweating freely when this job was finished.

"Say, is that a usual morning's task with the pack-animals?" asked Shefford.

"They're all pretty decent to-day, except Dynamite," replied Withers. "She's got to be worked out."

Shefford felt both amusement and consternation. The sun was just rising over the ramparts of the canyon, and he had already seen more difficult and dangerous work accomplished than half a dozen men of his type could do in a whole day. He liked the outlook of his new duty as Withers's assistant, but he felt helplessly inefficient. Still, all he needed was experience. He passed over what he anticipated would be pain and peril—the cost was of no moment.

Soon the pack-train was on the move, with the Indian leading. This morning Nack-yal began his strange swinging off to the left, precisely as he had done the day before. It got to be annoying to Shefford, and he lost patience with the mustang and jerked him sharply round. This, however, had no great effect upon Nack-yal.

As the train headed straight up the canyon Joe Lake dropped back to ride beside Shefford. The Mormon had been amiable and friendly.

"Flock of deer up that draw," he said, pointing up a narrow side canyon.

Shefford gazed to see a half-dozen small, brown, long-eared objects, very like burros, watching the pack-train pass.

"Are they deer?" he asked, delightedly.

"Sure are," replied Joe, sincerely. "Get down and shoot one. There's a rifle in your saddle-sheath."

Shefford had already discovered that he had been armed this morning, a matter which had caused him reflection. These animals certainly looked like deer; he had seen a few deer, though not in their native wild haunts; and he experienced the thrill of the hunter. Dismounting, he drew the rifle out of the sheath and started toward the little canyon.

"Hyar! Where you going with that gun?" yelled Withers. "That's a bunch of burros.... Joe's up to his old tricks. Shefford, look out for Joe!"

Rather sheepishly Shefford returned to his mustang and sheathed the rifle, and then took a long look at the animals up the draw. They, resembled deer, but upon second glance they surely were burros.

"Durn me! Now if I didn't think they sure were deer!" exclaimed Joe. He appeared absolutely sincere and innocent. Shefford hardly knew how to take this likable Mormon, but vowed he would be on his guard in the future.

Nas Ta Bega soon led the pack-train toward the left wall of the canyon, and evidently intended to scale it. Shefford could not see any trail, and the wall appeared steep and insurmountable. But upon nearing the cliff he saw a narrow broken trail leading zigzag up over smooth rock, weathered slope, and through cracks.

"Spread out, and careful now!" yelled Withers.

The need of both advices soon became manifest to Shefford. The burros started stones rolling, making danger for those below. Shefford dismounted and led Nack-yal and turned aside many a rolling rock. The Indian and the burros, with the red mule leading, climbed steadily. But the mustangs had trouble. Joe's spirited bay had to be coaxed to face the ascent; Nack-yal balked at every difficult step; and Dynamite slipped on a flat slant of rock and slid down forty feet. Withers and Lake with ropes hauled the mare out of the dangerous position. Shefford, who brought up the rear, saw all the action, and it was exciting, but his pleasure in the climb was spoiled by sight of blood and hair on the stones. The ascent was crooked, steep, and long, and when Shefford reached the top of the wall he was glad to rest. It made him gasp to look down and see what he had surmounted. The canyon floor, green and level, lay a thousand feet below; and the wild burros which had followed on the trail looked like rabbits.

Shefford mounted presently, and rode out upon a wide, smooth trail leading into a cedar forest. There were bunches of gray sage in the open places. The air was cool and crisp, laden with a sweet fragrance. He saw Lake and Withers bobbing along, now on one side of the trail, now on the other, and they kept to a steady trot. Occasionally the Indian and his bright-red saddle-blanket showed in an opening of the cedars.

It was level country, and there was nothing for Shefford to see except cedar and sage, an outcropping of red rock in places, and the winding trail. Mocking-birds made melody everywhere. Shefford seemed full of a strange pleasure, and the hours flew by. Nack-yal still wanted to be everlastingly turning off the trail, and, moreover, now he wanted to go faster. He was eager, restless, dissatisfied.

At noon the pack-train descended into a deep draw, well covered with cedar and sage. There was plenty of grass and shade, but no water. Shefford was surprised to see that every pack was removed; however, the roll of blankets was left on Dynamite.

The men made a fire and began to cook a noonday meal. Shefford, tired and warm, sat in a shady spot and watched. He had become all eyes. He had almost forgotten Fay Larkin; he had forgotten his trouble; and the present seemed sweet and full. Presently his ears were filled by a pattering roar and, looking up the draw, he saw two streams of sheep and goats coming down. Soon an Indian shepherd appeared, riding a fine mustang. A cream-colored colt bounded along behind, and presently a shaggy dog came in sight. The Indian dismounted at the camp, and his flock spread by in two white and black streams. The dog went with them. Withers and Joe shook hands with the Indian, whom Joe called "Navvy," and Shefford lost no time in doing likewise. Then Nas Ta Bega came in, and he and the Navajo talked. When the meal was ready all of them sat down round the canvas. The shepherd did not tie his horse.

Presently Shefford noticed that Nack-yal had returned to camp and was acting strangely. Evidently he was attracted by the Indian's mustang or the cream-colored colt. At any rate, Nack-yal hung around, tossed his head, whinnied in a low, nervous manner, and looked strangely eager and wild. Shefford was at first amused, then curious. Nack-yal approached too close to the mother of the colt, and she gave him a sounding kick in the ribs. Nack-yal uttered a plaintive snort and backed away, to stand, crestfallen, with all his eagerness and fire vanished.

Nas Ta Bega pointed to the mustang and said something in his own tongue. Then Withers addressed the visiting Indian, and they exchanged some words, whereupon the trader turned to Shefford:

"I bought Nack-yal from this Indian three years ago. This mare is Nack-yal's mother. He was born over here to the south. That's why he always swung left off the trail. He wanted to go home. Just now he recognized his mother and she whaled away and gave him a whack for his pains. She's got a colt now and probably didn't recognize Nack-yal. But he's broken-hearted."

The trader laughed, and Joe said, "You can't tell what these durn mustangs will do." Shefford felt sorry for Nack-yal, and when it came time to saddle him again found him easier to handle than ever before. Nack-yal stood with head down, broken-spirited.

Shefford was the first to ride up out of the draw, and once upon the top of the ridge he halted to gaze, wide-eyed and entranced. A rolling, endless plain sloped down beneath him, and led him on to a distant round-topped mountain. To the right a red canyon opened its jagged jaws, and away to the north rose a whorled and strange sea of curved ridges, crags, and domes.

Nas Ta Bega rode up then, leading the pack-train.

"Bi Nai, that is Na-tsis-an," he said, pointing to the mountain. "Navajo Mountain. And there in the north are the canyon."

Shefford followed the Indian down the trail and soon lost sight of that wide green-and-red wilderness. Nas Ta Bega turned at an intersecting trail, rode down into the canyon, and climbed out on the other side. Shefford got a glimpse now and then of the black dome of the mountain, but for the most part the distant points of the country were hidden. They crossed many trails, and went up and down the sides of many shallow canyon. Troops of wild mustangs whistled at them, stood on ridge-tops to watch, and then dashed away with manes and tails flying.

Withers rode forward presently and halted the pack-train. He had some conversation with Nas Ta Bega, whereupon the Indian turned his horse and trotted back, to disappear in the cedars.

"I'm some worried," explained Withers. "Joe thinks he saw a bunch of horsemen trailing us. My eyes are bad and I can't see far. The Indian will find out. I took a roundabout way to reach the village because I'm always dodging Shadd."

This communication lent an added zest to the journey. Shefford could hardly believe the truth that his eyes and his ears brought to his consciousness. He turned in behind Withers and rode down the rough trail, helping the mustang all in his power. It occurred to him that Nack-yal had been entirely different since that meeting with his mother in the draw. He turned no more off the trail; he answered readily to the rein; he did not look afar from every ridge. Shefford conceived a liking for the mustang.

Withers turned sidewise in his saddle and let his mustang pick the way.

"Another time we'll go up round the base of the mountain, where you can look down on the grandest scene in the world," said he. "Two hundred miles of wind-worn rock, all smooth and bare, without a single straight line—canyon, caves, bridges—the most wonderful country in the world! Even the Indians haven't explored it. It's haunted, for them, and they have strange gods. The Navajos will hunt on this side of the mountain, but not on the other. That north side is consecrated ground. My wife has long been trying to get the Navajos to tell her the secret of Nonnezoshe. Nonnezoshe means Rainbow Bridge. The Indians worship it, but as far as she can find out only a few have ever seen it. I imagine it'd be worth some trouble."

"Maybe that's the bridge Venters talked about—the one overarching the entrance to Surprise Valley," Said Shefford.

"It might be," replied the trader. "You've got a good chance of finding out. Nas Ta Bega is the man. You stick to that Indian. ... Well, we start down here into this canyon, and we go down some, I reckon. In half an hour you'll see sago-lilies and Indian paint-brush and vermilion cactus."

About the middle of the afternoon the pack-train and its drivers arrived at the hidden Mormon village. Nas Ta Bega had not returned from his scout back along the trail.

Shefford's sensibilities had all been overstrained, but he had left in him enthusiasm and appreciation that made the situation of this village a fairyland. It was a valley, a canyon floor, so long that he could not see the end, and perhaps a quarter of a mile wide. The air was hot, still, and sweetly odorous of unfamiliar flowers. Pinon and cedar trees surrounded the little log and stone houses, and along the walls of the canyon stood sharp-pointed, dark-green spruce-trees. These walls were singular of shape and color. They were not imposing in height, but they waved like the long, undulating swell of a sea. Every foot of surface was perfectly smooth, and the long curved lines of darker tinge that streaked the red followed the rounded line of the slope at the top. Far above, yet overhanging, were great yellow crags and peaks, and between these, still higher, showed the pine-fringed slope of Navajo Mountain with snow in the sheltered places, and glistening streams, like silver threads, running down.

All this Shefford noticed as he entered the valley from round a corner of wall. Upon nearer view he saw and heard a host of children, who, looking up to see the intruders, scattered like frightened quail. Long gray grass covered the ground, and here and there wide, smooth paths had been worn. A swift and murmuring brook ran through the middle of the valley, and its banks were bordered with flowers.

Withers led the way to one side near the wall, where a clump of cedar-trees and a dark, swift spring boiling out of the rocks and banks of amber moss with purple blossoms made a beautiful camp site. Here the mustangs were unsaddled and turned loose without hobbles. It was certainly unlikely that they would leave such a spot. Some of the burros were unpacked, and the others Withers drove off into the village.

"Sure's pretty nice," said Joe, wiping his sweaty face. "I'll never want to leave. It suits me to lie on this moss.... Take a drink of that spring."

Shefford complied with alacrity and found the water cool and sweet, and he seemed to feel it all through him. Then he returned to the mossy bank. He did not reply to Joe. In fact, all his faculties were absorbed in watching and feeling, and he lay there long after Joe went off to the village. The murmur of water, the hum of bees, the songs of strange birds, the sweet, warm air, the dreamy summer somnolence of the valley—all these added drowsiness to Shefford's weary lassitude, and he fell asleep. When he awoke Nas Ta Bega was sitting near him and Joe was busy near a camp-fire.

"Hello, Nas Ta Bega!" said Shefford. "Was there any one trailing us?"

The Navajo nodded.

Joe raised his head and with forceful brevity said, "Shadd."

"Shadd!" echoed Shefford, remembering the dark, sinister face of his visitor that night in the Sagi. "Joe, is it serious—his trailing us?"

"Well, I don't know how durn serious it is, but I'm scared to death," replied Lake. "He and his gang will hold us up somewhere on the way home."

Shefford regarded Joe with both concern and doubt. Joe's words were at variance with his looks.

"Say, pard, can you shoot a rifle?" queried Joe.

"Yes. I'm a fair shot at targets."

The Mormon nodded his head as if pleased. "That's good. These outlaws are all poor shots with a rifle. So 'm I. But I can handle a six-shooter. I reckon we'll make Shadd sweat if he pushes us."

Withers returned, driving the burros, all of which had been unpacked down to the saddles. Two gray-bearded men accompanied him. One of them appeared to be very old and venerable, and walked with a stick. The other had a sad-lined face and kind, mild blue eyes. Shefford observed that Lake seemed unusually respectful. Withers introduced these Mormons merely as Smith and Henninger. They were very cordial and pleasant in their greetings to Shefford. Presently another, somewhat younger, man joined the group, a stalwart, jovial fellow with ruddy face. There was certainly no mistaking his kindly welcome as he shook Shefford's hand. His name was Beal. The three stood round the camp-fire for a while, evidently glad of the presence of fellow-men and to hear news from the outside. Finally they went away, taking Joe with them. Withers took up the task of getting supper where Joe had been made to leave it.

"Shefford, listen," he said, presently, as he knelt before the fire. "I told them right out that you'd been a Gentile clergyman—that you'd gone back on your religion. It impressed them and you've been well received. I'll tell the same thing over at Stonebridge. You'll get in right. Of course I don't expect they'll make a Mormon of you. But they'll try to. Meanwhile you can be square and friendly all the time you're trying to find your Fay Larkin. To-morrow you'll meet some of the women. They're good souls, but, like any women, crazy for news. Think what it is to be shut up in here between these walls!"

"Withers, I'm intensely interested," replied Shefford, "and excited, too. Shall we stay here long?"

"I'll stay a couple of days, then go to Stonebridge with Joe. He'll come back here, and when you both feel like leaving, and if Nas Ta Bega thinks it safe, you'll take a trail over to some Indian hogans and pack me out a load of skins and blankets.... My boy, you've all the time there is, and I wish you luck. This isn't a bad place to loaf. I always get sentimental over here. Maybe it's the women. Some of them are pretty, and one of them—Shefford, they call her the Sago Lily. Her first name is Mary, I'm told. Don't know her last name. She's lovely. And I'll bet you forget Fay Larkin in a flash. Only—be careful. You drop in here with rather peculiar credentials, so to speak—as my helper and as a man with no religion! You'll not only be fully trusted, but you'll be welcome to these lonely women. So be careful. Remember it's my secret belief they are sealed wives and are visited occasionally at night by their husbands. I don't know this, but I believe it. And you're not supposed to dream of that."

"How many men in the village?" asked Shefford.

"Three. You met them."

"Have they wives?" asked Shefford, curiously.

"Wives! Well, I guess. But only one each that I know of. Joe Lake is the only unmarried Mormon I've met."

"And no men—strangers, cowboys, outlaws—ever come to this village?"

"Except to Indians, it seems to be a secret so far," replied the trader, earnestly. "But it can't be kept secret. I've said that time after time over in Stonebridge. With Mormons it's 'sufficient unto the day is the evil thereof.'"

"What'll happen when outsiders do learn and ride in here?"

"There'll be trouble—maybe bloodshed. Mormon women are absolutely good, but they're human, and want and need a little life. And, strange to say, Mormon men are pig-headedly jealous.... Why, if some of the cowboys I knew in Durango would ride over here there'd simply be hell. But that's a long way, and probably this village will be deserted before news of it ever reaches Colorado. There's more danger of Shadd and his gang coming in. Shadd's half Piute. He must know of this place. And he's got some white outlaws in his gang.... Come on. Grub's ready, and I'm too hungry to talk."

Later, when shadows began to gather in the valley and the lofty peaks above were gold in the sunset glow, Withers left camp to look after the straying mustangs, and Shefford strolled to and fro under the cedars. The lights and shades in the Sagi that first night had moved him to enthusiastic watchfulness, but here they were so weird and beautiful that he was enraptured. He actually saw great shafts of gold and shadows of purple streaming from the peaks down into the valley. It was day on the heights and twilight in the valley. The swiftly changing colors were like rainbows.

While he strolled up and down several women came to the spring and filled their buckets. They wore shawls or hoods and their garments were somber, but, nevertheless, they appeared to have youth and comeliness. They saw him, looked at him curiously, and then, without speaking, went back on the well-trodden path. Presently down the path appeared a woman—a girl in lighter garb. It was almost white. She was shapely and walked with free, graceful step, reminding him of the Indian girl, Glen Naspa. This one wore a hood shaped like a huge sunbonnet and it concealed her face. She carried a bucket. When she reached the spring and went down the few stone steps Shefford saw that she did not have on shoes. As she braced herself to lift the bucket her bare foot clung to the mossy stone. It was a strong, sinewy, beautiful foot, instinct with youth. He was curious enough, he thought, but the awakening artist in him made him more so. She dragged at the full bucket and had difficulty in lifting it out of the hole. Shefford strode forward and took the bucket-handle from her.

"Won't you let me help you?" he said, lifting the bucket. "Indeed—it's very heavy."

"Oh—thank you," she said, without raising her head. Her voice seemed singularly young and sweet. He had not heard a voice like it. She moved down the path and he walked beside her. He felt embarrassed, yet more curious than ever; he wanted to say something, to turn and look at her, but he kept on for a dozen paces without making up his mind.

Finally he said: "Do you really carry this heavy bucket? Why, it makes my arm ache."

"Twice every day—morning and evening," she replied. "I'm very strong."

Then he stole a look out of the corner of his eye, and, seeing that her face was hidden from him by the hood, he turned to observe her at better advantage. A long braid of hair hung down her back. In the twilight it gleamed dull gold. She came up to his shoulder. The sleeve nearest him was rolled up to her elbow, revealing a fine round arm. Her hand, like her foot, was brown, strong, and well shaped. It was a hand that had been developed by labor. She was full-bosomed, yet slender, and she walked with a free stride that made Shefford admire and wonder.

They passed several of the little stone and log houses, and women greeted them as they went by and children peered shyly from the doors. He kept trying to think of something to say, and, failing in that, determined to have one good look under the hood before he left her.

"You walk lame," she said, solicitously. "Let me carry the bucket now—please. My house is near."

"Am I lame?... Guess so, a little," he replied. "It was a hard ride for me. But I'll carry the bucket just the same."

They went on under some pinon-trees, down a path to a little house identical with the

433

others, except that it had a stone porch. Shefford smelled fragrant wood-smoke and saw a column curling from the low, flat, stone chimney. Then he set the bucket down on the porch. "Thank you, Mr. Shefford," she said. "You know my name?" he asked. "Yes. Mr. Withers spoke to my nearest neighbor and she told me."

"Oh, I see. And you—"

He did not go on and she did not reply. When she stepped upon the porch and turned he was able to see under the hood. The face there was in shadow, and for that very reason he answered to ungovernable impulse and took a step closer to her. Dark, grave, sad eyes looked down at him, and he felt as if he could never draw his own glance away. He seemed not to see the rest of her face, and yet felt that it was lovely. Then a downward movement of the hood hid from him the strange eyes and the shadowy loveliness.

"I—I beg your pardon," he said, quickly, drawing back. "I'm rude. ... Withers told me about a girl he called—he said looked like a sago-lily. That's no excuse to stare under your hood. But I—I was curious. I wondered if—"

He hesitated, realizing how foolish his talk was. She stood a moment, probably watching him, but he could not be sure, for her face was hidden.

"They call me that," she said. "But my name is Mary."

"Mary—what?" he asked.

"Just Mary," she said, simply. "Good night."

He did not say good night and could not have told why. She took up the bucket and went into the dark house. Shefford hurried away into the gathering darkness.

❧ 6 ☙

IN THE HIDDEN VALLEY

SHEFFORD HAD HARDLY SEEN her face, yet he was more interested in a woman than he had ever been before. Still, he reflected, as he returned to camp, he had been under a long strain, he was unduly excited by this new and adventurous life, and these, with the mystery of this village, were perhaps accountable for a state of mind that could not last.

He rolled in his blankets on the soft bed of moss and he saw the stars through the needle-like fringe of the pinyons. It seemed impossible to fall asleep. The two domed peaks split the sky, and back of them, looming dark and shadowy, rose the mountain. There was something cold, austere, and majestic in their lofty presence, and they made him feel alone, yet not alone. He raised himself to see the quiet forms of Withers and Nas Ta Bega prone in the starlight, and their slow, deep breathing was that of tired men. A bell on a mustang rang somewhere off in the valley and gave out a low, strange, reverberating echo from wall to wall. When it ceased a silence set in that was deader than any silence he had ever felt, but gradually he became aware of the low murmur of the brook. For the rest there was no sound of wind, no bark of dog or yelp of coyote, no sound of voice in the village.

He tried to sleep, but instead thought of this girl who was called the Sago Lily. He recalled everything incident to their meeting and the walk to her home. Her swift, free step, her graceful poise, her shapely form—the long braid of hair, dull gold in the twilight, the beautiful bare foot and the strong round arm—these he thought of and recalled vividly. But of her face he had no idea except the shadowy, haunting loveliness, and that grew more and more difficult to remember. The tone of her voice and what she had said—how the one had thrilled him and the other mystified! It was her voice that had most attracted him. There was something in it besides music—what, he could not tell—sadness, depth, something like that in Nas Ta Bega's beauty springing from disuse. But this seemed absurd. Why should he imagine her voice one that had not been used as freely as any other woman's? She was a Mormon; very likely, almost surely, she was a sealed wife. His interest, too, was absurd, and he tried to throw it off, or imagine it one he might have felt in any other of these strange women of the hidden village.

But Shefford's intelligence and his good sense, which became operative when he was fully

435

roused and set the situation clearly before his eyes, had no effect upon his deeper, mystic, and primitive feelings. He saw the truth and he felt something that he could not name. He would not be a fool, but there was no harm in dreaming. And unquestionably, beyond all doubt, the dream and the romance that had lured him to the wilderness were here; hanging over him like the shadows of the great peaks. His heart swelled with emotion when he thought of how the black and incessant despair of the past was gone. So he embraced any attraction that made him forget and think and feel; some instinct stronger than intelligence bade him drift.

Joe's rolling voice awoke him next morning and he rose with a singular zest. When or where in his life had he awakened in such a beautiful place? Almost he understood why Venters and Bess had been haunted by memories of Surprise Valley. The morning was clear, cool, sweet; the peaks were dim and soft in rosy cloud; shafts of golden sunlight shot down into the purple shadows. Mocking-birds were singing. His body was sore and tired from the unaccustomed travel, but his heart was full, happy. His spirit wanted to run, and he knew there was something out there waiting to meet it. The Indian and the trader and the Mormon all meant more to him this morning. He had grown a little overnight. Nas Ta Bega's deep "Bi Nai" rang in his ears, and the smiles of Withers and Joe were greetings. He had friends; he had work; and there was rich, strange, and helpful life to live. There was even a difference in the mustang Nack-yal. He came readily; he did not look wild; he had a friendly eye; and Shefford liked him more.

"What is there to do?" asked Shefford, feeling equal to a hundred tasks.

"No work," replied the trader, with a laugh, and he drew Shefford aside, "I'm in no hurry. I like it here. And Joe never wants to leave. To-day you can meet the women. Make yourself popular. I've already made you that. These women are most all young and lonesome. Talk to them. Make them like you. Then some day you may be safe to ask questions. Last night I wanted to ask old Mother Smith if she ever heard the name Fay Larkin. But I thought better of it. If there's a girl here or at Stonebridge of that name we'll learn it. If there's mystery we'd better go slow. Mormons are hell on secret and mystery, and to pry into their affairs is to queer yourself. My advice is—just be as nice as you can be, and let things happen."

Fay Larkin! All in a night Shefford had forgotten her. Why? He pondered over the matter, and then the old thrill, the old desire, came back.

"Shefford, what do you think Nas Ta Bega said to me last night?" asked Withers in lower voice.

"Haven't any idea," replied Shefford, curiously.

"We were sitting beside the fire. I saw you walking under the cedars. You seemed thoughtful. That keen Indian watched you, and he said to me in Navajo, 'Bi Nai has lost his God. He has come far to find a wife. Nas Ta Bega is his brother.'... He meant he'll find both God and wife for you. I don't know about that, but I say take the Indian as he thinks he is— your brother. Long before I knew Nas Ta Bega well my wife used to tell me about him. He's a sage and a poet—the very spirit of this desert. He's worth cultivating for his own sake. But more—remember, if Fay Larkin is still shut in that valley the Navajo will find her for you."

"I shall take Nas Ta Bega as my brother—and be proud," replied Shefford.

"There's another thing. Do you intend to confide in Joe?"

"I hadn't thought of that."

"Well, it might be a good plan. But wait until you know him better and he knows you. He's ready to fight for you now. He's taken your trouble to heart. You wouldn't think Joe is deeply religious. Yet he is. He may never breathe a word about religion to you.... Now, Shefford, go ahead. You've struck a trail. It's rough, but it'll make a man of you. It'll lead somewhere."

"I'm singularly fortunate—I—who had lost all friends. Withers, I am grateful. I'll prove it. I'll show—"

Withers's upheld hand checked further speech, and Shefford realized that beneath the rough exterior of this desert trader there was fine feeling. These men of crude toil and wild surroundings were beginning to loom up large in Shefford's mind.

The day began leisurely. The men were yet at breakfast when the women of the village began to come one by one to the spring. Joe Lake made friendly and joking remarks to each. And as each one passed on down the path he poised a biscuit in one hand and a cup of coffee in the other, and with his head cocked sidewise like an owl he said, "Reckon I've got to get me a woman like her."

Shefford saw and heard, yet he was all the time half unconsciously watching with strange eagerness for a white figure to appear. At last he saw her—the same girl with the hood, the same swift step. A little shock or quiver passed over him, and at the moment all that was explicable about it was something associated with regret.

Joe Lake whistled and stared.

"I haven't met her," he muttered.

"That's the Sago Lily," said Withers.

"Reckon I'm going to carry that bucket," went on Joe.

"And queer yourself with all the other women who've been to the spring? Don't do it, Joe," advised the trader.

"But her bucket's bigger," protested Joe, weakly.

"That's true. But you ought to know Mormons. If she'd come first, all right. As she didn't —why, don't single her out."

Joe kept his seat. The girl came to the spring. A low "good morning" came from under the hood. Then she filled her bucket and started home. Shefford observed that this time she wore moccasins and she carried the heavy bucket with ease. When she disappeared he had again the vague, inexplicable sensation of regret.

Joe Lake breathed heavily. "Reckon I've got to get me a woman like her," he said. But the former jocose tone was lacking and he appeared thoughtful.

Withers first took Shefford to the building used for a school. It was somewhat larger than the other houses, had only one room with two doors and several windows. It was full of children, of all sizes and ages, sitting on rude board benches.

There were half a hundred of them, sturdy, healthy, rosy boys and girls, clad in home-made garments. The young woman teacher was as embarrassed as her pupils were shy, and the visitors withdrew without having heard a word of lessons.

Withers then called upon Smith, Henninger, and Beal, and their wives. Shefford found himself cordially received, and what little he did say showed him how he would be listened to when he cared to talk. These folk were plain and kindly, and he found that there was nothing about them to dislike. The men appeared mild and quiet, and when not conversing seemed austere. The repose of the women was only on the surface; underneath he felt their intensity. Especially in many of the younger women, whom he met in the succeeding hour, did he feel this power of restrained emotion. This surprised him, as did also the fact that almost every one of them was attractive and some of them were exceedingly pretty. He became so interested in them all as a whole that he could not individualize one. They were as widely different in appearance and temperament as women of any other class, but it seemed to Shefford that one common trait united them—and it was a strange, checked yearning for something that he could not discover. Was it happiness? They certainly seemed to be happy, far more so than those millions of women who were chasing phantoms. Were they really sealed wives, as Withers believed, and was this unnatural wife-hood responsible for the strange intensity? At any rate he returned to camp with the conviction that he had stumbled upon a remarkable situation.

He had been told the last names of only three women, and their husbands were in the village. The names of the others were Ruth, Rebecca, Joan—he could not recall them all. They were the mothers of these beautiful children. The fathers, as far as he was concerned, were as intangible as myths. Shefford was an educated clergyman, a man of the world, and, as such, knew women in his way. Mormons might be strange and different, yet the fundamental truth was that all over the world mothers of children were wives; there was a relation between wife and mother that did not need to be named to be felt; and he divined from this that, whatever the situation of these lonely and hidden women, they knew themselves to be wives. Shefford absolutely satisfied himself on that score. If they were miserable they certainly did not show it, and the question came to him how just was the criticism of uninformed men? His judgment of Mormons had been established by what he had heard and read, rather than what he knew. He wanted now to have an open mind. He had studied the totemism and exogamy of the primitive races, and here was his opportunity to understand polygamy. One wife for one man—that was the law. Mormons broke it openly; Gentiles broke it secretly. Mormons acknowledged all their wives and protected their children; Gentiles acknowledged one wife only. Unquestionably the Mormons were wrong, but were not the Gentiles still more wrong?

. . . .

The following day Joe Lake appeared reluctant to start for Stonebridge with Withers.

"Joe, you'd better come along," said the trader, dryly. "I reckon you've seen a little too much of the Sago Lily."

Lake offered no reply, but it was evident from his sober face that Withers had not hit short of the mark. Withers rode off, with a parting word to Shefford, and finally Joe somberly mounted his bay and trotted down the valley. As Nas Ta Bega had gone off somewhere to visit Indians, Shefford was left alone.

He went into the village and made himself useful and agreeable. He made friends with the children and he talked to the women until he was hoarse. Their ignorance of the world was a spur to him, and never in his life had he had such an attentive audience. And as he showed no curiosity, asked no difficult questions, gradually what reserve he had noted wore away, and the end of the day saw him on a footing with them that Withers had predicted.

By the time several like days had passed it seemed from the interest and friendliness of these women that he might have lived long among them. He was possessed of wit and eloquence and information, which he freely gave, and not with selfish motive. He liked these women; he liked to see the somber shade pass from their faces, to see them brighten. He had met the girl Mary at the spring and along the path, but he had not yet seen her face. He was always looking for her, hoping to meet her, and confessed to himself that the best of the day for him were the morning and evening visits she made to the spring. Nevertheless, for some reason hard to divine, he was reluctant to seek her deliberately.

Always while he had listened to her neighbors' talk, he had hoped they might let fall something about her. But they did not. He received an impression that she was not so intimate with the others as he had supposed. They all made one big family. Still, she seemed a little outside. He could bring no proofs to strengthen this idea. He merely felt it, and many of his feelings were independent of intelligent reason. Something had been added to curiosity, that was sure.

It was his habit to call upon Mother Smith in the afternoons. From the first her talk to him hinted of a leaning toward thought of making him a Mormon. Her husband and the other men took up her cue and spoke of their religion, casually at first, but gradually opening their minds to free and simple discussion of their faith. Shefford lent respectful attention. He would rather have been a Mormon than an atheist, and apparently they considered him the latter, and were earnest to save his soul. Shefford knew that he could never be one any more than the other. He was just at sea. But he listened, and he found them simple in faith, blind, perhaps, but loyal and good. It was noteworthy that Mother Smith happened to be the only woman in the village who had ever mentioned religion to him. She was old, of a past generation; the young women belonged to the present. Shefford pondered the significant difference.

Every day made more steadfast his impression of the great mystery that was like a twining shadow round these women, yet in the same time many little ideas shifted and many new characteristics became manifest. This last was of course the result of acquaintance; he was learning more about the villagers. He gathered from keen interpretation of subtle words and looks that here in this lonely village, the same as in all the rest of the world where women were together, there were cliques, quarrels, dislikes, loves, and jealousies. The truth, once known to him, made him feel natural and fortified his confidence to meet the demands of an increasingly interesting position. He discovered, with a somewhat grim amusement, that a clergyman's experience in a church full of women had not been entirely useless.

One afternoon he let fall a careless remark that was a subtle question in regard to the girl Mary, whom Withers called the Sago Lily. In response he received an answer couched in the sweet poisoned honey of woman's jealousy. He said no more. Certain ideas of his were strengthened, and straightway he became thoughtful.

That afternoon late, as he did his camp chores, he watched for her. But she did not come. Then he decided to go to see her. But even the decision and the strange thrill it imparted did not change his reluctance.

Twilight was darkening the valley when he reached her house, and the shadows were thick under the pinyons. There was no light in the door or window. He saw a white shape on the porch, and as he came down the path it rose. It was the girl Mary, and she appeared startled.

"Good evening," he said. "It's Shefford. May I stay and talk a little while?"

She was silent for so long that he began to feel awkward.

"I'd be glad to have you," she replied, finally.

There was a bench on the porch, but he preferred to sit upon a blanket on the step.

"I've been getting acquainted with everybody—except you," he went on.

"I have been here," she replied.

That might have been a woman's speech, but it certainly had been made in a girl's voice. She was neither shy nor embarrassed nor self-conscious. As she stood back from him he could not see her face in the dense twilight.

"I've been wanting to call on you."

She made some slight movement. Shefford felt a strange calm, yet he knew the moment was big and potent.

"Won't you sit here?" he asked.

She complied with his wish, and then he saw her face, though dimly, in the twilight. And it struck him mute. But he had no glimpse such as had flashed upon him from under her hood that other night. He thought of a white flower in shadow, and received his first impression of the rare and perfect lily Withers had said graced the wild canyon. She was only a girl. She sat very still, looking straight before her, and seemed to be waiting, listening. Shefford saw the quick rise and fall of her bosom.

"I want to talk," he began, swiftly, hoping to put her at her ease. "Every one here has been good to me and I've talked—oh, for hours and hours. But the thing in my mind I haven't spoken of. I've never asked any questions. That makes my part so strange. I want to tell why I came out here. I need some one who will keep my secret, and perhaps help me.... Would you?"

"Yes, if I could," she replied.

"You see I've got to trust you, or one of these other women. You're all Mormons. I don't mean that's anything against you. I believe you're all good and noble. But the fact makes—well, makes a liberty of speech impossible. What can I do?"

Her silence probably meant that she did not know. Shefford sensed less strain in her and more excitement. He believed he was on the right track and did not regret his impulse. Even had he regretted it he would have gone on, for opposed to caution and intelligence was his driving mystic force.

Then he told her the truth about his boyhood, his ambition to be an artist, his renunciation to his father's hope, his career as a clergyman, his failure in religion, and the disgrace that had made him a wanderer.

"Oh—I'm sorry!" she said. The faint starlight shone on her face, in her eyes, and if he ever saw beauty and soul he saw them then. She seemed deeply moved. She had forgotten herself. She betrayed girlhood then—all the quick sympathy, the wonder, the sweetness of a heart innocent and untutored. She looked at him with great, starry, questioning eyes, as if they had just become aware of his presence, as if a man had been strange to her.

"Thank you. It's good of you to be sorry," he said. "My instinct guided me right. Perhaps you'll be my friend."

"I will be—if I can," she said.

"But CAN you be?"

"I don't know. I never had a friend. I... But, sir, I mustn't talk of myself.... Oh, I'm afraid I can't help you."

How strange the pathos of her voice! Almost he believed she was in need of help or sympathy or love. But he could not wholly trust a judgment formed from observation of a class different from hers.

"Maybe you CAN help me. Let's see," he said. "I don't seek to make you talk of yourself. But—you're a human being—a girl—almost a woman. You're not dumb. But even a nun can talk."

"A nun? What is that?"

"Well—a nun is a sister of mercy—a woman consecrated to God—who has renounced the world. In some ways you Mormon women here resemble nuns. It is sacrifice that nails you in this lonely valley.... You see—how I talk! One word, one thought brings another, and I speak what perhaps should be unsaid. And it's hard, because I feel I could unburden myself to you."

"Tell me what you want," she said.

Shefford hesitated, and became aware of the rapid pound of his heart. More than anything he wanted to be fair to this girl. He saw that she was warming to his influence. Her shadowy eyes were fixed upon him. The starlight, growing brighter, shone on her golden hair and white face.

"I'll tell you presently," he said. "I've trusted you. I'll trust you with all.... But let me have my own time. This is so strange a thing, my wanting to confide in you. It's selfish, perhaps. I have my own ax to grind. I hope I won't wrong you. That's why I'm going to be perfectly frank. I might wait for days to get better acquainted. But the impulse is on me. I've been so interested in all you Mormon women. The fact—the meaning of this hidden village is so—so terrible to me. But that's none of my business. I have spent my afternoons and evenings with these women at the different cottages. You do not mingle with them. They are lonely, but have not such loneliness as yours. I have passed here every night. No light—no sound. I can't help thinking. Don't censure me or be afraid or draw within yourself just because I must think. I may be all wrong. But I'm curious. I wonder about you. Who are you? Mary—Mary what? Maybe I really don't want to know. I came with selfish motive and now I'd like to—to —what shall I say? Make your life a little less lonely for the while I'm here. That's all. It needn't offend. And if you accept it, how much easier I can tell you my secret. You are a Mormon and I—well, I am only a wanderer in these wilds. But—we might help each other.... Have I made a mistake?"

"No—no," she cried, almost wildly.

"We can be friends then. You will trust me, help me?"

"Yes, if I dare."

"Surely you may dare what the other women would?"

She was silent.

And the wistfulness of her silence touched him. He felt contrition. He did not stop to analyze his own emotions, but he had an inkling that once this strange situation was ended he would have food for reflection. What struck him most now was the girl's blanched face, the strong, nervous clasp of her hands, the visible tumult of her bosom. Excitement alone could not be accountable for this. He had not divined the cause for such agitation. He was puzzled, troubled, and drawn irresistibly. He had not said what he had planned to say. The moment had given birth to his speech, and it had flowed. What was guiding him?

"Mary," he said, earnestly, "tell me—have you mother, father, sister, brother? Something prompts me to ask that."

"All dead—gone—years ago," she answered.

"How old are you?"

"Eighteen, I think. I'm not sure."

"You ARE lonely."

His words were gentle and divining.

"O God!" she cried. "Lonely!"

Then as a man in a dream he beheld her weeping. There was in her the unconsciousness of a child and the passion of a woman. He gazed out into the dark shadows and up at the white stars, and then at the bowed head with its mass of glinting hair. But her agitation was no longer strange to him. A few gentle and kind words had proved her undoing. He knew then that whatever her life was, no kindness or sympathy entered it. Presently she recovered, and sat as before, only whiter of face it seemed, and with something tragic in her dark eyes. She was growing cold and still again, aloof, more like those other Mormon women.

"I understand," he said. "I'm not sorry I spoke. I felt your trouble, whatever it is.... Do not retreat into your cold shell, I beg of you.... Let me trust you with my secret."

He saw her shake out of the cold apathy. She wavered. He felt an inexplicable sweetness in the power his voice seemed to have upon her. She bowed her head in acquiescence. And

Shefford began his story. Did she grow still, like stone, or was that only his vivid imagination? He told her of Venters and Bess—of Lassiter and Jane—of little Fay Larkin—of the romance, and then the tragedy of Surprise Valley.

"So, when my Church disowned me," he concluded, "I conceived the idea of wandering into the wilds of Utah to save Fay Larkin from that canyon prison. It grew to be the best and strongest desire of my life. I think if I could save her that it would save me. I never loved any girl. I can't say that I love Fay Larkin. How could I when I've never seen her—when she's only a dream girl? But I believe if she were to become a reality—a flesh-and-blood girl—that I would love her."

That was more than Shefford had ever confessed to any one, and it stirred him to his depths. Mary bent her head on her hands in strange, stonelike rigidity.

"So here I am in the canyon country," he continued. "Withers tells me it is a country of rainbows, both in the evanescent air and in the changeless stone. Always as a boy there had been for me some haunting promise, some treasure at the foot of the rainbow. I shall expect the curve of a rainbow to lead me down into Surprise Valley. A dreamer, you will call me. But I have had strange dreams come true.... Mary, do you think THIS dream will come true?"

She was silent so long that he repeated his question.

"Only—in heaven," she whispered.

He took her reply strangely and a chill crept over him.

"You think my plan to seek to strive, to find—you think that idle, vain?"

"I think it noble.... Thank God I've met a man like you!"

"Don't praise me!" he exclaimed, hastily. "Only help me.... Mary, will you answer a few little questions, if I swear by my honor I'll never reveal what you tell me?"

"I'll try."

He moistened his lips. Why did she seem so strange, so far away? The hovering shadows made him nervous. Always he had been afraid of the dark. His mood now admitted of unreal fancies.

"Have you ever heard of Fay Larkin?" he asked, very low.

"Yes."

"Was there only one Fay Larkin?"

"Only one."

"Did you—ever see her?"

"Yes," came the faint reply.

He was grateful. How she might be breaking faith with creed or duty! He had not dared to hope so much. All his inner being trembled at the portent of his next query. He had not dreamed it would be so hard to put, or would affect him so powerfully. A warmth, a glow, a happiness pervaded his spirit; and the chill, the gloom were as if they had never been.

"Where is Fay Larkin now?" he asked, huskily.

He bent over her, touched her, leaned close to catch her whisper.

"She is—dead!"

Slowly Shefford rose, with a sickening shock, and then in bitter pain he strode away into the starlight.

❦ 7 ❦

SAGO-LILIES

THE INDIAN RETURNED to camp that night, and early the next day, which was Sunday, Withers rode in, accompanied by a stout, gray-bearded personage wearing a long black coat.

"Bishop Kane, this is my new man, John Shefford," said the trader.

Shefford acknowledged the introduction with the respectful courtesy evidently in order, and found himself being studied intently by clear blue eyes. The bishop appeared old, dry, and absorbed in thought; he spoke quaintly, using in every speech some Biblical word or phrase; and he had an air of authority. He asked Shefford to hear him preach at the morning service, and then he went off into the village.

"Guess he liked your looks," remarked Withers.

"He certainly sized me up," replied Shefford.

"Well, what could you expect? Sure I never heard of a deal like this—a handsome young fellow left alone with a lot of pretty Mormon women! You'll understand when you learn to know Mormons. Bishop Kane's a square old chap. Crazy on religion, maybe, but otherwise he's a good fellow. I made the best stand I could for you. The Mormons over at Stonebridge were huffy because I hadn't consulted them before fetching you over here. If I had, of course you'd never have gotten here. It was Joe Lake who made it all right with them. Joe's well thought of, and he certainly stood up for you."

"I owe him something, then," replied Shefford. "Hope my obligations don't grow beyond me. Did you leave Joe at Stonebridge?"

"Yes. He wanted to stay, and I had work there that'll keep him awhile. Shefford, we got news of Shadd—bad news. The half-breed's cutting up rough. His gang shot up some Piutes over here across the line. Then he got run out of Durango a few weeks ago for murder. A posse of cowboys trailed him. But he slipped them. He's a fox. You know he was trailing us here. He left the trail, Nas Ta Bega said. I learned at Stonebridge that Shadd is well disposed toward Mormons. It takes the Mormons to handle Indians. Shadd knows of this village and that's why he shunted off our trail. But he might hang down in the pass and wait for us. I think I'd better go back to Kayenta alone, across country. You stay here till Joe and the Indian think it safe to leave. You'll be going up on the slope of

Navajo to load a pack-train, and from there it may be well to go down West canyon to Red Lake, and home over the divide, the way you came. Joe'll decide what's best. And you might as well buckle on a gun and get used to it. Sooner or later you'll have to shoot your way through."

Shefford did not respond with his usual enthusiasm, and the omission caused the trader to scrutinize him closely.

"What's the matter?" he queried. "There's no light in your eye to-day. You look a little shady."

"I didn't rest well last night," replied Shefford. "I'm depressed this morning. But I'll cheer up directly."

"Did you get along with the women?"

"Very well indeed. And I've enjoyed myself. It's a strange, beautiful place."

"Do you like the women?"

"Yes."

"Have you seen much of the Sago Lily?"

"No. I carried her bucket one night—and saw her only once again. I've been with the other women most of the time."

"It's just as well you didn't run often into Mary. Joe's sick over her. I never saw a girl with a face and form to equal hers. There's danger here for any man, Shefford. Even for you who think you've turned your back on the world! Any of these Mormon women may fall in love with you. They CAN'T love their husbands. That's how I figure it. Religion holds them, not love. And the peculiar thing is this: they're second, third, or fourth wives, all sealed. That means their husbands are old, have picked them out for youth and physical charms, have chosen the very opposite to their first wives, and then have hidden them here in this lonely hole.... Did you ever imagine so terrible a thing?"

"No, Withers, I did not."

"Maybe that's what depressed you. Anyway, my hunch is worth taking. Be as nice as you can, Shefford. Lord knows it would be good for these poor women if every last one of them fell in love with you. That won't hurt them so long as you keep your head. Savvy? Perhaps I seem rough and coarse to a man of your class. Well, that may be. But human nature is human nature. And in this strange and beautiful place you might love an Indian girl, let alone the Sago Lily. That's all. I sure feel better with that load off my conscience. Hope I don't offend."

"No indeed. I thank you, Withers," replied Shefford, with his hand on the trader's shoulder. "You are right to caution me. I seem to be wild—thirsting for adventure—chasing a gleam. In these unstable days I can't answer for my heart. But I can for my honor. These unfortunate women are as safe with me as—as they are with you and Joe."

Withers uttered a blunt laugh.

"See here, son, look things square in the eye. Men of violent, lonely, toilsome lives store up hunger for the love of woman. Love of a STRANGE woman, if you want to put it that way. It's nature. It seems all the beautiful young women in Utah are corralled in this valley. When I come over here I feel natural, but I'm not happy. I'd like to make love to—to that flower-faced girl. And I'm not ashamed to own it. I've told Molly, my wife, and she understands. As for Joe, it's much harder for him. Joe never has had a wife or sweetheart. I tell you he's sick, and if I'd stay here a month I'd be sick."

Withers had spoken with fire in his eyes, with grim humor on his lips, with uncompromising brutal truth. What he admitted was astounding to Shefford, but, once spoken, not at all strange. The trader was a man who spoke his inmost thought. And what he said suddenly focused Shefford's mental vision clear and whole upon the appalling significance of the tragedy of those women, especially of the girl whose life was lonelier, sadder, darker than that of the others.

"Withers, trust me," replied Shefford.

"All right. Make the best of a bad job," said the trader, and went off about his tasks.

Shefford and Withers attended the morning service, which was held in the school-house. Exclusive of the children every inhabitant of the village was there. The women, except the few eldest, were dressed in white and looked exceedingly well. Manifestly they had bestowed care upon this Sabbath morning's toilet. One thing surely this dress occasion brought out, and it was evidence that the Mormon women were not poor, whatever their misfortunes might be. Jewelry was not wanting, nor fine lace. And they all wore beautiful wild flowers of a kind unknown to Shefford. He received many a bright smile. He looked for Mary, hoping to see her face for the first time in the daylight, but she sat far forward and did not turn. He saw her graceful white neck, the fine lines of her throat, and her colorless cheek. He recognized her, yet in the light she seemed a stranger.

The service began with a short prayer and was followed by the singing of a hymn. Nowhere had Shefford heard better music or sweeter voices. How deeply they affected him! Had any man ever fallen into a stranger adventure than this? He had only to shut his eyes to believe it all a creation of his fancy—the square log cabin with its red mud between the chinks and a roof like an Indian hogan—the old bishop in his black coat, standing solemnly, his hand beating time to the tune—the few old women, dignified and stately—the many young women, fresh and handsome, lifting their voices.

Shefford listened intently to the bishop's sermon. In some respects it was the best he had ever heard. In others it was impossible for an intelligent man to regard seriously. It was very long, lasting an hour and a half, and the parts that were helpful to Shefford came from the experience and wisdom of a man who had grown old in the desert. The physical things that had molded characters of iron, the obstacles that only strong, patient men could have overcome, the making of homes in a wilderness, showed the greatness of this alien band of Mormons. Shefford conceded greatness to them. But the strange religion—the narrowing down of the world to the soil of Utah, the intimations of prophets on earth who had direct converse with God, the austere self-conscious omnipotence of this old bishop—these were matters that Shefford felt he must understand better, and see more favorably, if he were not to consider them impossible.

Immediately after the service, forgetting that his intention had been to get the long-waited-for look at Mary in the light of the sun, Shefford hurried back to camp and to a secluded spot among the cedars. Strikingly it had come to him that the fault he had found in Gentile religion he now found in the Mormon religion. An old question returned to haunt him—were all religions the same in blindness? As far as he could see, religion existed to uphold the founders of a Church, a creed. The Church of his own kind was a place where narrow men and women went to think of their own salvation. They did not go there to think of others. And now Shefford's keen mind saw something of Mormonism and found it wanting. Bishop Kane was a sincere, good, mistaken man. He believed what he preached, but that would not stand logic. He taught blindness and mostly it appeared to be directed at the women. Was there no religion divorced from power, no religion as good for one man as another, no religion in the spirit of brotherly love? Nas Ta Bega's "Bi Nai" (brother)—that was love, if not religion, and perhaps the one and the other were the same. Shefford kept in mind an intention to ask Nas Ta Bega what he thought of the Mormons.

Later, when opportunity afforded, he did speak to the Indian. Nas Ta Bega threw away his cigarette and made an impressive gesture that conveyed as much sorrow as scorn.

"The first Mormon said God spoke to him and told him to go to a certain place and dig. He went there and found the Book of Mormon. It said follow me, marry many wives, go into the desert and multiply, send your sons out into the world and bring us young women, many young women. And when the first Mormon became strong with many followers he said again: Give to me part of your labor—of your cattle and sheep—of your silver—that I may build me great cathedrals for you to worship in. And I will commune with God and make it right and good that you have more wives. That is Mormonism."

"Nas Ta Bega, you mean the Mormons are a great and good people blindly following a leader?"

"Yes. And the leader builds for himself—not for them."

"That is not religion. He has no God but himself."

"They have no God. They are blind like the Mokis who have the creeping growths on their eyes. They have no God they can see and hear and feel, who is with them day and night."

It was late in the afternoon when Bishop Kane rode through the camp and halted on his way to speak to Shefford. He was kind and fatherly. "Young man, are you open to faith?" he questioned gravely.

"I think I am," replied Shefford, thankful he could answer readily.

"Then come into the fold. You are a lost sheep. 'Away on the desert I heard its cry.'... God bless you. Visit me when you ride to Stonebridge."

He flicked his horse with a cedar branch and trotted away beside the trader, and presently the green-choked neck of the valley hid them from view. Shefford could not have said that he was glad to be left behind, and yet neither was he sorry.

That Sabbath evening as he sat quietly with Nas Ta Bega, watching the sunset gilding the peaks, he was visited by three of the young Mormon women—Ruth, Joan, and Hester. They deliberately sought him and merrily led him off to the village and to the evening service of singing and prayer. Afterward he was surrounded and made much of. He had been popular before, but this was different. When he thoughtfully wended his way campward under the quiet stars he realized that the coming of Bishop Kane had made a subtle change in the women. That change was at first hard to define, but from every point by which he approached it he came to the same conclusion—the bishop had not objected to his presence in the village. The women became natural, free, and unrestrained. A dozen or twenty young and attractive women thrown much into companionship with one man. He might become a Mormon. The idea made him laugh. But upon reflection it was not funny; it sobered him. What a situation! He felt instinctively that he ought to fly from this hidden valley. But he could not have done it, even had he not been in the trader's employ. The thing was provokingly seductive. It was like an Arabian Nights' tale. What could these strange, fatally bound women do? Would any one of them become involved in sweet toils such as were possible to him? He was no fool. Already eyes had flashed and lips had smiled.

A thousand like thoughts whirled through his mind. And when he had calmed down somewhat two things were not lost upon him—an intricate and fascinating situation, with no end to its possibilities, threatened and attracted him—and the certainty that, whatever change the bishop had inaugurated, it had made these poor women happier. The latter fact weighed more with Shefford than fears for himself. His word was given to Withers. He would have felt just the same without having bound himself. Still, in the light of the trader's blunt philosophy, and of his own assurance that he was no fool, Shefford felt it incumbent upon him to accept a belief that there were situations no man could resist without an anchor. The ingenuity of man could not have devised a stranger, a more enticing, a more overpoweringly fatal situation. Fatal in that it could not be left untried! Shefford gave in and clicked his teeth as he let himself go. And suddenly he thought of her whom these bitter women called the Sago Lily.

The regret that had been his returned with thought of her. The saddest disillusion of his life, the keenest disappointment, the strangest pain, would always be associated with her. He had meant to see her face once, clear in the sunlight, so that he could always remember it, and then never go near her again. And now it came to him that if he did see much of her these other women would find him like the stone wall in the valley. Folly! Perhaps it was, but she would be safe, maybe happier. When he decided, it was certain that he trembled.

Then he buried the memory of Fay Larkin.

Next day Shefford threw himself with all the boy left in him into the work and play of the village. He helped the women and made games for the children. And he talked or listened. In the early evening he called on Ruth, chatted awhile, and went on to see Joan, and from her to another. When the valley became shrouded in darkness he went unseen down the path to Mary's lonely home.

She was there, a white shadow against the black.

When she replied to his greeting her voice seemed full, broken, eager to express something that would not come. She was happier to see him than she should have been, Shefford thought. He talked, swiftly, eloquently, about whatever he believed would interest her. He stayed long, and finally left, not having seen her face except in pale starlight and shadow; and the strong clasp of her hand remained with him as he went away under the pinyons.

Days passed swiftly. Joe Lake did not return. The Indian rode in and out of camp, watered and guarded the pack-burros and the mustangs. Shefford grew strong and active. He made gardens for the women; he cut cords of fire-wood; he dammed the brook and made an irrigation ditch; he learned to love these fatherless children, and they loved him.

In the afternoons there was leisure for him and for the women. He had no favorites, and let the occasion decide what he should do and with whom he should be. They had little parties at the cottages and picnics under the cedars. He rode up and down the valley with Ruth, who could ride a horse as no other girl he had ever seen. He climbed with Hester. He walked with Joan. Mostly he contrived to include several at once in the little excursions, though it was not rare for him to be out alone with one.

It was not a game he was playing. More and more, as he learned to know these young women, he liked them better, he pitied them, he was good for them. It shamed him, hurt him, somehow, to see how they tried to forget something when they were with him. Not improbably a little of it was coquetry, as natural as a laugh to any pretty woman. But that was not what hurt him. It was to see Ruth or Rebecca, as the case might be, full of life and fun, thoroughly enjoying some jest or play, all of a sudden be strangely recalled from the wholesome pleasure of a girl to become a deep and somber woman. The crimes in the name of religion! How he thought of the blood and the ruin laid at the door of religion! He wondered if that were so with Nas Ta Bega's religion, and he meant to find out some day. The women he liked best he imagined the least religious, and they made less effort to attract him.

Every night in the dark he went to Mary's home and sat with her on the porch. He never went inside. For all he knew, his visits were unknown to her neighbors. Still, it did not matter to him if they found out. To her he could talk as he had never talked to any one. She liberated all his thought and fancy. He filled her mind.

As there had been a change in the other women, so was there in Mary; however, it had no relation to the bishop's visit. The time came when Shefford could not but see that she lived and dragged through the long day for the sake of those few hours in the shadow of the stars with him. She seldom spoke. She listened. Wonderful to him—sometimes she laughed—and it seemed the sound was a ghost of childhood pleasure. When he stopped to consider that she might fall in love with him he drove the thought from him. When he realized that his folly had become sweet and that the sweetness imperiously drew him, he likewise cast off that thought. The present was enough. And if he had any treasures of mind and heart he gave them to her.

She never asked him to stay, but she showed that she wanted him to. That made it hard to go. Still, he never stayed late. The moment of parting was like a break. Her good-by was sweet, low music; it lingered on his ear; it bade him come to-morrow night; and it sent him away into the valley to walk under the stars, a man fighting against himself.

One night at parting, as he tried to see her face in the wan glow of a clouded moon, he said:

"I've been trying to find a sago-lily."

"Have you never seen one?" she asked.

"No." He meant to say something with a double meaning, in reference to her face and the name of the flower, but her unconsciousness made him hold his tongue. She was wholly unlike the other women.

"I'll show you where the lilies grow," she said.

"When?"

"To-morrow. Early in the afternoon I'll come to the spring. Then I'll take you."

Next morning Joe Lake returned and imparted news that was perturbing to Shefford. Reports of Shadd had come in to Stonebridge from different Indian villages; Joe was not inclined to linger long at the camp, and favored taking the trail with the pack-train.

Shefford discovered that he did not want to leave the valley, and the knowledge made him reflective. That morning he did not go into the village, and stayed in camp alone. A depression weighed upon him. It was dispelled, however, early in the afternoon by the sight of a slender figure in white swiftly coming down the path to the spring. He had an appointment with Mary to go to see the sago lilies; everything else slipped his mind.

Mary wore the long black hood that effectually concealed her face. It made of her a woman, a Mormon woman, and strangely belied the lithe form and the braid of gold hair.

"Good day," she said, putting down her bucket. "Do you still want to go—to see the lilies?"

"Yes," replied Shefford, with a short laugh.

"Can you climb?"

"I'll go where you go."

Then she set off under the cedars and Shefford stalked at her side. He was aware that Nas Ta Bega watched them walk away. This day, so far, at least, Shefford did not feel talkative; and Mary had always been one who mostly listened. They came at length to a place where the wall rose in low, smooth swells, not steep, but certainly at an angle Shefford would not of his own accord have attempted to scale.

Light, quick, and sure as a mountain-sheep Mary went up the first swell to an offset above. Shefford, in amaze and admiration, watched the little moccasins as they flashed and held on to the smooth rock.

When he essayed to follow her he slipped and came to grief. A second attempt resulted in like failure. Then he backed away from the wall, to run forward fast and up the slope, only to slip, halfway up, and fall again.

He made light of the incident, but she was solicitous. When he assured her he was unhurt she said he had agreed to go where she went.

"But I'm not a—a bird," he protested.

"Take off your boots. Then you can climb. When we get over the wall it'll be easy," she said.

In his stocking-feet he had no great difficulty walking up the first bulge of the walls. And from there she led him up the strange waves of wind-worn rock. He could not attend to anything save the red, polished rock under him, and so saw little. The ascent was longer than he would have imagined, and steep enough to make him pant, but at last a huge round summit was reached.

From here he saw down into the valley where the village lay. But for the lazy columns of blue smoke curling up from the pinyons the place would have seemed uninhabited. The wall on the other side was about level with the one upon which he stood. Beyond rose other walls and cliffs, up and up to the great towering peaks between which the green-and-black mountain loomed. Facing the other way, Shefford had only a restricted view. There were low crags and smooth stone ridges, between which were aisles green with cedar and pinon. Shefford's companion headed toward one of these, and when he had followed her a few steps he could no longer see down into the valley. The Mormon village where she lived was as if it were lost, and when it vanished Shefford felt a difference. Scarcely had the thought passed when Mary removed the dark hood. Her small head glistened like gold in the sunlight.

Shefford caught up with her and walked at her side, but could not bring himself at once deliberately to look at her. They entered a narrow, low-walled lane where cedars and pinyons grew thickly, their fragrance heavy in the warm air, and flowers began to show in the grassy patches.

"This is Indian paint-brush," she said, pointing to little, low, scarlet flowers. A gray sage-bush with beautiful purple blossoms she called purple sage; another bush with yellow flowers she named buck-brush, and there were vermilion cacti and low, flat mounds of lavender daisies which she said had no name. A whole mossy bank was covered with lace like green leaves and tiny blossoms the color of violets, which she called loco.

"Loco? Is this what makes the horses go crazy when they eat it?" he asked.

"It is, indeed," she said, laughing.

When she laughed it was impossible not to look at her. She walked a little in advance. Her white cheek and temple seemed framed in the gold of her hair. How white her skin! But it was like pearl, faintly veined and flushed. The profile, clear-cut and pure, appeared cold, almost stern. He knew now that she was singularly beautiful, though he had yet to see her full face.

They walked on. Quite suddenly the lane opened out between two rounded bluffs, and Shefford looked down upon a grander and more awe-inspiring scene than ever he had viewed in his dreams.

What appeared to be a green mountainside sloped endlessly down to a plain, and that rolled and billowed away to a boundless region of strangely carved rock. The greatness of the scene could not be grasped in a glance. The slope was long; the plain not as level as it seemed to be on first sight; here and there round, red rocks, isolated and strange, like lonely castles, rose out of the green. Beyond the green all the earth seemed naked, showing smooth, glistening bones. It was a formidable wall of rock that flung itself up in the distance, carved into a thousand canyon and walls and domes and peaks, and there was not a straight nor a broken nor a jagged line in all that wildness. The color low down was red, dark blue, and purple in the clefts, yellow upon the heights, and in the distance rainbow-hued. A land of curves and color!

Shefford uttered an exclamation.

"That's Utah," said Mary. "I come often to sit here. You see that winding blue line. There.... That's San Juan canyon. And the other dark line, that's Escalante canyon. They wind down into this great purple chasm—'way over here to the left—and that's the Grand canyon. They say not even the Indians have been in there."

Shefford had nothing to say. The moment was one of subtle and vital assimilation. Such places as this to be unknown to men! What strength, what wonder, what help, what glory, just to sit there an hour, slowly and appallingly to realize! Something came to Shefford from the distance, out of the purple canyon and from those dim, wind-worn peaks. He resolved to come here to this promontory again and again, alone and in humble spirit, and learn to know why he had been silenced, why peace pervaded his soul.

It was with this emotion upon him that he turned to find his companion watching him. Then for the first time he saw her face fully, and was thrilled that chance had reserved the privilege for this moment. It was a girl's face he saw, flower-like, lovely and pure as a Madonna's, and strangely, tragically sad. The eyes were large, dark gray, the color of the sage. They were as clear as the air which made distant things close, and yet they seemed full of shadows, like a ruffled pool under midnight stars. They disturbed him. Her mouth had the sweet curves and redness of youth, but it showed bitterness, pain, and repression.

"Where are the sago-lilies?" he asked, suddenly.

"Farther down. It's too cold up here for them. Come," she said.

He followed her down a winding trail—down and down till the green plain rose to blot out the scrawled wall of rock, down into a verdant canyon where a brook made swift music over stones, where the air was sultry and hot, laden with the fragrant breath of flower and leaf. This was a canyon of summer, and it bloomed.

The girl bent and plucked something from the grass.

"Here's a white lily," she said. "There are three colors. The yellow and pink ones are deeper down in the canyon."

Shefford took the flower and regarded it with great interest. He had never seen such an exquisite thing. It had three large petals, curving cuplike, of a whiteness purer than new-fallen snow, and a heart of rich, warm gold. Its fragrance was so faint as to be almost indistinguishable, yet of a haunting, unforgettable sweetness. And even while he looked at it the petals drooped and their whiteness shaded and the gold paled. In a moment the flower was wilted.

"I don't like to pluck the lilies," said Mary. "They die so swiftly."

Shefford saw the white flowers everywhere in the open, sunny places along the brook. They swayed with stately grace in the slow, warm wind. They seemed like three-pointed stars shining out of the green. He bent over one with a particularly lofty stem, and after a close survey of it he rose to look at her face. His action was plainly one of comparison. She laughed and said it was foolish for the women to call her the Sago Lily. She had no coquetry; she spoke as she would have spoken of the stones at her feet; she did not know that she was beautiful. Shefford imagined there was some resemblance in her to the lily—the same whiteness, the same rich gold, and, more striking than either, a strange, rare quality of beauty, of life, intangible as something fleeting, the spirit that had swiftly faded from the plucked flower. Where had the girl been born—what had her life been? Shefford was intensely curious about her. She seemed as different from any other women he had known as this rare canyon lily was different from the tame flowers at home.

On the return up the slope she outstripped him. She climbed lightly and tirelessly. When he reached her upon the promontory there was a stain of red in her cheeks and her expression had changed.

"Let's go back up over the rocks," she said. "I've not climbed for—for so long."

"I'll go where you go," he replied.

Then she was off, and he followed. She took to the curves of the bare rocks and climbed. He sensed a spirit released in her. It was so strange, so keen, so wonderful to be with her, and when he did catch her he feared to speak lest he break this mood. Her eyes grew dark and daring, and often she stopped to look away across the wavy sea of stones to something beyond the great walls. When they got high the wind blew her hair loose and it flew out, a golden stream, with the sun bright upon it. He saw that she changed her direction, which had been in line with the two peaks, and now she climbed toward the heights. They came to a more difficult ascent, where the stone still held to the smooth curves, yet was marked by steep bulges and slants and crevices. Here she became a wild thing. She ran, she leaped, she would have left him far behind had he not called. Then she appeared to remember him and waited.

Her face had now lost its whiteness; it was flushed, rosy, warm.

"Where—did you—ever learn—to run over rocks—this way?" he panted.

"All my life I've climbed," she said. "Ah! it's so good to be up on the walls again—to feel the wind—to see!"

Thereafter he kept close to her, no matter what the effort. He would not miss a moment of her, if he could help it. She was wonderful. He imagined she must be like an Indian girl, or a savage who loved the lofty places and the silence. When she leaped she uttered a strange, low, sweet cry of wildness and exultation. Shefford guessed she was a girl freed from her prison, forgetting herself, living again youthful hours. Still she did not forget him. She waited for him at the bad places, lent him a strong hand, and sometimes let it stay long in his clasp. Tireless and agile, sure-footed as a goat, fleet and wild she leaped and climbed and ran until Shefford marveled at her. This adventure was indeed fulfilment of a dream. Perhaps she might lead him to the treasure at the foot of the rainbow. But that thought, sad with memory daring forth from its grave, was irrevocably linked with a girl who was dead. He could not remember her, in the presence of this wonderful creature who was as strange as she was beautiful. When Shefford reached for the brown hand stretched forth to help him in a leap, when he felt its strong clasp, the youth and vitality and life of it, he had the fear of a man who was running towards a precipice and who could not draw back. This was a climb, a lark, a wild race to the Mormon girl, bound now in the village, and by the very freedom of it she betrayed her bonds. To Shefford it was also a wild race, but toward one sure goal he dared not name.

They went on, and at length, hand in hand, even where no steep step or wide fissure gave reason for the clasp. But she seemed unconscious. They were nearing the last height, a bare eminence, when she broke from him and ran up the smooth stone. When he surmounted it she was standing on the very summit, her arms wide, her full breast heaving, her slender body straight as an Indian's, her hair flying in the wind and blazing in the sun. She seemed to embrace the west, to reach for something afar, to offer herself to the wind and distance. Her face was scarlet from the exertion of the climb, and her broad brow was moist. Her eyes had the piercing light of an eagle's, though now they were dark. Shefford instinctively grasped the essence of this strange spirit, primitive and wild. She was not the woman who had met him at the spring. She had dropped some side of her with that Mormon hood, and now she stood totally strange.

She belonged up here, he divined. She was a part of that wildness. She must have been born and brought up in loneliness, where the wind blew and the peaks loomed and silence held dominion. The sinking sun touched the rim of the distant wall, and as if in parting regret shone with renewed golden fire. And the girl was crowned as with a glory.

Shefford loved her then. Realizing it, he thought he might have loved her before, but that did not matter when he was certain of it now. He trembled a little, fearfully, though without regret. Everything pertaining to his desert experience had been strange—this the strangest of all.

The sun sank swiftly, and instantly there was a change in the golden light. Quickly it died out. The girl changed as swiftly. She seemed to remember herself, and sat down as if suddenly weary. Shefford went closer and seated himself beside her.

"The sun has set. We must go," she said. But she made no movement.

"Whenever you are ready," replied he.

Just as the blaze had died out of her eyes, so the flush faded out of her face. The whiteness stole back, and with it the sadness. He had to bite his tongue to keep from telling her what he felt, to keep from pouring out a thousand questions. But the privilege of having seen her, of having been with her when she had forgotten herself—that he believed was enough. It had been wonderful; it had made him love her But it need not add to the tragedy of her life, whatever that was. He tried to eliminate himself. And he watched her.

Her eyes were fixed upon the gold-rimmed ramparts of the distant wall in the west. Plain it was how she loved that wild upland. And there seemed to be some haunting memory of the past in her gaze—some happy part of life, agonizing to think of now.

"We must go," she said, and rose.

Shefford rose to accompany her. She looked at him, and her haunting eyes seemed to want him to know that he had helped her to forget the present, to remember girlhood, and that somehow she would always associate a wonderful happy afternoon with him. He divined that her silence then was a Mormon seal on lips.

"Mary, this has been the happiest, the best, the most revealing day of my life," he said, simply.

Swiftly, as if startled, she turned and faced down the slope. At the top of the wall above the village she put on the dark hood, and with it that somber something which was Mormon.

Twilight had descended into the valley, and shadows were so thick Shefford had difficulty in finding Mary's bucket. He filled it at the spring, and made offer to carry it home for her, which she declined.

"You'll come to-night—later?" she asked.

"Yes," he replied, hurriedly promising. Then he watched her white form slowly glide down the path to disappear in the shadows.

Nas Ta Bega and Joe were busy at the camp-fire. Shefford joined them. This night he was uncommunicative. Joe peered curiously at him in the flare of the blaze. Later, after the meal, when Shefford appeared restless and strode to and fro, Joe spoke up gruffly:

"Better hang round camp to-night."

Shefford heard, but did not heed. Nevertheless, the purport of the remark, which was either jealousy or admonition, haunted him with the possibility of its meaning.

He walked away from the camp-fire, under the dark pinyons, out into the starry open; and every step was hard to take, unless it pointed toward the home of the girl whose beauty and sadness and mystery had bewitched him. After what seemed hours he took the well-known path toward her cabin, and then every step seemed lighter. He divined he was rushing to some fate—he knew not what.

The porch was in shadow. He peered in vain for the white form against the dark background. In the silence he seemed to hear his heart-beats thick and muffled.

Some distance down the path he heard the sound of hoofs. Withdrawing into the gloom of a cedar, he watched. Soon he made out moving horses with riders. They filed past him to the number of half a score. Like a flash of fire the truth burned him. Mormons come for one of those mysterious night visits to sealed wives!

Shefford stalked far down the valley, into the lonely silence and the night shadows under the walls.

҂ 8 ҂

THE HOGAN OF NAS TA BEGA

The home of Nas Ta Bega lay far up the cedared slope, with the craggy yellow cliffs and the black canyon and the pine-fringed top of Navajo Mountain behind, and to the fore the vast, rolling descent of cedar groves and sage flats and sandy washes. No dim, dark range made bold outline along the horizon; the stretch of gray and purple and green extended to the blue line of sky.

Down the length of one sage level Shefford saw a long lane where the brush and the grass had been beaten flat. This, the Navajo said, was a track where the young braves had raced their mustangs and had striven for supremacy before the eyes of maidens and the old people of the tribe.

"Nas Ta Bega, did you ever race here?" asked Shefford.

"I am a chief by birth. But I was stolen from my home, and now I cannot ride well enough to race the braves of my tribe," the Indian replied, bitterly.

In another place Joe Lake halted his horse and called Shefford's attention to a big yellow rock lying along the trail. And then he spoke in Navajo to the Indian.

"I've heard of this stone—Isende Aha," said Joe, after Nas Ta Bega had spoken. "Get down, and let's see." Shefford dismounted, but the Indian kept his seat in the saddle.

Joe placed a big hand on the stone and tried to move it. According to Shefford's eye measurement the stone was nearly oval, perhaps three feet high, by a little over two in width. Joe threw off his sombrero, took a deep breath, and, bending over, clasped the stone in his arms. He was an exceedingly heavy and powerful man, and it was plain to Shefford that he meant to lift the stone if that were possible. Joe's broad shoulders strained, flattened; his arms bulged, his joints cracked, his neck corded, and his face turned black. By gigantic effort he lifted the stone and moved it about six inches. Then as he released his hold he fell, and when he sat up his face was wet with sweat.

"Try it," he said to Shefford, with his lazy smile. "See if you can heave it."

Shefford was strong, and there had been a time when he took pride in his strength. Something in Joe's supreme effort and in the gloom of the Indian's eyes made Shefford curious about this stone. He bent over and grasped it as Joe had done. He braced himself and

454

lifted with all his power, until a red blur obscured his sight and shooting stars seemed to explode in his head. But he could not even stir the stone.

"Shefford, maybe you'll be able to heft it some day," observed Joe. Then he pointed to the stone and addressed Nas Ta Bega.

The Indian shook his head and spoke for a moment.

"This is the Isende Aha of the Navajos," explained Joe. "The young braves are always trying to carry this stone. As soon as one of them can carry it he is a man. He who carries it farthest is the biggest man. And just so soon as any Indian can no longer lift it he is old. Nas Ta Bega says the stone has been carried two miles in his lifetime. His own father carried it the length of six steps."

"Well! It's plain to me that I am not a man," said Shefford, "or else I am old."

Joe Lake drawled his lazy laugh and, mounting, rode up the trail. But Shefford lingered beside the Indian.

"Bi Nai," said Nas Ta Bega, "I am a chief of my tribe, but I have never been a man. I never lifted that stone. See what the pale-face education has done for the Indian!"

The Navajo's bitterness made Shefford thoughtful. Could greater injury be done to man than this—to rob him of his heritage of strength?

Joe drove the bobbing pack-train of burros into the cedars where the smoke of the hogans curled upward, and soon the whistling of mustangs, the barking of dogs, the bleating of sheep, told of his reception. And presently Shefford was in the midst of an animated scene. Great, woolly, fierce dogs, like wolves, ran out to meet the visitors. Sheep and goats were everywhere, and little lambs scarcely able to walk, with others frisky and frolicsome. There were pure-white lambs, and some that appeared to be painted, and some so beautiful with their fleecy white all except black faces or ears or tails or feet. They ran right under Nack-yal's legs and bumped against Shefford, and kept bleating their thin-piped welcome. Under the cedars surrounding the several hogans were mustangs that took Shefford's eye. He saw an iron-gray with white mane and tail sweeping to the ground; and a fiery black, wilder than any other beast he had ever seen; and a pinto as wonderfully painted as the little lambs; and, most striking of all, a pure, cream-colored mustang with grace and fine lines and beautiful mane and tail, and, strange to see, eyes as blue as azure. This albino mustang came right up to Shefford, an action in singular contrast with that of the others, and showed a tame and friendly spirit toward him and Nack-yal. Indeed, Shefford had reason to feel ashamed of Nack-yal's temper or jealousy.

The first Indians to put in an appearance were a flock of children, half naked, with tangled manes of raven-black hair and skin like gold bronze. They appeared bold and shy by turns. Then a little, sinewy man, old and beaten and gray, came out of the principal hogan. He wore a blanket round his bent shoulders. His name was Hosteen Doetin, and it meant gentle man. His fine, old, wrinkled face lighted with a smile of kindly interest. His squaw followed him, and she was as venerable as he. Shefford caught a glimpse of the shy, dark Glen Naspa, Nas Ta Bega's sister, but she did not come out. Other Indians appeared, coming from adjacent hogans.

Nas Ta Bega turned the mustangs loose among those Shefford had noticed, and presently there rose a snorting, whistling, kicking, plunging melee. A cloud of dust hid them, and then a thudding of swift hoofs told of a run through the cedars. Joe Lake began picking over stacks of goat-skins and bags of wool that were piled against the hogan.

"Reckon we'll have one grand job packing out this load," he growled. "It's not so heavy, but awkward to pack."

It developed, presently, from talk with the old Navajo, that this pile was only a half of the load to be packed to Kayenta, and the other half was round the corner of the mountain in the camp of Piutes. Hosteen Doetin said he would send to the camp and have the Piutes bring their share over. The suggestion suited Joe, who wanted to save his burros as much as possible. Accordingly, a messenger was despatched to the Piute camp. And Shefford, with time on his hands and poignant memory to combat, decided to recall his keen interest in the Navajo, and learn, if possible, what the Indian's life was like. What would a day of his natural life be?

In the gray of dawn, when the hush of the desert night still lay deep over the land, the Navajo stirred in his blanket and began to chant to the morning light. It began very soft and low, a strange, broken murmur, like the music of a brook, and as it swelled that weird and mournful tone was slowly lost in one of hope and joy. The Indian's soul was coming out of night, blackness, the sleep that resembled death, into the day, the light that was life.

Then he stood in the door of his hogan, his blanket around him, and faced the east.

Night was lifting out of the clefts and ravines; the rolling cedar ridges and the sage flats were softly gray, with thin veils like smoke mysteriously rising and vanishing; the colorless rocks were changing. A long, horizon-wide gleam of light, rosiest in the center, lay low down in the east and momentarily brightened. One by one the stars in the deep-blue sky paled and went out and the blue dome changed and lightened. Night had vanished on invisible wings and silence broke to the music of a mockingbird. The rose in the east deepened; a wisp of cloud turned gold; dim distant mountains showed dark against the red; and low down in a notch a rim of fire appeared. Over the soft ridges and valleys crept a wondrous transfiguration. It was as if every blade of grass, every leaf of sage, every twig of cedar, the flowers, the trees, the rocks came to life at sight of the sun. The red disk rose, and a golden fire burned over the glowing face of that lonely waste.

The Navajo, dark, stately, inscrutable, faced the sun—his god. This was his Great Spirit. The desert was his mother, but the sun was his life. To the keeper of the winds and rains, to the master of light, to the maker of fire, to the giver of life the Navajo sent up his prayer:

> *Of all the good things of the Earth let me always have plenty.*
> *Of all the beautiful things of the Earth let me always have plenty.*
> *Peacefully let my horses go and peacefully let my sheep go.*
> *God of the Heavens, give me many sheep and horses.*
> *God of the Heavens, help me to talk straight.*
> *Goddess of the Earth, my Mother, let me walk straight.*
> *Now all is well, now all is well, now all is well, now all is well.*

Hope and faith were his.

A chief would be born to save the vanishing tribe of Navajos. A bride would rise from a wind—kiss of the lilies in the moonlight.

He drank from the clear, cold spring bubbling from under mossy rocks. He went into the cedars, and the tracks in the trails told him of the visitors of night. His mustangs whistled to him from the ridge-tops, standing clear with heads up and manes flying, and then trooped down through the sage. The shepherd-dogs, guardians of the flocks, barked him a welcome, and the sheep bleated and the lambs pattered round him.

In the hogan by the warm, red fire his women baked his bread and cooked his meat. And he satisfied his hunger. Then he took choice meat to the hogan of a sick relative, and joined in the song and the dance and the prayer that drove away the evil spirit of illness. Down in the valley, in a sandy, sunny place, was his corn-field, and here he turned in the water from the ditch, and worked awhile, and went his contented way.

He loved his people, his women, and his children. To his son he said: "Be bold and brave. Grow like the pine. Work and ride and play that you may be strong. Talk straight. Love your brother. Give half to your friend. Honor your mother that you may honor your wife. Pray and listen to your gods."

Then with his gun and his mustang he climbed the slope of the mountain. He loved the solitude, but he was never alone. There were voices on the wind and steps on his trail. The lofty pine, the lichened rock, the tiny bluebell, the seared crag—all whispered their secrets. For him their spirits spoke. In the morning light Old Stone Face, the mountain, was a red god calling him to the chase. He was a brother of the eagle, at home on the heights where the winds swept and the earth lay revealed below.

In the golden afternoon, with the warm sun on his back and the blue canyon at his feet, he knew the joy of doing nothing. He did not need rest, for he was never tired. The sage-sweet breath of the open was thick in his nostrils, the silence that had so many whisperings was all about him, the loneliness of the wild was his. His falcon eye saw mustang and sheep, the puff of dust down on the cedar level, the Indian riding on a distant ridge, the gray walls, and the blue clefts. Here was home, still free, still wild, still untainted. He saw with the eyes of his ancestors. He felt them around him. They had gone into the elements from which their voices came on the wind. They were the watchers on his trails.

At sunset he faced the west, and this was his prayer:

> *Great Spirit, God of my Fathers,*
> *Keep my horses in the night.*
> *Keep my sheep in the night.*
> *Keep my family in the night.*
> *Let me wake to the day.*
> *Let me be worthy of the light.*
> *Now all is well, now all is well,*
> *Now all is well, now all is well.*

And he watched the sun go down and the gold sink from the peaks and the red die out of the west and the gray shadows creep out of the canyon to meet the twilight and the slow, silent, mysterious approach of night with its gift of stars.

Night fell. The white stars blinked. The wind sighed in the cedars. The sheep bleated. The shepherd-dogs bayed the mourning coyotes. And the Indian lay down in his blankets with his dark face tranquil in the starlight. All was well in his lonely world. Phantoms hovered, illness lingered, injury and pain and death were there, the shadow of a strange white hand flitted across the face of the moon—but now all was well—the Navajo had prayed to the god of his Fathers. Now all was well!

And this, thought Shefford in revolt, was what the white man had killed in the Indian tribes, was reaching out now to kill in this wild remnant of the Navajos. The padre, the trapper, the trader, the prospector, and the missionary—so the white man had come, some of him good, no doubt, but more of him evil; and the young brave learned a thirst that could never be quenched at the cold, sweet spring of his forefathers, and the young maiden burned with a fever in her blood, and lost the sweet, strange, wild fancies of her tribe.

. . .

Joe Lake came to Shefford and said, "Withers told me you had a mix-up with a missionary at Red Lake."

"Yes, I regret to say," replied Shefford.

"About Glen Naspa?"

"Yes, Nas Ta Bega's sister."

"Withers just mentioned it. Who was the missionary?"

"Willetts, so Presbrey, the trader, said."

"What'd he look like?"

Shefford recalled the smooth, brown face, the dark eyes, the weak chin, the mild expression, and the soft, lax figure of the missionary.

"Can't tell by what you said," went on Joe. "But I'll bet a peso to a horse-hair that's the fellow who's been here. Old Hosteen Doetin just told me. First visits he ever had from the priest with the long gown. That's what he called the missionary. These old fellows will never forget what's come down from father to son about the Spanish padres. Well, anyway, Willetts has been here twice after Glen Naspa. The old chap is impressed, but he doesn't want to let the girl go. I'm inclined to think Glen Naspa would as lief go as stay. She may be a Navajo, but she's a girl. She won't talk much."

"Where's Nas Ta Bega?" asked Shefford.

"He rode off somewhere yesterday. Perhaps to the Piute camp. These Indians are slow. They may take a week to pack that load over here. But if Nas Ta Bega or some one doesn't come with a message to-day I'll ride over there myself."

"Joe, what do you think about this missionary?" queried Shefford, bluntly.

"Reckon there's not much to think, unless you see him or find out something. I heard of Willetts before Withers spoke of him. He's friendly with Mormons. I understand he's worked for Mormon interests, someway or other. That's on the quiet. Savvy? This matter of him coming after Glen Naspa, reckon that's all right. The missionaries all go after the young people. What'd be the use to try to convert the old Indians? No, the missionary's work is to educate the Indian, and, of course, the younger he is the better."

"You approve of the missionary?"

"Shefford, if you understood a Mormon you wouldn't ask that. Did you ever read or hear of Jacob Hamblin?... Well, he was a Mormon missionary among the Navajos. The Navajos were as fierce as Apaches till Hamblin worked among them. He made them friendly to the white man."

"That doesn't prove he made converts of them," replied Shefford, still bluntly.

"No. For the matter of that, Hamblin let religion alone. He made presents, then traded with them, then taught them useful knowledge. Mormon or not, Shefford, I'll admit this: a good man, strong with his body, and learned in ways with his hands, with some knowledge of medicine, can better the condition of these Indians. But just as soon as he begins to preach his religion, then his influence wanes. That's natural. These heathen have their ideals, their gods."

"Which the white man should leave them!" replied Shefford, feelingly.

"That's a matter of opinion. But don't let's argue.... Willetts is after Glen Naspa. And if I know Indian girls he'll persuade her to go to his school."

"Persuade her!" Then Shefford broke off and related the incident that had occurred at Red Lake.

"Reckon any means justifies the end," replied Joe, imperturbably. "Let him talk love to her or rope her or beat her, so long as he makes a Christian of her."

Shefford felt a hot flush and had difficulty in controlling himself. From this single point of view the Mormon was impossible to reason with.

"That, too, is a matter of opinion. We won't discuss it," continued Shefford. "But—if old Hosteen Doetin objects to the girl leaving, and if Nas Ta Bega does the same, won't that end the matter?"

"Reckon not. The end of the matter is Glen Naspa. If she wants to go she'll go."

Shefford thought best to drop the discussion. For the first time he had occasion to be repelled by something in this kind and genial Mormon, and he wanted to forget it. Just as he had never talked about men to the sealed wives in the hidden valley, so he could not talk of women to Joe Lake.

Nas Ta Bega did not return that day, but, next morning a messenger came calling Lake to the Piute camp. Shefford spent the morning high on the slope, learning more with every hour in the silence and loneliness, that he was stronger of soul than he had dared to hope, and that the added pain which had come to him could be borne.

Upon his return toward camp, in the cedar grove, he caught sight of Glen Naspa with a white man. They did not see him. When Shefford recognized Willetts an embarrassment as well as an instinct made him halt and step into a bushy, low-branched cedar. It was not his intention to spy on them. He merely wanted to avoid a meeting. But the missionary's hand on the girl's arm, and her up-lifted head, her pretty face, strange, intent, troubled, struck Shefford with an unusual and irresistible curiosity. Willetts was talking earnestly; Glen Naspa was listening intently. Shefford watched long enough to see that the girl loved the missionary, and that he reciprocated or was pretending. His manner scarcely savored of pretense, Shefford concluded, as he slipped away under the trees.

He did not go at once into camp. He felt troubled, and wished that he had not encountered the two. His duty in the matter, of course, was to tell Nas Ta Bega what he had seen. Upon reflection Shefford decided to give the missionary the benefit of a doubt; and if he really cared for the Indian girl, and admitted or betrayed it, to think all the better of him for the fact. Glen Naspa was certainly pretty enough, and probably lovable enough, to please any lonely man in this desert. The pain and the yearning in Shefford's heart made him lenient. He had to fight himself—not to forget, for that was impossible—but to keep rational and sane when a white flower-like face haunted him and a voice called.

The cracking of hard hoofs on stones caused him to turn toward camp, and as he emerged from the cedar grove he saw three Indian horsemen ride into the cleared space before the hogans. They were superbly mounted and well armed, and impressed him as being different from Navajos. Perhaps they were Piutes. They dismounted and led the mustangs down to the pool below the spring. Shefford saw another mustang, standing bridle down and carrying a pack behind the saddle. Some squaws with children hanging behind their skirts were standing at the door of Hosteen Doetin's hogan. Shefford glanced in to see Glen Naspa, pale, quiet, almost sullen. Willetts stood with his hands spread. The old Navajo's seamed face worked convulsively as he tried to lift his bent form to some semblance of dignity, and his voice rolled out, sonorously: "Me no savvy Jesus Christ! Me hungry! ... Me no eat Jesus Christ!"

Shefford drew back as if he had received a blow. That had been Hosteen Doetin's reply to the importunities of the missionary. The old Navajo could work no longer. His sons were gone. His squaw was worn out. He had no one save Glen Naspa to help him. She was young, strong. He was hungry. What was the white man's religion to him?

With long, swift stride Shefford entered the hogan. Willetts, seeing him, did not look so mild as Shefford had him pictured in memory, nor did he appear surprised. Shefford touched Hosteen Doetin's shoulder and said, "Tell me."

The aged Navajo lifted a shaking hand.

"Me no savvy Jesus Christ! Me hungry!... Me no eat Jesus Christ!"

Shefford then made signs that indicated the missionary's intention to take the girl away. "Him come—big talk—Jesus—all Jesus.... Me no want Glen Naspa go," replied the Indian.

Shefford turned to the missionary.

"Willetts, is he a relative of the girl?"

"There's some blood tie, I don't know what. But it's not close," replied Willetts.

"Then don't you think you'd better wait till Nas Ta Bega returns? He's her brother."

"What for?" demanded Willetts. "That Indian may be gone a week. She's willing to accompany the missionary."

Shefford looked at the girl.

"Glen Naspa, do you want to go?"

She was shy, ashamed, and silent, but manifestly willing to accompany the missionary. Shefford pondered a moment. How he hoped Nas Ta Bega would come back! It was thought of the Indian that made Shefford stubborn. What his stand ought to be was hard to define, unless he answered to impulse; and here in the wilds he had become imbued with the idea that his impulses and instincts were no longer false.

"Willetts, what do you want with the girl?" queried Shefford, coolly, and at the question he seemed to find himself. He peered deliberately and searchingly into the other's face. The missionary's gaze shifted and a tinge of red crept up from under his collar.

"Absurd thing to ask a missionary!" he burst out, impatiently.

"Do you care for Glen Naspa?"

"I care as God's disciple—who cares to save the soul of heathen," he replied, with the lofty tone of prayer.

"Has Glen Naspa no—no other interest in you—except to be taught religion?"

The missionary's face flamed, and his violent tremor showed that under his exterior there was a different man.

"What right have you to question me?" he demanded. "You're an adventurer—an outcast. I've my duty here. I'm a missionary with Church and state and government behind me."

"Yes, I'm an outcast," replied Shefford, bitterly. "And you may be all you say. But we're alone now out here on the desert. And this girl's brother is absent. You haven't answered me yet.... Is there anything between you and Glen Naspa except religion?"

"No, you insulting beggar?"

Shefford had forced the reply that he had expected and which damned the missionary beyond any consideration.

"Willetts, you are a liar!" said Shefford, steadily.

"And what are you?" cried Willetts, in shrill fury. "I've heard all about you. Heretic! Atheist! Driven from your Church! Hated and scorned for your blasphemy!"

Then he gave way to ungovernable rage, and cursed Shefford as a religious fanatic might have cursed the most debased sinners. Shefford heard with the blood beating, strangling the pulse in his ears. Somehow this missionary had learned his secret—most likely from the Mormons in Stonebridge. And the terms of disgrace were coals of fire upon Shefford's head. Strangely, however, he did not bow to them, as had been his humble act in the past, when his calumniators had arraigned and flayed him. Passion burned in him now, for the first time in his life, made a tiger of him. And these raw emotions, new to him, were difficult to control.

"You can't take the girl," he replied, when the other had ceased. "Not without her brother's consent."

"I will take her!"

Shefford threw him out of the hogan and strode after him. Willetts had stumbled. When he straightened up he was white and shaken. He groped for the bridle of his horse while keeping his eyes upon Shefford, and when he found it he whirled quickly, mounted, and rode off. Shefford saw him halt a moment under the cedars to speak with the three strange Indians, and then he galloped away. It came to Shefford then that he had been unconscious of the last strained moment of that encounter. He seemed all cold, tight, locked, and was amazed to find his hand on his gun. Verily the wild environment had liberated strange instincts and impulses, which he had answered. That he had no regrets proved how he had changed.

Shefford heard the old woman scolding. Peering into the hogan, he saw Glen Naspa flounce sullenly down, for all the world like any other thwarted girl. Hosteen Doetin came out and pointed down the slope at the departing missionary.

"Heap talk Jesus—all talk—all Jesus!" he exclaimed, contemptuously. Then he gave Shefford a hard rap on the chest. "Small talk—heap man!"

The matter appeared to be adjusted for the present. But Shefford felt that he had made a bitter enemy, and perhaps a powerful one.

He prepared and ate his supper alone that evening, for Joe Lake and Nas Ta Bega did not put in an appearance. He observed that the three strange Indians, whom he took for Piutes, kept to themselves, and, so far as he knew, had no intercourse with any one at the camp. This would not have seemed unusual, considering the taciturn habit of Indians, had he not remembered seeing Willetts speak to the trio. What had he to do with them? Shefford was considering the situation with vague doubts when, to his relief, the three strangers rode off into the twilight. Then he went to bed.

He was awakened by violence. It was the gray hour before dawn. Dark forms knelt over him. A cloth pressed down hard over his mouth: Strong hands bound it while other strong hands held him. He could not cry out. He could not struggle. A heavy weight, evidently a man, held down his feet. Then he was rolled over, securely bound, and carried, to be thrown like a sack over the back of a horse.

All this happened so swiftly as to be bewildering. He was too astounded to be frightened. As he hung head downward he saw the legs of a horse and a dim trail. A stirrup swung to and fro, hitting him in the face. He began to feel exceedingly uncomfortable, with a rush of blood to his head, and cramps in his arms and legs. This kept on and grew worse for what seemed a long time. Then the horse was stopped and a rude hand tumbled him to the ground. Again he was rolled over on his face. Strong fingers plucked at his clothes, and he believed he was being searched. His captors were as silent as if they had been dumb. He felt when they took his pocketbook and his knife and all that he had. Then they cut, tore, and stripped off all his clothing. He was lifted, carried a few steps, and dropped upon what seemed a soft, low mound, and left lying there, still tied and naked. Shefford heard the rustle of sage and the dull thud of hoofs as his assailants went away.

His first sensation was one of immeasurable relief. He had not been murdered. Robbery was nothing. And though roughly handled, he had not been hurt. He associated the assault with the three strange visitors of the preceding day. Still, he had no proof of that. Not the slightest clue remained to help him ascertain who had attacked him.

It might have been a short while or a long one, his mind was so filled with growing conjectures, but a time came when he felt cold. As he lay face down, only his back felt cold at first. He was grateful that he had not been thrown upon the rocks. The ground under him appeared soft, spongy, and gave somewhat as he breathed. He had really sunk down a little in this pile of soft earth. The day was not far off, as he could tell by the brightening of the gray. He began to suffer with the cold, and then slowly he seemed to freeze and grow numb. In an effort to roll over upon his back he discovered that his position, or his being bound, or the numbness of his muscles was responsible for the fact that he could not move. Here was a predicament. It began to look serious. What would a few hours of the powerful sun do to his uncovered skin? Somebody would trail and find him: still, he might not be found soon.

He saw the sky lighten, turn rosy and then gold. The sun shone upon him, but some time elapsed before he felt its warmth. All of a sudden a pain, like a sting, shot through his shoulder. He could not see what caused it; probably a bee. Then he felt another upon his leg, and about simultaneously with it a tiny, fiery stab in his side. A sickening sensation pervaded his body, slowly moving, as if poison had entered the blood of his veins. Then a puncture, as from a hot wire, entered the skin of his breast. Unmistakably it was a bite. By dint of great effort he twisted his head to see a big red ant on his breast. Then he heard a faint sound, so exceedingly faint that he could not tell what it was like. But presently his strained ears detected a low, swift, rustling, creeping sound, like the slipping rattle of an infinite number of tiny bits of moving gravel. Then it was a sound like the seeping of wind-blown sand. Several hot bites occurred at once. And then with his head twisted he saw a red stream of ants pour out of the mound and spill over his quivering flesh.

In an instant he realized his position. He had been dropped intentionally upon an ant-heap, which had sunk with his weight, wedging him between the crusts. At the mercy of those terrible desert ants! A frantic effort to roll out proved futile, as did another and another. His violent muscular contractions infuriated the ants, and in an instant he was writhing in pain so horrible and so unendurable that he nearly fainted. But he was too strong to faint suddenly. A bath of vitriol, a stripping of his skin and red embers of fire thrown upon raw flesh, could not have equaled this. There was fury in the bites and poison in the fangs of these ants. Was this an Indian's brutal trick or was it the missionary's revenge? Shefford realized that it would kill him soon. He sweat what seemed blood, although perhaps the blood came from the bites. A strange, hollow, buzzing roar filled his ears, and it must have been the pouring of the angry ants from their mound.

Then followed a time that was hell—worse than fire, for fire would have given merciful death—agony under which his physical being began spasmodically to jerk and retch—and his eyeballs turned and his breast caved in.

A cry rang through the roar in his ears. "Bi Nai! Bi Nai!"

His fading sight seemed to shade round the dark face of Nas Ta Bega.

Then powerful hands dragged him from the mound, through the grass and sage, rolled him over and over, and brushed his burning skin with strong, swift sweep.

𝔰𝔩 9 𝔰𝔩

IN THE DESERT CRUCIBLE

THAT HARD EXPERIENCE was but the beginning of many cruel trials for John Shefford.

He never knew who his assailants were, nor their motive other than robbery; and they had gotten little, for they had not found the large sum of money sewed in the lining of his coat. Joe Lake declared it was Shadd's work, and the Mormon showed the stern nature that lay hidden under his mild manner. Nas Ta Bega shook his head and would not tell what he thought. But a somber fire burned in his eyes.

The three started with a heavily laden pack-train and went down the mountain slope into West canyon. The second day they were shot at from the rim of the walls. Lake was wounded, hindering the swift flight necessary to escape deeper into the canyon. Here they hid for days, while the Mormon recovered and the Indian took stealthy trips to try to locate the enemy. Lack of water and grass for the burros drove them on. They climbed out of a side canyon, losing several burros on a rough trail, and had proceeded to within half a day's journey of Red Lake when they were attacked while making camp in a cedar grove. Shefford sustained an exceedingly painful injury to his leg, but, fortunately, the bullet went through without breaking a bone. With that burning pain there came to Shefford the meaning of fight, and his rifle grew hot in his hands. Night alone saved the trio from certain fatality. Under the cover of darkness the Indian helped Shefford to escape. Joe Lake looked out for himself. The pack-train was lost, and the mustangs, except Nack-yal.

Shefford learned what it meant to lie out at night, listening for pursuit, cold to his marrow, sick with dread, and enduring frightful pain from a ragged bullet-hole. Next day the Indian led him down into the red basin, where the sun shone hot and the sand reflected the heat. They had no water. A wind arose and the valley became a place of flying sand. Through a heavy, stifling pall Nas Ta Bega somehow got Shefford to the trading-post at Red Lake. Presbrey attended to Shefford's injury and made him comfortable. Next day Joe Lake limped in, surly and somber, with the news that Shadd and eight or ten of his outlaw gang had gotten away with the pack-train.

In short time Shefford was able to ride, and with his companions went over the pass to

Kayenta. Withers already knew of his loss, and all he said was that he hoped to meet Shadd some day.

Shefford showed a reluctance to go again to the hidden village in the silent canyon with the rounded walls. The trader appeared surprised, but did not press the point. And Shefford meant sooner or later to tell him, yet never quite reached the point. The early summer brought more work for the little post, and Shefford toiled with the others. He liked the outdoor tasks, and at night was grateful that he was too tired to think. Then followed trips to Durango and Bluff and Monticello. He rode fifty miles a day for many days. He knew how a man fares who packs light and rides far and fast. When the Indian was with him he got along well, but Nas Ta Bega would not go near the towns. Thus many mishaps were Shefford's fortune.

Many and many a mile he trailed his mustang, for Nack-yal never forgot the Sagi, and always headed for it when he broke his hobbles. Shefford accompanied an Indian teamster in to Durango with a wagon and four wild mustangs. Upon the return, with a heavy load of supplies, accident put Shefford in charge of the outfit. In despair he had to face the hardest task that could have been given him—to take care of a crippled Indian, catch, water, feed, harness, and drive four wild mustangs that did not know him and tried to kill him at every turn, and to get that precious load of supplies home to Kayenta. That he accomplished it proved to hint the possibilities of a man, for both endurance and patience. From that time he never gave up in the front of any duty.

In the absence of an available Indian he rode to Durango and back in record time. Upon one occasion he was lost in a canyon for days, with no food and little water. Upon another he went through a sand-storm in the open desert, facing it for forty miles and keeping to the trail; When he rode in to Kayenta that night the trader, in grim praise, said there was no worse to endure. At Monticello Shefford stood off a band of desperadoes, and this time Shefford experienced a strange, sickening shock in the wounding of a man. Later he had other fights, but in none of them did he know whether or not he had shed blood.

The heat of midsummer came, when the blistering sun shone, and a hot blast blew across the sand, and the furious storms made floods in the washes. Day and night Shefford was always in the open, and any one who had ever known him in the past would have failed to recognize him now.

In the early fall, with Nas Ta Bega as companion, he set out to the south of Kayenta upon long-neglected business of the trader. They visited Red Lake, Blue canyon, Keams canyon, Oribi, the Moki villages, Tuba, Moencopie, and Moen Ave. This trip took many weeks and gave Shefford all the opportunity he wanted to study the Indians, and the conditions nearer to the border of civilization. He learned the truth about the Indians and the missionaries.

Upon the return trip he rode over the trail he had followed alone to Red Lake and thence on to the Sagi, and it seemed that years had passed since he first entered this wild region which had come to be home, years that had molded him in the stern and fiery crucible of the desert.

STONEBRIDGE

In October Shefford arranged for a hunt in the Cresaw Mountains with Joe Lake and Nas Ta Bega. The Indian had gone home for a short visit, and upon his return the party expected to start. But Nas Ta Bega did not come back. Then the arrival of a Piute with news that excited Withers and greatly perturbed Lake convinced Shefford that something was wrong.

The little trading-post seldom saw such disorder; certainly Shefford had never known the trader to neglect work. Joe Lake threw a saddle on a mustang he would have scorned to notice in an ordinary moment, and without a word of explanation or farewell rode hard to the north on the Stonebridge trail.

Shefford had long since acquired patience. He was curious, but he did not care particularly what was in the wind. However, when Withers came out and sent an Indian to drive up the horses Shefford could not refrain from a query.

"I hate to tell you," replied the trader.

"Go on," added Shefford, quickly.

"Did I tell you about the government sending a Supreme Court judge out to Utah to prosecute the polygamists?"

"No," replied Shefford.

"I forgot to, I reckon. You've been away a lot. Well, there's been hell up in Utah for six months. Lately this judge and his men have worked down into southern Utah. He visited Bluff and Monticello a few weeks ago.... Now what do you think?"

"Withers! Is he coming to Stonebridge?"

"He's there now. Some one betrayed the whereabouts of the hidden village over in the canyon. All the women have been arrested and taken to Stonebridge. The trial begins to-day."

"Arrested!" echoed Shefford, blankly. "Those poor, lonely, good women? What on earth for?"

"Sealed wives!" exclaimed Withers, tersely. "This judge is after the polygamists. They say he's absolutely relentless."

"But—women can't be polygamists. Their husbands are the ones wanted."

"Sure. But the prosecutors have got to find the sealed wives—the second wives—to find the law-breaking husbands. That'll be a job, or I don't know Mormons.... Are you going to ride over to Stonebridge with me?"

Shefford shrank at the idea. Months of toil and pain and travail had not been enough to make him forget the strange girl he had loved. But he had remembered only at poignant intervals, and the lapse of time had made thought of her a dream like that sad dream which had lured him into the desert. With the query of the trader came a bitter-sweet regret.

"Better come with me," said Withers. "Have you forgotten the Sago Lily? She'll be put on trial.... That girl—that child!... Shefford, you know she hasn't any friends. And now no Mormon man are protect her, for fear of prosecution."

"I'll go," replied Shefford, shortly.

The Indian brought up the horses. Nack-yal was thin from his long travel during the hot summer, but he was as hard as iron, and the way he pointed his keen nose toward the Sagi showed how he wanted to make for the upland country, with its clear springs and valleys of grass. Withers mounted his bay and with a hurried farewell to his wife spurred the mustang into the trail. Shefford took time to get his weapons and the light pack he always carried, and then rode out after the trader.

The pace Withers set was the long, steady lope to which these Indian mustangs had been trained all their lives. In an hour they reached the mouth of the Sagi, and at sight of it it seemed to Shefford that the hard half-year of suffering since he had been there had disappeared. Withers, to Shefford's regret, did not enter the Sagi. He turned off to the north and took a wild trail into a split of the red wall, and wound in and out, and climbed a crack so narrow that the light was obscured and the cliffs could be reached from both sides of a horse.

Once up on the wild plateau, Shefford felt again in a different world from the barren desert he had lately known. The desert had crucified him and had left him to die or survive, according to his spirit and his strength. If he had loved the glare, the endless level, the deceiving distance, the shifting sand, it had certainly not been as he loved this softer, wilder, more intimate upland. With the red peaks shining up into the blue, and the fragrance of cedar and pinon, and the purple sage and flowers and grass and splash of clear water over stones—with these there came back to him something that he had lost and which had haunted him.

It seemed he had returned to this wild upland of color and canyon and lofty crags and green valleys and silent places with a spirit gained from victory over himself in the harsher and sterner desert below. And, strange to him, he found his old self, the dreamer, the artist, the lover of beauty, the searcher for he knew not what, come to meet him on the fragrant wind.

He felt this, saw the old wildness with glad eyes, yet the greater part of his mind was given over to the thought of the unfortunate women he expected to see in Stonebridge.

Withers was harder to follow, to keep up with, than an Indian. For one thing he was a steady and tireless rider, and for another there were times when he had no mercy on a horse. Then an Indian always found easier steps in a trail and shorter cuts. Withers put his mount to some bad slopes, and Shefford had no choice but to follow. But they crossed the great broken bench of upland without mishap, and came out upon a promontory of a plateau from which Shefford saw a wide valley and the dark-green alfalfa fields of Stonebridge.

Stonebridge lay in the center of a fertile valley surrounded by pink cliffs. It must have been a very old town, certainly far older than Bluff or Monticello, though smaller, and evidently it had been built to last. There was one main street, very wide, that divided the town and was crossed at right angles by a stream spanned by a small natural stone bridge. A line of poplar-trees shaded each foot-path. The little log cabins and stone houses and cottages were half hidden in foliage now tinted with autumn colors. Toward the center of the town the houses and stores and shops fronted upon the street and along one side of a green square, or plaza. Here were situated several edifices, the most prominent of which was a church built of wood, whitewashed, and remarkable, according to Withers, for the fact that not a nail had been used in its construction. Beyond the church was a large, low structure of stone, with a split-shingle roof, and evidently this was the town hall.

Shefford saw, before he reached the square, that this day in Stonebridge was one of singular action and excitement for a Mormon village. The town was full of people and, judging from the horses hitched everywhere and the big canvas-covered wagons, many of the people were visitors. A crowd surrounded the hall—a dusty, booted, spurred, shirt-sleeved and sombreroed assemblage that did not wear the hall-mark Shefford had come to associate with Mormons. They were riders, cowboys, horse-wranglers, and some of them Shefford had seen in Durango. Navajos and Piutes were present, also, but they loitered in the background.

Withers drew Shefford off to the side where, under a tree, they hitched their horses.

"Never saw Stonebridge full of a riffraff gang like this to-day," said Withers. "I'll bet the Mormons are wild. There's a tough outfit from Durango. If they can get anything to drink—or if they've got it—Stonebridge will see smoke to-day!... Come on. I'll get in that hall."

But before Withers reached the hall he started violently and pulled up short, then, with apparent unconcern, turned to lay a hand upon Shefford. The trader's face had blanched and his eyes grew hard and shiny, like flint. He gripped Shefford's arm.

"Look! Over to your left!" he whispered. "See that gang of Indians there—by the big wagon. See the short Indian with the chaps. He's got a face big as a ham, dark, fierce. That's Shadd!... You ought to know him. Shadd and his outfit here! How's that for nerve? But he pulls a rein with the Mormons."

Shefford's keen eye took in a lounging group of ten or twelve Indians and several white men. They did not present any great contrast to the other groups except that they were isolated, appeared quiet and watchful, and were all armed. A bunch of lean, racy mustangs, restive and spirited, stood near by in charge of an Indian. Shefford had to take a second and closer glance to distinguish the half-breed. At once he recognized in Shadd the broad-faced squat Indian who had paid him a threatening visit that night long ago in the mouth of the Sagi. A fire ran along Shefford's veins and seemed to concentrate in his breast. Shadd's dark, piercing eyes alighted upon Shefford and rested there. Then the half-breed spoke to one of his white outlaws and pointed at Shefford. His action attracted the attention of others in the gang, and for a moment Shefford and Withers were treated to a keen-eyed stare.

The trader cursed low. "Maybe I wouldn't like to mix it with that damned breed," he said. "But what chance have we with that gang? Besides, we're here on other and more important business. All the same, before I forget, let me remind you that Shadd has had you spotted ever since you came out here. A friendly Piute told me only lately. Shefford, did any Indian between here and Flagstaff ever see that bunch of money you persist in carrying?"

"Why, yes, I suppose so—'way back in Tuba, when I first came out," replied Shefford.

"Huh! Well, Shadd's after that.... Come on now, let's get inside the hall."

The crowd opened for the trader, who appeared to be known to everybody.

A huge man with a bushy beard blocked the way to a shut door.

"Hello, Meade!" said Withers. "Let us in."

The man opened the door, permitted Withers and Shefford to enter, and then closed it.

Shefford, coming out of the bright glare of sun into the hall, could not see distinctly at first. His eyes blurred. He heard a subdued murmur of many voices. Withers appeared to be affected with the same kind of blindness, for he stood bewildered a moment. But he recovered sooner than Shefford. Gradually the darkness shrouding many obscure forms lifted. Withers drew him through a crowd of men and women to one side of the hall, and squeezed along a wall to a railing where progress was stopped.

Then Shefford raised his head to look with bated breath and strange curiosity.

The hall was large and had many windows. Men were in consultation upon a platform. Women to the number of twenty sat close together upon benches. Back of them stood another crowd. But the women on the benches held Shefford's gaze. They were the prisoners. They made a somber group. Some were hooded, some veiled, all clad in dark garments except one on the front bench, and she was dressed in white. She wore a long hood that concealed her face. Shefford recognized the hood and then the slender shape. She was Mary—she whom her jealous neighbors had named the Sago Lily. At sight of her a sharp pain pierced Shefford's breast. His eyes were blurred when he forced them away from her, and it took a moment for him to see clearly.

Withers was whispering to him or to some one near at hand, but Shefford did not catch the meaning of what was said. He paid more attention; however, Withers ceased speaking. Shefford gazed upon the crowd back of him. The women were hooded and it was not possible to see what they looked like. There were many stalwart, clean-cut, young Mormons of Joe Lake's type, and these men appeared troubled, even distressed and at a loss. There was little about them resembling the stern, quiet, somber austerity of the more matured men, and nothing at all of the strange, aloof, serene impassiveness of the gray-bearded old patriarchs. These venerable men were the Mormons of the old school, the sons of the pioneers, the ruthless fanatics. Instinctively Shefford felt that it was in them that polygamy was embodied; they were the husbands of the sealed wives. He conceived an absorbing curiosity to learn if his instinct was correct; and hard upon that followed a hot, hateful eagerness to see which one was the husband of Mary.

"There's Bishop Kane," whispered Withers, nudging Shefford. "And there's Waggoner with him."

Shefford saw the bishop, and then beside him a man of striking presence.

"Who's Waggoner?" asked Shefford, as he looked.

"He owns more than any Mormon in southern Utah," replied the trader. "He's the biggest man in Stonebridge, that's sure. But I don't know his relation to the Church. They don't call him elder or bishop. But I'll bet he's some pumpkins. He never had any use for me or any Gentile. A close-fisted, tight-lipped Mormon—a skinflint if I ever saw one! Just look him over."

Shefford had been looking, and considered it unlikely that he would ever forget this individual called Waggoner. He seemed old, sixty at least, yet at that only in the prime of a wonderful physical life. Unlike most of the others, he wore his grizzled beard close-cropped, so close that it showed the lean, wolfish line of his jaw. All his features were of striking sharpness. His eyes, of a singularly brilliant blue, were yet cold and pale. The brow had a serious, thoughtful cast; long furrows sloped down the cheeks. It was a strange, secretive face, full of a power that Shefford had not seen in another man's, full of intelligence and thought that had not been used as Shefford had known them used among men. The face mystified him. It had so much more than the strange aloofness so characteristic of his fellows.

"Waggoner had five wives and fifty-five children before the law went into effect," whispered Withers. "Nobody knows and nobody will ever know how many he's got now. That's my private opinion."

Somehow, after Withers told that, Shefford seemed to understand the strange power in Waggoner's face. Absolutely it was not the force, the strength given to a man from his years of control of men. Shefford, long schooled now in his fair-mindedness, fought down the feelings of other years, and waited with patience. Who was he to judge Waggoner or any other Mormon? But whenever his glance strayed back to the quiet, slender form in white, when he realized again and again the appalling nature of this court, his heart beat heavy and labored within his breast.

Then a bustle among the men upon the platform appeared to indicate that proceedings were about to begin. Some men left the platform; several sat down at a table upon which were books and papers, and others remained standing. These last were all roughly garbed, in riding-boots and spurs, and Shefford's keen eye detected the bulge of hidden weapons. They looked like deputy-marshals upon duty.

Somebody whispered that the judge's name was Stone. The name fitted him. He was not young, and looked a man suited to the prosecution of these secret Mormons. He had a ponderous brow, a deep, cavernous eye that emitted gleams but betrayed no color or expression. His mouth was the saving human feature of his stony face.

Shefford took the man upon the judge's right hand to be a lawyer, and the one on his left an officer of court, perhaps a prosecuting attorney. Presently this fellow pounded upon the table and stood up as if to address a court-room. Certainly he silenced that hallful of people. Then he perfunctorily and briefly stated that certain women had been arrested upon suspicion of being sealed wives of Mormon polygamists, and were to be herewith tried by a judge of the United States Court. Shefford felt how the impressive words affected that silent hall of listeners, but he gathered from the brief preliminaries that the trial could not be otherwise than a crude, rapid investigation, and perhaps for that the more sinister.

The first woman on the foremost bench was led forward by a deputy to a vacant chair on the platform just in front of the judge's table. She was told to sit down, and showed no sign that she had heard. Then the judge courteously asked her to take the chair. She refused. And Stone nodded his head as if he had experienced that sort of thing before. He stroked his chin wearily, and Shefford conceived an idea that he was a kind man, if he was a relentless judge.

"Please remove your veil," requested the prosecutor.

The woman did so, and proved to be young and handsome. Shefford had a thrill as he recognized her. She was Ruth, who had been one of his best-known acquaintances in the hidden village. She was pale, angry, almost sullen, and her breast heaved. She had no shame, but she seemed to be outraged. Her dark eyes, scornful and blazing, passed over the judge and his assistants, and on to the crowd behind the railing. Shefford, keen as a blade, with all his faculties absorbed, fancied he saw Ruth stiffen and change slightly as her glance encountered some one in that crowd. Then the prosecutor in deliberate and chosen words enjoined her to kiss the Bible handed to her and swear to tell the truth. How strange for Shefford to see her kiss the book which he had studied for so many years! Stranger still to hear the low murmur from the listening audience as she took the oath!

"What is your name?" asked Judge Stone, leaning back and fixing the cavernous eyes upon her.

"Ruth Jones," was the cool reply.

"How old are you?"

"Twenty."

"Where were you born?" went on the judge. He allowed time for the clerk to record her answers.

"Panguitch, Utah."

"Were your parents Mormons?"

"Yes."

"Are you a Mormon?"

"Yes."

"Are you a married woman?"

"No."

The answer was instant, cold, final. It seemed to the truth. Almost Shefford believed she spoke truth. The judge stroked his chin and waited a moment, and then hesitatingly he went on.

"Have you—any children?"

"No." And the blazing eyes met the cavernous ones.

That about the children was true enough, Shefford thought, and he could have testified to it.

"You live in the hidden village near this town?"

"Yes."

"What is the name of this village?"

"It has none."

"Did you ever hear of Fre-donia, another village far west of here?"

"Yes."

"It is in Arizona, near the Utah line. There are few men there. Is it the same kind of village as this one in which you live?"

"Yes."

"What does Fre-donia mean? The name—has it any meaning?"

"It means free women."

The judge maintained silence for a moment, turned to whisper to his assistants, and presently, without glancing up, said to the woman:

"That will do."

Ruth was led back to the bench, and the woman next to her brought forward. This was a heavier person, with the figure and step of a matured woman. Upon removing her bonnet she showed the plain face of a woman of forty, and it was striking only in that strange, stony aloofness noted in the older men. Here, Shefford thought, was the real Mormon, different in a way he could not define from Ruth. This woman seated herself in the chair and calmly faced her prosecutors. She manifested no emotion whatever. Shefford remembered her and could not see any change in her deportment. This trial appeared to be of little moment to her and she took the oath as if doing so had been a habit all her life.

"What is your name?" asked Judge Stone, glancing up from a paper he held.

"Mary Danton."

"Family or married name?"

"My husband's name was Danton."

"Was. Is he living?"

"No."

"Where did you live when you were married to him?"

"In St. George, and later here in Stonebridge."

"You were both Mormons?"

"Yes."

"Did you have any children by him?"

"Yes."

"How many?"

"Two."

"Are they living?"

"One of them is living."

Judge Stone bent over his paper and then slowly raised his eyes to her face.

"Are you married now?"

"No."

Again the judge consulted his notes, and held a whispered colloquy with the two men at his table.

"Mrs. Danton, when you were arrested there were five children found in your home. To whom do they belong?"

"Me."

"Are you their mother?"

"Yes."

"Your husband Danton is the father of only one, the eldest, according to your former statement. Is that correct?"

"Yes."

"Who, then, is the father—or who are the fathers, of your other children?"

"I do not know."

She said it with the most stony-faced calmness, with utter disregard of what significance her words had. A strong, mystic wall of cold flint insulated her. Strangely it came to Shefford how impossible either to doubt or believe her. Yet he did both! Judge Stone showed a little heat.

"You don't know the father of one or all of these children?" he queried, with sharp rising inflection of voice.

"I do not."

"Madam, I beg to remind you that you are under oath."

The woman did not reply.

"These children are nameless, then—illegitimate?"

"They are."

"You swear you are not the sealed wife of some Mormon?"

"I swear."

"How do you live—maintain yourself?"

"I work."

"What at?"

"I weave, sew, bake, and work in my garden."

"My men made note of your large and comfortable cabin, even luxurious, considering this country. How is that?"

"My husband left me comfortable."

Judge Stone shook a warning finger at the defendant.

"Suppose I were to sentence you to jail for perjury? For a year? Far from your home and children! Would you speak—tell the truth?"

"I am telling the truth. I can't speak what I don't know.... Send me to jail."

Baffled, with despairing, angry impatience, Judge Stone waved the woman away.

"That will do for her. Fetch the next one," he said.

One after another he examined three more women, and arrived, by various questions and

ZANE GREY

answers different in tone and temper, at precisely the same point as had been made in the case of Mrs. Danton. Thereupon the proceedings rested a few moments while the judge consulted with his assistants.

Shefford was grateful for this respite. He had been worked up to an unusual degree of interest, and now, as the next Mormon woman to be examined was she whom he had loved and loved still, he felt rise in him emotion that threatened to make him conspicuous unless it could be hidden. The answers of these Mormon women had been not altogether unexpected by him, but once spoken in cold blood under oath, how tragic, how appallingly significant of the shadow, the mystery, the yoke that bound them! He was amazed, saddened. He felt bewildered. He needed to think out the meaning of the falsehoods of women he knew to be good and noble. Surely religion, instead of fear and loyalty, was the foundation and the strength of this disgrace, this sacrifice. Absolutely, shame was not in these women, though they swore to shameful facts. They had been coached to give these baffling answers, every one of which seemed to brand them, not the brazen mothers of illegitimate offspring, but faithful, unfortunate sealed wives. To Shefford the truth was not in their words, but it sat upon their somber brows.

Was it only his heightened imagination, or did the silence and the suspense grow more intense when a deputy led that dark-hooded, white-clad, slender woman to the defendant's chair? She did not walk with the poise that had been manifest in the other women, and she sank into the chair as if she could no longer stand.

"Please remove your hood," requested the prosecutor.

How well Shefford remembered the strong, shapely hands! He saw them tremble at the knot of ribbon, and that tremor was communicated to him in a sympathy which made his pulses beat. He held his breath while she removed the hood. And then there was revealed, he thought, the loveliest and the most tragic face that ever was seen in a court-room.

A low, whispering murmur that swelled like a wave ran through the hall. And by it Shefford divined, as clearly as if the fact had been blazoned on the walls, that Mary's face had been unknown to these villagers. But the name Sago Lily had not been unknown; Shefford heard it whispered on all sides.

The murmuring subsided. The judge and his assistants stared at Mary. As for Shefford, there was no need of his personal feeling to make the situation dramatic. Not improbably Judge Stone had tried many Mormon women. But manifestly this one was different. Unhooded, Mary appeared to be only a young girl, and a court, confronted suddenly with her youth and the suspicion attached to her, could not but have been shocked. Then her beauty made her seem, in that somber company, indeed the white flower for which she had been named. But, more likely, it was her agony that bound the court into silence which grew painful. Perhaps the thought that flashed into Shefford's mind was telepathic; it seemed to him that every watcher there realized that in this defendant the judge had a girl of softer mold, of different spirit, and from her the bitter truth could be wrung.

Mary faced the court and the crowd on that side of the platform. Unlike the other women, she did not look at or seem to see any one behind the railing. Shefford was absolutely sure there was not a man or a woman who caught her glance. She gazed afar, with eyes strained, humid, fearful.

When the prosecutor swore her to the oath her lips were seen to move, but no one heard her speak.

"What is your name?" asked the judge.

"Mary." Her voice was low, with a slight tremor.

"What's your other name?"

472

"I won't tell."

Her singular reply, the tones of her voice, her manner before the judge, marked her with strange simplicity. It was evident that she was not accustomed to questions.

"What were your parents' names?"

"I won't tell," she replied, very low.

Judge Stone did not press the point. Perhaps he wanted to make the examination as easy as possible for her or to wait till she showed more composure.

"Were your parents Mormons?" he went on.

"No, sir." She added the sir with a quaint respect, contrasting markedly with the short replies of the women before her.

"Then you were not born a Mormon?"

"No, sir."

"How old are you?"

"Seventeen or eighteen. I'm not sure."

"You don't know your exact age?"

"No."

"Where were you born?"

"I won't tell."

"Was it in Utah?"

"Yes, sir."

"How long have you lived in this state?"

"Always—except last year."

"And that's been over in the hidden village where you were arrested?"

"Yes."

"But you often visited here—this town Stonebridge?"

"I never was here—till yesterday."

Judge Stone regarded her as if his interest as a man was running counter to his duty as an officer. Suddenly he leaned forward.

"Are you a Mormon NOW?" he queried, forcibly.

"No, sir," she replied, and here her voice rose a little clearer.

It was an unexpected reply. Judge Stone stared at her. The low buzz ran through the listening crowd. And as for Shefford, he was astounded. When his wits flashed back and he weighed her words and saw in her face truth as clear as light, he had the strangest sensation of joy. Almost it flooded away the gloom and pain that attended this ordeal.

The judge bent his head to his assistants as if for counsel. All of them were eager where formerly they had been weary. Shefford glanced around at the dark and somber faces, and a slow wrath grew within him. Then he caught a glimpse of Waggoner. The steel-blue, piercing intensity of the Mormon's gaze impressed him at a moment when all that older generation of Mormons looked as hard and immutable as iron. Either Shefford was over-excited and mistaken or the hour had become fraught with greater suspense. The secret, the mystery, the power, the hate, the religion of a strange people were thick and tangible in that hall. For Shefford the feeling of the presence of Withers on his left was entirely different from that of the Mormon on his other side. If there was not a shadow there, then the sun did not shine so brightly as it had shone when he entered. The air seemed clogged with nameless passion.

"I gather that you've lived mostly in the country—away from people?" the judge began.

"Yes, sir," replied the girl.

"Do you know anything about the government of the United States?"

"No, sir."

He pondered again, evidently weighing his queries, leading up to the fatal and inevitable question.

Still, his interest in this particular defendant had become visible.

"Have you any idea of the consequences of perjury?"

"No, sir."

"Do you understand what perjury is?"

"It's to lie."

"Do you tell lies?"

"No, sir."

"Have you ever told a single lie?"

"Not—yet," she replied, almost whispering.

It was the answer of a child and affected the judge. He fussed with his papers. Perhaps his task was not easy; certainly it was not pleasant. Then he leaned forward again and fixed those deep, cavernous eyes upon the sad face.

"Do you understand what a sealed wife is?"

"I've never been told."

"But you know there are sealed wives in Utah?"

"Yes, sir; I've been told that."

Judge Stone halted there, watching her. The hall was silent except for faint rustlings and here and there deep breaths drawn guardedly. The vital question hung like a sword over the white-faced girl. Perhaps she divined its impending stroke, for she sat like a stone with dilating, appealing eyes upon her executioner.

"Are you a sealed wife?" he flung at her.

She could not answer at once. She made effort, but the words would not come. He flung the question again, sternly.

"No!" she cried.

And then there was silence. That poignant word quivered in Shefford's heart. He believed it was a lie. It seemed he would have known it if this hour was the first in which he had ever seen the girl. He heard, he felt, he sensed the fatal thing. The beautiful voice had lacked some quality before present. And the thing wanting was something subtle, an essence, a beautiful ring—the truth. What a hellish thing to make that pure girl a liar—a perjurer! The heat deep within Shefford kindled to fire.

"You are not married?" went on Judge Stone.

"No, sir," she answered, faintly.

"Have you ever been married?"

"No, sir."

"Do you expect ever to be married?"

"Oh! No, sir."

She was ashen pale now, quivering all over, with her strong hands clasping the black hood, and she could no longer meet the judge's glance.

"Have you—any—any children?" the judge asked, haltingly. It was a hard question to get out.

"No."

Judge Stone leaned far over the table, and that his face was purple showed Shefford he was a man. His big fist clenched.

"Girl, you're not going to swear you, too, were visited—over there by men... You're not going to swear that?"

"Oh—no, sir!"

Judge Stone settled back in his chair, and while he wiped his moist face that same foreboding murmur, almost a menace, moaned through the hall.

Shefford was sick in his soul and afraid of himself. He did not know this spirit that flamed up in him. His helplessness was a most hateful fact.

"Come—confess you are a sealed wife," called her interrogator.

She maintained silence, but shook her head.

Suddenly he seemed to leap forward.

"Unfortunate child! Confess."

That forced her to lift her head and face him, yet still she did not speak. It was the strength of despair. She could not endure much more.

"Who is your husband?" he thundered at her.

She rose wildly, terror-stricken. It was terror that dominated her, not of the stern judge, for she took a faltering step toward him, lifting a shaking hand, but of some one or of some thing far more terrible than any punishment she could have received in the sentence of a court. Still she was not proof against the judge's will. She had weakened, and the terror must have been because of that weakening.

"Who is the Mormon who visits you?" he thundered, relentlessly.

"I—never—knew—his—name.

"But you'd know his face. I'll arrest every Mormon in this country and bring him before you. You'd know his face?"

"Oh, I wouldn't. I COULDN'T TELL!... I—NEVER—SAW HIS FACE—IN THE LIGHT!"

The tragic beauty of her, the certainty of some monstrous crime to youth and innocence, the presence of an agony and terror that unfathomably seemed not to be for herself—these transfixed the court and the audience, and held them silenced, till she reached out blindly and then sank in a heap to the floor.

✣ II ✣

AFTER THE TRIAL

SHEFFORD MIGHT HAVE LEAPED over the railing but for Withers's restraining hand, and when there appeared to be some sign of kindness in those other women for the unconscious girl Shefford squeezed through the crowd and got out of the hall.

The gang outside that had been denied admittance pressed upon Shefford, with jest and curious query, and a good nature that jarred upon him. He was far from gentle as he jostled off the first importuning fellows; the others, gaping at him, opened a lane for him to pass through.

Then there was a hand laid on his shoulder that he did not shake off. Nas Ta Bega loomed dark and tall beside him. Neither the trader nor Joe Lake nor any white man Shefford had met influenced him as this Navajo.

"Nas Ta Bega! you here, too. I guess the whole country is here. We waited at Kayenta. What kept you so long?"

The Indian, always slow to answer, did not open his lips till he drew Shefford apart from the noisy crowd.

"Bi Nai, there is sorrow in the hogan of Hosteen Doetin," he said.

"Glen Naspa!" exclaimed Shefford.

"My sister is gone from the home of her brother. She went away alone in the summer."

"Blue canyon! She went to the missionary. Nas Ta Bega, I thought I saw her there. But I wasn't sure. I didn't want to make sure. I was afraid it might be true."

"A brave who loved my sister trailed her there."

"Nas Ta Bega, will you—will we go find her, take her home?"

"No. She will come home some day."

What bitter sadness and wisdom in his words!

"But, my friend, that damned missionary—" began Shefford, passionately. The Indian had met him at a bad hour.

"Willetts is here. I saw him go in there," interrupted Nas Ta Bega, and he pointed to the hall.

"Here! He gets around a good deal," declared Shefford. "Nas Ta Bega, what are you going to do to him?"

The Indian held his peace and there was no telling from his inscrutable face what might be in his mind. He was dark, impassive. He seemed a wise and bitter Indian, beyond any savagery of his tribe, and the suffering Shefford divined was deep.

"He'd better keep out of my sight," muttered Shefford, more to himself than to his companion.

"The half-breed is here," said Nas Ta Bega.

"Shadd? Yes, we saw him. There! He's still with his gang. Nas Ta Bega, what are they up to?"

"They will steal what they can."

"Withers says Shadd is friendly with the Mormons."

"Yes, and with the missionary, too."

"With Willetts?"

"I saw them talk together—strong talk."

"Strange. But maybe it's not so strange. Shadd is known well in Monticello and Bluff. He spends money there. They are afraid of him, but he's welcome just the same. Perhaps everybody knows him. It'd be like him to ride into Kayenta. But, Nas Ta Bega, I've got to look out for him, because Withers says he's after me."

"Bi Nai wears a scar that is proof," said the Indian.

"Then it must be he found out long ago I had a little money."

"It might be. But, Bi Nai, the half-breed has a strange step on your trail."

"What do you mean?" demanded Shefford.

"Nas Ta Bega cannot tell what he does not know," replied the Navajo. "Let that be. We shall know some day. Bi Nai, there is sorrow to tell that is not the Indian's.... Sorrow for my brother!"

Shefford lifted his eyes to the Indian's, and if he did not see sadness there he was much deceived.

"Bi Nai, long ago you told a story to the trader. Nas Ta Bega sat before the fire that night. You did not know he could understand your language. He listened. And he learned what brought you to the country of the Indian. That night he made you his brother.... All his lonely rides into the canyon have been to find the little golden-haired child, the lost girl—Fay Larkin.... Bi Nai, I have found the girl you wanted for your sweetheart."

Shefford was bereft of speech. He could not see steadily, and the last solemn words of the Indian seemed far away.

"Bi Nai, I have found Fay Larkin," repeated Nas Ta Bega.

"Fay Larkin!" gasped Shefford, shaking his head. "But—she's dead."

"It would be less sorrow for Bi Nai if she were dead."

Shefford clutched at the Indian. There was something terrible to be revealed. Like an aspen-leaf in the wind he shook all over. He divined the revelation—divined the coming blow—but that was as far as his mind got.

"She's in there," said the Indian, pointing toward hall.

"Fay Larkin?" whispered Shefford.

"Yes, Bi Nai."

"My God! HOW do you know? Oh, I could have seen. I've been blind. ... Tell me, Indian. Which one?"

"Fay Larkin is the Sago Lily."

• • •

Shefford strode away into a secluded corner of the Square, where in the shade and quiet of the trees he suffered a storm of heart and mind. During that short or long time—he had no idea how long—the Indian remained with him. He never lost the feeling of Nas Ta Bega close beside him. When the period of acute pain left him and some order began to replace the tumult in his mind he felt in Nas Ta Bega the same quality—silence or strength or help—that he had learned to feel in the deep canyon and the lofty crags. He realized then that the Indian was indeed a brother. And Shefford needed him. What he had to fight was more fatal than suffering and love—it was hate rising out of the unsuspected dark gulf of his heart—the instinct to kill—the murder in his soul. Only now did he come to understand Jane Withersteen's tragic story and the passion of Venters and what had made Lassiter a gun-man. The desert had transformed Shefford. The elements had entered into his muscle and bone, into the very fiber of his heart. Sun, wind, sand, cold, storm, space, stone, the poison cactus, the racking toil, the terrible loneliness—the iron of the desert man, the cruelty of the desert savage, the wildness of the mustang, the ferocity of hawk and wolf, the bitter struggle of every surviving thing—these were as if they had been melted and merged together and now made a dark and passionate stream that was his throbbing blood. He realized what he had become and gloried in it, yet there, looking on with grave and earnest eyes, was his old self, the man of reason, of intellect, of culture, who had been a good man despite the failure and shame of his life. And he gave heed to the voice of warning, of conscience. Not by revengefully seeking the Mormon who had ruined Fay Larkin and blindly dealing a wild justice could he help this unfortunate girl. This fierce, newborn strength and passion must be tempered by reason, lest he become merely elemental, a man answering wholly to primitive impulses. In the darkness of that hour he mined deep into his heart, understood himself, trembled at the thing he faced, and won his victory. He would go forth from that hour a man. He might fight, and perhaps there was death in the balance, but hate would never overthrow him.

Then when he looked at future action he felt a strange, unalterable purpose to save Fay Larkin. She was very young—seventeen or eighteen, she had said—and there could be, there must be some happiness before her. It had been his dream to chase a rainbow—it had been his determination to find her in the lost Surprise Valley. Well, he had found her. It never occurred to him to ask Nas Ta Bega how he had discovered that the Sago Lily was Fay Larkin. The wonder was, Shefford thought, that he had so long been blind himself. How simply everything worked out now! Every thought, every recollection of her was proof. Her strange beauty like that of the sweet and rare lily, her low voice that showed the habit of silence, her shapely hands with the clasp strong as a man's, her lithe form, her swift step, her wonderful agility upon the smooth, steep trails, and the wildness of her upon the heights, and the haunting, brooding shadow of her eyes when she gazed across the canyon—all these fitted so harmoniously the conception of a child lost in a beautiful Surprise Valley and growing up in its wildness and silence, tutored by the sad love of broken Jane and Lassiter. Yes, to save her had been Shefford's dream, and he had loved that dream. He had loved the dream and he had loved the child. The secret of her hiding-place as revealed by the story told him and his slow growth from dream to action—these had strangely given Fay Larkin to him. Then had come the bitter knowledge that she was dead. In the light of this subsequent revelation how easy to account for his loving Mary, too. Never would she be Mary again to him! Fay Larkin and the Sago Lily were one and the same. She was here, near him, and he was powerless for the present to help her or to reveal himself. She was held back there in that gloomy hall among those somber Mormons, alien to the women, bound in some fatal way to one of the men, and now, by reason of her weakness in the trial, surely to be hated. Thinking of her past and her present, of the future, and that secret Mormon whose face she had never seen, Shefford felt a sinking of his heart, a terrible cold pang in his breast, a fainting of his spirit. She had sworn she was no sealed wife. But had she not lied? So, then, how utterly powerless he was!

But here to save him, to uplift him, came that strange mystic insight which had been the gift of the desert to him. She was not dead. He had found her. What mattered obstacles, even that implacable creed to which she had been sacrificed, in the face of this blessed and overwhelming truth? It was as mighty as the love suddenly dawning upon him. A strong and terrible and deathly sweet wind seemed to fill his soul with the love of her. It was her fate that had drawn him; and now it was her agony, her innocence, her beauty, that bound him for all time. Patience and cunning and toil, passion and blood, the unquenchable spirit of a man to save—these were nothing to give—life itself were little, could he but free her.

Patience and cunning! His sharpening mind cut these out as his greatest assets for the present. And his thoughts flashed like light through his brain.... Judge Stone and his court would fail to convict any Mormon in Stonebridge, just the same as they had failed in the northern towns. They would go away, and Stonebridge would fall to the slow, sleepy tenor of its former way. The hidden village must become known to all men, honest and outlawed, in that country, but this fact would hardly make any quick change in the plans of the Mormons. They did not soon change. They would send the sealed wives back to the canyon and, after the excitement had died down, visit them as usual. Nothing, perhaps, would ever change these old Mormons but death.

Shefford resolved to remain in Stonebridge and ingratiate himself deeper into the regard of the Mormons. He would find work there, if the sealed wives were not returned to the hidden village. In case the women went back to the valley Shefford meant to resume his old duty of driving Withers's pack-trains. Wanting that opportunity, he would find some other work, some excuse to take him there. In due time he would reveal to Fay Larkin that he knew her. How the thought thrilled him! She might deny, might persist in her fear, might fight to keep her secret. But he would learn it—hear her story—hear what had become of Jane Withersteen and Lassiter—and if they were alive, which now he believed he would find them —and he would take them and Fay out of the country.

The duty, the great task, held a grim fascination for him. He had a foreboding of the cost; he had a dark realization of the force he meant to oppose. There were duty here and pity and unselfish love, but these alone did not actuate Shefford. Mystically fate seemed again to come like a gleam and bid him follow.

When Shefford and Nas Ta Bega returned to the town hall the trial had been ended, the hall was closed, and only a few Indians and cowboys remained in the square, and they were about to depart. On the street, however, and the paths and in the doorways of stores were knots of people, talking earnestly. Shefford walked up and down, hoping to meet Withers or Joe Lake. Nas Ta Bega said he would take the horses to water and feed and then return.

There were indications that Stonebridge might experience some of the excitement and perhaps violence common to towns like Monticello and Durango. There was only one saloon in Stonebridge, and it was full of roystering cowboys and horse-wranglers. Shefford saw the bunch of mustangs, in charge of the same Indian, that belonged to Shadd and his gang. The men were inside, drinking. Next door was a tavern called Hopewell House, a stone structure of some pretensions. There were Indians lounging outside. Shefford entered through a wide door and found himself in a large bare room, boarded like a loft, with no ceiling except the roof. The place was full of men and noise. Here he encountered Joe Lake talking to Bishop

Kane and other Mormons. Shefford got a friendly greeting from the bishop, and then was well received by the strangers, to whom Joe introduced him.

"Have you seen Withers?" asked Shefford.

"Reckon he's around somewhere," replied Joe. "Better hang up here, for he'll drop in sooner or later."

"When are you going back to Kayenta?" went on Shefford.

"Hard to say. We'll have to call off our hunt. Nas Ta Bega is here, too."

"Yes, I've been with him."

The older Mormons drew aside, and then Joe mentioned the fact that he was half starved. Shefford went with him into another clapboard room, which was evidently a dining-room. There were half a dozen men at the long table. The seat at the end was a box, and scarcely large enough or safe enough for Joe and Shefford, but they risked it.

"Saw you in the hall," said Joe. "Hell—wasn't it?"

"Joe, I never knew how much I dared say to you, so I don't talk much. But, it was hell," replied Shefford.

"You needn't be so scared of me," spoke up Joe, testily.

That was the first time Shefford had heard the Mormon speak that way.

"I'm not scared, Joe. But I like you—respect you. I can't say so much of—of your people."

"Did you stick out the whole mix?" asked Joe.

"No. I had enough when—when they got through with Mary." Shefford spoke low and dropped his head. He heard the Mormon grind his teeth. There was silence for a little space while neither man looked at the other.

"Reckon the judge was pretty decent," presently said Joe.

"Yes, I thought so. He might have—" But Shefford did not finish that sentence. "How'd the thing end?"

"It ended all right."

"Was there no conviction—no sentence?" Shefford felt a curious eagerness.

"Naw," he snorted. "That court might have saved its breath."

"I suppose. Well, Joe, between you and me, as old friends now, that trial established one fact, even if it couldn't be proved.... Those women are sealed wives."

Joe had no reply for that. He looked gloomy, and there was a stern line in his lips. To-day he seemed more like a Mormon.

"Judge Stone knew that as well as I knew," went on Shefford. "Any man of penetration could have seen it. What an ordeal that was for good women to go through! I know they're good. And there they were swearing to—"

"Didn't it make me sick?" interrupted Joe in a kind of growl. "Reckon it made Judge Stone sick, too. After Mary went under he conducted that trial like a man cuttin' out steers at a round-up. He wanted to get it over. He never forced any question.... Bad job to ride down Stonebridge way! It's out of creation. There's only six men in the party, with a poor lot of horses. Really, government officers or not, they're not safe. And they've taken a hunch."

"Have they left already?" inquired Shefford.

"Were packed an hour ago. I didn't see them go, but somebody said they went. Took the trail for Bluff, which sure is the only trail they could take, unless they wanted to go to Colorado by way of Kayenta. That might have been the safest trail."

"Joe, what might happen to them?" asked Shefford, quietly, with eyes on the Mormon.

"Aw, you know that rough trail. Bad on horses. Weathered slopes—slipping ledges—a rock might fall on you any time. Then Shadd's here with his gang. And bad Piutes."

"What became of the women?" Shefford asked, presently.

"They're around among friends."

"Where are their children?"

"Left over there with the old women. Couldn't be fetched over. But there are some pretty young babies in that bunch—need their mothers."

"I should—think so," replied Shefford, constrainedly. "When will their mothers get back to them?"

"To-night, maybe, if this mob of cow-punchers and wranglers get out of town.... It's a bad mix, Shefford, here's a hunch on that. These fellows will get full of whisky. And trouble might come if they—approach the women."

"You mean they might get drunk enough to take the oaths of those poor women—take the meaning literally—pretend to believe the women what they swore they were?"

"Reckon you've got the hunch," replied Joe, gloomily.

"My God! man, that would be horrible!" exclaimed Shefford.

"Horrible or not, it's liable to happen. The women can be kept here yet awhile. Reckon there won't be any trouble here. It'll be over there in the valley. Shefford, getting the women over there safe is a job that's been put to me. I've got a bunch of fellows already. Can I count on you? I'm glad to say you're well thought of. Bishop Kane liked you, and what he says goes."

"Yes, Joe, you can count on me," replied Shefford.

They finished their meal then and repaired to the big office-room of the house. Several groups of men were there and loud talk was going on outside. Shefford saw Withers talking to Bishop Kane and two other Mormons, both strangers to Shefford. The trader appeared to be speaking with unwonted force, emphasizing his words with energetic movements of his hands.

"Reckon something's up," whispered Joe, hoarsely. "It's been in the air all day."

Withers must have been watching for Shefford.

"Here's Shefford now," he said to the trio of Mormons, as Joe and Shefford reached the group. "I want you to hear him speak for himself."

"What's the matter?" asked Shefford.

"Give me a hunch and I'll put in my say-so," said Joe Lake.

"Shefford, it's the matter of a good name more than a job," replied the trader. "A little while back I told the bishop I meant to put you on the pack job over to the valley—same as when you first came to me. Well, the bishop was pleased and said he might put something in your way. Just now I ran in here to find you—not wanted. When I kicked I got the straight hunch. Willetts has said things about you. One of them—the one that sticks in my craw—was that you'd do anything, even pretend to be inclined toward Mormonism, just to be among those Mormon women over there. Willetts is your enemy. And he's worse than I thought. Now I want you to tell Bishop Kane why this missionary is bitter toward you."

"Gentlemen, I knocked him down," replied Shefford, simply.

"What for?" inquired the bishop, in surprise and curiosity.

Shefford related the incident which had occurred at Red Lake and that now seemed again to come forward fatefully.

"You insinuate he had evil intent toward the Indian girl?" queried Kane.

"I insinuate nothing. I merely state what led to my acting as I did."

"Principles of religion, sir?"

"No. A man's principles."

Withers interposed in his blunt way, "Bishop, did you ever see Glen Naspa?"

"No."

481

"She's the prettiest Navajo in the country. Willetts was after her, that's all."

"My dear man, I can't believe that of a Christian missionary. We've known Willetts for years. He's a man of influence. He has money back of him. He's doing a good work. You hint of a love relation."

"No, I don't hint," replied Withers, impatiently. "I know. It's not the first time I've known a missionary to do this sort of thing. Nor is it the first time for Willetts. Bishop Kane, I live among the Indians. I see a lot I never speak of. My work is to trade with the Indians, that's all. But I'll not have Willetts or any other damned hypocrite run down my friend here. John Shefford is the finest young man that ever came to me in the desert. And he's got to be put right before you all or I'll not set foot in Stonebridge again.... Willetts was after Glen Naspa. Shefford punched him. And later threw him out of the old Indian's hogan up on the mountain. That explains Willetts's enmity. He was after the girl."

"What's more, gentlemen, he GOT her," added Shefford. "Glen Naspa has not been home for six months. I saw her at Blue canyon.... I would like to face this Willetts before you all."

"Easy enough," replied Withers, with a grim chuckle. "He's just outside."

The trader went out; Joe Lake followed at his heels and the three Mormons were next; Shefford brought up the rear and lingered in the door while his eye swept the crowd of men and Indians. His feeling was in direct contrast to his movements. He felt the throbbing of fierce anger. But it seemed a face came between him and his passion—a sweet and tragic face that would have had power to check him in a vastly more critical moment than this. And in an instant he had himself in hand, and, strangely, suddenly felt the strength that had come to him.

Willetts stood in earnest colloquy with a short, squat Indian—the half-breed Shadd. They leaned against a hitching-rail. Other Indians were there, and outlaws. It was a mixed group, rough and hard-looking.

"Hey, Willetts!" called the trader, and his loud, ringing voice, not pleasant, stilled the movement and sound.

When Willetts turned, Shefford was half-way across the wide walk. The missionary not only saw him, but also Nas Ta Bega, who was striding forward. Joe Lake was ahead of the trader, the Mormons followed with decision, and they all confronted Willetts. He turned pale. Shadd had cautiously moved along the rail, nearer to his gang, and then they, with the others of the curious crowd, drew closer.

"Willetts, here's Shefford. Now say it to his face!" declared the trader. He was angry and evidently wanted the fact known, as well as the situation.

Willetts had paled, but he showed boldness. For an instant Shefford studied the smooth face, with its sloping lines, the dark, wine-colored eyes.

"Willetts, I understand you've maligned me to Bishop Kane and others," began Shefford, curtly.

"I called you an atheist," returned the missionary, harshly.

"Yes, and more than that. And I told these men WHY you vented your spite on me."

Willetts uttered a half-laugh, an uneasy, contemptuous expression of scorn and repudiation.

"The charges of such a man as you are can't hurt me," he said.

The man did not show fear so much as disgust at the meeting. He seemed to be absorbed in thought, yet no serious consideration of the situation made itself manifest. Shefford felt puzzled. Perhaps there was no fire to strike from this man. The desert had certainly not made him flint. He had not toiled or suffered or fought.

"But I can hurt you," thundered Shefford, with startling suddenness. "Here! Look at this

Indian! Do you know him? Glen Naspa's brother. Look at him. Let us see you face him while I accuse you.... You made love to Glen Naspa—took her from her home!"

"Harping infidel!" replied Willetts, hoarsely. "So that's your game. Well, Glen Naspa came to my school of her own accord and she will say so."

"Why will she? Because you blinded the simple Indian girl.... Willetts, I'll waste little more time on you."

And swift and light as a panther Shefford leaped upon the man and, fastening powerful hands round the thick neck, bore him to his knees and bent back his head over the rail. There was a convulsive struggle, a hard flinging of arms, a straining wrestle, and then Willetts was in a dreadful position. Shefford held him in iron grasp.

"You damned, white-livered hypocrite—I'm liable to kill you!" cried Shefford. "I watched you and Glen Naspa that day up on the mountain. I saw you embrace her. I saw that she loved you. Tell THAT, you liar! That'll be enough."

The face of the missionary turned purple as Shefford forced his head back over the rail.

"I'll kill you, man," repeated Shefford, piercingly. "Do you want to go to your God unprepared? Say you made love to Glen Naspa—tell that you persuaded her to leave her home. Quick!"

Willetts raised a shaking hand and then Shefford relaxed the paralyzing grip and let his head come forward. The half-strangled man gasped out a few incoherent words that his livid, guilty face made unnecessary.

Shefford gave him a shove and he fell into the dust at the feet of the Navajo.

"Gentlemen, I leave him to Nas Ta Bega," said Shefford, with a strange change from passion to calmness.

Late that night, when the roystering visitors had gone or were deep in drunken slumber, a melancholy and strange procession filed out of Stonebridge. Joe Lake and his armed comrades were escorting the Mormon women back to the hidden valley. They were mounted on burros and mustangs, and in all that dark and somber line there was only one figure which shone white under the pale moon.

At the starting, until that white-clad figure had appeared, Shefford's heart had seemed to be in his throat; and thereafter its beat was muffled and painful in his breast. Yet there was some sad sweetness in the knowledge that he could see her now, be near her, watch over her.

By and by the overcast clouds drifted and the moon shone bright. The night was still; the great dark mountain loomed to the stars; the numberless waves of rounded rock that must be crossed and circled lay deep in shadow. There was only a steady pattering of light hoofs.

Shefford's place was near the end of the line, and he kept well back, riding close to one woman and then another. No word was spoken. These sealed wives rode where their mounts were led or driven, as blind in their hoods as veiled Arab women in palanquins. And their heads drooped wearily and their shoulders bent, as if under a burden. It took an hour of steady riding to reach the ascent to the plateau, and here, with the beginning of rough and smooth and shadowed trail, the work of the escort began. The line lengthened out and each man kept to the several women assigned to him. Shefford had three, and one of them was the girl he loved. She rode as if the world and time and life were naught to her. As soon as he dared trust his voice and his control he meant to let her know the man whom perhaps she had not forgotten was there with her, a friend. Six months! It had been a lifetime to him. Surely eternity to her! Had she forgotten? He felt like a coward who had basely deserted her. Oh—had he only known!

She rode a burro that was slow, continually blocking the passage for those behind, and eventually it became lame. Thus the other women forged ahead. Shefford dismounted and stopped her burro. It was a moment before she noted the halt, and twice in that time Shefford tried to speak and failed. What poignant pain, regret, love made his utterance fail!

"Ride my horse," he finally said, and his voice was not like his own.

Obediently and wearily she dismounted from the burro and got up on Nack-yal. The stirrups were long for her and he had to change them. His fingers were all thumbs as he fumbled with the buckles.

Suddenly he became aware that there had been a subtle change in her. He knew it without looking up and he seemed to be unable to go on with his task. If his life had depended upon keeping his head lowered he could not have done it. The listlessness of her drooping form was no longer manifest. The peak of the dark hood pointed toward him. He knew then that she was gazing at him.

Never so long as he lived would that moment be forgotten! They were alone. The others had gotten so far ahead that no sound came back. The stillness was so deep it could be felt. The moon shone with white, cold radiance and the shining slopes of smooth stone waved away, crossed by shadows of pinyons.

Then she leaned a little toward him. One swift hand flew up to tear the black hood back so that she could see. In its place flashed her white face. And her eyes were like the night.

"YOU!" she whispered.

His blood came leaping to sting neck and cheek and temple. What dared he interpret from that single word? Could any other word have meant so much?

"No—one—else," he replied, unsteadily.

Her white hand flashed again to him, and he met it with his own. He felt himself standing cold and motionless in the moonlight. He saw her, wonderful, with the deep, shadowy eyes, and a silver sheen on her hair. And as he looked she released her hand and lifted it, with the other, to her hood. He saw the shiny hair darken and disappear—and then the lovely face with its sad eyes and tragic lips.

He drew Nack-yal's bridle forward, and led him up the moonlit trail.

THE REVELATION

THE FOLLOWING afternoon cowboys and horse-wranglers, keen-eyed as Indians for tracks and trails, began to arrive in the quiet valley to which the Mormon women had been returned.

Under every cedar clump there were hobbled horses, packs, and rolled bedding in tarpaulins. Shefford and Joe Lake had pitched camp in the old site near the spring. The other men of Joe's escort went to the homes of the women; and that afternoon, as the curious visitors began to arrive, these homes became barred and dark and quiet, as if they had been closed and deserted for the winter. Not a woman showed herself.

Shefford and Joe, by reason of the location of their camp and their alertness, met all the new-comers. The ride from Stonebridge was a long and hard one, calculated to wear off the effects of the whisky imbibed by the adventure-seekers. This fact alone saved the situation. Nevertheless, Joe expected trouble. Most of the visitors were decent, good-natured fellows, merely curious, and simple enough to believe that this really was what the Mormons had claimed—a village of free women. But there were those among them who were coarse, evil-minded, and dangerous.

By supper-time there were two dozen or more of these men in the valley, camped along the west wall. Fires were lighted, smoke curled up over the cedars, gay songs disturbed the usual serenity of the place. Later in the early twilight the curious visitors, by twos and threes, walked about the village, peering at the dark cabins and jesting among themselves. Joe had informed Shefford that all the women had been put in a limited number of cabins, so that they could be protected. So far as Shefford saw or heard there was no unpleasant incident in the village; however, as the sauntering visitors returned toward their camps they loitered at the spring, and here developments threatened.

In spite of the fact that the majority of these cowboys and their comrades were decent-minded and beginning to see the real relation of things, they were not disposed to be civil to Shefford. They were certainly not Mormons. And his position, apparently as a Gentile, among these Mormons was one open to criticism. They might have been jealous, too; at any rate, remarks were passed in his hearing, meant for his ears, that made it exceedingly trying for him not to resent. Moreover, Joe Lake's increasing impatience rendered the situation more difficult. Shefford welcomed the arrival of Nas Ta Bega. The Indian listened to the loud talk of several loungers round the camp-fire; and thereafter he was like Shefford's shadow, silent, somber, watchful.

Nevertheless, it did not happen to be one of the friendly and sarcastic cowboys that precipitated the crisis. A horse-wrangler named Hurley, a man of bad repute, as much outlaw as anything, took up the bantering.

"Say, Shefford, what in the hell's your job here, anyway?" he queried as he kicked a cedar branch into the camp-fire. The brightening blaze showed him swarthy, unshaven, a large-featured, ugly man.

"I've been doing odd jobs for Withers," replied Shefford. "Expect to drive pack-trains in here for a while."

"You must stand strong with these Mormons. Must be a Mormon yerself?"

"No," replied Shefford, briefly.

"Wal, I'm stuck on your job. Do you need a packer? I can throw a diamond-hitch better 'n any feller in this country."

"I don't need help."

"Mebbe you'll take me over to see the ladies," he went on, with a coarse laugh.

Shefford did not show that he had heard. Hurley waited, leering as looked from the keen listeners to Shefford.

"Want to have them all yerself, eh?" he jeered.

Shefford struck him—sent him tumbling heavily, like a log. Hurley, cursing as he half rose, jerked his gun out. Nas Ta Bega, swift as light, kicked the gun out of his hand. And Joe Lake picked it up.

Deliberately the Mormon cocked the weapon and stood over Hurley.

"Get up!" he ordered, and Shefford heard the ruthless Mormon in him then.

Hurley rose slowly. Then Joe prodded him in the middle with the cocked gun. Shefford startled, expected the gun to go off. So did the others, especially Hurley, who shrank in panic from the dark Mormon.

"Rustle!" said Joe, and gave the man a harder prod. Assuredly the gun did not have a hair-trigger.

"Joe, mebbe it's loaded!" protested one of the cowboys.

Hurley shrank back, and turned to hurry away, with Joe close after him. They disappeared in the darkness. A constrained silence was maintained around the camp-fire for a while. Presently some of the men walked off and others began to converse. Everybody heard the sound of hoofs passing down the trail. The patter ceased, and in a few moments Lake returned. He still carried Hurley's gun.

The crowd dispersed then. There was no indication of further trouble. However, Shefford and Joe and Nas Ta Bega divided the night in watches, so that some one would be wide awake.

Early next morning there was an exodus from the village of the better element among the visitors. "No fun hangin' round hyar," one of them expressed it, and as good-naturedly as they had come they rode away. Six or seven of the desperado class remained behind, bent on mischief; and they were reinforced by more arrivals from Stonebridge. They avoided the camp by the spring, and when Shefford and Lake attempted to go to them they gave them a wide berth. This caused Joe to assert that they were up to some dirty work. All morning they lounged around under the cedars, keeping out of sight, and evidently the reinforcement from Stonebridge had brought liquor. When they gathered together at their camp, half drunk, all noisy, some wanting to swagger off into the village and others trying to hold them back, Joe

Lake said, grimly, that somebody was going to get shot. Indeed, Shefford saw that there was every likelihood of bloodshed.

"Reckon we'd better take to one of the cabins," said Joe.

Thereupon the three repaired to the nearest cabin, and, entering, kept watch from the windows. During a couple of hours, however, they did not see or hear anything of the ruffians. Then came a shot from over in the village, a single yell, and, after that, a scattering volley. The silence and suspense which followed were finally broken by hoof-beats. Nas Ta Bega called Joe and Shefford to the window he had been stationed at. From here they saw the unwelcome visitors ride down the trail, to disappear in the cedars toward the outlet of the valley. Joe, who had numbered them, said that all but one of them had gone.

"Reckon he got it," added Joe.

So indeed it turned out; one of the men, a well-known rustler named Harker, had been killed, by whom no one seemed to know. He had brazenly tried to force his way into one of the houses, and the act had cost him his life. Naturally Shefford, never free from his civilized habit of thought, remarked apprehensively that he hoped this affair would not cause the poor women to be arrested again and haled before some rude court.

"Law!" grunted Joe. "There ain't any. The nearest sheriff is in Durango. That's Colorado. And he'd give us a medal for killing Harker. It was a good job, for it'll teach these rowdies a lesson."

Next day the old order of life was resumed in the village. And the arrival of a heavily laden pack-train, under the guidance of Withers, attested to the fact that the Mormons meant not only to continue to live in the valley, but also to build and plant and enlarge. This was good news to Shefford. At least the village could be made less lonely. And there was plenty of work to give him excuse for staying there. Furthermore, Withers brought a message form Bishop Kane to the effect that the young man was offered a place as teacher in the school, in co-operation with the Mormon teachers. Shefford experienced no twinge of conscience when he accepted.

It was the fourth evening after the never-to-be-forgotten moonlight ride to the valley that Shefford passed under the dark pinon-trees on his way to Fay Larkin's cottage. He paused in the gloom and memory beset him. The six months were annihilated, and it was the night he had fled. But now all was silent. He seemed to be trying to drag himself back. A beginning must be made. Only how to meet her—what to say—what to conceal!

He tapped on the door and she came out. After all, it was a meeting vastly different from what his feeling made him imagine it might have been. She was nervous, frightened, as were all the other women, for that matter. She was alone in the cottage. He made haste to reassure her about the improbability of any further trouble such as had befallen the last week. As he had always done on those former visits to her, he talked rapidly, using all his wit, and here his emotion made him eloquent; he avoided personalities, except to tell about his prospects of work in the village, and he sought above all to lead her mind from thought of herself and her condition. Before he left her he had the gladness of knowing he had succeeded.

When he said good night he felt the strange falsity of his position. He did not expect to be able to keep up the deception for long. That roused him, and half the night he lay awake, thinking. Next day he was the life of the work and study and play in that village. Kindness and good-will did not need inspiration, but it was keen, deep passion that made him a plotter for influence and friendship. Was there a woman in the village whom he might trust, in case he needed one? And his instinct guided him to her whom he had liked well—Ruth. Ruth Jones she had called herself at the trial, and when Shefford used the name she laughed mockingly. Ruth was not very religious, and sometimes she was bitter and hard. She wanted life, and here she was a prisoner in a lonely valley. She welcomed Shefford's visits. He imagined that she had slightly changed, and whether it was the added six months with its trouble and pain or a growing revolt he could not tell. After a time he divined that the inevitable retrogression had set in: she had not enough faith to uphold the burden she had accepted, nor the courage to cast it off. She was ready to love him. That did not frighten Shefford, and if she did love him he was not so sure it would not be an anchor for her. He saw her danger, and then he became what he had never really been in all the days of his ministry—the real helper. Unselfishly, for her sake, he found power to influence her; and selfishly, for the sake of Fay Larkin, he began slowly to win her to a possible need.

The days passed swiftly. Mormons came and went, though in the open day, as laborers; new cabins went up, and a store, and other improvements. Some part of every evening Shefford spent with Fay, and these visits were no longer unknown to the village. Women gossiped, in a friendly way about Shefford, but with jealous tongues about the girl. Joe Lake told Shefford the run of the village talk. Anything concerning the Sago Lily the droll Mormon took to heart. He had been hard hit, and admitted it. Sometimes he went with Shefford to call upon her, but he talked little and never remained long. Shefford had anticipated antagonism on the part of Joe; however, he did not find it.

Shefford really lived through the busy day for that hour with Fay in the twilight. And every evening seemed the same. He would find her in the dark, alone, silent, brooding, hopeless. Her mood did not puzzle him, but how to keep from plunging her deeper into despair baffled him. He exhausted all his powers trying to do for her what he had been able to do for Ruth. Yet he failed. Something had blunted her. The shadow of that baneful trial hovered over her, and he came to sense a strange terror in her. It was mostly always present. Was she thinking of Jane Withersteen and Lassiter, left dead or imprisoned in the valley from which she had been brought so mysteriously? Shefford wearied his brain revolving these questions. The fate of her friends, and the cross she bore—of these was tragedy born, but the terror—that Shefford divined came of waiting for the visit of the Mormon whose face she had never seen. Shefford prayed that he might never meet this man. Finally he grew desperate. When he first arrived at the girl's home she would speak, she showed gladness, relief, and then straightway she dropped back into the shadow of her gloom. When he got up to go then there was a wistfulness, an unspoken need, an unconscious reliance, in her reluctant good night.

Then the hour came when he reached his limit. He must begin his revelation.

"You never ask me anything—let alone about myself," he said.

"I'd like to hear," she replied, timidly.

"Do I strike you as an unhappy man?"

"No, indeed."

"Well, how DO I strike you?"

This was an entirely new tack he had veered to.

"Very good and kind to us women," she said.

"I don't know about that. If I am so, it doesn't bring me happiness. ... Do you remember what I told you once, about my being a preacher—disgrace, ruin, and all that—and my rainbow-chasing dream out here after a—a lost girl?"

"I—remember all—you said," she replied, very low.

"Listen." His voice was a little husky, but behind it there seemed a tide of resistless utterance. "Loss of faith and name did not send me to this wilderness. But I had love—love for that lost girl, Fay Larkin. I dreamed about her till I loved her. I dreamed that I would find her—my treasure—at the foot of a rainbow. Dreams!... When you told me she was dead I accepted that. There was truth in your voice. I respected your reticence. But something died in me then. I lost myself, the best of me, the good that might have uplifted me. I went away, down upon the barren desert, and there I rode and slept and grew into another and a harder man. Yet, strange to say, I never forgot her, though my dreams were done. As I toiled and suffered and changed I loved her—if not her, the thought of her—more and more. Now I have come back to these walled valleys—to the smell of pinon, to the flowers in the nooks, to the wind on the heights, to the silence and loneliness and beauty. And here the dreams come back and SHE is WITH me always. Her spirit is all that keeps me kind and good, as you say I am. But I suffer, I long for her alive. If I love her dead, how could I love her living! Always I torture myself with the vain dream that—that she MIGHT not be dead. I have never been anything but a dreamer. And here I go about my work by day and lie awake at night with that lost girl in my mind.... I love her. Does that seem strange to you? But it would not if you understood. Think. I had lost faith, hope. I set myself a great work—to find Fay Larkin. And by the fire and the iron and the blood that I felt it would cost to save her some faith must come to me again.... My work is undone—I've never saved her. But listen, how strange it is to feel—now—as I let myself go—that just the loving her and the living here in the wildness that holds her somewhere have brought me hope again. Some faith must come, too. It was through her that I met this Indian, Nas Ta Bega. He has saved my life—taught me much. What would I ever have learned of the naked and vast earth, of the sublimity of the wild uplands, of the storm and night and sun, if I had not followed a gleam she inspired? In my hunt for a lost girl perhaps I wandered into a place where I shall find a God and my salvation. Do you marvel that I love Fay Larkin—that she is not dead to me? Do you marvel that I love her, when I KNOW, were she alive, chained in a canyon, or bound, or lost in any way, my destiny would lead me to her, and she should be saved?"

Shefford ended, overcome with emotion. In the dusk he could not see the girl's face, but the white form that had drooped so listlessly seemed now charged by some vitalizing current. He knew he had spoken irrationally; still he held it no dishonor to have told her he loved her as one dead. If she took that love to the secret heart of living Fay Larkin, then perhaps a spirit might light in her darkened soul. He had no thought yet that Fay Larkin might ever belong to him. He divined a crime—he had seen her agony. And this avowal of his was only one step toward her deliverance.

Softly she rose, retreating into the shadow.

"Forgive me if I—I disturb you, distress you," he said. "I wanted to tell you. She was— somehow known to you. I am not happy. And are YOU happy?... Let her memory be a bond between us.... Good night."

"Good night."

Faintly as the faintest whisper breathed her reply, and, though it came from a child forced into womanhood, it whispered of girlhood not dead, of sweet incredulity, of amazed tumult, of a wondering, frantic desire to run and hide, of the bewilderment incident to a first hint of love.

Shefford walked away into the darkness. The whisper filled his soul. Had a word of love ever been spoken to that girl? Never—not the love which had been on his lips. Fay Larkin's lonely life spoke clearly in her whisper.

Next morning as the sun gilded the looming peaks and shafts of gold slanted into the valley she came swiftly down the path to the spring.

Shefford paused in his task of chopping wood. Joe Lake, on his knees, with his big hands in a pan of dough, lifted his head to stare. She had left off the somber black hood, and, although that made a vast difference in her, still it was not enough to account for what struck both men.

"Good morning," she called, brightly.

They both answered, but not spontaneously. She stopped at the spring and with one sweep of her strong arm filled the bucket and lifted it. Then she started back down the path and, pausing opposite the camp, set the bucket down.

"Joe, do you still pride yourself on your sour dough?" she asked.

"Reckon I do," replied Joe, with a grin.

"I've heard your boasts, but never tasted your bread," she went on.

"I'll ask you to eat with us some day."

"Don't forget," she replied.

And then shyly she looked at Shefford. She was like the fresh dawn, and the gold of the sun shone on her head.

"Have you chopped all that wood—so early?" she asked.

"Sure," replied Shefford, laughing. "I have to get up early to keep Joe from doing all the camp chores."

She smiled, and then to Shefford she seemed to gleam, to be radiant.

"It'd be a lovely morning to climb—'way high."

"Why—yes—it would," replied Shefford, awkwardly. "I wish I didn't have my work."

"Joe, will YOU climb with me some day?"

"I should smile I will," declared Joe.

"But I can run right up the walls."

"I reckon. Mary, it wouldn't surprise me to see you fly."

"Do you mean I'm like a canyon swallow or an angel?"

Then, as Joe stared speechlessly, she said good-by and, taking up the bucket, went on with her swift, graceful step.

"She's perked up," said the Mormon, staring after her. "Never heard her say more 'n yes or no till now."

"She did seem—bright," replied Shefford.

He was stunned. What had happened to her? To-day this girl had not been Mary, the sealed wife, or the Sago Lily, alien among Mormon women. Then it flashed upon him—she was Fay Larkin. She who had regarded herself as dead had come back to life. In one short night what had transformed her—what had taken place in her heart? Shefford dared not accept, nor allow lodgment in his mind, a thrilling idea that he had made her forget her misery.

"Shefford, did you ever see her like that?" asked Joe.

"Never."

"Haven't you—something to do with it?"

"Maybe I have. I—I hope so."

"Reckon you've seen how she's faded—since the trial?"

"No," replied Shefford, swiftly. "But I've not seen her face in daylight since then."

"Well, take my hunch," said Joe, soberly. "She's begun to fade like the canyon lily when it's broken. And she's going to die unless—"

"Why man!" ejaculated Shefford. "Didn't you see—"

"Sure I see," interrupted the Mormon. "I see a lot you don't. She's so white you can look through her. She's grown thin, all in a week. She doesn't eat. Oh, I know, because I've made it my business to find out. It's no news to the women. But they'd like to see her die. And she will die unless—"

"My God!" exclaimed Shefford, huskily. "I never noticed—I never thought.... Joe, hasn't she any friends?"

"Sure. You and Ruth—and me. Maybe Nas Ta Bega, too. He watches her a good deal."

"We can do so little, when she needs so much."

"Nobody can help her, unless it's you," went on the Mormon. "That's plain talk. She seemed different this morning. Why, she was alive—she talked—she smiled.... Shefford, if you cheer her up I'll go to hell for you!"

The big Mormon, on his knees, with his hands in a pan of dough, and his shirt all covered with flour, presented an incongruous figure of a man actuated by pathos and passion. Yet the contrast made his emotion all the simpler and stronger. Shefford grew closer to Joe in that moment.

"Why do you think *I* can cheer her, help her?" queried Shefford.

"I don't know. But she's different with you. It's not that you're a Gentile, though, for all the women are crazy about you. You talk to her. You have power over her, Shefford. I feel that. She's only a kid."

"Who is she, Joe? Where did she come from?" asked Shefford, very low, with his eyes cast down.

"I don't know. I can't find out. Nobody knows. It's a mystery—to all the younger Mormons, anyway."

Shefford burned to ask questions about the Mormon whose sealed wife the girl was, but he respected Joe too much to take advantage of him in a poignant moment like this. Besides, it was only jealousy that made him burn to know the Mormon's identity, and jealousy had become a creeping, insidious, growing fire. He would be wise not to add fuel to it. He rejected many things before he thought of one that he could voice to his friend.

"Joe, it's only her body that belongs to—to.... Her soul is lost to—"

"John Shefford, let that go. My mind's tired. I've been taught so and so, and I'm not bright.... But, after all, men are much alike. The thing with you and me is this—we don't want to see HER grave!"

Love spoke there. The Mormon had seized upon the single elemental point that concerned him and his friend in their relation to this unfortunate girl. His simple, powerful statement united them; it gave the lie to his hint of denseness; it stripped the truth naked. It was such a wonderful thought-provoking statement that Shefford needed time to ponder how deep the Mormon was. To what limit would he go? Did he mean that here, between two men who loved the same girl, class, duty, honor, creed were nothing if they stood in the way of her deliverance and her life?

"Joe Lake, you Mormons are impossible," said Shefford, deliberately. "You don't want to see her grave. So long as she lives—remains on the earth—white and gold like the flower you call her, that's enough for you. It's her body you think of. And that's the great and horrible error in your religion.... But death of the soul is infinitely worse than death of the body. I have been thinking of her soul.... So here we stand, you and I. You to save her life—I to save her soul! What will you do?"

"Why, John, I'd turn Gentile," he said, with terrible softness. It was a softness that scorned Shefford for asking, and likewise it flung defiance at his creed and into the face of hell.

Shefford felt the sting and the exaltation.

"And I'd be a Mormon," he said.

"All right. We understand each other. Reckon there won't be any call for such extremes. I haven't an idea what you mean—what can be done. But I say, go slow, so we won't all find graves. First cheer her up somehow. Make her want to live. But go slow, John. AND DON'T BE WITH HER LATE!"

That night Shefford found her waiting for him in the moonlight—a girl who was as transparent as crystal-clear water, who had left off the somber gloom with the black hood, who tremulously embraced happiness without knowing it, who was one moment timid and wild like a half-frightened fawn, and the next, exquisitely half-conscious of what it meant to be thought dead, but to be alive, to be awakening, wondering, palpitating, and to be loved.

Shefford lived the hour as a dream and went back to the quiet darkness under the cedars to lie wide-eyed, trying to recall all that she had said. For she had talked as if utterance had long been dammed behind a barrier of silence.

There followed other hours like that one, indescribable hours, so sweet they stung, and in which, keeping pace with his love, was the nobler stride of a spirit that more every day lightened her burden.

The thing he had to do, sooner or later, was to tell her he knew she was Fay Larkin, not dead, but alive, and that, not love nor religion, but sacrifice, nailed her down to her martyrdom. Many and many a time he had tried to force himself to tell her, only to fail. He hated to risk ending this sweet, strange, thoughtless, girlish mood of hers. It might not be soon won back—perhaps never. How could he tell what chains bound her? And so as he vacillated between Joe's cautious advice to go slow and his own pity the days and weeks slipped by.

One haunting fear kept him sleepless half the nights and sick even in his dreams, and it was that the Mormon whose sealed wife she was might come, surely would come, some night. Shefford could bear it. But what would that visit do to Fay Larkin? Shefford instinctively feared the awakening in the girl of womanhood, of deeper insight, of a spiritual realization of what she was, of a physical dawn.

He might have spared himself needless torture. One day Joe Lake eyed him with penetrating glance.

"Reckon you don't have to sleep right on that Stonebridge trail," said the Mormon, significantly.

Shefford felt the blood burn his neck and face. He had pulled his tarpaulin closer to the trail, and his motive was as an open page to the keen Mormon.

"Why?" asked Shefford.

"There won't be any Mormons riding in here soon—by night—to visit the women," replied Joe, bluntly. "Haven't you figured there might be government spies watching the trails?"

"No, I haven't."

"Well, take a hunch, then," added the Mormon, gruffly, and Shefford divined, as well as if he had been told, that warning word had gone to Stonebridge. Gone despite the fact that Nas Ta Bega had reported every trail free of watchers! There was no sign of any spies, cowboys, outlaws, or Indians in the vicinity of the valley. A passionate gratitude to the Mormon overcame Shefford; and the unreasonableness of it, the nature of it, perturbed him greatly. But, something hammered into his brain, if he loved one of these sealed wives, how could he help being jealous?

The result of Joe's hint was that Shefford put off the hour of revelation, lived in his dream, helped the girl grow farther and farther away from her trouble, until that inevitable hour arrived when he was driven by accumulated emotion as much as the exigency of the case.

He had not often walked with her beyond the dark shade of the pinyons round the cottage, but this night, when he knew he must tell her, he led her away down the path, through the cedar grove to the west end of the valley where it was wild and lonely and sad and silent.

The moon was full and the great peaks were crowned as with snow. A coyote uttered his cutting cry. There were a few melancholy notes from a night bird of the stone walls. The air was clear and cold, with a tang of frost in it. Shefford gazed about him at the vast, uplifted, insulating walls, and that feeling of his which was more than a sense told him how walls like these and the silence and shadow and mystery had been nearly all of Fay Larkin's life. He felt them all in her.

He stopped out in the open, near the line where dark shadow of the wall met the silver moonlight on the grass, and here, by a huge flat stone where he had come often alone and sometimes with Ruth, he faced Fay Larkin in the spirit to tell her gently that he knew her, and sternly to force her secret from her.

"Am I your friend?" he began.

"Ah!—my only friend," she said.

"Do you trust me, believe I mean well by you, want to help you?"

"Yes, indeed."

"Well, then, let me speak of you. You know one topic we've never touched upon. You!"

She was silent, and looked wonderingly, a little fearfully, at him, as if vague, disturbing thoughts were entering the fringe of her mind.

"Our friendship is a strange one, is it not?" he went on.

"How do I know? I never had any other friendship. What do you mean by strange?"

"Well, I'm a young man. You're a—a married woman. We are together a good deal—and like to be."

"Why is that strange?" she asked.

Suddenly Shefford realized that there was nothing strange in what was natural. A remnant of sophistication clung to him and that had spoken. He needed to speak to her in a way which in her simplicity she would understand.

"Never mind strange. Say that I am interested in you, and, as you're not happy, I want to help you. And say that your neighbors are curious and oppose my idea. Why do they?"

"They're jealous and want you themselves," she replied, with sweet directness. "They've said things I don't understand. But I felt they—they hated in me what would be all right in themselves."

Here to simplicity she added truth and wisdom, as an Indian might have expressed them. But shame was unknown to her, and she had as yet only vague perceptions of love and passion. Shefford began to realize the quickness of her mind, that she was indeed awakening.

"They are jealous—were jealous before I ever came here. That's only human nature. I was trying to get to a point. Your neighbors are curious. They oppose me. They hate you. It's all bound up in the—the fact of your difference from them, your youth, beauty, that you're not a Mormon, that you nearly betrayed their secret at the trial in Stonebridge."

"Please—please don't—speak of that!" she faltered.

"But I must," he replied, swiftly. "That trial was a torture to you. It revealed so much to me.... I know you are a sealed wife. I know there has been a crime. I know you've sacrificed yourself. I know that love and religion have nothing to do with—what you are.... Now, is not all that true?"

"I must not tell," she whispered.

"But I shall MAKE you tell," he replied, and his voice rang.

"Oh no, you cannot," she said.

"I can—with just one word!"

Her eyes were great, starry, shadowy gulfs, dark in the white beauty of her face. She was calm now. She had strength. She invited him to speak the word, and the wistful, tremulous quiver of her lips was for his earnest thought of her.

"Wait—a—little," said Shefford, unsteadily. "I'll come to that presently. Tell me this—have you ever thought of being free?"

"Free!" she echoed, and there was singular depth and richness in her voice. That was the first spark of fire he had struck from her. "Long ago, the minute I was unwatched, I'd have leaped from a wall had I dared. Oh, I wasn't afraid. I'd love to die that way. But I never dared."

"Why?" queried Shefford, piercingly.

She was silent then.

"Suppose I offered to give you freedom that meant life?"

"I—couldn't—take it."

"Why?"

"Oh, my friend, don't ask me any more."

"I know, I can see—you want to tell me—you need to tell."

"But I daren't."

"Won't you trust me?"

"I do—I do."

"Then tell me."

"No—no—oh no!"

The moment had come. How sad, tragic, yet glorious for him! It would be like a magic touch upon this lovely, cold, white ghost of Fay Larkin, transforming her into a living, breathing girl. He held his love as a thing aloof, and, as such, intangible because of the living death she believed she lived, it had no warmth and intimacy for them. What might it not become with a lightning flash of revelation? He dreaded, yet he was driven to speak. He waited, swallowing hard, fighting the tumultuous storm of emotion, and his eyes dimmed.

"What did I come to this country for?" he asked, suddenly, in ringing, powerful voice.

"To find a girl," she whispered.

"I've found her!"

She began to shake. He saw a white hand go to her breast.

"Where is Surprise Valley?... How were you taken from Jane Withersteen and Lassiter?... I know they're alive. But where?"

She seemed to turn to stone.

"Fay!—FAY LARKIN!... I KNOW YOU!" he cried, brokenly.

She slipped off the stone to her knees, swayed forward blindly with her hands reaching out, her head falling back to let the moon fall full upon the beautiful, snow-white, tragically convulsed face.

✣ 13 ✣

THE STORY OF SURPRISE VALLEY

"... Oh, I remember so well! Even now I dream of it sometimes. I hear the roll and crash of falling rock—like thunder.... We rode and rode. Then the horses fell. Uncle Jim took me in his arms and started up the cliff. Mother Jane climbed close after us. They kept looking back. Down there in the gray valley came the Mormons. I see the first one now. He rode a white horse. That was Tull. Oh, I remember so well! And I was five or six years old.

"We climbed up and up and into dark canyon and wound in and out. Then there was the narrow white trail, straight up, with the little cut steps and the great, red, ruined walls. I looked down over Uncle Jim's shoulder. I saw Mother Jane dragging herself up. Uncle Jim's blood spotted the trail. He reached a flat place at the top and fell with me. Mother Jane crawled up to us.

"Then she cried out and pointed. Tull was 'way below, climbing the trail. His men came behind him. Uncle Jim went to a great, tall rock and leaned against it. There was a bloody hole in his hand. He pushed the rock. It rolled down, banging the loose walls. They crashed and crashed—then all was terrible thunder and red smoke. I couldn't hear—I couldn't see.

"Uncle Jim carried me down and down out of the dark and dust into a beautiful valley all red and gold, with a wonderful arch of stone over the entrance.

"I don't remember well what happened then for what seemed a long, long time. I can feel how the place looked, but not so clear as it is now in my dreams. I seem to see myself with the dogs, and with Mother Jane, learning my letters, marking with red stone on the walls.

"But I remember now how I felt when I first understood we were shut in for ever. Shut in Surprise Valley where Venters had lived so long. I was glad. The Mormons would never get me. I was seven or eight years old then. From that time all is clear in my mind.

"Venters had left supplies and tools and grain and cattle and burros, so we had a good start to begin life there. He had killed off the wildcats and kept the coyotes out, so the rabbits and quail multiplied till there were thousands of them. We raised corn and fruit, and stored what we didn't use. Mother Jane taught me to read and write with the soft red stone that marked well on the walls.

"The years passed. We kept track of time pretty well. Uncle Jim's hair turned white and

Mother Jane grew gray. Every day was like the one before. Mother Jane cried sometimes and Uncle Jim was sad because they could never be able to get me out of the valley. It was long before they stopped looking and listening for some one. Venters would come back, Uncle Jim always said. But Mother Jane did not think so.

"I loved Surprise Valley. I wanted to stay there always. I remembered Cottonwoods, how the children there hated me, and I didn't want to go back. The only unhappy times I ever had in the valley were when Ring and Whitie, my dogs, grew old and died. I roamed the valley. I climbed to every nook upon the mossy ledges. I learned to run up the steep cliffs. I could almost stick on the straight walls. Mother Jane called me a wild girl. We had put away the clothes we wore when we got there, to save them, and we made clothes of skins. I always laughed when I thought of my little dress—how I grew out of it. I think Uncle Jim and Mother Jane talked less as the years went by. And after I'd learned all she could teach me we didn't talk much. I used to scream into the caves just to hear my voice, and the echoes would frighten me.

"The older I grew the more I was alone. I was always running round the valley. I would climb to a high place and sit there for hours, doing nothing. I just watched and listened. I used to stay in the cliff-dwellers' caves and wonder about them. I loved to be out in the wind. And my happiest time was in the summer storms with the thunder echoes under the walls. At evening it was such a quiet place—after the night bird's cry, no sound. The quiet made me sad but I loved it. I loved to watch the stars as I lay awake.

"So it was beautiful and happy for me there till—till...

"Two years or more ago there was a bad storm, and one of the great walls caved. The walls were always weathering, slipping. Many and many a time have I heard the rumble of an avalanche, but most of them were in other canyon. This slide in the valley made it possible, Uncle Jim said, for men to get down into the valley. But we could not climb out unless helped from above. Uncle Jim never rested well after that. But it never worried me.

"One day, over a year ago, while I was across the valley, I heard strange shouts, and then screams. I ran to our camp. I came upon men with ropes and guns. Uncle Jim was tied, and a rope was round his neck. Mother Jane was lying on the ground. I thought she was dead until I heard her moan. I was not afraid. I screamed and flew at Uncle Jim to tear the ropes off him. The men held me back. They called me a pretty cat. Then they talked together, and some were for hanging Lassiter—that was the first time I ever knew any name for him but Uncle Jim—and some were for leaving him in the valley. Finally they decided to hang him. But Mother Jane pleaded so and I screamed and fought so that they left off. Then they went away and we saw them climb out of the valley.

"Uncle Jim said they were Mormons, and some among them had been born in Cottonwoods. I was not told why they had such a terrible hate for him. He said they would come back and kill him. Uncle Jim had no guns to fight with.

"We watched and watched. In five days they did come back, with more men, and some of them wore black masks. They came to our cave with ropes and guns. One was tall. He had a cruel voice. The others ran to obey him. I could see white hair and sharp eyes behind the mask. The men caught me and brought me before him.

"He said Lassiter had killed many Mormons. He said Lassiter had killed his father and should be hanged. But Lassiter would be let live and Mother Jane could stay with him, both prisoners there in the valley, if I would marry the Mormon. I must marry him, accept the Mormon faith, and bring up my children as Mormons. If I refused they would hang Lassiter, leave the heretic Jane Withersteen alone in the valley, and take me and break me to their rule.

"I agreed. But Mother Jane absolutely forbade me to marry him. Then the Mormons took me away. It nearly killed me to leave Uncle Jim and Mother Jane. I was carried and lifted out of the valley, and rode a long way on a horse. They brought me here, to the cabin where I live, and I have never been away except that—that time—to—Stonebridge. Only little by little did I learn my position. Bishop Kane was kind, but stern, because I could not be quick to learn the faith.

"I am not a sealed wife. But they're trying to make me one. The master Mormon—he visited me often—at night—till lately. He threatened me. He never told me a name—except Saint George. I don't—know him—except his voice. I never—saw his face—in the light!"

Fay Larkin ended her story. Toward its close Shefford had grown involuntarily restless, and when her last tragic whisper ceased all his body seemed shaken with a terrible violence of his joy. He strode to and fro in the dark shadow of the stone. The receding blood left him cold, with a pricking, sickening sensation over his body, but there seemed to be an overwhelming tide accumulating deep in his breast—a tide of passion and pain. He dominated the passion, but the ache remained. And he returned to the quiet figure on the stone.

"Fay Larkin!" he exclaimed, with a deep breath of relief that the secret was disclosed. "So you're not a wife!... You're free! Thank Heaven! But I felt it was sacrifice. I knew there had been a crime. For crime it is. You child! You can't understand what crime. Oh, almost I wish you and Jane and Lassiter had never been found. But that's wrong of me. One year of agony —that shall not ruin your life. Fay, I will take you away."

"Where?" she whispered.

"Away from this Mormon country—to the East," he replied, and he spoke of what he had known, of travel, of cities, of people, of happiness possible for a young girl who had spent all her life hidden between the narrow walls of a silent, lonely valley—he spoke swiftly and eloquently till he lost his breath.

There was an instant of flashing wonder and joy on her white face, and then the radiance paled, the glow died. Her soul was the darker for that one strange, leaping glimpse of a glory not for such as she.

"I must stay here," she said, shudderingly.

"Fay!—How strange to SAY Fay aloud to YOU!—Fay, do you know the way to Surprise Valley?"

"I don't know where it is, but I could go straight to it," she replied.

"Take me there. Show me your beautiful valley. Let me see where you ran and climbed and spent so many lonely years."

"Ah, how I'd love to! But I dare not. And why should you want me to take you? We can run and climb here."

"I want to—I mean to save Jane Withersteen and Lassiter," he declared.

She uttered a little cry of pain. "Save them?"

"Yes, save them. Get them out of the valley, take them out of the country, far away where they and YOU—"

"But I can't go," she wailed. "I'm afraid. I'm bound. It CAN'T be broken. If I dared—if I tried to go they would catch me. They would hang Uncle Jim and leave Mother Jane alone there to starve."

"Fay, Lassiter and Jane both will starve—at least they will die there if we do not save them. You have been terribly wronged. You're a slave. You're not a wife."

"They—said I'll be burned in hell if I don't marry him.... Mother Jane never taught me about God. I don't know. But HE—he said God was there. I dare not break it."

"Fay, you have been deceived by old men. Let them have their creed. But YOU mustn't accept it."

"John, what is God to you?"

"Dear child, I—I am not sure of that myself," he replied, huskily. "When all this trouble is behind us, surely I can help you to understand and you can help me. The fact that you are alive—that Lassiter and Jane are alive—that I shall save you all—that lifts me up. I tell you—Fay Larkin will be my salvation."

"Your words trouble me. Oh, I shall be torn one way and another.... But, John, I daren't run away. I will not tell you where to find Lassiter and Mother Jane."

"I shall find them—I have the Indian. He found you for me. Nas Ta Bega will find Surprise Valley."

"Nas Ta Bega!... Oh, I remember. There was an Indian with the Mormons who found us. But he was a Piute."

"Nas Ta Bega never told me how he learned about you. That he learned was enough. And, Fay, he will find Surprise Valley. He will save Uncle Jim and Mother Jane."

Fay's hands clasped Shefford's in strong, trembling pressure; the tears streamed down her white cheeks; a tragic and eloquent joy convulsed her face.

"Oh, my friend, save them! But I can't go.... Let them keep me! Let him kill me!"

"Him! Fay—he shall not harm you," replied Shefford in passionate earnestness.

She caught the hand he had struck out with.

"You talk—you look like Uncle Jim when he spoke of the Mormons," she said. "Then I used to be afraid of him. He was so different. John, you must not do anything about me. Let me be. It's too late. He—and his men—they would hang you. And I couldn't bear that. I've enough to bear without losing my friend. Say you won't watch and wait—for—for him."

Shefford had to promise her. Like an Indian she gave expression to primitive feeling, for it certainly never occurred to her that, whatever Shefford might do, he was not the kind of man to wait in hiding for an enemy. Fay had faltered through her last speech and was now weak and nervous and frightened. Shefford took her back to the cabin.

"Fay, don't be distressed," he said. "I won't do anything right away. You can trust me. I won't be rash. I'll consult you before I make a move. I haven't any idea what I could do, anyway.... You must bear up. Why, it looks as if you're sorry I found you."

"Oh! I'm glad!" she whispered.

"Then if you're glad you mustn't break down this way again. Suppose some of the women happened to run into us."

"I won't again. It's only you—you surprised me so. I used to think how I'd like you to know—I wasn't really dead. But now—it's different. It hurts me here. Yet I'm glad—if my being alive makes you—a little happier."

Shefford felt that he had to go then. He could not trust himself any further.

"Good night, Fay," he said.

"Good night, John," she whispered. "I promise—to be good to-morrow."

She was crying softly when he left her. Twice he turned to see the dim, white, slender form against the gloom of the cabin. Then he went on under the pinyons, blindly down the path, with his heart as heavy as lead. That night as he rolled in his blanket and stretched wearily he felt that he would never be able to sleep. The wind in the cedars made him shiver. The great stars seemed relentless, passionless, white eyes, mocking his little destiny and his pain. The huge shadow of the mountain resembled the shadow of the insurmountable barrier between Fay and him.

. . .

Her pitiful, childish promise to be good was in his mind when he went to her home on the next night. He wondered how she would be, and he realized a desperate need of self-control.

But that night Fay Larkin was a different girl. In the dark, before she spoke, he felt a difference that afforded him surprise and relief. He greeted her as usual. And then it seemed, though not at all clearly, that he was listening to a girl, strangely and unconsciously glad to see him, who spoke with deeper note in her voice, who talked where always she had listened, whose sadness was there under an eagerness, a subdued gaiety as new to her, as sweet as it was bewildering. And he responded with emotion, so that the hour passed swiftly, and he found himself back in camp, in a kind of dream, unable to remember much of what she had said, sure only of this strange sweetness suddenly come to her.

Upon the following night, however, he discovered what had wrought this singular change in Fay Larkin. She loved him and she did not know it. How passionately sweet and sad and painful was that realization for Shefford! The hour spent with her then was only a moment.

He walked under the stars that night and they shed a glorious light upon him. He tried to think, to plan, but the sweetness of remembered word or look made mental effort almost impossible. He got as far as the thought that he would do well to drift, to wait till she learned she loved him, and then, perhaps, she could be persuaded to let him take her and Lassiter and Jane away together.

And from that night he went at his work and the part he played in the village with a zeal and a cunning that left him free to seek Fay when he chose.

Sometimes in the afternoon, always for a while in the evening, he was with her. They climbed the walls, and sat upon a lonely height to look afar; they walked under the stars, and the cedars, and the shadows of the great cliffs. She had a beautiful mind. Listening to her, he imagined he saw down into beautiful Surprise Valley with all its weird shadows, its colored walls and painted caves, its golden shafts of morning light and the red haze at sunset; and he felt the silence that must have been there, and the singing of the wind in the cliffs, and the sweetness and fragrance of the flowers, and the wildness of it all. Love had worked a marvelous transformation in this girl who had lived her life in a canyon. The burden upon her did not weigh heavily. She could not have an unhappy thought. She spoke of the village, of her Mormon companions, of daily happenings, of Stonebridge, of many things in a matter-of-fact way that showed how little they occupied her mind. She even spoke of sealed wives in a kind of dreamy abstraction. Something had possession of her, something as strong as the nature which had developed her, and in its power she, in her simplicity, was utterly unconscious, a watching and feeling girl. A strange, witching, radiant beauty lurked in her smile. And Shefford heard her laugh in his dreams.

The weeks slipped by. The black mountain took on a white cap of snow; in the early mornings there was ice in the crevices on the heights and frost in the valley. In the sheltered canyon where sunshine seemed to linger it was warm and pleasant, so that winter did not kill the flowers.

Shefford waited so long for Fay's awakening that he believed it would never come, and, believing, had not the heart to force it upon her. Then there was a growing fear with him. What would Fay Larkin do when she awakened to the truth? Fay was indeed like that white and fragile lily which bloomed in the silent, lonely canyon, but the same nature that had created it had created her. Would she droop as the lily would in a furnace blast? More than that, he feared a sudden flashing into life of strength, power, passion, hate. She did not hate yet because she did not yet realize love. She was utterly innocent of any wrong having been done her. More and more he began to fear, and a foreboding grew upon him. He made up his mind to broach the subject of Surprise Valley and of escaping with Lassiter and Jane; still, every time he was with Fay the girl and her beauty and her love were so wonderful that he put off the ordeal till the next night. As time flew by he excused his vacillation on the score that winter was not a good time to try to cross the desert. There was no grass for the mustangs, except in well-known valleys, and these he must shun. Spring would soon come. So the days passed, and he loved Fay more all the time, desperately living out to its limit the sweetness of every moment with her, and paying for his bliss in the increasing trouble that beset him when once away from her charm.

One starry night, about ten o'clock, he went, as was his custom, to drink at the spring. Upon his return to the cedars Nas Ta Bega, who slept under the same tree with him, had arisen, with his blanket hanging half off his shoulder.

"Listen," said the Indian.

Shefford took one glance at the dark, somber face, with its inscrutable eyes, now so strange and piercing, and then, with a kind of cold excitement, he faced the way the Indian looked, and listened. But he heard only the soft moan of the night wind in the cedars.

Nas Ta Bega kept the rigidity of his position for a moment, and then he relaxed, and stood at ease. Shefford knew the Indian had made a certainty of what must have been a doubtful sound. And Shefford leaned his ear to the wind and strained his hearing.

Then the soft night breeze brought a faint patter—the slow trot of horses on a hard trail. Some one was coming into the village at a late hour. Shefford thought of Joe Lake. But Joe lay right behind him, asleep in his blankets. It could not be Withers, for the trader was in Durango at that time. Shefford thought of Willetts and Shadd.

"Who's coming?" he asked low of the Indian.

Nas Ta Bega pointed down the trail without speaking.

Shefford peered through the white dim haze of starlight and presently he made out moving figures. Horses, with riders—a string of them—one—two—three—four—five—and he counted up to eleven. Eleven horsemen riding into the village! He was amazed, and suddenly keenly anxious. This visit might be one of Shadd's raids.

"Shadd's gang!" he whispered.

"No, Bi Nai," replied Nas Ta Bega, and he drew Shefford farther into the shade of the cedars. His voice, his action, the way he kept a hand on Shefford's shoulder, all this told much to the young man.

Mormons come on a night visit! Shefford realized it with a slight shock. Then swift as a lightning flash he was rent by another shock—one that brought cold moisture to his brow and to his heart a flame of hell.

He was shaking when he sank down to find the support of a log. Like a shadow the Indian silently moved away. Shefford watched the eleven horses pass the camp, go down the road, to disappear in the village. They vanished, and the soft clip-clops of hoofs died away. There was nothing left to prove he had not dreamed.

Nothing to prove it except this sudden terrible demoralization of his physical and spiritual being! While he peered out into the valley, toward the black patch of cedars and pinyons that hid the cabins, moments and moments passed, and in them he was gripped with cold and fire.

Was the Mormon who had abducted Fay—the man with the cruel voice—was he among those eleven horsemen? He might not have been. What a torturing hope! But vain—vain, for inevitably he must be among them. He was there in the cabin already. He had dismounted, tied his horse, had knocked on her door. Did he need to knock? No, he would go in, he would call her in that cruel voice, and then...

Shefford pulled a blanket from his bed and covered his cold and trembling body. He had sunk down off the log, was leaning back upon it. The stars were pale, far off, and the valley seemed unreal. He found himself listening—listening with sick and terrible earnestness, trying to hear against the thrum and beat of his heart, straining to catch a sound in all that cold, star-blanched, silent valley. But he could hear no sound. It was as if death held the valley in its perfect silence. How he hated that silence! There ought to have been a million horrible, bellowing demons making the night hideous. Did the stars serenely look down upon the lonely cabins of these exiles? Was there no thunderbolt to drop down from that dark and looming mountain upon the silent cabin where tragedy had entered? In all the world, under the sea, in the abysmal caves, in the vast spaces of the air, there was no such terrible silence as this. A scream, a long cry, a moan—these were natural to a woman, and why did not one of these sealed wives, why did not Fay Larkin, damn this everlasting acquiescent silence? Perhaps she would fly out of her cabin, come running along the path. Shefford peered into the bright patches of starlight and into the shadows of the cedars. But he saw no moving form in the open, no dim white shape against the gloom. And he heard no sound—not even a whisper of wind in the branches overhead.

Nas Ta Bega returned to the shade of the cedars and, lying down on his blankets, covered himself and went to sleep. The fact seemed to bring bitter reality to Shefford. Nothing was going to happen. The valley was to be the same this night as any other night. Shefford accepted the truth. He experienced a kind of self-pity. The night he had thought so much about, prepared for, and had forgotten had now arrived. Then he threw another blanket round him, and, cold, dark, grim, he faced that lonely vigil, meaning to sit there, wide-eyed, to endure and to wait.

Jealousy and pain, following his frenzy, abided with him long hours, and when they passed he divined that selfishness passed with them. What he suffered then was for Fay Larkin and for her sisters in misfortune. He grew big enough to pity these fanatics. The fiery, racing tide of blood that had made of him only an animal had cooled with thought of others. Still he feared that stultifying thing which must have been hate. What a tempest had raged within him! This blood of his, that had received a stronger strain from his desert life, might in a single moment flood out reason and intellect and make him a vengeful man. So in those starlit hours that dragged interminably he looked deep into his heart and tried to fortify himself against a dark and evil moment to come.

Midnight—and the valley seemed a tomb! Did he alone keep wakeful? The sky was a darker blue, the stars burned a whiter fire, the peaks stood looming and vast, tranquil sentinels of that valley, and the wind rose to sigh, to breathe, to mourn through the cedars. It was a sad music. The Indian lay prone, dark face to the stars. Joe Lake lay prone, sleeping as quietly, with his dark face exposed to the starlight. The gentle movement of the cedar branches changed the shape of the bright patches on the grass where shadow and light met. The walls of the valley waved upward, dark below and growing paler, to shine faintly at the rounded rims. And there was a tiny, silvery tinkle of running water over stones.

Here was a little nook of the vast world. Here were tranquillity, beauty, music, loneliness, life. Shefford wondered—did he alone keep watchful? Did he feel that he could see dark, wide eyes peering into the gloom? And it came to him after a time that he was not alone in his vigil, nor was Fay Larkin alone in her agony. There was some one else in the valley, a great and breathing and watchful spirit. It entered into Shefford's soul and he trembled. What had come to him? And he answered—only added pain and new love, and a strange strength from the firmament and the peaks and the silence and the shadows.

The bright belt with its three radiant stars sank behind the western wall and there was a paler gloom upon the valley.

Then a few lights twinkled in the darkness that enveloped the cabins; a woman's laugh strangely broke the silence, profaning it, giving the lie to that somber yoke which seemed to consist of the very shadows; the voices of men were heard, and then the slow clip-clop of trotting horses on the hard trail.

Shefford saw the Mormons file out into the paling starlight, ride down the valley, and vanish in the gray gloom. He was aware that the Indian sat up to watch the procession ride by, and that Joe turned over, as if disturbed.

One by one the stars went out. The valley became a place of gray shadows. In the east a light glowed. Shefford sat there, haggard and worn, watching the coming of the dawn, the kindling of the light; and had the power been his the dawn would never have broken and the rose and gold never have tipped the lofty peaks.

Shefford attended to his camp chores as usual. Several times he was aware of Joe's close scrutiny, and finally, without looking at him, Shefford told of the visit of the Mormons. A violent expulsion of breath was Joe's answer and it might have been a curse. Straightway Joe ceased his cheery whistling and became as somber as the Indian. The camp was silent; the men did not look at one another. While they sat at breakfast Shefford's back was turned toward the village—he had not looked in that direction since dawn.

"Ugh!" suddenly exclaimed Nas Ta Bega.

Joe Lake muttered low and deep, and this time there was no mistake about the nature of his speech. Shefford did not have the courage to turn to see what had caused these exclamations. He knew since today had dawned that there was calamity in the air.

"Shefford, I reckon if I know women there's a little hell coming to you," said the Mormon, significantly.

Shefford wheeled as if a powerful force had turned him on a pivot. He saw Fay Larkin. She seemed to be almost running. She was unhooded and her bright hair streamed down. Her swift, lithe action was without its usual grace. She looked wild, and she almost fell crossing the stepping-stones of the brook.

Joe hurried to meet her, took hold of her arm and spoke, but she did not seem to hear him. She drew him along with her, up the little bench under the cedars straight toward Shefford. Her face held a white, mute agony, as if in the hour of strife it had hardened into marble. But her eyes were dark-purple fire—windows of an extraordinarily intense and vital life. In one night the girl had become a woman. But the blight Shefford had dreaded to see— the withering of the exquisite soul and spirit and purity he had considered inevitable, just as inevitable as the death of something similar in the flower she resembled, when it was broken and defiled—nothing of this was manifest in her. Straight and swiftly she came to him back in the shade of the cedars and took hold of his hands.

"Last night—HE CAME!" she said.

"Yes—Fay—I—I know," replied Shefford, haltingly.

He was tremblingly conscious of amaze at her—of something wonderful in her. She did not heed Joe, who stepped aside a little; she did not see Nas Ta Bega, who sat motionless on a log, apparently oblivious to her presence.

"You knew he came?"

"Yes, Fay. I was awake when—they rode in. I watched them. I sat up all night. I saw them ride away."

"If you knew when he came why didn't you run to me—to get to me before he did?"

Her question was unanswerable. It had the force of a blow. It stunned him. Its sharp, frank directness sprang from a simplicity and a strength that had not been nurtured in the life he had lived. So far men had wandered from truth and nature!

"I came to you as soon as I was able," she went on. "I must have fainted. I just had to drag myself around.... And now I can tell you."

He was powerless to reply, as if she had put another unanswerable question. What did she mean to tell him? What might she not tell him? She loosed her hands from his and lifted them to his shoulders, and that was the first conscious action of feeling, of intimacy, which she had ever shown. It quite robbed Shefford of strength, and in spite of his sorrow there was an indefinable thrill in her touch. He looked at her, saw the white-and-gold beauty that was hers yesterday and seemed changed to-day, and he recognized Fay Larkin in a woman he did not know.

"Listen! He came—"

"Fay, don't—tell me," interrupted Shefford.

"I WILL tell you," she said.

Did the instinct of love teach her how to mitigate his pain? Shefford felt that, as he felt the new-born strength in her.

"Listen," she went on. "He came when I was undressing for bed. I heard the horse. He knocked on the door. Something terrible happened to me then. I felt sick and my head wasn't clear. I remember next—his being in the room—the lamp was out—I couldn't see very well. He thought I was sick and he gave me a drink and let the air blow in on me through the window. I remember I lay back in the chair and I thought. And I listened. When would you come? I didn't feel that you could leave me there alone with him. For his coming was different this time. That pain like a blade in my side!... When it came I was not the same. I loved you. I understood then. I belonged to you. I couldn't let him touch me. I had never been his wife. When I realized this—that he was there, that you might suffer for it—I cried right out.

"He thought I was sick. He worked over me. He gave me medicine. And then he prayed. I saw him, in the dark, on his knees, praying for me. That seemed strange. Yet he was kind, so kind that I begged him to let me go. I was not a Mormon. I couldn't marry him. I begged him to let me go.

"Then he thought I had been deceiving him. He fell into a fury. He talked for a long time. He called upon God to visit my sins upon me. He tried to make me pray. But I wouldn't. And then I fought him. I'd have screamed for you had he not smothered me. I got weak.... And you never came. I know I thought you would come. But you didn't. Then I—I gave out. And after—some time—I must have fainted."

"Fay! For Heaven's sake, how could I come to you?" burst out Shefford, hoarse and white with remorse, passion, pain.

"If I'm any man's wife I'm yours. It's a thing you FEEL, isn't it? I know that now.... But I want to know what to do?"

"Fay!" he cried, huskily.

"I'm sick of it all. If it weren't for you I'd climb the wall and throw myself off. That would be easy for me. I'd love to die that way. All my life I've been high up on the walls. To fall would be nothing!"

"Oh, you mustn't talk like that!"

"Do you love me?" she asked, with a low and deathless sweetness.

"Love you? With all my heart! Nothing can change that!"

"Do you want me—as you used to want the Fay Larkin lost in Surprise Valley? Do you love me that way? I understand things better than before, but still—not all. I AM Fay Larkin. I think I must have dreamed of you all my life. I was glad when you came here. I've been happy lately. I forgot—till last night. Maybe it needed that to make me see I've loved you all the time.... And I fought him like a wildcat!... Tell me the truth. I feel I'm yours. Is that true? If I'm not—I'll not live another hour. Something holds me up. I am the same.... Do you want me?"

"Yes, Fay Larkin, I want you," replied Shefford, steadily, with his grip on her arms.

"Then take me away. I don't want to live here another hour."

"Fay, I'll take you. But it can't be done at once. We must plan. I need help. There are Lassiter and Jane to get out of Surprise Valley. Give me time, dear—give me time. It'll be a hard job. And we must plan so we can positively get away. Give me time, Fay."

"Suppose HE comes back?" she queried, with a singular depth of voice.

"We'll have to risk that," replied Shefford, miserably. "But—he won't come soon."

"He said he would," she flashed.

Shefford seemed to freeze inwardly with her words. Love had made her a woman and now the woman in her was speaking. She saw the truth as he could not see it. And the truth was nature. She had been hidden all her life from the world, from knowledge as he had it, yet when love betrayed her womanhood to her she acquired all its subtlety.

"If I wait and he DOES come will you keep me from him?" she asked.

"How can I? I'm staking all on the chance of his not coming soon. ... But, Fay, if he DOES come and I don't give up our secret—how on earth can I keep you from him?" demanded Shefford.

"If you love me you will do it," she said, as simply as if she were fate.

"But how?" cried Shefford, almost beside himself.

"You are a man. Any man would save the woman who loves him from—from—Oh, from a beast!... How would Lassiter do it?"

"Lassiter!"

"YOU CAN KILL HIM!"

It was there, deep and full in her voice, the strength of the elemental forces that had surrounded her, primitive passion and hate and love, as they were in woman in the beginning.

"My God!" Shefford cried aloud with his spirit when all that was red in him sprang again into a flame of hell. That was what had been wrong with him last night. He could kill this stealthy night-rider, and now, face to face with Fay, who had never been so beautiful and wonderful as in this hour when she made love the only and the sacred thing of life, now he had it in him to kill. Yet, murder—even to kill a brute—that was not for John Shefford, not the way for him to save a woman. Reason and wisdom still fought the passion in him. If he could but cling to them—have them with him in the dark and contending hour!

She leaned against him now, exhausted, her soul in her eyes, and they saw only him. Shefford was all but powerless to resist the longing to take her into his arms, to hold her to his heart, to let himself go. Did not her love give her to him? Shefford gazed helplessly at the stricken Joe Lake, at the somber Indian, as if from them he expected help.

"I know him now," said Fay, breaking the silence with startling suddenness.

"What!"

"I've seen him in the light. I flashed a candle in his face. I saw it. I know him now. He was there at Stonebridge with us, and I never knew him. But I know him now. His name is—"

"For God's sake don't tell me who he is!" implored Shefford.

Ignorance was Shefford's safeguard against himself. To make a name of this heretofore intangible man, to give him an identity apart from the crowd, to be able to recognize him— that for Shefford would be fatal.

"Fay—tell me—no more," he said, brokenly. "I love you and I will give you my life. Trust me. I swear I'll save you."

"Will you take me away soon?"

"Yes."

She appeared satisfied with that and dropped her hands and moved back from him. A light flitted over her white face, and her eyes grew dark and humid, losing their fire in changing, shadowing thought of submission, of trust, of hope.

"I can lead you to Surprise Valley," she said. "I feel the way. It's there!" And she pointed to the west.

"Fay, we'll go—soon. I must plan. I'll see you to-night. Then we'll talk. Run home now, before some of the women see you here."

She said good-by and started away under the cedars, out into the open where her hair shone like gold in the sunlight, and she took the stepping-stones with her old free grace, and strode down the path swift and lithe as an Indian. Once she turned to wave a hand.

Shefford watched her with a torture of pride, love, hope, and fear contending within him.

❧ 14 ❧

THE NAVAJO

THAT MORNING a Piute rode into the valley.

Shefford recognized him as the brave who had been in love with Glen Naspa. The moment Nas Ta Bega saw this visitor he made a singular motion with his hands—a motion that somehow to Shefford suggested despair—and then he waited, somber and statuesque, for the messenger to come to him. It was the Piute who did all the talking, and that was brief. Then the Navajo stood motionless, with his hands crossed over his breast. Shefford drew near and waited.

"Bi Nai," said the Navajo, "Nas Ta Bega said his sister would come home some day.... Glen Naspa is in the hogan of her grandfather."

He spoke in his usual slow, guttural voice, and he might have been bronze for all the emotion he expressed; yet Shefford instinctively felt the despair that had been hinted to him, and he put his hand on the Indian's shoulder.

"If I am the Navajo's brother, then I am brother to Glen Naspa," he said. "I will go with you to the hogan of Hosteen Doetin."

Nas Ta Bega went away into the valley for the horses. Shefford hurried to the village, made his excuses at the school, and then called to explain to Fay that trouble of some kind had come to the Indian.

Soon afterward he was riding Nack-yal on the rough and winding trail up through the broken country of cliffs and canyon to the great league-long sage and cedar slope of the mountain. It was weeks since he had ridden the mustang. Nack-yal was fat and lazy. He loved his master, but he did not like the climb, and so fell far behind the lean and wiry pony that carried Nas Ta Bega. The sage levels were as purple as the haze of the distance, and there was a bitter-sweet tang on the strong, cool wind. The sun was gold behind the dark line of fringe on the mountain-top. A flock of sheep swept down one of the sage levels, looking like a narrow stream of white and black and brown. It was always amazing for Shefford to see how swiftly these Navajo sheep grazed along. Wild mustangs plunged out of the cedar clumps and stood upon the ridges, whistling defiance or curiosity, and their manes and tails waved in the wind.

Shefford mounted slowly to the cedar bench in the midst of which were hidden the few hogans. And he halted at the edge to dismount and take a look at that downward-sweeping world of color, of wide space, at the wild desert upland which from there unrolled its magnificent panorama.

Then he passed on into the cedars. How strange to hear the lambs bleating again! Lambing-time had come early, but still spring was there in the new green of grass, in the bright upland flower. He led his mustang out of the cedars into the cleared circle. It was full of colts and lambs, and there were the shepherd-dogs and a few old rams and ewes. But the circle was a quiet place this day. There were no Indians in sight. Shefford loosened the saddle-girths on Nack-yal and, leaving him to graze, went toward the hogan of Hosteen Doetin. A blanket was hung across the door. Shefford heard a low chanting. He waited beside the door till the covering was pulled in, then he entered.

Hosteen Doetin met him, clasped his hand. The old Navajo could not speak; his fine face was working in grief; tears streamed from his dim old eyes and rolled down his wrinkled cheeks. His sorrow was no different from a white man's sorrow. Beyond him Shefford saw Nas Ta Bega standing with folded arms, somehow terrible in his somber impassiveness. At his feet crouched the old woman, Hosteen Doetin's wife, and beside her, prone and quiet, half covered with a blanket, lay Glen Naspa.

She was dead. To Shefford she seemed older than when he had last seen her. And she was beautiful. Calm, cold, dark, with only bitter lips to give the lie to peace! There was a story in those lips.

At her side, half hidden under the fold of blanket, lay a tiny bundle. Its human shape startled Shefford. Then he did not need to be told the tragedy. When he looked again at Glen Naspa's face he seemed to understand all that had made her older, to feel the pain that had lined and set her lips.

She was dead, and she was the last of Nas Ta Bega's family. In the old grandfather's agony, in the wild chant of the stricken grandmother, in the brother's stern and terrible calmness Shefford felt more than the death of a loved one. The shadow of ruin, of doom, of death hovered over the girl and her family and her tribe and her race. There was no consolation to offer these relatives of Glen Naspa. Shefford took one more fascinated gaze at her dark, eloquent, prophetic face, at the tragic tiny shape by her side, and then with bowed head he left the hogan.

Outside he paced to and fro, with an aching heart for Nas Ta Bega, with something of the white man's burden of crime toward the Indian weighing upon his soul.

Old Hosteen Doetin came to him with shaking hands and words memorable of the time Glen Naspa left his hogan.

"Me no savvy Jesus Christ. Me hungry. Me no eat Jesus Christ!"

That seemed to be all of his trouble that he could express to Shefford. He could not understand the religion of the missionary, this Jesus Christ who had called his granddaughter away. And the great fear of an old Indian was not death, but hunger. Shefford remembered a custom of the Navajos, a thing barbarous looked at with a white man's mind. If an old Indian failed on a long march he was inclosed by a wall of stones, given plenty to eat and drink, and left there to die in the desert. Not death did he fear, but hunger! Old Hosteen Doetin expected to starve, now that the young and strong squaw of his family was gone.

Shefford spoke in his halting Navajo and assured the old Indian that Nas Ta Bega would never let him starve.

At sunset Shefford stood with Nas Ta Bega facing the west. The Indian was magnificent in repose. He watched the sun go down upon the day that had seen the burial of the last of his family. He resembled an impassive destiny, upon which no shocks fell. He had the light of that flaring golden sky in his face, the majesty of the mountain in his mien, the silence of the great gulf below on his lips. This educated Navajo, who had reverted to the life of his ancestors, found in the wildness and loneliness of his environment a strength no white teaching could ever have given him. Shefford sensed in him a measureless grief, an impenetrable gloom, a tragic acceptance of the meaning of Glen Naspa's ruin and death—the vanishing of his race from the earth. Death had written the law of such bitter truth round Glen Naspa's lips, and the same truth was here in the grandeur and gloom of the Navajo.

"Bi Nai," he said, with the beautiful sonorous roll in his voice, "Glen Naspa is in her grave and there are no paths to the place of her sleep. Glen Naspa is gone."

"Gone! Where? Nas Ta Bega, remember I lost my own faith, and I have not yet learned yours."

"The Navajo has one mother—the earth. Her body has gone to the earth and it will become dust. But her spirit is in the air. It shall whisper to me from the wind. I shall hear it on running waters. It will hide in the morning music of a mocking-bird and in the lonely night cry of the canyon hawk. Her blood will go to make the red of the Indian flowers and her soul will rest at midnight in the lily that opens only to the moon. She will wait in the shadow for me, and live in the great mountain that is my home, and for ever step behind me on the trail."

"You will kill Willetts?" demanded Shefford.

"The Navajo will not seek the missionary."

"But if you meet him you'll kill him?"

"Bi Nai, would Nas Ta Bega kill after it is too late? What good could come? The Navajo is above revenge."

"If he crosses my trail I think I couldn't help but kill him," muttered Shefford in a passion that wrung the threat from him.

The Indian put his arm round the white man's shoulders.

"Bi Nai, long ago I made you my brother. And now you make me your brother. Is it not so? Glen Naspa's spirit calls for wisdom, not revenge. Willetts must be a bad man. But we'll let him live. Life will punish him. Who knows if he was all to blame? Glen Naspa was only one pretty Indian girl. There are many white men in the desert. She loved a white man when she was a baby. The thing was a curse. ... Listen, Bi Nai, and the Navajo will talk.

"Many years ago the Spanish padres, the first white men, came into the land of the Indian. Their search was for gold. But they were not wicked men. They did not steal and kill. They taught the Indian many useful things. They brought him horses. But when they went away they left him unsatisfied with his life and his god.

"Then came the pioneers. They crossed the great river and took the pasture-lands and the hunting-grounds of the Indian. They drove him backward, and the Indian grew sullen. He began to fight. The white man's government made treaties with the Indian, and these were broken. Then war came—fierce and bloody war. The Indian was driven to the waste places. The stream of pioneers, like a march of ants, spread on into the desert. Every valley where grass grew, every river, became a place for farms and towns. Cattle choked the water-holes where the buffalo and deer had once gone to drink. The forests in the hills were cut and the springs dried up. And the pioneers followed to the edge of the desert.

"Then came the prospectors, mad, like the padres for the gleam of gold. The day was not long enough for them to dig in the creeks and the canyon; they worked in the night. And they brought weapons and rum to the Indian, to buy from him the secret of the places where the shining gold lay hidden.

"Then came the traders. And they traded with the Indian. They gave him little for much, and that little changed his life. He learned a taste for the sweet foods of the white man. Because he could trade for a sack of flour he worked less in the field. And the very fiber of his bones softened.

"Then came the missionaries. They were proselytizers for converts to their religion. The missionaries are good men. There may be a bad missionary, like Willetts, the same as there are bad men in other callings, or bad Indians. They say Shadd is a half-breed. But the Piutes can tell you he is a full-blood, and he, like me, was sent to a white man's school. In the beginning the missionaries did well for the Indian. They taught him cleaner ways of living, better farming, useful work with tools—many good things. But the wrong to the Indian was the undermining of his faith. It was not humanity that sent the missionary to the Indian. Humanity would have helped the Indian in his ignorance of sickness and work, and left him his god. For to trouble the Indian about his god worked at the roots of his nature.

"The beauty of the Indian's life is in his love of the open, of all that is nature, of silence, freedom, wildness. It is a beauty of mind and soul. The Indian would have been content to watch and feel. To a white man he might be dirty and lazy—content to dream life away without trouble or what the white man calls evolution. The Indian might seem cruel because he leaves his old father out in the desert to die. But the old man wants to die that way, alone with his spirits and the sunset. And the white man's medicine keeps his old father alive days and days after he ought to be dead. Which is more cruel? The Navajos used to fight with other tribes, and then they were stronger men than they are to-day.

"But leaving religion, greed, and war out of the question, contact with the white man would alone have ruined the Indian. The Indian and the white man cannot mix. The Indian brave learns the habits of the white man, acquires his diseases, and has not the mind or body to withstand them. The Indian girl learns to love the white man—and that is death of her Indian soul, if not of life.

"So the red man is passing. Tribes once powerful have died in the life of Nas Ta Bega. The curse of the white man is already heavy upon my race in the south. Here in the north, in the wildest corner of the desert, chased here by the great soldier, Carson, the Navajo has made his last stand.

"Bi Nai, you have seen the shadow in the hogan of Hosteen Doetin. Glen Naspa has gone to her grave, and no sisters, no children, will make paths to the place of her sleep. Nas Ta Bega will never have a wife—a child. He sees the end. It is the sunset of the Navajo.... Bi Nai, the Navajo is dying—dying—dying!"

WILD JUSTICE

A CRESCENT MOON hung above the lofty peak over the valley and a train of white stars ran along the bold rim of the western wall. A few young frogs peeped plaintively. The night was cool, yet had a touch of balmy spring, and a sweeter fragrance, as if the cedars and pinyons had freshened in the warm sun of that day.

Shefford and Fay were walking in the aisles of moonlight and the patches of shade, and Nas Ta Bega, more than ever a shadow of his white brother, followed them silently.

"Fay, it's growing late. Feel the dew?" said Shefford. "Come, I must take you back."

"But the time's so short. I have said nothing that I wanted to say," she replied.

"Say it quickly, then, as we go."

"After all, it's only—will you take me away soon?"

"Yes, very soon. The Indian and I have talked. But we've made no plan yet. There are only three ways to get out of this country. By Stonebridge, by Kayenta and Durango, and by Red Lake. We must choose one. All are dangerous. We must lose time finding Surprise Valley. I hoped the Indian could find it. Then we'd bring Lassiter and Jane here and hide them near till dark, then take you and go. That would give us a night's start. But you must help us to Surprise Valley."

"I can go right to it, blindfolded, or in the dark.... Oh, John, hurry! I dread the wait. He might come again."

"Joe says—they won't come very soon."

"Is it far—where we're going—out of the country?"

"Ten days' hard riding."

"Oh! That night ride to and from Stonebridge nearly killed me. But I could walk very far, and climb for ever."

"Fay, we'll get out of the country if I have to carry you."

When they arrived at the cabin Fay turned on the porch step and, with her face nearer a level with his, white and sweet in the moonlight, with her eyes shining and unfathomable, she was more than beautiful.

"You've never been inside my house," she said. "Come in. I've something for you."

"But it's late," he remonstrated. "I suppose you've got me a cake or pie—something to eat. You women all think Joe and I have to be fed."

"No. You'd never guess. Come in," she said, and the rare smile on her face was something Shefford would have gone far to see.

"Well, then, for a minute."

He crossed the porch, the threshold, and entered her home. Her dim, white shape moved in the darkness. And he followed into a room where the moon shone through the open window, giving soft, mellow, shadowy light. He discerned objects, but not clearly, for his senses seemed absorbed in the strange warmth and intimacy of being for the first time with her in her home.

"No, it's not good to eat," she said, and her laugh was happy. "Here—"

Suddenly she abruptly ceased speaking. Shefford saw her plainly, and the slender form had stiffened, alert and strained. She was listening.

"What was that?" she whispered.

"I didn't hear anything," he whispered back.

He stepped softly nearer the open window and listened.

Clip-clop! clip-clop! clip-clop! Hard hoofs on the hard path outside!

A strong and rippling thrill went over Shefford. In the soft light her eyes seemed unnaturally large and black and fearful.

Clip-clop! clip-clop!

The horse stopped outside. Then followed a metallic clink of spur against stirrup—thud of boots on hard ground—heavy footsteps upon the porch.

A swift, cold contraction of throat, of breast, convulsed Shefford. His only thought was that he could not think.

"Ho—Mary!"

A voice liberated both Shefford's muscle and mind—a voice of strange, vibrant power. Authority of religion and cruelty of will—these Mormon attributes constituted that power. And Shefford suffered a transformation which must have been ordered by demons. That sudden flame seemed to curl and twine and shoot along his veins with blasting force. A rancorous and terrible cry leaped to his lips.

"Ho—Mary!" Then came a heavy tread across the threshold of the outer room.

Shefford dared not look at Fay. Yet, dimly, from the corner of his eye, he saw her, a pale shadow, turned to stone, with her arms out. If he looked, if he made sure of that, he was lost. When had he drawn his gun? It was there, a dark and glinting thing in his hand. He must fly —not through cowardice and fear, but because in one more moment he would kill a man. Swift as the thought he dove through the open window. And, leaping up, he ran under the dark pinyons toward camp.

Joe Lake had been out late himself. He sat by the fire, smoking his pipe. He must have seen or heard Shefford coming, for he rose with unwonted alacrity, and he kicked the smoldering logs into a flickering blaze.

Shefford, realizing his deliverance, came panting, staggering into the light. The Mormon uttered an exclamation. Then he spoke, anxiously, but what he said was not clear in Shefford's thick and throbbing ears. He dropped his pipe, a sign of perturbation, and he stared.

But Shefford, without a word, lunged swiftly away into the shadow of the cedars. He found relief in action. He began a steep ascent of the east wall, a dangerous slant he had never dared even in daylight, and he climbed it without a slip. Danger, steep walls, perilous heights, night, and black canyon the same—these he never thought of. But something drove him to desperate effort, that the hours might seem short.

The red sun was tipping the eastern wall when he returned to camp, and he was neither calm nor sure of himself nor ready for sleep or food. Only he had put the night behind him.

The Indian showed no surprise. But Joe Lake's jaw dropped and his eyes rolled. Moreover, Joe bore a singular aspect, the exact nature of which did not at once dawn upon Shefford.

"By God! you've got nerve—or you're crazy!" he ejaculated, hoarsely.

Then it was Shefford's turn to stare. The Mormon was haggard, grieved, frightened, and utterly amazed. He appeared to be trying to make certain of Shefford's being there in the flesh and then to find reason for it.

"I've no nerve and I am crazy," replied Shefford. "But, Joe—what do you mean? Why do you look at me like that?"

"I reckon if I get your horse that'll square us. Did you come back for him? You'd better hit the trail quick."

"It's you now who're crazy," burst out Shefford.

"Wish to God I was," replied Joe.

It was then Shefford realized catastrophe, and cold fear gnawed at his vitals, so that he was sick.

"Joe, what has happened?" he asked, with the blood thick in his heart.

"Hadn't you better tell me?" demanded the Mormon, and a red wave blotted out the haggard shade of his face.

"You talk like a fool," said Shefford, sharply, and he strode right up to Joe.

"See here, Shefford, we've been pards. You're making it hard for me. Reckon you ain't square."

Shefford shot out a long arm and his hand clutched the Mormon's burly shoulder.

"Why am I not square? What do you mean?"

Joe swallowed hard and gave himself a shake. Then he eyed his comrade steadily.

"I was afraid you'd kill him. I reckon I can't blame you. I'll help you get away. And I'm a Mormon! Do you take the hunch?... But don't deny you killed him!"

"Killed whom?" gasped Shefford.

"Her husband!"

Shefford seemed stricken by a slow, paralyzing horror. The Mormon's changing face grew huge and indistinct and awful in his sight. He was clutched and shaken in Joe's rude hands, yet scarcely felt them. Joe seemed to be bellowing at him, but the voice was far off. Then Shefford began to see, to hear through some cold and terrible deadness that had come between him and everything.

"Say YOU killed him!" hoarsely supplicated the Mormon.

Shefford had not yet control of speech. Something in his gaze appeared to drive Joe frantic.

"Damn you! Tell me quick. Say YOU killed him!... If you want to know my stand, why, I'm glad!... Shefford, don't look so stony! ... For HER sake, say you killed him!"

Shefford stood with a face as gray and still as stone. With a groan the Mormon drew away from him and sank upon a log. He bowed his head; his broad shoulders heaved; husky sounds came from him. Then with a violent wrench he plunged to his feet and shook himself like a huge, savage dog.

"Reckon it's no time to weaken," he said, huskily, and with the words a dark, hard, somber bitterness came to his face.

"Where—is—she?" whispered Shefford.

"Shut up in the school-house," he replied.

"Did she—did she—"

"She neither denied nor confessed."

"Have you—seen her?"

"Yes."

"How did—she look?"

"Cool and quiet as the Indian there.... Game as hell! She always had stuff in her."

"Oh, Joe!... It's unbelievable!" cried Shefford. "That lovely, innocent girl! She couldn't—she couldn't."

"She's fixed him. Don't think of that. It's too late. We ought to have saved her."

"God!... She begged me to hurry—to take her away."

"Think what we can do NOW to save her," cut in the Mormon.

Shefford sustained a vivifying shock. "To save her?" he echoed.

"Think, man!"

"Joe, I can hit the trail and let you tell them I killed him," burst out Shefford in panting excitement.

"Reckon I can."

"So help me God I'll do it!"

The Mormon turned a dark and austere glance upon Shefford.

"You mustn't leave her. She killed him for your sake.... You must fight for her now—save her—take her away."

"But the law!"

"Law!" scoffed Joe. "In these wilds men get killed and there's no law. But if she's taken back to Stonebridge those iron-jawed old Mormons will make law enough to—to... Shefford, the thing is—get her away. Once out of the country, she's safe. Mormons keep their secrets."

"I'll take her. Joe, will you help me?"

Shefford, even in his agitation, felt the Mormon's silence to be a consent that need not have been asked. And Shefford had a passionate gratefulness toward his comrade. That stultifying and blinding prejudice which had always seemed to remove a Mormon outside the pale of certain virtue suffered final eclipse; and Joe Lake stood out a man, strange and crude, but with a heart and a soul.

"Joe, tell me what to do," said Shefford, with a simplicity that meant he needed only to be directed.

"Pull yourself together. Get your nerve back," replied Joe. "Reckon you'd better show yourself over there. No one saw you come in this morning—your absence from camp isn't known. It's better you seem curious and shocked like the rest of us. Come on. We'll go over. And afterward we'll get the Indian, and plan."

They left camp and, crossing the brook, took the shaded path toward the village. Hope of saving Fay, the need of all his strength and nerve and cunning to effect that end, gave Shefford the supreme courage to overcome his horror and fear. On that short walk under the pinyons to Fay's cabin he had suffered many changes of emotion, but never anything like this change which made him fierce and strong to fight, deep and crafty to plan, hard as iron to endure.

The village appeared very quiet, though groups of women stood at the doors of cabins. If they talked, it was very low. Henninger and Smith, two of the three Mormon men living in the village, were standing before the closed door of the school-house. A tigerish feeling thrilled Shefford when he saw them on guard there. Shefford purposely avoided looking at Fay's cabin as long as he could keep from it. When he had to look he saw several hooded, whispering women in the yard, and Beal, the other Mormon man, standing in the cabin door. Upon the porch lay the long shape of a man, covered with blankets.

Shefford experienced a horrible curiosity.

"Say, Beal, I've fetched Shefford over," said Lake. "He's pretty much cut up."

Beal wagged a solemn head, but said nothing. His mind seemed absent or steeped in gloom, and he looked up as one silently praying.

Joe Lake strode upon the little porch and, reaching down, he stripped the blanket from the shrouded form.

Shefford saw a sharp, cold, ghastly face. "WAGGONER!" he whispered.

"Yes," replied Lake.

Waggoner! Shefford remembered the strange power in his face, and, now that life had gone, that power was stripped of all disguise. Death, in Shefford's years of ministry, had lain under his gaze many times and in a multiplicity of aspects, but never before had he seen it stamped so strangely. Shefford did not need to be told that here was a man who believed he had conversed with God on earth, who believed he had a divine right to rule women, who had a will that would not yield itself to death utterly. Waggoner, then, was the devil who had come masked to Surprise Valley, had forced a martyrdom upon Fay Larkin. And this was the Mormon who had made Fay Larkin a murderess. Shefford had hated him living, and now he hated him dead. Death here was robbed of all nobility, of pathos, of majesty. It was only retribution. Wild justice! But alas! that it had to be meted out by a white-soled girl whose innocence was as great as the unconscious savagery which she had assimilated from her lonely and wild environment. Shefford laid a despairing curse upon his own head, and a terrible remorse knocked at his heart. He had left her alone, this girl in whom love had made the great change—like a coward he had left her alone. That curse he visited upon himself because he had been the spirit and the motive of this wild justice, and his should have been the deed.

Joe Lake touched Shefford's arm and pointed at the haft of a knife protruding from Waggoner's breast. It was a wooden haft. Shefford had seen it before somewhere.

Then he was struck with what perhaps Joe meant him to see—the singular impression the haft gave of one sweeping, accurate, powerful stroke. A strong arm had driven that blade home. The haft was sunk deep; there was a little depression in the cloth; no blood showed; and the weapon looked as if it could not be pulled out. Shefford's thought went fatally and irresistibly to Fay Larkin's strong arm. He saw her flash that white arm and lift the heavy bucket from the spring with an ease he wondered at. He felt the strong clasp of her hand as she had given it to him in a flying leap across a crevice upon the walls. Yes, her fine hand and the round, strong arm possessed the strength to have given that blade its singular directness and force. The marvel was not in the physical action. It hid inscrutably in the mystery of deadly passion rising out of a gentle and sad heart.

Joe Lake drew up the blanket and shut from Shefford's fascinated gaze that spare form, that accusing knife, that face of strange, cruel power.

"Anybody been sent for?" asked Lake of Beal.

"Yes. An Indian boy went for the Piute. We'll send him to Stonebridge," replied the Mormon.

"How soon do you expect any one here from Stonebridge?"

"To-morrow, mebbe by noon."

"Meantime what's to be done with—this?"

"Elder Smith thinks the body should stay right here where it fell till they come from Stonebridge."

"Waggoner was found here, then?"

"Right here."

"Who found him?"

"Mother Smith. She came over early. An' the sight made her scream. The women all came runnin'. Mother Smith had to be put to bed."

"Who found—Mary?"

"See here, Joe, I told you all I knowed once before," replied the Mormon, testily.

"I've forgotten. Was sort of bewildered. Tell me again.... Who found—her?"

"The women folks. She laid right inside the door, in a dead faint. She hadn't undressed. There was blood on her hands an' a cut or scratch. The women fetched her to. But she wouldn't talk. Then Elder Smith come an' took her. They've got her locked up."

Then Joe led Shefford away from the cabin farther on into the village. When they were halted by the somber, grieving women it was Joe who did the talking. They passed the school-house, and here Shefford quickened his step. He could scarcely bear the feeling that rushed over him. And the Mormon gripped his arm as if he understood.

"Shefford, which one of these younger women do you reckon your best friend? Ruth?" asked Lake, earnestly.

"Ruth, by all means. Just lately I haven't seen her often. But we've been close friends. I think she'd do much for me."

"Maybe there'll be a chance to find out. Maybe we'll need Ruth. Let's have a word with her. I haven't seen her out among the women."

They stopped at the door of Ruth's cabin. It was closed. When Joe knocked there came a sound of footsteps inside, a hand drew aside the window-blind, and presently the door opened. Ruth stood there, dressed in somber hue. She was a pretty, slender, blue-eyed, brown-haired young woman.

Shefford imagined from her pallor and the set look of shock upon her face, that the tragedy had affected her more powerfully than it had the other women. When he remembered that she had been more friendly with Fay Larkin than any other neighbor, he made sure he was right in his conjecture.

"Come in," was Ruth's greeting.

"No. We just wanted to say a word. I noticed you've not been out. Do you know—all about it?"

She gave them a strange glance.

"Any of the women folks been in?" added Joe.

"Hester ran over. She told me through the window. Then I barred my door to keep the other women out."

"What for?" asked Joe, curiously.

"Please come in," she said, in reply.

They entered, and she closed the door after them. The change that came over her then was the loosing of restraint.

"Joe—what will they do with Mary?" she queried, tensely.

The Mormon studied her with dark, speculative eyes. "Hang her!" he rejoined in brutal harshness.

"O Mother of Saints!" she cried, and her hands went up.

"You're sorry for Mary, then?" asked Joe, bluntly.

"My heart is breaking for her."

"Well, so's Shefford's," said the Mormon, huskily. "And mine's kind of damn shaky."

Ruth glided to Shefford with a woman's swift softness.

"You've been my good—my best friend. You were hers, too. Oh, I know! ... Can't you do something for her?"

"I hope to God I can," replied Shefford.

Then the three stood looking from one to the other, in a strong and subtly realizing moment drawn together.

"Ruth," whispered Joe, hoarsely, and then he glanced fearfully around, at the window and door, as if listeners were there. It was certain that his dark face had paled. He tried to whisper more, only to fail. Shefford divined the weight of Mormonism that burdened Joe Lake then. Joe was faithful to a love for Fay Larkin, noble in friendship to Shefford, desperate in a bitter strait with his own manliness, but the power of that creed by which he had been raised struck his lips mute. For to speak on meant to be false to that creed. Already in his heart he had decided, yet he could not voice the thing.

"Ruth"—Shefford took up the Mormon's unfinished whisper—"if we plan to save her—if we need you—will you help?"

Ruth turned white, but an instant and splendid fire shone in her eyes.

"Try me," she whispered back. "I'll change places with her—so you can get her away. They can't do much to me."

Shefford wrung her hands. Joe licked his lips and found his voice: "We'll come back later." Then he led the way out and Shefford followed. They were silent all the way back to camp.

Nas Ta Bega sat in repose where they had left him, a thoughtful, somber figure. Shefford went directly to the Indian, and Joe tarried at the camp-fire, where he raked out some red embers and put one upon the bowl of his pipe. He puffed clouds of white smoke, then found a seat beside the others.

"Shefford, go ahead. Talk. It'll take a deal of talk. I'll listen. Then I'll talk. It'll be Nas Ta Bega who makes the plan out of it all."

Shefford launched himself so swiftly that he scarcely talked coherently. But he made clear the points that he must save Fay, get her away from the village, let her lead him to Surprise Valley, rescue Lassiter and Jane Withersteen, and take them all out of the country.

Joe Lake dubiously shook his head. Manifestly the Surprise Valley part of the situation presented a new and serious obstacle. It changed the whole thing. To try to take the three out by way of Kayenta and Durango was not to be thought of, for reasons he briefly stated. The Red Lake trail was the only one left, and if that were taken the chances were against Shefford. It was five days over sand to Red Lake—impossible to hide a trail—and even with a day's start Shefford could not escape the hard-riding men who would come from Stonebridge. Besides, after reaching Red Lake, there were days and days of desert-travel needful to avoid places like Blue canyon, Tuba, Moencopie, and the Indian villages.

"We'll have to risk all that," declared Shefford, desperately.

"It's a fool risk," retorted Joe. "Listen. By tomorrow noon all of Stonebridge, more or less, will be riding in here. You've got to get away to-night with the girl—or never! And to-morrow you've got to find that Lassiter and the woman in Surprise Valley. This valley must be back, deep in the canyon country. Well, you've got to come out this way again. No trail through here would be safe. Why, you'd put all your heads in a rope!... You mustn't come through this way. It'll have to be tried across country, off the trails, and that means hell—day-

and-night travel, no camp, no feed for horses—maybe no water. Then you'll have the best trackers in Utah like hounds on your trail."

When the Mormon ceased his forceful speech there was a silence fraught with hopeless meaning. He bowed his head in gloom. Shefford, growing sick again to his marrow, fought a cold, hateful sense of despair.

"Bi Nai!" In his extremity he called to the Indian.

"The Navajo has heard," replied Nas Ta Bega, strangely speaking in his own language.

With a long, slow heave of breast Shefford felt his despair leave him. In the Indian lay his salvation. He knew it. Joe Lake caught the subtle spirit of the moment and looked up eagerly.

Nas Ta Bega stretched an arm toward the east, and spoke in Navajo. But Shefford, owing to the hurry and excitement of his mind, could not translate. Joe Lake listened, gave a violent start, leaped up with all his big frame quivering, and then fired question after question at the Indian. When the Navajo had replied to all, Joe drew himself up as if facing an irrevocable decision which would wring his very soul. What did he cast off in that moment? What did he grapple with? Shefford had no means to tell, except by the instinct which baffled him. But whether the Mormon's trial was one of spiritual rending or the natural physical fear of a perilous, virtually impossible venture, the fact was he was magnificent in his acceptance of it. He turned to Shefford, white, cold, yet glowing.

"Nas Ta Bega believes he can take you down a canyon to the big river—the Colorado. He knows the head of this canyon. Nonnezoshe Boco it's called—canyon of the rainbow bridge. He has never been down it. Only two or three living Indians have ever seen the great stone bridge. But all have heard of it. They worship it as a god. There's water runs down this canyon and water runs to the river. Nas Ta Bega thinks he can take you down to the river."

"Go on," cried Shefford breathlessly, as Joe paused.

"The Indian plans this way. God, it's great!... If only I can do my end!... He plans to take mustangs to-day and wait with them for you to-night or to-morrow till you come with the girl. You'll go get Lassiter and the woman out of Surprise Valley. Then you'll strike east for Nonnezoshe Boco. If possible, you must take a pack of grub. You may be days going down— and waiting for me at the mouth of the canyon, at the river."

"Joe! Where will you be?"

"I'll ride like hell for Kayenta, get another horse there, and ride like hell for the San Juan River. There's a big flatboat at the Durango crossing. I'll go down the San Juan in that—into the big river. I'll drift down by day, tie up by night, and watch for you at the mouth of every canyon till I come to Nonnezoshe Boco."

Shefford could not believe the evidence of his ears. He knew the treacherous San Juan River. He had heard of the great, sweeping, terrible red Colorado and its roaring rapids.

"Oh, it seems impossible!" he gasped. "You'll just lose your life for nothing."

"The Indian will turn the trick, I tell you. Take my hunch. It's nothing for me to drift down a swift river. I worked a ferry-boat once."

Shefford, to whom flying straws would have seemed stable, caught the inflection of defiance and daring and hope of the Mormon's spirit.

"What then—after you meet us at the mouth of Nonnezoshe Boco?" he queried.

"We'll all drift down to Lee's Ferry. That's at the head of Marble canyon. We'll get out on the south side of the river, thus avoiding any Mormons at the ferry. Nas Ta Bega knows the country. It's open desert—on the other side of these plateaus. He can get horses from Navajos. Then you'll strike south for Willow Springs."

"Willow Springs? That's Presbrey's trading-post," said Shefford.

"Never met him. But he'll see you safe out of the Painted Desert. ... The thing that worries me most is how not to miss you all at the mouth of Nonnezoshe. You must have sharp eyes. But I forget the Indian. A bird couldn't pass him.... And suppose Nonnezoshe Boco has a steep-walled, narrow mouth opening into a rapids!... Whew! Well, the Indian will figure that, too. Now, let's put our heads together and plan how to turn this end of the trick here. Getting the girl!"

After a short colloquy it was arranged that Shefford would go to Ruth and talk to her of the aid she had promised. Joe averred that this aid could be best given by Ruth going in her somber gown and hood to the school-house, and there, while Joe and Shefford engaged the guards outside, she would change apparel and places with Fay and let her come forth.

"What'll they do to Ruth?" demanded Shefford. "We can't accept her sacrifice if she's to suffer—or be punished."

"Reckon Ruth has a strong hunch that she can get away with it. Did you notice how strange she said that? Well, they can't do much to her. The bishop may damn her soul. But —Ruth—"

Here Lake hesitated and broke off. Not improbably he had meant to say that of all the Mormon women in the valley Ruth was the least likely to suffer from punishment inflicted upon her soul.

"Anyway, it's our only chance," went on Joe, "unless we kill a couple of men. Ruth will gladly take what comes to help you."

"All right; I consent," replied Shefford, with emotion. "And now after she comes out—the supposed Ruth—what then?"

"You can be natural-like. Go with her back to Ruth's cabin. Then stroll off into the cedars. Then climb the west wall. Meanwhile Nas Ta Bega will ride off with a pack of grub and Nack-yal and several other mustangs. He'll wait for you or you'll wait for him, as the case may be, at some appointed place. When you're gone I'll jump my horse and hit the trail for Kayenta and the San Juan."

"Very well; that's settled," said Shefford, soberly. "I'll go at once to see Ruth. You and Nas Ta Bega decide on where I'm to meet him."

"Reckon you'd do just as well to walk round and come up to Ruth's from the other side— instead of going through the village," suggested Joe.

Shefford approached Ruth's cabin in a roundabout way; nevertheless, she saw him coming before he got there and, opening the door, stood pale, composed, and quietly bade him enter. Briefly, in low and earnest voice, Shefford acquainted her with the plan.

"You love her so much," she said, wistfully, wonderingly.

"Indeed I do. Is it too much to ask of you to do this thing?" he asked.

"Do it?" she queried, with a flash of spirit. "Of course I'll do it."

"Ruth, I can't thank you. I can't. I've only a faint idea what you're risking. That distresses me. I'm afraid of what may happen to you."

She gave him another of the strange glances. "I don't risk so much as you think," she said, significantly.

"Why?"

She came close to him, and her hands clasped his arms and she looked up at him, her eyes darkening and her face growing paler. "Will you swear to keep my secret?" she asked, very low.

"Yes, I swear."

"I was one of Waggoner's sealed wives!"

"God Almighty!" broke out Shefford, utterly overwhelmed.

"Yes. That's why I say I don't risk so much. I will make up a story to tell the bishop and everybody. I'll tell that Waggoner was jealous, that he was brutal to Mary, that I believed she was goaded to her mad deed, that I thought she ought to be free. They'll be terrible. But what can they do to me? My husband is dead... and if I have to go to hell to keep from marrying another married Mormon, I'll go!"

In that low, passionate utterance Shefford read the death-blow to the old Mormon polygamous creed. In the uplift of his spirit, in the joy at this revelation, he almost forgot the stern matter at hand. Ruth and Joe Lake belonged to a younger generation of Mormons. Their nobility in this instance was in part a revolt at the conditions of their lives. Doubt was knocking at Joe Lake's heart, and conviction had come to this young sealed wife, bitter and hopeless while she had been fettered, strong and mounting now that she was free. In a flash of inspiration Shefford saw the old order changing. The Mormon creed might survive, but that part of it which was an affront to nature, a horrible yoke on women's necks, was doomed. It could not live. It could never have survived more than a generation or two of religious fanatics. Shefford had marked a different force and religious fervor in the younger Mormons, and now he understood them.

"Ruth, you talk wildly," he said. "But I understand. I see. You are free and you're going to stay free.... It stuns me to think of that man of many wives. What did you feel when you were told he was dead?"

"I dare not think of that. It makes me—wicked. And he was good to me.... Listen. Last night about midnight he came to my window and woke me. I got up and let him in. He was in a terrible state. I thought he was crazy. He walked the floor and called on his saints and prayed. When I wanted to light a lamp he wouldn't let me. He was afraid I'd see his face. But I saw well enough in the moonlight. And I knew something had happened. So I soothed and coaxed him. He had been a man as close-mouthed as a stone. Yet then I got him to talk.... He had gone to Mary's, and upon entering, thought he heard some one with her. She didn't answer him at first. When he found her in her bedroom she was like a ghost. He accused her. Her silence made him furious. Then he berated her, brought down the wrath of God upon her, threatened her with damnation. All of which she never seemed to hear. But when he tried to touch her she flew at him like a she-panther. That's what he called her. She said she'd kill him! And she drove him out of her house.... He was all weak and unstrung, and I believe scared, too, when he came to me. She must have been a fury. Those quiet, gentle women are furies when they're once roused. Well, I was hours up with him and finally he got over it. He didn't pray any more. He paced the room. It was just daybreak when he said the wrath of God had come to him. I tried to keep him from going back to Mary. But he went.... An hour later the women ran to tell me he had been found dead at Mary's door."

"Ruth—she was mad—driven—she didn't know what she—was doing," said Shefford, brokenly.

"She was always a strange girl, more like an Indian than any one I ever knew. We called her the Sago Lily. I gave her the name. She was so sweet, lovely, white and gold, like those flowers.... And to think! Oh, it's horrible for her! You must save her. If you get her away there never will be anything come of it. The Mormons will hush it up."

"Ruth, time is flying," rejoined Shefford, hurriedly. "I must go back to Joe. You be ready for us when we come. Wear something loose, easily thrown off, and don't forget the long hood."

"I'll be ready and watching," she said. "The sooner the better, I'd say."

He left her and returned toward camp in the same circling route by which he had come. The Indian had disappeared and so had his mustang. This significant fact augmented

Shefford's hurried, thrilling excitement. But one glance at Joe's face changed all that to a sudden numbness, a sinking of his heart.

"What is it?" he queried.

"Look there!" exclaimed the Mormon.

Shefford's quick eye caught sight of horses and men down the valley. He saw several Indians and three or four white men. They were making camp.

"Who are they?" demanded Shefford.

"Shadd and some of his gang. Reckon that Piute told the news. By to-morrow the valley will be full as a horse-wrangler's corral.... Lucky Nas Ta Bega got away before that gang rode in. Now things won't look as queer as they might have looked. The Indian took a pack of grub, six mustangs, and my guns. Then there was your rifle in your saddle-sheath. So you'll be well heeled in case you come to close quarters. Reckon you can look for a running fight. For now, as soon as your flight is discovered, Shadd will hit your trail. He's in with the Mormons. You know him—what you'll have to deal with. But the advantage will all be yours. You can ambush the trail."

"We're in for it. And the sooner we're off the better," replied Shefford, grimly.

"Reckon that's gospel. Well—come on!"

The Mormon strode off, and Shefford, catching up with him, kept at his side. Shefford's mind was full, but Joe's dark and gloomy face did not invite communication. They entered the pinon grove and passed the cabin where the tragedy had been enacted. A tarpaulin had been stretched across the front porch. Beal was not in sight, nor were any of the women.

"I forgot," said Shefford, suddenly. "Where am I to meet the Indian?"

"Climb the west wall, back of camp," replied Joe. "Nas Ta Bega took the Stonebridge trail. But he'll leave that, climb the rocks, then hide the outfit and come back to watch for you. Reckon he'll see you when you top the wall."

They passed on into the heart of the village. Joe tarried at the window of a cabin, and passed a few remarks to a woman there, and then he inquired for Mother Smith at her house. When they left here the Mormon gave Shefford a nudge. Then they separated, Joe going toward the school-house, while Shefford bent his steps in the direction of Ruth's home.

Her door opened before he had a chance to knock. He entered. Ruth, white and resolute, greeted him with a wistful smile.

"All ready?" she asked.

"Yes. Are you?" he replied, low-voiced.

"I've only to put on my hood. I think luck favors you. Hester was here and she said Elder Smith told some one that Mary hadn't been offered anything to eat yet. So I'm taking her a little. It'll be a good excuse for me to get in the school-house to see her. I can throw off this dress and she can put it on in a minute. Then the hood. I mustn't forget to hide her golden hair. You know how it flies. But this is a big hood.... Well, I'm ready now. And—this 's our last time together."

"Ruth, what can I say—how can I thank you?"

"I don't want any thanks. It'll be something to think of always—to make me happy.... Only I'd like to feel you—you cared a little."

The wistful smile was there, a tremor on the sad lips, and a shadow of soul-hunger in her eyes. Shefford did not misunderstand her. She did not mean love, although it was a yearning for real love that she mutely expressed.

"Care! I shall care all my life," he said, with strong feeling. "I shall never forget you."

"It's not likely I'll forget you.... Good-by, John!"

Shefford took her in his arms and held her close. "Ruth—good-by!" he said, huskily.

Then he released her. She adjusted the hood and, taking up a little tray which held food covered with a napkin, she turned to the door. He opened it and they went out.

They did not speak another word.

It was not a long walk from Ruth's home to the school-house, yet if it were to be measured by Shefford's emotion the distance would have been unending. The sacrifice offered by Ruth and Joe would have been noble under any circumstances had they been Gentiles or persons with no particular religion, but, considering that they were Mormons, that Ruth had been a sealed-wife, that Joe had been brought up under the strange, secret, and binding creed, their action was no less than tremendous in its import. Shefford took it to mean vastly more than loyalty to him and pity for Fay Larkin. As Ruth and Joe had arisen to this height, so perhaps would other young Mormons, have arisen. It needed only the situation, the climax, to focus these long-insulated, slow-developing and inquiring minds upon the truth—that one wife, one mother of children, for one man at one time was a law of nature, love, and righteousness. Shefford felt as if he were marching with the whole younger generation of Mormons, as if somehow he had been a humble instrument in the working out of their destiny, in the awakening that was to eliminate from their religion the only thing which kept it from being as good for man, and perhaps as true, as any other religion.

And then suddenly he turned the corner of school-house to encounter Joe talking with the Mormon Henninger. Elder Smith was not present.

"Why, hello, Ruth!" greeted Joe. "You've fetched Mary some dinner. Now that's good of you."

"May I go in?" asked Ruth.

"Reckon so," replied Henninger, scratching his head. He appeared to be tractable, and probably was good-natured under pleasant conditions. "She ought to have somethin' to eat. An' nobody 'pears—to have remembered that—we're so set up."

He unbarred the huge, clumsy door and allowed Ruth to pass in.

"Joe, you can go in if you want," he said. "But hurry out before Elder Smith comes back from his dinner."

Joe mumbled something, gave a husky cough, and then went in.

Shefford experienced great difficulty in presenting to this mild Mormon a natural and unagitated front. When all his internal structure seemed to be in a state of turmoil he did not see how it was possible to keep the fact from showing in his face. So he turned away and took aimless steps here and there.

"'Pears like we'd hev rain," observed Henninger. "It's right warm an' them clouds are onseasonable."

"Yes," replied Shefford. "Hope so. A little rain would be good for the grass."

"Joe tells me Shadd rode in, an' some of his fellers."

"So I see. About eight in the party."

Shefford was gritting his teeth and preparing to endure the ordeal of controlling his mind and expression when the door opened and Joe stalked out. He had his sombrero pulled down so that it hid the upper half of his face. His lips were a shade off healthy color. He stood there with his back to the door.

"Say, what Mary needs is quiet—to be left alone," he said. "Ruth says if she rests, sleeps a little, she won't get fever.... Henninger, don't let anybody disturb her till night."

"All right, Joe," replied the Mormon. "An' I take it good of Ruth an' you to concern yourselves."

A slight tap on the inside of the door sent Shefford's pulses to throbbing. Joe opened it with a strong and vigorous sweep that meant more than the mere action.

"Ruth—reckon you didn't stay long," he said, and his voice rang clear. "Sure you feel sick and weak. Why, seeing her flustered even me!"

A slender, dark-garbed woman wearing a long black hood stepped uncertainly out. She appeared to be Ruth. Shefford's heart stood still because she looked so like Ruth. But she did not step steadily, she seemed dazed, she did not raise the hooded head.

"Go home," said Joe, and his voice rang a little louder. "Take her home, Shefford. Or, better, walk her round some. She's faintish .... And see here, Henninger—"

Shefford led the girl away with a hand in apparent carelessness on her arm. After a few rods she walked with a freer step and then a swifter. He found it necessary to make that hold on her arm a real one, so as to keep her from walking too fast. No one, however, appeared to observe them. When they passed Ruth's house then Shefford began to lose his fear that this was not Fay Larkin. He was far from being calm or clear-sighted. He thought he recognized that free step; nevertheless, he could not make sure. When they passed under the trees, crossed the brook, and turned down along the west wall, then doubt ceased in Shefford's mind. He knew this was not Ruth. Still, so strange was his agitation, so keen his suspense, that he needed confirmation of ear, of eye. He wanted to hear her voice, to see her face. Yet just as strangely there was a twist of feeling, a reluctance, a sadness that kept off the moment.

They reached the low, slow-swelling slant of wall and started to ascend. How impossible not to recognize Fay Larkin now in that swift grace and skill on the steep wall! Still, though he knew her, he perversely clung to the unreality of the moment. But when a long braid of dead-gold hair tumbled from under the hood, then his heart leaped. That identified Fay Larkin. He had freed her. He was taking her away. Then a sadness embittered his joy.

As always before, she distanced him in the ascent to the top. She went on without looking back. But Shefford had an irresistible desire to took again and the last time at this valley where he had suffered and loved so much.

✿ 16 ✿

SURPRISE VALLEY

FROM THE SUMMIT of the wall the plateau waved away in red and yellow ridges, with here and there little valleys green with cedar and pinon.

Upon one of these ridges, silhouetted against the sky, appeared the stalking figure of the Indian. He had espied the fugitives. He disappeared in a niche, and presently came again into view round a corner of cliff. Here he waited, and soon Shefford and Fay joined him.

"Bi Nai, it is well," he said.

Shefford eagerly asked for the horses, and Nas Ta Bega silently pointed down the niche, which was evidently an opening into one of the shallow canyon. Then he led the way, walking swiftly. It was Shefford, and not Fay, who had difficulty in keeping close to him. This speed caused Shefford to become more alive to the business, instead of the feeling, of the flight. The Indian entered a crack between low cliffs—a very narrow canyon full of rocks and clumps of cedars—and in a half-hour or less he came to where the mustangs were halted among some cedars. Three of the mustangs, including Nack-yal, were saddled; one bore a small pack, and the remaining two had blankets strapped on their backs.

"Fay, can you ride in that long skirt?" asked Shefford. How strange it seemed that his first words to her were practical when all his impassioned thought had been only mute! But the instant he spoke he experienced a relief, a relaxation.

"I'll take it off," replied Fay, just as practically. And in a twinkling she slipped out of both waist and skirt. She had worn them over the short white-flannel dress with which Shefford had grown familiar.

As Nack-yal appeared to be the safest mustang for her to ride, Shefford helped her upon him and then attended to the stirrups. When he had adjusted them to the proper length he drew the bridle over Nack-yal's head and, upon handing it to her, found himself suddenly looking into her face. She had taken off the hood, too. The instant there eyes met he realized that she was strangely afraid to meet his glance, as he was to meet hers. That seemed natural. But her face was flushed and there were unmistakable signs upon it of growing excitement, of mounting happiness. Save for that fugitive glance she would have been the Fay Larkin of yesterday. How he had expected her to look he did not know, but it was not like this. And never had he felt her strange quality of simplicity so powerfully.

"Have you ever been here—through this little canyon?" he asked.

"Oh yes, lots of times."

"You'll be able to lead us to Surprise Valley, you think?"

"I know it. I shall see Uncle Jim and Mother Jane before sunset!"

"I hope—you do," he replied, a little shakily. "Perhaps we'd better not tell them of the—the—about what happened last night."

Her beautiful, grave, and troubled glance returned to meet his, and he received a shock that he considered was amaze. And after more swift consideration he believed he was amazed because that look, instead of betraying fear or gloom or any haunting shadow of darkness, betrayed apprehension for him—grave, sweet, troubled love for him. She was not thinking of herself at all—of what he might think of her, of a possible gulf between them, of a vast and terrible change in the relation of soul to soul. He experienced a profound gladness. Though he could not understand her, he was happy that the horror of Waggoner's death had escaped her. He loved her, he meant to give his life to her, and right then and there he accepted the burden of her deed and meant to bear it without ever letting her know of the shadow between them.

"Fay, we'll forget—what's behind us," he said. "Now to find Surprise Valley. Lead on. Nack-yal is gentle. Pull him the way you want to go. We'll follow."

Shefford mounted the other saddled mustang, and they set off, Fay in advance. Presently they rode out of this canyon up to level cedar-patched, solid rock, and here Fay turned straight west. Evidently she had been over the ground before. The heights to which he had climbed with her were up to the left, great slopes and looming promontories. And the course she chose was as level and easy as any he could have picked out in that direction.

When a mile or more of this up-and-down travel had been traversed Fay halted and appeared to be at fault. The plateau was losing its rounded, smooth, wavy characteristics, and to the west grew bolder, more rugged, more cut up into low crags and buttes. After a long, sweeping glance Fay headed straight for this rougher country. Thereafter from time to time she repeated this action.

"Fay, how do you know you're going in the right direction?" asked Shefford, anxiously.

"I never forget any ground I've been over. I keep my eyes close ahead. All that seems strange to me is the wrong way. What I've seen, before must be the right way, because I saw it when they brought me from Surprise Valley."

Shefford had to acknowledge that she was following an Indian's instinct for ground he had once covered.

Still Shefford began to worry, and finally dropped back to question Nas Ta Bega.

"Bi Nai, she has the eye of a Navajo," replied the Indian. "Look! Iron-shod horses have passed here. See the marks in the stone?"

Shefford indeed made out faint cut tracks that would have escaped his own sight. They had been made long ago, but they were unmistakable.

"She's following the trail by memory—she must remember the stones, trees, sage, cactus," said Shefford in surprise.

"Pictures in her mind," replied the Indian.

Thereafter the farther she progressed the less at fault she appeared and the faster she traveled. She made several miles an hour, and about the middle of the afternoon entered upon the more broken region of the plateau. View became restricted. Low walls, and ruined cliffs of red rock with cedars at their base, and gullies growing into canyon and canyon opening into larger ones—these were passed and crossed and climbed and rimmed in travel that grew more difficult as the going became wilder. Then there was a steady ascent, up and up all the time, though not steep, until another level, green with cedar and pinon, was reached.

It reminded Shefford of the forest near the mouth of the Sagi. It was so dense he could not see far ahead of Fay, and often he lost sight of her entirely. Presently he rode out of the forest into a strip of purple sage. It ended abruptly, and above that abrupt line, seemingly far away, rose a long, red wall. Instantly he recognized that to be the opposite wall of a canyon which as yet he could not see.

Fay was acting strangely and he hurried forward. She slipped off Nack-yal and fell, sprang up and ran wildly, to stand upon a promontory, her arms uplifted, her hair a mass of moving gold in the wind, her attitude one of wild and eloquent significance.

Shefford ran, too, and as he ran the red wall in his eager sight seemed to enlarge downward, deeper and deeper, and then it merged into a strip of green.

Suddenly beneath him yawned a red-walled gulf, a deceiving gulf seen through transparent haze, a softly shining green-and-white valley, strange, wild, beautiful, like a picture in his memory.

"Surprise Valley!" he cried, in wondering recognition.

Fay Larkin waved her arms as if they were wings to carry her swiftly downward, and her plaintive cry fitted the wildness of her manner and the lonely height where she leaned.

Shefford drew her back from the rim.

"Fay, we are here," he said. "I recognize the valley. I miss only one thing—the arch of stone."

His words seemed to recall her to reality.

"The arch? That fell when the wall slipped, in the great avalanche. See! There is the place. We can get down there. Oh, let us hurry!"

The Indian reached the rim and his falcon gaze swept the valley. "Ugh!" he exclaimed. He, too, recognized the valley that he had vainly sought for half a year.

"Bring the lassos," said Shefford.

With Fay leading, they followed the rim toward the head of the valley. Here the wall had caved in, and there was a slope of jumbled rock a thousand feet wide and more than that in depth. It was easy to descend because there were so many rocks waist-high that afforded a handhold. Shefford marked, however, that Fay never took advantage of these. More than once he paused to watch her. Swiftly she went down; she stepped from rock to rock; lightly she crossed cracks and pits; she ran along the sharp and broken edge of a long ledge; she poised on a pointed stone and, sure-footed as a mountain-sheep, she sprang to another that had scarce surface for a foothold; her moccasins flashed, seemed to hold wondrously on any angle; and when a rock tipped or slipped with her she leaped to a surer stand. Shefford watched her performance, so swift, agile, so perfectly balanced, showing such wonderful accord between eye and foot; and then when he swept his gaze down upon that wild valley where she had roamed alone for twelve years he marveled no more.

The farther down he got the greater became the size of rocks, until he found himself amid huge pieces of cliff as large as houses. He lost sight of Fay entirely, and he anxiously threaded a narrow, winding, descending way between the broken masses. Finally he came out upon flat rock again. Fay stood on another rim, looking down. He saw that the slide had moved far out into the valley, and the lower part of it consisted of great sections of wall. In fact, the base of the great wall had just moved out with the avalanche, and this much of it held its vertical

ZANE GREY

position. Looking upward, Shefford was astounded and thrilled to see how far he had
descended, how the walls leaned like a great, wide, curving, continuous rim of mountain.

"Here! Here!" called Fay. "Here's where they got down—where they brought me up. Here
are the sticks they used. They stuck them in this crack, down to that ledge."

Shefford ran to her side and looked down. There was a narrow split in this section of wall
and it was perhaps sixty feet in depth. The floor of rock below led out in a ledge, with a sheer
drop to the valley level.

As Shefford gazed, pondering on a way to descend lower, the Indian reached his side. He
had no sooner looked than he proceeded to act. Selecting one of the sticks, which were strong
pieces of cedar, well hewn and trimmed, he jammed it between the walls of the crack till it
stuck fast. Then sitting astride this one he jammed in another some three feet below. When he
got down upon that one it was necessary for Shefford to drop him a third stick. In a
comparatively short time the Indian reached the ledge below. Then he called for the lassos.
Shefford threw them down. His next move was an attempt to assist Fay, but she slipped out
of his grasp and descended the ladder with a swiftness that made him hold his breath. Still,
when his turn came, her spirit so governed him that he went down as swiftly, and even
leaped sheer the last ten feet.

Nas Ta Bega and Fay were leaning over the ledge.

"Here's the place," she said, excitedly. "Let me down on the rope."

It took two thirty-foot lassos tied together to reach the floor of the valley. Shefford folded
his vest, put it round Fay, and slipped a loop of the lasso under her arms. Then he and Nas Ta
Bega lowered her to the grass below. Fay, throwing off the loop, bounded away like a wild
creature, uttering the strangest cries he had ever heard, and she disappeared along the wall.

"I'll go down," said Shefford to the Indian. "You stay here to help pull us up."

Hand over hand Shefford descended, and when his feet touched the grass he experienced
a shock of the most singular exultation.

"In Surprise Valley!" he breathed, softly. The dream that had come to him with his
friend's story, the years of waiting, wondering, and then the long, fruitless, hopeless search in
the desert uplands—these were in his mind as he turned along the wall where Fay had
disappeared. He faced a wide terrace, green with grass and moss and starry with strange
white flowers, and dark-foliaged, spear-pointed spruce-trees. Below the terrace sloped a
bench covered with thick copse, and this merged into a forest of dwarf oaks, and beyond that
was a beautiful strip of white aspens, their leaves quivering in the stillness. The air was close,
sweet, warm, fragrant, and remarkably dry. It reminded him of the air he had smelled in dry
caves under cliffs. He reached a point from where he saw a meadow dotted with red-and-
white-spotted cattle and little black burros. There were many of them. And he remembered
with a start the agony of toil and peril Venters had endured bringing the progenitors of this
stock into the valley. What a strange, wild, beautiful story it all was! But a story connected
with this valley could not have been otherwise.

Beyond the meadow, on the other side of the valley, extended the forest, and that ended in
the rising bench of thicket, which gave place to green slope and mossy terrace of sharp-
tipped spruces—and all this led the eye irresistibly up to the red wall where a vast, dark,
wonderful cavern yawned, with its rust-colored streaks of stain on the wall, and the queer
little houses of the cliff-dwellers, with their black, vacant, silent windows speaking so
weirdly of the unknown past.

Shefford passed a place where the ground had been cultivated, but not as recently as the
last six months. There was a scant shock of corn and many meager standing stalks. He
became aware of a low, whining hum and a fragrance overpowering in its sweetness. And

there round another corner of wall he came upon an orchard all pink and white in blossom and melodious with the buzz and hum of innumerable bees.

He crossed a little stream that had been dammed, went along a pond, down beside an irrigation-ditch that furnished water to orchard and vineyard, and from there he strode into a beautiful cove between two jutting corners of red wall. It was level and green and the spruces stood gracefully everywhere. Beyond their dark trunks he saw caves in the wall.

Suddenly the fragrance of blossom was overwhelmed by the stronger fragrance of smoke from a wood fire. Swiftly he strode under the spruces. Quail fluttered before him as tame as chickens. Big gray rabbits scarcely moved out of his way. The branches above him were full of mockingbirds. And then—there before him stood three figures.

Fay Larkin was held close to the side of a magnificent woman, barbarously clad in garments made of skins and pieces of blanket. Her face worked in noble emotion. Shefford seemed to see the ghost of that fair beauty Venters had said was Jane Withersteen's. Her hair was gray. Near her stood a lean, stoop-shouldered man whose long hair was perfectly white. His gaunt face was bare of beard. It had strange, sloping, sad lines. And he was staring with mild, surprised eyes.

The moment held Shefford mute till sight of Fay Larkin's tear-wet face broke the spell. He leaped forward and his strong hands reached for the woman and the man.

"Jane Withersteen!... Lassiter! I have found you!"

"Oh, sir, who are you?" she cried, with rich and deep and quivering voice. "This child came running—screaming. She could not speak. We thought she had gone mad—and escaped to come back to us."

"I am John Shefford," he replied, swiftly. "I am a friend of Bern Venters—of his wife Bess. I learned your story. I came west. I've searched a year. I found Fay. And we've come to take you away."

"You found Fay? But that masked Mormon who forced her to sacrifice herself to save us!... What of him? It's not been so many long years—I remember what my father was—and Dyer and Tull—all those cruel churchmen."

"Waggoner is dead," replied Shefford.

"Dead? She is free! Oh, what—how did he die?"

"He was killed."

"Who did it?"

"That's no matter," replied Shefford, stonily, and he met her gaze with steady eyes. "He's out of the way. Fay was never his wife. Fay's free. We've come to take you out of the country. We must hurry. We'll be tracked—pursued. But we've horses and an Indian guide. We'll get away.... I think it better to leave here at once. There's no telling how soon we'll be hunted. Get what things you want to take with you."

"Oh—yes—Mother Jane, let us hurry!" cried Fay. "I'm so full—I can't talk—my heart hurts so!"

Jane Withersteen's face shone with an exceedingly radiant light, and a glory blended with a terrible fear in her eyes.

"Fay! my little Fay!"

Lassiter had stood there with his mild, clear blue eyes upon Shefford.

"I shore am glad to see you—all," he drawled, and extended his hand as if the meeting were casual. "What'd you say your name was?"

Shefford repeated it as he met the proffered hand.

"How's Bern an' Bess?" Lassiter inquired.

"They were well, prosperous, happy when last I saw them.... They had a baby."

"Now ain't thet fine?... Jane, did you hear? Bess has a baby. An', Jane, didn't I always say Bern would come back to get us out? Shore it's just the same."

How cool, easy, slow, and mild this Lassiter seemed! Had the man grown old, Shefford wondered? The past to him manifestly was only yesterday, and the danger of the present was as nothing. Looking in Lassiter's face, Shefford was baffled. If he had not remembered the greatness of this old gun-man he might have believed that the lonely years in the valley had unbalanced his mind. In an hour like this coolness seemed inexplicable—assuredly would have been impossible in an ordinary man. Yet what hid behind that drawling coolness? What was the meaning of those long, sloping, shadowy lines of the face? What spirit lay in the deep, mild, clear eyes? Shefford experienced a sudden check to what had been his first growing impression of a drifting, broken old man.

"Lassiter, pack what little you can carry—mustn't be much—and we'll get out of here," said Shefford.

"I shore will. Reckon I ain't a-goin' to need a pack-train. We saved the clothes we wore in here. Jane never thought it no use. But I figgered we might need them some day. They won't be stylish, but I reckon they'll do better 'n these skins. An' there's an old coat thet was Venters's."

The mild, dreamy look became intensified in Lassiter's eyes.

"Did Venters have any hosses when you knowed him?" he asked.

"He had a farm full of horses," replied Shefford, with a smile. "And there were two blacks —the grandest horses I ever saw. Black Star and Night! You remember, Lassiter?"

"Shore. I was wonderin' if he got the blacks out. They must be growin' old by now.... Grand hosses, they was. But Jane had another hoss, a big devil of a sorrel. His name was Wrangle. Did Venters ever tell you about him—an' thet race with Jerry Card?"

"A hundred times!" replied Shefford.

"Wrangle run the blacks off their legs. But Jane never would believe thet. An' I couldn't change her all these years.... Reckon mebbe we'll get to see them blacks?"

"Indeed, I hope—I believe you will," replied Shefford, feelingly.

"Shore won't thet be fine. Jane, did you hear? Black Star an' Night are livin' an' we'll get to see them."

But Jane Withersteen only clasped Fay in her arms, and looked at Lassiter with wet and glistening eyes.

Shefford told them to hurry and come to the cliff where the ascent from the valley was to be made. He thought best to leave them alone to make their preparations and bid farewell to the cavern home they had known for so long.

Then he strolled back along the wall, loitering here to gaze into a cave, and there to study crude red paintings in the nooks. And sometimes he halted thoughtfully and did not see anything. At length he rounded a corner of cliff to espy Nas Ta Bega sitting upon the ledge, reposeful and watchful as usual. Shefford told the Indian they would be climbing out soon, and then he sat down to wait and let his gaze rove over the valley.

He might have sat there a long while, so sad and reflective and wondering was his thought, but it seemed a very short time till Fay came in sight with her free, swift grace, and Lassiter and Jane some distance behind. Jane carried a small bundle and Lassiter had a sack over his shoulder that appeared no inconsiderable burden.

"Them beans shore is heavy," he drawled, as he deposited the sack upon the ground.

Shefford curiously took hold of the sack and was amazed to find that a second and hard muscular effort was required to lift it.

"Beans?" he queried.

"Shore," replied Lassiter.

"That's the heaviest sack of beans I ever saw. Why—it's not possible it can be.... Lassiter, we've a long, rough trail. We've got to pack light—"

"Wal, I ain't a-goin' to leave this here sack behind. Reckon I've been all of twelve years in fillin' it," he declared, mildly.

Shefford could only stare at him.

"Fay may need them beans," went on Lassiter.

"Why?"

"Because they're gold."

"Gold!" ejaculated Shefford.

"Shore. An' they represent some work. Twelve years of diggin' an' washin'!"

Shefford laughed constrainedly. "Well, Lassiter, that alters the case considerably. A sack of gold nuggets or grains, or beans, as you call them, certainly must not be left behind.... Come, now, we'll tackle this climbing job."

He called up to the Indian and, grasping the rope, began to walk up the first slant, and then by dint of hand-over-hand effort and climbing with knees and feet he succeeded, with Nas Ta Bega's help, in making the ledge. Then he let down the rope to haul up the sack and bundle. That done, he directed Fay to fasten the noose round her as he had fixed it before. When she had complied he called to her to hold herself out from the wall while he and Nas Ta Bega hauled her up.

"Hold the rope tight," replied Fay, "I'll walk up."

And to Shefford's amaze and admiration, she virtually walked up that almost perpendicular wall by slipping her hands along the rope and stepping as she pulled herself up. There, if never before, he saw the fruit of her years of experience on steep slopes. Only such experience could have made the feat possible.

Jane had to be hauled up, and the task was a painful one for her. Lassiter's turn came then, and he showed more strength and agility than Shefford had supposed him capable of. From the ledge they turned their attention to the narrow crack with its ladder of sticks. Fay had already ascended and now hung over the rim, her white face and golden hair framed vividly in the narrow stream of blue sky above.

"Mother Jane! Uncle Jim! You are so slow," she called.

"Wal, Fay, we haven't been second cousins to a canyon squirrel all these years," replied Lassiter.

This upper half of the climb bid fair to be as difficult for Jane, if not so painful, as the lower. It was necessary for the Indian to go up and drop the rope, which was looped around her, and then, with him pulling from above and Shefford assisting Jane as she climbed, she was finally gotten up without mishap. When Lassiter reached the level they rested a little while and then faced the great slide of jumbled rocks. Fay led the way, light, supple, tireless, and Shefford never ceased looking at her. At last they surmounted the long slope and, winding along the rim, reached the point where Fay had led out of the cedars.

Nas Ta Bega, then, was the one to whom Shefford looked for every decision or action of the immediate future. The Indian said he had seen a pool of water in a rocky hole, that the day was spent, that here was a little grass for the mustangs, and it would be well to camp right there. So while Nas Ta Bega attended to the mustangs Shefford set about such preparations for camp and supper as their light pack afforded. The question of beds was easily answered, for the mats of soft needles under pinon and cedar would be comfortable places to sleep.

When Shefford felt free again the sun was setting. Lassiter and Jane were walking under the trees. The Indian had returned to camp. But Fay was missing. Shefford imagined he knew where to find her, and upon going to the edge of the forest he saw her sitting on the promontory. He approached her, drawn in spite of a feeling that perhaps he ought to stay away.

"Fay, would you rather be alone?" he asked.

His voice startled her.

"I want you," she replied, and held out her hand.

Taking it in his own, he sat beside her.

The red sun was at their backs. Surprise Valley lay hazy, dusky, shadowy beneath them. The opposite wall seemed fired by crimson flame, save far down at its base, which the sun no longer touched. And the dark line of red slowly rose, encroaching upon the bright crimson. Changing, transparent, yet dusky veils seemed to float between the walls; long, red rays, where the sun shone through notch or crack in the rim, split the darker spaces; deep down at the floor the forest darkened, the strip of aspen paled, the meadow turned gray; and all under the shelves and in the great caverns a purple gloom deepened. Then the sun set. And swiftly twilight was there below while day lingered above. On the opposite wall the fire died and the stone grew cold.

A canyon night-hawk voiced his lonely, weird, and melancholy cry, and it seemed to pierce and mark the silence.

A pale star, peering out of a sky that had begun to turn blue, marked the end of twilight. And all the purple shadows moved and hovered and changed till, softly and mysteriously, they embraced black night.

Beautiful, wild, strange, silent Surprise Valley! Shefford saw it before and beneath him, a dark abyss now, the abode of loneliness. He imagined faintly what was in Fay Larkin's heart. For the last time she had seen the sun set there and night come with its dead silence and sweet mystery and phantom shadows, its velvet blue sky and white trains of stars.

He, who had dreamed and longed and searched, found that the hour had been incalculable for him in its import.

17

THE TRAIL TO NONNEZOSHE

WHEN SHEFFORD AWOKE next morning and sat up on his bed of pinon boughs the dawn had broken cold with a ruddy gold brightness under the trees. Nas Ta Bega and Lassiter were busy around a camp-fire; the mustangs were haltered near by; Jane Withersteen combed out her long, tangled tresses with a crude wooden comb; and Fay Larkin was not in sight. As she had been missing from the group at sunset, so she was now at sunrise. Shefford went out to take his last look at Surprise Valley.

On the evening before the valley had been a place of dusky red veils and purple shadows, and now it was pink-walled, clear and rosy and green and white, with wonderful shafts of gold slanting down from the notched eastern rim. Fay stood on the promontory, and Shefford did not break the spell of her silent farewell to her wild home. A strange emotion abided with him and he knew he would always, all his life, regret leaving Surprise Valley.

Then the Indian called.

"Come, Fay," said Shefford, gently.

And she turned away with dark, haunted eyes and a white, still face.

The somber Indian gave a silent gesture for Shefford to make haste. While they had breakfast the mustangs were saddled and packed. And soon all was in readiness for the flight. Fay was given Nack-yal, Jane the saddled horse Shefford had ridden, and Lassiter the Indian's roan. Shefford and Nas Ta Bega were to ride the blanketed mustangs, and the sixth and last one bore the pack. Nas Ta Bega set off, leading this horse; the others of the party lined in behind, with Shefford at the rear.

Nas Ta Bega led at a brisk trot, and sometimes, on level stretches of ground, at an easy canter; and Shefford had a grim realization of what this flight was going to be for these three fugitives, now so unaccustomed to riding. Jane and Lassiter, however, needed no watching, and showed they had never forgotten how to manage a horse. The Indian back-trailed yesterday's path for an hour, then headed west to the left, and entered a low pass. All parts of this plateau country looked alike, and Shefford was at some pains to tell the difference of this strange ground from that which he had been over. In another hour they got out of the rugged, broken rock to the wind-worn and smooth, shallow canyon. Shefford calculated that

531

they were coming to the end of the plateau. The low walls slanted lower; the canyon made a turn; Nas Ta Bega disappeared; and then the others of the party. When Shefford turned the corner of wall he saw a short strip of bare, rocky ground with only sky beyond. The Indian and his followers had halted in a group. Shefford rode to them, halted himself, and in one sweeping glance realized the meaning of their silent gaze. But immediately Nas Ta Bega started down; and the mustangs, without word or touch, followed him. Shefford, however, lingered on the promontory.

His gaze seemed impelled and held by things afar—the great yellow-and-purple corrugated world of distance, now on a level with his eyes. He was drawn by the beauty and the grandeur of that scene and transfixed by the realization that he had dared to venture to find a way through this vast, wild, and upflung fastness. He kept looking afar, sweeping the three-quartered circle of horizon till his judgment of distance was confounded and his sense of proportion dwarfed one moment and magnified the next. Then he withdrew his fascinated gaze to adopt the Indian's method of studying unlimited spaces in the desert—to look with slow, contracted eyes from near to far.

His companions had begun to zigzag down a long slope, bare of rock, with yellow gravel patches showing between the scant strips of green, and here and there a scrub-cedar. Half a mile down, the slope merged into green level. But close, keen gaze made out this level to be a rolling plain, growing darker green, with blue lines of ravines, and thin, undefined spaces that might be mirage. Miles and miles it swept and relied and heaved to lose its waves in apparent darker level. A round, red rock stood isolated, marking the end of the barren plain, and farther on were other round rocks, all isolated, all of different shape. They resembled huge grazing cattle. But as Shefford gazed, and his sight gained strength from steadily holding it to separate features these rocks were strangely magnified. They grew and grew into mounds, castles, domes, crags—great, red, wind-carved buttes. One by one they drew his gaze to the wall of upflung rock. He seemed to see a thousand domes of a thousand shapes and colors, and among them a thousand blue clefts, each one a little mark in his sight, yet which he knew was a canyon. So far he gained some idea of what he saw. But beyond this wide area of curved lines rose another wall, dwarfing the lower, dark red, horizon—long, magnificent in frowning boldness, and because of its limitless deceiving surfaces, breaks, and lines, incomprehensible to the sight of man. Away to the eastward began a winding, ragged, blue line, looping back upon itself, and then winding away again, growing wider and bluer. This line was the San Juan canyon. Where was Joe Lake at that moment? Had he embarked yet on the river—did that blue line, so faint, so deceiving, hold him and the boat? Almost it was impossible to believe. Shefford followed the blue line all its length, a hundred miles, he fancied, down toward the west where it joined a dark, purple, shadowy cleft. And this was the Grand canyon of the Colorado. Shefford's eye swept along with that winding mark, farther and farther to the west, round to the left, until the cleft, growing larger and coming closer, losing its deception, was seen to be a wild and winding canyon. Still farther to the left, as he swung in fascinated gaze, it split the wonderful wall—a vast plateau now with great red peaks and yellow mesas. The canyon was full of purple smoke. It turned, it gaped, it lost itself and showed again in that chaos of a million cliffs. And then farther on it became again a cleft, a purple line, at last to fail entirely in deceiving distance.

Shefford imagined there was no scene in all the world to equal that. The tranquillity of lesser spaces was not here manifest. Sound, movement, life, seemed to have no fitness here. Ruin was there and desolation and decay. The meaning of the ages was flung at him, and a man became nothing. When he had gazed at the San Juan canyon he had been appalled at the nature of Joe Lake's Herculean task. He had lost hope, faith. The thing was not possible. But when Shefford gazed at that sublime and majestic wilderness, in which the Grand canyon was only a dim line, he strangely lost his terror and something else came to him from across the shining spaces. If Nas Ta Bega led them safely down to the river, if Joe Lake met them at the mouth of Nonnezoshe Boco, if they survived the rapids of that terrible gorge, then Shefford would have to face his soul and the meaning of this spirit that breathed on the wind.

He urged his mustang to the descent of the slope, and as he went down, slowly drawing nearer to the other fugitives, his mind alternated between this strange intimation of faith, this subtle uplift of his spirit, and the growing gloom and shadow in his love for Fay Larkin. Not that he loved her less, but more! A possible God hovering near him, like the Indian's spirit-step on the trail, made his soul the darker for Fay's crime, and he saw with light, with deeper sadness, with sterner truth.

More than once the Indian turned on his mustang to look up the slope and the light flashed from his dark, somber face. Shefford instinctively looked back himself, and then realized the unconscious motive of the action. Deep within him there had been a premonition of certain pursuit, and the Indian's reiterated backward glance had at length brought the feeling upward. Thereafter, as they descended, Shefford gradually added to his already wrought emotions a mounting anxiety.

No sign of a trail showed where the base of the slope rolled out to meet the green plain. The earth was gravelly, with dark patches of heavy silt, almost like cinders; and round, black rocks, flinty and glassy, cracked away from the hoofs of the mustangs. There was a level bench a mile wide, then a ravine, and then an ascent, and after that, rounded ridge and ravine, one after the other, like huge swells of a monstrous sea. Indian paint-brush vied in its scarlet hue with the deep magenta of cactus. There was no sage. Soapweed and meager grass and a bunch of cactus here and there lent the green to that barren; and it was green only at a distance. Nas Ta Bega kept on a steady, even trot. The sun climbed. The wind rose and whipped dust from under the mustangs.

Shefford looked back often, and the farther out in the plain he reached the higher loomed the plateau they had descended; and as he faced ahead again the lower sank the red-domed and castled horizon to the fore. The ravines became deeper, with dry rock bottoms, and the ridge-tops sharper, with outcroppings of yellow, crumbling ledges. Once across the central depression of that plain a gradual ascent became evident, and the round rocks grew clearer in sight, began to rise shine and grow. And thereafter every slope brought them nearer.

The sun was straight overhead and hot when Nas Ta Bega halted the party under the first lonely scrub-cedar. They all dismounted to stretch their limbs, and rest the horses. It was not a talkative group, Lassiter's comments on the never-ending green plain elicited no response. Jane Withersteen looked afar with the past in her eyes. Shefford felt Fay's wistful glance and could not meet it; indeed, he seemed to want to hide something from her. The Indian bent a falcon gaze on the distant slope, and Shefford did not like that intent, searching, steadfast watchfulness. Suddenly Nas Ta Bega stiffened and whipped the halter he held.

"Ugh!" he exclaimed.

All eyes followed the direction of his dark hand. Puffs of dust rose from the base of the long slope they had descended; tiny dark specks moved with the pace of a snail.

"Shadd!" added the Indian.

"I expected it," said Shefford, darkly, as he rose.

"An' who's Shadd?" drawled Lassiter in his cool, slow speech.

Briefly Shefford explained, and then, looking at Nas Ta Bega, he added:

"The hardest-riding outfit in the country! We can't get away from them."

Jane Withersteen was silent, but Fay uttered a low cry. Shefford did not look at either of them. The Indian began swiftly to tighten the saddle-cinches of his roan, and Shefford did likewise for Nack-yal. Then Shefford drew his rifle out of the saddle-sheath and Joe Lake's big guns from the saddle-bag.

"Here, Lassiter, maybe you haven't forgotten how to use these," he said.

The old gun-man started as if he had seen ghosts. His hands grew clawlike as he reached for the guns. He threw open the cylinders, spilled out the shells, snapped back the cylinders. Then he went through motions too swift for Shefford to follow. But Shefford heard the hammers falling so swiftly they blended their clicks almost in one sound. Lassiter reloaded the guns with a speed comparable with the other actions. A remarkable transformation had come over him. He did not seem the same man. The mild eyes had changed; the long, shadowy, sloping lines were tense cords; and there was a cold, ashy shade on his face.

"Twelve years!" he muttered to himself. "I dropped them old guns back there where I rolled the rock.... Twelve years!"

Shefford realized the twelve years were as if they had never been. And he would rather have had this old gun-man with him than a dozen ordinary men.

The Indian spoke rapidly in Navajo, saying that once in the rocks they were safe. Then, after another look at the distant dust-puffs, he wheeled his mustang.

It was doubtful if the party could have kept near him had they been responsible for the gait of their mounts. The fact was that the way the Indian called to his mustang or some leadership in the one rode drew the others to a like trot or climb or canter. For a long time Shefford did not turn round; he knew what to expect. And when he did turn he was startled at the gain made by the pursuers. But he was encouraged as well by the looming, red, rounded peaks seemingly now so close. He could see the dark splits between the sloping curved walls, the pinon patches in the amphitheater under the circled walls. That was a wild place they were approaching, and, once in there, he believed pursuit would be useless. However, there were miles to go still, and those hard-riding devils behind made alarming decrease in the intervening distance. Shefford could see the horses plainly now. How they made the dust fly! He counted up to six—and then the dust and moving line caused the others to be indistinguishable.

At last only a long, gently rising slope separated the fugitives from that labyrinthine network of wildly carved rock. But it was the clear air that made the distance seem short. Mile after mile the mustangs climbed, and when they were perhaps half-way across that last slope to the rocks the first horse of the pursuers mounted to the level behind. In a few moments the whole band was strung out in sight. Nas Ta Bega kept his mustang at a steady walk, in spite of the gaining pursuers. There came a point, however, when the Indian, reaching comparatively level ground, put his mount to a swinging canter. The other mustangs broke into the same gait.

It became a race then, with the couple of miles between fugitives and pursuers only imperceptibly lessened. Nas Ta Bega had saved his mustangs and Shadd had ridden his to the limit. Shefford kept looking back, gripping his rifle, hoping it would not come to a fight, yet slowly losing that reluctance.

Sage began to show on the slope, and other kinds of brush and cedars straggled everywhere. The great rocks loomed closer, the red color mixed with yellow, and the slopes lengthening out, not so steep, yet infinitely longer than they had seemed at a distance.

Shefford ceased to feel the dry wind in his face. They were already in the lee of the wall. He could see the rock-squirrels scampering to their holes. The mustangs valiantly held to the gait, and at last the Indian disappeared between two rounded comers of cliff. The others were close behind. Shefford wheeled once more. Shadd and his gang were a mile in the rear, but coming fast, despite winded horses.

Shefford rode around the wall into a widening space thick with cedars. It ended in a bare slope of smooth rock. Here the Indian dismounted. When the others came up with him he told them to lead their horses and follow. Then he began the ascent of the rock.

It was smooth and hard, though not slippery. There was not a crack. Shefford did not see a broken piece of stone. Nas Ta Bega climbed straight up for a while, and then wound around a swell, to turn this way and that, always going up. Shefford began to see similar mounds of rock all around him, of every shape that could be called a curve. There were yellow domes far above, and small red domes far below. Ridges ran from one hill of rock to another. There were no abrupt breaks, but holes and pits and caves were everywhere, and occasionally, deep down, an amphitheater green with cedar and pinon. The Indian appeared to have a clear idea of where he wanted to go, though there was no vestige of a trail on those bare slopes. At length Shefford was high enough to see back upon the plain, but the pursuers were no longer in sight.

Nas Ta Bega led to the top of that wall, only to disclose to his followers another and a higher wall beyond, with a ridged, bare, wild, and scalloped depression between. Here footing began to be precarious for both man and beast. When the ascent of the second wall began it was necessary to zigzag up, slowly and carefully, taking advantage of every level bulge or depression. They must have consumed half an hour mounting this slope to the summit. Once there, Shefford drew a sharp breath with both backward and forward glances. Shadd and his gang, in single file, showed dark upon the bare stone ridge behind. And to the fore there twisted and dropped and curved the most dangerous slopes Shefford had ever seen. The fugitives had reached the height of stone wall, of the divide, and many of the drops upon this side were perpendicular and too steep to see the bottom.

Nas Ta Bega led along the ridge-top and then started down, following the waves in the rock. He came out upon a round promontory from which there could not have been any turning of a horse. The long slant leading down was at an angle Shefford declared impossible for the animals. Yet the Indian started down. His mustang needed urging, but at last edged upon the steep descent. Shefford and the others had to hold back and wait. It was thrilling to see the intelligent mustang. He did not step. He slid his fore hoofs a few inches at a time and kept directly behind the Indian. If he fell he would knock Nas Ta Bega off his feet and they would both roll down together. There was no doubt in Shefford's mind that the mustang knew this as well as the Indian. Foot by foot they worked down to a swelling bulge, and here Nas Ta Bega left his mustang and came back for the pack-horse. It was even more difficult to get this beast down. Then the Indian called for Lassiter and Jane and Fay to come down. Shefford began to keep a sharp lookout behind and above, and did not see how the three fared on the slope, but evidently there was no mishap. Nas Ta Bega mounted the slope again, and at the moment sight of Shadd's dark bays silhouetted against the sky caused Shefford to call out:

"We've got to hurry!"

The Indian led one mustang and called to the others. Shefford stepped close behind. They went down in single file, inch by inch, foot by foot, and safely reached the comparative level below.

"Shadd's gang are riding their horses up and down these walls!" exclaimed Shefford.

"Shore," replied Lassiter.

Both the women were silent.

Nas Ta Bega led the way swiftly to the right. He rounded a huge dome, climbed a low, rolling ridge, descended and ascended, and came out upon the rim of a steep-walled amphitheater. Along the rim was a yard-wide level, with the chasm to the left and steep slope to the right. There was no time to flinch at the danger, when an even greater danger menaced from the rear. Nas Ta Bega led, and his mustang kept at his heels. One misstep would have plunged the animal to his death. But he was surefooted and his confidence helped the others. At the apex of the curve the only course led away from the rim, and here there was no level. Four of the mustangs slipped and slid down the smooth rock until they stopped in a shallow depression. It cost time to get them out, to straighten pack and saddles. Shefford thought he heard a yell in the rear, but he could not see anything of the gang.

They rounded this precipice only to face a worse one. Shefford's nerve was sorely tried when he saw steep slants everywhere, all apparently leading down into chasms, and no place a man, let alone a horse, could put a foot with safety. Nevertheless the imperturbable Indian never slacked his pace. Always he appeared to find a way, and he never had to turn back. His winding course, however, did not now cover much distance in a straight line, and herein lay the greatest peril. Any moment Shadd and his men might come within range.

Upon a particularly tedious and dangerous side of rocky hill the fugitives lost so much time that Shefford grew exceedingly alarmed. Still, they accomplished it without accident, and their pursuers did not heave in sight. Perhaps they were having trouble in a bad place.

The afternoon was waning. The red sun hung low above the yellow mesa to the left, and there was a perceptible shading of light.

At last Nas Ta Bega came to a place that halted him. It did not look so bad as places they had successfully passed. Yet upon closer study Shefford did not see how they were to get around the neck of the gully at their feet. Presently the Indian put the bridle over the head of his mustang and left him free. He did likewise for two more mustangs, while Lassiter and Shefford rendered a like service to theirs. Then the Indian started down, with his mustang following him. The pack-animal came next, then Fay and Nack-yal, then Lassiter and his mount, with Jane and hers next, and Shefford last. They followed the Indian, picking their steps swiftly, looking nowhere except at the stone under their feet. The right side of the chasm was rimmed, the curve at the head crossed, and then the real peril of this trap had to be faced. It was a narrow slant of ledge, doubling back parallel with the course already traversed.

A sharp warning cry from Nas Ta Bega scarcely prepared Shefford for hoarse yells, and then a rattling rifle-volley from the top of the slope opposite. Bullets thudded on the cliff, whipped up red dust, and spanged and droned away.

Fay Larkin screamed and staggered back against the wall. Nack-yal was hit, and with frightened snort he reared, pawed the air, and came down, pounding the stone. The mustang behind him went to his knees, sank with his head over the rim, and, slipping off, plunged into the depths. In an instant a dull crash came up.

For a moment there was imminent peril for the horses, more in the yawning hole than in the spanging of badly aimed bullets. Lassiter drew Jane up a little slope out of the way of the frightened mustangs, and Shefford, risking his neck, rushed to Fay. She was holding her arm, which was bleeding. Unheeding the rain of bullets, he half carried, half dragged her along the slope of the low bluff, where he hid behind a corner till the Indian drove the mustangs round it. Shefford's swift fingers were wet and red with the blood from Fay's arm when he had bound the wound with his scarf. Lassiter had gotten around with Jane and was calling Shefford to hurry.

It had been Shefford's idea to halt there and fight. But he did not want to send Fay on alone, so he hurried ahead with her. The Indian had the horses going fast on a long level, overhung by bulging wall. Lassiter and Jane were looking back. Shefford, becoming aware of a steep slope to his left, looked down to see a narrow chasm and great crevices in the cliffs, with bunches of cedars here and there.

Presently Nas Ta Bega disappeared with the mustangs. He had evidently turned off to go down behind the split cliffs. Shefford and Fay caught up with Lassiter and Jane, and, panting, hurrying, looking backward and then forward, they kept on, as best they could, in the Indian's course. Shefford made sure they had lost him, when he appeared down to the left. Then they all ran to catch up with him. They went around the chasm, and then through one of the narrow cracks to come out upon the rim, among cedars. Here the Indian waited for them. He pointed down another long swell of naked stone to a narrow green split which was evidently different from all these curved pits and holes and abysses, for this one had straight walls and wound away out of sight. It was the head of a canyon.

"Nonnezoshe Boco!" said the Indian.

"Nas Ta Bega, go on!" replied Shefford. "When Shadd comes out on that slope above he can't see you—where you go down. Hurry on with the horses and women. Lassiter, you go with them. And if Shadd passes me and comes up with you—do your best.... I'm going to ambush that Piute and his gang!"

"Shore you've picked out a good place," replied Lassiter.

In another moment Shefford was alone. He heard the light, soft pat and slide of the hoofs of the mustangs as they went down. Presently that sound ceased.

He looked at the red stain on his hands—from the blood of the girl he loved. And he had to stifle a terrible wrath that shook his frame. In regard to Shadd's pursuit, it had not been blood that he had feared, but capture for Fay. He and Nas Ta Bega might have expected a shot if they resisted, but to wound that unfortunate girl—it made a tiger out of him. When he had stilled the emotions that weakened and shook him and reached cold and implacable control of himself, he crawled under the cedars to the rim and, well hidden, he watched and waited.

Shadd appeared to be slow for the first time since he had been sighted. With keen eyes Shefford watched the corner where he and the others had escaped from that murderous volley. But Shadd did not come.

The sun had lost its warmth and was tipping the lofty mesa to his right. Soon twilight would make travel on those walls more perilous and darkness would make it impossible. Shadd must hurry or abandon the pursuit for that day. Shefford found himself grimly hopeful.

Suddenly he heard the click of hoofs. It came, faint yet clear, on the still air. He glued his sight upon that corner where he expected the pursuers to appear. More cracks of hoofs pierced his ear, clearer and sharper this time. Presently he gathered that they could not possibly come from beyond the corner he was watching. So he looked far to the left of that place, seeing no one, then far to the right. Out over a bulge of stone he caught sight of the bobbing head of a horse—then another—and still another.

He was astounded. Shadd had gone below that place where the attack had been made and he had come up this steep slope. More horses appeared—to the number of eight. Shefford easily recognized a low, broad, squat rider to be Shadd. Assuredly the Piute did not know this country. Possibly, however, he had feared an ambush. But Shefford grew convinced that Shadd had not expected an ambush, or at least did not fear it, and had mistaken the Indian's course. Moreover, if he led his gang a few rods farther up that slope he would do worse than make a mistake—he would be facing a double peril.

What fearless horsemen these Indians were! Shadd was mounted, as were three others of his gang. Evidently the white men, the outlaws, were the ones on foot. Shefford thrilled and his veins stung when he saw these pursuers come passing what he considered the danger mark. But manifestly they could not see their danger. Assuredly they were aware of the chasm; however, the level upon which they were advancing narrowed gradually, and they could not tell that very soon they could not go any farther nor could they turn back. The alternative was to climb the slope, and that was a desperate chance.

They came up, now about on a level with Shefford, and perhaps three hundred yards distant. He gripped his rifle with a fatal assurance that he could kill one of them now. Still he waited. Curiosity consumed him because every foot they advanced heightened their peril. Shefford wondered if Shadd would have chosen that course if he had not supposed the Navajo had chosen it first. It was plain that one of the walking Piutes stooped now and then to examine the rock. He was looking for some faint sign of a horse track.

Shadd halted within two hundred yards of where Shefford lay hidden. His keen eye had caught the significance of the narrowing level before he had reached the end. He pointed and spoke. Shefford heard his voice. The others replied. They all looked up at the steep slope, down into the chasm right below them, and across into the cedars. The Piute in the rear succeeded in turning his horse, went back, and began to circle up the slope. The others entered into an argument and they became more closely grouped upon the narrow bench. Their mustangs were lean, wiry, wild, vicious, and Shefford calculated grimly upon what a stampede might mean in that position.

Then Shadd turned his mustang up the slope. Like a goat he climbed. Another Indian in the rear succeeded in pivoting his steed and started back, apparently to circle round and up. The others of the gang appeared uncertain. They yelled hoarsely at Shadd, who halted on the steep slant some twenty paces above them. He spoke and made motions that evidently meant the climb was easy enough. It looked easy for him. His dark face flashed red in the rays of the sun.

At this critical moment Shefford decided to fire. He meant to kill Shadd, hoping if the leader was gone the others would abandon the pursuit. The rifle wavered a little as he aimed, then grew still. He fired. Shadd never flinched. But the fiery mustang, perhaps wounded, certainly terrified, plunged down with piercing, horrid scream. Shadd fell under him. Shrill yells rent the air. Like a thunderbolt the sliding horse was upon men and animals below.

A heavy shock, wild snorts, upflinging heads and hoofs, a terrible tramping, thudding, shrieking melee, then a brown, twisting, tangled mass shot down the slant over the rim!

Shefford dazedly thought he saw men running. He did see plunging horses. One slipped, fell, rolled, and went into the chasm.

Then up from the depths came a crash, a long, slipping roar. In another instant there was a lighter crash and a lighter sliding roar.

Two horses, shaking, paralyzed with fear, were left upon the narrow level. Beyond them a couple of men were crawling along the stone. Up on the level stood the two Indians, holding down frightened horses, and staring at the fatal slope.

And Shefford lay there under the cedar, in the ghastly grip of the moment, hardly comprehending that his ill-aimed shot had been a thunderbolt.

He did not think of shooting at the Piutes; they, however, recovering from their shock, evidently feared the ambush, for they swiftly drew up the slope and passed out of sight. The frightened horses below whistled and tramped along the lower level, finally vanishing. There was nothing left on the bare wall to prove to Shefford that it had been the scene of swift and tragic death. He leaned from his covert and peered over the rim. Hundreds of feet below he saw dark growths of pinyons. There was no sign of a pile of horses and men, and then he realized that he could not tell the number that had perished. The swift finale had been as stunning to him as if lightning had struck near him.

Suddenly it flashed over him what state of suspense and torture Fay and Jane must be in at that very moment. And, leaping up, he ran out of the cedars to the slope behind and hurried down at risk of limb. The sun had set by this time. He hoped he could catch up with the party before dark. He went straight down, and the end of the slope was a smooth, low wall. The Indian must have descended with the horses at some other point. The canyon was about fifty yards wide and it headed under the great slope of Navajo Mountain. These smooth, rounded walls appeared to end at its low rim.

Shefford slid down upon a grassy bank, and finding the tracks of the horses, he followed them. They led along the wall. As soon as he had assured himself that Nas Ta Bega had gone down the canyon he abandoned the tracks and pushed ahead swiftly. He heard the soft rush of running water. In the center of the canyon wound heavy lines of bright-green foliage, bordering a rocky brook. The air was close, warm, and sweet with perfume of flowers. The walls were low and shelving, and soon lost that rounded appearance peculiar to the wind-worn slopes above. Shefford came to where the horses had plowed down a gravelly bank into the clear, swift water of the brook. The little pools of water were still muddy. Shefford drank, finding the water cold and sweet, without the bitter bite of alkali. He crossed and pushed on, running on the grassy levels. Flowers were everywhere, but he did not notice them particularly. The canyon made many leisurely turns, and its size, if it enlarged at all, was not perceptible to him yet. The rims above him were perhaps fifty feet high. Cottonwood-trees began to appear along the brook, and blossoming buck-brush in the corners of wall.

He had traveled perhaps a mile when Nas Ta Bega, appearing to come out of the thicket, confronted him.

"Hello!" called Shefford. "Where're Fay—and the others?"

The Indian made a gesture that signified the rest of the party were beyond a little way. Shefford took Nas Ta Bega's arm, and as they walked, and he panted for breath, he told what had happened back on the slopes.

The Indian made one of his singular speaking sweeps of hand, and he scrutinized Shefford's face, but he received the news in silence. They turned a corner of wall, crossed a wide, shallow, boulder-strewn place in the brook, and mounted the bank to a thicket. Beyond this, from a clump of cottonwoods, Lassiter strode out with a gun in each hand. He had been hiding.

"Shore I'm glad to see you," he said, and the eyes that piercingly fixed on Shefford were now as keen as formerly they had been mild.

"Gone! Lassiter—they're gone," broke out Shefford. "Where's Fay—and Jane?"

Lassiter called, and presently the women came out of the thick brake, and Fay bounded forward with her swift stride, while Jane followed with eager step and anxious face. Then they all surrounded Shefford.

"It was Shadd—and his gang," panted Shefford. "Eight in all. Three or four Piutes—the others outlaws. They lost track of us. Went below the place—where they shot at us. And they came up—on a bad slope."

Shefford described the slope and the deep chasm and how Shadd led up to the point where he saw his mistake and then how the catastrophe fell.

"I shot—and missed," repeated Shefford, with the sweat in beads on his pale face. "I missed Shadd. Maybe I hit the horse. He plunged—reared—fell back—a terrible fall—right upon that bunch of horses and men below.... In a horrible, wrestling, screaming tangle they slid over the rim! I don't know how many. I saw some men running along. I saw three other horses plunging. One slipped and went over. ... I have no idea how many, but Shadd and some of his gang went to destruction."

"Shore thet's fine!" said Lassiter. "But mebbe I won't get to use them guns, after all."

"Hardly on that gang," laughed Shefford. "The two Piutes and what others escaped turned back. Maybe they'll meet a posse of Mormons—for of course the Mormons will track us, too—and come back to where Shadd lost his life. That's an awful place. Even the Piute got lost—couldn't follow Nas Ta Bega. It would take any pursuers some time to find how we got in here. I believe we need not fear further pursuit. Certainly not to-night or to-morrow. Then we'll be far down the canyon."

When Shefford concluded his earnest remarks the faces of Fay and Jane had lost the signs of suppressed dread.

"Nas Ta Bega, make camp here," said Shefford. "Water—wood—grass—why, this 's something like.... Fay, how's your arm?"

"It hurts," she replied, simply.

"Come with me down to the brook and let me wash and bind it properly."

They went, and she sat upon a stone while he knelt beside her and untied his scarf from her arm. As the blood had hardened, it was necessary to slit her sleeve to the shoulder. Using his scarf, he washed the blood from the wound, and found it to be merely a cut, a groove, on the surface.

"That's nothing," Shefford said, lightly. "It'll heal in a day. But there'll always be a scar. And when we—we get back to civilization, and you wear a pretty gown without sleeves, people will wonder what made this mark on your beautiful arm."

Fay looked at him with wonderful eyes. "Do women wear gowns without sleeves?" she asked.

"They do."

"Have I a—beautiful arm?"

She stretched it out, white, blue-veined, the skin fine as satin, the lines graceful and flowing, a round, firm, strong arm.

"The most beautiful I ever saw," he replied.

But the pleasure his compliment gave her was not communicated to him. His last impression of that right arm had been of its strength, and his mind flashed with lightning swiftness to a picture that haunted him—Waggoner lying dead on the porch with that powerfully driven knife in his breast. Shefford shuddered through all his being. Would this phantom come often to him like that? Hurriedly he bound up her arm with the scarf and did not look at her, and was conscious that she felt a subtle change in him.

The short twilight ended with the fugitives comfortable in a camp that for natural features could not have been improved upon. Darkness found Fay and Jane asleep on a soft mossy bed, a blanket tucked around them, and their faces still and beautiful in the flickering camp-fire light. Lassiter did not linger long awake. Nas Ta Bega, seeing Shefford's excessive fatigue, urged him to sleep. Shefford demurred, insisting that he share the night-watch. But Nas Ta Bega, by agreeing that Shefford might have the following night's duty, prevailed upon him.

Shefford seemed to shut his eyes upon darkness and to open them immediately to the light. The stream of blue sky above, the gold tints on the western rim, the rosy, brightening colors down in the canyon, were proofs of the sunrise. This morning Nas Ta Bega proceeded leisurely, and his manner was comforting. When all was in readiness for a start he gave the mustang he had ridden to Shefford, and walked, leading the pack-animal.

The mode of travel here was a selection of the best levels, the best places to cross the brook, the best banks to climb, and it was a process of continual repetition. As the Indian picked out the course and the mustangs followed his lead there was nothing for Shefford to do but take his choice between reflection that seemed predisposed toward gloom and an absorption in the beauty, color, wildness, and changing character of Nonnezoshe Boco.

Assuredly his experience in the desert did not count in it a trip down into a strange, beautiful, lost canyon such as this. It did not widen, though the walls grew higher. They began to lean and bulge, and the narrow strip of sky above resembled a flowing blue river. Huge caverns had been hollowed out by some work of nature, what, he could not tell, though he was sure it could not have been wind. And when the brook ran close under one of these overhanging places the running water made a singular, indescribable sound. A crack from a hoof on a stone rang like a hollow bell and echoed from wall to wall. And the croak of a frog—the only living creature he had so far noted in the canyon—was a weird and melancholy thing.

Fay rode close to him, and his heart seemed to rejoice when she spoke, when she showed how she wanted to be near him, yet, try as he might, he could not respond. His speech to her —what little there was—did not come spontaneously. And he suffered a remorse that he could not be honestly natural to her. Then he would drive away the encroaching gloom, trusting that a little time would dispel it.

"We are deeper down than Surprise Valley," said Fay.

"How do you know?" he asked.

"Here are the pink and yellow sago-lilies. You remember we went once to find the white ones? I have found white lilies in Surprise Valley, but never any pink or yellow."

Shefford had seen flowers all along the green banks, but he had not marked the lilies. Here he dismounted and gathered several. They were larger than the white ones of higher altitudes, of the same exquisite beauty and fragility, of such rare pink and yellow hues as he had never seen. He gave the flowers to Fay.

"They bloom only where it's always summer," she said.

That expressed their nature. They were the orchids of the summer canyon. They stood up everywhere starlike out of the green. It was impossible to prevent the mustangs treading them under hoof. And as the canyon deepened, and many little springs added their tiny volume to the brook, every grassy bench was dotted with lilies, like a green sky star-spangled. And this increasing luxuriance manifested itself in the banks of purple moss and clumps of lavender daisies and great clusters of yellow violets. The brook was lined by blossoming buck-rush; the rocky corners showed the crimson and magenta of cactus; ledges were green with shining moss that sparkled with little white flowers. The hum of bees filled the air.

But by and by this green and colorful and verdant beauty, the almost level floor of the canyon, the banks of soft earth, the thickets and the clumps of cotton-woods, the shelving caverns and the bulging walls—these features gradually were lost, and Nonnezoshe Boco began to deepen in bare red and white stone steps, the walls sheered away from one another, breaking into sections and ledges, and rising higher and higher, and there began to be manifested a dark and solemn concordance with the nature that had created this rent in the earth.

There was a stretch of miles where steep steps in hard red rock alternated with long levels of round boulders. Here one by one the mustangs went lame. And the fugitives, dismounting to spare the faithful beasts, slipped and stumbled over these loose and treacherous stones.

ZANE GREY

Fay was the only one who did not show distress. She was glad to be on foot again and the rolling boulders were as stable as solid rock for her.

The hours passed; the toil increased; the progress diminished; one of the mustangs failed entirely and was left; and all the while the dimensions of Nonnezoshe Boco magnified and its character changed. It became a thousand-foot walled canyon, leaning, broken, threatening, with great yellow slides blocking passage, with huge sections split off from the main wall, with immense dark and gloomy caverns. Strangely, it had no intersecting canyon. It jealously guarded its secret. Its unusual formations of cavern and pillar and half-arch led the mind to expect any monstrous stone-shape left by an avalanche or cataclysm.

Down and down the fugitives toiled. And now the stream-bed was bare of boulders, and the banks of earth. The floods that had rolled down that canyon had here borne away every loose thing. All the floor was bare red and white stone, polished, glistening, slippery, affording treacherous foothold. And the time came when Nas Ta Bega abandoned the stream-bed to take to the rock-strewn and cactus-covered ledges above.

Jane gave out and had to be assisted upon the weary mustang. Fay was persuaded to mount Nack-yal again. Lassiter plodded along. The Indian bent tired steps far in front. And Shefford traveled on after him, footsore and hot.

The canyon widened ahead into a great, ragged, iron-hued amphitheater, and from there apparently turned abruptly at right angles. Sunset rimmed the walls. Shefford wondered dully when the Indian would halt to camp. And he dragged himself onward with eyes down on the rough ground.

When he raised them again the Indian stood on a point of slope with folded arms, gazing down where the canyon veered. Something in Nas Ta Bega's pose quickened Shefford's pulse and then his steps. He reached the Indian and the point where he, too, could see beyond that vast jutting wall that had obstructed his view.

A mile beyond all was bright with the colors of sunset, and spanning the canyon in the graceful shape arid beautiful hues of a rainbow was a magnificent stone bridge.

"Nonnezoshe!" exclaimed the Navajo, with a deep and sonorous roll in his voice.

18

AT THE FOOT OF THE RAINBOW

THE RAINBOW BRIDGE was the one great natural phenomenon, the one grand spectacle, which Shefford had ever seen that did not at first give vague disappointment, a confounding of reality, a disenchantment of contrast with what the mind had conceived.

But this thing was glorious. It silenced him, yet did not awe or stun. His body and brain, weary and dull from the toil of travel, received a singular and revivifying freshness. He had a strange, mystic perception of this rosy-hued stupendous arch of stone, as if in a former life it had been a goal he could not reach. This wonder of nature, though all-satisfying, all-fulfilling to his artist's soul, could not be a resting-place for him, a destination where something awaited him, a height he must scale to find peace, the end of his strife. But it seemed all these. He could not understand his perception or his emotion. Still, here at last, apparently, was the rainbow of his boyish dreams and of his manhood—a rainbow magnified even beyond those dreams, no longer transparent and ethereal, but solidified, a thing of ages, sweeping up majestically from the red walls, its iris-hued arch against the blue sky.

Nas Ta Bega led on down the ledge and Shefford plodded thoughtfully after him. The others followed. A jutting corner of wall again hid the canyon. The Indian was working round to circle the huge amphitheater. It was slow, irritating, strenuous toil, for the way was on a steep slant, rough and loose and dragging. The rocks were as hard and jagged as lava. And the cactus further hindered progress. When at last the long half-circle had been accomplished the golden and rosy lights had faded.

Again the canyon opened to view. All the walls were pale and steely and the stone bridge loomed dark. Nas Ta Bega said camp would be made at the bridge, which was now close. Just before they reached it the Navajo halted with one of his singular actions. Then he stood motionless. Shefford realized that Nas Ta Bega was saying his prayer to this great stone god. Presently the Indian motioned for Shefford to lead the others and the horses on under the bridge. Shefford did so, and, upon turning, was amazed to see the Indian climbing the steep and difficult slope on the other side. All the party watched him until he disappeared behind the huge base of cliff that supported the arch. Shefford selected a level place for camp, some few rods away, and here, with Lassiter, unsaddled and unpacked the lame, drooping

543

mustangs. When this was done twilight had fallen. Nas Ta Bega appeared, coming down the steep slope on this side of the bridge. Then Shefford divined why the Navajo had made that arduous climb. He would not go under the bridge. Nonnezoshe was a Navajo god. And Nas Ta Bega, though educated as a white man, was true to the superstition of his ancestors.

Nas Ta Bega turned the mustangs loose to fare for what scant grass grew on bench and slope. Firewood was even harder to find than grass. When the camp duties had been performed and the simple meal eaten there was gloom gathering in the canyon and the stars had begun to blink in the pale strip of blue above the lofty walls. The place was oppressive and the fugitives mostly silent. Shefford spread a bed of blankets for the women, and Jane at once lay wearily down. Fay stood beside the flickering fire, and Shefford felt her watching him. He was conscious of a desire to get away from her haunting gaze. To the gentle good-night he bade her she made no response.

Shefford moved away into a strange dark shadow cast by the bridge against the pale starlight. It was a weird, black belt, where he imagined he was invisible, but out of which he could see. There was a slab of rock near the foot of the bridge, and here Shefford composed himself to watch, to feel, to think the unknown thing that seemed to be inevitably coming to him.

A slight stiffening of his neck made him aware that he had been continually looking up at the looming arch. And he found that insensibly it had changed and grown. It had never seemed the same any two moments, but that was not what he meant. Near at hand it was too vast a thing for immediate comprehension. He wanted to ponder on what had formed it—to reflect upon its meaning as to age and force of nature, yet all he could do at each moment was to see. White stars hung along the dark curved line. The rim of the arch seemed to shine. The moon must be up there somewhere. The far side of the canyon was now a blank, black wall. Over its towering rim showed a pale glow. It brightened. The shades in the canyon lightened, then a white disk of moon peered over the dark line. The bridge turned to silver, and the gloomy, shadowy belt it had cast blanched and vanished.

Shefford became aware of the presence of Nas Ta Bega. Dark, silent, statuesque, with inscrutable eyes uplifted, with all that was spiritual of the Indian suggested by a somber and tranquil knowledge of his place there, he represented the same to Shefford as a solitary figure of human life brought out the greatness of a great picture. Nonnezoshe Boco needed life, wild life, life of its millions of years—and here stood the dark and silent Indian.

There was a surge in Shefford's heart and in his mind a perception of a moment of incalculable change to his soul. And at that moment Fay Larkin stole like a phantom to his side and stood there with her uncovered head shining and her white face lovely in the moonlight.

"May I stay with you—a little?" she asked, wistfully. "I can't sleep."

"Surely you may," he replied. "Does your arm hurt too badly, or are you too tired to sleep?"

"No—it's this place. I—I—can't tell you how I feel."

But the feeling was there in her eyes for Shefford to read. Had he too great an emotion—did he read too much—did he add from his soul? For him the wild, starry, haunted eyes mirrored all that he had seen and felt under Nonnezoshe. And for herself they shone eloquently of courage and love.

"I need to talk—and I don't know how," she said.

He was silent, but he took her hands and drew her closer.

"Why are you so—so different?" she asked, bravely.

"Different?" he echoed.

"Yes. You are kind—you speak the same to me as you used to. But since we started you've been different, somehow."

"Fay, think how hard and dangerous the trip's been! I've been worried—and sick with dread—with—Oh, you can't imagine the strain I'm under! How could I be my old self?"

"It isn't worry I mean."

He was too miserable to try to find out what she did mean; besides, he believed, if he let himself think about it, he would know what troubled her.

"I—I am almost happy," she said, softly.

"Fay!... Aren't you at all afraid?"

"No. You'll take care of me.... Do—do you love me—like you did before?"

"Why, child! Of course—I love you," he replied, brokenly, and he drew her closer. He had never embraced her, never kissed her. But there was a whiteness about her then—a wraith—a something from her soul, and he could only gaze at her.

"I love you," she whispered. "I thought I knew it that—that night. But I'm only finding it out now.... And somehow I had to tell you here."

"Fay, I haven't said much to you," he said, hurriedly, huskily. "I haven't had a chance. I love you. I—I ask you—will you be my wife?"

"Of course," she said, simply, but the white, moon-blanched face colored with a dark and leaping blush.

"We'll be married as soon as we get out of the desert," he went on. "And we'll forget—all —all that's happened. You're so young. You'll forget."

"I'd forgotten already, till this difference came in you. And pretty soon—when I can say something more to you—I'll forget all except Surprise Valley—and my evenings in the starlight with you."

"Say it then—quick!"

She was leaning against him, holding his hands in her strong clasp, soulful, tender, almost passionate.

"You couldn't help it.... I'm to blame.... I remember what I said."

"What?" he queried in amaze.

"'YOU CAN KILL HIM!'... I said that. I made you kill him."

"Kill—whom?" cried Shefford.

"Waggoner. I'm to blame.... That must be what's made you different. And, oh, I've wanted you to know it's all my fault.... But I wouldn't be sorry if you weren't.... I'm glad he's dead."

"YOU—THINK—I—" Shefford's gasping whisper failed in the shock of the revelation that Fay believed he had killed Waggoner. Then with the inference came the staggering truth —her guiltlessness; and a paralyzing joy held him stricken.

A powerful hand fell upon Shefford's shoulder, startling him. Nas Ta Bega stood there, looking down upon him and Fay. Never had the Indian seemed so dark, inscrutable of face. But in his magnificent bearing, in the spirit that Shefford sensed in him, there were nobility and power and a strange pride.

The Indian kept one hand on Shefford's shoulder, and with the other he struck himself on the breast. The action was that of an Indian, impressive and stern, significant of an Indian's prowess.

"My God!" breathed Shefford, very low.

"Oh, what does he mean?" cried Fay.

Shefford held her with shaking hands, trying to speak, to fight a way out of these stultifying emotions.

"Nas Ta Bega—you heard. She thinks—I killed Waggoner!"

All about the Navajo then was dark and solemn disproof of her belief. He did not need to speak. His repetition of that savage, almost boastful blow on his breast added only to the dignity, and not to the denial, of a warrior.

"Fay, he means he killed the Mormon," said Shefford. "He must have, for I did not!"

"Ah!" murmured Fay, and she leaned to him with passionate, quivering gladness. It was the woman—the human—the soul born in her that came uppermost then; now, when there was no direct call to the wild and elemental in her nature, she showed a heart above revenge, the instinct of a saving right, of truth as Shefford knew them. He took her into his arms and never had he loved her so well.

"Nas Ta Bega, you killed the Mormon," declared Shefford, with a voice that had gained strength. No silent Indian suggestion of a deed would suffice in that moment. Shefford needed to hear the Navajo speak—to have Fay hear him speak. "Nas Ta Bega, I know I understand. But tell her. Speak so she will know. Tell it as a white man would!"

"I heard her cry out," replied the Indian, in his slow English. "I waited. When he came I killed him."

A poignant why was wrenched from Shefford. Nas Ta Bega stood silent.

"BI NAI!" And when that sonorous Indian name rolled in dignity from his lips he silently stalked away into the gloom. That was his answer to the white man.

Shefford bent over Fay, and as the strain on him broke he held her closer and closer and his tears streamed down and his voice broke in exclamations of tenderness and thanksgiving. It did not matter what she had thought, but she must never know what he had thought. He clasped her as something precious he had lost and regained. He was shaken with a passion of remorse. How could he have believed Fay Larkin guilty of murder? Women less wild and less justified than she had been driven to such a deed, yet how could he have believed it of her, when for two days he had been with her, had seen her face, and deep into her eyes? There was mystery in his very blindness. He cast the whole thought from him for ever. There was no shadow between Fay and him. He had found her. He had saved her. She was free. She was innocent. And suddenly, as he seemed delivered from contending tumults within, he became aware that it was no unresponsive creature he had folded to his breast.

He became suddenly alive to the warm, throbbing contact of her bosom, to her strong arms clinging round his neck, to her closed eyes, to the rapt whiteness of her face. And he bent to cold lips that seemed to receive his first kisses as new and strange; but tremulously changed, at last to meet his own, and then to burn with sweet and thrilling fire.

"My darling, my dream's come true," he said. "You are my treasure. I found you here at the foot of the rainbow!... What if it is a stone rainbow—if all is not as I had dreamed? I followed a gleam. And it's led me to love and faith!"

Hours afterward Shefford walked alone to and fro under the bridge. His trouble had given place to serenity. But this night of nights he must live out wide-eyed to its end.

The moon had long since crossed the streak of star-fired blue above and the canyon was black in shadow. At times a current of wind, with all the strangeness of that strange country in its hollow moan, rushed through the great stone arch. At other times there was silence such as Shefford imagined dwelt deep under this rocky world. At still other times an owl hooted, and the sound was nameless. But it had a mocking echo that never ended. An echo of night, silence, gloom, melancholy death, age, eternity!

The Indian lay asleep with his dark face upturned, and the other sleepers lay calm and white in the starlight.

Shefford saw in them the meaning of life and the past—the illimitable train of faces that had shone the stars. There was a spirit in the canyon, and whether or not it was what the Navajo embodied in the great Nonnezoshe, or the life of this present, or the death of the ages, or the nature so magnificently manifested in those silent, dreaming waiting walls—the truth for Shefford was that this spirit was God.

Life was eternal. Man's immortality lay in himself. Love of a woman was hope—happiness. Brotherhood—that mystic and grand "Bi Nai!" of the Navajo—that was religion.

🎇 19 🎇

THE GRAND CANYON OF THE
COLORADO

THE NIGHT PASSED, the gloom turned gray, the dawn stole cool and pale into the canyon. When Nas Ta Bega drove the mustangs into camp the lofty ramparts of the walls were rimmed with gold and the dark arch of Nonnezoshe began to lose its steely gray.

The women had rested well and were in better condition to travel. Jane was cheerful and Fay radiant one moment and in a dream the next. She was beginning to live in that wonderful future. They talked more than usual at breakfast, and Lassiter made droll remarks. Shefford, with his great and haunting trouble ended for ever, with now only danger to face ahead, was a different man, but thoughtful and quiet.

This morning the Indian leisurely made preparations for the start. For all the concern he showed he might have known every foot of the canyon below Nonnezoshe. But, for Shefford, with the dawn had returned anxiety, a restless feeling of the need of hurry. What obstacles, what impassable gorges, might lie between this bridge and the river! The Indian's inscrutable serenity and Fay's trust, her radiance, the exquisite glow upon her face, sustained Shefford and gave him patience to endure and conceal his dread.

At length the flight was resumed, with Nas Ta Bega leading on foot, and Shefford walking in the rear. A quarter of a mile below camp the Indian led down a declivity into the bottom of the narrow gorge, where the stream ran. He did not gaze backward for a last glance at Nonnezoshe; nor did Jane or Lassiter. Fay, however, checked Nack-yal at the rim of the descent and turned to look behind. Shefford contrasted her tremulous smile, her half-happy good-by to this place, with the white stillness of her face when she had bade farewell to Surprise Valley. Then she rode Nack-yal down into the gorge.

Shefford knew that this would be his last look at the rainbow bridge. As he gazed the tip of the great arch lost its cold, dark stone color and began to shine. The sun had just arisen high enough over some low break in the wall to reach the bridge. Shefford watched. Slowly, in wondrous transformation, the gold and blue and rose and pink and purple blended their hues, softly, mistily, cloudily, until once again the arch was a rainbow.

Ages before life had evolved upon the earth it had spread its grand arch from wall to wall, black and mystic at night, transparent and rosy in the sunrise, at sunset a flaming curve limned against the heavens. When the race of man had passed it would, perhaps, stand there still. It was not for many eyes to see. Only by toil, sweat, endurance, blood, could any man ever look at Nonnezoshe. So it would always be alone, grand, silent, beautiful, unintelligible.

Shefford bade Nonnezoshe a mute, reverent farewell. Then plunging down the weathered slope of the gorge to the stream below, he hurried forward to join the others. They had progressed much farther than he imagined they would have, and this was owing to the fact that the floor of the gorge afforded easy travel. It was gravel on rock bottom, tortuous, but open, with infrequent and shallow downward steps. The stream did not now rush and boil along and tumble over rock-encumbered ledges. In corners the water collected in round, green, eddying pools. There were patches of grass and willows and mounds of moss. Shefford's surprise equaled his relief, for he believed that the violent descent of Nonnezoshe Boco had been passed. Any turn now, he imagined, might bring the party out upon the river. When he caught up with them he imparted this conviction, which was received with cheer. The hopes of all, except the Indian, seemed mounting; and if he ever hoped or despaired it was never manifest.

Shefford's anticipation, however, was not soon realized. The fugitives traveled miles farther down Nonnezoshe Boco, and the only changes were that the walls of the lower gorge heightened and merged into those above and that these upper ones towered ever loftier. Shefford had to throw his head straight back to look up at the rims, and the narrow strip of sky was now indeed a flowing stream of blue.

Difficult steps were met, too, yet nothing compared to those of the upper canyon. Shefford calculated that this day's travel had advanced several hours; and more than ever now he was anticipating the mouth of Nonnezoshe Boco. Still another hour went by. And then came striking changes. The canyon narrowed till the walls were scarcely twenty paces apart; the color of stone grew dark red above and black down low; the light of day became shadowed, and the floor was a level, gravelly, winding lane, with the stream meandering slowly and silently.

Suddenly the Indian halted. He turned his ear down the canyon lane. He had heard something. The others grouped round him, but did not hear a sound except the soft flow of water and the heave of the mustangs. Then the Indian went on. Presently he halted again. And again he listened. This time he threw up his head and upon his dark face shone a light which might have been pride.

"Tse ko-n-tsa-igi," he said.

The others could not understand, but they were impressed.

"Shore he means somethin' big," drawled Lassiter.

"Oh, what did he say?" queried Fay in eagerness.

"Nas Ta Bega, tell us," said Shefford. "We are full of hope."

"Grand canyon," replied the Indian.

"How do you know?" asked Shefford.

"I hear the roar of the river."

But Shefford, listen as he might, could not hear it. They traveled on, winding down the wonderful lane. Every once in a while Shefford lagged behind, let the others pass out of hearing, and then he listened. At last he was rewarded. Low and deep, dull and strange, with some quality to incite dread, came a roar. Thereafter, at intervals, usually at turns in the canyon, and when a faint stir of warm air fanned his cheeks, he heard the sound, growing clearer and louder.

He rounded an abrupt corner to have the roar suddenly fill his ears, to see the lane extend straight to a ragged vent, and beyond that, at some distance, a dark, ragged, bulging wall, like iron. As he hurried forward he was surprised to find that the noise did not increase. Here it kept a strange uniformity of tone and volume. The others of the party passed out of the mouth of Nonnezoshe Boco in advance of Shefford, and when he reached it they were grouped upon a bank of sand. A dark-red canyon yawned before them, and through it slid the strangest river Shefford had ever seen. At first glance he imagined the strangeness consisted of the dark-red color of the water, but at the second he was not so sure. All the others, except Nas Ta Bega, eyed the river blankly, as if they did not know what to think. The roar came from round a huge bulging wall downstream. Up the canyon, half a mile, at another turn, there was a leaping rapid of dirty red-white waves and the sound of this, probably, was drowned in the unseen but nearer rapid.

"This is the Grand canyon of the Colorado," said Shefford. "We've come out at the mouth of Nonnezoshe Boco.... And now to wait for Joe Lake!"

They made camp on a dry, level sand-bar under a shelving wall. Nas Ta Bega collected a pile of driftwood to be used for fire, and then he took the mustangs back up the side canyon to find grass for them. Lassiter appeared unusually quiet, and soon passed from weary rest on the sand to deep slumber. Fay and Jane succumbed to an exhaustion that manifested itself the moment relaxation set in, and they, too, fell asleep. Shefford patrolled the long strip of sand under the wall, and watched up the river for Joe Lake. The Indian returned and went along the river, climbed over the jutting, sharp slopes that reached into the water, and passed out of sight up-stream toward the rapid.

Shefford had a sense that the river and the canyon were too magnificent to be compared with others. Still, all his emotions and sensations had been so wrought upon, he seemed not to have any left by which he might judge of what constituted the difference. He would wait. He had a grim conviction that before he was safely out of this earth-riven crack he would know. One thing, however, struck him, and it was that up the canyon, high over the lower walls, hazy and blue, stood other walls, and beyond and above them, dim in purple distance, upreared still other walls. The haze and the blue and the purple meant great distance, and, likewise, the height seemed incomparable.

The red river attracted him most. Since this was the medium by which he must escape with his party, it was natural that it absorbed him, to the neglect of the gigantic cliffs. And the more he watched the river, studied it, listened to it, imagined its nature, its power, its restlessness, the more he dreaded it. As the hours of the afternoon wore away, and he strolled along and rested on the banks, his first impressions, and what he realized might be his truest ones, were gradually lost. He could not bring them back. The river was changing, deceitful. It worked upon his mind. The low, hollow roar filled his ears and seemed to mock him. Then he endeavored to stop thinking about it, to confine his attention to the gap up-stream where sooner or later he prayed that Joe Lake and his boat would appear. But, though he controlled his gaze, he could not his thought, and his strange, impondering dread of the river augmented.

The afternoon waned. Nas Ta Bega came back to camp and said any likelihood of Joe's arrival was past for that day. Shefford could not get over an impression of strangeness—of the impossibility of the reality presented to his naked eyes. These lonely fugitives in the huge-walled canyon waiting for a boatman to come down that river! Strange and wild—those were the words which, inadequately at best, suited this country and the situations it produced.

After supper he and Fay walked along the bars of smooth, red sand. There were a few moments when the distant peaks and domes and turrets were glorified in changing sunset hues. But the beauty was fleeting. Fay still showed lassitude. She was quiet, yet cheerful, and the sweetness of her smile, her absolute trust in him, stirred and strengthened anew his spirit. Yet he suffered torture when he thought of trusting Fay's life, her soul, and her beauty to this strange red river.

Night brought him relief. He could not see the river; only the low roar made its presence known out there in the shadows. And, there being no need to stay awake, he dropped at once into heavy slumber. He was roused by hands dragging at him. Nas Ta Bega bent over him. It was broad daylight. The yellow wall high above was glistening. A fire was crackling and pleasant odors were wafted to him. Fay and Jane and Lassiter sat around the tarpaulin at breakfast. After the meal suspense and strain were manifested in all the fugitives, even the imperturbable Indian being more than usually watchful. His eyes scarcely ever left the black gap where the river slid round the turn above. Soon, as on the preceding day, he disappeared up the ragged, iron-bound shore. There was scarcely an attempt at conversation. A controlling thought bound that group into silence—if Joe Lake was ever going to come he would come to-day.

Shefford asked himself a hundred times if it were possible, and his answer seemed to be in the low, sullen, muffled roar of the river. And as the morning wore on toward noon his dread deepened until all chance appeared hopeless. Already he had begun to have vague and unformed and disquieting ideas of the only avenue of escape left—to return up Nonnezoshe Boco—and that would be to enter a trap.

Suddenly a piercing cry pealed down the canyon. It was followed by echoes, weird and strange, that clapped from wall to wall in mocking concatenation. Nas Ta Bega appeared high on the ragged slope. The cry had been the Indian's. He swept an arm out, pointing up-stream, and stood like a statue on the iron rocks.

Shefford's keen gaze sighted a moving something in the bend of the river. It was long, low, dark, and flat, with a lighter object upright in the middle. A boat and a man!

"Joe! It's Joe!" yelled Shefford, madly. "There!... Look!"

Jane and Fay were on their knees in the sand, clasping each other, pale faces toward that bend in the river.

Shefford ran up the shore toward the Indian. He climbed the jutting slant of rock. The boat was now full in the turn—it moved faster—it was nearing the smooth incline above the rapid. There! it glided down—heaved darkly up—settled back—and disappeared in the frothy, muddy roughness of water. Shefford held his breath and watched. A dark, bobbing object showed, vanished, showed again to enlarge—to take the shape of a big flatboat—and then it rode the swift, choppy current out of the lower end of the rapid.

Nas Ta Bega began to make violent motions, and Shefford, taking his cue, frantically waved his red scarf. There was a five-mile-an-hour current right before them, and Joe must needs see them so that he might sheer the huge and clumsy craft into the shore before it drifted too far down.

Presently Joe did see them. He appeared to be half-naked; he raised aloft both arms, and bellowed down the canyon. The echoes boomed from wall to wall, every one stronger with the deep, hoarse triumph in the Mormon's voice, till they passed on, growing weaker, to die away in the roar of the river below. Then Joe bent to a long oar that appeared to be fastened to the stern of the boat, and the craft drifted out of the swifter current toward the shore. It reached a point opposite to where Shefford and the Indian waited, and, though Joe made prodigious efforts, it slid on. Still, it also drifted shoreward, and half-way down to the mouth of Nonnezoshe Boco Joe threw the end of a rope to the Indian.

"Ho! Ho!" yelled the Mormon, again setting into motion the fiendish echoes. He was naked to the waist; he had lost flesh; he was haggard, worn, dirty, wet. While he pulled on a shirt Nas Ta Bega made the rope fast to a snag of a log of driftwood embedded in the sand, and the boat swung to shore. It was perhaps thirty feet long by half as many wide, crudely built of rough-hewn boards. The steering-gear was a long pole with a plank nailed to the end. The craft was empty save for another pole and plank, Joe's coat, and a broken-handled shovel. There were water and sand on the flooring. Joe stepped ashore and he was gripped first by Shefford and then by the Indian. He was an unkempt and gaunt giant, yet how steadfast and reliable, how grimly strong to inspire hope!

"Reckon most of me's here," he said in reply to greetings. "I've had water aplenty. My God! I've had WATER!" He rolled out a grim laugh. "But no grub for three days.... Forgot to fetch some!"

How practical he was! He told Fay she looked good for sore eyes, but he needed a biscuit most of all. There was just a second of singular hesitation when he faced Lassiter, and then the big, strong hand of the young Mormon went out to meet the old gunman's. While they fed him and he ate like a starved man Shefford told of the flight from the village, the rescuing of Jane and Lassiter from Surprise Valley, the descent from the plateau, the catastrophe to Shadd's gang—and, concluding, Shefford, without any explanation, told that Nas Ta Bega had killed the Mormon Waggoner.

"Reckon I had that figured," replied Joe. "First off. I didn't think so.... So Shadd went over the cliff. That's good riddance. It beats me, though. Never knew that Piute's like with a horse. And he had some grand horses in his outfit. Pity about them."

Later when Joe had a moment alone with Shefford he explained that during his ride to Kayenta he had realized Fay's innocence and who had been responsible for the tragedy. He took Withers, the trader, into his confidence, and they planned a story, which Withers was to carry to Stonebridge, that would exculpate Fay and Shefford of anything more serious than flight. If Shefford got Fay safely out of the country at once that would end the matter for all concerned.

"Reckon I'm some ferry-boatman, too—a FAIRY boatman. Haw! Haw!" he added. "And we're going through.... Now I want you to help me rig this tarpaulin up over the bow of the boat. If we can fix it up strong it'll keep the waves from curling over. They filled her four times for me."

They folded the tarpaulin three times, and with stout pieces of split plank and horseshoe nails from Shefford's saddle-bags and pieces of rope they rigged up a screen around bow and front corners.

Nas Ta Bega put the saddles in the boat. The mustangs were far up Nonnezoshe Boco and would work their way back to green and luxuriant canyons. The Indian said they would soon become wild and would never be found. Shefford regretted Nack-yal, but was glad the faithful little mustang would be free in one of those beautiful canyons.

"Reckon we'd better be off," called Joe. "All aboard!" He placed Fay and Jane in a corner of the bow, where they would be spared sight of the rapids. Shefford loosed the rope and sprang aboard. "Pard," said Joe, "it's one hell of a river! And now with the snow melting up in the mountains it's twenty feet above normal and rising fast. But that's well for us. It covers the stones in the rapids. If it hadn't been in flood Joe would be an angel now!"

The boat cleared the sand, lazily wheeled in the eddying water, and suddenly seemed caught by some powerful gliding force. When it swept out beyond the jutting wall Shefford saw a quarter of a mile of sliding water that appeared to end abruptly. Beyond lengthened out the gigantic gap between the black and frowning cliffs.

"Wow!" ejaculated Joe. "Drops out of sight there. But that one ain't much. I can tell by the roar. When you see my hair stand up straight—then watch out!... Lassiter, you look after the women. Shefford, you stand ready to bail out with the shovel, for we'll sure ship water. Nas Ta Bega, you help here with the oar."

The roar became a heavy, continuous rumble; the current quickened; little streaks and ridges seemed to race along the boat; strange gurglings rose from under the bow. Shefford stood on tiptoe to see the break in the river below. Swiftly it came into sight—a wonderful, long, smooth, red slant of water, a swelling mound, a huge back-curling wave, another and another, a sea of frothy, uplifting crests, leaping and tumbling and diminishing down to the narrowing apex of the rapid. It was a frightful sight, yet it thrilled Shefford. Joe worked the steering-oar back and forth and headed the boat straight for the middle of the incline. The boat reached the round rim, gracefully dipped with a heavy sop, and went shooting down. The wind blew wet in Shefford's face. He stood erect, thrilling, fascinated, frightened. Then he seemed to feel himself lifted; the curling wave leaped at the boat; there was a shock that laid him flat; and when he rose to his knees all about him was roar and spray and leaping, muddy waves. Shock after shock jarred the boat. Splashes of water stung his face. And then the jar and the motion, the confusion and roar, gradually lessened until presently Shefford rose to see smooth water ahead and the long, trembling rapid behind.

"Get busy, bailer," yelled Joe. "Pretty soon you'll be glad you have to bail—so you can't see!"

There were several inches of water in the bottom of the boat and Shefford learned for the first time the expediency of a shovel in the art of bailing.

"That tarpaulin worked powerful good," went on Joe. "And it saves the women. Now if it just don't bust on a big wave! That one back there was little."

When Shefford had scooped out all the water he went forward to see how Fay and Jane and Lassiter had fared. The women were pale, but composed. They had covered their heads.

"But the dreadful roar!" exclaimed Fay.

Lassiter looked shaken for once.

"Shore I'd rather taken a chance meetin' them Mormons on the way out," he said.

Shefford spoke with an encouraging assurance which he did not himself feel. Almost at the moment he marked a silence that had fallen into the canyon; then it broke to a low, dull, strange roar.

"Aha! Hear that?" The Mormon shook his shaggy head. "Reckon we're in Cataract canyon. We'll be standing on end from now on. Hang on to her, boys!"

Danger of this unusual kind had brought out a peculiar levity in the somber Mormon—a kind of wild, gay excitement. His eyes rolled as he watched the river ahead and he puffed out his cheek with his tongue.

The rugged, overhanging walls of the canyon grew sinister in Shefford's sight. They were jaws. And the river—that made him shudder to look down into it. The little whirling pits were eyes peering into his, and they raced on with the boat, disappeared, and came again, always with the little, hollow gurgles.

The craft drifted swiftly and the roar increased. Another rapid seemed to move up into view. It came at a bend in the canyon. When the breeze struck Shefford's cheeks he did not this time experience exhilaration. The current accelerated its sliding motion and bore the flatboat straight for the middle of the curve. Shefford saw the bend, a long, dark, narrow, gloomy canyon, and a stretch of contending waters, then, crouching low, he waited for the dip, the race, the shock. They came—the last stopping the boat—throwing it aloft—letting it drop—and crests of angry waves curled over the side. Shefford, kneeling, felt the water slap around him, and in his ears was a deafening roar. There were endless moments of strife and hell and flying darkness of spray all about him, and under him the rocking boat. When they lessened—ceased in violence—he stood ankle-deep in water, and then madly he began to bail.

Another roar deadened his ears, but he did not look up from his toil. And when he had to get down to avoid the pitch he closed his eyes. That rapid passed and with more water to bail, he resumed his share in the manning of the crude craft. It was more than a share—a tremendous responsibility to which he bent with all his might. He heard Joe yell—and again —and again. He heard the increasing roars one after another till they seemed one continuous bellow. He felt the shock, the pitch, the beating waves, and then the lessening power of sound and current. That set him to his task. Always in these long intervals of toil he seemed to see, without looking up, the growing proportions of the canyon. And the river had become a living, terrible thing. The intervals of his tireless effort when he scooped the water overboard were fleeting, and the rides through rapid after rapid were endless periods of waiting terror. His spirit and his hope were overwhelmed by the rush and roar and fury.

Then, as he worked, there came a change—a rest to deafened ears—a stretch of river that seemed quiet after chaos—and here for the first time he bailed the boat clear of water.

Jane and Fay were huddled in a corner, with the flapping tarpaulin now half fallen over them. They were wet and muddy. Lassiter crouched like a man dazed by a bad dream, and his white hair hung, stained and bedraggled, over his face. The Indian and the Mormon, grim, hard, worn, stood silent at the oar.

The afternoon was far advanced and the sun had already descended below the western ramparts. A cool breeze blew up the canyon, laden with a sound that was the same, yet not the same, as those low, dull roars which Shefford dreaded more and more.

Joe Lake turned his ear to the breeze. A stronger puff brought a heavy, quivering rumble. This time he did not vent his gay and wild defiance to the river. He bent lower—listened. Then as the rumble became a strange, deep, reverberating roll, as if the monstrous river were rolling huge stones down a subterranean canyon, Shefford saw with dilating eyes that the Mormon's hair was rising stiff upon his head.

"Hear that!" said Joe, turning an ashen face to Shefford. "We'll drop off the earth now. Hang on to the girl, so if we go you can go together.... And, pard, if you've a God—pray!"

Nas Ta Bega faced the bend from whence that rumble came, and he was the same dark, inscrutable, impassive Indian as of old. What was death to him?

Shefford felt the strong, rushing love of life surge in him, and it was not for himself he thought, but for Fay and the happiness she merited. He went to her, patted the covered head, and tried with words choking in his throat to give hope. And he leaned with hands gripping the gunwale, with eyes wide open, ready for the unknown.

The river made a quick turn and from round the bend rumbled a terrible uproar. The current racing that way was divided or uncertain, and it gave strange motion to the boat. Joe and Nas Ta Bega shoved desperately upon the oar, all to no purpose. The currents had their will. The bow of the boat took the place of the stern. Then swift at the head of a curved incline it shot beyond the bulging wall.

And Shefford saw an awful place before them. The canyon had narrowed to half its width, and turned almost at right angles. The huge clamor of appalling sound came from under the cliff where the swollen river had to pass and where there was not space. The rapid rushed in gigantic swells right upon the wall, boomed against it, climbed and spread and fell away, to recede and gather new impetus, to leap madly on down the canyon.

Shefford went to his knees, clasped Fay, and Jane, too. But facing this appalling thing he had to look. Courage and despair came to him at the last. This must be the end. With long, buoyant swing the boat sailed down, shot over the first waves, was caught and lifted upon the great swell and impelled straight toward the cliff. Huge whirlpools raced alongside, and from them came a horrible, engulfing roar. Monstrous bulges rose on the other side. All the stupendous power of that mighty river of downward-rushing silt swung the boat aloft, up and up, as the swell climbed the wall. Shefford, with transfixed eyes and harrowed soul, watched the wet black wall. It loomed down upon him. The stern of the boat went high. Then when the crash that meant doom seemed imminent the swell spread and fell back from the wall and the boat never struck at all. By some miraculous chance it had been favored by a strange and momentary receding of the huge spent swell. Then it slid back, was caught and whirled by the current into a red, frothy, up-flung rapids below. Shefford bowed his head over Fay and saw no more, nor felt nor heard. What seemed a long time after that the broken voice of the Mormon recalled him to his labors.

The boat was half full of water. Nas Ta Bega scooped out great sheets of it with his hands. Shefford sprang to aid him, found the shovel, and plunged into the task. Slowly but surely they emptied the boat. And then Shefford saw that twilight had fallen. Joe was working the craft toward a narrow bank of sand, to which, presently, they came, and the Indian sprang out to moor to a rock.

The fugitives went ashore and, weary and silent and drenched, they dropped in the warm sand.

But Shefford could not sleep. The river kept him awake. In the distance it rumbled, low, deep, reverberating, and near at hand it was a thing of mutable mood. It moaned, whined, mocked, and laughed. It had the soul of a devil. It was a river that had cut its way to the bowels of the earth, and its nature was destructive. It harbored no life. Fighting its way through those dead walls, cutting and tearing and wearing, its heavy burden of silt was death, destruction, and decay. A silent river, a murmuring, strange, fierce, terrible, thundering river of the desert! Even in the dark it seemed to wear the hue of blood.

All night long Shefford heard it, and toward the dark hours before dawn, when a restless, broken sleep came to him, his dreams were dreams of a river of sounds.

All the beautiful sounds he knew and loved he heard—the sigh of the wind in the pines, the mourn of the wolf, the cry of the laughing-gull, the murmur of running brooks, the song of a child, the whisper of a woman. And there were the boom of the surf, the roar of the north wind in the forest, the roll of thunder. And there were the sounds not of earth—a river of the universe rolling the planets, engulfing the stars, pouring the sea of blue into infinite space.

Night with its fitful dreams passed. Dawn lifted the ebony gloom out of the canyon and sunlight far up on the ramparts renewed Shefford's spirit. He rose and awoke the others. Fay's wistful smile still held its faith. They ate of the gritty, water-soaked food. Then they embarked. The current carried them swiftly down and out of hearing of the last rapid. The character of the river and the canyon changed. The current lessened to a slow, smooth, silent, eddying flow. The walls grew straight, sheer, gloomy, and vast. Shefford noted these features, but he was listening so hard for the roar of the next rapid that he scarcely appreciated them. All the fugitives were listening. Every bend in the canyon—and now the turns were numerous—might hold a rapid. Shefford strained his ears. He imagined the low, dull, strange rumble. He had it in his ears, yet there was the growing sensation of silence.

"Shore this 's a dead place," muttered Lassiter.

"She's only slowed up for a bigger plunge," replied Joe. "Listen! Hear that?"

But there was no true sound, Joe only imagined what he expected and hated and dreaded to hear.

Mile after mile they drifted through the silent gloom between those vast and magnificent walls. After the speed, the turmoil, the whirling, shrieking, thundering, the never-ceasing sound and change and motion of the rapids above, this slow, quiet drifting, this utter, absolute silence, these eddying stretches of still water below, worked strangely upon Shefford's mind and he feared he was going mad.

There was no change to the silence, no help for the slow drift, no lessening of the strain. And the hours of the day passed as moments, the sun crossed the blue gap above, the golden lights hung on the upper walls, the gloom returned, and still there was only the dead, vast, insupportable silence.

There came bends where the current quickened, ripples widened, long lanes of little waves roughened the surface, but they made no sound.

And then the fugitives turned through a V-shaped vent in the canyon. The ponderous walls sheered away from the river. There was space and sunshine, and far beyond this league-wide open rose vermilion-colored cliffs. A mile below the river disappeared in a dark, boxlike passage from which came a rumble that made Shefford's flesh creep.

The Mormon flung high his arms and let out the stentorian yell that had rolled down to the fugitives as they waited at the mouth of Nonnezoshe Boco. But now it had a wilder, more exultant note. Strange how he shifted his gaze to Fay Larkin!

"Girl! Get up and look!" he called. "The Ferry! The Ferry!"

Then he bent his brawny back over the steering-oar, and the clumsy craft slowly turned toward the left-hand shore, where a long, low bank of green willows and cottonwoods gave welcome relief to the eyes. Upon the opposite side of the river Shefford saw a boat, similar to the one he was in, moored to the bank.

"Shore, if I ain't losin' my eyes, I seen an Injun with a red blanket," said Lassiter.

"Yes, Lassiter," cried Shefford. "Look, Fay! Look, Jane! See! Indians—hogans—mustangs —there above the green bank!"

The boat glided slowly shoreward. And the deep, hungry, terrible rumble of the remorseless river became something no more to dread.

❧ 20 ❧

WILLOW SPRINGS

Two days' travel from the river, along the saw-toothed range of Echo Cliffs, stood Presbrey's trading-post, a little red-stone square house in a green and pretty valley called Willow Springs.

It was nearing the time of sunset—that gorgeous hour of color in the Painted Desert—when Shefford and his party rode down upon the post.

The scene lacked the wildness characteristic of Kayenta or Red Lake. There were wagons and teams, white men and Indians, burros, sheep, lambs, mustangs saddled and unsaddled, dogs, and chickens. A young, sweet-faced woman stood in the door of the post and she it was who first sighted the fugitives. Presbrey was weighing bags of wool on a scale, and when she called he lazily turned, as if to wonder at her eagerness.

Then he flung up his head, with its shock of heavy hair, in a start of surprise, and his florid face lost its lazy indolence to become wreathed in a huge smile.

"Haven't seen a white person in six months!" was his extraordinary greeting.

An hour later Shefford, clean-shaven, comfortably clothed once more, found himself a different man; and when he saw Fay in white again, with a new and indefinable light shining through that old, haunting shadow in her eyes, then the world changed and he embraced perfect happiness.

There was a dinner such as Shefford had not seen for many a day, and such as Fay had never seen, and that brought to Jane Withersteen's eyes the dreamy memory of the bountiful feasts which, long years ago, had been her pride. And there was a story told to the curious trader and his kind wife—a story with its beginning back in those past years, of riders of the purple sage, of Fay Larkin as a child and then as a wild girl in Surprise Valley, of the flight down Nonnezoshe Boco an the canyon, of a great Mormon and a noble Indian.

Presbrey stared with his deep-set eyes and wagged his tousled head and stared again; then with the quick perception of the practical desert man he said:

"I'm sending teamsters in to Flagstaff to-morrow. Wife and I will go along with you. We've light wagons. Three days, maybe—or four—and we'll be there.... Shefford, I'm going to see you marry Fay Larkin!"

557

Fay and Jane and Lassiter showed strangely against this background of approaching civilization. And Shefford realized more than ever the loneliness and isolation and wildness of so many years for them.

When the women had retired Shefford and the men talked a while. Then Joe Lake rose to stretch his big frame.

"Friends, reckon I'm all in," he said. "Good night." In passing he laid a heavy hand on Shefford's shoulder. "Well, you got out. I've only a queer notion how. But SOME ONE besides an Indian and a Mormon guided you out!... Be good to the girl.... Good-by, pard!"

Shefford grasped the big hand and in the emotion of the moment did not catch the significance of Joe's last words.

Later Shefford stepped outside into the starlight for a few moments' quiet walk and thought before he went to bed. It was a white night. The coyotes were yelping. The stars shone steadfast, bright, cold. Nas Ta Bega stalked out of the shadow of the house and joined Shefford. They walked in silence. Shefford's heart was too full for utterance and the Indian seldom spoke at any time. When Shefford was ready to go in Nas Ta Bega extended his hand.

"Good-by—Bi Nai!" he said, strangely, using English and Navajo in what Shefford supposed to be merely good night. The starlight shone full upon the dark, inscrutable face of the Indian. Shefford bade him good night and then watched him stride away in the silver gloom.

But next morning Shefford understood. Nas Ta Bega and Joe Lake were gone. It was a shock to Shefford. Yet what could he have said to either? Joe had shirked saying good-by to him and Fay. And the Indian had gone out of Shefford's life as he had come into it.

What these two men represented in Shefford's uplift was too great for the present to define, but they and the desert that had developed them had taught him the meaning of life. He might fail often, since failure was the lot of his kind, but could he ever fail again in faith in man or God while he had mind to remember the Indian and the Mormon?

Still, though he placed them on a noble height and loved them well, there would always abide with him a sorrow for the Mormon and a sleepless and eternal regret for that Indian on his lonely cedar slope with the spirits of his vanishing race calling him.

Willow Springs appeared to be a lively place that morning. Presbrey was gay and his sweet-faced wife was excited. The teamsters were a jolly, whistling lot. And the lean mustangs kicked and bit at one another. The trader had brought out two light wagons for the trip, and, after the manner of desert men, desired to start at sunrise.

Far across the Painted Desert towered the San Francisco peaks, black-timbered, blue-canyoned, purple-hazed, with white snow, like the clouds, around their summits.

Jane Withersteen looked at the radiant Fay and lived again in her happiness. And at last excitement had been communicated to the old gun-man.

"Shore we're goin' to live with Fay an' John, an' be near Venters an' Bess, an' see the blacks again, Jane.... An' Venters will tell you, as he did me, how Wrangle run Black Star off his legs!"

All connected with that early start was sweet, sad, hopeful.

And so they rode away from Willow Springs, through the green fields of alfalfa and cotton wood, down the valley with its smoking hogans and whistling mustangs and scarlet-blanketed Indians, and out upon the bare, ridgy, colorful desert toward the rosy sunrise.

EPILOGUE

ON THE OUTSKIRTS of a little town in Illinois there was a farm of rolling pasture-land. And here a beautiful meadow, green and red in clover, merged upon an orchard in the midst of which a brown-tiled roof showed above the trees.

One afternoon in May a group of people, strangely agitated, walked down a shady lane toward the meadow.

"Wal, Jane, I always knew we'd get a look at them hosses again—I shore knew," Lassiter was saying in the same old, cool, careless drawl. But his clawlike hands shook a little.

"Oh! will they know me?" asked Jane Withersteen, turning to a stalwart man—no other than the dark-faced Venters, her rider of other days.

"Know you? I'll bet they will," replied Venters. "What do you say, Bess?"

The shadow brightened in Bess's somber blue eyes, as if his words had recalled her from a sad and memorable past.

"Black Star will know her, surely," replied Bess. "Sometimes he points his nose toward the west and watches as if he saw the purple slopes and smelt the sage of Utah! He has never forgotten. But Night has grown deaf and partly blind of late. I doubt if he'd remember."

Shefford and Fay walked arm in arm in the background.

Out in the meadow two horses were grazing. They were sleek, shiny, long-maned, long-tailed, black as coal, and, though old, still splendid in every line.

"Do you remember them?" whispered Shefford.

"Oh, I only needed to see Black Star," murmured Fay, her voice quivering. "I can remember being lifted on his back.... How strange! It seems so long ago.... Look! Mother Jane is going out to them."

Jane Withersteen advanced alone through the clover, and it was with unsteady steps. Presently she halted. What glorious and bitter memories were expressed in her strange, poignant call!

Black Star started and swept up his noble head and looked. But Night went on calmly grazing. Then Jane called again—the same strange call, only louder, and this time broken. Black Star raised his head higher and he whistled a piercing blast. He saw Jane; he knew her

559

as he had remembered the call; and he came pounding toward her. She met him, encircled his neck with her arms, and buried her face in his mane.

"Shore I reckon I'd better never say any more about Wrangle runnin' the blacks off their legs thet time," muttered Lassiter, as if to himself.

"Lassiter, you only dreamed that race," replied Venters, with a smile.

"Oh, Bern, isn't it good that Black Star remembered her—that she'll have him—something left of her old home?" asked Bess, wistfully.

"Indeed it is good. But, Bess, Jane Withersteen will find a new spirit and new happiness here."

Jane came toward them, leading both horses. "Dear friends, I am happy. To-day I bury all regrets. Of the past I shall remember only—my riders of the purple sage."

Venters smiled his gladness. "And you—Lassiter—what shall you remember?" he queried.

The old gun-man looked at Jane and then at his clawlike hands and then at Fay. His eyes lost their shadow and began to twinkle.

"Wal, I rolled a stone once, but I reckon now thet time Wrangle—"

"Lassiter, I said you dreamed that race. Wrangle never beat the blacks," interrupted Venters.... "And you, Fay, what shall you remember?"

"Surprise Valley," replied Fay, dreamily.

"And you—Shefford?"

Shefford shook his head. For him there could never be one memory only. In his heart there would never change or die memories of the wild uplands, of the great towers and walls, of the golden sunsets on the canyon ramparts, of the silent, fragrant valleys where the cedars and the sago-lilies grew, of those starlit nights when his love and faith awoke, of grand and lonely Nonnezoshe, of that red, sullen, thundering, mysterious Colorado River, of a wonderful Indian and a noble Mormon—of all that was embodied for him in the meaning of the rainbow trail.

Made in the USA
Coppell, TX
01 September 2023

21092871R00329